MONEY
AND THE ECONOMY
Third Edition

MONEY AND THE ECONOMY

Third Edition

John J. Klein GEORGIA STATE UNIVERSITY

HARCOURT BRACE JOVANOVICH, INC.
New York   Chicago   San Francisco   Atlanta

To Sylvia and Leslie

ISBN: 0-15-564004-6

Library of Congress Catalog Card Number: 73-13183

Printed in the United States of America

Preface

For me, the purpose of education is to develop civilized, reasoning minds. Students of economics need to understand economic institutions and problems and should have the analytical equipment to evaluate them, but it is important for all of us, students and teachers alike, to see the relationships between the conditions of man and his intellectual heritage. It is with these ends in mind that I have written this book. In each edition I have striven for a balance of analysis, description of institutions, history of policy, and history of thought.

At a more pedantic level this textbook is designed to fill the needs of the junior-senior course in money and banking. It is primarily written for two types of student: the liberal arts student who takes only one course in money and banking and the business student who studies money and banking in those economics and finance departments that stress finance and the economy rather than bank management. For both, the book provides a basic but rigorous exposition of financial institutions, theoretical analysis, and economic policy.

I believe that a textbook should be addressed primarily to the student rather than the professional. It should be clear, self-contained, self-explanatory, as well as timely and challenging. The only prerequisite for this book is the principles of economics course. I have assumed no knowledge of statistics and calculus in order to make the book accessible to as wide a range of students as possible. This has made the book more difficult to write, but I trust that both the rigor and the humanity of the economics discipline show through the literary and general behavior equation approach I have followed.

The theme of the book is that money and other financial assets play an important role in the economy. With historical perspective, the book discusses the operation of the financial system and presents a critical analysis of monetary theory and policy. It is divided into five parts. Part I, "Money and Private Financial Institutions," examines the private financial institutions that determine the volume and composition of our various monetary resources. Emphasis is placed on financial institutions as potential sources of economic disturbance. Part II, "Money and Government," offers a concise history of central banking in the United States and evaluates the federal government's attempts over the years to regulate money in order to prevent the extremes of inflation and deflation. Part III, a brief one-chapter section, deals with portfolio theory and presents the relationship between individual portfolio decisions and interest rates. Part IV, "Money and Aggregate Economic Activity," traces the historical development of monetary theory and posits a contemporary framework of analysis for studying the impact of money supply and demand forces upon economic activity. Part V, "Money and Economic Policy," uses the analytical framework developed in Part IV to evaluate various alternative monetary, fiscal, and international economic policies. Current wage-price control policies are only briefly considered since they are more appropriately examined in the macroeconomic theory course.

It is my hope that the student will emerge from his reading of this book not with a financier's view of the system, or with the Federal Reserve's view, or with the bias of any school of economic theory, but rather with a well-integrated, overall perception of the financial system and the theory on which it is based. Although both my value judgments and professional judgments are evident throughout the book, I trust I have given a balanced view of monetary economics.

I have tried in the third edition, as in the first two, to provide both a sense of historical perspective and a feeling for contemporary monetary theory and policy. Overall, the outline of the book remains much the same. This edition is one chapter shorter than the second edition, but is really longer. Such a feat has been accomplished by three structural changes: (1) the consolidation of Chapters 5 and 6 of the second edition into one chapter, "Commercial Bank Sources and Uses of Funds," (2) the introduction of an entirely new chapter, "Financial Markets and Portfolio Decisions," and (3) the elimination of Chapter 22 of the second edition ("Alternative Monetary Theories") and the inclusion of much of its subject matter in Chapters 21 and 26. I feel that these changes have helped to clarify the relationship between theory and policy. In addition, each chapter has been carefully reviewed; numerous deletions, modifications, and additions have been made, and completely new material appears in almost every chapter. A small but useful feature, new to this edition, is the inclusion of a structural outline at the beginning of each chapter.

Irving Fisher's views on interest and the neo-Keynesian portfolio approach receive particular emphasis in the third edition. This apparent ambivalence between the monetarism of Milton Friedman and the Keynesianism of portfolio theorists reflects my own increasing eclecticism.

My gratitude extends to many people. A detailed and extremely useful critique of the manuscript was provided by Joseph Perry. Eugene Lerner and Rubin Saposnik read and commented upon portions of the manuscript. Victor Andrews made suggestions that proved helpful in the preparation of Chapter 15. James Crawford gave me encouragement and assistance.

I want to thank my wife, Sylvia, who again served as editor at home and made this edition more readable.

Among my past and current graduate students who provided challenges as well as assistance are Lloyd Blackwell, Richard Cebula, Forest Denman, James Esslinger, Donald Hudson, Gary Leff, Charles Lee, Daniel McCarty, and Thomas Pearson. I am also grateful to the excellent research assistants I have had over the years. In chronological order they are Frank McGrath, Neal McKenzie, Joseph Prinzinger, Robert Pierce, and Ray Popovic.

I must also express appreciation to Helen Gatlin for providing clerical assistance and to Wanda Botelho who typed large portions of the manuscript.

JOHN J. KLEIN

Contents

List of Tables

List of Figures

MONEY
AND THE ECONOMY

Third Edition

1 Introduction

The economist is concerned with how man makes his living. How the individual earns his income, how businesses use resources to produce goods and services, and how the economy as a whole functions are all important aspects of the study of economics. It is for many of us a fascinating and stimulating discipline, for separate individuals and separate businesses from thousands of political communities somehow manage to work together to produce the goods and services that satisfy people's basic wants.

How does the economy accomplish this? Part of the answer lies in the fact that our economy runs on money. Individuals use money to purchase goods and services. Businesses use it to expand production. National governments use it to satisfy social wants.

Money does not always function properly, of course. There are times when businesses, individuals, and governments all feel that there is a shortage of funds. This may happen during periods of either recession or inflation. In periods of recession people with insufficient incomes and monetary resources are forced to reduce their spending. This, in turn, results in a decreased demand for goods, lower production, and fewer jobs. On the other hand, during periods of inflation almost everyone may be employed and earning apparently adequate incomes but still feel that their incomes and monetary resources are inadequate in light of rapidly rising prices.

How do such paradoxical situations arise? *Money and the Economy* will concentrate on problems of this sort. The theme of the book is that money is important for the economy. Along with other forms of wealth holding, money influences interest rates and spending; it thereby has a significant impact on aggregate economic activity.

WHAT IS MONEY?

Definitions of money abound. It is sometimes defined in terms of the job it does. As we shall see shortly, it serves as a medium of exchange, a store of value, a standard of deferred payments, a unit of account, and a means of paying off debt. Money may also be defined according to its physical properties. Sometimes it is coin, paper currency, and checking deposits. It may exist in many other forms, however. In Europe, for example, after

2

World War II, cigarettes were widely used as a medium of exchange, since the supply of currency was so abundant and prices were rising so rapidly that currency had little actual value. In addition, gold, silver, wampum, stone, and even leather have been considered money.

Money Defined

For our purposes, the most suitable definition of money is one that focuses on the primary use to which money is put in the American economy, as follows: *money is anything generally acceptable as a means of paying off debt*. The term "paying off debt" is emphasized in our definition because in most economic transactions a debt is created and subsequently extinguished. Businesses seldom make immediate payment for goods and services. Similarly, individuals often are not billed for goods and services they have purchased until the end of the month. Here too a debt arises and is subsequently extinguished through the use of either checking deposits or currency. Even when one purchases groceries at a grocery store a momentary debt is created, which is, of course, immediately extinguished by a cash payment to the clerk.

Before any item can function as money it must be "generally acceptable," and to retain this quality of acceptability, must exhibit some degree of stability in value over time. History is full of examples of monies that lost their value and were consequently abandoned. Money must have stable purchasing power in order to retain the public's faith.

The Uses of Money

Money as a medium of exchange. Money is used principally in the payment of debts incurred when goods and services are purchased. Most of us use our productive resources to acquire money and, in turn, use money to purchase goods and services. In reality, then, goods and services are exchanged for goods and services. Money merely facilitates this exchange. For this reason it is often called a *medium of exchange*.

Why do we need a medium of exchange? Consider for a moment what the economy would be like without money. How would one exchange goods for goods? Some people might answer that there need be no exchange of goods. Let everyone produce what he needs for himself. But this would overlook the tremendous advantages of specialization. Obviously, some men can make shoes better than others; some can produce machines more efficiently; others are talented in the arts. The total production in an economy will usually be greater when everyone is doing that job for which his talents and training best suit him. Civilization depends upon specialization for its very existence. Men have long recognized its importance. Even Plato argued ". . . we must infer that all things are produced more plentifully and easily and of a better quality when one man does one thing which is natural to him and does it at the right time, and leaves other things."[1]

Imagine, then, a specialized economy with no money. Goods would have to be exchanged by direct barter. The producer of shoes who wanted food would have to find a producer of food who wanted shoes. This is known as *double coincidence of wants.* If there were thousands of goods produced and desired, it would be almost impossible to arrange the necessary number of exchanges. One would also have to work out innumerable ratios of exchange of one good for another. How many shoes must one give up to acquire cars, stockings, bread, etc.—and vice versa? If there were just 1,000 commodities in the economy, there would have to be almost 500,000 rates of exchange between the goods.[2] Obviously, much time and many valuable resources would be used in barter exchange instead of in the production of real goods and services.

Money eliminates all the complexities of making barter transactions. One need no longer seek out those who have the goods one needs and who also desire the goods one has produced. Instead, goods may be exchanged for money and the money may then be used to buy other goods and services. We ". . . give money in exchange for goods to those who desire to sell and . . . take money from those who desire to buy."[3] Much wasted effort in exchanging goods for goods is thus eliminated, and the total production of the economy can be substantially increased.

Money as a unit of account. In a money economy, all goods and services have a price, which is stated uniformly in terms of the amount of money that must be given to acquire them. Thus it may also be said that money acts as a *unit of account.* The dollar, the peso, the lira, the franc, the Deutsche mark, the hwan, the yen, the ruble, are all units of account. The things that function as money—in our economy, currency and demand deposits—are also counted in terms of the unit of account. Thus, the unit of account is simply an abstract measure of value, just as the pound and the ounce are abstract measures of weight.

Money as a store of value. People want money not only for the goods and services that they purchase today but also for the goods and services they will want to buy in the future. In addition, many people hold money as a precaution against such contingencies as the loss of a job, the destruction of a home by fire, a medical emergency, etc. Of course, money is only one way of storing up the ability to buy goods and services. Other examples are stocks, bonds, and life insurance policies. However, these must first be

[1] Plato. *The Republic,* Book II. In Robert Hutchins, ed. *Great Books of the Western World* (Encyclopedia Britannica, Inc., 1952), Vol. 7, p. 317.
[2] The formula $n(n-1)/2$, where n refers to the number of goods, may be used to determine the number of different ratios of exchange. This formula is the standard expression for the number of possible combinations of n items taken two at a time.
[3] Plato, *op. cit.,* p. 317.

converted into money before goods can actually be purchased. Thus money is sometimes said to be the most *liquid* of the various types of claims over future goods and services because it is the one thing that can be used immediately to acquire them.

Money as a standard of deferred payments. Another function of money is to serve as a *standard of deferred payments*. This role is an outgrowth of the use of money as a means of paying debt and as a unit of account. Contracts are often written providing for future payments to be made in specific sums of money. A bond, for example, is the contractual promise of a corporation to make periodic interest payments to bondholders and to redeem the bond at full face value at some specified time in the future. It is agreed that interest on bonds and the principal when due are to be paid in the form of money. Thus money is both the standard by which deferred payments of bond interest are to be reckoned and the means by which these payments are to be made.

Types of Money

In our economy, hand-to-hand currency and checking deposits are considered money, since nearly everyone will accept them in payment of debt.

Hand-to-hand currency. Hand-to-hand currency consists of coins and paper currency. Coins may be either full bodied or token. In the United States our unit of account, the dollar, is defined by law as being equal to a specific amount of a commodity. This commodity is gold and the dollar is legally defined as being equal to 1/42.22 of an ounce of gold. If gold coins circulated in the United States, and if the amount of gold contained in the coins were equal in value to their legally stated face value, then our coins would be *full-bodied money*. However, gold does not circulate in the United States as money. Some of our coins do contain silver, but in such small amounts that the market value is less than the face value of the coins. Hence all our coins are *token coins*. The market value of the commodities of which the coins are made is much less than the value of the coins as money.

Paper currency may be either *representative full-bodied paper money* or *fiat money*. Paper money is full bodied when it represents a claim to a specific amount of a commodity, such as gold or silver. Fiat money, on the other hand, is irredeemable. All paper currency in the United States is now fiat. It cannot be redeemed in either gold or silver. Until 1933, gold certificates could be redeemed in full-bodied gold coins. Until 1968, silver certificates could be redeemed in silver bullion at the U.S. Treasury.

Since none of our hand-to-hand currency is full bodied, why are people willing to accept it? As we shall see in subsequent chapters, hand-to-hand currency is accepted as a medium of exchange because it has a high degree of stability in value. It has this stability because our monetary authorities effectively limit its quantity.

Checking deposits. It is readily apparent why coin and paper currency are money; however, it is not so obvious why checking deposits are also considered money. Checking deposits are money because they function like currency. They serve as a medium of exchange and their quantity is limited by our monetary authority, the Federal Reserve. By far the greater volume of all monetary transactions in the economy involves the use of checks. The extensive utilization of checking deposits, or demand deposits, as they are more correctly called, is illustrated by the fact that the Federal Reserve banks handle almost $4.0 trillion worth of checks a year.[4]

Demand deposits are very nearly as liquid as currency. The average man, even when he questions the credit-worthiness of a check user, will still be willing to accept a cashier's check from him in lieu of a personal check. The checks themselves are not money. They are the means by which people transfer the ownership of demand deposits when making purchases and paying off debt. The creation of demand deposits and their use as money will be discussed extensively in subsequent chapters.

MONEY AND STABLE PURCHASING POWER

We have previously noted that, in order to retain acceptability, money must exhibit stability in value. Its purchasing power must not diminish over time. For example, consider the effect on the pensioner who is receiving an annual pension of $1,500 when the price level suddenly doubles. The purchasing power of the income from his pension and whatever savings he has is cut in half. The human misery that this entails is not something hypothetical, but very real. Imagine what would have happened to you and your family if you had lived in the Deep South from January of 1861 to January of 1864, when prices rose 27.8 times,[5] or in Germany from August 1922 to November 1923, when prices rose 1.02×10^{10}, over ten billion times. After World War II in Hungary, from August 1945 to July 1946, prices rose by 3.81×10^{27}![6]

How do such tremendous price increases, and consequent reductions in the purchasing power of money, occur? Several possible answers to that question will be considered later. For the moment, however, suffice it to say that these price-level increases were associated with a money stock that went "out of order." For example, in the Confederacy the money stock increased 11.6 times during the previously mentioned period.[7] In

---

[4] Board of Governors of the Federal Reserve System. *Annual Report* (1972), p. 242.

[5] Eugene M. Lerner, "Money, Prices, and Wages in the Confederacy, 1861–65." *Journal of Political Economy* (1955), p. 29.

[6] Phillip Cagan. "The Monetary Dynamics of Hyperinflation." *Studies in the Quantity Theory of Money,* Milton Friedman, ed. (University of Chicago Press, 1956), p. 26.

[7] Lerner, *op. cit.,* p. 21.

Germany after World War I it increased 7.32×10^9, and in Hungary after World War II 1.19×10^{25}.[8]

On the other hand, do periods of price deflation and accompanying increases in the value of money lead to any lessening of economic distress? Apparently not, since unemployment and a drop in production have usually accompanied price declines in the modern world. For example, in the United States from 1929 to 1933 the price level dropped some 25 percent.[9] Thus, a dollar spent in 1929 would have bought $1.33 worth of goods in 1933, yet unemployment rose from a yearly average of 1,550,000 to 12,830,000 in that period.[10] Real output in America dropped in that same period by 30 percent.[11] These decreases in the price level and real output were accompanied by a 27 percent fall in the money stock.[12]

Thus we can see that money does not always have stable purchasing power. The ability of money to command goods and services decreases with inflation and increases with deflation. This change in the value of money is usually accompanied by employment, output, and money stock changes. Normally, a dollar can buy tomorrow about as much as it can buy today, but over longer periods—particularly when we encounter wars and depressions—the value of money may change significantly.

Table 1–1 shows how consumer prices in the United States have varied from 1929 through 1973. Here we see how prices dipped during the early

TABLE 1–1 THE CONSUMER PRICE INDEX, 1929–73
(1967 = 100)

YEAR	INDEX	YEAR	INDEX	YEAR	INDEX
1929	51.3	1944	52.7	1959	87.3
1930	50.0	1945	53.9	1960	88.7
1931	45.6	1946	58.5	1961	89.6
1932	40.9	1947	66.9	1962	90.6
1933	38.8	1948	72.1	1963	91.7
1934	40.1	1949	71.4	1964	92.9
1935	41.1	1950	72.1	1965	94.5
1936	41.5	1951	77.8	1966	97.2
1937	43.0	1952	79.5	1967	100.0
1938	42.2	1953	80.1	1968	104.2
1939	41.6	1954	80.5	1969	109.8
1940	42.0	1955	80.2	1970	116.3
1941	44.1	1956	81.4	1971	121.3
1942	48.8	1957	84.3	1972	125.3
1943	51.8	1958	86.6	1973*	132.0

* Estimated by author.

SOURCE: *Economic Report of the President* (1973), p. 244.

[8] Cagan, *op. cit.*, p. 26.
[9] *Economic Report of the President* (1973), p. 244.
[10] *Ibid.*, p. 220.
[11] *Ibid.*, p. 194.
[12] Milton Friedman and Anna Schwartz. *A Monetary History of the United States, 1867–1960* (Princeton University Press, 1963), Table A-1.

years of the depression and then leveled off until World War II, when prices began a marked rise until the recession of 1948–49. The consumers' price index again surged upward during the Korean conflict. Price stability characterized the 1953–54 recession. From 1955 through 1965 we experienced a gradual rise in prices, one which amounted to only 18 percent during the whole period — a remarkable record of stability among contemporary economies. However, beginning in 1966 the rise of prices in the United States accelerated, this change being associated with an escalating Vietnam war effort, deficit finance, and sharp increases in the stock of money. More will be said about these events in later chapters.

The behavior of prices in other countries has often been disasterous compared with price fluctuations in the United States. Yet it is important to recognize the distress inherent in either inflation or deflation, even in the United States. In economies as complex as those of the modern world, society must regulate money and spending to ensure a relatively stable price level. Serious damage may be done to the economy if money is either issued to excess or not issued and spent in sufficient quantities.

Part I MONEY AND PRIVATE FINANCIAL INSTITUTIONS

2 Money and Liquid Wealth in the United States

Chapter 1 stressed that money and its relative stability in purchasing power are important for the economy. Money is unique by comparison with other assets in the economy because it is the only financial asset that can be used directly in the purchase of goods and services. One of the central themes of this book is that variations in the demand for and supply of money are closely associated with changes in aggregate economic activity. It must nevertheless be stressed that money is only one form in which people may hold wealth. People must make portfolio decisions: they must determine how much of their wealth they wish to hold in the form of money; how much they wish to hold in such financial assets as stocks, bonds, and savings accounts; and how much they wish to hold in such real wealth forms as real estate, capital goods, etc. Thus, part of the study of monetary economics consists of examining the decisions people make concerning their asset choices. This is considered in Chapters 15 and 26. In addition, Chapters 3 through 7, as well as Chapter 15, examine private financial institutions and the assets that form the financial environment within which people and businesses make their portfolio choices. As is to be expected in a book dealing with a unique asset — money, the emphasis is upon commercial banks.

The present chapter sets the stage for our later work by examining how money fits into a general scheme of property holding. We shall see how it differs from other forms of wealth and how these other forms influence money. In addition we shall describe the currency component of our money stock in some detail.

WEALTH AND CLAIMS TO WEALTH

Individual Wealth

The wealth of an individual consists of the total value of his physical goods (*real wealth*) and the total amount of his claims to real wealth (*liquid wealth*). When held in the form of money, wealth represents generalized purchasing power — the ability to buy goods and services today and in the future. Money is only one of the forms in which an individual may choose to hold his liquid wealth. Among the alternatives to money are such claims to wealth as certificates of deposit and savings accounts in commercial banks, savings deposits in mutual banks, savings and loan share accounts, the stocks and bonds of private businesses and governments, and the cash value of life insurance policies.

What determines the distribution of an individual's wealth-holding among the various forms of liquid wealth? The question is a difficult one. The alternatives chosen depend on individual tastes and preferences, the rate of interest, expectations concerning future prices of goods versus liquid assets, or simply the amount of these items that one already has. For example, a decline in interest rates may well induce people to hold more money and stocks relative to bonds, other things being equal. If prices are expected to rise, it should be advantageous to reduce one's money holdings and bonds in order to acquire goods that will shortly cost considerably more. If an individual's money holdings have increased relative to other forms of wealth, then he may feel able to purchase additional goods and services. Later chapters will provide a more detailed analysis of the fluctuations in the demand for various forms of wealth.

The Wealth of a Nation

The wealth of a nation is not computed in the same way as the wealth of an individual. On the national level, one cannot arrive at a total by adding up the amount of real and liquid wealth in the economy. To do so would be double counting, since *liquid wealth* represents only a *claim to physical goods*. The individual can add to his total real wealth by converting his liquid wealth into physical goods, but this is impossible for the economy as a whole. Were everyone to convert his claims to wealth into real goods, there would still be no more real goods than existed before the conversion, since there is only one stock of physical goods. The ultimate amount of real wealth in an economy depends not upon claims to wealth but upon productive resources and technology.

Nor does the aggregate amount of liquid wealth in the country equal the aggregate amount of real wealth. Liquid and real wealth are not created in the same way. As already indicated, real wealth is created in the productive process. Liquid wealth, on the other hand, is created when individuals or institutions such as businesses and governments issue and sell obligations. The funds received from the sale of these obligations may be used to help in the creation of real wealth through production, to purchase existent real goods, to purchase other forms of liquid wealth, or they may simply be held idle.

THE LIQUID WEALTH SYSTEM OF THE UNITED STATES

The liquid wealth forms of a nation may be classified according to degrees of *liquidity*, by which we mean the relative ability of a liquid asset to be converted into money rapidly and without loss. Liquid assets that may be converted into money very rapidly and with little or no loss are known as *near monies*. Assets other than those that are near monies are not as reliable a source of funds. For example, an asset such as common stock, whose price can fluctuate widely, cannot be expected to provide a fixed number of dollars in the future.

This does not mean that other forms of liquid wealth are unimportant. Actually there are many markets for financial instruments such as treasury bills, commercial paper, bankers' acceptances, etc. Some discussion of these markets will be found in subsequent chapters. First it is important to understand the relationship between money and near monies. As will be explained more fully in Chapters 7 and 26, many economists believe that the creation of close money substitutes significantly weakens the effectiveness of monetary policy. Table 2–1 lists the forms of liquid wealth that possess a high degree of liquidity.

Money as a Form of Wealth

The most liquid asset is, of course, money itself, since it can be used immediately without loss to purchase goods and services. Our total *money stock* consists of all currency and commercial bank demand deposits not owned by the Treasury, the Federal Reserve banks, or commercial banks. It is owned and held by private individuals, businesses, state and local governments, and nonbank financial institutions such as savings and loan associations, mutual savings banks, foreign banks, and insurance companies. This listing of those who own money is sometimes called "the nonbank public," sometimes simply "the public."

Table 2–1 shows that the currency holdings of the nonbank public dur-

TABLE 2-1 MONEY AND NEAR-MONEY HOLDINGS OF THE NONBANK PUBLIC
MARCH 1973
(IN BILLIONS OF DOLLARS)

FORM OF LIQUID WEALTH	AMOUNT	
Currency	57.3	
Demand deposits*	196.7	
Total money stock		254.0
Time deposits in commercial banks	331.4	
Time deposits in mutual savings banks	93.5	
Savings and loan shares	214.3	
Total time deposits and savings and loan shares		639.2
Savings bonds held by individuals	58.5	
Marketable and convertible U.S. government securities	128.3	
Total U.S. government securities		186.8
Cash value of life insurance		193.0
Total money and near-money holdings of the nonbank public		1,273.0

* Other than domestic interbank deposits and U.S. government, less cash items in process of collection and F. R. float.
SOURCE: Computed from *Federal Reserve Bulletin* (June 1973), pp. A-16, 37, 38, 42, 43.

ing March 1973 were $57.3 billion, whereas the total holdings of demand deposits amounted to $196.7 billion. Demand-deposit money is thus clearly the more important component of our money stock. The phrase *commercial bank demand deposits* does not mean that the banking system owns these deposits; rather, it means that the deposits are *liabilities* of the banking system. This type of money is owned by the nonbank public and owed to them by the commercial banks. Furthermore, as we shall discuss in greater detail in later chapters, the deposits do not exist physically; they are bookkeeping claims of the nonbank public on the banking system.

Demand-deposit claims on the banking system may be transferred from one part of the nonbank public to another by the use of checks. This happens whenever a debt is paid off or when goods and services are purchased with checks. In addition, people often demand currency from the banks in exchange for their demand deposits. How can the banks meet these demands when the amount of currency available in the economic system amounts to only a fraction of total demand-deposit liabilities? Fortunately, the number of demands for currency at any one time is generally offset by the number of deposits. If this were not the case, a cash drain from the banking system might occur, causing economic distress. However, it is very unlikely that people in our economy will ever again sustain significant losses on their demand-deposit holdings. The existence of deposit insurance almost precludes bank panics that occur when too many people attempt to convert their deposits (either demand or time deposits) into currency at the same time. Deposits are insured up to a limit of $20,000 by the Federal Deposit Insurance Corporation. Only $1.5 billion of the demand-deposit liabilities of the commercial banks are not insured by the FDIC.[1]

Time Deposits as a Form of Wealth

Time deposits of various sorts are another part of the nonbank public's total wealth. Savings and loan share accounts and time deposits in commercial and mutual savings banks constitute almost 50 percent of our total money and near-money holdings. Most of these forms of time deposits are also insured by some agency of the federal government. For example, mutual savings bank time deposits are insured by the FDIC, and the Federal Savings and Loan Insurance Corporation insures the share accounts of most savings and loan associations.

How do time deposits differ from demand deposits? Why cannot the former be included in the money stock? There is usually no possibility of loss on time deposits, and they can be used quickly to make payments. There are, however, a number of important differences between time and checking deposits that should be noted.

[1] *Federal Reserve Bulletin* (June 1973), p. A-21.

First, time deposits need not be paid on demand. The debtor institutions can legally require the holder of a time deposit to give 30 days notice of a withdrawal, provided that the time deposit is in the form of a savings account.[2] For all practical purposes, however, this is not an important distinguishing feature of savings accounts because most financial institutions do redeem these accounts on demand. Competitive conditions are such that a required 30-day waiting period could be enforced only if all debtor institutions followed this practice.

Second, interest is paid on time deposits. The law does not permit the payment of interest on checking accounts.

Third, and most important, time-deposit accounts must first be converted into either currency or checking deposits before they can be used as money. They cannot be used directly to purchase goods or services.

There are also a number of differences in form between the various kinds of time deposits that will affect the volume of money and total liquid wealth differently when the deposits are converted into money. For example, when a savings and loan share account is converted into money there will be no change in the money holdings of the nonbank public, but there will be a reduction in the total volume of liquid wealth. Assume that you have a $1,000 savings account with a savings and loan association. Your ownership of the account means that you have a claim on the assets of the association. Hence your ownership claim is equal in value to a certain percentage of what the association owns. What will happen if you decide to convert that claim into money? The savings and loan association will either give you currency or write a check on its checking account at a commercial bank. There will thus be a transfer of money holdings from one part of the nonbank public (the savings and loan association) to another part (you). The total volume of money in the economy remains the same. On the other hand, your claim to the assets of the association will have been reduced. You no longer have a share account. As a result the total liquid wealth of the economy will have been reduced. This transaction may be formulated in terms of the entire economy as follows: money + savings and loan shares + other forms of liquid wealth = total liquid wealth.[3] When savings and loan shares are converted into money, the total amount of money remains the same, but total savings and loan shares decrease. Therefore, total liquid wealth decreases.

When holders of mutual savings bank time deposits decide to convert their deposits into money, the effects are exactly the same as when savings

[2] The 30-day requirement applies to time deposits that are savings and loan share accounts, mutual savings bank time-deposit accounts, and commercial bank time deposits that are in the form of savings accounts. Most people maintain savings accounts at commercial banks, but some hold other forms of time deposits that have variable maturities. Corporations are prohibited by law from owning savings accounts, but they do own significant numbers of other types of time deposits at commercial banks. A more detailed discussion of the various forms of time deposits will be found in Chapters 5 and 7.

[3] See Table 2–1 for a list of near monies.

and loan shares are converted, since mutual savings banks are part of the nonbank public. The effects are entirely different, however, when the holder of a time deposit with a commercial bank demands money in place of his time deposit. For example, assume a depositor wishes to transfer his $1,000 account from an interest-earning savings account to a demand deposit. The commercial bank simply creates a new checking-deposit account for him in that amount. It switches his savings account to demand deposits. The amount of money in the economy has therefore increased by $1,000, since time deposits are not considered money. Total liquid wealth remains the same, however, and no member of the nonbank public has lost purchasing power. The results are the same if the depositor wants currency. The bank gives up an asset, vault cash, in return for a reduction in time-deposit liabilities. It should be noted that currency held by the commercial banking system as vault cash is neither money nor part of the liquid-wealth system of the nonbank public. Vault cash is not owned by the nonbank public and hence cannot be used to purchase goods and services until distributed to the public by banks.

The T-Account as a Tool of Analysis

The T-account can be effectively used to illustrate the examples discussed in the preceding section. The T-account shows the change in a balance sheet that occurs as a result of a transaction. Briefly, the balance sheet is a means of showing, at a moment in time, the balance between what one owns (*assets*) and what one owes (*liabilities plus capital accounts*). These are always equal. On the asset side of the balance sheet are such items as cash assets, security holdings, and furniture. Liabilities would include demand deposits, time deposits, borrowings, and securities issued, such as bonds. Examples of capital accounts are the book value of common stock issued by a corporation to its owners and earned surplus. (A more complete discussion of the nature of the balance sheet will be found in Chapter 5.) These simple rules will help you correctly analyze the elementary T-accounts and balance sheets that will follow:

1. Assets must always equal liabilities plus capital accounts.
2. If assets increase or decrease in their total size, then there must be a corresponding increase or decrease in the sum of liabilities plus capital accounts.
3. If there is an increase or decrease in the total liabilities and capital accounts, there must be a corresponding increase or decrease in the total size of assets.
4. An increase in one type of asset item means a decrease in some other asset or an increase in a liability and capital-account item.
5. A decrease in an asset means an increase in the value of some other asset or a decrease in a liability and capital account.

6. An increase in a liability or capital account means a decrease in some other liability or capital account or an increase in an asset.

7. A decrease in a liability or capital account means an increase in some other liability or capital account or a decrease in an asset.

For example, take the case in which the depositor in a commercial bank wanted to convert his $1,000 time deposit into a demand deposit:

BALANCE-SHEET CHANGES FOR DEPOSITOR

ASSETS		LIABILITIES + CAPITAL ACCOUNTS	
Demand deposits	+$1,000		
Time deposits	−$1,000		

BALANCE-SHEET CHANGES FOR COMMERCIAL BANK A

ASSETS		LIABILITIES + CAPITAL ACCOUNTS	
		Demand deposits	+$1,000
		Time deposits	−$1,000

Here we see that the depositor has changed the nature of his assets — an increase in one type of asset has meant a decrease in another. The bank, on the other hand, has experienced a decrease in one type of its liability and an increase in another type.

The analysis becomes somewhat more complicated in the case of a depositor in a savings and loan association who wants to convert his savings and loan shares into a demand-deposit account:

BALANCE-SHEET CHANGES FOR DEPOSITOR

ASSETS		LIABILITIES + CAPITAL ACCOUNTS	
Savings capital	−$1,000		
Demand deposits	+$1,000		

BALANCE-SHEET CHANGES FOR THE COMMERCIAL BANKING SYSTEM

ASSETS		LIABILITIES + CAPITAL ACCOUNTS	
		Demand deposits (of savings and loan association)	−$1,000
		Demand deposits (of depositor)	+$1,000

BALANCE-SHEET CHANGES FOR THE SAVINGS AND LOAN ASSOCIATION

ASSETS		LIABILITIES + CAPITAL ACCOUNTS	
Demand deposits	−$1,000	Savings capital	−$1,000

Here we see that there has been no change in the stock of money, but that total liquid wealth has decreased by $1,000 due to the reduced amount of savings capital. The commercial banking system, which formerly owed money to the savings and loan association, now owes it to the private individual depositor.

U.S. Government Securities as a Form of Wealth

Quantitatively, United States government securities are some three-fourths as important a form of liquid wealth as money itself. In March of 1973, government securities held by the nonbank public totaled $186.8 billion, whereas the stock of money was $254.0 billion.

Government securities are basically of two types: nonmarketable and marketable.

Nonmarketable securities cannot be transferred from one owner to another. To get back one's financial investment, the securities must be returned to the original issuer. Savings bonds are the principal type of nonmarketable securities held by individuals. They presently yield 5.5 percent interest at maturity. Thus, if a $25 bond were purchased for $18.75, in five years and ten months it could be redeemed for $25, or the purchase price plus the accumulated interest. There is no possibility of loss on these securities, except that which may occur in purchasing power if the price level in the economy increases sharply. However, these securities are redeemable upon demand only after they have been held by the purchaser for more than 60 days. Thus, during the initial period of ownership, they are not as liquid as other forms of near money.

Marketable securities, on the other hand, are transferable. The market for them is composed of the nonbank public, commercial banks, and various agencies of the federal government itself. For example, the Federal Reserve banks alone owned some $74.3 billion of these securities in March 1973.[4]

The market price for U.S. government securities is ultimately determined by the market forces of supply and demand. If the securities are held until maturity—that is, until the time when the United States Treasury is obligated to redeem them—there is no possibility of loss. Normally they are not redeemable before maturity, however. If one chooses to regain one's financial investment prior to the redemption date, they must be sold on the open market for what they will bring. Thus there may be a gain or a loss. Short-term securities that can be redeemed within one year are usually not subject to wide fluctuations in value. Longer-term securities, however, may appreciate or depreciate in value significantly, depending upon market conditions. United States government securities yielding 3 percent and due in 1995 were selling at $748 in April of 1973 for example.[5] This means that a $1,000 security of this type, if purchased when first issued for about $1,000, could be sold on the open market for only $748,

[4] *Federal Reserve Bulletin* (May 1973), p. A-12.
[5] *Wall Street Journal* (April 5, 1973), p. 25.

which is a substantial loss. For this reason, marketable public securities are not usually considered to be good near monies: one can be certain of not incurring a loss only if they are held to maturity. On the other hand, they are immediately marketable and thus highly liquid. The funds obtained from the sale of securities may be used immediately to pay off debt or to purchase goods and services.

When nonmarketable U.S. government securities are converted into money, the stock of money increases without changing the total of liquid wealth. The Treasury redeems these securities by drawing on its own deposit balances (which are not part of the money stock). This leads to an increase in the deposit balances of the nonbank public. If the Treasury redeems marketable securities at maturity, the results are the same. Results will vary, however, when marketable securities are bought and sold on the open market. For example, assume that one individual buys a security from another for $900:

BALANCE-SHEET CHANGES FOR INDIVIDUAL 1

ASSETS		LIABILITIES + CAPITAL ACCOUNTS
Demand deposits	−$900	
U.S. securities	+$900	

BALANCE-SHEET CHANGES FOR INDIVIDUAL 2

ASSETS		LIABILITIES + CAPITAL ACCOUNTS
Demand deposits	+$900	
U.S. securities	−$900	

BALANCE-SHEET CHANGES FOR THE COMMERCIAL BANKING SYSTEM

ASSETS	LIABILITIES + CAPITAL ACCOUNTS	
	Demand deposits (of Individual 1)	−$900
	Demand deposits (of Individual 2)	+$900

Individual 1, who purchases the security, does so by writing a $900 check on his checking account. Individual 2 receives the check, deposits it in his checking account, and turns the security over to the new owner, Individual 1. The whole transaction takes place within the nonbank public. Thus there is no change in total money holdings or in total liquid wealth of the nonbank public. There is merely a redistribution. Nor is there a change in the total liabilities of the commercial banking system.

The results are different when the banking system purchases the security. Assume that the security is sold by Individual 1 to the banking system for $900:

BALANCE-SHEET CHANGES FOR INDIVIDUAL 1

ASSETS		LIABILITIES + CAPITAL ACCOUNTS
U.S. securities	−$900	
Demand deposits	+$900	

BALANCE-SHEET CHANGES FOR THE COMMERCIAL BANKING SYSTEM

ASSETS		LIABILITIES + CAPITAL ACCOUNTS	
U.S. securities	+$900	Demand deposits (of Individual 1)	+$900

The banking system creates a demand deposit for the seller of the security, thus increasing the total money holdings of the nonbank public. Total liquid wealth remains unchanged, however, since the U.S. security component of the nonbank public's assets decreases by the same amount that deposits increase.

We have included U.S. government securities among the principal forms of the nonbank public's liquid-wealth holdings. Why not include privately issued stocks and bonds also? For several reasons. First, privately issued securities exhibit considerable variation in price depending upon (1) the financial condition of the firm issuing the securities and (2) the business prospects for the economy and the industry in general. If the firm has had stable earnings, the chances are good that its securities will sell well. But a brief setback in earnings or a decline in the demand for the products of the firm can initiate a wave of security sales, driving bond and stock prices down and causing security holders to suffer extensive capital losses. Thus, the liquidity of these securities — their ability to be converted into money quickly and without loss — is seriously hampered. Marketability is uncertain. Similarly, even with adequate earnings and good prospects, a firm may have difficulty marketing its securities if it is small or if its success depends on a few key individuals. The securities of larger, better-established firms will frequently command a higher price than those of smaller, younger corporations.

The prevailing rate of interest is another factor that influences the price of both public and private securities. If prevailing interest rates are higher than rates in the past, then previously issued securities must be sold by their holders at a lower price. There is an inverse relationship between interest rates and bond prices.[6] This factor also tends to reduce the liquidity of private and public securities.

Finally, private securities have less secure backing than federal securities. The U.S. government stands behind its securities, but only the issuing corporations guarantee private stocks and bonds. No one doubts the permanence of the government or its ability to redeem securities. Few enterprises exhibit such permanence or inspire such confidence.

---

[6] This will be examined in more detail in Chapter 20.

Life Insurance as a Form of Liquid Wealth

The cash value of life insurance is another type of near money. As long as the insurance company remains in business, the policyholder can, within a matter of days, either acquire the cash surrender value of his policy or borrow on the basis of that value. Since life insurance companies are classified as part of the nonbank public, there is no change in the stock of money when policyholders choose to convert their life insurance into money. There is, however, a decrease in total liquid wealth. The policyholder also suffers a small loss by converting to cash. He loses insurance protection and the excess of premium payments over the cash value of the policy.

Summary

So far in Chapter 2 we have (1) classified the liquid-wealth system of the United States by degrees of liquidity and (2) developed the T-account as a tool of analysis. Insured time deposits, savings and loan shares, and U.S. savings bonds are the safest and most liquid near monies available. There is virtually no possiblity of loss and they may be quickly converted into cash. Life insurance policies and marketable U.S. government securities, while usually safe and quickly convertible, are less safe as near monies because of possible losses. Table 2–2 summarizes the effects that the conversion of near monies has upon the stock of money and total liquid wealth. In a later chapter we will consider the importance of these liquid-wealth holdings for aggregate economic activity.

CURRENCY IN THE UNITED STATES

The American unit of account is the dollar, which is divisible into 100 cents. Coins are made in convenient divisibles of 100: 1, 5, 10, 25, 50, and 100 cents. Similarly, paper comes in convenient 1, 5, 10, 20, 50, and 100

TABLE 2–2 PROBABLE EFFECTS ON THE STOCK OF MONEY AND TOTAL LIQUID WEALTH FOLLOWING CONVERSION OF NEAR MONIES INTO MONEY

FORM OF NEAR MONEY CONVERTED	DIRECTION OF CHANGE OF STOCK OF MONEY	DIRECTION OF CHANGE OF TOTAL LIQUID WEALTH
Time deposits in commercial banks	+	0
Time deposits in mutual savings banks	0	−
Savings and loan shares	0	−
Savings bonds	+	0
Marketable U.S. government securities	+*	0*
	0†	0†
Cash value of life insurance	0	−

* If redeemed by the U.S. government or purchased by the banking system.
† If purchased by other members of the nonbank public.

dollar denominations. In 1969, the Federal Reserve discontinued the issuance of 500, 1,000, 5,000, and 10,000 dollar denomination notes due to a decline in their use. All this currency must, by law, be accepted by creditors in payment of debt. It is, in other words, *legal tender*. The other component of our money stock, demand deposits, is *not* legal tender; it is only a generally accepted substitute for it. Issuing currency and defining the unit of account are the prerogatives of the federal government.

The Federal Reserve Note

Table 2–3 shows the present composition of currency in the United States. Clearly the most important type of currency is the Federal Reserve note, which is issued in denominations of $1 and up. These notes make up almost 90 percent of the total currency in circulation. They are liabilities of the Federal Reserve banks that issue them.

The backing of Federal Reserve notes consists of gold certificates, U.S. government securities and other assets held by the Federal Reserve banks, almost all the collateral being in the form of U.S. government securities. This does not mean, however, that you can convert your Federal Reserve notes into any of these assets merely by presenting them at any Federal Reserve bank. Currency is redeemed by the Federal Reserve banks with currency. What is it, then, that makes Federal Reserve notes "good"? Three things: (1) they are legal tender, (2) the public has faith in them, and (3) the Federal Reserve banks issue and retire currency only in response to the demands of the public.

TABLE 2–3   UNITED STATES CURRENCY IN CIRCULATION,
FEBRUARY 28, 1973
(IN MILLIONS OF DOLLARS)

KIND OF CURRENCY*		AMOUNT
Coins		
Dollars	675	
Fractional coin	6,599	
Total amount of coins		7,274
Paper currency — Treasury		
United States notes	320	
In process of retirement	290	
Total amount of Treasury paper currency		610
Paper currency — Federal Reserve		
Federal Reserve notes		56,428
Total currency in circulation		64,312
Currency in commercial bank vaults		− 8,388
Currency in circulation outside commercial bank vaults		55,924

* Includes all currency outside the Treasury and Federal Reserve banks.
SOURCE: *Federal Reserve Bulletin* (March 1973), pp. A-16 and A-17.

Assume, for example, that the public demand for currency in the form of Federal Reserve notes rises by $1 million. How may the public get this additional amount? By writing checks out to "cash" at commercial banks. This causes the banks to lose both a liability, demand deposits, and an asset, vault cash:

BALANCE-SHEET CHANGES FOR THE COMMERCIAL BANKING SYSTEM

ASSETS		LIABILITIES + CAPITAL ACCOUNTS	
Vault cash	−$1,000,000	Demand deposits	−$1,000,000

BALANCE-SHEET CHANGES FOR THE NONBANK PUBLIC

ASSETS		LIABILITIES + CAPITAL ACCOUNTS	
Demand deposits	−$1,000,000		
Currency	+$1,000,000		

Commercial banks now need to replenish their depleted currency holdings. Where do they get the currency? From the Federal Reserve banks. Commercial banks exchange their reserve accounts (checking deposits at the Federal Reserve banks owned by commercial banks and owed to them by the Federal Reserve banks) at the Federal Reserve banks for currency. The Federal Reserve banks then issue and turn over to the commercial banks the desired type of currency (in this case, Federal Reserve notes of various denominations). This transaction appears as follows:

BALANCE-SHEET CHANGES FOR THE COMMERCIAL BANKING SYSTEM

ASSETS		LIABILITIES + CAPITAL ACCOUNTS	
Reserves with Federal Reserve banks	−$1,000,000		
Vault cash	+$1,000,000		

BALANCE-SHEET CHANGES FOR THE FEDERAL RESERVE BANKS

ASSETS		LIABILITIES + CAPITAL ACCOUNTS	
		Member bank reserves	−$1,000,000
		Federal Reserve notes	+$1,000,000

When the public wants less currency than it has, this process is reversed. People exchange currency for increased deposits at the commercial banks. The commercial banks, with excess holdings of vault cash, return currency to the Federal Reserve banks, thus increasing commercial bank reserve accounts. The Federal Reserve banks then retire the currency that has been returned.

Treasury Currency

Together the Treasury and the Federal Reserve monopolize currency issue. There are two types of Treasury currency: coin and paper. Coin amounts to 11 percent of the total amount of currency in circulation. Treasury paper currency is now barely 1 percent of all currency. Coins are issued by the Treasury Department in response to the needs of the public for "change."

United States notes are the other type of Treasury currency. They were first issued during the Civil War, and the quantity available is limited. Some $320 million of these notes are presently in circulation; they now come only in $5 denominations. All other types of Treasury paper currency, including silver certificates, are being retired.

Treasury currency gets into circulation in much the same manner as Federal Reserve notes. When there is a need for currency, commercial banks may procure Treasury money from the Federal Reserve banks. There is this difference, however: since the Federal Reserve banks do not issue Treasury currency, they are giving up an asset, one that they previously purchased from the Treasury at face value.

The Nature of Our Currency System

This discussion points up an important characteristic of our currency system. In the United States, changes in the amount and composition of currency occur almost exclusively in response to the demands of the public. There are no accompanying changes in the money stock. When the amount of currency in the economy increases, there is a corresponding decrease in demand-deposit money. When the supply of currency decreases, demand-deposit money increases. This causes a constant redistribution of the components of the money stock, but not a change in the total stock itself. This is true whether the redistribution involves Treasury currency or Federal Reserve notes. *The United States government does not issue currency to defray its own expenses or to finance its own operations.*

In other words, the United States has a self-regulatory paper currency system. It is a "paper" system because currency is the money of ultimate redemption. Coin and paper-currency holdings of United States citizens are redeemable in coin and paper currency. It is a self-regulatory system because the money stock does not change when the currency total changes.

Data Sources

Board of Governors of the Federal Reserve System. *Federal Reserve Bulletin* (monthly).

_____. *Annual Reports.*
_____. *Banking and Monetary Statistics* (Washington, D.C., 1943).
_____. *All Bank Statistics United States 1896–1955* (Washington, D.C., 1959).
Comptroller of the Currency. *Annual Reports.*
Economic Report of the President (annual).
Federal Deposit Insurance Corporation. *Annual Reports.*
U.S. Department of Commerce. *Survey of Current Business* (monthly).

3 Finance, Commercial Banks, and the Economy

Economists frequently use income and employment statistics to measure the economic importance of a given industry. These statistics are thought to reveal the extent to which economic activities contribute to the national economy. As we shall see, this is *not* the way to assess the importance of the financial sector of the economy. Rather, one needs to examine the relationship of the financial sector to the flow of funds through the economy — to the saving-investment process.

This chapter first examines some income and employment statistics, and then presents flow-of-funds statistics so that the overall importance of the financial sector of the economy can be assessed more accurately. Some special characteristics of the commercial banking system — our most important financial subsector — are then discussed. Chapters 4, 5, and 6, respectively, study commercial bank structure, sources and uses of funds, and creation of money. Finally, in Chapter 7, other financial subsectors and financial markets are examined in some detail.

FINANCE IN THE ECONOMY

Table 3–1 shows the contributions of various industries to the national income and employment in 1971. Ranking these different sectors in order of their contributions, we have:

INCOME	EMPLOYMENT
Manufacturing	Manufacturing
Government	Government
Wholesale and retail trade	Wholesale and retail trade
Services	Services
Finance	Contract construction
Contract construction	Finance
Communications and public utilities	Transportation
Transportation	Communications and public utilities
Agriculture	Agriculture
Mining	Mining

The income and the employment statistics in Table 3–1 tell the same story: quantitatively the manufacturing, government, wholesale and retail

TABLE 3-1 UNITED STATES NATIONAL INCOME AND EMPLOYMENT BY INDUSTRY, 1971

	INCOME CONTRIBUTED BY EACH SECTOR		FULL-TIME EQUIVALENT EMPLOYEES	
	(IN MILLIONS OF DOLLARS)	(IN PERCENT)	(IN THOUSANDS)	(IN PERCENT)
Agriculture, forestry, and fisheries	26,508	3.1	1,363	1.9
Mining	7,642	0.9	617	0.9
Contract construction	46,509	5.4	3,532	5.0
Manufacturing	223,167	26.1	18,574	26.1
Wholesale and retail trade	130,780	15.3	13.135	18.5
Finance, insurance, and real estate	98,717	11.5	3,454	4.9
Transportation	32,510	3.8	2,381	3.4
Communications and public utilities	34,498	4.0	1,815	2.6
Services	110,589	12.9	11,882	16.7
Government and government enterprise	137,885	16.1	14,386	20.2
Other	6,943	0.8	4	.0
All industries (total)	855,748	99.9*	71,143	100.2*

* Totals may differ due to rounding.
SOURCE: Office of Business Economics, U.S. Department of Commerce. *Survey of Current Business* (July 1972), pp. 20 and 40.

trade, and service sectors of the economy are by far the most significant contributors to income and employment, with the financial sector ranking about midway. In 1971, the financial sector was the source of only 11.5 percent of income and 4.9 percent of employment.

Why, then, is the financial sector of the economy thought to be so important? The answer is simple: *it is our most important creator of liquid assets and it is also the principal lender in U.S. credit markets.* As Table 2–1 showed, the financial institutions most influential in creating liquid assets were commercial banks, savings institutions, and insurance companies. A further indication of the importance of financial institutions is shown in Table 3–2, which presents data on the total funds advanced to borrowers in 1970 and 1971. Here we see that commercial banks, savings institutions, and insurance companies advanced $103.4 billion in 1971. All funds advanced directly in credit markets to the nonfinancial sectors in 1971 were $142.9 billion. Clearly, the quantitative impact of financial institutions on economic activity is tremendous.

Financial institutions act as financial intermediaries: they collect funds from savers and lend them to borrowers. As households and businesses receive income, they frequently save more than they spend. The funds that are saved may be held idle in the form of noninterest earning money, or they may be lent to others in the economy. The provision of funds by households and businesses may be *direct*, as in the case of an individual

TABLE 3-2 FUNDS RAISED AND ADVANCED IN U.S. CREDIT MARKETS, 1970 AND 1971

(IN BILLIONS OF DOLLARS)	1970	1971
Total funds raised by nonfinancial sectors	101.6	156.3
U.S. government	12.8	25.5
Foreign	3.0	5.6
State and local government	13.9	20.6
Households	22.3	41.6
Corporate business	39.8	48.6
Nonfarm, noncorporate business	6.4	10.3
Farm	3.2	4.1
Total funds advanced in credit markets to nonfinancial sectors	94.7*	142.9*
Advanced by:		
U.S. government	2.8	3.2
U.S. government-sponsored credit agencies	9.9	2.8
Federal Reserve	5.0	8.8
Foreign	10.3	26.4
Commercial banking	31.6	49.8
Savings institutions	16.6	41.6
Insurance and pension funds	17.6	12.0
Other finance	4.5	2.3
Private, domestic, nonfinancial investors: direct lending	7.0	4.2

* This total is less than the items listed below since some funds advanced to financial sectors are included in the detailed breakdown.
SOURCE: *Federal Reserve Bulletin* (June 1973), pp. A-70, 71.

purchasing a newly issued stock or bond, or it may be *indirect*. When it is indirect, what frequently occurs is that the saver (be it a business or an individual) purchases a liquid asset from a financial institution. A savings account may be set up for an individual at a commercial bank or a savings and loan association, for example, or a certificate of deposit may be purchased at a commercial bank, and so forth. In any event, the financial institution acquires funds that must be put to use, since interest must be paid on the outstanding savings accounts and certificates. The financial institution thus lends to those who are seeking funds. They lend to home builders, corporations seeking funds for construction purposes, householders who want to borrow to make consumer-durable purchases, etc.

Imagine how complex the lending of funds would be if there were no financial intermediaries. Those with idle funds and those with a need to borrow would have to seek each other out. Just as in the case of the barter economy discussed in Chapter 1, a double coincidence of wants would have to be established—not in goods, but in money instead. Financial intermediaries help to eliminate these complexities. By collecting funds from thousands of savers, they are able to lend to both small and large demanders of funds.

The lending decisions of the various financial intermediaries help to determine the growth path of the economy. Although decisions regarding the direction and timing of future expenditures are initially dictated by business and consumer desires, financial institutions, acting as sources of funds, often indirectly shape those decisions. Whether they make loans to business and consumers or extend real-estate credit, financial institutions help to determine the uses to which much of our money will be put. By making one form of loan or security purchase and not another, they influence the nature of expenditures. As money on loan is spent by borrowers, the demand for certain goods and services is increased. This in turn may stimulate investment in plant and equipment in the industries most affected by the increased demand. The economy's overall level of prosperity, its rate of growth, the level of employment, the rate of inflation, and the composition of the nation's output are all heavily influenced by the financial sector and the rate at which it finances various activities. Unlike other industrial sectors, therefore, the financial sector cannot be accurately evaluated in terms of its contributions to income and employment; it must be judged in terms of its functions.

THE COMMERCIAL BANKING SYSTEM

Distinguishing Characteristics

Like other financial institutions, commercial banks make loans and investments, take deposits, act as securities underwriters and brokers, provide safety-deposit facilities, and administer estates. Unlike other financial institutions, however, they also *create and destroy money* and *allow their creditors to transfer claims to money through the use of checks.* No other financial institution is presently able to do this.

When a bank makes a loan, it gives the borrower either a deposit or cash. Most people and businesses prefer deposits to cash because they are more convenient. A deposit is money created by the bank. For example, if someone borrows $500 from Bank A to finance emergency medical payments, the T-account entries will look like this:

BALANCE-SHEET CHANGES FOR COMMERCIAL BANK A

ASSETS		LIABILITIES + CAPITAL ACCOUNTS	
Loans to individuals	+$500	Demand deposits	+$500

Thus, in making a loan, the commercial bank has created money. *As long as the total loan volume is increased,* the stock of money *is increased.* Given stable prices, the ability of the public to purchase goods and services will thus be enhanced.

Similarly, when a borrower repays a loan, he does so with cash or by check. The majority of loan repayments are negotiated by check. On repayment, Bank A's balance sheet will show:

BALANCE-SHEET CHANGES FOR COMMERCIAL BANK A

ASSETS		LIABILITIES + CAPITAL ACCOUNTS	
Loans to individuals	−$500	Demand deposits	−$500

Here money has been destroyed.[1]

What is the difference when a borrower obtains a loan from a consumer finance company rather than from a bank? Assume that the finance company gives the borrower a check. This check is not money created by the finance company; it is simply a check written on its account at a commercial bank.[2] The balance-sheet changes that take place are:

BALANCE-SHEET CHANGES FOR CONSUMER FINANCE COMPANY

ASSETS		LIABILITIES + CAPITAL ACCOUNTS	
Demand deposits	−$500		
Loans	+$500		

BALANCE-SHEET CHANGES FOR THE COMMERCIAL BANKING SYSTEM

ASSETS	LIABILITIES + CAPITAL ACCOUNTS	
	Demand deposits (of consumer finance company)	−$500
	Demand deposits (of individual borrower)	+$500

The individual borrower deposits the check in his own account at the bank with which he does business. Subsequently, he writes out checks on his increased demand-deposit account. Thus, there has been only a transfer of deposits from one part of the nonbank public to another. Likewise, when the loan is repaid, there is no corresponding reduction of the money supply.

Other financial institutions are in a position similar to that of the consumer finance company. When they make loans and investments they are merely transferring their money holdings. Only commercial banks can create and destroy money because only they are permitted to allow creditors to transfer claims through the use of checks. In addition, only commercial banks among financial institutions have liabilities legally payable on demand.

---

[1] We are assuming for simplicity that the bank collected interest on the loan in advance. Also, note that the effects of these transactions on the stock of money would be the same if people took cash instead of deposits. Vault cash is not part of the money stock; hence if it is given to a borrower by the bank, the money holdings of the nonbank public increase. Chapter 6 examines the mechanics of the creation and destruction of money in more detail.

[2] It is assumed here that the finance company has adequate funds to engage in lending and therefore need not borrow from the banking system.

Special Responsibility of the Commercial Banking System

The commercial banking system shares one very important characteristic with other members of the financial sector and the rest of the business community — the desire to maximize profits and to expand its share of the market. Commercial banks are profit-seeking enterprises. As such, they share with other businesses the same set of expectations concerning the "health" of the economy. When the consensus among businessmen is that the future will be prosperous, businesses generally expand their operations. When the economy is expected to take a turn for the worse, businesses usually limit their plans for expansion, hire fewer new workers, and may even contract their work force. Commercial banks follow suit. They tend to expand their loans during periods of economic upturn and contract loans (or at least contract the growth rate of loans) during an economic downturn. In the absence of compensating actions by government, this expansion and contraction of loans results in a parallel expansion and contraction of the deposit part of our money stock.

This in turn means that, in periods of economic upturn, commercial banks add to the money stock and thereby help to expand the demand for goods and services. However, once the economy arrives at full employment of men and resources, a continued expansion of loans and deposits simply adds to price-level increases. When full employment is reached, it is difficult to increase real production, except by increasing the utilization of men and equipment through a longer work week, adding a number of retired people, women, and students to the work force, or bringing obsolete machinery back into production.

On the other hand, if banks contract loans in periods of mild economic decline, experience shows that we are not likely to have a drop in the price level. Prices in the United States seem to have some downward "stickiness." As a consequence, the reduced amount of deposits accompanying the reduction in loans usually tends to aggravate the downturn in demand and output.

In short, banks share the general business outlook on economic conditions. *Commercial banks, in the absence of regulation, tend to intensify whatever phase of the business cycle is current. They do this through their unique ability to create and destroy money when making loans and investments.*

The real bills doctrine. An individual banker may counter the preceding analysis by arguing that all he really does is respond to the loan demands of the public, that he supplies credit and money according to the needs of trade. His standards with respect to granting loans do not change. Rather, when people want more funds in periods of upturn, he supplies them. In periods of decline, fewer loans are made because fewer loans are requested. Furthermore, he contends, this is a safe loan policy. On business loans, for example, the borrower uses the funds to purchase productive resources. Shortly after the loan is made, the business borrower will have produced the goods that are to be sold. The proceeds from the sale of the goods can then be used to repay the loan. This line of reasoning is sometimes called the *commercial loan theory of banking* or the *real bills doctrine*.

There are two loopholes in this line of reasoning. First, though it may be neither intentional nor conscious, such a procedure usually involves disproportionate stringency during periods of declining business activity. What may appear to be a sound loan on the upward side of the business cycle may not appear safe on the downward side. In periods of economic decline, banks examine their loan applications more carefully, in addition to reducing the amount of loans in response to the increased reluctance of businesses and individuals to borrow. This places additional downward pressure on loans, when what is needed in a period of decline may well be added demand, further expansion of loans, and an increase in the money stock.

Second, although many loans are granted on the basis of future production, no increase in production may occur if the economy is in a period of full employment. During upswings demand may outrun production. The future production on which banks base their loans may never materialize because resources are already being used to the fullest extent possible. All that a business can do is use its borrowed funds to bid resources away from other enterprises. Thus, a shift in the type but not in the total amount of production takes place. In addition, prices of resources, and hence of final goods and services, are bid up. If a business wants to renew its loan in the future to facilitate production, it will have to borrow an amount larger than the initial loan to meet increased costs. A vicious circle of increased borrowing and rising prices may easily ensue.

Bank responsibilities and federal regulation. This analysis suggests that normal commercial bank loan operations can perversely affect the economy at both ends of the cycle, either worsening recession or feeding inflation. Yet commercial banks are given the right to create demand deposits, which constitute the major part of our money supply. Almost 80 percent of our money is in this form, and about 90 percent of all transactions in the economy are check transactions. For this reason, banks have a responsibility that transcends that of other business enterprises. They are responsible for the creation, destruction, and administration of our money. As a consequence, they are also responsible to a great extent for the welfare of the economy.

This dual responsibility—to itself as a business enterprise and to the nation—puts a tremendous burden on the individual commercial bank. If it acts in the national interest, it may hurt its competitive position. If its lending policy is conservative during periods of prosperity and full employment, it reduces its potential profits since borrowers will seek funds from competing banks and savings institutions. If its lending policy is liberal during periods of recession, unpaid loans may weaken its financial soundness. On the other hand, if it acts purely on the basis of self-interest, it may worsen the national economic picture.

Because of the contradictory nature of this dual responsibility, the government exercises considerable control over the commercial banking system. As we shall see later, various governmental regulatory agencies, such as the Federal Reserve, the Federal Deposit Insurance Corporation, the Comptroller of the Currency, and comparable state agencies are all engaged in the business of regulating commercial banks. Some supervisory agencies are concerned solely with banks as businesses, seeing to it that they operate in the interest of their stockholders. Others, such as the Federal Reserve, are concerned with maintaining employment levels, stimulating economic growth, and holding the price line. These latter agencies regulate commercial banks and their money-creating activities with an eye to the national interest.[3] This permits the banks to act in their own interest without too much concern for the national welfare. The ultimate responsibility for the safety of the money stock and aggregate economic activity rests with the federal government.

---

[3] As previously indicated, other financial institutions also affect the national economy. Because of this, some economists argue that these institutions should also be subject to extensive regulation. This point is discussed further in Chapters 7 and 26.

4 The Structure of the Commercial Banking System

TYPES OF BANKS

TYPES OF BANKING

MEMBER AND NONMEMBER BANKS

MEMBER BANK REQUIREMENTS AND PRIVILEGES

The Capital Requirement
The Par Collection Requirement
Other Member Bank Obligations and Privileges
Advantages of Nonmember Bank Status

NATIONAL AND STATE BANKS

National Bank Charter Requirements

INSURED AND NONINSURED BANKS

THE AMERICAN BANKING SYSTEM: TYPES OF OPERATION

Unit and Branch Banking
Arguments for and against Branch Banking
Chain Banking
Group Banking
   The one-bank holding company
Correspondent Banking
Conclusion

The commercial banking system of the United States is composed of more than 13,800 banks. Listed below are the types of banks and the types of banking with which we will be concerned in this chapter. Having defined our terms, we will then proceed to examine the structure of our banking system in some detail.

TYPES OF BANKS

Member bank. A bank that is a member of the Federal Reserve System. Member banks are classified by the system as Reserve city or country banks.

Nonmember bank. A bank that is not a member of the Federal Reserve System.

National bank. A bank that holds a charter from the federal government. National banks must be members of the Federal Reserve System.

State bank. A bank that has a state charter. State banks may or may not be members of the Federal Reserve System.

Insured bank. A bank whose deposits are insured by the Federal Deposit Insurance Corporation. All member banks must be so insured.

Noninsured bank. A bank whose deposits are not insured by the Federal Deposit Insurance Corporation.

TYPES OF BANKING

Unit banking. The operation of only one banking office by a commercial bank.

Branch banking. The operation of two or more banking offices by a commercial bank.

Chain banking. The association of a number of commercial banks through an interlocking directorate.

Group banking. The control of two or more banks by a holding company with a controlling interest in the stock of the banks.

Correspondent banking. Commercial bank maintenance of checking-deposit accounts with another bank in return for such services as bond and security purchases and check clearance.

MEMBER AND NONMEMBER BANKS

Table 4–1 summarizes changes in commercial bank membership in the Federal Reserve System between December 1947 and June 1972. Of the 13,875 commercial banks in the United States and its possessions in 1972, only 5,714, or 41 percent, were member banks. These member banks accounted for 80 percent of demand deposits, however, and 76 percent of commercial bank time-deposit liabilities. Their average total deposit liabilities amounted to $69 million, whereas those of nonmember banks came to only $14 million. Clearly, member banks figure more importantly in the economy than nonmember banks.

Despite this quantitative importance of member banks, the trend in Federal Reserve membership has been downward for several decades. Member banks accounted for 49 percent of all banks and 85 percent of all bank demand deposits in 1947. Since 1947, the number of consolidations and mergers among existing members has been greater than the number of new members created. There has also been some tendency for small member banks to withdraw from the system and to operate as insured nonmember banks. In addition, most newly formed banks have been small nonmember banks. This gradually increasing significance of nonmember banks has led the Federal Reserve to request that Congress require nonmember banks to join the Federal Reserve System. As will be noted in Chapter 12, the Federal Reserve apparently fears that its control over the economy will be weakened should nonmember banks continue to grow, relative to member banks.

The total number of banks in the economy has also declined. The biggest drop in the twentieth century, of course, came when the large-scale bank failures of the depression thirties cut the number of banks almost in half.

TABLE 4–1 COMMERCIAL BANKS IN THE UNITED STATES AND POSSESSIONS, DECEMBER 31, 1947 AND JUNE 30, 1972

TYPE OF BANK	NUMBER 1947	NUMBER 1972	DEMAND DEPOSITS (IN MILLIONS OF DOLLARS)* 1947	1972	TIME DEPOSITS (IN MILLIONS OF DOLLARS)* 1947	1972
Member Banks						
National	5,005	4,606	53,541	128,454	19,278	170,586
State	1,918	1,108	27,068	43,965	9,062	53,331
Total member banks	6,923	5,714	80,609	172,419	28,340	223,917
Nonmember Banks						
Insured state	6,478	7,955	12,366	45,222	6,558	67,934
Noninsured state	783	206	1,392	1,409	478	1,258
Total nonmember banks	7,261	8,161	13,758	46,631	7,036	69,192
Total commercial banks	14,184	13,875	94,367	219,050	35,376	293,109

* Excluding U.S. government and interbank deposits.
SOURCE: *Federal Reserve Bulletin* (March 1973), pp. A-20–23.

TABLE 4–2 NUMBER OF COMMERCIAL BANK BRANCHES, ADDITIONAL OFFICES, AND FACILITIES, 1947–72*

YEAR	TOTAL	MEMBER			NONMEMBER		
		Total	*National*	*State*	*Total*	*Insured*	*Noninsured*
Dec. 31, 1947	4,161	3,051	1,870	1,181	1,110	1,043	67
Dec. 31, 1951	5,153	3,837	2,370	1,467	1,316	1,275	41
Dec. 31, 1956	7,589	5,886	3,809	2,077	1,703	1,666	37
Dec. 31, 1961	11,353	8,899	6,044	2,855	2,454	2,410	44
Dec. 31, 1966	16,908	13,129	9,611	3,518	3,779	3,717	62
Dec. 31, 1972	24,622	17,954	13,974	3,980	6,668	6,623	45

* Figures do not include the head office of the banks.
SOURCE: *Federal Reserve Bulletin* (March 1973), p. A-98.

Since the end of World War II, the number of banks has declined only slightly; all of the decrease occurred in the 1950s, principally through absorptions, consolidations, and mergers. The decrease in banks stopped in the early 1960s, possibly as a result of (1) some reduction in the regulatory barriers to bank formation and (2) relative prosperity and economic growth as well as low unemployment levels stimulating the formation of new banks.

Accompanying the halt in the decrease of banks in the 1960s was a sharp acceleration in the number of banking offices in the United States, with almost two-thirds of this increase being in the number of offices and branches operated by member banks. Table 4–2 shows the number of branches, additional offices, and facilities operated by commercial banks at selected end-of-year intervals between 1947 and 1972. Here we see, for example, that the increase in the total number of offices (excluding head offices) from 1961 through 1966 was greater than the total number of offices in 1951. This trend continued into the 1970s. Apparently most of the need for additional banking facilities in our expanding economy has been met recently through an expansion of bank branches rather than via new bank entries. Just as there was some reduction of barriers to bank entry in the 1960s, there was a change in the laws of many states concerning branch banking. With the urbanization of the suburbs, state banking laws permitted banks to follow their customers into the suburbs. For example, in New York and Georgia, banks were permitted to establish branches in adjacent counties, in contrast to earlier prohibitions on branching across county lines.

MEMBER BANK REQUIREMENTS AND PRIVILEGES

Banks wishing to become members of the Federal Reserve System must meet certain standards. They must (1) have sufficient capital relative to assets and deposit liabilities and (2) redeem at par all checks drawn by their depositors and presented by out-of-town banks for collection. In addition, the banks' past operations, their solvency, and their managerial talent must be satisfactory to the Federal Reserve. Many banks do not meet these requirements and must therefore remain outside the system. However, if a bank applies for and receives a national charter from the Comptroller of the Currency, membership in the Reserve System is automatic.

The Capital Requirement

The ratio of deposits to capital accounts is thought to be an important measure of bank solvency by bankers. A low ratio indicates sound investment policies. The higher the ratio, the smaller the presumable margin of safety for depositors, although, almost always, bank supervisors will step in prior to actual insolvency. In those few cases where banks are forced to liquidate, the average depositor need not fear for the safety of his funds, since deposit insurance is likely to cover any losses. Liquidation is particularly painful to bank directors and stockholders, who are not protected by deposit insurance. When a bank fails, creditors have first claim to the assets of the corporation; stockholders have only a residual claim. Deposit claims constitute almost all the liabilities of a commercial bank. If capital accounts are low in relation to these claims, nearly all the assets of the bank would have to be used to meet them in the event of liquidation. Furthermore, when corporate assets are sold in liquidation, they usually do not bring their full book value; if there is a high deposit/capital ratio, all creditor claims may not be met.

It is the responsibility of the Federal Reserve System and other examining groups to see that commercial banks do not engage in unsound practices that might lead to insolvency. A low deposit/capital ratio coupled with sound assets may serve to protect both depositors and stockholders. Once each year, the examining authorities carefully study the qualitative composition of assets as well as the deposit/capital ratio. Cash, deposits with Federal Reserve banks, and short-term U.S. government securities are considered very good assets since they involve almost no risk of loss.

In recent years, the deposit/capital ratio for all commercial banks has been about 10/1.[1] There have been few bank failures. In addition, the number of annual absorptions and mergers of commercial banks is low relative to the total number of banks in the banking system. Neither the present ratio nor any other ratio is necessarily a safe one, however. One study shows that the deposit/capital ratio and other measures of bank solvency ". . . do a relatively poor job of measuring capital adequacy."[2] Another study concludes "About all that can be said for government regulation of bank capital is that it may have prevented bankers from responding completely to the incentive they face to substitute deposit insur-

---

[1] *Federal Reserve Bulletin* (March 1973), p. A-20.
[2] Richard V. Cotter. "Capital Ratios and Capital Adequacies." *The National Banking Review* (1966), p. 345.

ance for capital."[3] Evidently further research is needed to establish more relevant measures for determining the adequacy of capital requirements.

The Par Collection Requirement

Any bank that is a member of the Federal Reserve System must remit checks drawn on it at par. Nonmember banks wishing to use Federal Reserve check-clearing facilities must also remit at par.[4] Banks that do not do so are called *nonpar* banks. They cannot be members of the Federal Reserve System, and the Federal Reserve banks will not accept their checks for collection.

Only a small and declining number of banks are nonpar. In 1954 there were 1,787 nonpar banks; by the end of 1968, there were only 932. Since then the decrease has been even more marked, until, by the end of 1972, only 179 nonpar banks were in existence.[5] These banks represent less than 2 percent of the total number of banks in the United States, and they control an even smaller percentage of total bank-deposit liabilities. Although nonpar banks are not particularly important in the national economy, some are important regionally, especially in the South where they are concentrated. States still having nonpar banks in 1972 were Arkansas, Louisiana, North Carolina, South Carolina, and Texas.[6]

Nonpar banks usually impose a minimum "exchange charge" of 0.1 percent on checks presented for collection by out-of-town banks. Thus, on a $1,000 check, a nonpar bank will remit only $999. Any checks drawn on and presented at a nonpar bank, however, will be paid at par.

Why do some commercial banks choose to operate in this manner? Nonpar bankers argue that an exchange charge is required to cover the costs of making payment to large out-of-town banks since expensive checking-deposit accounts must be maintained with them. This is hardly a valid argument, however, because local banks must maintain deposit balances with out-of-town banks anyway in order to collect on the deposit of checks drawn on these banks. The real reason for remaining nonpar is that the exchange charge is profitable. Since checks sent to the par banks for collection are paid at par, whereas checks drawn on nonpar banks are paid at less than par, a profit margin exists. Nonpar banks are typically small, rural banks that are not as efficient as the city banks, nor as skilled in making profitable investments; hence, some have come to rely on the exchange charge as a source of earnings. Furthermore, they are often located in one-bank towns where there is little competitive pressure to force them to abandon their nonpar status.

---

[3] Sam Peltzman. "Capital Investment in Commercial Banking and Its Relationship to Portfolio Regulation." *Journal of Political Economy* (1970), p. 20.

[4] For a more complete account of the process of check clearing and collection, see Chapter 9.

[5] *Federal Reserve Bulletin* (February 1955), p. 209; (February 1969), p. A-95; and (March 1973), p. A-99.

[6] *Federal Reserve Bulletin* (March 1973), p. A-99.

Other Member Bank Obligations and Privileges

Banks that are members of the Federal Reserve System must also meet certain other requirements. First, they must be insured by the Federal Deposit Insurance Corporation. This becomes automatic with system membership. Second, they are subject to periodic examination by the Reserve System. (Actually the Federal Reserve usually examines only state member banks, since national banks are examined by the Comptroller of the Currency.) Third, they must subscribe to the Federal Reserve bank stock. At present, a member bank must subscribe to an amount of stock equal in value to 3 percent of its own capital accounts. The Board of Governors of the Federal Reserve System may increase this requirement by as much as an additional 3 percent. Finally, member banks must maintain a certain level of reserves.

This *reserve requirement* is a *ratio* of *vault cash plus deposits at the Federal Reserve Bank* to the bank's *deposit liabilities.* The amount of reserves required to back demand-deposit liabilities at banks designated as Reserve city banks by the Federal Reserve System is now 17.5 percent for banks with demand-deposit liabilities in excess of $400 million. For banks designated as country banks—those with demand deposits less than $400 million—the reserve requirements for demand-deposit liabilities now vary from 8 to 13 percent, depending upon the size of their deposit liabilities. The requirement is 3 percent for savings accounts in all member commercial banks. The reserve requirement for other types of time deposits is 3 percent for all banks having these deposits in amounts less than $5 million; and 5 percent where these deposits exceed $5 million.[7]

Reserve System membership carries with it certain privileges. Member banks may (1) have their checks cleared and collected free of cost by the Federal Reserve banks, (2) obtain currency free of charge, (3) obtain loans and advances from the Reserve banks, (4) receive a 6 percent dividend on their holdings of Reserve bank stock, and (5) participate in the selection of six of the nine directors of each district Federal Reserve bank. In addition, a bank gains a certain amount of prestige merely by being a member bank.

Advantages of Nonmember Bank Status

Nonmember banks are typically small banks that either do not meet the Federal Reserve membership requirements or do not care to become members. There are a number of reasons why a bank may not become a member. First, its capital accounts simply may be too small to meet the requirements set by the System. The capital requirements set by the Federal Reserve are stiffer than those set by the FDIC for nonmember, insured banks. Second, some state banking authorities set lower reserve requirements for nonmember banks than the Federal Reserve sets for

---

[7] *Federal Reserve Bulletin* (June 1973), p. A-9.

member banks. State bank reserve requirements are generally some ratio of *vault cash plus deposits at other commercial banks* (and, in some instances, plus certain types of U.S. government securities) to *deposit liabilities*. Member banks, on the other hand, are not permitted to count deposits at other commercial banks as part of their reserves. In short, nonmember banks in some states do not need to keep as large a percentage of their monetary resources idle as do member banks. This is not generally the case, however, since in about half the states today reserve requirements for nonmember banks are higher and more restrictive than those for member banks.

A third advantage of nonmembership is that a bank is subject to audit by one less supervisory agency than a member bank: it is not audited by the Federal Reserve.

Fourth, many nonmember banks, particularly those that remit at par, are able to obtain most of the advantages of membership, without any of its responsibilities, by maintaining checking-deposit balances with large "city correspondents" (in some instances, with a Federal Reserve bank). The correspondent banks are almost always member banks and can use the facilities of the Federal Reserve banks to clear checks, obtain currency, and arrange for loans on behalf of nonmember banks.

Finally, banks that are nonpar banks may not wish to relinquish their profitable exchange charge.

NATIONAL AND STATE BANKS

During 1972 there were 4,606 national banks, 1,108 state member banks and 8,161 state nonmember banks. The average deposit liability of national banks at that time was $65 million, as against $23 million for state banks. As previously indicated, average deposit liabilities were $69 million for member banks and $14 million for nonmember banks. Although one would also expect the deposit liabilities of state member banks to average less than those of the national banks, this is not the case. The average deposit liability of national banks in 1972 was $65 million; for state member banks, the figure came to $88 million.

There appear to be two principal reasons for the larger size of deposit liabilities in state member banks. One concerns the prestige factor. Many small banks apparently feel that they need "national" status in order to maintain their competitive position. Small "storefront" national banks are not uncommon in small rural communities, for example. Many of these banks have held their charters since the early days of the national banking system and are now reluctant to relinquish their national status. The officers of these banks believe that changing to a state charter would cause their customers to transfer deposits to larger banks in the big city. Thus, many national banks are quite small. On the other hand, a number of very large banks feel that the advantages of a state charter outweigh this prestige factor. Some of these banks—principally the large downtown New York City banks, whose operations are international in scope—are so well known that a national charter would add little to their already high prestige. Typically, state banking authorities are more permissive in the nature of the banking practices in which they permit banks to engage. This provides an incentive for both large and small banks to prefer state charters.

The mid-1960s saw some increase in the number of national banks as a result of the liberalization of rules concerning national bank operations that took place when James Saxon was Comptroller of the Currency. The Chase Manhattan Bank, for example, became a national bank in 1965 when its directors felt that national bank rules had become more flexible than those of New York State banking authorities. National banks have the ability to sell unsecured promissory notes, to go into equipment leasing, and to act as factors (i.e., to purchase directly business accounts receivable), whereas New York State banking rules do not permit such operations. Since 1967, however, national bank growth has declined, partly as a result of a change in policy by succeeding Comptrollers of the Currency and partly due to a reexamination of bank operation standards by state banking authorities.

National Bank Charter Requirements

The capital requirements for national banks vary with the size of the city in which the bank is located, as follows:

POPULATION	CAPITAL REQUIREMENT
Under 6,000	$ 50,000
6,000–50,000	100,000
Over 50,000	200,000

The capital requirement for new state banks, on the other hand, is usually $25,000, although some states have larger requirements. These formal requirements are so low as to be unimportant in the actual charter-granting decision by the Comptroller of the Currency or by the state banking authorities. In fact, the legal capital requirements for national banks are the same as they were in the nineteenth century.

Today the Comptroller of the Currency and the various state banking departments rely upon a variety of criteria when judging an application for a charter. Among these are (1) the access of the community to other banking facilities, (2) the need of the community for additional banking facilities, (3) the talent of the managers of the proposed bank, (4) the adequacy of the proposed capital size of the bank relative to its estimated deposits, (5) the effects of the proposed bank upon banking competition in the community, and (6) the ability of the bank to have projected earnings sufficient to cover the expenses of bank operations.

INSURED AND NONINSURED BANKS

Almost all commercial banks in the United States are insured. In 1972, only 206 banks—under 2 percent—were not insured by the FDIC. Their deposits totaled only 0.5 percent of all deposit liabilities. However, not all deposits of insured banks are covered by deposit insurance; the FDIC insures deposits only up to $20,000 per account. Typically, the smaller the bank, the smaller the average deposit size and the greater the fraction of deposits insured. In spite of less than 100 percent deposit coverage, we find that, since 1934, 99.7 percent of the depositors of failed banks have fully recovered their funds.[8]

Banks that are members of the Federal Reserve System are automatically covered by deposit insurance. Nonmember banks are insured only after examination by the FDIC, which bases its decision on (1) the financial condition of the bank, (2) its prospective earnings, (3) its managerial talent, and (4) the needs of the community. The standards for FDIC coverage are thus much the same as those for national and member bank status.

Insured banks are under certain obligations to the FDIC. They are subject to periodic FDIC examination,[9] they must secure FDIC permission before merging with another bank,[10] and they must pay an annual assessment fee.[11]

THE AMERICAN BANKING SYSTEM: TYPES OF OPERATION

Unit and Branch Banking

Most American banks operate only one office and are not controlled by any other bank or corporation. This is known as unit banking. At the end of 1972, the United States had 13,928 banks, of which 9,817 were unit banks and 4,111 were banks operating a total of 24,622 branches.[12] In contrast, foreign banks have developed extensive systems of multiple banking offices.

[8] Federal Deposit Insurance Corporation. *Annual Report* (1971), p. 4.

[9] In practice, the FDIC examines only state nonmember insured banks directly. The Comptroller of the Currency and the Federal Reserve bank authorities examine all member banks and the FDIC simply reviews their reports.

[10] If the resulting bank is to be national, permission for a merger must be obtained from the Comptroller of the Currency. If the new bank is to be a state member bank, the Board of Governors of the Federal Reserve must give its approval. If the bank is to be a nonmember insured bank, the FDIC must give its consent. Notice that the approving agency in the case of consolidation is the same as the examining agency for each class of bank.

[11] The assessment rate is $\frac{1}{12}$ of 1 percent of total assessable deposits. Actually, the amount paid by the banks does not equal this rate. After deducting its expenses and losses from the total amount due according to the assessment rate, the FDIC credits two-thirds of what is left to the insured banks. The total amount collected from deposit-insurance assessments from 1933, when the FDIC was created, through 1971 amounted to only $3.02 billion, while deposit-insurance losses were even less ($75.6 million). (Federal Deposit Insurance Corporation. *Annual Report* (1971), p. 23.)

[12] *Federal Reserve Bulletin* (March 1973), p. A-98.

BRANCHES
65
347
3,176
469
99
108
142
165
237
567
89
1,224
359
179
459
100
148
89
887
589
303
412
671
361
414
781
1,254
369
69
1,097
140
2,556
1,370
1,826
528
286
179
29
43
123
329
73
17
100
10
45
72
71
86
6
2
23,080

ican tradition of free enterprise has encouraged
ιy small banks. In addition, until recently large
tes were underpopulated. The great distances
:rs, the difficulties in travel and communication,
ι nature of the economy all fostered the develop-
ly owned, operated, and controlled. By 1921, for
)76 banks operating only 1,455 branches.[13] The
ɔf the twenties and thirties demonstrated all too
ere were too many small and inefficient banks.
‹ing," state and national authorities made it more
ɔanks. Today, banking remains a "free" field for
extent that the authorities believe we need addi-
charter, a new bank should prove that a need for
at it is capable of meeting that need. For this
ative stability in the total number of banks during
ιll decline that has occurred is a result of the fact
ɔeen more mergers than newly chartered banks.
e the result of FDIC efforts to have small, inef-
‹en over by larger banks.

nomy, a need arises for more banking facilities.
has been met in recent years, not through the es-
ɔers of new banks, but through the establishment
ιf branches by existing banks. Branch banks are
neet the needs of the community than unit banks
ncial resources at their disposal. Some state stat-
ɔ encourage unit banking and discourage other
ιs. In addition, the Supreme Court ruled in 1963
ject to the antitrust laws.[14] Today bank mergers
ιg company formations and acquisitions are sub-
ιe Sherman and Clayton Acts.

the status of unit and branch banking in the
ɔy-state basis. Here we see that unit banking is
third of the states. In those states with extensive
we find that expansion is limited. Almost one-
ιmple, permit a bank to establish a branch only
ιty or, at best, in a contiguous county.

ι to national as well as to state banks. United
" only in the sense that they have a charter from
ιrrency. They are still allowed to operate only
ate. No bank is permitted to establish branches
its home office is located,[15] and, under present

rporation. *Annual Report* (1960), p. 29.
ɔhia National Bank et al., 374 U.S. 321 (1963).
s not apply to the establishment of branches in U.S. terri-

TABLE 4-3 NUMBER OF COMMERCIAL BANKING OFFICES IN THE UN
DECEMBER 31, 1971

STATE AND TYPE OF BANKING	ALL OFFICES	UNIT BANKS	BANKS OPERATING BRANCHES
Statewide Branching			
Alaska	76	4	7
Arizona	360	3	10
California	3,328	34	118
Connecticut	532	17	46
Delaware	117	9	9
District of Columbia	122	1	13
Hawaii	152	2	8
Idaho	189	10	14
Maine	281	11	33
Maryland	679	41	71
Nevada	97	2	6
North Carolina	1,319	30	65
Oregon	405	15	31
Rhode Island	192	0	13
South Carolina	558	34	65
South Dakota	259	120	39
Utah	198	29	21
Vermont	131	17	25
Virginia	1,132	87	158
Washington	681	42	50
Limited Branching			
Alabama	576	177	96
Georgia	846	297	137
Indiana	1,079	209	199
Kentucky	704	200	143
Louisiana	649	99	136
Massachusetts	939	36	122
Michigan	1,585	122	209
Mississippi	552	68	115
New Hampshire	143	42	32
New Jersey	1,308	43	168
New Mexico	208	16	52
New York	2,867	120	191
Ohio	1,884	223	291
Pennsylvania	2,280	203	251
Tennessee	838	159	151
Wisconsin	897	436	175
Unit Banking			
Arkansas	432	163	90
Colorado	307	253	25
Florida	583	501	39
Illinois	1,257	1,016	118
Iowa	995	446	220
Kansas	676	532	71
Minnesota	748	718	13
Missouri	772	574	98
Montana	154	134	10
Nebraska	488	400	43
North Dakota	241	117	52
Oklahoma	508	369	68
Texas	1,301	1,134	81
West Virginia	205	193	6
Wyoming	73	69	2
United States	36,903	9,577	4,206

SOURCE: Federal Deposit Insurance Corporation. *Annual Report* (1971), pp. 186–93.

regulations, a national bank is allowed to establish branches only to the extent permitted by the statutes of the state where it is located.

Even when a state does permit extensive branch banking, a national bank is not authorized to establish an unlimited number of offices. It must file an application with the Comptroller of the Currency for permission to establish each branch. When an application is presented, it is studied with a view not only to the need for the branch, but also to the potential effects on bank competition and concentration. Not every branch application is approved. During 1971, for example, some 1,157 applications were filed with the Comptroller of the Currency. Of these, 786 were approved, 104 were rejected, and 27 were withdrawn. The remaining 240 were still in process at the end of the year.[16]

Arguments for and against Branch Banking

A number of arguments may be advanced against branch banking. One has already been mentioned: branch banking leads to a concentration of economic power and lessens competition. The following arguments are also frequently cited: first, branch banks draw funds away from local areas and channel them into the big cities. Second, the unit bank can make loan decisions more quickly; branch managers must consult the home office before making loans over a certain amount. Third, the unit bank is best equipped to make correct loan and investment decisions because its managers are more aware of local conditions; branch managers are frequently out-of-towners without a "feeling" for the community and its problems. Finally, the unit bank is able to meet almost any legitimate financial need of the local business community through its correspondent arrangements with large city banks.

Proponents of branch banking, on the other hand, counter with these arguments: first, the competitive position of large banks has, if anything, worsened in recent years. With city populations moving to the suburbs, banks in outlying areas have grown more rapidly than large city banks, even those with branches. The city banks have often been prevented from expanding into suburban districts by the restrictive prohibitions against branch banking. As a result, these suburban banks are not faced with competition. This monopoly of banking power increases with the distance from competing financial centers and is particularly strong in "one-bank" communities. Banks in these areas frequently charge more for loans and pay less interest than banks in areas where alternative banking facilities are available.

Second, those in favor of branch banking argue that the unit bank is frequently too small to handle the large borrower. Nor can it provide skilled banking services, such as investment counseling, which the branch bank can provide through its contact with the home office.

---

[16] Comptroller of the Currency. *Annual Report* (1971), p. 11.

Third, a large branch bank is usually financially sounder and more efficiently managed than a unit bank. Most bank mergers in recent years have been between large banks and small, weak banks, and most of these smaller banks have been unit banks. For example, in 1971, 118 banks having resources of $4.3 billion were absorbed by 99 banks having resources of $38.4 billion. Prior to these transactions the number of offices operated by the absorbing banks was 2,530. The absorbed banks had operated a total of 407 offices. After absorption, 2,944 were in operation.[17]

Finally, when a branch needs funds, it is able to acquire them through the home office from branches that have a surplus. Hence, a branch may immediately draw upon the resources of the whole bank. Unit banks, on the other hand, may be embarrassed by a shortage of loan funds.

Certainly there are valid points on each side in this controversy. The unit bank probably does know the needs of the community best and through its correspondents is able to provide almost as many services as a large branch bank. At the same time, the unit bank tends to be monopolistic wherever there is a lack of competing bank facilities. The large bank and its branches, in competition with other large banks and their branches, do provide a greater variety of services. In addition, they charge relatively low interest rates on loans and pay close to the maximum interest allowed on deposits. Economic research tends to support the view that branch banking enhances rather than lessens competition. For example, one study

. . . suggests that neither in terms of number of competitors, nor concentration (measures of actual competition), nor in terms of the condition of entry (potential competition) have the structures of local banking markets been adversely affected by branch banking in the United States. The weight of evidence suggests that, to the contrary, market structures are adversely affected by restrictions on branch banking.[18]

Chain Banking

Chain banking is a term used to describe the association of a number of commercial banks through an interlocking directorate. It is not an important feature of American banking. Each bank in a chain is counted as a separate bank; some may operate branches. Control over the chain is exercised by an individual or a group of individuals who own stock in or are directors of the separate banks in the chain. This type of banking originated in the 1880s in the South and central Northwest and reached the peak of its popularity around 1920. Since then chain banking has declined markedly, primarily because of a shift from individual to corporate control.

[17] Federal Deposit Insurance Corporation, *Annual Report* (1971), p. 14.
[18] Bernard Shullin and Paul M. Horvitz. "Branch Banking and the Structure of Competition." *The National Banking Review* (1964), p. 341.

Group Banking

Group banking usually exists in one of two forms. In one, a nonbanking corporation, sometimes called a *bancorporation,* owns the stock of the constituent banks and acts as the controlling agency. In the other, one bank controls the stock of the other banks in the group. Both of these are holding company arrangements. Each bank in a group is *counted as a separate bank; some even operate branches.*[19]

The arguments for and against group banking are similar to those for and against branch banking. One side contends that group banking concentrates banking power, decreases competition, and is neither concerned nor able to cope with the problems of the small financial centers. The other side argues that the bank holding company has all the advantages of branch banking (increased competition and a sounder financial structure) plus local participation through local boards of directors.

For many years there was little growth in bank holding companies; if anything they declined in importance from the mid-1930s until the 1950s. This stagnation in bank holding company formation was surprising since the holding company device provided a more advantageous form of expansion than branch banking. Bank holding companies could establish systems that crossed city, county, and even state lines—the only way that banks were able to operate offices across state lines. In addition, the lack of growth of bank holding companies was surprising because there were few legal prohibitions on this type of bank expansion. Despite forces that should have facilitated bank holding company expansion, other forces restrained group banking growth: first, liberalization of branch banking laws in some states led some banking groups to convert to branch bank systems. Second, in 1938, President Roosevelt publicly advocated the abolition of bank holding companies—a proposal that placed the status of group banking in a position of uncertainty until the passage of the Bank Holding Company Act of 1956. During the intervening 18 years, unit banking interests waged an extensive campaign against group banking.

The Bank Holding Company Act of 1956 was designed to be restrictive—to regulate bank holding company expansion. In the process of imposing these regulations, it clarified the status of group banking and thereby fostered its growth. According to the original provisions of this act, all bank holding companies owning 25 or more percent of the voting stock of two or more banks were required to (1) register with the Board of Governors of the Federal Reserve System, (2) obtain the permission of the board prior to the purchase of additional bank voting stock, and (3) hold no stock in subsidiaries that were not engaged in banking. In addition, the law barred bank holding companies from acquiring banks across state lines.

---

[19] This means that single banks will be counted as unit banks, while those operating branches will be counted as branch banks. Our method of counting banks, therefore, fails to distinguish clearly between unit, branch, chain, and group banking.

(Bank holding companies that had acquired banks across state lines prior to 1956 were permitted to continue their ownership.)

An expansion in the importance of the bank holding company followed the passage of the Bank Holding Company Act of 1956. As of December 31, 1970, there were 121 registered bank holding companies operating 895 banks and 3,260 branches. These groups accounted for 11.8 percent of all bank offices and held 16.2 percent of all deposits in the United States.[20] As recently as 1963, holding companies had accounted for only 6.5 percent of all bank offices and had held only 8 percent of all bank deposits.[21] Holding companies thus doubled in importance in less than a decade. Even these figures understate the growth of bank holding companies, however.

This growth in holding companies was of two types: the multibank holding company and the one-bank holding company. Multibank holding companies were devised to help banks expand geographically. Sometimes the multibank holding company held less than 25 percent of the stock of its subsidiaries and therefore was not affected by the provisions of the 1956 act. This loophole was closed by the Bank Holding Company Act Amendments of 1970. The 1956 act now applies to bank holding companies that own less than 25 percent of a bank's stock and yet exercise control over the subsidiary as well. As a result of these changes, we now have a more accurate picture of the importance of bank holding companies. On December 31, 1972, there were 1,607 bank holding companies operating 2,720 banks and 13,441 branches. Those groups held 61.5 percent of all U.S. bank deposits.[22]

The one-bank holding company. The Bank Holding Company Act of 1956 did not cover holding companies that controlled only one bank. This was an intentional omission on the part of Congress in order to avoid placing regulatory hardships upon small, family-owned companies operating several types of businesses, only one of which was a bank. The exemption of these banks from regulation produced a phenomenal growth of one-bank holding companies.

Many one-bank holding companies are small; others are large, but the bank whose stock is controlled by the holding company accounts for a minor part of the latter's activity. Numerous one-bank holding companies, however, are formed by large banks themselves, each bank being the principal affiliate. In these cases, the other subsidiary companies are frequently financial in nature. Insurance companies and factors (companies that purchase the accounts receivable of other firms) are examples of firms that may be part of a bank-dominated, one-bank holding company. The purpose of such a corporate structure is to permit commercial banks to diversify

[20] *Federal Reserve Bulletin* (August 1971), p. A-98. The data cover only those groups where the holding company controls 25 percent or more of the voting stock.
[21] *Federal Reserve Bulletin* (June 1964), p. 783.
[22] *Federal Reserve Bulletin* (June 1973), p. A-104.

their operations. Given the rapid growth of the one-bank holding company form of banking business, it was feared that banking would become concentrated and that bank competition would be lessened. Because of these forces, Congress amended the Bank Holding Act of 1956 in 1970, making all types of bank holding companies subject to its provisions.

Correspondent Banking

A correspondent bank is one that maintains deposit accounts for other, usually smaller, customer banks. These deposits are called *interbank deposits.* As of February 28, 1973, there were $33.4 billion in interbank deposits — $29.5 and $3.9 billion of this amount, respectively, in demand and time deposits.[23]

Maintaining these accounts benefits both the correspondent and customer banks. To the correspondent bank, the deposit is a source of funds like any other new deposit; thus, when a small bank with excess funds makes a new interbank deposit of $1,000, the T-account entries are as follows:

BALANCE-SHEET CHANGES FOR A LARGE MEMBER BANK

ASSETS		LIABILITIES + CAPITAL ACCOUNTS	
Cash assets	+$1,000	Interbank deposits	+$1,000

The large bank, on the basis of increased cash assets, is now in a position to expand its loans and deposits.[24] The total cash assets of the small bank, however, remain unchanged. To the small bank a deposit with a correspondent bank is as good as cash, since it is subject to call on demand.

Small banks maintain these deposit balances because of the variety of services provided by the larger banks. Among these are (1) the clearing and collection of checks for both member and nonmember banks, (2) security analysis, (3) the handling of bond and security purchases, (4) currency shipments, (5) participation in loans that the small banks cannot handle alone, (6) the making of loans to customer banks, and (7) the providing of foreign monies (exchange) so that the customers of small banks may buy and sell abroad.

Conclusion

If there is one conclusion to be drawn from the preceding description of the structure of banking, it is that many types of banking structures are possible. The American banking structure is fluid; changes are continually

---

[23] *Federal Reserve Bulletin* (March 1973), p. A-20.
[24] A more complete account of deposit creation will be given in Chapter 6.

taking place in response to changing economic, competitive, and legal environments.

Supplementary Readings

The Administrator of National Banks, United States Treasury. *Studies in Banking Competition and the Banking Structure.* Articles reprinted from the *National Banking Review* (Washington, D.C., 1966).

Alhadeff, David A. *Monopoly and Competition in Banking* (University of California Press, 1954).

"Recent Changes in the Structure of Commercial Banking." *Federal Reserve Bulletin* (1970), pp. 195–210.

Fraser, Donald R., and Rose, Peter S. "Bank Entry and Bank Performance." *Journal of Finance* (1972), pp. 65–78.

Salley, Charles D. "1970 Bank Holding Company Amendments: What is 'Closely Related to Banking?'" *Monthly Review* (Federal Reserve Bank of Atlanta, 1971), pp. 98–106.

5 Commercial Bank Sources and Uses of Funds

THE BALANCE SHEET FOR A REPRESENTATIVE COMMERCIAL BANK

LIABILITIES AND CAPITAL ACCOUNTS

How Liabilities and Capital Accounts Provide Funds
Composition and Size of Bank Sources of Funds
  Demand deposits
  Interbank demand deposits
  Time deposits
  Borrowings
  Capital accounts

THE NATURE OF COMMERCIAL BANK USES OF FUNDS

Cash Assets
  Commercial and industrial loans
  Agriculture credit
  Real-estate credit
  Consumer credit
  Other lending activity
Investments
  U.S. government securities
  The "lock-in" effect
  State and local government securities
  Other securities
  Federal funds sold

BANK EARNINGS AND PROFIT MAXIMIZATION

A Banking Industry Dilemma—Earnings versus safety

BANK OPERATIONS AND THE NATIONAL ECONOMY

Competition between Commercial Banks and
    Nonbank Financial Institutions for Funds
  Periods of relative decline by commercial banks
  Periods of relative growth for commercial banks
  Conclusion
The Behavior of Bank Loans and Investments and
    Gross National Product
The Commercial Banking System's Role in
    Economic Fluctuations

In preceding chapters, we have examined the structure of commercial banking and the relative importance of the financial community to the U.S. economy. We have seen that commercial banks differ from other members of the financial community in their unique ability to create and destroy money. In Chapter 6 we will investigate this peculiar money-creating ability of the commercial banking system in some detail, but first we shall study commercial bank operations as they are summarized on a bank balance sheet, focusing upon the sources and uses of commercial bank funds. What are the sources of funds? To what uses do banks put these funds? Are they invested in securities, loans, or real estate, or are they merely held idle in the form of cash? What do the differing sources and uses of funds mean for the national economy and for bank earnings and operations? These are some of the questions we will be concerned with in this chapter.

THE BALANCE SHEET FOR A REPRESENTATIVE COMMERCIAL BANK

The balance sheet of a commercial bank shows its financial position at a moment in time. Table 5–1 gives a simplified, hypothetical balance sheet for a typical commercial bank.

The *asset* side of the balance sheet shows what the bank owns; that is, the uses, to which it has put its funds. Here we see that the bank has $1 million in *cash assets*, consisting of cash in its own vaults and demand deposits maintained with other banks. These are idle assets, for they do not enhance the bank's earning powers and are kept on hand primarily to meet reserve requirements and the cash demands of depositors.

Almost one-third of our typical bank's assets are in the form of *security holdings*, primarily U.S. government securities. In addition, banks hold substantial quantities of state and local government securities. Banks view government securities as secondary reserves, since they are easily marketable and can be converted to cash quickly to meet depositor demands. Relatively small quantities of privately-issued stocks and bonds are held.

The largest category of assets for our bank is *loans and discounts*, composed primarily of real-estate loans, business loans, and loans to individuals. This is the most profitable and the most important use to which com-

TABLE 5-1 BALANCE SHEET FOR A TYPICAL COMMERCIAL BANK

ASSETS		LIABILITIES + CAPITAL ACCOUNTS	
Cash assets	$1,000,000	Demand deposits	$2,500,000
Securities	2,000,000	Time deposits	2,900,000
Loans and discounts	3,000,000	Miscellaneous liabilities	200,000
Miscellaneous assets	100,000	Capital accounts	500,000
Total	$6,100,000	Total	$6,100,000

mercial banks can put their funds and is the principal source of their earnings.

Miscellaneous assets is a catchall category representing all nonincome-yielding assets, such as the book value of the bank's premises, furniture, and fixtures.

Claims of creditors to the assets of a bank are termed *liabilities*; residual claims of stockholders, on the other hand, are termed *capital accounts*. Both liabilities and capital accounts are sources of funds. As they increase, banks are provided with the funds that enable them to acquire earning assets.

We have said that *demand deposits* are claims upon the commercial bank that may be transferred on demand by the use of checks. The owners of these checking-deposit accounts are the depositors. Because any amount of these liabilities may be demanded in cash by depositors at any given time, commercial banks must maintain assets that can be quickly liquidated to meet the current demand. Cash assets and U.S. government securities usually perform this function.

Time deposits, the other form of deposits on our hypothetical balance sheet, are *not* legally subject to call upon the demand. Nevertheless, time deposits are a method of holding idle funds, since they yield interest to the depositors. They are an important source of funds because banks are not asked to redeem time deposits as often as demand deposits. Banks need not maintain as large idle cash reserves to cover time deposits as they must to cover demand deposits.

Miscellaneous liabilities consist mainly of borrowings which arise when a bank borrows funds from other commercial banks or from Federal Reserve banks. Also included under miscellaneous liabilities are such unpaid items as taxes, interest, and wages.

Capital accounts, the last item on the bank's balance sheet, consist of surplus and the par value of the bank's common and preferred stock. Most of the surplus is created when the bank makes profits on its loans and investments.

LIABILITIES AND CAPITAL ACCOUNTS

We began our discussion of commercial bank operations with the balance sheet because it serves as a convenient outline of the more detailed discussion that follows. We shall now examine the right-hand side of the balance sheet. First, we shall see how liabilities and capital accounts provide funds for the commercial bank. Second, we shall examine the composition and size of the banking system's sources of funds.

How Liabilities and Capital Accounts Provide Funds

When a commercial bank accepts deposits, sells stock, or borrows funds, it is provided with funds that it can use to expand its holdings of earning assets. For example, when an individual deposits $1,000 in cash in either his checking- or his savings-deposit account, the bank acquires an asset— $1,000 in cash—and also a liability, since it is liable to the depositor for the amount of his deposit. The T-account entries for this transaction are:

BALANCE-SHEET CHANGES FOR COMMERCIAL BANK A

ASSETS		LIABILITIES + CAPITAL ACCOUNTS	
Reserves (vault cash)	+$1,000	Deposits	+$1,000

The asset entry is recorded as an increase in reserves because vault cash is usually part of a bank's reserves. If a check drawn on some other bank is deposited, the T-account entries are the same as above, because once the check written on the other bank is collected, the reserves of Bank A will increase, while the bank on which the check was drawn will experience a decrease in reserves.

Very much the same thing occurs when a bank issues stock. If it sells the new stock for $1,000 cash, reserves are increased by $1,000, as is common stock under capital accounts. The entries for such a transaction are:

BALANCE-SHEET CHANGES FOR COMMERCIAL BANK A

ASSETS		LIABILITIES + CAPITAL ACCOUNTS	
Reserves	+$1,000	Common stock	+$1,000

Likewise, if the stock is paid for with a check drawn on another commercial bank, both reserves and common stock increase by $1,000.[1] The other bank, of course, is faced with a decrease in reserves. *The reserves that the acquiring bank receives provide it with the basis for an expansion of its earning assets.*

A bank, however, will not receive cash or deposits drawn on other banks when it sells stock to its own depositors. Banks frequently attempt to in-

---

[1] If it happens that the stock is sold for more than its par value, common stock increases by $1,000, and surplus increases by the difference between the amount received by the bank and the par value of the stock; reserves will increase by the amount of the proceeds from the sale of the stock. On the other hand, if the stock sells for less than its par value, surplus will be reduced by the amount that the par value exceeds the receipts from the sale of the stock, and common stock will be increased by the par value of the stock; reserves will increase by the amount received from the stock sale.

duce their depositors to become stockholders. Although this does not provide banks with additional funds, their lending abilities are enhanced nonetheless. Assume that a depositor of Bank A purchases $1,000 in Bank A stock by drawing $1,000 from his checking-deposit account. The T-account entries are:

BALANCE-SHEET CHANGES FOR COMMERCIAL BANK A

ASSETS	LIABILITIES + CAPITAL ACCOUNTS	
	Demand deposits	−$1,000
	Common stock	+$1,000

Note that no change has occurred in assets. The bank has not acquired funds through the sale of stock. Nevertheless, its lending ability has increased because its deposit liabilities have decreased. A commercial bank must maintain reserves, as we have seen, to cover its demand-deposit liabilities. If demand deposits decrease, the bank will have more reserves relative to demand-deposit liabilities than before and may, accordingly, grant new loans and create new deposits.

Commercial banks also obtain funds by borrowing. If a bank wants to increase its lending operations or feels that it is short of funds, it may borrow funds from its district Federal Reserve bank, other banks, or in the Euro-dollar market (which is discussed later in the chapter). In any of these cases, the T-account entries for the borrowing bank are usually:

BALANCE-SHEET CHANGES FOR COMMERCIAL BANK A

ASSETS		LIABILITIES + CAPITAL ACCOUNTS	
Reserves	+$1,000	Borrowings	+$1,000

Commercial banks and other business institutions differ in their use of funds. When a *nonbanking business enterprise* receives additional money from operations, from sales of stock, or from outside lenders, it is likely to spend this money sooner or later to acquire income-producing assets. If the money is used to purchase a $50,000 machine, this increase in the company's income-producing assets is accompanied by an equal decrease in its cash holdings. The balance-sheet changes are recorded in items (a) and (b) below:

BALANCE-SHEET CHANGES FOR COMPANY A

ASSETS		LIABILITIES + CAPITAL ACCOUNTS
Cash	−$50,000 (a)	
Plant and equipment	+$50,000 (b)	
Cash	−$50,000 (c)	
Loans	+$50,000 (d)	

If Company A were to extend a $50,000 loan to some other business, there would normally be an equal and offsetting increase and decrease in the corresponding asset items also. This is illustrated by the changes in (c) and (d) in the balance sheet above.

When a *commercial bank* receives additional funds from new deposits, borrowings, or sales of stock, however, it does not use its cash increase directly to make loans and investments. As mentioned previously, when a commercial bank grants a loan, it acquires an asset—an interest-earning loan—and it creates a demand-deposit liability for its customer. For Bank A, the entries would be:

BALANCE-SHEET CHANGES FOR COMMERCIAL BANK A

ASSETS		LIABILITIES + CAPITAL ACCOUNTS	
Loans	+$50,000	Demand deposits	+$50,000

An increase in demand-deposit liabilities necessitates an increase in bank reserves to back these additional liabilities. Consequently, banks add additional incoming funds to reserves, instead of lending them or investing them directly. When the bank has more reserves than it needs to meet its legal reserve requirement, it may then expand its loans by the amount permitted by its excess reserves.

Most borrowers find demand deposits more convenient than cash for borrowing all but very small amounts. When a cash loan is made, however, the bank uses its vault cash reserves directly. Thus, in such a case, the bank's reserves will decline by an amount equal to the loan.

Generally a bank should not expand its loans and create new deposits beyond an amount equal to its excess reserves. A fuller discussion of excess reserves will appear in Chapter 6, but for the present we may define *excess reserves as the amount by which the reserves of a bank exceed what it legally must have to back its outstanding deposit liabilities.*

This general rule is important. When a commercial bank lends and creates deposits, it cannot expect its borrowers to do business only with those firms and individuals that maintain accounts with it. If Individual 1 borrows $1,000 from Bank A, he is quite likely to use the money to purchase goods or services from Individual 2, who maintains deposit balances with another bank, Bank B. Hence, when Individual 1 writes a check, that check will find its way into the deposit account of Individual 2, increasing the reserves of Bank B, while Bank A loses reserves. The appropriate T-account entries are:

BALANCE-SHEET CHANGES FOR COMMERCIAL BANK A

ASSETS		LIABILITIES + CAPITAL ACCOUNTS	
Loans	+$1,000 (a)	Demand deposits of Individual 1	+$1,000 (a)
Reserves	−$1,000 (b)	Demand deposits of Individual 1	−$1,000 (b)

BALANCE-SHEET CHANGES FOR COMMERCIAL BANK B

ASSETS		LIABILITIES + CAPITAL ACCOUNTS
Reserves	+$1,000 (b)	Demand deposits of Individual 2 +$1,000 (b)

Entries labeled (a) show the results of Bank A's loan to Individual 1. Entries labeled (b) show the effects of Individual 1's purchase of $1,000 worth of goods and services from Individual 2, who deposits the check in his account with Bank B. Bank B in turn collects $1,000 from Bank A, and the checking account of Individual 1 is decreased.

If Bank A had had only $500 in excess reserves, it would now be $500 short of its legal reserve requirement and probably would be forced to reduce its loans or borrow additional reserves from a Federal Reserve bank. Either alternative is costly, however, since the Federal Reserve banks charge for borrowed reserves and since fewer loans mean less income.

We can see, therefore, that a commercial bank should expect to lose reserves to other banks when it makes a loan. Hence, it should expand loans and investments only by an amount equal to its excess reserves. Thus an increase in funds that increases excess reserves indirectly permits the bank to expand its loans and investments. A stable volume of funds means that the bank should maintain about the same volume of loans and investments, since continuous repayment of outstanding loans enables it to make new loans even though it is not receiving additional excess reserves.

There appears to be a paradox in this line of reasoning, however. Demand-deposit liabilities of a commercial bank have been described as *a source of funds*. While it is true that deposits of checks drawn on other banks or deposits of cash provide funds that enable a bank to make loans and create additional demand deposits, these additional deposits are *not* sources of funds. Only a *primary deposit,* a deposit that increases the bank's holding of reserves, provides a bank with additional funds. Deposits created when a bank makes loans are called *derivative deposits.* Derivative deposits can become sources of funds only when they are used—and then they increase the reserves and deposits of some *other* bank, as described in the last T-account illustration under entry (b).

Composition and Size of Bank Sources of Funds

Table 5–2 shows that time deposits are the chief source of bank funds. They comprise 43.2 percent of all liabilities and capital accounts. Demand deposits are the second largest source of funds, accounting for 40.2 percent of liabilities and capital accounts. Only 7.1 percent of the total are in the form of capital accounts.

Individuals, partnerships, and corporations, the federal government, state and local governments, and American and foreign banks all own demand deposits in U.S. banks. More than 75 percent of these deposits are

TABLE 5-2 ALL COMMERCIAL BANK LIABILITIES AND CAPITAL ACCOUNTS, DECEMBER 31, 1972

TYPE OF LIABILITY OR CAPITAL ACCOUNT	AMOUNT (IN MILLIONS OF DOLLARS)	PERCENT OF TOTAL
Demand deposits		
Interbank		
Domestic	29,971	
Foreign	3,883	
U.S. government	10,875	
State and local government	18,588	
Certified and officers' checks, etc.	11,685	
Individuals, partnerships, and corporations	221,950	
Total	296,952	40.2
Time deposits		
Interbank	4,194	
U.S. government and Postal Savings	606	
State and local government	37,161	
Individuals, partnerships, and corporations	277,683	
Total	319,644	43.2
Borrowings	38,083	5.2
Other liabilities	31,696	4.3
Capital accounts	52,658	7.1
Total liabilities and capital accounts	739,033	100.1*

* Figures do not total 100.0 due to rounding.
SOURCE: *Federal Reserve Bulletin* (June 1973), pp. A-18 and A-25.

held by individuals, partnerships, and corporations. This group also owns over 87 percent of all time deposits. The federal government and domestic commercial banks keep almost all their funds in the form of demand deposits. State and local governments, on the other hand, maintain substantial amounts in time deposits, principally for the purpose of earning interest.

Demand deposits. The demand deposits owned by individuals, businesses, and state and local governments are usually held for *transaction* purposes — that is, in order to have money readily available for the purchase of goods and services. Deposits held at commercial banks by the federal government, on the other hand, are not used to purchase goods and services; the Treasury uses its balances with the Federal Reserve banks for this purpose.

The Treasury's deposit balances at commercial banks are called *Tax and Loan Accounts*. These balances normally increase as commercial banks sell U.S. government savings bonds, as they purchase new issues of government securities, and as employers make social security and income-withholding payments. The purpose of these accounts is to help banks avoid the reserve losses that would otherwise occur when the private sector of the economy makes payments to the government.

Tax and Loan Accounts decrease when the Treasury orders the commercial banks to transfer a portion of the accumulated deposits to the U.S. government balances with the Federal Reserve banks. This is reflected on the balance sheets as follows:

BALANCE-SHEET CHANGES FOR THE COMMERCIAL BANKING SYSTEM

ASSETS		LIABILITIES + CAPITAL ACCOUNTS
Reserves	−$1,000,000	U.S. government demand deposits −$1,000,000

BALANCE-SHEET CHANGES FOR THE FEDERAL RESERVE BANKS

ASSETS	LIABILITIES + CAPITAL ACCOUNTS
	Deposits Member bank reserves −$1,000,000 U.S. government general account +$1,000,000

The Treasury orders this type of decrease in its balances at commercial banks when the government needs money to meet its obligations. This is generally done at regular intervals. As the preceding T-account entries show, banks lose reserves when the Treasury balances are transferred to the Federal Reserve banks. As the Treasury spends funds, however, bank reserves are built up again. In the meantime, to offset possible adverse economic repercussions of this decrease in reserves, the Federal Open Market Committee usually provides banks with additional reserves from other sources. (More will be said of this in Chapter 12.)

Interbank demand deposits. As we have seen (page 51), interbank demand deposits are maintained at large banks by small banks in return for a variety of services. The interbank deposits are important as a source of funds for the large banks—as these deposits increase, so do reserves.[2]

Time Deposits. Time deposits, which constitute the most important source of funds for commercial banks, have increased in significance over the last several decades. Adjusted demand deposits increased from $87.1 billion at the end of 1947 to $212.1 billion at the end of 1972, an increase of almost 150 percent. In that period, however, all commercial bank time deposits increased from $35.4 to $314.9 billion—almost 900 percent.[3]

[2] It should be noted that interbank demand deposits are excluded from the data on the money stock in Table 2–1.

[3] *Federal Reserve Bulletin* (June 1973), p. A-23. Adjusted demand deposits include all demand deposits other than interbank and U.S. government deposits, less cash items in process of collection. Commercial bank time deposits include all commercial bank time deposits other than interbank and Treasurer's open-account deposits and those of the Postal Savings System.

The increased interest yield now allowed by the Federal Reserve is one significant reason for this growth of time deposits. The yield on these deposits has increased relative to yields on nonbank financial assets, making time deposits a more attractive form of savings. As a consequence, more time deposits and fewer other liquid assets are demanded. Under the Federal Reserve's "Regulation Q," the maximum interest rate payable on time deposits from 1936 to 1957 was 2.5 percent.[4] This was raised to 3 percent in 1957, and to 4 percent in 1962. In the last decade the Federal Reserve has used "Regulation Q" eight times to change the interest rates payable on time deposits. These more recent changes have been closely connected with Federal Reserve implementation of monetary policy. (A full discussion will be found in Chapter 12). Another reason for the increase in time deposits is that commercial banks are more actively working to acquire this source of funds. Reserve requirements for time deposits are lower than those for demand deposits. Consequently, from every new deposit invested in time deposits instead of checking deposits, the bank is able to create a substantially greater amount of loans and demand deposits.

What forms do time deposits take? Principally three: savings deposits, certificates of deposit, and open-account time deposits. Of these, *savings deposits* are the most familiar. These accounts, held mainly by individuals, are payable upon presentation of a passbook and are usually paid on demand. Few banks enforce the legal 30-day waiting period.

Businesses may not hold savings deposits, but they may invest idle funds in time certificates of deposit or in open-account time deposits. *Certificates of deposit* (CDs) are for fixed amounts and are issued in both single and multiple maturities ranging from 30 days to as many as four years. They may or may not be negotiable and are offered by banks to both their corporate and noncorporate customers. Certificates of deposit first became important in 1961, when large money-market banks in New York City began to offer them in readily marketable form. Until the mid-1960s, business enterprises were the principal purchasers of these certificates. Since that time, however, the number of individual purchasers has grown appreciably because of the increased yield on these securities relative to competing liquid assets. It is interesting to note that the yield on certificates of deposit has even increased relative to the yield on savings accounts. As a result of this higher yield, commercial bank CD liabilities have increased relative to savings accounts.

Open-account time deposits are similar to time certificates of deposit in that payment will not be made by the bank until some specific maturity date. On the other hand, open-account deposits are not for fixed amounts; they may be increased. A Christmas club savings account is one example of an open-account time deposit.

---

[4] Under the provisions of Regulation Q, the Board of Governors sets the maximum interest rates payable on savings and other time deposits.

Borrowings. Borrowings, as previously indicated, are liabilities that a bank incurs when it borrows funds from other commercial banks, in the Euro-dollar market, or from the Federal Reserve district banks. Borrowings usually take place when banks are temporarily deficient in reserves or when they wish to expand earning assets. Some 5 percent of bank liabilities and capital accounts are in this form.

Borrowing funds from other commercial banks is called trading in the *federal funds market*. "Federal Funds are immediately available Federal Reserve funds, and are essentially titles to reserve balances of member banks at the Federal Reserve banks."[5]

Banks that are short of reserves will borrow funds—generally for very short periods, such as a single day—from banks with excess reserves. Since excess reserves yield no income, banks are willing to lend them for a short time at a positive yield. The federal funds market has become increasingly important since the late 1950s. Federal Reserve use of monetary controls to restrict the reserves available to the banking system has forced a more efficient use of existing reserves and has thus encouraged borrowing in the federal funds market. Trading in federal funds was formerly limited to very large banks, with the amounts involved in excess of $1 million. Now, however, small banks have become active in the market.

The placement of *Euro-dollars* by overseas branches with their American head office is another source of additional reserves for some commercial banks. Euro-dollars are created when the ownership of demand-deposit liabilities at American banks is transferred to foreign banks. Assume, for example, that a holder of demand deposits in an American commercial bank makes a deposit in a foreign bank and wants to keep the claim denominated in dollars. The foreign bank gains an asset (deposits at an American bank) and creates a liability (usually time deposits denominated in dollars) which it owes to the depositor. If the foreign bank then sells its Euro-dollar holdings on an American bank to a foreign branch of another U.S. bank, the Euro-dollars are now owned by the foreign branch of an American bank. The dollars, of course, are still in the United States as liabilities of some American bank. The foreign branch that owns the Euro-dollars will now transfer the ownership to its home office in the United States. The home office will seek payment and, in so doing, will acquire reserves from the American bank whose deposit liabilities had served as Euro-dollars.

American banks need not purchase Euro-dollars from foreign banks. They may also borrow them. Such transactions are generally conducted on an overnight basis with a resultant increase in the reserve assets and borrowing liabilities of the borrowing banks.

Finally, as already indicated, commercial banks that are members of the

[5] Parker B. Willis. *The Federal Funds Market—Its Origin and Development,* Third Edition (Federal Reserve Bank of Boston, 1968), p. 1.

Federal Reserve system can borrow additional dollars from district Federal Reserve banks. Member bank borrowings are discussed in depth in Chapter 11 and will not be considered any further at this point.

Capital accounts. Capital accounts consist of the sum of a bank's stock (par value), surplus, undivided profits, and special reserve accounts. Capital stock increases when a bank issues new stock. Surplus changes when a bank receives more or less than par value from the proceeds of the sale of newly-issued stock. Surplus also changes when the directors of the bank vote to change undistributed profits. For example, if the directors decide to increase capital surplus by a given amount, they do so by reducing undistributed profits by that amount. National banks are required to keep their capital surplus equal to the value of their outstanding stock. Undivided profits are profits remaining after dividend payments have been made. They increase when profits on bank operations are not entirely distributed to stockholders and decrease when there are operational losses. Banks frequently reduce the size of undivided profits by setting up reserve accounts to cover losses on loans and investments. Actually, this involves no transfer of cash or setting aside of funds. A reserve account is merely a segregation of undivided profits designed to reduce stockholder claims to these profits.

As mentioned earlier in this chapter, the total of capital accounts is simply a measure of the claims of stockholders to the assets of the bank. Thus, accounts such as surplus and undivided profits are claims to bank assets. The bank does not segregate any of its cash assets for the purpose of distributing them to stockholders. If the bank has earnings, it is highly probable that it will reinvest most of the funds in income-producing assets such as loans or securities. Profitable banks generally pay dividends, but the total of dividends is substantially less than the total of profits.

The relative importance of capital accounts as a source of funds has remained approximately the same in recent years. The ratio of capital accounts to assets was 0.071 in 1972. While their relative importance remained at about the same level during the 1960s and early 1970s, the total value of capital accounts increased along with the total growth in commercial bank assets. Most of the absolute increase in commercial bank capital accounts can be accounted for by a rise in retained profits rather than by any significant increase in oustanding common stock. Common stock today constitutes approximately 25 percent of total commercial bank capital accounts.[6]

There are numerous reasons for this limited volume of new bank common stock sales. First, there is the memory of the Great Depression. The number of U.S. banks was cut almost in half between 1929 and 1933, and earnings were poor throughout the 1930s. Second, many small banks

---

[6] Federal Deposit Insurance Corporation. *Annual Report* (1971).

are either family dominated or controlled by a small group of individuals who do not want to expand bank ownership for fear of losing control. Third, *bank earnings are low in comparison with many other industries.* Member bank net income after taxes as a percentage of total assets and of capital accounts was 0.81 and 10.54 percent, respectively, in 1972.[7] This third factor has probably been the source of most of the difficulty in expanding stock ownership.

THE NATURE OF COMMERCIAL BANK USES OF FUNDS

The asset side of a commercial bank's balance sheet indicates the many ways in which the bank is able to employ available funds. It may hold funds idle, it may extend credit to business firms, consumers, farmers, financial institutions, and buyers of real estate, and it may invest in corporate and government securities. As one study pointed out, a

. . . characteristic of commercial banks is the multifunctional nature of their lending and investing. In contrast, savings banks and nonbank financial institutions are essentially specialized institutions, although a few lend to more than one category of borrower. Commercial banks, on the other hand, deal in a wide variety of debts and accommodate all types of borrowers.[8]

Table 5–3 shows the asset side of the combined balance sheets of all commercial banks in the United States at the end of 1972. The liability and capital account data for these banks were given in Table 5–2.

Cash Assets

Cash assets consist of reserves with the Federal Reserve banks, vault cash (currency and coin), balances with domestic banks, and other cash assets (a very small amount of deposit balances held with foreign banks and a large volume of cash items in process of collection).

Cash assets, as indicated earlier, have several functions. First, member banks can meet their legal reserve requirements with vault cash and with deposits at the Federal Reserve banks; nonmember banks can usually meet state requirements by vault cash and deposits with other domestic banks. Second, cash assets, in the form of vault cash, provide banks with funds to meet the demands of depositors for cash. And third, cash assets, in the form of deposit balances with the Federal Reserve and other banks, are used to redeem checks drawn on a bank by its customers and presented for collection by other banks.

Cash items in process of collection are the value of checks drawn on

---

[7] *Federal Reserve Bulletin* (May 1973), pp. A-107 and A-108.
[8] The American Bankers Association. *The Commercial Banking Industry* (Prentice-Hall, 1962), p. 1.

TABLE 5-3 ALL COMMERCIAL BANK ASSETS, DECEMBER 31, 1972

ASSETS	AMOUNT (IN MILLIONS OF DOLLARS)	PERCENT OF TOTAL
Cash assets		
Reserves with Federal Reserve banks	26,070	
Currency and coin	8,666	
Balances with domestic banks	32,185	
Other	46,207	
Total cash assets	113,128	15.3
Loans		
Commercial and industrial	132,701	
Agricultural	14,314	
For purchasing or carrying securities		
To brokers and dealers	11,316	
To others	4,491	
To financial institutions		
To banks	6,585	
To others	23,402	
Real estate	98,382	
Other loans to individuals	87,232	
Other	10,171	
Total loans	388,593*	52.6
Investments		
U.S. government securities	67,028	
Bills		
Certificates		
Notes		
Bonds		
State and local government securities	89,504	
Other securities	27,579	
Total investments	184,111	24.9
Federal Funds Sold	26,662	3.6
Other assets	26,539	3.6
Total assets	739,033	100.0

* Total differs due to rounding.
SOURCE: *Federal Reserve Bulletin* (June 1973), pp. A-18, A-22, and A-24.

other banks and not yet collected. These cash assets are not considered usable as a source of funds. Bankers realize that the items that they have for collection on other banks will probably be matched by the checks that other banks will present.

Finally, some banks use their cash assets to secure valuable services from larger city banks and from foreign banks. Smaller banks, for example, often leave substantial sums of money on deposit with large city banks in return for such services as security analysis, the handling of bond and security purchases, the clearing and collection of checks, and participation in loans that the small banks cannot handle alone. Thus, interbank deposits represent another function of cash assets.

Bank Loans

Bank loans are distinguished from investments in that they are generally made directly to a bank's customers; bank investments are usually made indirectly, through the various securities markets. Loans are the largest category, accounting for more than 50 percent of all bank assets, and are extremely diverse, as Table 5–3 shows.

Commercial and industrial loans. The greater part of commercial bank lending has traditionally taken the form of commercial and industrial loans. These loans are extended to manufacturing, mining, wholesale trade, retail trade, transportation, public utility, construction, and service concerns. In short, commercial and industrial loans are made to all types of business enterprises except competing financial institutions and farms, which are covered by other types of loans.

Commercial loans may be *secured* or *unsecured,* and they may be of any duration. Most are secured. The collateral may consist of plant and equipment, accounts receivable,[9] merchandise inventory, or even the stock and bond holdings of the borrowing firm.

One important unsecured loan made by a commercial bank is that created when a firm draws on its *line of credit.* Only firms with excellent credit ratings are granted a line. Under the terms of this arrangement, a business enterprise may borrow up to a predetermined limit, provided that it maintains a compensating balance—usually around 10 percent of the line—and repays the loan annually. Assume, for example, that a firm has a $100,000 line of credit and a 10 percent, compensating-balance requirement. To utilize the line, it must maintain an average deposit account of $10,000 with the lending bank. Having a line of credit, however, does not necessarily mean that the firm has borrowed from the bank. Only when the line is used is a debt created and interest collected by the lending bank. Many firms rarely use their lines, maintaining them simply for purposes of prestige or to have funds available in case of an emergency.

Commercial loans are often designed to provide businesses with funds to take care of temporary discrepancies between receipts and expenditures. For example, a business may borrow to meet a monthly payroll and repay the loan through the month as receipts come in. Or a retailer may borrow substantial amounts in the fall of the year to build up inventories, in anticipation of heavy Christmas sales. When a business borrows for a *seasonal* reason such as this, the maturity of the loan is usually short. On the other hand, when a firm borrows to expand plant and equipment, the loan is likely to be made for a longer period.

As previously indicated, the maturity of both secured and unsecured loans varies considerably, although unsecured loans generally have a

---

[9] An account receivable is created when a firm delivers merchandise to the purchaser with payment to be made at some future date.

shorter life. Most commercial and industrial loans mature within a year, but some have maturities ranging from one to ten years. Those that mature in more than a year are called *term loans*.

Agricultural credit. This is another form of credit extended by commercial banks to borrowers. Although less than 4 percent of all bank loans are agricultural, nevertheless, these loans provide an important source of funds for the agricultural sector of the economy and represent a major source of earnings for a large number of U.S. commercial banks.

Agricultural loans are generally seasonal and are made principally to provide the farmer with money for current expenses. However, banks also provide farmers with funds to buy livestock and machinery, and these loans usually have a longer maturity than those designed to meet current expenses. Still other loans are made to repay debts and to finance real-estate purchases.

Real-estate credit. Real-estate credit is the second most important type of credit extended by commercial banks. Some 25 percent of all bank loans are mortgage loans, and most of these are for residential construction. Since real-estate assets purchased by the borrowers have a long life, the maturity of mortgage loans usually runs from 10 to 25 years.

Many commercial banks compete aggressively for mortgage loans, which, because of their long maturities, provide a steady source of income. Mortgage loans have, in fact, acquired great importance for banks since the end of World War II. In 1972, for example, commercial banks had $98.3 billion in mortgages, contrasted with only $4.8 billion in mortgages in 1945. Some $51.1 billion were uninsured conventional mortgage loans; an additional $10.6 billion were insured and guaranteed by the government.[10] The Federal Housing Administration and the Veterans Administration underwite many different types of mortgages for residential construction and insure remodeling and rehabilitation loans. FHA and VA mortgage insurance removes almost all risk for lenders, thus encouraging the expansion of mortgage credit. However, bank holdings of conventional mortage loans have grown more rapidly than VA and FHA guaranteed loans, principally because of higher interest yields.

Consumer credit. Loans to consumers are another important use of commercial bank funds. Most of the $87.2 billion listed under "Other loans to individuals" in Table 5–3 consists of consumer loans. These are quite varied and may be made on an installment or a noninstallment basis. Banks lend funds to finance the purchase of automobiles and make other "personal" loans for repairs and modernization or for the purchase of various

---

[10] *Federal Reserve Bulletin* (May 1972), p. A-52 and (June 1973), p. A-50.

TABLE 5-4 CONSUMER CREDIT, DECEMBER 31, 1972
(IN MILLIONS OF DOLLARS)

TYPE OF CREDIT	TOTAL CREDIT	CREDIT HELD BY COMMERCIAL BANKS
Installment		
Automobile paper	44,129	27,096
Other consumer goods paper	40,080	16,196
Repair and modernization loans	6,201	3,544
Personal loans	36,922	12,947
Total	127,332	59,783
Noninstallment		
Single payment loans	12,256	10,857
Charge accounts	9,002	— *
Service credit	8,974	—
Total	30,232	10,857
Total consumer credit	157,564	70,640

* Bank credit card accounts outstanding are included in estimates of installment credit outstanding.
SOURCE: *Federal Reserve Bulletin* (March 1973), pp. A-56 and A-57.

consumer durables. In addition to making direct loans to consumers, banks also purchase installment paper created by the sellers of consumer goods.

Table 5-4 shows the amount of consumer credit outstanding in the economy in 1972 and the relative importance of commercial banks as sources of this type of credit. Out of a total $157.6 billion in consumer credit in 1972, $70.6 billion was furnished by commercial banks. Collectively, they are the largest supplier of consumer credit in the economy. Finance companies, credit unions, and retail outlets follow in that order as additional suppliers of consumer credit.

This strong position of commercial banks in consumer credit is a relatively recent phenomenon which, for the most part, has developed since the 1930s. Because the credit demands of traditional business borrowers during the Depression were weak, commercial banks increased the variety of their lending activities, particularly in the area of consumer credit. By 1939, commercial banks accounted for 24 percent of all consumer credit. This figure has continued to grow until presently banks extend almost 40 percent of total consumer credit.

Other lending activity. Banks lend to one another and to various financial intermediaries, too. For example, finance companies, which make personal loans to individuals, may borrow from commercial banks. There are many other ways in which commercial banks lend to competing financial institutions. The amount of loans to financial intermediaries in 1972 was $23.4 billion.

Banks also lend to brokers, dealers, and individual purchasers of securities. The total volume of such loans in 1972 was $15.8 billion. When individuals wish to purchase stock but have insufficient funds to cover the full purchase price, they may borrow up to a certain percentage of that purchase price from the bank. The Federal Reserve determines how high this maximum percentage or *margin* may be.[11] Banks also lend directly to securities brokers.

Investments

Commercial bank holdings of investments (see Table 5–3) consist primarily of U.S. government securities. In 1972, commercial banks held $67.0 billion in U.S. government securities, representing approximately 9 percent of all bank assets. In addition, banks held $89.5 billion in state and local government securities and $27.6 billion in other securities.

U.S. government securities. Commercial banks purchase U.S. government securities for a variety of reasons. First, they are very safe; there is no risk that the U.S. government, like a private borrower, may fail to meet its obligations. Second, they are highly liquid: there is a wide market for these securities, and banks in need of cash can quickly find purchasers for their security holdings. Third, banks are permitted to use U.S. government securities as collateral when borrowing reserves from the Federal Reserve banks. Finally, banks earn interest on their security holdings. *In short, commercial banks purchase and hold U.S. government securities because they are safe, highly liquid, interest-yielding assets.*

The "lock-in effect." This is not to say, of course, that banks never lose money on U.S. government securities. While there is no risk of default on the part of the government, the danger does exist that a commercial bank will lose on its security holdings if they are sold prior to maturity. But a security sold prior to maturity may occasionally lead to a capital gain, and a bond purchased at less than par may yield a profit when redeemed. For example, when a bank purchases a $1,000, 3 percent U.S. government security at time of issue for $1,000 and interest rates on comparable U.S. government securities subsequently increase to 3.5 percent, the market price of the 3 percent security will decline. For a 3 percent, $1,000 security to be sold in the face of such competition, its price must be sufficiently low to give the purchaser the same return on his investment that he could get on a 3.5 percent security. How much of a loss will the bank suffer? The $1,000, 3 percent security yields $30, and $30 is 3.5 percent of $857. Hence, figuring backward, the old security probably cannot be sold for more than $857. Therefore, if the bank that originally purchased the security for $1,000 decides to sell at this point, it will lose $143 on the transaction. On the other hand, if the security had been purchased when it was selling at less than par, the purchasing bank would have gained either by

---

[11] We will discuss margin requirements in Chapter 12.

holding it until maturity or by selling it when interest rates on comparable securities had eased and their prices had consequently risen.

In short, when government bonds held by commercial banks have a lower nominal interest yield than is currently available on comparable new security issues, the older bonds can no longer be described as highly liquid. They can no longer be quickly converted into cash assets without substantial loss. To break even, the banks must hold the bonds until maturity or until such time as their prices again increase. This situation leads to what economists call the *lock-in effect*.[12] The hypothesis is that, rather than suffer a loss, commercial banks will hold on to their government securities. In effect, they are "locked in" to their investments in these securities.[13] Furthermore, with funds tied up in U.S. government securities, banks will be unable to expand loans. In a period of full employment and rising prices, this restraint on bank lending is thought to be a deterrent to inflation.

If it is true that holding U.S. government securities tends to restrain commercial bank lending operations in periods of rising interest rates and strong demands for loans, why do banks bother to hold them at all? For reasons already given: they are safe investments and may be used as collateral when borrowing reserves. Furthermore, almost a third of the U.S. government securities held by banks mature in less than one year. Most government bills mature in 90 to 92 days, most certificates in less than a year, most notes in one to five years, and most bonds at the end of five years. Banks with a high proportion of short-term U.S. government securities in their investment portfolios can frequently overcome the lock-in effect in periods of inflation by gradually replacing some of these securities as they come due with high-yield private investments and loans. Caution must be observed, however, since private securities and loans involve more risk and can be illiquid on the downward side of the business cycle.

State and local government securities. Investment in state and local government securities represents the final major use of commercial bank funds. Approximately 12 percent of all bank assets are in this form.

Since state and local government securities are tax exempt, they are a highly attractive investment for commercial banks and for persons in high income-tax brackets. The after-tax yield of these securities is generally higher than that of comparable nontax-exempt securities. Thus, if a tax-exempt security yields 4 percent, the actual return to the security holder is substantially higher than that on a comparable taxable investment. For example, if the bondholder is a bank in the 48 percent corporation-income-tax bracket, a 4 percent tax-exempt security is equivalent to a 7.7 percent tax-

[12] "The Influence of Monetary Policy on Lenders and Borrowers." *Federal Reserve Bulletin* (May 1953); and "The Lock-in Effect: Bank Reactions to Security Losses." *Monthly Review* (Federal Reserve Bank of Kansas City, June 1960).
[13] Actually, commercial banks are only occasionally locked in (See Table 5–7).

able security.[14] For this reason, tax-exempt securities tend to carry lower nominal yields than private securities of comparable face value. This difference in nominal yields tends to diminish the difference in actual yields of taxable and tax-exempt securities with the same face value.

Nevertheless, the actual yields of most tax-exempt securities are higher than the after-tax yields of taxable securities of comparable face value, largely for competitive reasons. A large volume of municipal securities has been issued since World War II to pay for expansion in educational, sewage, water, electric, and gas facilities to meet the needs of our rapidly growing population. Local governments, in order to increase their ability to obtain funds, must offer higher yields. Thus, a favorable spread is maintained by state and local governments between the after-tax yields on taxable securities and the yields on tax-exempt securities.

Investment in state and local government securities by commercial banks does pose several problems, however. Banks are subject to community pressures to purchase securities that may be somewhat risky. Also, the market for tax-exempt securities is limited, with banks and individuals in high income-tax brackets the principal purchasers. This limited market means that the relative liquidity of these securities is reduced. Consequently, when banks purchase tax-exempt securities, they tend to hold them to maturity.

Other securities. Commercial banks purchase a limited number of privately-issued securities, primarily corporate bonds. Government agencies closely regulate such bank purchases, and banks are not permitted to buy stocks as investments.

Federal funds sold. Federal Funds Sold correspond to the borrowing of reserves in the federal funds market discussed earlier. Banks that borrow reserves acquire an asset (reserves) and a liability (borrowings). Selling (lending) banks acquire an asset (Federal Funds Sold) and lose an asset (reserves). All of these transactions are reversed when the borrowing bank repays the selling bank.

BANK EARNINGS AND PROFIT MAXIMIZATION

A bank's revenue is derived almost exclusively from its earning assets — its loans and investments. Table 5–5 categorizes and then accounts for bank sources of income in 1972. We see that 60 percent of all bank operating income in 1972 resulted from loans. Bank ownership of securities

---

[14] A $1,000, 4 percent tax-exempt security yields $40 per year. What rate of interest would a $1,000 security subject to tax have to yield for the bondholder to be left with $40 after taxes? Let x be the rate of interest. Then $(1,000) (x) - (.48) (\$1,000) (x) = \$40$; solving for x, we get 7.7 percent.

TABLE 5-5 INCOME, EXPENSES, AND DIVIDENDS OF INSURED COMMERCIAL BANKS, 1972 (IN THOUSANDS OF DOLLARS)

ITEM	ALL INSURED BANKS	INSURED NONMEMBER BANKS	ALL MEMBER BANKS
Operating income — Total	**40,055,267**	**8,720,739**	**31,334,528**
Loans:			
Interest and fees	25,441,739	5,444,681	19,997,058
Federal funds sold and securities purchased with resale agreement	1,022,955	229,087	793,868
Securities — Interest and dividends:			
U.S. Treasury securities	3,375,749	963,710	2,412,040
Other U.S. government securities (agencies and corporations)	1,142,498	412,665	729,834
Obligations of states and political subdivisions	3,488,847	779,919	2,708,928
All other securities	318,675	84,854	233,821
Trust department income	1,366,160	97,270	1,268,890
Service charges on deposit accounts	1,255,423	351,242	904,182
Other charges, fees, etc.	1,078,369	214,809	863,560
Other operating income:			
On trading account, net	257,174	3,006	254,168
Other	1,307,677	139,496	1,168,181
Operating expenses — Total	**32,826,740**	**7,187,850**	**25,638,890**
Salaries and wages of officers and employees	7,713,325	1,693,028	6,020,297
Officer and employee benefits	1,323,050	250,021	1,073,029
Interest paid on:			
Time and savings deposits	13,776,156	3,263,234	10,512,922
Federal funds purchased and securities sold with repurchase agreement	1,424,763	37,496	1,387,267
Other borrowed money	114,613	12,549	102,064
Capital notes and debentures	212,220	28,672	183,548
Occupancy expense of bank premises, net	1,573,976	314,572	1,259,404
Furniture, equipment, etc.	1,082,486	234,804	847,681
Provision for loan losses	962,808	195,941	766,868
Other operating expenses	4,643,343	1,157,533	3,485,811
Income before income taxes and securities gains or losses	**7,228,527**	**1,532,889**	**5,695,638**
Applicable income taxes	1,707,342	351,732	1,355,609
Income before securities gains or losses	5,521,185	1,181,156	4,340,029
Net securities gains or losses (−) after taxes	90,061	43,586	46,475
Extraordinary charges (−) or credits after taxes	17,899	4,151	13,748
Less minority interest in consolidated subsidiaries	663	294	370
Net income	**5,628,482**	**1,228,600**	**4,399,882**
Cash dividends declared			
On common stock	2,186,666	350,317	1,836,349
On preferred stock	3,813	954	2,859

SOURCE: *Federal Reserve Bulletin* (May 1973), p. A-96.

provided another 20 percent. In comparison, all other sources of income were relatively insignificant.

It may seem peculiar that bank loans earned three times as much as investments, despite the fact that the dollar volume of the former was double that of the latter. The differing characteristics of these assets are responsible for this striking difference in return. Loans are held primarily for return, whereas investments are held primarily for safety and liquidity. Since investments are less risky and more liquid than loans, their yield is lower. To put it another way, the higher interest returns on loans are a way of compensating commercial banks for the risks they assume.

How did commercial banks dispose of this income in 1972? A quarter of it provided wages and salaries. Taxes took another 4 percent. The 34 percent of income used to pay interest on time deposits represents a marked increase over previous interest costs. In 1963, for example, interest paid on time deposits was only 25 percent of total income.[15] This change is attributable in part to increased interest rates on commercial bank time deposits and in part to a sharp rise in the total volume of time-deposit liabilities as a result of their higher yields.

A Banking Industry Dilemma—Earnings versus Safety

Commercial banks, like other businesses, are private, profit-seeking corporations. They can be expected to try to maximize profits, hopefully in a manner that is consistent with bank safety. Compared with other industries, however, banks have a low but steady level of earnings.

To raise earnings, banks must grant more loans and make more investments, and in order to do this they must have more funds (reserves). Additional usable reserves for the commercial banking system are provided only when the monetary authorities lower reserve requirements or purchase U.S. government securities on the open market. Thus, the commercial banking system must depend upon the decisions of regulatory agencies to grant needed additional reserves.

How can banks increase earnings and profits when additional reserves are not available to them? One obvious solution is to reduce expenses. In a competitive industry like banking, however, most firms are already striving for reduced costs. Another alternative is to engage in more aggressive *liability management*. By selling more certificates of deposit, offering the legal maximum on all types of time deposits, borrowing in the federal funds market, acquiring Euro-dollars, and having nonbank subsidiaries sell commercial paper, the individual commercial bank is able to acquire additional reserves—but these procedures simply benefit some banks at the expense of others.

Yet another alternative available for increasing profits is to change the composition of the bank asset portfolio—that is, to improve on bank *asset*

---

[15] Federal Deposit Insurance Corporation. *Annual Report* (1963), p. 153.

management. This alternative usually involves making relatively more high-income producing loans and investments. Higher-yielding loans and investments, however, are likely to be risky. An increased proportion of risk assets in a bank portfolio will impair the quality of that bank's assets in the view of government supervisory agencies.

For several decades, bank secondary reserves in the form of U.S. government securities have declined relative to deposits, as has the ratio of capital accounts to risk assets in the form of bank loans. In addition, the ratio of loans to deposits has increased. These are all signs of increased risk. Nevertheless, deposit insurance in recent decades has resulted in a very low rate of bank failure and deposit loss.

Ultimately, the solution to what many bankers view as serious problems—a high proportion of risk assets and inadequate bank capital—appears to lie in the creation of more usable reserves by the Federal Reserve System. With increased reserves, banks would be able to make more loans and investments, increase earnings, and thereby induce greater stock sales. The ratio of capital accounts to assets would rise, providing a greater margin of protection for bank depositors. The wisdom of such an approach, of course, depends upon the national economic situation.

BANK OPERATIONS AND THE NATIONAL ECONOMY

The contribution of the commercial banking system to economic growth and stability depends in large part upon the sources and uses of bank funds. To help promote growth, banks need expanding sources of funds. To help maintain economic stability, bank operations should not intensify economic fluctuations. Yet, as banks pursue the profit motive, they may contribute to a destabilization of the economy. And when banks are not successful in acquiring expanding sources of funds, profits are low. These are some of the enigmas posed by banks in their dual role of money creators and profit-seeking business enterprises. In this section, we shall examine in some depth the problems bank operations pose, both for banks and for the national economy.

Competition between Commercial Banks and Nonbank Financial Institutions for Funds

Periods of relative decline by commercial banks. Table 5–6 shows the rate of growth in the financial assets of various financial institutions for selected periods from 1945 through 1972. The period ending around 1960 was one of relative decline for commercial banks as direct contributors to the pecuniary assets of the economy. This decline can be partly attributed to the characteristic that sets commercial banks apart from other financial institutions: their creation and administration of the principal part of our money stock—demand deposits. The level of economic activity is closely related to the stock of money. When the money supply is allowed to

TABLE 5–6 FINANCIAL INSTITUTION GROWTH OF ASSETS,
PERCENT INCREASE FOR SELECTED PERIODS, 1945–72*

PERIOD	COMMERCIAL BANKS	MUTUAL SAVINGS BANKS	LIFE INSURANCE COMPANIES	SAVINGS AND LOAN ASSOCIATIONS
1945–60	60.7	139.2	166.9	717.1
1960–61	8.2	5.6	6.1	14.9
1961–62	6.7	7.7	5.1	14.0
1962–63	5.3	7.8	5.9	14.9
1963–64	10.9	9.1	5.9	11.0
1964–65	8.7	7.4	6.3	8.6
1965–66	6.9	4.7	5.1	3.4
1966–67	11.8	8.8	6.1	7.2
1967–68	11.0	7.2	5.8	6.5
1968–69	6.0	4.2	5.1	6.1
1969–70	8.6	6.5	5.1	8.7
1970–71	11.1	13.1	6.9	17.1
1971–72	11.8	12.4	7.8	18.0

* All computations are based on end-of-year figures.
SOURCE: Computed from *Federal Reserve Bulletin* (October 1961), p. 1197; (February 1964), p. 190; (March 1966), p. 368; (January 1968), p. A-19; (April 1969), pp. A-35 and A-36; (March 1973), pp. A-20, A-39, and A-40.

increase rapidly, inflation generally follows. Depressions, on the other hand, are usually accompanied by a fall in the stock of money. In our economy the monetary authorities attempt to prevent inflation and recession by manipulating interest rates and the money supply. To affect the money stock, the Federal Reserve regulates the reserve position of the commercial banking system. In periods of high employment, it limits the ability of commercial banks to create demand deposits. When these limitations are imposed upon the banking system, borrowers turn to other lending institutions. This worsens the competitive position of the commercial banks.

When one borrows from a lender other than a commercial bank, money is not created. These financial institutions lend funds directly, usually in the form of demand deposits at commercial banks. For example, the balance-sheet changes that occur when other financial institutions lend $10,000 are:

BALANCE-SHEET CHANGES FOR NONBANK LENDING INSTITUTIONS

ASSETS	LIABILITIES + CAPITAL ACCOUNTS
Demand deposits at commercial banks −$10,000 Loans and investments +$10,000	

BALANCE-SHEET CHANGES FOR THE COMMERCIAL BANKING SYSTEM

ASSETS	LIABILITIES + CAPITAL ACCOUNTS
	Demand deposits of the nonbank lending institutions −$10,000 Demand deposits of the borrowers +$10,000

As a result, the dollar volume of loans and investments made by commercial banks decreases in relation to those of other institutions, although for the economy as a whole there is an increase in economic activity. The total of the money stock is unchanged but there has been an increase in its turnover. In other words, the *velocity* with which the money stock changes hands in the economy has increased.

Other lending institutions obtain funds for loans by successfully competing with commercial banks for the idle cash and deposits of individuals in the economy. For example, here is what happens to the balance sheet when a depositor in a commercial bank is induced to switch $1,000 from deposits (either time or demand) in a commercial bank to a savings and loan share account:

BALANCE-SHEET CHANGES FOR THE COMMERCIAL BANKING SYSTEM

ASSETS	LIABILITIES + CAPITAL ACCOUNTS
	Deposits of individual depositor −$1,000
	Deposits of savings and loan association +$1,000

BALANCE-SHEET CHANGES FOR THE SAVINGS AND LOAN ASSOCIATION

ASSETS	LIABILITIES + CAPITAL ACCOUNTS
Deposits at the commercial banking system +$1,000	Savings and loan share accounts +$1,000

The savings and loan association is now in a position to lend, and will probably choose to make a mortgage loan.

In a period of full employment and rising prices when this situation prevails throughout the economy, there is an added incentive for the monetary authorities to impose tighter controls. The Federal Reserve System can be expected to restrict commercial bank lending activity in hopes of causing interest rate increases that will discourage borrowers. Thus, the main brunt of monetary restraints may be borne by the commercial banking system. The effects of such action on other financial institutions will be only indirect—that is, their lending activities will be curtailed only to the extent that rising interest rates will also discourage borrowers from seeking funds at their institutions.

Periods of relative growth for commercial banks. Table 5–6 also shows that mutual savings bank and life insurance company assets grew somewhat less rapidly than commercial bank assets during 1960–72. Only savings and loan association assets grew more rapidly, and their growth slowed relative to commercial bank assets from 1964 through 1970. The relative growth in commercial bank assets during the late 1960s is partly attributable to a change in Federal Reserve policy. The Federal Reserve increasingly used Regulation Q to regulate the maximum rates payable by commercial banks on time deposits, raising these rates relative to those payable by nonbank financial institutions such as savings and loan associations. The result was a marked increase in outstanding certificates of deposit issued by commercial banks. Many members of the nonbank public increased their rate of purchase of CDs, decreased their investments in other near-money forms issued by nonbank financial institutions, and, in some instances, actually converted their near-money holdings into CDs.

When this occurs, severe contractionary pressures are felt by the non-bank financial institutions that created the near-money forms. People with claims on these institutions will demand payment. To make payment, the institutions must draw down their own checking-deposit accounts at commercial banks. When these funds are then used to purchase certificates of deposit issued by commercial banks, the net effect will be an increase in commercial bank time-deposit liabilities. For example, the balance-sheet changes that take place when individuals switch $1,000 from savings and loan share accounts to time deposits at commercial banks are:

BALANCE-SHEET CHANGES FOR THE COMMERCIAL BANKING SYSTEM

ASSETS	LIABILITIES + CAPITAL ACCOUNTS
	Demand deposits of savings and loan association −$1,000 Time deposits of individual depositor +$1,000

BALANCE-SHEET CHANGES FOR THE SAVINGS AND LOAN ASSOCIATION

ASSETS	LIABILITIES + CAPITAL ACCOUNTS
Demand deposits at the commercial banking system −$1,000	Savings and loan share accounts −$1,000

As a result, commercial bank demand deposits decrease. The total wealth holdings of those members of the nonbank public who are not financial institutions remain the same, but the composition of their liquid-wealth holdings changes as a result of the decrease in the liabilities of nonbank financial institutions and the increase in commercial bank time deposits. Since the demand deposits that are destroyed are those of the nonbank financial institutions, and since these deposits serve as their cash reserves, any reduction constitutes a decrease in reserves and thus in their lending ability. The Federal Reserve action increasing maximum interest rates on time deposits thus may ultimately be deflationary, since the reduction in lending will serve to contract the demand for goods and services.

At the same time it should be noted that commercial bank reserve positions will have improved because of the lower reserve requirements for time deposits relative to demand deposits. To the extent that commercial banks previously were rationing credit because of reserve limitations, they may now expand loans and investments and, accordingly, demand deposits.

These newly created demand deposits are most likely to be active deposits that add to the demand for goods and services. The final result will be a total of demand and time deposits at commercial banks greater than that which existed prior to the rise in interest rates, but a somewhat smaller volume of demand deposits. The Federal Reserve, of course, is well aware of the liberalizing effect of higher interest rates and has used other measures to restrict the scope of expansion by the commercial banking system. Overall, the effect of Federal Reserve action in the late 1960s was to increase the rate of growth of commercial banks relative to other financial institutions while slowing the growth of demand during a period of high employment and rising prices.

Conclusion. The fact that much of monetary policy directly affects only commercial banks limits their ability to compete for funds. Ironically, the tighter the restraint placed by the Federal Reserve on commercial banks, the less direct control it may have over the economy. Increased lending activity by nonbank financial institutions increases the demand for goods and services just as commercial bank loans do, and the Federal Reserve has little direct control over these nonbank institutions. However, the activities of nonbank financial institutions can be indirectly controlled through the use of Regulation Q to raise the interest rates paid by commercial banks on CDs relative to the rates paid by nonbank financial institutions on their liabilities.

The Behavior of Bank Loans and Investments and Gross National Product

Table 5–7, which compares the growth of commercial bank loans, security investments, and demand deposits with the growth of gross national product from 1951 to 1973, shows the close relationship between bank loan and investment activity and the condition of the economy. The growth of bank loans slackened in the recession years—1954, 1958, 1961, and 1970. Gross national product remained steady in 1954 and 1958, and increased slowly in the recessions of 1961 and 1970. Bank investments, on the other hand, rose substantially in each of these years. The 1970 figure in Table 5–7 on investment in U.S. government securities does not reflect the increase in these holdings that took place in 1970 because the midyear figure is given. The full impact of the 1970 recession was not felt until later in the year, at which time banks increased their holdings of U.S. government securities. Conversely, during economic recovery and prosperity, as was dramatized by the boom of 1973, bank loans increased rapidly, while investments declined somewhat or grew slowly. (The years 1962, 1967, and 1971, as we shall discuss in a moment, were exceptions.)

For the most part, Federal Reserve monetary policy during this period was one of ease in the recession years and gradually increasing restraint

TABLE 5-7 COMMERCIAL BANK LOANS, U.S. GOVERNMENT SECURITIES, OTHER SECURITIES, AND DEMAND DEPOSITS AT MIDYEAR, 1951–73; GROSS NATIONAL PRODUCT, 1951–73 (IN BILLIONS OF DOLLARS)

YEAR	COMMERCIAL BANK LOANS	U.S. GOVERNMENT SECURITIES	OTHER SECURITIES	DEMAND DEPOSITS*	GROSS NATIONAL PRODUCT
1951	54.8	58.5	12.7	96.3	328.4
1952	59.2	61.2	14.0	103.4	345.5
1953	65.0	58.6	14.3	105.7	364.6
1954	67.3	63.5	15.5	107.0	364.8
1955	75.2	63.3	16.8	113.0	398.0
1956	86.9	56.6	16.5	115.8	419.2
1957	93.3	55.5	16.8	115.7	441.1
1958	93.6	64.2	20.1	117.1	447.3
1959	104.5	60.9	20.6	121.6	483.6
1960	114.8	54.2	19.9	119.5	503.8
1961	118.0	61.8	22.1	125.2	520.1
1962	129.2	64.4	27.0	128.8	560.3
1963	145.0	63.5	32.4	133.6	590.5
1964	164.5	59.3	36.4	135.6	632.4
1965	188.6	56.9	44.2	145.3	684.9
1966	212.0	53.5	48.8	153.8	749.9
1967	224.0	54.2	56.7	161.0	793.9
1968	244.6	58.6	64.4	177.8	864.2
1969	283.9	54.0	72.4	193.8	929.1
1970	296.1	51.6	75.6	193.0	974.1
1971	322.9	60.3	97.4	206.9	1,046.8
1972	370.9	60.3	111.5	219.1	1,151.8
1973	447.9	56.9	119.7	223.7	1,290.0

* Excluding interbank and U.S government demand deposits.
SOURCE: Board of Governors of the Federal Reserve System. *Supplement to Banking and Monetary Statistics,* Section 1 (1962), pp. 26–28, and *Federal Reserve Bulletins* (December 1962), p. 1650; (June 1963), p. 808; (December 1964), p. 1554; (December 1965), p. 1742; (January 1967), p. 102; (December 1967), p. 2092; (June 1968, May 1969 and 1970), p. A-19; (May 1971, 1972, and 1973), p. A-20; (August 1973), p. A-20. (See Table 19-1 for gross national product sources.)

through recovery and prosperity. This policy was based on the theory that in recession we need an expansion of loans, and in prosperity some restraint on lending. Yet the actual situation was the reverse of that hoped for by monetary theorists. Why? Bankers argue that loan volume does *not* grow during recessions because demand is slack. As a result, banks place additional funds in safe investments such as U.S. government securities. With prosperity, however, the demand for loans *increases* sharply. Banks are eager to expand their loan volume to increase their earnings, but restriction of bank reserve positions by the Federal Reserve may prevent this. Consequently, banks cut back on their investments in low-interest-yielding government securities in order to make more profitable use of their funds in loans. Thus, we find that in years of relative prosperity, bank investments usually remain comparatively steady or grow slowly.

Exceptions to this rule occurred in 1962, 1967, and 1971. Although the economy was in some respects prosperous in 1962, the Federal Reserve retained an expansive monetary policy because of continued high unemployment levels. This permitted banks to expand both loans and investments. In addition, most of the growth in investments that year was in state and local government securities. Banks exhibited a strong demand for these tax-exempt securities because they needed high-interest, long-term investments to provide funds to meet rising interest charges on an increasing volume of time deposits. The year 1967, unlike 1962, was very prosperous overall. Stimulated by the Vietnam war, the economy was growing, and prices and employment were rising — particularly in the latter half of that year. There was some slack in the economy early in the year. The result was a comparatively easy monetary policy, designed in part to stimulate the housing market which had been hurt by the tight money policies of 1966. Banks, as in some other periods of prosperity, expanded both loans and investments. Almost all of the increase in investments was again in highly profitable state and local tax-exempt securities. In some ways, the year 1971 was comparable to 1962, a year of recovery with an easy monetary policy, but a continued unemployment level that hovered around 6 percent. The net effect was rising loans, increased demand deposits, a small increase in bank holdings of U.S. government securities, and a sharp rise in bank holdings of state and local government securities.

For the period 1951–73 as a whole, bank uses of funds were expansive. Loans increased from $54.8 to $447.9 billion, or more than 700 percent. Investments, however, rose only from $71.2 to $176.6 billion, or 148 percent. Thus, bank loans, which tend to stimulate demand in the economy more than bank investments, increased more than four times as much as investments. The government securities component of investments varied contracyclically during these years, but the period as a whole showed almost no change in the total of these holdings. Demand deposits increased only 132 percent, yet gross national product rose more than 290 percent. This means that bank loan and investment activity, coupled with federal monetary restraint, resulted more in an increased *use* than in an increased *volume* of demand deposits. The monetary restraints imposed by the federal authorities cause banks to economize on the creation of demand deposits. This is what the Federal Reserve wants to accomplish. But such Federal Reserve action could be self-defeating since the velocity of money increases. The following section discusses this more fully.

The Commercial Banking System's Role in Economic Fluctuations

The manner in which commercial banks build up loans and decrease investment growth in periods of prosperity and hold down the level of loans and increase investment growth in recessions suggests the following conclusions concerning the role of the commercial banking system during economic fluctuations.

First, it shows that banking activities as a whole are not always effectively circumscribed by the "lock-in effect." Banks may readily decrease investments in periods of prosperity by failing to reinvest as bonds mature or by selling off some of their holdings. And they apparently have not been afraid to do so, even taking, in some cases, a capital loss in order to unload securities.

Second, commercial bank loan creation in periods of recovery helps to increase demand deposits and stimulates demand, output, and employment in the economy. Demand deposits have grown in the last two decades and — aside from the relatively prosperous Vietnam war period — most of the growth has come in the year or two following each recession. These were periods of monetary ease, when commercial banks had adequate reserves.

Third, when banks put their funds in investments rather than in loans during recessions, it slows the pace of recovery. The money balances held by borrowers are active and stimulate the economy, but the money balances used in the purchase and sale of securities are relatively inactive. This behavior by banks is justified; available funds go into securities in part because of the lack of qualified borrowers. The alternative would be for banks to hold excess reserves. Since putting funds into securities tends to push down interest rates, it contributes more to recovery than would a policy of holding excess reserves.

Finally, commercial bank activity may also have an adverse effect on the economy during periods of high employment, rapidly growing gross national product, and rising prices. In these periods, banks are able to avoid monetary restrictions by reducing investment growth and increasing loans. This transfers money balances from security purchasers (relatively inactive spenders) to borrowers (active spenders). Thus, even with no change in the money supply, bank loan and investment policy may increase inflationary pressures by increasing the velocity of money and thus the demand for goods.

A balance-sheet transaction may be used to illustrate this last situation:

BALANCE-SHEET CHANGES FOR THE COMMERCIAL BANKING SYSTEM

ASSETS		LIABILITIES + CAPITAL ACCOUNTS
Investments	−$1,000,000 (a)	Demand deposits of security purchasers −$1,000,000 (a)
Loans	+$1,000,000 (b)	Demand deposits of borrowers +$1,000,000 (b)
		Demand deposits of sellers of goods to borrowers +$1,000,000 (c)
		Demand deposits of borrowers −$1,000,000 (c)

Transaction (a) records a sale of securities by the commercial banks. Those who purchase the securities from the banks do so by drawing down their checking accounts. This reduces the demand-deposit liabilities of the commercial banking system, thus freeing reserves. The banks can then use these reserves to back new loans; the new deposits created by these loans are recorded in transaction (b). Bank loans and the demand-deposit accounts of borrowers are increased by $1 million. Subsequently, the borrowers purchase goods and services, and the $1 million in demand deposits is transferred to the sellers of goods and services. This is recorded in transaction (c).

Thus, despite Federal Reserve monetary controls, commercial banks may intensify, rather than dampen, the cyclical swings of the economy.

Supplementary Readings

American Bankers Association. *The Commercial Banking Industry* (Prentice-Hall, 1962), Chapters 2, 4–8, 10.

Anderson, Leonall and Albert Burger. "Asset Management and Commercial Bank Portfolio Behavior: Theory and Practice." *Journal of Finance* (1969), pp. 207–222.

Dill, Arnold. "Liability Management Banking—Its Growth and Impact," *Monthly Review* (Federal Reserve Bank of Atlanta, 1971).

Gramley, L. E., and S. B. Chase. "Time Deposits in Monetary Analysis." *Federal Reserve Bulletin* (1965), pp. 1093–1101.

Melnik, Arie. "Short Run Determinants of Commercial Bank Investment Portfolios: An Empirical Analysis." *Journal of Finance* (1970), pp. 639–49.

Theilman, Ward. "Commercial Bank Liability Management and Monetary Control." *Journal of Financial and Quantitative Analysis* (1970), pp. 329–40.

6 Commercial Banks
and the Creation of Money

CREATION AND DESTRUCTION OF DEPOSITS BY INDIVIDUAL BANKS

Creation of Deposits
  Primary deposits
  Derivative deposits
Destruction of Deposits

**LIMITATIONS TO INDIVIDUAL BANK DEPOSIT CREATING
AND DESTROYING ABILITIES**

Deposit Creation and the Reserve Requirement
Deposit Destruction and the Reserve Requirement
How a Bank Obtains Additional Reserves
Other Factors Affecting Commercial Bank Deposit Creation
  The demand for currency
  The demand for time deposits
  Favorable and adverse clearing balances
  Willingness to borrow and lend
  The unpredictability of business conditions
  Government economic policy
  Summary

**CREATION AND DESTRUCTION OF DEPOSITS BY
THE COMMERCIAL BANKING SYSTEM**

Banking System Creation of Deposits
Banking System Destruction of Deposits
A Shorthand Formula to Predict the Deposit Creation
and Destruction Potential of the Commercial Banking System
Banking System Deposit Creation and Destruction
Under Relaxed Assumptions
  Cash drains and influxes
  Excess reserves
  Time deposits

THE TOTAL STOCK OF MONEY

Predicting Changes in the Stock of Money
Predicting the Stock of Money from High-Powered Money

SUMMARY AND PREVIEW

Appendix: The Derivation of Deposit, Money, and Loan Multipliers
The Derivation of Deposit Multipliers
The Derivation of Money Multiplier Equation 6–10
The Derivation of a Bank Credit Multiplier

$\mathbf{P}$receding chapters have repeatedly emphasized the importance of the commercial banking system in the creation and destruction of the principal component of our nation's money supply – demand deposits. It has been explained that individual commercial banks create deposits when they accept new deposits, grant loans, or make investments. This chapter will demonstrate how this is done. Deposit creation will then be studied from the larger perspective of the entire banking system.

CREATION AND DESTRUCTION OF DEPOSITS BY INDIVIDUAL BANKS

Creation of Deposits

Primary deposits. A commercial bank creates deposits when it accepts *deposits of cash.* Assume that Individual 1 deposits $1,000 in currency with Bank A. This results in a $1,000 increase in Bank A's reserves (since vault cash is part of a bank's reserves) and a $1,000 increase in its deposit liabilities:

BALANCE-SHEET CHANGES FOR COMMERCIAL BANK A

ASSETS		LIABILITIES + CAPITAL ACCOUNTS	
Reserves	+$1,000	Deposits of Individual 1	+$1,000

The deposits thus created are called *primary deposits* because they result from the deposit of cash.

Primary deposits may also result from the *deposit of checks drawn on other banks.* These checks will also increase the reserves of the receiving bank. Suppose that Individual 1 wishes to deposit a $1,000 bonus check from his employer. If the individual makes the deposit with Bank A but the employer has written the check on the company account at Bank B, the appropriate balance-sheet changes, after the check has cleared,[1] are:

---

[1] Check clearing is discussed in Chapter 9.

BALANCE-SHEET CHANGES FOR COMMERCIAL BANK A

ASSETS		LIABILITIES + CAPITAL ACCOUNTS	
Reserves	+$1,000	Deposits of Individual 1	+$1,000

BALANCE-SHEET CHANGES FOR COMMERCIAL BANK B

ASSETS		LIABILITIES + CAPITAL ACCOUNTS	
Reserves	−$1,000	Demand deposits of employer	−$1,000

Notice that no distinction is made between the time and demand deposits of Individual 1, since he may choose to increase either account.

What are the overall effects of the creation of these primary deposits upon the total money stock? If Individual 1 chooses to keep his funds in the form of demand deposits, the money stock is not affected. A cash deposit decreases the currency holdings of the nonbank public, but it increases demand deposits. Thus, there is no change in the total money stock. Similarly, when demand deposits are transferred from one part of the nonbank public (the employer) to another part (Individual 1), there is no effect on the total money stock. On the other hand, if Individual 1 puts his cash in a time deposit, there is a *decrease* on total money stock. Before time deposits become active money, before they may be used in the purchase of goods and services, they must be converted into either currency or demand deposits. Time deposits, therefore, are not considered part of the money stock. In either case, the total *liquid wealth* holdings of the nonbank public undergo no change, however, because both time and demand deposits are part of liquid wealth.

Derivative deposits. When commercial banks make *loans and investments*, deposits are also created. Assume that Individual 1 borrows $1,000 from Bank A. He will probably receive the proceeds of the loan in the form of a demand-deposit increase.[2] Thus, bank loans and demand deposits increase by $1,000:

BALANCE-SHEET CHANGES FOR COMMERCIAL BANK A

ASSETS		LIABILITIES + CAPITAL ACCOUNTS	
Loans	+$1,000	Demand deposits of Individual 1	+$1,000

[2] Of course, the borrower always has the option of increasing his time deposits. If he does so, total bank deposit liabilities increase but there is no increase in the money stock. Total liquid wealth increases because of the increase in time deposits. This sequence of events, however, is unlikely to occur because people generally borrow either to make purchases or to repay debts.

These newly created deposits are called *derivative deposits*. They increase the money stock and liquid-wealth holdings of the economy, and they contribute to economic expansion by increasing spending power. They do *not* increase the reserves of the lending bank, however.

Investment expansion also causes an increase in the money stock. Suppose that Bank A increases its holdings of securities by $10,000 and pays for them by writing a cashier's check on itself. If the seller of the securities deposits the check in his checking account at Bank B, this will increase Bank B's reserves and decrease Bank A's reserves:

BALANCE-SHEET CHANGES FOR COMMERCIAL BANK A

ASSETS		LIABILITIES + CAPITAL ACCOUNTS
Reserves	−$10,000	
Securities	+$10,000	

BALANCE-SHEET CHANGES FOR COMMERCIAL BANK B

ASSETS		LIABILITIES + CAPITAL ACCOUNTS	
Reserves	+$10,000	Demand deposits of securities-seller	+$10,000

For the banking system as a whole, both demand-deposit liabilities and security holdings have increased, but reserves remain unchanged. Thus, although the money holdings of the nonbank public have increased, Bank A's purchase of securities has brought about no change in the total liquid wealth of the nonbank public.

Are the deposits created in the second transaction primary or derivative? From the point of view of Bank B, they are primary deposits because they increased reserves by an amount equal to the increase in deposit liability. From the perspective of the whole banking system, however, they are derivative deposits because there has been no increase of the total volume of bank reserves.

Destruction of Deposits

Commercial bank demand deposits are destroyed when cash is withdrawn, when loans are repaid, when bank investments are sold, and when reserves decline.

Assume that Individual 1 needs additional cash for vacation expenses and draws $1,000 from his checking account:

BALANCE-SHEET CHANGES FOR COMMERCIAL BANK A

ASSETS		LIABILITIES + CAPITAL ACCOUNTS	
Reserves	−$1,000	Demand deposits of Individual 1	−$1,000

As the balance-sheet changes above reflect, the bank loses reserves and deposit liabilities. The nonbank public experiences no change either in the money stock or in liquid wealth; it has merely exchanged one form of money (demand deposits) for another (currency). This bank and the banking system as a whole have lost reserves, however. Hence, as we shall discuss shortly, commercial bank lending activity will be restricted.

A bank also loses reserves and deposits when its depositors write checks payable to persons maintaining accounts with other banks. This was the situation confronting Bank B in the illustration on page 86. When the employer paid Individual 1, a primary deposit was made at Bank A. As a consequence, Bank B's deposit liability and its reserves were diminished.

Loan repayments also cause deposits to be destroyed. Assume that Individual 1 repays a $1,000 loan with Bank A by drawing down his checking account. The T-account entries would be:

BALANCE-SHEET CHANGES FOR COMMERCIAL BANK A

ASSETS		LIABILITIES + CAPITAL ACCOUNTS	
Loans	−$1,000	Demand deposits of Individual 1	−$1,000

If the loan is repaid with checks drawn on other banks, $1,000 in demand deposits is still destroyed from the point of view of the entire banking system. Bank A does not experience this loss directly, however:

BALANCE-SHEET CHANGES FOR COMMERCIAL BANK A

ASSETS		LIABILITIES + CAPITAL ACCOUNTS
Reserves	+$1,000	
Loans	−$1,000	

BALANCE-SHEET CHANGES FOR THE REST OF THE COMMERCIAL BANKING SYSTEM

ASSETS		LIABILITIES + CAPITAL ACCOUNTS	
Reserves	−$1,000	Demand deposits	−$1,000

Finally, deposits are destroyed when banks reduce their investments. Suppose, for example, that Bank A sells $10,000 in U.S. government securities. If the purchasers are members of the nonbank public, payment usually is made with checks drawn on commercial banks. Assume that Bank A sells the securities and that depositors of Bank B are the ultimate purchasers. The balance-sheet changes for this transaction are:

BALANCE-SHEET CHANGES FOR COMMERCIAL BANK A

ASSETS		LIABILITIES + CAPITAL ACCOUNTS
Reserves	+$10,000	
U.S. government securities	−$10,000	

BALANCE-SHEET CHANGES FOR COMMERCIAL BANK B

ASSETS		LIABILITIES + CAPITAL ACCOUNTS	
Reserves	−$10,000	Demand deposits	−$10,000

Here the money supply of the nonbank public has decreased, while total liquid wealth and the reserves of the banking system remain unchanged.

LIMITATIONS TO INDIVIDUAL BANK DEPOSIT CREATING AND DESTROYING ABILITIES

Deposit Creation and the Reserve Requirement

The ability of an individual commercial bank to create deposits is not unlimited. The reserve requirement and the volume of each bank's reserves restrict its power to create deposits.

The reserve requirement is the legally required ratio of those cash assets defined by law as reserves to deposit liabilities. Reserves are divided into two categories: required and excess. *Required reserves* are those which a bank must have to meet its reserve requirement. *Excess reserves* are the amount of reserves that a bank has in excess of its required amount. When required reserves exceed actual reserves, the bank has a *deficiency* (or *shortage*) *of reserves*.

Assume, for example, that a bank has $1 million in reserves, a 20 percent reserve requirement, and $4 million in deposit liabilities. The bank's required reserves are $800,000. Since its actual reserves are $1 million, the bank has $200,000 in excess reserves. On the basis of this volume of excess reserves, it may expand loans and investments by $200,000 and create up to $200,000 in demand deposits. Of course, the bank could expand beyond this amount, but it would consider this a very risky policy. On the basis of past experience, the bank expects to lose reserves in an amount equal to its loan and investment expansion, unless it has a favorable clearing balance—as we shall discuss in a moment.

What would happen if some of the givens in this illustration changed? If the volume of reserves increases by $50,000 because of loan repayments, the lending and money-creating ability of our bank increases by $50,000. Similarly, if the legal reserve requirement drops to 15 percent, then the excess reserves of our bank increase from $200,000 to $400,000. In general terms, the lower the reserve requirement, the greater the amount of excess reserves and hence the greater the lending and money-creating ability of the bank. Also, the greater the volume of reserves available to meet a fixed reserve requirement, the greater the volume of excess reserves and hence the greater the lending and money-creating abilities of the bank.

Deposit Destruction and the Reserve Requirement

If a bank becomes deficient in reserves, it will stop expanding loans and investments, and may even cut back on loans and investments outstanding. For example, if the bank discussed in the preceding section had had $600,000 instead of $1 million in reserves, it would have had a $200,000 shortage of reserves. In such a situation, the bank might refuse to renew $100,000 in loans and might sell $100,000 in investments. If those who repay the loans and purchase the investments do so with checks drawn on other banks, these other banks will have lost reserves and Bank A will no longer be deficient in reserves:

BALANCE-SHEET CHANGES FOR COMMERCIAL BANK A

ASSETS		LIABILITIES + CAPITAL ACCOUNTS
Reserves	+$200,000	
Loans	−$100,000	
Investments	−$100,000	

However, these methods of meeting reserve requirements have several shortcomings. First, it is not good business practice to refuse to renew loans for customers—this can hurt future lending opportunities since borrowers may decide to go elsewhere for a loan in a subsequent period when the bank has adequate excess reserves. Second, too great a reduction of investments may jeopardize the safety and liquidity of the bank. Third, a reduction of loans lowers bank earnings. And, finally, if those who repay loans do so with checks drawn on the deficient bank itself, a contraction in an amount *greater* than the deficiency of reserves will be necessary:

BALANCE-SHEET CHANGES FOR COMMERCIAL BANK A

ASSETS		LIABILITIES + CAPITAL ACCOUNTS	
Loans	−$200,000	Demand deposits	−$200,000

Addenda: Original deficiency of reserves	$200,000
Reduction in required reserves	$ 40,000
New deficiency of reserves	$160,000

When depositors repay $200,000 in loans, a corresponding amount of demand deposits is destroyed. With $200,000 less in deposit liabilities, the required reserves of the bank are reduced by 20 percent of $200,000, or $40,000. Thus, there is still a shortage of reserves amounting to $160,000.

To make up a $200,000 deficiency in required reserves in this fashion, the bank would have to reduce its loans by $1 million:

BALANCE-SHEET CHANGES FOR COMMERCIAL BANK A

ASSETS		LIABILITIES + CAPITAL ACCOUNTS	
Loans	−$1,000,000	Demand deposits	−$1,000,000

Addenda: Original deficiency of reserves $200,000
Reduction in required reserves $200,000
New deficiency of reserves 0

Thus, to improve Bank A's reserve position by not making new loans once the old loans have been repaid, the total dollar volume of loans must be reduced by an amount *five times as large* as the initial deficiency in reserves: *required reserves are reduced only by $1 for every $5 decrease in deposit liabilities when the reserve requirement is 20 percent.* The reason for this is quite simple: since $200,000 in reserves represents 20 percent, or one-fifth, of a given amount of demand deposits, it will take $200,000 in demand deposits multiplied by the reciprocal of one-fifth (5) to restore an equivalent amount in lost reserves.

How a Bank Obtains Additional Reserves

For the reasons just discussed, banks try not to rely solely on contracting loans and investments to eliminate deficiencies in reserves. Instead, they use a variety of techniques. They may *reduce investments* slightly to bring in some reserves from other banks, and they may also *reduce loans* by granting fewer new loans than are currently running off. (This will bring in some reserves and lower deposit liabilities, since some loans will be repaid with checks drawn on other banks.) But there are other ways to increase reserves. If the shortage appears temporary, a bank may borrow reserves from other banks. As pointed out earlier in discussing the *federal funds market,* banks with a surplus of excess reserves are generally willing to lend them to other banks for short periods. These excess reserves, maintained at Federal Reserve banks in the form of deposit balances, are usually loaned to deficient banks on an overnight basis. Banks may also borrow reserves from their district Federal Reserve banks, which almost always meet legitimate requests for borrowings.

When banks *borrow reserves from other banks or from their district Federal Reserve bank,* the balance-sheet entries are:

BALANCE-SHEET CHANGES FOR COMMERCIAL BANK A

ASSETS		LIABILITIES + CAPITAL ACCOUNTS	
Reserves	+$200,000	Borrowings	+$200,000

Thus, Bank A's $200,000 deficiency in reserves is removed without re-
ducing its earning assets. The borrowed funds will have to be repaid with
interest, of course, but the borrowing bank hopes that future operations
will provide the means of repayment. Borrowing reserves permits banks
with temporary reserve deficiencies to provide their customers with credit
continuity.

As we discussed in Chapter 5, *Euro-dollars* are another source of
reserves for individual commercial banks. When Euro-dollars are purchased or borrowed, the bank acquiring the dollars experiences an increase
in its reserves and in its liabilities due to foreign branches or other banks.
The balance sheet entries are the same as those just shown for the borrowing of funds in the federal funds market. Reserves for all commercial
banks are unchanged by such actions. The reserves acquired are those of
American commercial banks whose demand deposits serve as Euro-dollars.

While Euro-dollar borrowing is in many ways comparable to the borrowing of reserves from other commercial banks or from Federal Reserve
banks, there is one important difference: banks are required to maintain
reserves against Euro-dollar borrowings. Thus, if a bank borrows $1 mil-
lion in Euro-dollars, not all of its reserve increase is directly usable. If the
reserve requirement against Euro-dollars is, say, 20 percent, then only
$800,000 is usable to satisfy the reserve requirement against bank demand-
and time-deposit liabilities. Until 1973 reserve requirements against Euro-
dollars were higher than those required to cover demand and time deposits.
Beginning in June of 1973, the reserve requirement for Euro-dollars was 8
percent. Typically, only large banks are very actively engaged in the search
for additional reserves in the Euro-dollar market.

Short-term promises to pay called *commercial paper* are still another
source of funds for large commercial banks. They are issued and sold by
bank holding companies and their nonbank affiliates. When, for example,
nonbank affiliates sell commercial paper, it is paid for with checks drawn
on the commercial banks of the purchasers of the paper. These checks are
deposited in the checking accounts of the nonbank affiliates at the commercial bank affiliate of the bank holding company. The commercial bank accepting the deposits acquires reserves from the banks on which the checks
were drawn. The nonbank affiliates then purchase loans and investments
held by the affiliate bank. When we combine the balance sheets of the affiliate bank and its nonbank affiliates, we find, on balance, that there are more
reserves available to the commercial bank and that there is an increase in
commercial paper liabilities. This is illustrated for a $1 million sale of com-
mercial paper in the following entries:

BALANCE-SHEET CHANGES FOR NONBANK AFFILIATES

ASSETS		LIABILITIES + CAPITAL ACCOUNTS	
Demand deposits	+$1,000,000 (a)	Commercial paper	+$1,000,000 (a)
Demand deposits	−$1,000,000 (b)		
Loans and Investments	+$1,000,000 (b)		

BALANCE-SHEET CHANGES FOR COMMERCIAL BANK AFFILIATE

ASSETS		LIABILITIES + CAPITAL ACCOUNTS	
Reserves	+$1,000,000 (a)	Demand deposits	+$1,000,000 (a)
Loans and Investments	−$1,000,000 (b)	Demand deposits	−$1,000,000 (b)

The (a) entries show the effects of the sale of the commercial paper, while the (b) entries show the effects of the purchase of the commercial bank loans and investments by its nonbank affiliates. The net effect, as in the case of the federal funds and the Euro-dollar markets, is a redistribution of reserves from other commercial banks to the acquiring banks. Since 1970 the Federal Reserve has required that commercial paper created in the above manner be subject to the same reserve requirements as certificates of deposit. There was an abrupt drop in bank-related commercial paper immediately following this action, but the level of such paper stabilized in subsequent years.

You will also recall from Chapter 5 that *demand deposits* are a source of funds for banks. If a bank in the process of competing for funds makes its demand deposit liabilities more attractive to depositors, it acquires reserve funds that formerly belonged to other banks. One means of doing this is to reduce service charges on checking-deposit accounts. Of course, if a bank's competitors follow suit, the edge gained by the bank initially lowering service charges will probably be eliminated.

A final technique widely used by banks to acquire additional reserve funds is the effort to increase the attractiveness of commercial bank *time deposits*. This force will be discussed in the following section.

What is important for us to recognize at this point is that, *aside from the borrowing of reserves from Federal Reserve banks, all of the techniques that banks use to acquire additional reserves lead to no change in the reserves of all commercial banks.* The Euro-dollar market, the sale of commercial paper, the sale of loans and investments, the efforts to attract additional demand- and time-deposit sources of funds, etc., all redistribute a given volume of bank reserves among the commercial banks.

Other Factors Affecting Commercial Bank Deposit Creation

Many other factors affect the ability of a commercial bank to create and destroy demand-deposit money. Some of the more important factors are (1) the demands of the nonbank public for currency, (2) the relative preferences of the nonbank public for time and demand deposits, (3) the bank's clearing balances, (4) the willingness of the bank to lend and the borrower to borrow, (5) the unpredictability of business conditions, and (6) government economic policy

The demand for currency. The reserve position of a commercial bank, and, for that matter, of the whole banking system, depends in part upon the willingness of the nonbank public to maintain its present distribution of currency and demand deposits. When people decide that they need more currency, they draw down their deposit balances. This reduces commercial bank reserves and deposits by an equal amount. The effect of a $1,000 cash withdrawal upon a bank that has extended as many loans as its reserves will permit and that is faced with a 20 percent reserve requirement is shown in the following T-account entry:

BALANCE-SHEET CHANGES FOR COMMERCIAL BANK A

ASSETS		LIABILITIES + CAPITAL ACCOUNTS	
Reserves	−$1,000	Demand deposits	−$1,000

Addenda: Change in reserves   −$1,000
         Change in required reserves   −$ 200
         Overall change in excess reserves   −$ 800

Since only 20 percent of $1,000. or $200, was required to back the $1,000 in demand-deposit liabilities, required reserves decrease by only $200. On balance, the bank is short $800 in reserves. To make up this deficiency, it must either contract loans, investments, and deposits, or borrow additional reserves. This type of currency drain is usually seasonal; more currency is needed during vacation periods, for example, when people travel, and during the Christmas season, when people make more cash purchases than usual. Fortunately, the Federal Reserve System generally provides banks with the needed reserves in such periods.

During other periods — for example, following the holiday seasons — there are sizable influxes of currency into the banking system, and reserves, excess reserves, and deposits all increase. This would seem to be an ideal time for commercial banks to expand their loans. Unfortunately, the demand for loans typically falls off during these same periods. In addition, the Federal Reserve usually takes measures to mop up the excess reserves.

The demand for time deposits. Up to this point in the chapter, we have seldom distinguished between the reserve requirements for demand and time deposits, in order to keep the numerical illustrations comparatively simple. As we know from earlier chapters, reserve requirements vary a great deal, depending on the location of the bank and the type of deposit. In 1973, for example, the reserve requirements were 3 and 8 percent for various types of time deposits at member banks, 8 to 13.5 percent for demand deposits at country banks, and 18 percent for demand deposits at reserve city banks. This difference in reserve requirements means that commercial bank reserve positions are weakened by a switch from time to demand deposits. Suppose, for example, that reserve requirements are 4 percent for time deposits and 15 percent for demand deposits, and that

Bank A is initially loaned up. If depositors should decide to increase their demand deposits by $100,000 and decrease their time deposits by an equal amount, the result would be a shortage in reserves:

BALANCE-SHEET CHANGES FOR COMMERCIAL BANK A

ASSETS		LIABILITIES + CAPITAL ACCOUNTS	
		Demand deposits	+$100,000
		Time deposits	−$100,000
Addenda: Change in existing amount of reserves	0		
Change in required reserves	+$11,000		

Bank A is now deficient in reserves by $11,000. The reduction in time deposits releases $4,000 in required reserves, but the demand-deposit increase calls for an additional $15,000 in reserves. The net effect is that Bank A needs $11,000 more in reserves.

On the other hand, when a bank's customers decide to shift funds from demand to time deposits, the reserve position of the bank is improved since the amount of reserves released by the reduction in demand deposits is greater than the amount of reserves required to back the new time deposits.

Similarly, a bank may gain reserves by making its time deposits more attractive than those of its competitors. A bank can do this by raising the interest on various classes of certificates of deposit, subject to whatever interest ceilings are imposed by the bank regulatory agencies.

Favorable and adverse clearing balances. A bank continually receives checks drawn on other banks. Conversely, it is also continually redeeming checks presented for collection by other banks. If the total value of the checks a bank redeems is less than the value of the checks it presents for collection, then that bank is said to have a *favorable clearing balance.* If the reverse is true, then the bank has an *adverse clearing balance.*

A bank that continues to experience a favorable clearing balance over a period of time is in a position to expand loans and deposits beyond its excess reserves. On the other hand, if it regularly has an adverse clearing balance, it must limit its expansion of loans and deposits to an amount less than the volume of its excess reserves.

Assume, for example, that Bank A has $10,000 in excess reserves, a 20 percent reserve requirement, and a consistently favorable clearing balance equal in value to 2 percent of its newly created demand deposits. What additional volume of loans and deposits can the bank create? Without a favorable or an adverse clearing balance it could create $10,000 in loans and deposits—the amount of its excess reserves. With a favorable balance, a $10,000 deposit creation would lead to a $200 deposit return to the bank. Thus, the bank can create more than $10,000 in deposits. It can create additional deposits equal to 1/0.984 times the volume of excess reserves,[3] or $163.

The following T-account entries show the effects of Bank A's expanding loans by 1/0.984 times its excess reserves when the new loan is made:

BALANCE-SHEET CHANGES FOR COMMERCIAL BANK A

ASSETS		LIABILITIES + CAPITAL ACCOUNTS	
Loans	+$10,163	Demand deposits	+$10,163

and when all its checks have been cleared:

BALANCE-SHEET CHANGES FOR COMMERCIAL BANK A

ASSETS		LIABILITIES + CAPITAL ACCOUNTS	
Reserves	−$9,960	Demand deposits	−$9,960

Addenda: Net increase in demand deposits after all transactions	$ 203
Net increase in required reserves	$ 40
Net decrease in total reserves	$ 9,960
Former volume of excess reserves	$10,000
New volume of excess reserves	0

The checks presented by other banks for collection are 2 percent less than the volume of newly created deposits. Hence, total deposit liabilities are $203 greater than they were at the start of these transactions and required reserves have increased by $40. The bank lost $9,960 in reserves. Without the favorable clearing balance the bank would have lost $10,000 in reserves.[4] Thus, a favorable clearing balance of 2 percent enabled the bank to expand loans and deposits beyond its excess reserves.

Other banks are not so fortunate, however. If one bank has a favorable balance, another bank must have an adverse balance. Thus, for the entire banking system there can be neither a favorable nor an adverse clearing position.

---

[3] The figure 1/0.984 is based on the following formula:

$$p = \frac{1}{1 - q + (r)(q)}$$

where r is the reserve requirement, q is the percentage of new deposits that return to the bank, and p is that multiple of its excess reserves by which the bank may expand its loans and deposits. As study of the formula shows, q acts as an expansive force on deposit creation, while r acts as a contractive force. As deposits return to the bank, the reserve requirement calls for an increase in required reserves.

This same formula is used when a bank has an adverse clearing balance. In this case p and r have the same meaning, but q now refers to the percentage by which checks drawn on the bank exceed the volume of newly created deposits. Under these circumstances, q takes a negative value and tends to hold down deposit creation, while r, the reserve requirement, helps maintain it.

[4] All amounts less than $1 have been dropped.

To the individual bank, however, an adverse clearing balance means that it cannot create loans and deposits to the full extent of its excess reserves. Assume that Bank B has excess reserves of $10,000, a reserve requirement of 20 percent, and a consistently adverse clearing balance equal to 2 percent of its newly created deposits. This bank would experience difficulty if it expanded to the extent of its excess reserves. If it expanded loans and deposits by $10,000, for example, it would lose $10,200 in reserves. Therefore, using the formula in footnote 3, Bank B should expand demand deposits by only 1/1.016 times its excess reserves. When the new loan is made, loans and deposits will rise:

BALANCE-SHEET CHANGES FOR COMMERCIAL BANK B

ASSETS		LIABILITIES + CAPITAL ACCOUNTS	
Loans	+$9,843	Demand deposits	+$9,843

When all its checks have been cleared, the result will be:

BALANCE-SHEET CHANGES FOR COMMERCIAL BANK B

ASSETS		LIABILITIES + CAPITAL ACCOUNTS	
Reserves	−$10,040	Demand deposits	−$10,040

Addenda: Net decrease in demand deposits after all transactions	$ 197
Net decrease in required reserves	$ 39
Net decrease in total reserves	$10,040
Former volume of excess reserves	$10,000
New volume of excess reserves	0

Various factors affect the clearing position of a bank. For instance, a bank located in an economically developing area may expect to gain reserves at the expense of banks in areas of declining economic activity. This shifting of reserves to a growing area is considered necessary by the banks whose resources are increased, of course. Growing areas generally experience a shortage of funds, since the demand for loans is strong relative to the supply. A bank with increasing loans and reserves is not necessarily one with a favorable clearing balance, however. Extensive lending activity may produce an adverse clearing balance: if a bank is rapidly expanding credit, it can usually expect sharp drains on its reserves. On the other hand, banks that make few loans may find their reserves rising. Thus, the movement of reserves to a district with a growing economy may simply offset losses attributable to the increased volume of bank lending.

Willingness to borrow and lend. Changes in the reserve requirement, in the demand for currency, in the demand for time deposits, and in clearing balances all tend to affect a commercial bank's reserve position and thus its ability to create money. In addition, the extent to which a bank creates new deposits through loans also depends on its own willingness to lend and upon the demands of borrowers. For example, banks are more willing to lend when there is prosperity in the community and the economy. In recession, they generally follow a more cautious lending policy, expanding investments instead.

Although most banks tend to vary the size of their loan and investment portfolios according to changes in the business cycle, there are, of course, many differences among individual banks. Some have a fundamentally conservative lending policy and keep a relatively large proportion of their assets in safe investments. Others follow a more liberal lending policy.

The attitude of borrowers is also important. When businesses expect a decline in sales, for example, they borrow less and repay loans. If economic conditions are expected to improve, however, businesses want to be prepared for the anticipated increase in demand. They borrow more from banks in order to build up inventories.

The unpredictability of business conditions. Although a bank may expect transfers from time to demand deposits, cash drains, and adverse clearing balances to confront it regularly, it cannot always predict the size and timing of these occurrences. Random disturbances, such as unanticipated cash drains, occur frequently. Since these disturbances cannot always be precisely anticipated, a bank must set aside a certain proportion of its excess reserves to meet these contingencies.

Small banks lack the skilled personnel and the specialized knowledge of the money markets that large banks have. As a result, small banks are not as well able to economize on reserves; often they must maintain substantial amounts of excess reserves as precautionary balances. The large banks must maintain precautionary balances, too, but these balances can be smaller relative to deposit liabilities. Regularly maintained precautionary balances of excess reserves do help to cover the unexpected demands for cash and reserve losses, but they also reduce the lending potential of the bank because they do not permit it to expand to the full extent of its excess reserves.

Government economic policy. In many ways, government economic policy is the single most important determinant of the commercial bank's power to create money. When it feels economic expansion is necessary, the federal government attempts to stimulate the economy through various agencies. The Federal Reserve System, for example, may lower the reserve requirement for member banks. This action will directly increase the lending ability of each member bank. Their improved reserve position, of course, does not guarantee that the banks will actually increase their lending activities, but it is a step in the right direction.

The Federal Reserve may also aggressively expand its holdings of U.S. government securities. When this happens, commercial bank reserves increase: the sellers of the securities receive checks drawn on the Federal Reserve banks and deposit them in checking accounts at commercial banks.[5] Although this action is expansive, its effects are not felt directly by every bank. Only those banks whose depositors have sold securities to the Federal Reserve are affected initially. Other banks may be affected indirectly, depending on the lending actions of the banks that receive the additional reserves.

Other government agencies also help to stimulate the economy. Their actions affect commercial banks only indirectly, however. For example, the federal government may increase its rate of spending. If the government demand for goods and services is increased in this fashion, businesses may be stimulated to borrow at commercial banks to meet this added demand. Hence, there may be increased willingness to borrow, resulting in even more lending activity. Also, bank reserves may increase as businesses deposit checks received from the government in payment for its increased orders of goods and services. These checks are usually drawn on U.S. Treasury accounts at the Federal Reserve banks. The deposit of these checks with commercial banks increases both their deposit liabilities and their reserves. Suppose, for example, that the federal government increases its spending by $50 million in an effort to stimulate the economy:

BALANCE-SHEET CHANGES FOR THE FEDERAL RESERVE BANKS

ASSETS	LIABILITIES + CAPITAL ACCOUNTS

	Deposits
	  Member bank reserves +$50,000,000
	  U.S. Treasurer−general account
	                                      −$50,000,000

BALANCE-SHEET CHANGES FOR THE COMMERCIAL BANKING SYSTEM

ASSETS		LIABILITIES + CAPITAL ACCOUNTS	
Reserves	+$50,000,000	Demand deposits	+$50,000,000

The checks deposited by businesses were drawn on the government accounts at the Federal Reserve banks. When commercial banks present these checks for collection, the Federal Reserve banks pay them by increasing commercial bank reserve accounts and decreasing the Treasury deposit accounts. Not all banks participate in the initial increase in reserves. As the banks that receive these additional reserves expand loans and investments, however, other banks will receive increased reserves and deposits.

During prosperity and inflation, government economic policy may be contractionary rather than expansionary: the Federal Reserve may attempt

[5] This type of action by the Federal Reserve System is called an *open-market* operation. See Chapter 12 for a full discussion.

to restrain inflationary pressures in the economy by restricting commercial bank lending. For example, it may sell U.S. government securities to the nonbank public. The purchasers of the securities will pay for them with checks drawn on their demand-deposit accounts at commercial banks. The Federal Reserve banks, when they receive these checks, will collect by lowering the reserve balances of member banks. The Federal Reserve could also raise reserve requirements to reduce inflationary pressure, but this is not the normal procedure.

Federal government spending may also be restricted in a period of inflation, since a decrease in the government's demand for goods and services can normally be expected to reduce spending and borrowing by the nonbank public. Also, as the rate of federal spending decreases, government receipts relative to expenditures tend to increase. Thus, Treasury balances with the Federal Reserve banks increase, while commercial bank reserves and deposit liabilities diminish.

Summary.   Thus far, Chapter 6 has dealt with some of the more important factors influencing the ability of a commercial bank to create money. Our analysis has concentrated on *potential* influences on bank money creation, and our focus, for the most part, has been on the individual bank. The ability of a commercial bank to create demand-deposit money depends principally on its reserve position. In general, a bank may create demand deposits in an amount equal to its excess reserves. Whether the bank actually expands deposits to this extent depends on its willingness to lend, the demand for loans, its clearing balances, and its precautionary margin of excess reserves. If the bank has a shortage of reserves, it must either contract its loans and investments or obtain additional reserves. Both government economic policy and changes in the demand for time deposits and currency affect banks principally by altering their reserve position.

CREATION AND DESTRUCTION OF DEPOSITS BY THE COMMERCIAL BANKING SYSTEM

The ability of the entire banking system to create and destroy money differs from that of the individual bank. It is true that the ability of the banking system to create and destroy money, like that of individual banks, depends upon reserve positions. But the individual bank may safely create new deposits only to the extent of its excess reserves, whereas the banking system may create new deposits by *a multiple of* banking system *excess reserves.*

Banking System Creation of Deposits

To illustrate the money-creating ability of the commercial banking system, let us begin by making the following assumptions: (1) the reserve requirement is 20 percent, (2) the deposit liabilities of the banking system are $140 billion, (3) the reserves of the banking system are $28 billion, (4) there is normally no cash drain or influx, (5) unless otherwise specified, all transactions are by check, (6) there are no time deposits, (7) banks require no minimum precautionary reserve balances, and (8) monetary-fiscal policy is neutral in its effects on commercial bank lending and investing activities. Under these conditions, banks would be loaned up; required reserves would thus equal actual reserves.

Now, imagine that there is a $100 million influx of cash into the banking system. These cash deposits increase both commercial bank reserves and demand-deposit liabilities by $100 million. Required reserves increase by $20 million. Excess reserves are no longer zero; they now amount to $80 million. What will happen to the lending and money-creating ability of the commercial banking system?

Initially, the banks will increase deposits only by the amount of their excess reserves, $80 million. They expect to lose their excess reserves to other banks as borrowers pay off debts to depositors of other banks. This will not cause a loss in reserves for the entire banking system, however. Because the reserves remain in the system, deposit creation will continue to occur. As the newly created funds are spent, other banks receive these reserves and create new primary deposits to the extent of $80 million. These banks now have excess reserves. With $80 million more in deposits and reserves, they have $64 million in excess reserves and may create additional deposits to this amount.

Summarizing the discussion up to this point in T-account form, we have:

1. A hypothetical initial balance sheet for the commercial banking system when loaned up:

BALANCE-SHEET FOR THE COMMERCIAL BANKING SYSTEM
(IN BILLIONS OF DOLLARS)

ASSETS		LIABILITIES + CAPITAL ACCOUNTS	
Reserves	$ 28	Demand deposits	$140
Other assets	$122	Other liabilities and capital accounts	$ 10

2. Balance-sheet changes that occur when people make cash deposits of $100 million (we will call banks receiving these deposits Group 1 banks):

BALANCE-SHEET CHANGES FOR GROUP 1 BANKS
(IN MILLIONS OF DOLLARS)

ASSETS		LIABILITIES + CAPITAL ACCOUNTS	
Reserves	+$100	Demand deposits	+$100

BALANCE-SHEET CHANGES FOR THE COMMERCIAL BANKING SYSTEM
(IN MILLIONS OF DOLLARS)

ASSETS		LIABILITIES + CAPITAL ACCOUNTS	
Reserves	+$100	Demand deposits	+$100

3. Balance-sheet changes that occur when the banks acquiring the $100 million in cash deposits create loans and derivative deposits:

BALANCE-SHEET CHANGES FOR GROUP 1 BANKS
(IN MILLIONS OF DOLLARS)

ASSETS		LIABILITIES + CAPITAL ACCOUNTS	
Loans	+$80	Demand deposits	+$80

BALANCE-SHEET CHANGES FOR THE COMMERCIAL BANKING SYSTEM
(IN MILLIONS OF DOLLARS)

ASSETS		LIABILITIES + CAPITAL ACCOUNTS	
Loans	+$80	Demand deposits	+$80

4. Balance-sheet changes that occur when the newly created deposits are spent and passed to other (Group 2) banks:

BALANCE-SHEET CHANGES FOR GROUP 1 BANKS
(IN MILLIONS OF DOLLARS)

ASSETS		LIABILITIES + CAPITAL ACCOUNTS	
Reserves	−$80	Demand deposits	−$80

BALANCE-SHEET CHANGES FOR GROUP 2 BANKS
(IN MILLIONS OF DOLLARS)

ASSETS		LIABILITIES + CAPITAL ACCOUNTS	
Reserves	+$80	Demand deposits	+$80

BALANCE-SHEET CHANGES FOR THE COMMERCIAL BANKING SYSTEM

ASSETS	LIABILITIES + CAPITAL ACCOUNTS
0	0

5. Balance-sheet changes that occur when Group 2 banks create loans and deposits:

BALANCE-SHEET CHANGES FOR GROUP 2 BANKS
(IN MILLIONS OF DOLLARS)

ASSETS		LIABILITIES + CAPITAL ACCOUNTS	
Loans	+$64	Demand deposits	+$64

BALANCE-SHEET CHANGES FOR THE COMMERCIAL BANKING SYSTEM
(IN MILLIONS OF DOLLARS)

ASSETS		LIABILITIES + CAPITAL ACCOUNTS	
Loans	+$64	Demand deposits	+$64

The above entries show that $100 million, $80 million, and $64 million in new demand deposits have successively been created. Theoretically, in the banking system as a whole, banks will continue to create deposits in this fashion until all the excess reserves in the system become required reserves. Under our assumptions, this point will be reached when the total of the newly created deposits is five times the initial increase in reserves of the commercial banking system. This means that *the banking system as a whole, with an initial increase in reserves of $100 million, can theoretically expand deposits by $500 million.* Since, in our illustration, the first $100 million created were primary deposits, the remaining $400 million will be, in a general sense, *derivative deposits* created when banks make loans and investments in that amount. Thus, the total nonbank public holdings of money will increase by $400 million.

The essential difference between deposit creation by individual banks and deposit creation by the banking system is this. When the *individual bank* makes investments, it expects to lose an equal amount of reserves; when it makes loans and creates deposit liabilities, it also expects to lose reserves equal to the amount of those deposit liabilities. When the *banking system* makes loans and investments and creates demand-deposit money, however, *there is no change in reserves*—they are merely redistributed among the various banks in the system.

Banking System Destruction of Deposits

The banking system, like individual banks, must contract deposits when it is short of reserves. Unlike an individual bank, however, it must contract deposits by *a multiple of the deficiency of reserves.* An individual bank may make up its shortage of reserves by obtaining reserves from other banks, reducing loans and investments, acquiring Euro-dollars, and borrowing reserves in the federal funds market. Such actions by individual banks, however, will not relieve a systemwide shortage of reserves. Instead, they will only make the problems of other banks more severe. This is particularly true when the Federal Reserve, for purposes of restraining inflation, fails to provide commercial banks with additional reserves.

To explain the multiple destruction of deposits that occurs in the commercial banking system, let us start with the same initial set of assumptions we used in illustrating the multiple expansion of deposits. The banking system is initially loaned up. Now, let us imagine that there is an increase in the reserve requirement from 20 to 21 percent. Let us assume further that additional reserves are not available. What will happen in the banking system?

To begin with, the required amount of reserves increases from $28 to $29.4 billion. With only $28 billion in reserves, banks now have a $1.4 billion deficiency of reserves. The system must therefore contract its loans and investments. Assume that the banks try to obtain additional reserves by lowering their investment holdings. Since each bank will try to acquire enough additional reserves to remove its own deficiency, each will contract its investments by that amount. Thus, all banks together sell off investments worth $1.4 billion. The purchasers of the investments will probably be members of the nonbank public, since it is unlikely that banks, being short of reserves, will be buying any securities. When the nonbank public pays for the securities with checks written on its demand-deposit accounts, the commercial banking system's deposit liabilities will contract by $1.4 billion, but the banks will have been unsuccessful in their attempt to get additional reserves:

BALANCE-SHEET CHANGES FOR THE COMMERCIAL BANKING SYSTEM
(IN BILLIONS OF DOLLARS)

ASSETS		LIABILITIES + CAPITAL ACCOUNTS	
Investments	−$1.4	Demand deposits	−$1.4

Addenda: Initial shortage of reserves $1.4
Decrease in required reserves after decrease in demand deposits $0.294
New deficiency of reserves $1.106

The sale of securities results in no change in reserves for the banking system. The parallel decrease in demand-deposit liabilities, however, reduces required reserves by 21 percent of $1.4 billion, or $294 million. Thus, the banking system is still $1.106 billion short in its reserves.

Given our assumptions, the banking system will continue to contract. Another means of contraction open to banks is loan reduction. As loans come due, depositors usually repay with demand deposits. If, prior to loan repayment, depositors build up their accounts with creditor banks by depositing checks received from others who have accounts with other banks, the creditor banks acquire reserves. These banks also lose reserves, however, since other banks are in approximately the same position. With a $1.106 billion shortage of reserves, all banks together may reduce loans and deposits by $1.106 billion. Are banks still short of reserves? Yes, because a $1.106 billion deposit reduction reduces required reserves by only 21 percent of $1.106 billion, or $232.26 million. The deposit, investment, and loan contraction must continue.

At this point deposits have already dropped by $1.4 and $1.106 billion, a multiple of the initial $1.4 billion shortage in reserves. They must continue to fall, however, until the overall decrease in demand deposits equals

1/0.21 times $1.4 billion, or $6.67 billion. Only when demand-deposit liabilities are reduced by a total of $6.67 billion will the original $1.4 billion shortage be made up:

BALANCE-SHEET CHANGES FOR THE COMMERCIAL BANKING SYSTEM
(IN BILLIONS OF DOLLARS)

ASSETS		LIABILITIES + CAPITAL ACCOUNTS	
Loans and investments	−$6.67	Demand deposits	−$6.67

Addenda: Decrease in required reserves (0.21)($6.67) = $1.4
           Initial deficiency of reserves $1.4
           Present level of excess reserves   0

A Shorthand Formula to Predict the Deposit Creation and Destruction Potential of the Commercial Banking System

The results of the preceding analysis may be more readily obtained by means of the formula

$$D = \frac{R}{r} \qquad\qquad [6\text{–}1]$$

where r is the reserve requirement, R is the volume of reserves in the commercial banking system, and D is the amount of demand deposits that a given volume of reserves (R) can support. For example, if R is $28 billion and r is 20 percent, then D is $140 billion — the initial demand-deposit figure given on page 101.

As long as R and r are unchanged, the maximum volume of deposits the banking system may maintain will be $140 billion. But if r were to increase to 21 percent, for example, D would then equal $133.33 billion. A 1 percent increase in the reserve requirement would thus lead to a $6.67 billion drop in deposits, as we saw above. On the other hand, a 1 percent decrease in the reserve requirement would lead to a $7.368 billion increase in deposit liabilities:

$$D = \frac{\$28 \text{ billion}}{0.19} = \$147.368 \text{ billion}$$

Given any value of r, the formula will indicate to what level deposits may expand. There is no requirement that the banking system must expand to this extent, of course, but the profit motive may encourage it to do so.

This formula may also be used to demonstrate the effects of a change in the volume of reserves R. For example, if the level of reserves is increased by $100 million, the lending ability of the banking system is increased by $500 million:

$$D = \frac{\$28.1 \text{ billion}}{0.20} = \$140.5 \text{ billion}$$

Similarly, a $100 million decrease in reserves would lead to a $500 million decrease in lending ability.

Banking System Deposit Creation and Destruction Under Relaxed Assumptions

The assumptions used to illustrate bank deposit creation and destruction capabilities in the preceding discussion are quite unrealistic, of course. They simply show the theoretical extent to which a given level of reserves and a given reserve requirement can be used to support deposits. In this section we will consider what happens when certain limiting assumptions are relaxed.

Cash drains and influxes. The nonbank public tends to maintain a relatively stable ratio of currency to deposits; an increase in nonbank public demand-deposit holdings is typically accompanied by an increased demand for currency. This tends to modify the potential increase in deposits and loans. When deposits contract, nonbank public holdings of currency also tend to decrease; currency flows into the banking system, building up commercial bank reserves.

Ironically, the very lending activities of banks that lead to deposit creation tend to restrain the money-creating abilities of the banking system. When banks make loans, for example, some people prefer cash and others both cash and deposits. Withdrawals of cash reduce the system's reserves and hence its lending and money-creating abilities. If businesses taking out loans for payroll purposes do so in the form of deposits, cash withdrawals also take place. Employees generally have a higher ratio of cash to deposits than do employers; paychecks are usually converted into both cash and deposits by employees.

On the other hand, when loans are repaid, they are not repaid solely with demand deposits. Instead, some portion of the repayments are in cash. This means that loan repayment usually leads to reserve increases for the banking system. If banks reduce investments, some security purchasers will use cash. This also leads to reserve increases. Thus, if banks contract because of a reserve deficiency, the extent to which they must contract will be reduced by the resultant cash inflow.

The ability of the banking system to create and destroy money, with this change in assumptions, is now determined by R, the level of reserves; r, the reserve requirement; and c, the ratio of currency to deposits desired by the nonbank public. Changes in the volume of demand deposits that can be maintained by the banking system, *given changes in reserves,* are governed by the equation

$$\Delta D = \frac{\Delta A}{r + c} \qquad [6\text{--}2]$$

where ΔD is the change in demand-deposit liabilities and ΔA is some beginning change in the volume of reserves.

Assume that R originally equals $28 billion, r is 0.20, c is 0.10, and that R then increases by $1 billion (that is, $\Delta A = \$1$ billion). Using equation 6–1, we can determine that reserves of $28 billion can support $140 billion in deposits, and reserves of $29 billion can support $145 billion. However, this new higher level of $29 billion in reserves is unlikely to be maintained, since the cash drain created when banks grant loans holds down the money-creating ability of the banking system. With c at 0.10, for every $1 billion increase in demand-deposit liabilities, the banking system must allow for a $100 million cash drain, which means, of course, a withdrawal of $100 million from commercial bank reserves. If banks were to attempt to expand deposits by $5 billion on the basis of the $1 billion in additional reserves, they would experience a $500 million loss in cash reserves. This would leave them, on balance, with $4.5 billion in additional demand-deposit liabilities and only $500 million in additional reserves, whereas legally $900 million in additional reserves would be required. Using equation 6–2, we can determine to what extent banks can safely expand demand deposits, given an initial $1 billion increase in reserves. Thus,

$$\Delta D = \frac{\$1 \text{ billion}}{0.20 + 0.10} = \$3.33 \text{ billion}$$

If banks expand demand deposits by $3.33 billion, they will lose $333 million of the initial $1 billion increment in reserves and be left with $667 million in reserves to cover the 0.20 reserve requirement against the newly created demand deposits. Bank loan and investment expansion during this time will total $3.66 billion: $3.33 billion extended to those customers who took deposits and $.33 billion extended to those who took currency. Equation 6–1 now gives

$$D = \frac{\$28.66 \text{ billion}}{0.20} = \$143.333 \text{ billion}$$

On the other hand, if R were initially *reduced* by $1 billion, the resultant cash inflow would hold down the potential deposit destruction to $3.333 billion.

Excess reserves. Many banks maintain precautionary and working balances of excess reserves, thus further reducing the extent to which the banking system can create and destroy demand deposits. Assume that $R = \$28$ billion, $r = 0.20$, $c = 0.10$, and that banks wish to have excess reserves equal to 5 percent of their demand-deposit liabilities. Let the symbol i' represent this percentage. The formula for the volume of demand deposits that the banking system can support now becomes

$$D = \frac{R}{r + i'} \qquad\qquad [6\text{–}3]$$

Thus, in terms of our hypothetical situation,

$$D = \frac{\$28 \text{ billion}}{0.20 + 0.05} = \$112 \text{ billion}$$

Now, suppose that R increases by an initial $1 billion ($\Delta A = \$1$ billion). Banks must now maintain reserves sufficient to cover the reserve requirement, precautionary demands for excess reserves, and the cash drain. As a consequence, the formula for changes in the volume of demand deposits that can be supported by the banking system, given changes in reserves, is now

$$\Delta D = \frac{\Delta A}{r + c + i'} \qquad [6\text{-}4]$$

Again, in terms of our hypothetical situation,

$$\Delta D = \frac{\$1 \text{ billion}}{0.20 + 0.10 + 0.05} = \$2.857 \text{ billion}$$

For every $1 billion increase in demand-deposit liabilities, the banking system must allow for a $100 million cash drain and also build up excess reserves by $50 million. Consequently, banks will create a maximum of only $2.857 billion in new deposits.

On the other hand, a $1 billion decrease in reserves results in a $2.857 billion drop in deposits, rather than a $5 billion drop. Thus, the tendency of banks to maintain working balances of excess reserves dampens both the money-creating and the money-destroying capacities of the banking system.

Time deposits. Banks create both time and demand deposits. Equations 6–1 and 6–3, however, are applicable only for a banking system with no time deposits. We need to know the volume of reserves required to cover time deposits before we can determine the ability of the banking system to create demand-deposit money.

Let r be the reserve requirement for demand deposits, r' the reserve requirement for time deposits, and TD the volume of time deposits. If $r' = 0.05$ and $TD = \$100$ billion, then $5 billion in reserves is needed to meet the reserve requirement for time deposits. If total reserves R are $30 billion, then $25 billion in reserves is available to support demand deposits. Thus, the formula for the demand-deposit supporting ability of the commercial banking system is

$$D = \frac{R - r'(TD)}{r + i'} \qquad [6\text{-}5]$$

If $R = \$30$ billion, then $D = \$100.0$ billion:

$$D = \frac{\$30 \text{ billion} - (0.05)(\$100 \text{ billion})}{0.20 + 0.05} = \frac{\$25.0 \text{ billion}}{0.25} = \$100.0 \text{ billion}$$

In recent decades the demand for commercial bank time deposits has gradually increased relative to the demand for demand deposits. This trend, as noted in Chapter 5, is in part a result of increased interest yields on time deposits. During any comparatively short period of time, however, the ratio of time to demand deposits changes slowly. This means that, for the short run, we can assume that the nonbank public desires a constant ratio of time to demand deposits. Let us call this desired ratio t. We now have another tool for predicting the volume of demand deposits that a given volume of bank reserves can support. The new equation is

$$D = \frac{R}{r + r't + i'}$$ [6–6]

If $R = \$30$ billion, $r = 0.20$, $r' = 0.05$, $t = 1$, and $i' = 0.05$, then

$$D = \frac{\$30 \text{ billion}}{0.20 + (0.05)(1) + 0.05} = \$100.0 \text{ billion}$$

The same result followed from equation 6–5.

Now suppose that R increases by an initial \$1 billion ($\Delta A = \$1$ billion). In addition to maintaining reserves sufficient to cover required reserves for demand deposits ($r = 0.20$), the drain ($c = 0.10$), and desired excess reserves ($i' = 0.05$), banks must have enough reserves to cover the potential increase in time as well as in demand deposits. As the deposit holdings of people expand with bank lending activity, people want additional currency, checking-deposit accounts, and time deposits. The formula for the change in demand deposits that can be supported by an initial change in reserves is

$$\Delta D = \frac{\Delta A}{r + r't + c + i'}$$ [6–7]

In terms of the aforementioned change in reserves (\$1 billion), we have

$$\Delta D = \frac{\$1 \text{ billion}}{0.20 + (0.05)(1) + (0.10) + (0.05)} = \$2.5 \text{ billion}$$

Hence, banks can maintain \$2.5 billion more in demand deposits. They will also maintain \$2.5 billion more in time deposits because $t = 1$. The nonbank public, in addition to owning \$2.5 billion more in each type of deposit (demand and time), will hold \$250 million more in currency. The total volume of loan and investment expansion by the commercial banking system will equal the sum of these three items, or \$5.25 billion. If there had been an initial decrease in reserves, the above figures would have been negative.

If t were 0, then the preceding illustration would yield

$$\Delta D = \frac{\$1 \text{ billion}}{0.20 + 0.10 + 0.05} = \$2.86 \text{ billion}$$

Demand-deposit money would increase \$2.86 billion, currency holdings would rise $286 million, and total loans would increase by $3.146 billion. By comparing this with the preceding result of $2.5 billion, we can see that the tendency of the nonbank public to maintain time deposits increases the volume of loans banks can make, but reduces the money-creating (and destroying) ability of the commercial banking system.

Overall, the greater the t and the larger the r', the lower is the ability of the banking system to create additional demand deposits. The reverse is also true. These statements should not be taken too literally, however, for, as previously indicated, if people can be persuaded to switch from demand to time deposits, the ability of the banking system to make loans and create deposits (both demand and time) is increased. A switch from demand to time deposits allows some portion of R to become excess reserves, since the reserve requirement for time deposits is lower than that for demand deposits. Clearly, if there are more time deposits, fewer demand deposits can be maintained; but the total dollar volume of time and demand deposits becomes greater as bank loans and investments expand.[6]

THE TOTAL STOCK OF MONEY

Predicting Changes in the Stock of Money

The analysis just developed showed how much demand-deposit money can be created by the commercial banking system. Demand deposits, of course, are only part of the money stock; the total amount of money that can be used in transactions consists of both demand deposits and currency. To derive an equation for the money stock M we simply add currency C to equation 6–6 for demand deposits D. If $M = D + C$, then

$$M = \frac{R}{r + r't + i'} + C$$

Since $c = C/D$, it follows that $C = cD$ and

$$M = \frac{R}{r + r't + i'} + \frac{cR}{r + r't + i'}$$

Hence

$$M = R \left(\frac{1 + c}{r + r't + i'} \right) \qquad [6\text{–}8]$$

The term $(1 + c/r + r't + i')$ in equation 6–8 is a *money multiplier*. It tells us how much money will exist in the economy, given some particular volume of reserves R, and given the values of c, r, r', t, and i'. Should these values equal those in our illustration concerning time deposits in the

---

[6] The deposit supporting equations developed here are more formally derived in the appendix to this chapter.

previous section of this chapter, we have

$$M = \$30 \text{ billion} \left(\frac{1 + 0.10}{0.20 + (0.05)(1) + 0.05} \right) =$$

$$\$30 \text{ billion} \left(\frac{1.1}{0.30} \right) = \$110 \text{ billion}$$

The volume of demand-deposit money is $100 billion and the volume of currency holdings is $10 billion.

Equation 6-8 cannot be used to predict the change in money that will follow from some initial change in bank reserves, however. To predict changes in the stock of money, we must expand equation 6–7. If we let the symbol Δ represent change, then $\Delta M = \Delta D + \Delta C$ and

$$\Delta M = \frac{\Delta A}{r + r't + c + i'} + \Delta C$$

Since $c = \Delta C / \Delta D$, then $\Delta C = c\Delta D$ and

$$\Delta M = \frac{\Delta A}{r + r't + c + i'} + \frac{c\Delta A}{r + r't + c + i'}$$

Hence:

$$\Delta M = \Delta A \left(\frac{1 + c}{r + r't + c + i'} \right) \qquad [6\text{–}9]$$

The term $(1 + c/r + r't + c + i')$ in equation 6–9 is another money multiplier. It tells us how much of a change in money will follow from some initial change in bank reserves. For example, if there is a $1 billion drop in bank reserves, we have

$$\Delta M = \$1 \text{ billion} \left(\frac{1 + 0.10}{0.20 + (0.5)(1) + 0.10 + 0.05} \right) = \$2.75 \text{ billion}$$

The change in demand deposits is a decrease of $2.5 billion and the drop in currency holdings is $250 million. *When bank reserves change, people change both their currency and demand-deposit holdings. As noted in our earlier discussions, bank time deposits, loans, and investments also change.*

Predicting the Stock of Money from High-Powered Money

The preceding equations predicted the stock of money and changes in the stock of money based upon bank reserves and money multipliers. These predictions can also be based upon a slightly different equation.[7]

Bank reserves R are a form of high-powered money — that is, they sup-

---

[7] The money multiplier equation given in the following discussion is more formally derived in the appendix to this chapter.

port a volume of deposits (D and TD) that are a multiple of R. Currency holdings C of the public are also high-powered in that if they were converted into reserves R they could support a multiple of themselves. Let the symbol H stand for high-powered money and equal R plus C. Then the equation for the money supply is

$$M = H \left(\frac{1+c}{r + r't + c + i'} \right) \qquad [6\text{--}10]$$

Substituting the values of our earlier example into this equation yields

$$M = (\$30\,\text{billion}\,(R) + \$10\,\text{billion}\,(C)) \left(\frac{1 + 0.10}{0.20 + (0.05)(1) + 0.10 + 0.05} \right)$$

$$= (\$40\,\text{billion}) \left(\frac{1.10}{0.40} \right) = \$110\,\text{billion}$$

This is the same result given by equation 6–8.

Equation 6–10 is a more powerful tool, however, because it can be used directly to yield a new money stock figure, given some change in high-powered money. Assume, for example, that H decreases by \$1 billion. Then

$$M = (\$39\,\text{billion}) \left(\frac{1.10}{0.40} \right) = \$107.25\,\text{billion}$$

Thus the stock of money has dropped by \$2.75 billion, the same result that was given by equation 6–9.

SUMMARY AND PREVIEW

It has been demonstrated that the ability of the banking system to create and destroy demand-deposit money depends on (1) r, the reserve requirement for demand deposits, (2) r', the reserve requirement for time deposits, (3) R, the volume of reserves, (4) t, the ratio of time deposits to demand deposits desired by the nonbank public, (5) c, the ratio of currency to demand deposits desired by the nonbank public, (6) i', the ratio of excess reserves to demand deposits desired by commercial banks. These six variables are all direct determinants of D, the volume of demand deposits that the banking system may maintain. Changes in any of the variables will change D. (Equations 6–6 and 6–7 incorporate all of these determinants.)

Three determinants of D, r, r', and R, are controlled by the monetary authorities. The current values of these variables are easy to ascertain.[8]

---

[8] There is, it is true, a spectrum of reserve requirements for demand deposits. They differ for country member banks and reserve city member banks, as well as for member and non-member banks. Yet, by calculating the percentage of deposits subject to each of the differing requirements, it is possible to calculate an average reserve requirement for the commercial banking system. For example, if 75 percent of deposits is subject to a 10 percent requirement and the remaining 25 percent of deposits to a 20 percent requirement, the average reserve requirement r would be 12.5 percent.

Two determinants, t and c, are determined by the nonbank public. One determinant, i', is controlled by the commercial banking system. To explain and predict movements in the stock of money successfully, we must understand how the banking system and the nonbank public react to changes in excess reserves and in our monetary base R.

Finally, in this chapter we have seen how it is possible to predict the total money supply from the volume of high-powered money and the various money multipliers. These tools of analysis will be important in the discussion that follows later in the book.

Chapter 20 is devoted in part to a study of contemporary money supply and demand theory. It develops behavior relationships, showing how the bank system and the public react to changes in economic conditions and the monetary base. Before we turn to this study, however, it is essential that we first understand the influence of other financial institutions and monetary authorities on our monetary resources. This will be discussed in Chapters 7–15.

Supplementary Readings

Burger, Albert. *The Money Supply Process* (Wadsworth, 1971).

Crick, W. F. "The Genesis of Bank Deposits." Reprinted in American Economic Association, *Readings in Monetary Theory* (Irwin, 1951), pp. 41–53.

Guttentag, Jack M., and Robert Lindsay. "The Uniqueness of Commercial Banks." *Journal of Political Economy* (1968), pp. 991–1014.

Orr, Daniel, and W. J. Mellon. "Stochastic Reserve Losses and Bank Credit." *American Economic Review* (1961), pp. 614–23.

APPENDIX
THE DERIVATION OF DEPOSIT, MONEY, AND LOAN MULTIPLIERS

Chapter 6 was concerned with the logic of how the commercial banking system, in contrast with an individual bank, creates and destroys money. Various equations to predict the volume of demand deposits and the stock of money were presented. Part of the discussion was also concerned with how bank loans and investments change in conjunction with deposits. This appendix is intended to give the formal derivations of deposit, money, and credit multiplier equations.

The Derivation of Deposit Multipliers

Let D, R, ΔA, r, r', t, c, and i' be defined as in Chapter 6. Assume that banks always expand demand deposits to the amount that they are able to maintain. From this it follows that bank actual reserve holdings R will equal the amount banks wish to hold.

To meet the legal reserve requirement the banking system must have sufficient reserves to cover its demand deposits, its time deposits, and its own desire for excess reserves. Thus, the amount of reserves that the banking system must have is

$$R = rD + r'TD + i'D$$

Since $t = TD/D$, it follows that $R = rD + r'tD + i'D$. Combining the terms in this equation somewhat differently tells us how much in demand deposits the banking system can support:

$$D = \frac{R}{r + r't + i'} \qquad [6\text{-}6]$$

From this we can also discover how much in time deposits the banking system can support. Since $D = TD/t$, we have

$$R = r\left(\frac{TD}{t}\right) + r't\left(\frac{TD}{t}\right) + i'\left(\frac{TD}{t}\right)$$

Thus

$$TD = \frac{Rt}{r + r't + i'} \qquad [6\text{-}11]$$

Now posit some initial change in bank reserves ΔA. This change in reserves must be sufficient to cover cash drain, desired excess reserves, and the increase in required reserves that occurs as banks expand demand and time deposits. Thus

$$\Delta A = r\Delta D + r'\Delta TD + \Delta C + i'\Delta D$$

Since $t = \Delta TD/\Delta D$, it follows that $\Delta TD = t\Delta D$. Also, since $c = \Delta C/\Delta D$, it follows[1] that $\Delta C = c\Delta D$. Hence

$$\Delta A = r\Delta D + r't\Delta D + c\Delta D + i'\Delta D$$

and

$$\Delta D = \frac{\Delta A}{r + r't + c + i'} \qquad [6\text{-}7]$$

From the preceding we can also derive the change in time deposits the banking system can support. Since $\Delta D = \Delta TD/t$ and $\Delta C = c(\Delta TD/t)$, the equation for the change in time deposits can be derived as follows:

$$\Delta A = r\left(\frac{\Delta TD}{t}\right) + r'\Delta TD + c\left(\frac{\Delta TD}{t}\right) + i'\left(\frac{\Delta TD}{t}\right)$$

$$\Delta A = \Delta TD\left(\frac{r + r't + c + i'}{t}\right)$$

$$\Delta TD = \frac{t\Delta A}{r + r't + c + i'} \qquad [6\text{-}12]$$

[1] We shall assume that $t = TD/D = \Delta TD/\Delta D$ and $c = C/D = \Delta C/\Delta D$.

The change in all bank deposits is the sum of equations 6–7 and 6–12, or

$$\Delta D + \Delta TD = \Delta A \left(\frac{1+t}{r + r't + c + i'} \right) \qquad [6\text{--}13]$$

The Derivation of Money Multiplier Equation 6–10[2]

In Chapter 6, two money multiplier equations (6–8 and 6–9) were formally derived. It remains to derive equation 6–10 — our most important money multiplier. Equation 6–10 is superior to equation 6–8 since it shows not only the volume of M, but also how to derive directly the new volume of money balances when we change either component of high-powered money $(H = R + C)$. What multiple of H will M always be? Let the symbol m represent this multiplier. Then

$$M = Hm$$

and

$$m = \frac{M}{H}$$

Since $M = D + C$ and $H = R + C$, it follows that

$$m = \frac{D + C}{R + C}$$

We know from equation 6–6 that

$$D = \frac{R}{r + r't + i'} \qquad [6\text{--}6]$$

Thus

$$R = D(r + r't + i')$$

and

$$m = \frac{D + C}{D(r + r't + i') + C}$$

Multiplying this by $\dfrac{1/D}{1/D} = 1$, we have

$$m = \frac{(1/D)(D+C)}{(1/D)[D(r + r't + i') + C]} = \frac{D/D + C/D}{(D/D)(r + r't + i') + C/D}$$

Since $C/D = c$, it follows that

$$m = \frac{1 + c}{r + r't + c + i'}$$

[2] I am grateful to Thomas Pearson, graduate student in economics at Georgia State University (1970–73), for preparing this solution to equation 6–10.

Substituting this expression in $M = Hm$ yields equation 6–10:

$$M = H \left(\frac{1 + c}{r + r't + c + i'} \right)$$

The Derivation of a Bank Credit Multiplier

Chapter 6 argued that loan and investment changes would ensue from a change in bank reserve positions. Here we will develop a bank credit multiplier that predicts changes in the total of bank loans and investments.

Throughout this derivation, it is important to remember that some borrowers take cash and others take either demand or time deposits. Let ΔL refer to the change in bank loans and investments. Then the change in credit is as follows:

$$\Delta L = \Delta D + \Delta TD + \Delta C$$

$$\Delta D = \frac{\Delta A}{r + r't + c + i'} \qquad [6\text{–}7]$$

$$\Delta TD = \frac{\Delta TD}{\Delta D} (\Delta D) = t\Delta D$$

$$\Delta C = \frac{\Delta C}{\Delta D} (\Delta D) = c\Delta D$$

$$\Delta L = \Delta D + t\Delta D + c\Delta D$$

$$\Delta L = \Delta D(1 + t + c)$$

$$\Delta L = \Delta A \left(\frac{1 + t + c}{r + r't + c + i'} \right) \qquad [6\text{–}14]$$

Assume that ΔA is $1 billion and that the other parameters have the values assumed in the last part of Chapter 6. Then

$$\Delta L = \$1 \text{ billion} \left(\frac{1 + 1 + 0.10}{0.20 + (0.05)(1) + 0.10 + 0.05} \right)$$

$$= \$1 \text{ billion} \left(\frac{2.1}{0.40} \right) = \$5.25 \text{ billion}$$

It will be recalled from our earlier illustrations that $\Delta D = \$2.5$ billion, $\Delta C = \$250$ million, and $\Delta TD = \$2.5$ billion; these amounts add up to the total change in credit or $5.25 billion.

7 Nonbank Financial Institutions: Sources and Uses of Funds

As commercial banks, in the process of increasing and decreasing their loans and investments, create and destroy money, they measurably affect economic growth. Commercial banks are not the only private financial institutions that help determine the rate of progress of the economy, however. Other financial institutions create and destroy financial assets that compete with currency and bank deposits as forms of liquid wealth. The greater the success of these nonbank institutions in attracting funds, the greater is the total liquid wealth of the nonbank public and the weaker is the direct control of our monetary authorities over the economy.

Previous chapters examined some of the problems that are created for banks and for the economy in general because the principal regulatory devices used by the monetary authorities have their initial impact on commercial banks. This chapter briefly discusses various competing financial institutions—institutions that, it is sometimes claimed, escape the brunt of monetary controls. We shall first study institutions that create assets with a high degree of liquidity—mutual savings banks, savings and loan associations, and life insurance companies. Other financial institutions will then be considered. Finally, the relationship between these nonbank financial institutions and the national economy will be examined. (Government financial institutions will be treated in later chapters.)

PRINCIPAL NONBANK FINANCIAL INSTITUTIONS

Mutual Savings Banks

Mutual savings banks, like commercial banks, create time deposits in large volume. However, this is where the similarity ends. Whereas commercial banks create both time and demand deposits, mutual savings banks today create only time deposits. These deposits arise when individuals deposit cash or checks drawn on commercial banks. Although all time deposits are legally subject to withdrawal only after notice, in practice depositors at mutual savings banks, like those at commercial banks, need give no advance notice.

As Table 7–1 indicates, deposits are the principal source of funds for mutual savings banks. They constituted more than 90 percent of total

TABLE 7–1 MUTUAL SAVINGS BANKS, SOURCES AND USES OF FUNDS,
DECEMBER 31, 1972
(IN BILLIONS OF DOLLARS)

Assets (*uses of funds*)	
Financial assets	
Mortgage loans	67.4
Other loans	3.0
U.S. government securities	3.5
State and local securities	0.9
Corporate and other securities	21.9
Total	96.7
Cash assets	1.7
Other assets	2.1
Total	100.5*
Liabilities and surplus accounts (*sources of funds*)	
Deposits	91.4
Other liabilities	2.0
General reserve accounts	6.9
Total	100.3*

* Totals differ due to rounding.
SOURCE: *Federal Reserve Bulletin* (March 1973), p. A-39.

mutual savings bank liabilities and surplus accounts in December 1972; the remaining 10 percent of funds was provided by other liabilities and surplus accounts.[1]

Mortgages and other investments represent the principal uses to which mutual savings banks put their funds. In December 1972, more than 67 percent of their assets was in the form of mortgages, and an additional 26 percent was in federal, state, local, and corporate securities. Only 1.7 percent of mutual savings bank assets was in the form of cash. This appears to be a dangerously low ratio of cash assets to deposits (0.018) when contrasted with the reserve requirement commercial banks must maintain. For institutions like mutual savings banks, however, this is not a dangerous ratio.

Mutual savings banks were initially established to provide a safe place for small savers to keep their funds. These savings banks soon found that they did not have to maintain a large volume of cash because their funds had such a slow turnover rate. Furthermore, mutual savings banks have traditionally maintained a very conservative investment policy; they almost never make risky loans which could sustain a loss. Thus, although their assets are quite illiquid, their slow rate of deposit turnover and the fact that two-thirds of them have deposit insurance with the Federal Deposit Insurance Corporation preclude the probability of substantial losses on those assets during periods of relative prosperity.

[1] We use the term "surplus accounts" rather than "capital accounts" since mutual savings banks, like other *mutual* organizations, have no stockholders. Surplus arises when operations are profitable.

Mutual savings banks have had an excellent record of performance. Even during the depression of the 1930s, few failed. Yet, despite this favorable record, they have not increased in number, and, while their assets have increased substantially, mutual savings bank assets have not risen as quickly as those of other nonbank financial institutions. Only commercial bank financial asset growth has been slower than the asset growth of mutual savings banks. What accounts for this relatively slow rate of growth? The principal reason is probably regional character.

Mutual savings banks are almost exclusively a phenomenon of the Middle Atlantic and New England states. They were first started there in the early 1800s. As the economy expanded in the nineteenth and twentieth centuries, the mutual savings form of financial institution did not expand geographically. Today there are only about 500 mutual savings banks.

Another factor limiting the growth of mutual savings banks has been the competition they face from savings and loan associations. As already mentioned, mutual savings banks were initially formed to provide a place of safekeeping for the funds of small savers. Safety being their primary consideration, little thought was given to the investment of funds for earnings; they preferred to make short-term mortgage loans and required relatively large down payments. Today, many mutual savings banks have departed from this tradition and now make long-term mortgage loans with low down payments. However, long before mutual banks became competitive, savings and loan associations dominated this field of lending and they also offered strong competition in obtaining deposits. The dividend return on savings and loan share accounts is often a bit higher than the interest return from competing mutual savings bank deposit accounts.

Savings and Loan Associations

In contrast to the limited number of mutual savings banks, there are about 6,000 savings and loan associations, these being specifically organized for the purpose of making mortgage loans. Table 7-2 shows that out of a total of $243.6 billion in assets in 1972, $206.4 billion was in the form of mortgages. Cash assets amounted to 1.1 percent of all assets. Savings and loan share accounts are the principal source of funds. Purchasers of these accounts often believe that they are the same as savings accounts with commercial and mutual savings banks. This is not usually true, however. In a savings and loan association a depositor usually owns *a share of the assets* of the association. Fortunately, this ownership is not the same as ownership in a corporation. To obtain cash for one's stock in a corporation the owner must sell the stock and, since the market price of corporate securities varies, the owner may sustain a loss. This is not usually possible with the shares of a savings and loan association, which ordinarily carries some type of insurance. Those associations regulated by the Federal Home Loan Bank Board, for example, have their share accounts insured by the Federal Savings and Loan Insurance Corporation.

TABLE 7–2 SAVINGS AND LOAN ASSOCIATIONS, SOURCES AND USES OF
FUNDS, DECEMBER 31, 1972
(IN BILLIONS OF DOLLARS)

Assets (uses of funds)	
Mortgages	206.4
Investment securities	21.8
Cash	2.7
Other	12.7
Total	243.6*
Liabilities (sources of funds)	
Savings capital	207.3
Reserves and undivided profits	14.7
Borrowed money	9.8
Loans in process	6.2
Other	5.5
Total	243.5

* Figures differ due to rounding.
SOURCE: *Federal Reserve Bulletin* (March 1973), p. A-40.

It should be observed that a few savings and loan associations do have a
corporate form of ownership. These institutions issue stock that is regularly traded in the securities market. The savings accounts that are sources
of funds for these corporations are liabilities and are thus comparable to
the savings deposits created by commercial and mutual savings banks.

Like mutual savings banks, savings banks, savings and loan associations
receive their funds in the form of cash or checks drawn on commercial
banks. When the associations accept these deposits and create savings and
loan share accounts, the volume of near money in the economy is increased. The funds received by the associations are then deposited in their
checking accounts at commercial banks and are subsequently used to make
mortgage loans or to purchase some other type of asset, such as U.S. government securities.

When mortgage loans made by savings and loan associations are received by borrowers, the funds become active money and stimulate demand and spending. Thus, these associations act as financial intermediaries; they help to transfer funds from those who save (the holders of
savings and loan share accounts) to those who borrow (the mortgagors). In
this fashion, funds pass from less active to more active spenders and, in the
process, the volume of liquid wealth and the claims to money in the
economy increase.

Until 1965, savings and loan associations grew faster in recent decades
than almost any other type of financial institution. Their growth during this
period was probably attributable to their active lending habits and to
usually higher dividend rates than the interest rates paid by competing
mutual savings banks and commercial banks.

Another reason often suggested for the rapid growth of savings and loan
associations in recent years is the fact that they are not subject to the same
type of reserve requirements as commercial banks. There is quite a bit of

truth in this argument. Savings and loan associations use cash holdings directly when redeeming share accounts. When additional funds are needed to redeem share accounts, the associations can either sell U.S. government security holdings or secure loans from a Federal Home Loan bank (if the association is a member of the Federal Home Loan Bank System), using their mortgage holdings as collateral. Furthermore, savings and loan associations seem to have little reluctance toward borrowing.

At the present time, savings and loan associations that are members of the Federal Home Loan Bank System operate under a liquidity reserve requirement of 5.5 percent. The Federal Home Loan Bank Board is authorized to vary this requirement from 4 to 8 percent of each association's savings and loan share accounts. The assets that satisfy this requirement are demand deposits, cash, certain types of time deposits, U.S. government securities, other federal agency securities, and various state and local government securities. Prior to 1966, if a savings and loan association's actual ratio of reserves to savings capital dropped beneath the requirement, it was forced to stop making loans. This regulation was dropped in 1966, making savings and loan mortgage lending more comparable to commercial bank lending behavior. In addition, the lending territory of savings and loan associations has been extended from 50 to 100 miles. Since 1971, savings and loan associations have been able to make mortgage loans on a nationwide basis up to 10 percent of their assets. However, they are still not comparable to commercial banks, which make a variety of loans and have different reserve requirements.

Cash deposits with a Federal Home Loan Bank and U.S. government securities are the principal assets used to meet the FHLB requirement. Were savings and loan associations subject to the same reserve requirements as Federal Reserve member banks, however, only cash assets could be used as reserves. This means that in December 1972 savings and loan associations would have needed $24.9 billion in cash assets instead of the $2.7 billion[2] they did maintain. This would seem to give savings and loan associations some competitive advantage over commercial banks, but the manipulation of Regulation Q by the Federal Reserve since the mid-1960s reduced this advantage. In addition, the Federal Home Loan Bank Board has moved toward a position of supplementing Federal Reserve control policies in the last decade.

Life Insurance Companies

Life insurance companies, with $239.4 billion in assets in 1972,[3] are the third most important financial subsector of the economy. Both commercial

---

[2] Assuming that the average reserve requirement on commercial bank time and demand deposits for member banks in 1972 was 12 percent.

[3] See Table 7–3.

banks and savings and loan associations have a larger volume of assets than life insurance companies.

Like other savings institutions, life insurance companies are financial intermediaries. They collect savings and use these funds to make investments. Thus, the process of getting funds from the ultimate lenders (savers) to the borrowers is considerably eased.

The principal sources of life insurance company funds are the premiums they collect from the sale of life insurance, annuities, and accident and health insurance. Term life insurance and accident-and-health insurance policies provide the insured with protection. Annuities and nonterm life insurance not only provide protection but also add to the volume of near monies in the economy as the policies acquire a cash surrender value, thus increasing total claims to the stock of money.

Life insurance companies generally put their funds to work in long-term investments, primarily mortgage loans and corporate bonds. Table 7–3 shows that life insurance company holdings of mortgages in December 1972 totaled $77.3 billion, or 32 percent of assets. Holdings of corporate bonds amounted to $86.6 billion, or 36 percent of assets. Life insurance companies put a large percentage of their funds into these long-term assets because they provide a steady source of revenue that can be used to meet benefit payments. Mortality tables enable insurance companies to predict approximately how much in benefits they will have to pay each year and reduce the need for a large volume of short-term assets that can be converted into cash quickly to meet unanticipated expenses.

The purchase of large quantities of long-term corporate securities by life

TABLE 7–3 LIFE INSURANCE COMPANY ASSETS, DECEMBER 31, 1972
(IN BILLIONS OF DOLLARS)

Government securities	
United States	4.3
State and local	3.5
Foreign	3.4
Total	11.1*
Business securities	
Bonds	86.6
Stocks	26.4
Total	113.0
Mortgages	77.3
Real estate	7.3
Policy loans	18.0
Other assets	12.7
Total assets	239.4

* Total differs due to rounding.
SOURCE: *Federal Reserve Bulletin* (March 1973), p. A-39.

insurance companies may well have a significant impact on the direction of growth in the U.S. economy. Long-term funds are used primarily for expansion of plant and equipment—a major source of economic growth. There are four main sources of such funds: retained earnings, depreciation, proceeds from the sale of bonds, and proceeds from the sale of stock. What proportion of these funds is supplied by life insurance companies? Of a total of $231.6 billion in outstanding corporate and foreign bonds in 1971, $79.3 billion were held by life insurance companies.[4] No other financial or nonfinancial sector of the economy holds more privately-issued bonds than do life insurance companies. Household and state and local government retirement fund sectors, which held $47.5 and $36.2 billion in these securities, respectively, in 1971,[5] are the second and third most important holders of privately-issued bonds.

Life insurance company holdings of corporate stock are comparatively small relative to bond holdings. Most states have legal limits to the amount of stock a life insurance company may hold. In New York, for example, a life insurance company can invest no more than 5 percent of its assets in corporate common stock. Life insurance companies purchased $3.6 billion of net stock issues in 1971.[6]

In what types of businesses do life insurance companies tend to invest? They hold a small number of railroad bonds, but, for the most part, they direct their funds toward utilities and such industrials as chemicals, machinery, and petroleum. The concentrations in these areas depend largely upon yield and the demand for funds by business. The issues purchased today tend to be direct placements; life insurance companies are purchasing fewer and fewer public issues.

OTHER NONBANK FINANCIAL INSTITUTIONS

A host of other financial institutions also provide funds for individuals and businesses. Some, like credit unions and pension funds, are principally savings institutions. Others, such as finance companies, do not collect savings, but act as intermediaries between borrowers and savers nonetheless. In fact, finance companies themselves often borrow from other financial institutions, using the proceeds of the borrowings to lend to consumers.

Credit Unions

A credit union is a savings institution that collects funds by selling shares to its members. This is comparable to the method of collecting funds employed by savings and loan associations, but the uses to which the two

---

[4] *Federal Reserve Bulletin* (June 1972), p. A-73.14.
[5] *Ibid.*
[6] *Ibid.*, p. A-73.7.

institutions put their funds differ sharply. Savings and loan associations make loans, principally long-term mortgage loans, to many different qualified borrowers, while credit unions lend on a short-term basis to a very restricted group—the members themselves.

Membership in a credit union is limited to a specific group of people. The group may consist of the members of a religious organization located in a particular community or members of the same occupational group. In the United States, 56.5 percent of all credit union members are industrial employees; an additional 15.0 percent are government employees.[7]

In recent years, these unions have experienced phenomenal growth. Their financial assets grew from $5.0 billion in 1960 to $18.3 in 1971.[8] No other type of savings institution has experienced a faster rate of growth in recent decades, but the relative importance of the credit union as a financial institution is still minor.

Credit union assets consist primarily of short-term loans to members. Unlike other savings institutions, credit unions concentrate on consumer installment debt. Out of a total $96.1 billion in installment credit held by financial institutions in April 1972, some $14.5 billion was held by credit unions. Only commercial banks (which held $47.1 billion) and finance companies ($32.5 billion) held more installment credit.[9] Most credit union lending takes the form of automobile, home-improvement, and debt consolidation loans. There are more than 20,000 credit unions, most of them quite small in asset size.

Until the 1970s the major problem facing credit union members was their lack of savings protection when compared to that provided for depositors in commercial and mutual savings banks by the FDIC and for shareholders in federal savings and loan associations by the Federal Savings and Loan Insurance Corporation. As a result, the risk attached to holding credit union shares was greater than for holding other forms of liquid wealth. Now, however, most credit union savings are insured by the National Credit Union Association.

Pension Funds

Pension funds are designed to provide income for people after retirement. There are two types of pension plans, *insured* and *uninsured*. Insured plans are administered by insurance companies; uninsured plans are administered by corporations, unions, or appointed trustees. In either plan, funds are supplied by both employer and employee contributions. Uninsured plans have become increasingly popular in recent decades, largely because of the legal limitations on insurance company investment in

---

[7] *Credit Union Yearbook* (1972), p. 7.
[8] *Federal Reserve Bulletin* (June 1972), p. A-73.19.
[9] *Ibid.*, p. A-56.

TABLE 7–4 INSURANCE SECTOR: FINANCIAL ASSETS FOR PRIVATE PENSION FUNDS, STATE AND LOCAL GOVERNMENT RETIREMENT FUNDS, AND OTHER INSURANCE COMPANIES, DECEMBER 31, 1971
(IN BILLIONS OF DOLLARS)

TYPE OF ASSET AND LIABILITY	PRIVATE PENSION FUNDS	STATE AND LOCAL GOVERNMENT RETIREMENT FUNDS	OTHER INSURANCE COMPANIES*
Total financial assets	128.4	64.8†	54.6†
Demand deposits and currency	1.6	.5	1.5
Corporate shares	86.6	11.2	15.5
Other credit market investments			
U.S. government securities	2.7	6.0	3.9
State and local obligations		1.9	19.3
Corporate bonds	29.0	36.2	9.3
Home mortgages	3.7		
Mortgages		7.1	
Commercial mortgages			.3
Trade credit			4.9
Other	4.8	2.0	

* Fire, casualty, and other companies.
† Totals may differ due to rounding.
Later data not available as of July 1973.
SOURCE: *Federal Reserve Bulletin* (June 1972), p. A-73.20.

common stock. This has made the uninsured plans, which are not ordinarily subject to such legal regulations, more attractive.

Pension plans may be *funded* or *nonfunded*. Companies with nonfunded plans meet pension payment requirements out of current income; in funded plans, funds are collected and invested to help meet future benefit payments. If the plan is insured, these funds are put to the same uses as other funds available to life insurance companies. Uses of funds in uninsured pension plans differ markedly, however. Table 7–4 lists the total financial assets of uninsured private pension funds as of December 1971. Out of a total $128.4 billion of financial assets, some $115.6 billion, or 90 percent, were in the form of corporate stocks and bonds. In the same year, by way of comparison, life insurance company holdings of corporate stocks and bonds amounted to only 47 percent of their total financial assets. The contrast is even more striking when we compare corporate stock holdings. Life insurance company holdings of stocks were only 9 percent of financial assets; uninsured private pension plans, however, held $86.6 billion, or 68 percent, of their financial assets in this form.[10] The reason for these differences, as previously indicated, are the legal restrictions imposed upon life insurance company stock investment. In a period of relative prosperity, such as that of the last 30 years, stocks usually appreciate in value and hence are a more attractive investment than bonds. Thus, there is a strong inducement to invest pension plan funds in stocks.

[10] *Ibid.*, p. A-73.20.

State and local government retirement funds. Various governmental bodies provide other types of pension plans. The most familiar is the social security retirement fund established by the federal government. The funds for social security benefits come from social security taxes on employers and employees. Idle funds are invested, primarily in U.S. government securities.

State and local government retirement funds, along with private pension funds, provide an important source of funds for corporate enterprise. Whereas the private plans have relatively more funds in stocks, the state and local government plans are concentrated in corporate bonds, having some 56 percent of all their financial assets in this form. These state and local retirement plans are often very much like funded private plans. The funds for state and local retirement plans come from employee payroll deductions, state and local government contributions, and income earned from the securities held by the retirement funds. Should an employee leave the government employment prior to meeting retirement requirements, he generally has a right to remove only his own direct contributions from the retirement fund.

Other Insurance Companies

Other insurance companies consist primarily of fire and casualty firms. Like life insurance companies, their sources of funds are principally premium payments, but unlike life insurance companies, they obtain substantial funds from capital accounts.

Fire and casualty insurance companies also differ sharply from life insurance companies in their use of funds. Their principal financial investments consist of high-yield state and local government obligations and corporate stocks, in contrast to the concentration of life insurance company funds in mortgages and corporate bonds.

Nonlife insurance company assets are also more liquid. As shown in Table 7–4, a total of $5.4 billion, or 10 percent, of fire and casualty financial assets were in the form of demand deposits and U.S. government securities in 1971. In contrast, life insurance companies had only 5 percent of their financial assets in this form.[11]

This difference is largely attributable to the nature of the financial obligations that the respective institutions are likely to incur. Life insurance companies can predict their total future financial responsibilities with a high degree of accuracy on the basis of mortality tables, and hence need not keep as many funds in highly liquid form. Fire and casualty companies, on the other hand, cannot know in advance the claims that will be made in a given year as a result, for example, of fire or the vagaries of the weather. Although increases in aggregate liability payments may be expected from

[11] *Ibid.*

year to year, this is of little assistance to the individual insurance company. Its power to predict the volume of future claims is limited. As a consequence, fire and casualty companies tend to concentrate more funds in assets that can quickly be converted into cash, such as demand deposits and government securities.

Finance Companies

Finance companies differ from the other financial institutions we have discussed principally in their sources of funds. Commercial banks, savings banks, savings and loan associations, and credit unions all receive their funds from depositors and shareholders and, in the process, create near monies. Life insurance companies receive their funds principally from premium payments; other insurance companies receive their funds from premium payments and capital accounts. Finance companies, however, obtain their funds principally from *borrowings* and *capital accounts.*

The two most important types of finance companies are consumer finance and sales finance companies. Consumer finance companies deal directly with the public; they usually make installment loans for the purchase of automobiles and consumer durables. Although the proceeds of the

TABLE 7-5 FINANCIAL ASSETS AND LIABILITIES FOR FINANCE COMPANIES, DECEMBER 31, 1971

(IN BILLIONS OF DOLLARS)

TYPE OF ASSET AND LIABILITY	FINANCE COMPANIES
Financial assets	
Demand deposits and currency	3.9
U.S. government securities	—
State and local obligations	—
Corporate bonds	—
Corporate stock	—
Open market paper	—
Home mortgages	7.0
Consumer credit	32.1
Other loans	21.3
Security credit (to others)	—
Total	64.4
Liabilities	
Corporate bonds	26.7
Bank loans	13.3
Other loans (open market paper)	21.1
Security credit (to brokers and dealers)	—
Taxes payable	0.3
Total	61.4

Later data not available as of July 1973.

SOURCE: *Federal Reserve Bulletin* (June 1972), p. A-73.21.

loans usually are used for a specified purchase, the actual loan is generally unsecured.

Sales finance companies, on the other hand, normally do not deal directly with the public. Instead, they purchase installment contracts from sellers of goods and services. The sale of these obligations to a finance company provides the retailer with funds that he can use immediately in his business operation and frees him from the expense and bother of collecting install-ment payments. Most installment-contract purchases are in the field of au-tomobile financing. Sales finance companies frequently lend directly to au-tomobile dealers at relatively low rates of interest, permitting the dealers to build up their stock of automobiles. Once the cars are sold, a dealer may extinguish the debt either by paying cash or by selling the installment con-tracts of his customers.

Table 7–5 shows the overwhelming importance of consumer credit as a use of funds for finance companies. At the end of 1971, the financial assets of finance companies amounted to $64.4 billion; 50 percent of this was in consumer credit. Total assets, however, were actually somewhat higher because of land and building ownership. Financial liabilities at the end of 1971 were $61.4 billion.

As is shown in Table 7–6, in December 1972 finance companies ac-counted for over $32.1 billion in installment debt, out of a total of $127.3 billion. Commercial banks, of course, held the largest amount — $59.8 bil-lion; this is to be expected, since commercial banks hold the largest volume of financial assets of any financial institution in the economy. Consumer credit is less important, however, for commercial banks than for finance companies. Commerical banks provide a wide variety of financial services for the public; finance companies specialize in consumer credit.

Open-End and Closed-End Investment Companies

Open-end investment companies, commonly called *mutual funds*, are yet another economically important financial institution. These companies ob-tain funds by selling their stock directly to the public. The proceeds are then used to purchase the stocks and bonds of other corporations.

Mutual funds issue new stock to meet the demands of the public. This stock may be purchased only from the investment company itself. When a stockholder wishes to redeem his shares, he does so by selling them back to the company. Thus, annual variations in the amount of open-end invest-ment company stock outstanding depend upon the difference between new stock sales and stock redemptions. In 1972, open-end investment compa-nies sold $4.892 billion of their own shares, while they retired $6.563 billion, leaving a net decrease of $1.671 billion.[12]

Obviously, such an excess of redemptions over sales constitutes a de-

---

[12] *Federal Reserve Bulletin* (March 1973), p. A-49.

TABLE 7–6 CONSUMER CREDIT, DECEMBER 31, 1972
(IN MILLIONS OF DOLLARS)

TYPE OF CREDIT AND INSTITUTION	AMOUNT	
Installment credit		
Commercial banks		
Automobile paper	27,096	
Other consumer goods paper	16,196	
Repair and modernization loans	3,544	
Personal loans	12,947	
Total		59,783
Finance companies		
Automobile paper	10,174	
Other consumer goods paper	6,505	
Repair and modernization loans	497	
Personal loans	14,912	
Total		32,088
Credit unions and others		
Automobile paper	6,598	
Other consumer goods paper	1,690	
Repair and modernization loans	2,160	
Personal loans	9,063	
Total		19,511
Retail outlets		
Automobile dealers	261	
Other retail outlets	15,689	
Total		15,950
Total installment credit		127,332
Noninstallment credit		
Single payment loans		
Commercial banks	10,857	
Other financial institutions	1,399	
Total		12,256
Charge accounts		
Retail outlets	7,055	
Credit cards (nonbank)	1,947	
Total		9,002
Service credit		8,974
Total noninstallment credit		30,232
Total consumer credit		157,564

SOURCE: *Federal Reserve Bulletin* (March 1973), pp. A-55 and A-56.

crease in shares outstanding. It does *not* mean that the liquid wealth of mutual fund stockholders has decreased, however. Mutual fund shares decrease in value only when the company sustains a loss on its investments in the stock of other companies.

Because of the large volume of funds they receive, open-end investment companies are able to purchase the stocks of diverse firms. Presumably this lessens the possibility of loss attendant upon holdings concentrated in particular stocks. However, a falling market can undermine the greater part of an open-end company's portfolio of stock investments. On the other hand, if the market is rising, as has been usual during recent decades, the value of an open-end investment company's stock investments will increase and the value of its own stock will rise, too. Mutual fund investment company assets have risen in market value from $17.0 billion at the end of 1960 to $59.8 billion at the end of 1972. Part of this $42.8 billion increase is attributable to a rise in net sales of mutual fund stocks amounting to $20.2 billion. The remaining $22.6 billion increase in market value of assets, however, is almost wholly due to the increased value of the stock investments made by these companies.[13]

How liquid a form of wealth are mutual fund shares? Clearly, the possibility of loss and the lack of any federal insurance on this type of asset indicate a small degree of liquidity. Nonetheless, such stocks may be fairly good investments during an extended period of economic prosperity.

Closed-end investment companies issue only a fixed amount of stock — not directly available to the public — which is usually sold through an investment bank. Once the stock has been purchased, it can then be resold through some form of stock exchange to individual purchasers; it cannot be resold to the company. Data on these companies are relatively incomplete, and therefore they will not be discussed further here. Closed-end and open-end investment companies are comparable, however, in that their fundamental purpose is to make earnings by wise investments in stocks of other corporations.

NONBANK FINANCIAL INSTITUTIONS AND THE ECONOMY

Most nonbank financial institutions are intermediaries that help channel funds from savers to borrowers. This is certainly a useful and, apparently, innocent function. However, financial intermediaries also create problems for the economy.[14]

Weakening the Effectiveness of Monetary Controls

Nonbank financial institutions create forms of liquid wealth (near monies) that compete with money. There are many forms of wealth; although real and liquid wealth are the two inclusive categories, people are confronted with choices between alternative forms of both liquid and nonliquid wealth. As pointed out in Chapter 5, the more successful nonbank financial institutions are in inducing people to maintain their liquid wealth holdings in the form of savings bank deposits, savings and loan

---

[13] *Ibid.*, p. A-49. Market value is the market value at the end of the period less current liabilities.

[14] Economists have discussed these problems extensively in the last two decades. Prominent among those associated with the ideas developed here are John Gurley and Edward Shaw. For an excellent theoretical discussion of their views see John G. Gurley and Edward S. Shaw. *Money in a Theory of Finance* (Brookings Institution, 1960).

association share accounts, or life insurance policies *instead of money*, the weaker is the control of our monetary authorities over the economy. Monetary policy usually affects only commercial banks directly. Thus the operations of nonbank financial institutions pose one problem: in the absence of effective monetary regulation, they may be responsible for an apparent weakening of our economic control mechanism.

Increased Velocity in Periods of Prosperity

A second problem arising out of increased nonbank financial institution operations is that of increased spending during periods of economic boom, when what is needed is a decrease in spending. Our monetary authorities attempt to dampen spending and hence reduce the demand for goods by limiting commercial bank lending activity. If, at the same time, savers are induced to switch from holding demand- or time-deposit accounts at commercial banks to the liquid wealth forms created by nonbank savings institutions, however, funds may become activated. Savings institutions do not hold their increased money balances idle: they lend them to consumers in the form of installment loans, to home buyers for home construction and improvement, or to businesses for capital expenditures. When the borrowed funds are spent, spending and the demand for goods and services rise. In a relatively high-employment economy, spending and demand may rise faster than the ability of the economy to meet this demand, resulting in an increase in prices rather than in the output of goods and services.

There does not have to be a change in the stock of money for this to occur — merely an increase in its use. A rise in the velocity of the circulation of money has the same effect as does the spending of an increased stock of money — its raises total spending. Nonbank financial institutions contribute to these inflationary pressures by helping to transfer money balances from savers, who are not active spenders, to actively spending borrowers.

There is some evidence that increases in the velocity of money underlay a substantial part of the price and output rises of the last several decades. Consider 1950 through 1972 — a remarkable period of sustained economic growth with brief pauses during four recessions. The stock of money increased from $118 billion to $256 billion. Gross national product rose from $285 billion to $1,152 billion. The income velocity of money — or the number of times that the stock of money is spent on gross national product during a year — is computed by dividing the gross national product by the stock of money figure for the year in question. Applying this measure to the case in hand, we find that income velocity increased from 2.4 in 1950 to 4.5 in 1972. So while gross national product increased 300 percent, the stock of money only rose 116 percent. Money therefore had to circulate more rapidly, and, indeed, velocity increased almost 90 percent. Thus, increased money stock and velocity were almost of equal importance to the growth in gross national product from 1950 to 1972.

Some of the increase in velocity in this period was attributable to the increased funds available to nonbank financial intermediaries. Increased funds mean increased lending. The relatively rapid growth rate of these institutions, as shown earlier in Table 5–6, supports this view. As indicated in Chapter 5, however, they grew more slowly than commercial banks after 1964, due to the effective use of Regulation Q by the Federal Reserve. Although nonbank financial institution growth contributed significantly to velocity increases, this contribution was not as important after 1964. The nonbank public apparently responded to changing interest rate differentials among financial institutions by altering the composition of its liquid wealth holdings.

Obviously, increased loan activity by commercial banks in periods of prosperity was another source of increased spending. Householders also tended to increase their rate of spending during these periods. What happened as a result? All this increased spending of a slowly rising money stock led to an increase in both output and the price of goods and services. As the economy approached full employment, the effects were concentrated more and more in price-level increases.

It should be emphasized, however, that commercial banks and nonbank financial intermediaries affect the velocity of money in somewhat different ways. Nonbank intermediaries make relatively few changes in the composition of their earning asset portfolios over the business cycle. Their acquisition of these assets is closely tied to current fund inflows, and these in turn reflect the reaction of the general public to interest rates and other factors that are set largely according to long-run growth considerations, rather than cyclical ones. *Thus, the destabilizing effects of nonbank financial intermediaries on the business cycle are primarily the result of an increase in the volume of their holdings of earning assets, rather than a change in the composition of these assets.* Commercial banks, on the other hand, vary the composition of their portfolios with the cycle, thereby intensifying it. They can engage in both asset and liability management because of their wide range of sources and uses of funds. Other financial intermediaries are more specialized in their sources and uses of funds.

Multiplication of Claims to Real Wealth

A third problem created by the growth of nonbank financial institutions is the multiplication of claims to real wealth in the economy. It has already been observed that the claims created by these institutions make monetary control more difficult. Liquid wealth is only a claim to real wealth. While an increase in the volume of liquid wealth may induce increased spending, and hence increased output, the mere multiplication of claims in itself does not increase the physical volume of real wealth in the economy.

Furthermore, real wealth can be purchased only with money. The more other forms of liquid wealth increase relative to money, the more difficult it may become to convert them into money. For example, in periods of rapidly rising prices, people may come to expect a continuation of rising prices. As a consequence most forms of liquid wealth, including money itself, will begin losing purchasing power. There may then be an attempt to "get out of" liquid wealth and "into" money for the ultimate purpose of "getting into" goods. The total amount of liquid wealth, however, is several times the volume of money in the economy. Hence, not all claims to money can actually be redeemed. A concerted attempt by the American public to transform a major portion of their liquid wealth holdings into money could conceivably result in a financial chaos comparable to that in the early 1930s.

Fortunately, several forms of nonmonetary liquid wealth—such as time deposits in commercial and mutual savings banks and savings and loan association and credit union share accounts—carry some form of federal insurance. Although the present assets of the federal insuring corporations are inadequate to meet all possible demands for converting insured liquid wealth into money, economists generally believe that the mere existence of this insurance may prevent the public from starting a financial panic. This "psychological" restraint on panics, however, applies only to recessions. What about "runs" on financial institutions that might occur with the expectation of sharply rising prices? Deposit insurance would do little good, because people would be demanding money in order to spend it and insurance would not restrain them from converting near money into money. Hopefully, we shall not be confronted with this situation if the relatively conservative monetary-fiscal policies of the two decades are continued. It is usually only when a nation's spending and money-creating activities are unrestrained that great inflations occur and there is a general abandonment of both money and other liquid wealth holdings.

Disintermediation

Another circumstance under which people may wish to "get out of" near monies created by nonbank financial institutions and "into" money occurs when interest yields on other forms of liquid wealth such as treasury bills rise above the interest rates on savings deposits. This process, known as *disintermediation*, may even affect commercial banks. Disintermediation sometimes occurs in periods of credit restraint; 1966, 1969, and 1973 provide the most recent examples. When people decide to reduce their savings deposits at nonbank financial institutions, they acquire funds that were serving as reserves for those institutions and thereby force a contraction of lending activity. Subsequently, the money acquired is used to purchase such financial assets as treasury bills. The housing industry, which needs mortgage funds provided by such nonbank financial institutions as savings and loan associations, is severely hampered. Businesses and individuals may also decide to redeem certificates of deposit issued by commercial banks and purchase treasury bills or commercial paper issued by other businesses instead. This action reduces bank time deposits and increases demand deposits which require higher levels of reserves. The effect is a reduction in bank lending activity. These contractionary forces may cool an economic boom, but they create serious adjustment problems for banks, other savings institutions, and the housing industry.

Our monetary authorities have the delicate job of restraining a boom without causing a contraction or disintermediation. For example, in July of 1973 it was feared that rising interest rates in the economy would cause disintermediation. To offset this possibility, the Federal Reserve lifted interest rate ceilings payable on time deposits at member banks. The FDIC took similar actions for nonmember banks and mutual savings banks, and the Federal Home Loan Bank made the same changes for savings and loan associations. In spite of this action, by the fall of 1973 many savings institutions reported significant fund losses — disintermediation was very much in evidence.

SUMMARY

Sources and Uses of Funds

We have now briefly examined the sources and uses of funds of our major financial institutions. The results of this survey are summarized in Table 7–7. In general, those financial institutions that receive a large portion of their funds from savers — mutual savings banks, savings and loan associations, and life insurance companies — use these funds to make long-term investments. Credit unions are a clear-cut exception. They appear to fill a gap left by the other financial institutions: no other credit institution concentrates on extending short-term credit to small savers in the relatively low-income groups.

Those financial institutions that receive a large fraction of their funds from capital accounts and borrowings tend to put their funds to uses that produce a high yield but are also highly liquid. Financial institutions that need funds on short notice to pay casualty claims (fire and casualty insurance companies), to repay borrowings (finance companies), or to redeem shares of stock (open-end investment companies) tend to invest their funds in highly liquid assets that can quickly be converted into cash. Of course, these assets are also somewhat risky, which accounts for their relatively high yield. Principal among these uses of funds are corporate stock and consumer credit. Uninsured pension funds are, to a certain extent, an exception. They receive their funds from premium payments and are able to predict with considerable accuracy their annual need for funds. Nevertheless, these pension funds tend to invest in both stocks and bonds, one important reason probably being the high yield obtainable from stocks in our relatively prosperous postwar era.

The sources and uses of commercial bank funds differ sharply from those

TABLE 7–7 PRINCIPAL SOURCES AND USES OF FUNDS, BY TYPE OF FINANCIAL INSTITUTION

TYPE OF FINANCIAL INSTITUTION	PRINCIPAL SOURCES OF FUNDS	PRINCIPAL USES OF FUNDS
Commercial banks	Demand deposits Time deposits	Commercial and industrial loans Real-estate loans Consumer credit U.S. government bonds U.S. government short-term securities State and local government securities Cash assets
Mutual savings banks	Deposits	Mortgages
Savings and loan associations	Savings capital	Mortgages
Life insurance companies	Premium payments Earnings	Corporate bonds Mortgages
Credit unions	Savings capital	Consumer credit
Pension funds (noninsured)	Premium payments	Corporate stock Corporate bonds
State and local government retirement funds	Payroll deductions	Corporate bonds Corporate stock
Other insurance companies	Premium payments Capital accounts	Corporate stock State and local government securities Corporate bonds
Finance companies	Borrowings Capital accounts	Consumer credit
Investment companies	Capital accounts	Corporate stock

of other financial institutions, mainly because banks in the United States provide such a wide range of services for their customers. Demand-deposit accounts, which can be converted into cash on demand, force banks to hold large amounts of highly-liquid assets, such as short-term government securities, commercial and industrial loans, and consumer credit. On the other hand, time-deposit accounts such as savings deposits, which have a relatively slow turnover rate, permit banks to invest in relatively safe, long-term, interest-yielding assets such as real estate loans and U.S. government bonds.

Problems Posed by Financial Intermediaries

The weakening of effective monetary controls, the increase in the velocity of money in periods of prosperity, disintermediation, and the multiplication of claims to real wealth are not problems created by nonbank financial institutions alone. Commercial banks, individuals, and government are all to some extent "responsible." A further exploration of these problems is reserved for the theory and policy discussion in Parts IV and V.

Supplementary Readings

Benston, George J. "Savings Banking and the Public Interest." *Journal of Money, Credit and Banking* (1972), pp. 133–226.

Bloch, Ernest. "Two Decades of Evolution of Financial Institutions and Public Policy." *Journal of Money, Credit and Banking* (1971), pp. 555–70.

Gurley, John G., and Edward S. Shaw. *Money in a Theory of Finance* (Brookings Institution, 1960).

Tobin, James, and William C. Brainard. "Financial Intermediaries and the Effectiveness of Monetary Controls." *American Economic Association Papers and Proceedings* (1963), pp. 383–400.

Part II MONEY AND GOVERNMENT

8 The Historical Development of Banking in the United States

MONETARY STANDARDS IN THE UNITED STATES

The Period of Bimetallism
  1792–1834
  Gresham's law
  1834–61
  1861–73
The Silver Question
The Gold Standard
  1873–1933
  1933; 1934–73

BANKING IN THE UNITED STATES FROM 1791 TO 1913

The First Bank of the United States, 1791–1811
State Banking, 1811–16
The Second Bank of the United States, 1816–36
State Banking, 1836–63
  The Suffolk System
  The Safety Fund System
  Free banking
  The Independent Treasury System
  Money and state banking
The National Banking System, 1863–1913
Principal Provisions of the National Banking Acts
  The granting of charters
  Capital requirements
  Government security deposits and bank notes
  Reserve requirements
  Other charter provisions
The Tax on State Bank Note Issues; Renewed Growth of State Banking
Principal Defects of the National Banking System
  Inelasticity of bank note issue
  Pyramiding of reserves
  Rigid reserve requirements
  Inadequate check-clearing facilities
Establishment of the Federal Reserve System
Federal Reserve Correction of National Bank Deficiencies
Early Shortcomings of the Federal Reserve System
  The lack of deposit insurance
  Early acceptance of the "real bills doctrine"
  A shortage of contracyclical policy instruments
  Coordination problems

Money consists of currency created by the federal government and demand deposits created by the commercial banking system. From the earliest days of our nation's history, our government has attempted to regulate money. At various times in our history Congress has placed the United States on bimetallic, gold coin, paper, and modified gold monetary standards. Congress has also created the First Bank of the United States, the Second Bank of the United States, the National Banking System, and, finally, our present Federal Reserve System. This chapter briefly examines the historical development of monetary standards and banking in the United States, with emphasis on the shaping influence of the government. The intent is to give some flavor of the historical problems we have faced and to set the stage for a consideration of contemporary monetary problems.

MONETARY STANDARDS IN THE UNITED STATES

The dollar is the unit of account in the United States. All debts, prices, and types of money are counted in terms of the dollar. Once a price for a good is established, we know how much money must be given up to acquire the good. Today the dollar is an abstract unit of account: its measure of value no longer domestically tied to a specific commodity. Officially the dollar is tied to gold: an ounce of gold is defined by law as being worth $42.22. However, no form of money, currency or deposits, can be redeemed in gold by citizens of the United States. Currency is our money of ultimate redemption. For this reason we say that the United States presently has an *internal paper standard;* that is, money can be redeemed only by currency, most of which is in the form of paper currency. Externally, of course, the United States is on the *gold standard,* since foreign government claims on the United States may be met in gold.

This distinction between our internal and external monetary standards has prevailed since the passage of the Gold Reserve Act of 1934. It has taken a long time for this characteristic of the contemporary American economy to be recognized by the general public, however. The Federal Reserve until recently printed currency bearing the designation, "will pay to the bearer on demand ____ dollars." Currently, however, Federal

Reserve notes simply state, "⎯⎯ dollars," The designation "will pay to the bearer on demand" has been dropped in recognition of the fact that currency, not gold, is the actual money of ultimate redemption. Nonetheless, this change in the labeling of our currency caused considerable consternation among Congressmen.

U.S. currency and the unit of account have not always been divorced internally from specific commodities such as gold or silver. This is a comparatively recent development, which began on a permanent basis in 1934. For most of its history, the United States has been on some type of metallic standard.

The Period of Bimetallism

1792–1834. Under a bimetallic standard, the unit of account is tied to two money metals — usually gold and silver. The first monetary standard in the United States was bimetallic. The *Coinage Act of 1792* defined the dollar as being equal either to 371.25 grains of silver or to 24.75 grains of gold. This meant that anyone bringing gold or silver to the mint could have it coined without charge. The legally defined mint ratio of silver to gold was 15 to 1 (371.25/24.75 = 15). A given amount of gold was, therefore, legally worth 15 times as much as an equal amount of silver. At that time, however, the actual market exchange ratio of silver to gold was about 15.5 to 1. Thus, Congress undervalued gold and overvalued silver and, as a consequence, only one money metal — silver — circulated in the United States. The intent of Congress had clearly been that both gold and silver coin should circulate, however, since the amount of either metal in the United States was insufficient by itself to meet domestic currency needs. If the bimetallic standard had legally priced gold and silver closer to the market ratio, both metals would probably have circulated, but the disparity between the mint and world ratios for gold and silver drove gold from circulation. Since gold in the United States was worth less at the mint than in the world market, little gold was brought to the mint for coinage. Silver, however, brought a high price at the mint and so a large amount of silver coinage took place.

Other circumstances combined to prevent even the freshly minted silver coin from having a wide circulation within the United States. American silver dollars found their way into the West Indies where both Spanish and American silver dollars circulated side by side, each equally acceptable. Unworn Spanish dollars were actually heavier than American silver dollars, however, so a trade in Spanish and American silver dollars developed. American dollars were exchanged for the Spanish dollars with the heavier silver content. The heavier Spanish dollars were then melted and minted in the United States into a greater number of new American silver dollars; these then flowed back to the West Indies. A flow of American silver dollars to the West Indies and a return flow of a roughly equivalent number of Spanish dollars to the United States developed. As a result, American silver dollars failed to circulate in the United States. Lower-denomination American coin and lightweight worn foreign coin circulated in the United States.[1] To put a halt to the outflow of silver caused by the failure of American silver dollars to remain in circulation in the United States, the Treasury stopped coining silver dollars in 1805. This suspension continued until 1834, and silver dollars were not minted for general circulation again until 1840. There was a general shortage of specie throughout this whole period, relieved in part by the circulation of small-denomination bank notes.

Gresham's law. The reasons for the outflow of gold and high-denomination silver coin during this period may also be explained by a principle called *Gresham's law* which states that "bad money drives out good." This simply means that a money form will be used where its value is the greatest. Under the bimetallic standard, when the mint ratio departs from the market ratio, there will tend to be an outflow of one money metal to where its value is greatest. Gold was undervalued in the United States from 1792 to 1834, so it flowed abroad. Silver was overvalued in the United States during the same period, so it flowed into the United States. The heavier weight of Spanish silver dollars offset this inflow, however, and led to an outflow of the lighter-weight American dollars to the West Indies.

During the period *1792 to 1834,* therefore, the *United States was legally on a bimetallic standard,* but *in fact, it was on a silver standard.* The currency in circulation consisted of worn foreign coin, small-denomination American coin, and bank notes. (More will be said about bank notes in a subsequent section of this chapter.) Gold virtually disappeared from circulation, particularly in the last decade of this period.

1834–61. Legally, bimetallism continued in the United States from 1834 to 1861, but during this period the standard became a *de facto gold standard.* This began in 1834 when Congress changed the legal ratio of silver to gold. Silver was kept at 371.25 grains to the dollar, but gold was changed to 23.22 grains to the dollar. This boosted the mint ratio to approximately 16 to 1. Congress hoped that the new mint ratio would return the United States to a de facto bimetallic standard, but again Congress miscalculated. The United States was too small a nation at the time to dominate the world price of gold and silver; changes in the American mint ratio had little influence on world gold and silver market prices. Since the market ratio of gold to silver was still approximately 15.5 to 1, gold became overvalued and silver undervalued in the United States. Some circulation of silver did continue in this period of a de facto gold standard, however.

---

[1] At that time it was legally permissible for foreign coin to circulate freely in the United States. This privilege was gradually restricted and finally terminated in 1857.

Now gold was brought to the U.S. mint for coining instead of silver. The outflow of large-denomination silver coins increased. Small-denomination silver coins remained in circulation, but there was little new minting of silver coin which contributed to a shortage of low-denomination coin. It was impractical to mint low-denomination gold coins; since the mint price of gold was 16 times that of silver, a low-denomination gold coin would have had to be either very small in size or a mixture of a small amount of gold and a large amount of some other metal. Hence, to increase the amount of coins in circulation, Congress reduced the silver content of subsidiary silver coins in 1853. From that date to the present, our subsidiary silver coin has not contained an amount of silver equal in value to the face value of the coin.

1861–73. The United States officially continued on a bimetallic standard until 1873. From 1861 to 1879, however, we were actually on a *paper standard*. Faced with the necessity of financing the Northern war effort, Congress authorized the Treasury to issue $450 million in "greenbacks," an irredeemable paper currency designed to serve as legal tender. It was not until 1879 that redemption of these greenbacks in gold specie was permitted. Greenbacks are now known as "United States notes" and are still being issued today. (The total amount of outstanding United States notes is limited by law to $323 million, however.) Coin was also in short supply during this period. People hoarded coin during the Civil War and, for a time, postage stamps were used to make change. Subsequently the Treasury issued fractional 3¢, 5¢, 10¢, 25¢, and 50c notes to facilitate making change.

The Silver Question

The United States continued on a de facto paper standard from 1873 to 1879, but the period of the legal gold standard started prior to the resumption of specie payments in 1879. The Coinage Act of 1873 made no provision for coining silver dollars. In effect, this failure to provide for silver coinage put the United States on a legal gold standard, although low-denomination subsidiary silver coin could still be minted.

At the time this action meant little, since greenbacks were not being redeemed in either gold or silver. It came to have meaning, however, when, due to a sharp increase in world silver production, there was a fall in the market price of silver. This produced a clamor for "free silver" and a silver standard in the United States. The agitation was so strong that silver purchase acts were passed in 1878 and 1890, providing that the Treasury should purchase silver at a given price and issue silver coin and silver certificates.

The silver purchase acts of 1878 and 1890 were the first of a long series of acts designed to protect silver-producing interests in the United States.

Additional silver purchase acts were passed in 1893, 1918, 1934, 1939, and 1946, providing a firm market price for silver producers. Whenever the market price of silver fell beneath the Treasury buying price, producers could sell their output to the Treasury. This policy of protection continued until 1963, when Congress repealed the silver purchase acts and permitted the Federal Reserve to replace silver certificates with Federal Reserve notes. Silver is now used only in 'Eisenhower' dollars. Actually, the concessions previously made to the silver interests by the various silver purchase acts were comparatively minor. Silver-backed currency and silver coin were generally a small part of our total currency supply.

The almost complete abandonment of silver as a money metal is related to the coin shortage of the early 1960s. Silver, as noted, was used as backing for silver certificates and in coin. Dimes, quarters, and half dollars contained 90 percent silver. But due to heavy and increasing industrial use of silver in the 1960s, world market prices rose as high as $1.75 per ounce of silver in 1967. Since the Treasury support price was only $.90 an ounce and its selling price $1.29 an ounce, it paid to buy silver from the Treasury and sell it to industrial users. Treasury silver stocks dropped. Accordingly, the government replaced circulating silver certificates with Federal Reserve notes and passed the Coinage Act of 1965, which removed all silver from dimes and quarters and reduced the silver content of the half dollar from 90 to 40 percent. Beginning in 1970, the silver content of the half dollar was also removed. Finally, in 1971 the Treasury began minting dollar coins for the first time since 1935. Some of these new dollar coins or 'Ike' dollars have no silver content, while others are 40 percent silver.

It should be noted that the Treasury now makes a substantial profit, called *seigniorage,* on coin production. Since the cost of producing coin is less than the face value of the coin, the Treasury makes a profit when it sells coin to the Federal Reserve at face value.

The Gold Standard

1873–1933. Although the United States was legally on the gold standard in 1873, the de facto paper standard continued until 1879. The Resumption Act of 1875 required that the U.S. Treasury begin the redemption of greenbacks in 1879. This action placed the United States on both *a legal and a de facto gold standard.* Gold coins were minted and gold certificates were issued, fully backed by gold held in the Treasury.

There was some doubt as to the legality of the gold standard, however, as widespread demands for "free silver" during this period indicated. The controversy was finally settled by the Gold Standard Act of 1900, which explicitly stated that the United States, like the leading European powers, was on a gold standard. The United States continued on this standard until 1933. With the exception of the World War I period of 1917–19, U.S. currency could be redeemed in gold until 1933.

1933; 1934–73. Until 1933, gold coins, gold certificates, Federal Reserve notes, and the various forms of Treasury currency circulated in the United States. All were considered legal tender. The volume of gold coins and gold certificates in circulation, however, tended to diminish after the establishment of the Federal Reserve System. After 1917, member banks were required to keep all of their reserves in the form of deposits with the Federal Reserve banks. This caused a large transfer of gold from the vaults of member banks to those of the Federal Reserve banks. In addition, the Federal Reserve replaced gold certificates in circulation with its own Federal Reserve notes. These actions led to a reduction of the amount of gold and gold certificates in circulation.

In the 1930s it became increasingly difficult for the large industrialized nations to remain on the gold standard. The depression caused the principal trading nations of the world to abandon the gold standard in favor of monetary policies more conducive to internal economic stability. By 1933, the United States was one of the few nations continuing on the gold standard, but widespread bank failures in that year caused our government to abandon the gold standard as well. The nonbank public and the commercial banks were required to turn in all holdings of gold coin, bullion, and certificates to the Federal Reserve banks (with the unpublished loophole of allowing private citizens to keep their gold coin in coin collections). This action took us off the gold standard internally. In addition, the United States stopped exporting gold, taking us off the gold standard externally. Thus, in 1933, the United States went on *a legal and de facto paper standard both domestically and externally*. Obligations could only be redeemed in paper currency.

In *1934* the United States returned to a gold standard, but one which may be more accurately described as a *modified gold standard*. Prior to 1934, an ounce of gold was legally worth $20.67. The new legal price of gold as set forth in the Gold Reserve Act of 1934 was $35 an ounce.

The Gold Reserve Act of 1934 also prohibited any further gold coinage, and declared all gold certificates to be the property of the Federal Reserve and all gold coin and bullion to be the property of the U.S. Treasury. As a result, gold coin and gold certificates are no longer used for transactions within the United States.

Gold certificates, like silver certificates, are legal tender; however, this provision allows them to be converted only into Federal Reserve notes and prevents currency collectors from being in violation of the law. The private sector of the economy is prohibited from owning gold except as jewelry, in coin collections, or for industrial purposes. Paper currency is now the money of ultimate redemption. Thus the United States has been on *a de facto paper standard internally since 1934,* even though the dollar is still legally defined as having a gold content.

The Gold Reserve Act of 1934 also authorized the Treasury to regulate the export of gold. Since that time the Treasury, aside from a short period in 1971–72, has used gold to settle international claims on American dollars. This means that the United States is on both *a legal and a de facto gold standard in international transactions.*

During 1971, there were strong pressures for a devaluation of the American dollar. These pressures, coming from international money markets, were due primarily to U.S. inflation, large deficits in the U.S. balance of payments, and private speculation in gold. As a result, the Treasury refused to use gold to settle foreign government claims on American dollars. In effect, this meant that during a period in 1971–72, the United States was on a *de facto paper standard even in international transactions.* This situation was terminated early in 1972 when Congress officially devalued the American dollar by making the legal price of gold $38 an ounce. Once again the United States was on a legal and de facto gold standard in international transactions. Unfortunately, the change in the legal price of gold did little to relieve international money market pressures on the dollar and the United States again devalued, this time making gold worth $42.22 an ounce. Conditions in 1973 were extremely confusing (to both international bankers and economic scholars), and the price of gold in the London private bullion market reached $125 an ounce. (A detailed discussion of international financial conditions is found in Chapter 24.)

BANKING IN THE UNITED STATES
FROM 1791 TO 1913

The First Bank of the United States, 1791–1811

Congress has often readjusted our monetary standard: principal changes have occurred in 1834, 1861, 1873, 1879, 1933, 1934, 1972, and 1973. Similarly, the development of banking in the United States has been shaped largely by governmental action.

In 1791, Congress chartered the First Bank of the United States. The establishment of this bank was due largely to the efforts of Alexander Hamilton, our first Secretary of the Treasury, and other advocates of a central banking institution.

At that time, there were only three commercial banks in the United States and their ability to issue currency was limited; state governments were forbidden to print currency at all. The bimetallic standard was still being moved through Congress under Hamilton's guidance, and coinage of gold and silver by the U.S. mint would not begin until after the Mint Act of 1792. The consequence was a general shortage of money. The First Bank of the United States was designed to be a source of currency convertible into specie and to operate both as commercial bank and as fiscal agent for the U.S. government.

The First Bank of the United States received its charter from Congress in 1791 and began operations with its head office in Philadelphia. In time, it operated eight branches in important domestic trading centers. In brief, the principal provisions of the charter authorized the First Bank to (1) have a capitalization of $10 million (25,000 shares were to be issued with a value of $400 each, of which $2 million in stock was to be purchased by the government and the remaining $8 million was to be sold to the public; foreigners could own stock, but only U.S. citizens could vote their shares), (2) issue up to $10 million in paper currency in denominations of $5 and up (these notes were the equivalent of legal tender because they could be used to pay debts to the U.S. government), (3) receive deposits, (4) make loans, (5) act as fiscal agent for the federal government, and (6) act as a clearing mechanism for other banks. Among the restrictions placed on the First Bank was the provision that forbade loans on real estate and commodities, preventing the Bank from engaging in speculative ventures that had frequently been the downfall of less well managed state banks.

Opposition to the establishment of the Bank was strong. Thomas Jefferson, a leading opponent, argued that the First Bank was unconstitutional. Others contended that the Bank would inhibit the development of private banking in the United States, that it would be a monopoly and abrogate the powers of state governments. Even after it was chartered, the First Bank of the United States encountered strong opposition. Rural interests in need of easy credit to meet the demands for funds in the expanding frontier areas, farm debtors, commercial banks, and even commercial business enterprises interested in low cost sources of funds were particularly vocal in their opposition.

The Bank's unwillingness to accept the notes of banks that refused to redeem their notes in specie (gold and silver) made it difficult for many commercial banks to expand loans. Banks at that time created bank notes in much the same way as they create demand deposits today.[2] Each commercial bank could create paper currency (bank notes) when extending loans. Borrowers usually took the proceeds of their loans in the form of bank notes rather than in specie. As these bank notes were spent, they passed into circulation in the economy. The notes were liabilities of the issuing bank and were presumedly redeemable in gold and silver coin. If the issuing bank had a good reputation and adequate specie reserves to cover demands for specie, its notes achieved a wide circulation. On the other hand, a bank that was illiquid, made risky loans, overextended note issues relative to specie holdings, or made it difficult for noteholders to redeem its currency soon found that its notes became generally unacceptable. By refusing to accept and redeem the notes of overextended banks, the First Bank of the United States hoped to restrain excessive issues of state bank notes. State bank opposition to this restraint was strong.

In addition, the First Bank's combination of public and private functions aroused state bank resentment. The First Bank was the only private commercial bank operating with a national charter. It also acted as a central

---

[2] Today, only the Federal Reserve and the U.S. Treasury can create paper money.

bank by regulating state bank note issues and as fiscal agent for the Treasury by holding federal funds. State banks felt that this represented unfair competition.

There were also many who objected to the large volume of Bank stock held by foreigners, even though this stock did not carry voting privileges. In sum, the opposition to the Bank was so strong that Congress failed to renew its charter in 1811. The First Bank of the United States, by assuming the responsibilities of a central bank in regulating the nation's currency, had run counter to rural interests, proponents of state rights, commercial business interests, and commercial banks.

State Banking, 1811–16

When the First Bank of the United States closed its doors for the last time in 1811, the restraint on unsound bank note issues was eliminated. The United States then entered a period of rapid state bank growth: the number of commercial banks rose from 88 in 1811 to 246 in 1816. Bank mismanagement also increased, however.

Speculative excesses occurred and inflation ensued. By 1814, paper currency had been issued to excess and state banks were no longer able to redeem notes in specie. It has been estimated that the volume of state bank notes in circulation tripled from 1811 to 1816.[3] In addition, during this period, there was some increase in the use of bank deposit money, much of which was created by the very banks issuing paper money to excess.

Not all of this financial difficulty was caused by the closing of the First Bank. This was also the period of the Napoleonic Wars, in which the United States became involved through the War of 1812. Europe, too, was experiencing currency problems. For example, from 1797 to 1821 the Bank of England refused to redeem its notes in specie; overissue of notes made it impossible to maintain redemption of notes in specie, and inflation followed. The American experience was not unique.

The absence of a central bank hampered the financing of the War of 1812. The Treasury could have refused to accept depreciated state bank notes in payment of debt, but it did not choose to do so. Instead, it tried to persuade state banks to resume specie payments, an effort which proved unsuccessful. Part of these difficulties, therefore, appear to have arisen because the Treasury failed to act as a monetary authority in the absence of a central bank.

The Second Bank of the United States, 1816–36

The drive for specie resumption led to the establishment of the Second Bank of the United States in 1816. The charter provisions passed by Congress were not unlike those of the First Bank. The major difference

[3] Leon M. Schur. "The Second Bank of the United States and the Inflation after the War of 1812." *Journal of Political Economy* (1960), pp. 118–34.

between the two banks was that the Second Bank was larger; its capitalization was greater, and it eventually operated a total of 25 branches.

The principal charter provisions authorized the Second Bank to (1) have a capitalization of $35 million, 20 percent going to the government and 80 percent to the public, (2) issue up to $35 million in paper currency in denominations of $5 and up (like those of the First bank, these notes were to be legal tender for payments of debts to the U.S. government), (3) receive deposits, (4) make loans, (5) act as fiscal agent for the federal government, and (6) act as a clearing mechanism for other banks. The charter was to run for 20 years.

The Second Bank had an even stormier history than the First. In its early years, the Second Bank was badly managed. Loans were made to stockholders who used stock as collateral. Investments were expanded too swiftly; the Second Bank's own note issue was increased too quickly. The Bank's first president, William Jones, a political appointee who was not a banker, actually speculated in the Bank's stock. Jones finally resigned in 1818 and Langdon Cheeves, another nonbanker, became the Bank's second president. Cheeves was successful in bringing some stability to operations, however.

Although the Second Bank of the United States was mismanaged in its early years, the principal charge leveled against it was that it failed to prevent inflation in 1817 and 1818. You will recall that one of the primary reasons for establishing the Second Bank had been to put a stop to the inflation that had been caused by the excessive issue of state bank notes. This inflation was not halted by the founding of the Second Bank. Part of the blame, however, has to be placed upon the Secretary of the Treasury, William Crawford, who pressured the Second Bank into accepting the notes of banks with questionable reserves. Crawford was primarily interested in minimizing losses to the Treasury that could result from the closing of overextended state banks.[4]

The Second Bank finally began to follow a restrictive policy in the latter part of 1818. It refused to accept the notes of state banks that did not redeem in specie, and it also restricted its own lending activity. The Second Bank took these actions chiefly because its own specie reserve position was in danger. Unfortunately, the timing of this restrictive action was bad: it intensified a sharp economic contraction that subsequently occurred in 1818 and 1820. This depression of 1818–20 was probably initiated by a drop in the foreign demand for agricultural goods, but the decrease in the stock of money resulting from the Bank's restrictive policy certainly accelerated the depression. At the time, however, the Second Bank received almost all of the blame for the depression. The opposition even went so far as to instigate an attempt to revoke the bank's charter, but this proved unsuccessful.

---

[4] *Ibid.,* p. 120.

From 1820 on, the Second Bank operated on a relatively sound basis, particularly after Nicholas Biddle became its president in 1823. Biddle operated the Bank both as a private profit-making commercial bank and as a central bank for the nation. He tried to restrain excessive state bank note issues and deposit creation, particularly in southern and western banks, and, with increased Bank pressure, resumption of specie payments became fairly widespread.

With the election of Andrew Jackson to the presidency in 1828, political difficulties again beset the Second Bank. Jackson was sympathetic to southern and western interests which were mistrustful of eastern bankers, among other things.

In 1832, four years prior to charter expiration, Congress rechartered the Second Bank, but Jackson vetoed the bill. In 1833, Jackson transferred federal deposits from the Second Bank to various private "pet banks." Biddle countered this action by contracting the Second Bank's assets and demand liabilities.[5] The result was a nationwide economic contraction. Needless to say, there was no renewal of the Bank's charter when it expired in 1836.[6] This "bank war" between Biddle and Jackson spelled the end of central banking and the end of branch banking in the United States until the establishment of the Federal Reserve System in 1913.

State Banking, 1836–63

The period from 1836 to 1863 was an era of state banking. Most legitimate banks operated on charters obtained from state legislatures or state banking authorities. There was no one central banking authority charged with supervising the stability of state bank notes and deposits or with regulating speculative lending operations by commercial banks.

As a result, financial chaos existed throughout most of this period. The number of banks increased rapidly in good times and decreased rapidly in recession; successive price inflations and deflations occurred. Many unsound loans were made, including illegal loans to stockholders. It was not uncommon for banks to have inadequate specie reserves, so that they were unable to redeem their bank note and deposit liabilities in specie. In fact, payment of specie was almost completely suspended from 1837 to 1842. The variety of bank notes in circulation ran into the thousands, and many of these, as might be expected, were counterfeit. Books published describing which notes were good and which were bad were out-of-date even before they were printed.

---

[5] For a discussion of this period see Jacob P. Meerman. "The Climax of the Bank War: Biddle's Contraction, 1833–34." *Journal of Political Economy* (1963), pp. 378–88. Also Peter Temin. "The Economic Consequences of the Bank War." *Journal of Political Economy* (1968), pp. 257–74.

[6] For some years, the Bank tried to operate with a Pennsylvania charter, but it finally failed in 1841.

Attempts to reform and regulate the banking system were primarily regional efforts that did little to improve the nationwide banking problem. The three main programs of reform were (1) the Suffolk System, (2) the Safety Fund System, and (3) free banking.

The Suffolk System. The Suffolk System was established in New England as early as 1824. Prior to 1824, bank notes moved toward Boston because of its financial importance in the New England area. Frequently, the notes of these outside banks did not circulate at par, whereas the notes of most Boston banks did. In fact, the more difficult it was for Boston banks to redeem the notes of outside banks, the greater the discount from par those notes bore.

Thus, in conformity with Gresham's law, the good notes of the Boston banks were driven from circulation. People hoarded the notes of the Boston banks and used the depreciated currency of distant banks in their daily transactions. Under the Suffolk System—set up to remedy this situation—banks outside of Boston that wished to have their notes redeemed at par within the Boston area were required to maintain at least a $2,000 redemption-fund account with the Suffolk bank. All notes of non-Boston banks received by Boston banks were to be cleared by the Suffolk bank. If the "outside" banks refused to join the Suffolk System, the Suffolk bank would collect a large volume of their notes and then request redemption in specie. Naturally any bank with inadequate specie reserves was unable to meet such a sudden large demand for specie. In this fashion the Suffolk System rather effectively eliminated most speculative and excessive note issues from the New England area. Eventually almost all New England commercial banks became members of the system, and only with the establishment of the National Banking System in 1863 was the need for the Suffolk System eliminated.

The Safety Fund System. The Safety Fund System was set up in 1829 by the New York State legislature. The principal function of this system was to protect depositors in the event of bank failure. Each bank in New York that was to receive a new charter or that requested renewal of its old one by the legislature was required to contribute an amount of money to the fund (to be held by the State Treasury) equal to 3 percent of its capital stock. Payments from the fund were to be made to creditors of banks that failed.

The Safety Fund System worked successfully while bank failures were not widespread. With the demise of the Second Bank of the United States in 1836, however, bank failures became more frequent—particularly during the 1837–42 recession—and the Safety Fund soon found it did not have adequate funds to meet the claims of the creditors of all the banks that failed during this period. Legislation was then passed limiting insurance to the claims of noteholders only, rather than to all creditors. The Fund continued to operate under this new arrangement for several decades, but it rapidly diminished in importance after 1846.

There are several reasons why the Safety Fund System gradually became less important. First, bank failures from 1837 to 1842 demonstrated that it was unlikely that a fund limited in scope to a small area of the country would be able to stave off nationwide financial panic. Second, New York adopted "free banking" in 1838, and new banks were no longer required to obtain their charters from the state legislature, as banks that were members of the Fund had had to do. Finally, the establishment of the National Banking System in 1863 provided nationwide note stability.

Although the Safety Fund soon became relatively unimportant, it was the first major attempt in our banking system to insure bank creditors. Today, of course, Federal Reserve notes are legal tender, and for funds on deposit we have a nationwide system of deposit insurance under the auspices of the Federal Deposit Insurance Corporation.

Free banking. Free banking was another answer to the excesses of state banking. Free banking began in the State of New York with the passage of the Free Banking Act of 1838. (A similar program was adopted at about the same time in Michigan.) Under the New York plan, any group of people could set up a bank, provided they deposited various state and United States bonds with the State Comptroller in an amount equal to the volume of notes to be issued. In the event of bank failure, the comptroller was to pay the noteholders out of the proceeds of the sale of those assets deposited with him. The purpose of the act was to standardize procedures for the establishment of banks and to free banks from dependency upon the whims and political pressures of state legislatures. No longer, for example, could legislators demand bank stock in exchange for their vote in favor of granting a bank a charter.

Some 15 states adopted free-banking laws prior to 1860. One difficulty with the free-banking system of this period was that it was frequently too easy for individuals to set up banks that complied with state requirements. Reserve requirements often did not exist, or were far too lenient. As a result, too many banks were established within a relatively short period of time, many of them with inadequate specie reserves.

Thus, *in the period of state banking from 1836 to 1863, the absence of a uniform currency and a central bank led to financial chaos.* A tremendous number of varying bank notes were in circulation, many of them counterfeit; deposits were created to excess; charters granted too freely. As a consequence, too many banks were weak and badly managed, and too many risky loans were made. Efforts at reform were regional in scope and thus unable to offer a solution to the national banking problem.

The Independent Treasury System. Much of this difficulty was caused by the closing of the Second Bank of the United States. At the time it was thought that the Treasury could regulate the banking system effectively by keeping government funds in various "pet banks" which were supposed to maintain separate specie reserves to cover Treasury deposits. Frequently, however, these banks used Treasury deposits as a basis for expanding their own loans and note issues. Consequently, when these banks experienced financial difficulty, the Treasury often discovered that its funds could not be withdrawn.

Finally, the Treasury itself lost confidence in the "pet banks," and, after various abortive regulatory attempts, Congress set up the *Independent Treasury System* in 1846. Under this system, a series of subtreasuries were established in various cities across the nation in which the Treasury could amass its funds. In doing this, the Treasury gave up what few powers of monetary regulation it had had. Instead of using its deposits to keep state bank notes safe throughout the nation, it now confined itself to safe-guarding its own funds. The Independent Treasury System did, in fact, safeguard federal funds, but it left the banking system totally unregulated in the process—and it created some new difficulties.

For example, Treasury tax collections and Treasury expenditures did not coincide. When collections temporarily exceeded payments, a surplus arose and funds were withdrawn from the economy and held by the Treasury. This reduced the amount of specie reserves held by commercial banks and thereby lessened their ability to redeem notes and deposits. On the other hand, when Treasury payments exceeded tax collections, an increased amount of funds would flow to the banking system and provide the basis for bank note, deposit, and loan expansion, some of it speculative.

The Independent Treasury System continued to operate until 1920. As early as 1863, however, the Treasury was again permitted to keep funds in commercial banks as well as its own Independent Treasury System. Gradually the Treasury began to realize that its deposits at commercial banks should be used in a way that would not affect bank specie reserves adversely.

While the period from 1836 to 1863 has been described as one of financial chaos, it must be recognized that the financial system did not collapse during these years. Many banks had specie reserves adequate to cover their bank notes and deposits. Regionally, the liabilities of even financially unsound banks were accepted as a medium of payment. Due to the shortage of silver coin, low-denomination bank notes continued to be accepted. As indicated earlier in our discussion of monetary standards, silver was undervalued at the mint with a consequent shortage of coin in circulation—a shortage not relieved until 1853 when Congress reduced the silver content of coin. After the establishment of the Independent Treasury System in 1846 and the 1848 gold discoveries in California, there was some tendency to substitute specie for bank notes and deposits.[7]

---

[7] For an excellent summary of the changes discussed here, see Edward J. Stevens. "Composition of the Money Stock Prior to the Civil War." *Journal of Money, Credit and Banking* (1971), pp. 84–101.

Money and state banking. Overall, the period of state banking can be divided into two subperiods with respect to stock of money changes. Following the close of the Second Bank of the United States, the stock of money decreased from $276 million in 1836 to $158 million in 1842—a very deflationary decline. Beginning in 1843, the money stock gradually increased until 1848—the year of the California gold discoveries—after which there was a sharp increase in monetary growth until the pre-Civil War high of $611 million was reached in 1856.[8]

The National Banking System, 1863–1913

The shortcomings of state banking were obvious. The problem was how to rectify the situation. There was considerable pressure for bank reform, but it was not until the Civil War that this agitation brought positive results with the passage of the National Banking Acts of 1863 and 1864. These acts did not reinstate centralized regulation of banking, but they did correct some of the deficiencies of state banking.

The National Banking Acts were designed to meet two broad goals: (1) to establish a safe currency system, and (2) to assist the Treasury in financing the Civil War. It is probable that the financial pressure of the war caused this banking legislation to be passed. According to the terms of these acts, national banks were to be established that would issue paper currency and provide a market for U.S. government securities. As it developed, the national banks did not purchase a large volume of U.S. government securities during the Civil War and therefore never became a principal source of funds for the Treasury.

The national banks, which, taken together, constituted the National Banking System, did provide a safe currency system for the United States, however. This was accomplished by limiting the amount of notes that national banks could issue to a maximum of 90 percent of their holdings on U.S. government securities. Since the federal government had budget surpluses throughout much of the time the National Banking System existed, there were several reductions in national debt which limited the supply of notes and contributed to their safety.

Principal Provisions of the National Banking Acts

In addition to a provision for the issuance of bank notes based upon U.S. government security holdings, the National Banking Acts of 1863 and 1864 contained provisions concerning the chartering of banks, capital requirements, government security holdings, reserve requirements, and bank lending operations.

[8] The figures cited are those of Peter Temin. *The Jacksonian Economy* (W. W. Norton and Company, 1969). These figures, along with other estimates, can be found in Milton Friedman and Anna Schwartz. *Monetary Statistics of the United States* (National Bureau of Economic Research, 1970), pp. 231–32.

The granting of charters. Under the National Banking Acts, any group of five or more persons could apply for a charter from the Comptroller of the Currency in Washington, D.C. In essence, this amounted to a new system of free banking, although the Comptroller was often strict in his granting of charters. Banks receiving their charters from the Comptroller were called "national banks," to distinguish them from "state banks" which received their charters from state banking authorities. This distinction between state and national banks remains with us today, as we have already seen in Chapter 4.

Capital requirements. The minimum capital requirements for the establishment of national banks were (1) $50,000 for banks in cities with less than 6,000 inhabitants, (2) $100,000 for banks in cities with 6,000 to 50,000 inhabitants, and (3) $200,000 for banks in cities with still larger populations. These requirements still apply to national banks today.

Some 50 percent of capital had to be paid to the bank's managers before the bank could begin operations. Each share had a par value of $100, and stockholders were subject to double liability—that is, if the bank failed, the stockholder could be required to pay an amount of money equal to his original stock purchase. The funds were to be used to meet the claims of the bank's creditors. This provision is no longer in effect.

Government security deposits and bank notes. Prior to beginning operations, a bank was required to deliver a given volume of U.S. government securities to the U.S. Treasury. These securities had to have a value of $30,000 or one-third the value of the bank's capital stock, depending upon which figure was larger. Once the bonds were delivered to the Treasury, the banks could start issuing national bank notes in an amount equal to 90 percent of the value of the securities. In 1900, banks were permitted to issue an amount of notes equal to a full 100 percent of the value of the securities. In addition, each national bank was obligated to redeem the notes of any other national bank at par.

Although each national bank was authorized to issue notes if it met the preceding requirements, the U.S. Treasury actually printed the currency in order to minimize the risk of counterfeiting.

These notes were not legal tender, but, since they could be used to pay federal taxes at par, they were the equivalent of legal tender just as the earlier notes of the First and Second Banks of the United States had been. Congress did not officially declare national bank notes to be legal tender until 1933. Today a few national bank notes are still in circulation, but they are being retired; no national bank notes have been issued since 1935. Private commercial banks are no longer permitted to issue paper currency. Today only the Federal Reserve and the U.S. Treasury are authorized to issue paper currency and coin money.

To further insure the safety of national bank notes, Congress provided in the National Banking Acts of 1863 and 1864 that no bank could issue notes in excess of the volume of its own stock and that the total volume of national bank notes could not exceed $300 million. A particular bank's share in the $300 million depended upon its size and location. These limitations were removed in 1875.

In the event of the failure of a national bank, the Comptroller of the Currency was authorized to sell the securities deposited by that bank and to use the proceeds to redeem its notes. In addition, the national banks were required to maintain a "redemption fund" with the Comptroller equal to 5 percent of their outstanding notes.

Reserve requirements. Initially national banks had one set of reserve requirements for both notes and deposit liabilities. The reserve requirements stipulated that banks designated as *central reserve city* and *reserve city* banks maintain reserves equal in value to 25 percent of their bank-note and deposit liabilities. Banks in other cities, called *country banks,* were to maintain reserves of 15 percent against their notes and deposits. At first, New York was the only central reserve city. By 1887, however, Chicago and St. Louis were also included in this category.

The reserves of central reserve city banks were to be vault cash in the form of "lawful money"—that is, legal tender specie and Treasury currency. National bank notes, of course, could not be used as reserves. Reserve city banks, on the other hand, needed to keep only one-half of their reserve requirement in the form of vault cash. The remaining portion could be in the form of deposits with central reserve city banks. The terms were even more lenient for country banks: only 40 percent of their reserves had to be in the form of vault cash; the remaining 60 percent could be in the form of deposits with either reserve city or central reserve city banks.

In 1874, the reserve requirement for notes was dropped altogether and reserves were only required for deposits. As we shall discuss in a moment, the composition of the assets used to satisfy the reserve requirement turned out to be one of the principal shortcomings of the National Banking System.

Other charter provisions. The major limitation on the lending activity of national bank was the banning of real-estate loans—a rule no longer in effect today. In addition, loans to any one borrower could not exceed 10 percent of the value of the capital stock of the bank, a regulation that still applies to national banks. Finally, national banks were permitted to serve as fiscal agents of the U.S. government.

The Tax on State Bank Note Issues;
Renewed Growth of State Banking

The National Banking Acts of 1863 and 1864 succeeded in providing a safe, uniform currency. Although the number of state banks declined markedly in the face of competition from national banks, those state banks remaining in operation continued to issue paper currency and many of these issued excessive amounts of notes. Thus the National Banking Acts did not substantially improve the quality of *all* bank note issues. To correct this deficiency, Congress passed an act in 1865 that placed a 10 percent annual tax on all state bank note issues. This tax was so prohibitive that within a few years all state bank note issues were withdrawn from circulation, and the number of state banks declined sharply.

The National Banking System did not spell the end of state banking, however. Banks had always considered the right of note issue a fundamental prerequisite for banking, but a revolution occurring in the banking habits of businesses and individuals soon invalidated that assumption. Following the Civil War, increasing use was made of deposit money; people found it more convenient to use demand deposits as a medium of exchange. State banks soon discovered that they could continue operations by creating deposits rather than currency. Bank customers seeking loans were willing to accept demand deposits in lieu of bank notes and, except for periods of financial panic, the turnover of deposits proved quite predictable. Thus, state banks could operate much as they always had, but with reserves a fraction of deposits instead of a fraction of notes and deposits. Once the banks became accustomed to operating under these new conditions, the number of state banks increased markedly. The number of national banks continued to mount also, but at a substantially slower rate than state banks.

Although many of the new state banks felt it would be advantageous to gain the right of note issue and prestige by becoming national banks, there were several distinct advantages to holding a state charter. The rules and regulations of state authorities were more lenient than those of the Comptroller of the Currency; reserve requirements and required capitalization were usually lower for state than for national banks; and state banks could make real-estate loans, whereas national banks could not.

Principal Defects of the National Banking System

Inelasticity of bank note issue. The National Banking System did not provide for the needed seasonal, cyclical, or secular variation in currency. At seasonal peaks of business activity, for example, more currency and deposit money are needed. The volume of national bank notes was tied to the national debt, however, and the national debt was determined by federal surpluses and deficits—not by seasonal business activity—leaving no room for a seasonal expansion of the currency supply.

More important than the seasonal inelasticity of national bank note issues was the cyclical and secular inelasticity of national bank notes. As the economy expands on the upward swing of the cycle, more currency is needed to carry on business activity. To the extent that expansion of business is in real output, an increase in money helps to finance the rise in economic activity. A growing economy needs additional currency and deposits to carry on a growing volume of transactions. Under the National Banking System, however, there was no mechanism for automatic note expansion. In point of fact, during the upward phase of the cycle, the federal government often found itself with a surplus which it used to retire part of the national debt. As national debt was retired, of course, the support for national bank notes decreased and their volume had to be reduced. Treasury surpluses were common throughout the 1880s and, as a consequence, the volume of national bank notes fell from $339 million in 1880 to a low of $165 million in 1891.[9] Surpluses were not as frequent in later years, and by 1913 the volume of national bank notes had climbed to $745 million.[10] Thus national bank note variations were geared to changes in the national debt, rather than to the economy's need for currency.

Other forms of currency did not have the desired elasticity in this period either. The volume of gold and silver coins in circulation depended upon both foreign and domestic production of the money metals. This was also true of gold and silver certificates, since they had to be backed fully by money metals. The greenbacks issued during the Civil War, which we call United States notes today, were limited in amount by act of Congress. These limitations, together with the limits placed upon national bank note expansion, effectively prevented the needed flexibility in our paper currency and coinage.

Pyramiding of reserves. Another major shortcoming of the National Banking System was that it made possible a pyramiding of reserves. It will be recalled that, legally, the reserves of national banks consisted of vault cash and deposits at other national banks. The *ultimate reserves* of all national banks, however, consisted of only vault cash and did not include deposits at other banks, since only vault cash could be used to redeem deposit liabilities.

Nonetheless, as country and reserve city banks made cash deposits with either reserve city or central reserve city banks, the total volume of reserves held by national banks increased, and, accordingly, the loan- and demand-deposit–creating ability of the banking system also rose.

Assume, for example, that country banks had $1 million in vault cash and no deposits at other banks. Since country banks could maintain as much as three-fifths of their reserves as deposits at noncountry national banks, under these conditions country banks could transfer $600,000 in cash to reserve city banks. Assume that country banks deposited $600,000 in cash with reserve city banks, as shown by the entries labeled (a) in the following T-account:

[9] Milton Friedman and Anna Schwartz. *A Monetary History of the United States, 1867–1960* (National Bureau of Economic Research, 1963), p. 131.
[10] *Ibid.,* p. 180.

BALANCE-SHEET CHANGES FOR COUNTRY BANKS

ASSETS		LIABILITIES + CAPITAL ACCOUNTS
Reserves		
Vault cash	−$600,000 (a)	
Deposits at reserve		
city banks	+$600,000 (a)	

BALANCE-SHEET CHANGES FOR RESERVE CITY BANKS

ASSETS		LIABILITIES + CAPITAL ACCOUNTS	
Reserves		Demand deposits due	
Vault cash	+$600,000 (a)	country banks	+$600,000 (a)
Vault cash	−$300,000 (b)		
Deposits at central			
reserve city banks	+$300,000 (b)		

BALANCE-SHEET CHANGES FOR CENTRAL RESERVE CITY BANKS

ASSETS		LIABILITIES + CAPITAL ACCOUNTS	
Reserves		Demand deposits due	
Vault cash	+$300,000 (b)	reserve city banks	+$300,000 (b)

Country bank total reserves have not changed, but those of reserve city banks have risen by $600,000.

The process need not stop here. Reserve city banks were required to keep at least one-half of their reserves in the form of vault cash. Thus, reserve city banks could now transfer $300,000 in cash to deposit accounts at central reserve city banks. This transaction, as shown in the entries labeled (b) above, results in another increase in reserves: central reserve city bank reserves have increased by $300,000. Thus, the initial $1 million in vault cash reserves has been pyramided to $1 million in vault cash reserves and $900,000 in reserves in the form of deposits at other banks.

So far this caused no economic difficulties. However, if reserve city and central reserve city banks expand loans and deposits on the basis of these increased reserves, then, in the event of a call for cash from other banks, there could well be a shortage of cash reserves. A shortage of cash reserves could force banks to suspend specie payments and this might precipitate financial panic. As the knowledge of a lack of liquidity became general, people would fear for the safety of their deposits and demand more cash, thus placing an added strain on the resources of the banking system. The financial panics of 1873, 1884, 1893, and 1907 were in large part an outgrowth of such reserve pyramiding and excessive deposit creation by reserve city and central reserve city banks. These panics were triggered by the currency drains that took place in periods of relative prosperity when banks were loaned up.

These difficulties could have been avoided if reserve city and central reserve city banks had kept enough vault cash on hand to back the deposit liabilities they owed other banks. Instead, as reserve city and central reserve city banks received cash deposits from other banks, they tended to consider this cash as part of their own reserves, and expanded loans and deposits as if they were receiving cash deposits from individuals. This is not to say that reserve city banks did not recognize their responsibility for maintaining funds to cover the deposits due other banks. City banks—particularly the large New York banks—were fully aware of this responsibility. As private profit-seeking corporations in a highly competitive industry, however, they felt obliged to keep their excess reserve positions low. Possible demands for cash by other banks were covered by the New York banks through call loans to stockholders. When pressed for funds from other banks, the New York banks could "call" back their funds from the brokers. These call loans were considered highly liquid.

The problem was, however, that if there were a widespread demand for cash throughout the economy, these call loans would prove to be nonliquid. Stockbrokers would not be able to get funds without selling stocks and causing a collapse of stock prices. Financial panic would follow in either case. Frequently these calls for cash would come when lending activity was high. Country banks would call for funds when farmers needed cash to help harvest and distribute crops in the fall. At the same time, however, central reserve city and reserve city banks were faced with loan demands from their own seasonal borrowers. No central bank existed to provide additional funds at such times.

Knowing this to be the case, why didn't the banks keep all reserves in cash form? Primarily for two reasons. First, until 1934, demand deposits accrued interest and were therefore a source of earnings for banks with temporarily idle funds. Second, country banks maintained deposits with reserve city banks to secure the advantages of correspondent banking.

Another problem related to the pyramiding of reserves was the lack of any means of accumulating cash for the purpose of helping a bank in an emergency. Each bank was prohibited from drawing down its vault cash beneath the required level. In effect, cash reserves were frozen at each national bank. As a result, although one bank might have a large volume of vault cash, it could not send any substantial amount to a bank in difficulty if this would entail a reduction in its own vault cash beneath the legal minimum. Once a bank's vault cash had sunk to its legal minimum, it had to close its vaults even if it had more than enough cash to cover a bank run.

Thus, under the National Banking System, cash flowed toward central reserve city and reserve city banks and, as this occurred, the loans and deposits of these banks increased. When the depositing country banks converted their deposits into cash, however, reserve city and central reserve city banks were forced to contract these loans and investments in order to reestablish a favorable reserve position. If they were unable to do so, they suspended cash payment and precipitated a financial panic.

Rigid reserve requirements. A third shortcoming of the National Banking System was that for the time that a bank was short of reserves, it was required to suspend the granting of new loans. This regulation created uncertainty for both borrowers and bank managers. Just when the demand for borrowing was strong, banks frequently had to halt the granting of new loans.

Inadequate check-clearing facilities. Finally, the clearing and collection mechanism for checks employed by the National Banking System was archaic. There was no central check-clearing agency comparable to that presently maintained by the Federal Reserve System.[11] With a unit banking system consisting of thousands of banks, checks had to be cleared through an elaborate network of correspondent banking relationships. If the United States had followed the example set by many European countries and had only a few banks with many branch offices, the need for adequate check-clearing facilities would not have been so important. As it was, however, the correspondent clearing facilities were cumbersome. The cost of transferring funds between distant points was expensive, long delays frequently occurred in check clearing, and many banks did not redeem out-of-town checks at par.

Establishment of the Federal Reserve System

The shortcomings of the National Banking System became increasingly apparent with each successive financial panic. After the panic of 1907, a National Monetary Commission was set up to study the situation. On the basis of its findings, the Commission submitted the *Aldrich Plan* for bank reform to Congress in 1910, calling for the creation of a National Reserve Association to act as a central bank for the United States.

The Aldrich Plan, largely backed by the Republican party, encountered widespread opposition and was not brought out of committee by a Democratic House of Representatives. Reform legislation was needed, however, and Congress finally passed the Federal Reserve Act in 1913 (largely a House bill) establishing the Federal Reserve System.

As originally conceived, the Federal Reserve System was designed not as a single strong central bank but as a federation of largely autonomous regional central banks. Each regional bank was to be responsive to the unique needs of its area. It was hoped that this federated system could avoid the charge of "monopoly." People at that time feared centralization, as many do even today, equating it with authoritarianism and lack of individual freedom. But in spite of the adverse experiences with state banking and the National Banking System, the public was not yet ready to accept central bank regulation. Many feared that under a centralized system the

---

[11] This mechanism will be described in Chapter 9.

unit banks would be dominated by eastern banking interests; anything akin to either the First or Second Bank of the United States would have met fierce opposition.

This reluctance to accept a system of central banking in order to provide the economy with safe banks and a sound currency was a peculiarly American attitude. Other advanced nations of the Western world had long possessed central banks, some of which were even engaged in commercial banking, as the First and Second Banks of the United States had been. The Bank of England, established in 1694, had a virtual monopoly of note issue very early in its history. The Bank of France, founded in 1800, had an extensive commercial banking operation organized along branch banking lines. The German Reichsbank, set up in 1875, was actually an outgrowth of the Bank of Prussia, which was founded in 1765. Other European nations had long operated similar institutions.

The commercial banking systems of most of these nations differed from that of the United States, however, in that they were generally dominated by a few large banks with extensive branch networks. Europeans were accustomed to big, powerful banks, and this may have made it easier for them to accept regulation from a strong central bank. The American tradition of small unit banking, of laissez faire, of private enterprise, made us naturally suspicious of any agency that appeared to foster bigness and regulation.

Federal Reserve Correction of National Bank Deficiencies

The Federal Reserve System was initially established to correct the deficiencies of the National Banking System; it was not specifically designed for purposes of economic stabilization—the Federal Reserve System's most important function today.

How did the Federal Reserve correct the shortcomings of the National Banking System? *First,* it introduced a mechanism for correcting inelasticity in the currency supply. Federal Reserve banks were authorized to issue a new type of bank note—Federal Reserve notes. Member banks could use their deposit accounts at Federal Reserve banks to acquire additional Federal Reserve notes as needed. If a bank's deposits at Federal Reserve banks were insufficient for this purpose, it could borrow from the Federal Reserve banks. Thus, commercial banks could always obtain additional currency from the Federal Reserve System. It was thought that this would help to avoid the financial panics that had previously occurred when commercial bank customers feared that currency would not be available on demand. The new currency could also expand and contract to suit the demands of the public. The Federal Reserve Act did not eliminate other forms of currency, however; it simply *added* an *elastic* currency, Federal Reserve notes. Today Federal Reserve notes have become our principal currency form.

Second, pyramiding of reserves became impossible for member banks.

All national banks were required to become members of the new Federal Reserve System. Member banks maintained reserve deposit accounts with the Federal Reserve banks; deposits at other commercial banks no longer counted as member bank reserves. The Federal Reserve banks, in sharp contrast to central reserve city national banks, did not also operate as private commercial banks. Thus, when the district Federal Reserve banks received cash deposits from member banks, no expansion of loans and deposits could take place in the private sector of the economy.

Third, the Federal Reserve banks were to operate as banks for commercial banks. If commercial banks were short of reserves, they could borrow from the Federal Reserve. This meant that member banks did not have to stop extending loans because they were temporarily deficient of reserves.

Fourth, the Federal Reserve banks provided an efficient mechanism for clearing and collecting checks throughout the country (as we will see shortly in Chapter 9).

Early Shortcomings of the Federal Reserve System

The lack of deposit insurance. Although the Federal Reserve System was able to solve many of the problems of the National Banking System, it also had defects of its own. For example, the Federal Reserve System did not make provisions for the safety of demand-deposit money. It took the depression of the 1930s to initiate this needed reform, which resulted in the establishment of the Federal Deposit Insurance Corporation in 1934. Deposit insurance now extends beyond commercial banks. Today almost all the deposit and savings liabilities of mutual savings banks, savings and loan associations, and credit unions are insured by some federal agency.

Early acceptance of the "real bills doctrine." Judging by the terms of the Federal Reserve Act of 1913, it was not recognized at the time that a central bank also has the important responsibility of stabilizing the economy. The Federal Reserve was originally viewed simply as a banker's bank. Reserve banks were to be sources of currency and funds to meet the credit needs of the commercial banking system. This was a recurrent theme throughout the aforementioned corrections to National Banking System deficiencies. The Federal Reserve Act provided that the Federal Reserve banks "discount notes, drafts, and bills of exchange issued or drawn for agricultural, industrial, or commercial purposes, or the proceeds of which have been used for such purposes. . . ."[12] This feature was included not only to protect banks and businesses in crisis, but also to take care of ordinary business needs for funds.

This amounted to an acceptance of the "real bills doctrine" or the "commercial loan theory of banking" which was briefly described in Chapter 3.

---

[12] Federal Reserve Board, *Annual Report* (1914), p. 17.

In essence, it was thought that, since the production of real goods was believed to be the real source of funds for loan repayment, the debts or "paper" of its customers that a bank put up for borrowed funds should arise out of current production. As was discussed previously, however, loans can prove illiquid in times of economic stress. Furthermore, expanding and contracting loans in accord with the "needs of trade" is a procyclical action. If full employment is reached, then the needed funds finance the operation of firms that successfully bid productive resources away from their competitors. Total output, however, remains unchanged. Thus, applying the real bills doctrine in periods of full employment only adds to inflationary pressures.

Fortunately, as early as the 1920s, the Federal Reserve recognized the potential dangers of following the real bills doctrine and began to develop a sense of responsibility for the stabilization of economic activity. Evidence of increased awareness of the need to stabilize economic activity is shown by the early contracyclical behavior of discount rates. Chapter 11 will deal with discount rates in depth, but for the present it will suffice to define the *discount rate* as the "price" that a Federal Reserve bank charges member banks who borrow reserves. In general, from 1917 to 1932, the Federal Reserve banks moved discount rates contracyclically. When discount rates were raised it was hoped that banks would hold down the growth of reserve borrowing and thereby restrain demand expansion in the economy. The reduction of discount rates, it was hoped, would encourage banks to lend. From 1933 through 1951 discount rates were low — first, because of the depression and, subsequently, because of an inappropriately easy monetary policy designed to support the government bond market during and immediately after World War II.

A shortage of contracyclical policy instruments. Many economists believe that the depression of the thirties demonstrated that there was a shortage of contracyclical monetary tools at the disposal of the Federal Reserve. Accordingly, in the 1930s, the powers of the Federal Reserve were expanded to include variable reserve requirements and open market operations. Unfortunately, these instruments were not used to counter economic fluctuations until the 1950s, and thereby contributed to what is generally regarded as the failure of the Federal Reserve to formulate an effective monetary policy during the interim period. (All of these problems will be considered further in Chapters 11 and 12.)

Coordination problems. In addition, the federated structure of the system created policy coordination problems. At first, the Federal Reserve Bank of New York tended to dominate the system, but soon the other district Federal Reserve banks sought to exercise more authority of their own. These organizational difficulties were resolved in the 1930s with the creation of our present Board of Governors.

As subsequent chapters will demonstrate, the Federal Reserve System has proved to be a valuable institution that has sometimes been able to adapt successfully to changing economic circumstances. However much economists may disagree concerning the system's effectiveness, it can at least be said that the Federal Reserve has become aware of its responsibility for promoting economic stability.

Supplementary Readings

Friedman, Milton, and Anna Schwartz. *A Monetary History of the United States, 1867–1960* (National Bureau of Economic Research, 1963).

Hammond, Bray. *Banks and Politics in America from the Revolution to the Civil War* (Princeton University Press, 1957).

Linke, Charles M. "The Evolution of Interest Rate Regulation on Commercial Bank Deposits in the United States." *National Banking Review* (1966), pp. 449–69.

Martin, David A. "Bimetallism in the United States before 1850." *Journal of Political Economy* (1968), pp. 428–42.

Spengler, Joseph J. "Coin Shortage: Modern and Pre-Modern." *National Banking Review* (1965), pp. 201–16.

Stevens, Edward J. "Composition of the Money Stock Prior to the Civil War." *Journal of Money, Credit and Banking* (1971), pp. 84–101.

9 The Structure and Nonregulatory Functions of the Federal Reserve System

THE STRUCTURE OF THE FEDERAL RESERVE SYSTEM

Board of Governors
  Policy actions
  Actions to enhance domestic competition in banking
  Routine administrative actions
  Bank examination and supervision
  The board and legislation
Federal Open Market Committee
Federal Advisory Council
The Federal Reserve Banks
Member Banks

NONREGULATORY FUNCTIONS OF THE FEDERAL RESERVE BANKS

Maintenance of Member Reserve Accounts
Check-clearing and Collection Operations by
    the Federal Reserve System
  A checkless society?
Fiscal and Foreign Agent Functions of
    the Federal Reserve Banks

SUMMARY

As presently constituted, the Federal Reserve acts as a central bank for the United States. Its primary function is to contribute to the stabilization of the domestic economy through the manipulation of money and credit. Its goals are stable prices, high employment levels, and economic growth. As subsequent chapters will show, however, these goals may be mutually contradictory. A fourth major objective of contemporary central banking policy is to influence the flow of goods and money between domestic and foreign markets, but its overriding concern is to help achieve a prosperous and growing domestic economy. No longer is the Federal Reserve concerned merely with maintaining an elastic currency or being a banker's bank.

Later chapters discuss in detail how the Federal Reserve System attempts to achieve its goals through the administration of monetary policy and these chapters summarize the contemporary controversy on economic policy. The scope of this chapter, however, is limited to an examination of the structure of the system and its nonregulatory functions.

THE STRUCTURE OF THE FEDERAL RESERVE SYSTEM

There are five principal elements in the organizational structure of the Federal Reserve System: (1) the Board of Governors, (2) the Federal Open Market Committee, (3) the Federal Advisory Council, (4) the twelve Federal Reserve banks and their branches, and (5) the member banks.

Board of Governors

The Board of Governors is the single most important part of the Federal Reserve System. It consists of seven men appointed to 14-year terms by the president with the approval of the U.S. Senate. Members may not serve for more than one full 14-year term and no more than one member can come from each Federal Reserve district. The president selects the chairman and vice-chairman of the board from among the board members; each serves a term of four years.

The members of the board are ultimately responsible for the operations of the entire Federal Reserve System. They formulate monetary policy and decide whether it will be restrictive or expansionary. In addition, the Board of Governors has more routine duties: it supervises the Federal Reserve banks, regulates member banks, interprets the Federal Reserve Act, and issues various regulations under the Act.

The varied nature of the activities of the Board of Governors is well illustrated by the following resume of some of its activities during 1972.[1]

Policy actions. 1. In March 1972, in a move designed to strengthen the U.S. balance of payments, the Board of Governors amended voluntary Foreign Credit Restraint Guidelines to prevent subsidiary banks in a holding company from consolidating a newly acquired lending ceiling with the ceilings of other banks in the same holding company. This action was intended to limit expansion of foreign lending by U.S. banks.

2. In April, the board adopted a number of regulatory changes to broaden the coverage of and tighten its control over the use of credit in stock market transactions.

3. In May, the board's statement on nondiscriminatory real estate financing went into effect. Banks making real estate loans are now required to display a public notice that they are in compliance with the Civil Rights Act of 1968.

4. In July, the Federal Reserve entered the foreign exchange market by selling German marks and buying dollars — an action intended to strengthen the dollar in international money markets.

5. In November, the board revised reserve requirements for all member banks, making the requirements dependent on bank size. This action was designed to reduce inequities in reserve requirements based upon bank location. Frequently, country banks, with lower reserve requirements, were located in areas of rapid growth such as the metropolitan suburbs. With population shifts, these country banks attracted reserves from the larger reserve city banks located in the downtown financial centers. The loss of reserves, coupled with higher reserve requirements and limitations on expansion via increased branch banking, had effectively reduced the growth rate of many reserve city banks. The uniform reserve requirements were intended to permit the reserve city banks to compete more effectively with country banks for deposits and loans.

6. In November, margin requirements for the purchase of stock were raised. This measure was designed to reduce lending for stock purchases.

Actions to enhance domestic competition in banking. The board issued numerous orders under the Bank Merger Act approving and disapproving proposed mergers in 1972. In the same year, it issued orders under the Bank Holding Company Act approving and disapproving applications for the establishment of bank holding companies.

---

[1] Compiled from *Federal Reserve Bulletin* (1972).

Routine administrative actions. 1. The board admitted various state banks to membership in the Federal Reserve System.

2. It appointed Federal Reserve bank directors and branch directors, and also made a number of staff changes.

3. The Board of Governors regularly revised various regulations and interpreted the Federal Reserve Act.

4. In February, the board announced approval of guidelines to be used in establishing regional centers for the overnight processing and settlement of checks. The ultimate end of this program is to facilitate check clearing and to reduce *float*.[2]

Bank examination and supervision. 1. The board's Division of Supervision and Regulation examines all state member banks at least once a year. The board does not normally examine national banks, since the Office of the Comptroller of the Currency makes copies of its own examinations available to the board.

2. The board's Division of Federal Reserve Bank Operations examines the Federal Reserve banks and their branches and facilities.

The board and legislation. The chairman and members of the Board of Governors frequently appeared before Congress to state their opinions on proposed banking and economic policy legislation. In March 1972, for example, the board argued for the passage of the Par Value Modification Act. The Act officially raised the price of gold from $35 to $38 dollars an ounce and was intended to help alleviate U.S. balance of payments difficulties.

These were just some of the actions taken by the Board of Governors in 1972. In addition, the members of the board served on the Federal Open Market Committee where they exerted a dominant influence over our most important instrument of monetary policy—the purchase and sale of U.S. government securities by the Federal Reserve banks.

Federal Open Market Committee

The Federal Open Market Committee or FOMC consists of 12 members, seven of whom are the members of the Board of Governors. Thus, the board (if it is in agreement) has a controlling voice in FOMC deliberations. The remaining five members are the presidents of five of our 12 Federal Reserve banks. The president of the Federal Reserve Bank of New York is vice-chairman of the committee and serves as a permanent member because of the crucial role of the New York bank in the purchase and sale of securities. The other four positions on the committee are rotated among the remaining Federal Reserve bank presidents. The chairman

---

[2] A discussion of the relationship between bank reserves and float will appear in Chapter 10.

of the committee is the chairman of the Board of Governors. Although only five Federal Reserve bank presidents are members of the Federal Open Market Committee, in practice all 12 presidents attend committee meetings.

The FOMC meets approximately every four weeks for the purpose of determining Federal Reserve policy with respect to the purchase and sale of securities — principally U.S. government securities — on the open market. Open market policy decisions are crucial for the economy because, as Chapter 10 will demonstrate, open market transactions in government securities by the Federal Reserve banks strongly influence the reserve position of the commercial banking system and, thus, are an important instrument of control over the money supply. In addition, the FOMC directs the purchase and sale of foreign currencies by Federal Reserve banks.

The FOMC is a policy setting organization and does not itself execute the policies that it selects as most appropriate for the current economic situation. Responsibility for the actual purchase and sale of securities and currencies lies with the manager of the System Open Market Account and the special manager in foreign currency at the Federal Reserve Bank of New York. Since New York is the center of the government securities and foreign exchange markets in the United States, all private government securities dealers have their main offices there. Securities and currencies purchased by the New York bank are apportioned among all the Federal Reserve banks according to each bank's share of total Fed assets.

Policy directives are formulated at each meeting of the FOMC. They are usually very broad in scope. For example, an economic policy statement issued to the Federal Reserve Bank of New York on October 17, 1972, stated:

The information reviewed at this meeting suggests a substantial increase in real output of goods and services in the third quarter, although well below the unusually large rise recorded in the second quarter. In September, wages and prices advanced moderately, while the unemployment rate remained substantial. In the U.S. balance of payments, the current account deficit has been largely offset by capital inflows in recent weeks, and the central bank reserves of most industrial countries have continued to change little. In August, the excess of U.S. merchandise imports over exports declined somewhat.

The narrowly and broadly defined money stock expanded at moderate rates in August and September, following large increases in July, but the bank credit proxy continued to grow rapidly. Since mid-September, short-term interest rates have increased somewhat, while yields on most long-term securities have changed little.

In light of the foregoing developments, it is the policy of the Federal Open Market Committee to foster financial conditions conducive to sustainable real economic growth and increased employment, abatement of inflationary pressures, and attainment of reasonable equilibrium in the country's balance of payments.

To implement this policy, while taking account of the effects of possible bank regulatory changes, treasury financing operations, and developments in credit markets, the Committee seeks to achieve bank reserve and money market conditions that will support more moderate growth in monetary aggregates over the months ahead than recorded in the third quarter.[3]

With such a broad directive the account manager and special manager have a great deal of latitude in executing FOMC policies. Since they are in day to day contact with the foreign currency and government securities markets, they are continually receiving information on the various forces directly affecting commercial bank reserve positions and the U.S. balance-of-payments situation. Consequently, within the context of current directives, they may need to make rapid adjustments to offset undesired changes in our reserve and currency positions. For example, the directive just quoted implies that for reasons of domestic policy Federal Reserve bank holdings of U.S. government securities should be increased more moderately. Yet, at a given time the account manager actually may be reducing these holdings to offset other forces that may be operating on commercial bank reserves. What is needed under such a directive is not an actual expansion in Federal Reserve holdings of securities, but a small *net expansion of commercial bank excess reserves.* This is just one aspect of Federal Reserve open market operations.

Federal Advisory Council

The Federal Advisory Council consists of 12 members, one from each Federal Reserve district. Each member is selected by his district Federal Reserve bank and is usually a representative banker from the district. The council is strictly an advisory group, meeting at least four times a year to survey general business conditions in the economy and to formulate appropriate policy recommendations to be presented at meetings with the Board of Governors. There is no obligation on the part of the board to execute the recommendations of the council, however.

Today it can be argued that there is little reason to continue the council because it has no powers. Originally, however, there was some justification for its establishment. When the Federal Reserve Act was passed, many commercial banks opposed the formation of a Federal Reserve Board; bankers felt that the board would not be responsive to their interests and needs. Consequently, the Federal Advisory Council was set up to provide the banking industry with a means of directly informing the Federal Reserve Board of its needs and wishes.

The Federal Reserve Banks

Geographically, the United States is divided into 12 Federal Reserve districts, each with a Federal Reserve bank and branches. There are 24

[3] *Federal Reserve Bulletin* (January 1973), pp. 17–18.

branch offices and two bank facilities, scattered throughout the various districts.

As Figure 9–1 indicates, Federal Reserve banks are located in Boston, New York, Philadelphia, Cleveland, Richmond, Atlanta, Chicago, St. Louis, Minneapolis, Kansas City, Dallas, and San Francisco. These 12 banks vary greatly in size. As Table 9–1 shows, the Federal Reserve Bank of New York is the largest, with total assets of $24.7 billion in February 1973. This is to be expected, since New York is the money market center

Figure 9–1 Boundaries of the Federal Reserve districts and their branch territories.

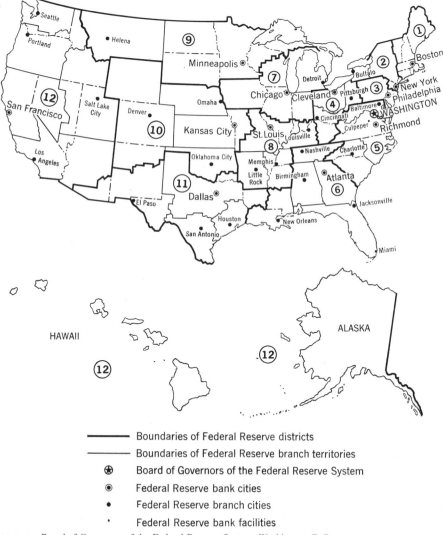

——————— Boundaries of Federal Reserve districts

——————— Boundaries of Federal Reserve branch territories

⊛ Board of Governors of the Federal Reserve System

◉ Federal Reserve bank cities

• Federal Reserve branch cities

· Federal Reserve bank facilities

SOURCE: Board of Governors of the Federal Reserve System, Washington, D.C.

TABLE 9-1 FEDERAL RESERVE BANK ASSETS, FEBRUARY 28, 1973

(IN MILLIONS OF DOLLARS)

DISTRICT NUMBER	FEDERAL RESERVE BANK	ASSETS
1	Boston	4,659
2	New York	24,694
3	Philadelphia	5,170
4	Cleveland	7,147
5	Richmond	7,665
6	Atlanta	5,896
7	Chicago	15,620
8	St. Louis	3,747
9	Minneapolis	2,279
10	Kansas City	4,181
11	Dallas	4,545
12	San Francisco	13,627
	Total	99,230

SOURCE: *Federal Reserve Bulletin* (March 1973), p. A-13.

of the nation. The Federal Reserve banks of Chicago and San Francisco are the next largest, with $15.6 and $13.6 billion in assets, respectively. The smallest is the Federal Reserve Bank of Minneapolis, with $2.3 billion in assets. These differences in size among district Reserve banks conform roughly to the percentage of total commercial bank assets within each district. Although initially it was hoped that the Federal Reserve banks would be approximately equal in size, such equality was impossible because of the concentration of financial business in a limited number of cities.

The decentralized character of the Federal Reserve System is an outgrowth of the traditional conflict between those who advocate local banking autonomy and those who argue for a more efficient centralized system. Local banking interests were quite vocal when the Federal Reserve Act was passed in 1913, and it was thought that local needs would be served best by regional Federal Reserve banks that were loosely federated under the Federal Reserve Board. Thus, at one time, each Federal Reserve bank had a substantial amount of authority in its district. This gradually changed as the need for more centralized operations became apparent. The Banking Act of 1935 recognized the need for centralization by giving the new Board of Governors of the Federal Reserve System strong powers.

Today, the principal function of each Federal Reserve bank is to supervise the operations of the member banks within its own district. The district Federal Reserve banks maintain member bank reserve deposits, clear and collect checks for member banks, lend them reserves, and supply them with currency. In addition, each district bank sets the discount rate for its district; this power, however, is subject to review by the Board of Governors.

Each Federal Reserve bank has the same type of administrative structure, supervised by Class A, Class B, and Class C directors. There are a total of nine directors in one Reserve bank, three of each class. Class A and Class B directors are selected by the member banks of the district. Two directors, one Class A and one Class B, are chosen by the small banks of the district, two are chosen by the medium-sized banks, and two by the large banks. Class A directors may be bankers. Class B directors must not be bankers, but should be actively engaged in commerce, agriculture, or industry in the district. The remaining three directors (Class C) are chosen by the Board of Governors, which appoints a Class C director as chairman and another as deputy chairman of the board of directors. Class C directors cannot be actively engaged in the banking business. The directors of each district bank formulate policy for the bank and appoint its president and vice-president, as well as certain other employees. The appointment of these bank officials, however, is subject to approval by the Board of Governors.

Each Federal Reserve bank is a corporation chartered by the federal government. Its stockholders are the member banks. Ownership of district Federal Reserve bank stock is a requirement for commercial banks that wish to be members of the system. The amount of stock held by a member bank must, at present, equal 3 percent of its capital accounts. Thus, the amount of Federal Reserve bank stock subscribed to by member banks varies as member bank capital accounts change and as the number of member banks in the system changes.

Although a Federal Reserve bank is in fact a corporation, it is unlike a private corporation in many ways. A Federal Reserve bank's fundamental purpose is to regulate the operations of the member banks in its district within the confines of the monetary policies articulated by the Board of Governors. Hence, Federal Reserve banks are not profit-seeking corporations. True, a Federal Reserve bank does make profits in the course of its operations. By law, however, stockholders (member banks) receive dividends equal to only 6 percent of the value of their subscription to Federal Reserve bank stock; member banks have no claim to additional dividends. Nor do they have a residual claim to the assets of a Federal Reserve bank. In addition, ownership of Federal Reserve bank stock, unlike the common stock of most corporations, is not transferable; there is no market for the stocks of the Federal Reserve banks. In the event of liquidation, the total value of the surplus and the par value of the common stock (assuming the Federal Reserve bank assets would yield their book value) would go the the U.S. government. Such a liquidation, however, is highly unlikely, given our tradition of at least some decentralization in central banking activities.

Member Banks

The last and most numerous component of the Federal Reserve System is, of course, the member banks themselves. Member banks are private, profit-seeking corporations, which, like all commercial banks, possess the unique ability to create and destroy money in the process of making loans and investments. Although they constitute only 41 percent of all commercial banks in the United States, member banks account for 80 percent of bank demand-deposit liabilities. (Member bank characteristics were discussed at length in Chapter 4.) These banks, of course, are the most important element of the Federal Reserve System since it is through regulating the financial position of member banks that the Federal Reserve Board attempts to stabilize economic conditions. The manipulative actions of the board and member bank reactions are analyzed in depth in Chapters 11 and 12.

NONREGULATORY FUNCTIONS OF THE FEDERAL RESERVE BANKS

Many of the functions performed by the Federal Reserve banks are not directly connected with the implementation of monetary policy. Three of these services have already been mentioned: (1) creating reserves for member banks, (2) supplying member banks with currency, and (3) clearing and collecting checks. These are all portions of the main function of a Federal Reserve bank — the maintenance of member bank reserve deposits. A fourth nonregulatory function of the Federal Reserve banks is to act as fiscal agents of the U.S. government.

Maintenance of Member Reserve Accounts

Each member bank is required to maintain reserves in the form of vault cash and deposits at its district Federal Reserve bank. These deposits do more than merely meet legal reserve requirements. Far from lying idle, reserve deposits at Federal Reserve banks are constantly increasing and decreasing. The activity of these accounts demands careful supervision by both the member banks and the Federal Reserve banks to ensure that minimum member bank reserve requirements are met.

How are these accounts employed? First, they are used in the *creation of reserves* for member banks by the Federal Reserve banks. Member banks are usually able to borrow from their district Federal Reserve bank to meet temporary shortages of reserves, provided they have the proper collateral. Frequent trips by a member to the "discount window," however, may cause the Federal Reserve bank to restrict the amount it will lend a particular bank.[4] When it lends reserves, the Federal Reserve bank simply increases the member bank's deposit balance. *These reserves are created by the Federal Reserve bank, just as commercial banks create demand*

---

[4] Federal Reserve banks do not normally discount eligible paper or make advances to member banks automatically; the time-honored position of the Federal Reserve has been that its discount facilities are available to member banks as a privilege, not as a right. During 1968, however, the Federal Reserve proposed an extensive redesign of its discount mechanism — a proposal still not implemented at the time of this writing (1973). As a result, some Federal Reserve lending of reserves to commercial banks may become automatic. A more extensive discussion of these proposed changes in the discount mechanism will be found in Chapter 11.

deposits when they extend loans. The Federal Reserve banks do not lend the reserves of one commercial bank to another; this is impossible, because a liability is a recognition of what one owes others. When the member bank repays the loan, it uses its reserve account. Member bank borrowing of reserves is discussed at greater length in Chapter 10.

Second, *member bank reserve deposit accounts are the mechanism through which the economy is supplied with currency.* As described in Chapter 2, when the nonbank public's demand for currency increases, commercial bank demand-deposit liabilities and vault cash holdings are reduced. Where do the commercial banks obtain currency to meet the increased demand? Nonmember banks buy it from member banks, who in turn purchase it from the Federal Reserve banks. Member banks "purchase" currency by accepting a decrease in their reserve accounts at Federal Reserve banks. When there is a subsequent influx of currency into the banking system, the excess currency is returned to the Federal Reserve banks and member bank reserve deposits are increased.

Third, *banks with excess funds in their reserve accounts may lend this excess to banks with a shortage of reserves.* Negotiations of this sort take place in the *federal funds market.* The reserve accounts of lending banks are reduced and those of borrowing banks are increased. (The federal funds market was discussed in Chapter 5.)

Fourth, when overseas branches place Euro-dollars with their home offices in the United States, these banks' reserve positions are enhanced. *The Federal Reserve increases the accounts of American banks by the amount of the Euro-dollar placement.* (The Euro-dollar was discussed in Chapter 6.)

Fifth, when *the Treasury transfers funds* from its accounts at member banks to its general accounts at Federal Reserve banks, member bank reserve deposits are decreased. This is discussed more fully in Chapter 10.

Finally, many *checks are cleared and collected* through member bank reserve accounts. This is one of the most valuable functions that a Federal Reserve bank performs for member banks. A member bank's reserve deposits are increased when it sends checks drawn on other banks to the Federal Reserve bank for collection. Conversely, its reserve account is decreased when checks written by its depositors are presented for collection to the Federal Reserve banks by other member banks.

Check-clearing and Collection Operations by the Federal Reserve System

The volume of Federal Reserve bank check-clearing operations is almost staggering. In 1972, Federal Reserve banks handled 8,453,733,000 packages of non-U.S. government checks valued at $3,317,873,664,000.[5] The bulk of these checks are now processed electronically.

[5] Board of Governors of the Federal Reserve System. *Annual Report* (1972), p. 242.

The nationwide clearing and processing of checks was one of the principal functions the Federal Reserve System was designed to perform under the Federal Reserve Act, and it has been quite successful in fulfilling this task. Here is how the process works. Assume that a businessman in New York has sold goods valued at $1,000 to someone in Chicago. The buyer pays for the goods with a check drawn on a Chicago member bank. The New York businessman then deposits the check with his bank in New York City. Assuming that the New York bank is also a member bank, there are several changes that may occur on its balance sheet.

If the Chicago bank is a customer bank, then the New York bank may simply increase the deposit account of the seller who presented the $1,000 check and, at the same time, reduce the deposit account of the Chicago bank. The check is then returned to the Chicago bank, which in turn reduces the account of the person who wrote the check. The net result of this transaction for the commercial banking system is that the Chicago bank will have lost an asset – deposits with the New York bank.

If the Chicago bank is not a customer bank, the check-clearing and collection procedure is considerably more complicated. First, there are the balance-sheet changes that occur upon deposit of the check by the seller. These are shown as entries (a) below:

BALANCE-SHEET CHANGES FOR NEW YORK CITY MEMBER BANK

ASSETS		LIABILITIES + CAPITAL ACCOUNTS	
Due from banks	+$1,000 (a)	Demand deposits	+$1,000 (a)
Due from banks	−$1,000 (b)		
Reserves	+$1,000 (b)		

The New York bank sends the check to the Federal Reserve Bank of New York for collection, resulting in a change in its balance sheet:

BALANCE-SHEET CHANGES FOR THE FEDERAL RESERVE BANK
OF NEW YORK

ASSETS	LIABILITIES + CAPITAL ACCOUNTS	
Cash items in process of collection +$1,000 (a)	Deferred availability cash items	+$1,000 (a)
	Deferred availability cash items	−$1,000 (b)
	Member bank reserve deposits	+$1,000 (b)

Entries labeled (a) show that the Federal Reserve Bank of New York has received a check (cash items in process of collection), the value of which has not yet been credited to the account of the New York City member bank (deferred availability cash items). Shortly after the Federal Reserve

Bank of New York receives the check, it increases the reserve account of the New York member bank.[6] The balance sheet of the New York City bank is now adjusted to show that its reserve position has increased (recorded as entries (b) on the New York member bank balance sheet above). The balance sheet of the Federal Reserve Bank of New York has also changed (recorded as entries (b) on the balance sheet of the Federal Reserve Bank of New York above).

The Federal Reserve Bank of New York must still collect on the $1,000 check. If the member bank on which the check is drawn were a member bank in District Number 2 (the district of the Federal Reserve Bank of New York), it would have a reserve deposit account with the Federal Reserve Bank of New York. The reserve account of the member bank would be reduced, as would cash items in process of collection. But, in our example, the member bank on which the check is drawn is in District Number 7. Under these circumstances, the Federal Reserve Bank of New York must send the check to the Federal Reserve Bank of Chicago for collection. The Federal Reserve Bank of Chicago, in turn, lowers the reserve deposit account of the Chicago member bank and forwards the check to it. The Chicago member bank lowers the deposit account of the businessman who first wrote the check. The balance-sheet changes for this member bank are as follows:

BALANCE-SHEET CHANGES FOR THE CHICAGO MEMBER BANK

ASSETS		LIABILITIES + CAPITAL ACCOUNTS	
Reserves	−$1,000	Demand deposits	−$1,000

Thus, the check has traveled from the Chicago businessman to the New York businessman, to the New York member bank, to the Federal Reserve Bank of New York, to the Federal Reserve Bank of Chicago, to the Chicago member bank, and back again to the Chicago businessman. The demand deposits of the New York businessman have increased; those of the Chicago businessman have decreased. The New York member bank has gained reserves; the Chicago member bank has lost reserves.

There is still one debt created during this process that remains unresolved. The Federal Reserve Bank of New York sent the check to the Federal Reserve Bank of Chicago for collection. Since the check was written on a bank in District 7, the Federal Reserve Bank of Chicago now owes $1,000 to the Federal Reserve Bank of New York. Debts of this type

---

[6] Usually, a Federal Reserve bank increases the reserve deposit account of a member bank before it collects on a check. As a result, cash items in process of collection are normally greater than deferred availability cash items. The difference between these two items, known as "Federal Reserve float," affects commercial bank reserve positions. The influence of "float" on the economy will be discussed more fully in Chapter 10.

among Federal Reserve banks are cleared through the System's *Interdistrict Settlement Fund*. Each Federal Reserve bank owns gold certificates on deposit with the Interdistrict Settlement Fund in Washington, D.C. When one Federal Reserve bank is in debt to another, its gold certificate fund is reduced by the amount of the debt. In turn, the gold certificate holdings of the creditor Federal Reserve bank are increased. This transaction is recorded on the balance sheets of the Federal Reserve banks and the Interdistrict Settlement Fund as follows:

BALANCE-SHEET CHANGES FOR THE FEDERAL RESERVE BANK
OF CHICAGO

ASSETS		LIABILITIES + CAPITAL ACCOUNTS	
Gold certificate account	−$1,000	Member bank reserve deposits	−$1,000

BALANCE-SHEET CHANGES FOR THE FEDERAL RESERVE BANK
OF NEW YORK

ASSETS		LIABILITIES + CAPITAL ACCOUNTS	
Gold certificate account	+$1,000	Member bank reserve deposits	+$1,000

BALANCE-SHEET CHANGES FOR THE INTERDISTRICT SETTLEMENT FUND

ASSETS	LIABILITIES + CAPITAL ACCOUNTS	
	Gold certificate accounts	
	Federal Reserve Bank of Chicago	−$1,000
	Federal Reserve Bank of New York	+$1,000

Gold certificate assets and member bank reserves have decreased at the Federal Reserve Bank of Chicago; they have increased at the Federal Reserve Bank of New York.

As complicated as the preceding illustration of check-clearing procedures may seem, it is a very simple one compared to the overall check-clearing process. Remember that trillions of dollars worth of checks are cleared by the Federal Reserve banks each year. Checks are continually flowing back and forth in the economy. The preceding illustration merely showed the movement of one check through the clearing system. In practice, each member bank presents checks to its Federal Reserve bank daily for collection and also has checks presented to it for collection. Thus, member bank reserve changes reflect *net flows* of checks. If the value of the checks a member bank presents for collection is greater than the value of the checks forwarded to it for collection, its reserves increase. If not, it loses reserves.

Similarly, gold certificate funds continually shift from one Federal Reserve bank to another. Each Federal Reserve bank daily forwards checks to the other 11 Federal Reserve banks, and in turn has checks presented to it. When the total value of checks forwarded by one Federal Reserve bank to other Federal Reserve banks exceeds the value of those presented, it gains gold certificates.

The clearing and collection of checks by the Federal Reserve are not the only check-clearing mechanisms in the economy. There is often a clearing-house for banks having head offices within a particular city. Representatives of these banks meet daily in the clearinghouse and present checks to one another for collection. Debts that exist between the banks are then extinguished by a transfer of reserve balances from debtor to creditor banks. If the clearing is not transacted with Federal Reserve funds, the payment may be made to a city correspondent; this increases the accounts of creditor banks and lowers those of the debtor banks.

The Federal Reserve clears and collects checks for nonmember banks as well as for member banks. Typically, when a Federal Reserve bank receives checks written on accounts in nonmember banks, it increases the accounts of the depositing member banks. The checks are then forwarded to those member banks that serve as correspondents for the nonmember banks. The reserve deposits of these member banks are decreased, and, in turn, the correspondent member banks decrease the demand-deposit balances of the nonmember banks. As indicated in Chapter 4, a Federal Reserve bank will perform this function for a nonmember bank only when the nonmember bank is on the par list.

A checkless society? The increased use of credit cards and the introduction of computer technology into banking in recent years may portend the demise of checks as the means of transferring demand-deposit liabilities and may well make the check-clearing process just described an anachronism.

At present, credit cards are simply another form of charge account. Both are means of regularizing payments. Without the charge privilege, transactions must be completed immediately, using either cash or checks. With the charge privilege, a debt is created that is subsequently extinguished, again using either currency or demand-deposit money. Most firms have regular billing procedures; hence, debtors can predict when payments must be made and creditors can forecast receipts with some degree of accuracy. This means, of course, that increased use of credit cards and charge accounts leads to a greater regularization of payments and receipts, reducing the need to accumulate cash to meet unforeseen contingencies. This in turn means a decrease in the amount of money needed, an increase in the velocity of the circulation of money, and a rise in the demand for goods and services. Overall, this has been the trend for some time in the United States.

Combining the credit card with the computer could change this payment technique, in addition to further regularizing the payment process. Bank computer systems could maintain the payments into and out of demand-deposit accounts for all bank customers in the economy. This should make it possible to eliminate checks as a means of transferring deposit balances. For example, a customer making a purchase would present his credit card and, using the seller's computer (which would be tied into the banking system computer), make immediate payment by directing the computer to transfer funds from his demand-deposit account to that of the payee; he could charge the purchase and/or arrange for installment credit by instructing the computer to transfer funds at the end of the charge period or when installments are due. No check would be sent to the payee, whose account would automatically be increased at the time specified. The computer would record the transaction and continuously update the customer's account.

A similar procedure takes place today when individuals instruct their creditors, such as the telephone company, to forward bills directly to their bank. Checks are not used, since the creditor is paid automatically by the bank.

Business payments could also be made using computers. Credit cards would not have to be involved; business and bank computers could be tied together. Thus, when one business needed to make a payment to another, it could instruct its bank through the computer to transfer funds from its account to the account of the creditor business. Electronic direct deposit of payrolls is also feasible.

Such a system is obviously far in the future. With a unit banking system of 13,900 commercial banks, it would obviously be difficult to tie all banks in the country into a centralized clearing and payments network. But it is feasible for large businesses and large banks in major financial centers to develop computerized communications. Many banking systems in Europe, where there are only a few commercial banks maintaining widespread branch bank networks, have operated on a comparable basis for decades. These European systems are not computerized. Rather, theirs is what is called a "giro" system, where the payer instructs his bank whom to pay and in what amounts. The first step in the development of a bank computer structure in the United States will be the computerization of all check clearing and collections by the Federal Reserve banks for member banks, as described in the following paragraph.[7]

The computers of banks can be tied into those of the Federal Reserve. When commercial bank computers report to the Federal Reserve that net claims against other banks have increased, the Fed's computers can automatically increase the reserve accounts of the creditor banks and decrease those of the debtor banks. All this information on payments will automatically be fed into each bank's equipment; there will be no need for float.[8]

---

[7] The developments discussed here are examples of institutional influences on the velocity of money. A more complete discussion of these forces will be found in Chapter 17.

[8] See Chapter 10 for discussion of float.

This type of *electronic* clearinghouse is now being established within the Federal Reserve System. As noted earlier, the Fed is setting up regional centers for the overnight processing and settlement of checks.

Fiscal and Foreign Agent Functions of the Federal Reserve Banks

The Federal Reserve banks also serve as fiscal agents and depositories for the U.S. government. In this capacity they maintain checking-deposit accounts for the Treasury Department. Almost all Treasury payments are made by drawing down these accounts. As these payments are made, the deposit accounts of the nonbank public are increased. As member banks forward government checks to the Federal Reserve for collection, member bank reserves are increased.

On the other hand, when the Treasury receives tax revenues and funds from the sale of government securities, this money is placed in its tax and loan accounts at commercial banks. Subsequently, as funds are needed to cover government payments, money is periodically transferred to the Treasury deposit accounts with the Fed. When this happens, member bank reserves are decreased and Treasury deposit accounts are increased.

Treasury payments and receipts do not coincide; this is the principal reason for the maintenance of tax and loan accounts by the Treasury at commercial banks. If all tax receipts were immediately placed in the Treasury's general accounts with the Federal Reserve banks, a serious drain would occur in commercial bank reserves as depositors made tax payments. In the absence of open market purchases by the Federal Reserve banks, this would force a contraction in commercial bank lending operations.

Not only do the Federal Reserve banks clear and collect checks for the Treasury, they also assist in public debt transactions. Federal Reserve banks act as agents in the sale of new U.S. government securities, processing the applications of purchasers of new security issues, delivering the securities, and receiving payment for them.

The Federal Reserve's responsibilities as fiscal agent and depository for the U.S. government extend beyond handling the financial transactions of the U.S. Treasury. The Federal Reserve banks also act as depositories and fiscal agents for such agencies as the FDIC, Federal Home Loan Banks, Federal Savings and Loan Insurance Corporation, Public Housing Administration, Small Business Administration, Federal National Mortgage Association, and Commodity Credit Corporation. In addition, Federal Reserve banks act as fiscal agents for those government agencies that guarantee loans to contractors and subcontractors engaged in the production and delivery of goods vital to national defense.

The activity of the U.S. government deposit accounts maintained with the Federal Reserve banks is intense. In 1972 the Federal Reserve banks handled 617,408,000 packages of treasury checks having a total value of $235,163,523,000.[9] In 1972, the general accounts of the U.S. government averaged $1,850.5 million.[10] Dividing the value of U.S. government check handlings by the average size of the U.S. general accounts gives us a measure of the turnover of federal government balances – 127. This is a very high turnover rate, many times that of individual deposit accounts at many commercial banks. In June 1972, the annual rate of demand-deposit turnover was 200 in New York, the most active financial center, but was only 59 elsewhere.[11]

Finally, the Federal Reserve banks perform valuable services in the area of international economic relations. They are authorized to act as depositories for such agencies as the International Monetary Fund and the International Bank for Reconstruction and Development. In addition, Federal Reserve banks are empowered to accept deposits of foreign monetary authorities. In practice the Federal Reserve Bank of New York conducts most foreign operations for all the Federal Reserve banks; foreign deposits are recorded on the balance sheet of each Federal Reserve bank in proportion to its share of total Fed assets.

The Federal Reserve Bank of New York also buys and sells foreign currencies for the U.S. government. Until recently this type of intervention in the exchange market was done not to influence exchange rates, but simply to provide the government with the foreign currency it needed for operations abroad. Now, however, it has an economic regulatory purpose as well – to alleviate the pressure on the U.S. balance of payments. The special-accounts manager handles all purchases and sales of foreign currency for the FOMC.

SUMMARY

This chapter has described the structure and nonregulatory functions of the Federal Reserve. We have seen that the Board of Governors is the most important regulatory body of the Federal Reserve System; it is ultimately responsible for the determination of national monetary policy. The various Federal Reserve banks carry out the board's economic and regulatory policies and, in turn, regulate the operations of the member banks. Actually, the member banks themselves are the most significant component of the Federal Reserve System, for they alone deal with the American public. In extending credit and creating money in their daily operations, they serve as the instruments by which Federal Reserve policy is executed.

Of the various Federal Reserve banks, the New York bank is the most

[9] Board of Governors of the Federal Reserve System. *Annual Report* (1972), p. 242.
[10] Computed by adding the average U.S. Treasurer monthly deposits for the period of January 1972 through December 1972 and dividing the total by 12. Data is taken from the *Federal Reserve Bulletin* tables on member bank reserves.
[11] *Federal Reserve Bulletin* (August 1972), p. A-15.

important. Because of its location in the nation's principal financial center, it acts for the other Reserve banks and the FOMC in the purchase and sale of U.S. government securities and foreign exchange.

All Federal Reserve banks provide member banks with important services, too. These are (1) the maintenance of member bank reserve deposit accounts, (2) the clearing and collection of checks, (3) the supplying of currency, and (4) the lending of reserves.

The Federal Reserve banks are the fiscal agents of the U.S. government. Member banks also provide services for the government by maintaining tax and loan accounts for the Treasury and assisting in the sale of and payment of interest on government securities.

Supplementary Readings

Board of Governors of the Federal Reserve System. *The Federal Reserve System: Purposes and Functions* (Washington, D.C., 1963), Chapters 2 and 17.

————. *Bank Credit-Card and Check-Credit Plans* (July 1968).

Mitchell, George W. "Effects of Automation on the Structure and Function of Banking." *American Economic Association Papers and Proceedings* (1966), pp. 159–67.

Ritter, L. S., and T. R. Atkinson. "Monetary Theory and Policy in the Payments System of the Future." *Journal of Money, Credit and Banking* (1970), pp. 493–503.

Treiber, William F. "The Changing Banking Scene." Federal Reserve Bank of New York. *Monthly Review* (1972), pp. 135–39.

10 Assets and Liabilities of the Federal Reserve Banks

FEDERAL RESERVE BANK ASSETS

Gold Certificates
Special Drawing Rights Certificate Account
Other Cash
Loans to Member Banks
Acceptances
U.S. Government Securities
Float
Other Assets

FEDERAL RESERVE BANK LIABILITIES

Federal Reserve Notes
Deposits
  Member bank reserves
  U.S. Treasurer general account
  Foreign deposits
  Other deposits

CAPITAL ACCOUNTS

Capital Paid In
Surplus

SUMMARY

Chapter 6 stressed the importance of the reserve position of commercial banks as the basis for credit extension and money creation. This chapter discusses how variations in the assets and liabilities of the Federal Reserve banks may alter commercial bank reserves and hence the lending ability of the commercial banking system. The emphasis is not upon how the Board of Governors, through a manipulation of Federal Reserve bank assets and liabilities, may affect commercial bank reserves and hence economic activity, however. Instead, we are concerned with the alterations in commercial bank reserves that are caused by changes in Federal Reserve bank assets and liabilities. Chapters 11 and 12 will then examine the instruments of Federal Reserve policy and explain how they may be manipulated so as to effect alternative policy goals.

FEDERAL RESERVE BANK ASSETS

Gold Certificates

Table 10-1 is a detailed balance sheet for all Federal Reserve banks as of December 31, 1972. The first asset of major importance on the balance sheet is that of gold certificates.

Gold certificates formerly were used to satisfy a reserve requirement for Federal Reserve notes and deposits. Each Federal Reserve bank was required to maintain reserves in gold certificates of not less than 25 percent against its deposits and of not less than 25 percent against its Federal Reserve notes. The first reserve requirement was eliminated in early 1965; the second requirement in 1968. Both were eliminated because a diminishing U.S. gold supply had virtually eliminated the excess reserve position of the Federal Reserve.

Today gold certificates along with U.S. government securities serve as collateral for Federal Reserve bank liabilities. There is no requirement that these gold certificates must be equal in value to a required percentage of Federal Reserve bank liabilities, however. In addition to serving as collateral, gold certificate funds continue to be used in the *Interdistrict Settlement Fund,* as described in Chapter 9.

The Federal Reserve banks obtain gold certificates by purchasing them

TABLE 10-1 DETAILED STATEMENT OF CONDITION OF ALL FEDERAL RESERVE
BANKS COMBINED, DECEMBER 31, 1972
(IN THOUSANDS OF DOLLARS)

Assets			
Gold certificates on hand		1,278	
Gold certificates due from U.S. Treasury:			
Interdistrict settlement fund		7,741,121	
Federal Reserve agents' fund		2,561,000	
Total gold certificate account			**10,303,399***
Special Drawing Rights certificate account			**400,000**
Federal Reserve notes of other Federal Reserve banks			**1,158,876**
Other cash:			
United States notes		279	
Silver certificates		102	
National bank notes and Federal Reserve bank notes		133	
Coin		312,709	
Total other cash			**313,223**
Loans to member banks secured by			
U.S. government and agency obligations	877,554		
Other eligible paper	1,049,380		
Other paper	54,020	1,980,954	
Loans to others		—	
Foreign loans on gold		—	
Total loans		**1,980,954**	
Acceptances:			
Bought outright		**70,461**	
Held under repurchase agreement		**36,306**	
Federal agency obligations:			
Bought outright		**1,311,364**	
Held under repurchase agreement		**13,000**	
U.S. government securities:			
Bought outright:			
Bills	**29,664,685**		
Certificates	—		
Notes	**36,681,435**		
Bonds	**3,462,370**		
Total bought outright		**69,808,490**	
Held under repurchase agreement		**97,500**	
Total U.S. government securities		**69,905,990**	
Total loans and securities			**73,318,075**
Cash items in process of collection:			
Transit items		8,443,753	
Exchanges for clearing house		345,850	
Other cash items		1,992,928	
Total cash items in process of collection			**10,782,531**
Bank premises:			
Land		64,865	
Buildings (including vaults)	130,810		
Fixed machinery and equipment	81,036		
Construction account	37,980		
Total buildings	249,826		
Less depreciation allowances	120,829	128,999	
Total bank premises			**193,864**
Other assets:			
Claims account closed banks		0	
Denominated in foreign currencies		192,341	
Gold due from U.S. Treasury for account International			
Monetary Fund		0	

TABLE 10-1 (Continued)

Reimbursable expenses and other items receivable	11,892	
Interest accrued	680,072	
Premium on securities	73,447	
Deferred charges	4,552	
Real estate acquired for banking-house purposes	3,055	
Suspense account	88,978	
All other	11,114	
Total other assets		**1,065,451**
Total assets		**97,535,419**

Liabilities

F.R. notes:			
Outstanding (issued to F.R. banks)		62,490,095	
Less: Held by issuing F.R. banks	2,557,634		
Forwarded for redemption	19,321	2,576,955	
F.R. notes, net (includes notes held by U.S. Treasury and by F.R. banks other than issuing Bank)			**59,913,140**
Deposits:			
Member bank reserves		**25,505,891**	
U.S. Treasurer – General account		**1,855,609**	
Foreign		**324,629**	
Other deposits:			
Nonmember bank – Clearing accounts	38,172		
Officers' and certified checks	16,148		
Reserves of corporations doing foreign banking or financing	74,575		
International organizations	123,684		
Secretary of Treasury special account	267,860		
All other	321,663		
Total other deposits		**842,102**	
Total deposits			**28,528,231**
Deferred availability cash items			**6,954,086**
Other liabilities:			
Accrued dividends unpaid		0	
Unearned discount		346	
Discount on securities		531,303	
Sundry items payable		15,823	
Suspense accounts		6,696	
All other		104	
Total other liabilities			**554,272**
Total liabilities			**95,949,729**

Capital accounts

Capital paid in	**792,845**
Surplus	**792,845**
Other capital accounts†	**–**
Total liabilities and capital accounts	**97,535,419**
Contingent liability on acceptances purchased for foreign correspondents	**179,011**

* Amounts in boldface type indicate items shown in the board's weekly statement of condition of the F.R. banks.

† During the year this item includes the net of earnings, expenses, profit and loss items, and accrued dividends which are closed out on Dec. 31.

SOURCE: Board of Governors of the Federal Reserve System. *Annual Report* (1972), pp. 228–29, Table 1.

as they are issued by the U.S. Treasury. Conversely, the banks lower their holdings of gold certificates by selling them back to the Treasury. The Federal Reserve banks may not legally own gold; they may only hold gold certificates—claims to the gold held by the U.S. Treasury. As a rule, Federal Reserve bank holdings of gold certificates increase and decrease in volume according to the amount of gold owned by the Treasury. Commercial bank reserves also usually increase and decrease in proportion to Treasury gold holdings.

Increases in Treasury gold holdings occur when the U.S. government buys gold from foreign governments. When a foreign government sells gold to the U.S. Treasury, Federal Reserve banks decrease the checking-deposit account of the Treasury and raise that of the foreign government.[1] Assume, for example, that gold is purchased by the Treasury at a cost of $1 million. The effects on the Federal Reserve banks are shown by the entries labeled (a) on the balance sheet below:

BALANCE-SHEET CHANGES FOR THE FEDERAL RESERVE BANKS

ASSETS		LIABILITIES + CAPITAL ACCOUNTS	
Gold certificate account	+$1,000,000 (b)	Deposits	
		U.S. Treasurer	−$1,000,000 (a)
		Foreign	+$1,000,000 (a)
		U.S. Treasurer	+$1,000,000 (b)
		Foreign	−$1,000,000 (c)
		Member bank reserves	+$1,000,000 (c)

The Treasury then issues gold certificates in an amount equal to the value of the gold purchase. These certificates are added to the gold certificates that the Treasury already holds for the Federal Reserve banks, and the banks in turn increase the deposit accounts of the Treasury. These transactions are recorded by the entries labeled (b) above.

Thus far there has been no change in commercial bank reserves. A change occurs only as the foreign government spends the funds in the United States or transfers them to deposit accounts with U.S. commercial banks. Then there is a decrease in foreign deposits and a corresponding increase in member bank reserves (as shown by entries (c) on the balance sheet). Member bank deposit liabilities also increase. These deposits will be held either by foreigners or by U.S. citizens who have sold goods and services to foreigners.

Until 1968, the Treasury also bought gold from domestic producers. The balance-sheet entries resulting from a domestic transaction were roughly the same as those shown in the preceding illustration. There was one difference, however. Because the gold producers deposited the checks they received

---

[1] Actually all transactions of this type are handled by the Federal Reserve Bank of New York.

from the Treasury in deposit accounts at commercial banks, which in turn collected on the checks by forwarding them to the Federal Reserve banks, member bank reserves increased directly. When the Treasury issued the gold certificates, gold certificate reserves and Treasury deposits again increased.

The Treasury also experiences drains on its gold supply. A foreign government, for example, may choose to convert its holdings in U.S. currency on deposit with commercial banks into gold in order to change this money into another currency. Using checks written on deposit accounts with commercial banks, the foreign government will probably first build up its deposit accounts at the Federal Reserve Bank of New York. This will decrease both commercial bank deposit liabilities and reserves by an equal amount, thereby reducing both commercial bank required and excess reserves. Subsequently, the foreign government will use its increase deposit accounts at the Federal Reserve Bank of New York to purchase the desired gold from the Treasury. Thus, foreign deposits with the New York bank are reduced and treasury deposits increased. Lower treasury gold holdings mean reduced gold certificate claims to gold, however. Consequently, the Treasury will then withdraw gold certificates in an amount equal to the gold drain, thus decreasing Treasury deposits. The results of a $1 million purchase of gold by a foreign government can be shown as balance-sheet changes by reversing the plus and minus entries on the preceding balance sheet for the Federal Reserve banks.

The gold certificate holdings of the Federal Reserve banks increase and decrease according to the amount of gold held by the U.S. Treasury. This, in turn, means that commercial bank reserves generally increase as treasury gold holdings increase and decrease as those treasury gold holdings decrease. Hence, if the effects of a change in the gold supply upon commercial bank reserves are viewed as undesirable in light of the general economic situation, the Federal Reserve will take action to offset these efforts, usually through the purchase and sale of U.S. government securities. As a matter of fact, the Fed usually takes such action whenever commercial bank reserves fluctuate beyond a certain point because of forces over which the Federal Reserve banks have no direct control. A change in our gold stock is merely one of these forces.

Our gold stock has been directly affected by our balance of payments.[2] In the 1960s and early 1970s, foreign dollar claims against the United States exceeded the claims of the United States against foreign countries. As a result, some foreign nations chose to take part of their additional claims in the form of gold rather than in increased holdings of dollars in U.S. commercial banks. Thus, we experienced gold losses and gold certificate reductions. Had the Federal Reserve not taken action, these forces

---

[2] See Chapter 24 for a discussion of the balance of payments.

would have reduced commercial bank reserves and lending ability. Due to new international agreements (to be discussed in Chapters 23 and 24), these gold losses terminated in 1968.

Special Drawing Rights Certificate Account

Special Drawing Rights (SDR) certificates are a recent addition to the balance sheet of the Federal Reserve banks. These certificates are an outgrowth of our operations in international money markets and our membership in the International Monetary Fund (IMF). Chapter 24 discusses these operations and their relationship to the facilitation of international trade and financial transactions. At present we are interested in placing SDR certificates within the perspective of their influence on the balance sheet of the Federal Reserve banks and on member bank reserves.

Federal Reserve operations involving SDR certificates are almost identical to those involving gold certificates. SDR certificates are purchased by the Fed primarily on the initiative of the U.S. Treasury. From time to time, the U.S. Treasury receives allocations of SDRs from the IMF. When there is a deficit in the U.S. balance of payments, the Treasury may choose to monetize a portion of these allocations by issuing SDR certificates which the Federal Reserve is obligated to purchase (actually, the Federal Reserve Bank of New York undertakes the operation). This increases a special Treasury checking account at the Fed. When the Treasury writes checks on this account, they find their way into foreign deposit accounts at commercial banks in the United States. When the member banks deposit these checks at Federal Reserve banks, member bank reserves increase.

The effects of the above SDR operations are shown in the following T-account entries:

BALANCE-SHEET CHANGES FOR THE FEDERAL RESERVE BANKS

ASSETS		LIABILITIES + CAPITAL ACCOUNTS	
SDR certificate account	+$1,000,000 (a)	Deposits	
		U.S. Treasurer	+$1,000,000 (a)
		Member bank reserves	+$1,000,000 (b)
		U.S. Treasurer	−$1,000,000 (b)

The (a) entries show the effects of the sale of SDR certificates by the Treasury to the Fed. The (b) entries show the effects of the use of the special account by the Treasury.

Other Cash

"Other cash" consists of Federal Reserve bank holdings of treasury currency. Two circumstances may lead to an increase in this balance-sheet item: (1) an issuance of new currency (usually token coin) by the Treasury which is purchased by the Federal Reserve banks, or (2) a return of treasury currency to the Federal Reserve banks by member banks. On the other hand, a retirement of currency by the Treasury or a demand for treasury currency by commercial banks would lead to a decrease in Federal Reserve holdings of "other cash."

When the Treasury issues new paper currency and mints new coins, the Federal Reserve banks are required to purchase the currency from the Treasury. Payment is made by increasing treasury deposit accounts. Similarly, when the Treasury retires currency, it does so by drawing down its deposit accounts at the Federal Reserve banks. At present a substantial volume of treasury currency is being withdrawn from circulation. Most treasury paper currency has been replaced by Federal Reserve notes. This action, as we pointed out in Chapter 8, has eliminated silver as a money metal in the United States. United States notes and token coin are the main forms of treasury currency still in use.

The issuance and retirement of Treasury currency have no direct effect on member bank reserves. Indirectly, however, there is some effect. When the Treasury spends the deposits it receives from a sale of currency to the Federal Reserve banks, the deposit liabilities and reserve deposits of member banks increase. The checks written by the Treasury are received by the nonbank public and deposited in commercial bank demand-deposit accounts. Commercial banks then send the checks to the Fed for collection. Federal Reserve banks in turn increase member bank reserve deposits and lower treasury deposits.

On the other hand, when member banks request additional treasury currency or send unneeded treasury currency to the Federal Reserve banks, the total value of member bank reserves is in no way affected. Only a change in the composition of member bank reserves takes place. Member bank reserves consist of both vault cash and reserve deposits at the Federal Reserve banks. A shipment of treasury currency to the Federal Reserve banks by member banks decreases the amount of reserves held in the form of vault cash, but the Federal Reserve banks make payment by increasing member bank reserve deposits.

Fluctuations in the amount of treasury currency holdings at the Federal Reserve banks, like changes in gold certificate holdings, are variables over which the Federal Reserve has no direct control.

Loans to Member Banks

Federal Reserve bank loans to member banks are a factor over which the Reserve banks do have some control. These loans usually arise when member banks borrow reserves. There are three principal types: (1) discounts and advances secured by eligible paper, (2) advances secured by U.S. government securities, and (3) advances secured to the satisfaction of the lending Federal Reserve bank.

Discounts are made when member banks sell "eligible paper" to a Federal Reserve bank. Eligible paper consists of notes, drafts, and bills of exchange arising out of agricultural, industrial, and commercial loans made by the borrowing bank. Such paper, at the time of discount, must have a maturity of less than 90 days, except for agricultural paper and some types of bankers' acceptances, which may have a maturity of nine months. For instance, if the paper has a value of $1 million and the current discount rate is 3 percent, the Federal Reserve bank pays for the paper by increasing the member bank's reserve deposits by $992,500. If the member bank wants an *advance* (rather than a discount) secured by eligible paper, the member bank's reserve deposits are still increased by $992,500.[3] The member bank must subsequently repay the advance, however, since it still owns the paper.

The total volume of discounts and advances based on eligible paper is actually very small. Almost all member bank borrowing of reserves takes the form of advances secured by U.S. government securities. Here, the security is a promissory note signed by the bank, which deposits U.S. government securities as collateral with the lending Federal Reserve bank. The reserve deposit account of the member bank is increased by the amount of the loan less the interest charged. Thus, discounts of eligible paper and advances secured by government securities are mechanically identical.

The third way in which a member bank may borrow reserves is through advances secured "to the satisfaction of the lending bank." This means that member banks may borrow reserves even if they do not wish to secure the advances with eligible paper or U.S. government securities. The lending Federal Reserve bank will determine what other assets are acceptable as collateral. The maximum maturity of such a loan, however, is four months. Advances of this sort also carry a penalty rate of interest, which is usually $\frac{1}{2}$ percent higher than the discount rate of advances secured by U.S. government securities. When the Federal Reserve banks received authority in 1935 to make this type of loan to member banks, it was expected that such borrowing would only be done under exceptional circumstances. Instead, it has now become a normal procedure.

Generally, banks apply for one of these three types of loans either to meet a deficiency of reserves or to increase their level of reserves prior to expanding loans and investments. Most loans of reserves are of short duration—about half mature within 15 days and almost all the remainder within 90 days. Many banks make frequent trips to the "discount window." As mentioned in Chapter 9, the Federal Reserve banks are usually ready to grant such loans to member banks, but the loans are not extended automatically. In practice, the Fed does not control the volume of member bank borrowings so much by loan limitation as by manipulation of the discount

---

[3] An annual discount cost of 3 percent will amount to $7,500 for 90 days.

rate. If the Board of Governors believes that the lending activity of the commercial banking system should be restricted, it may increase the discount rate. On the other hand, if an increase in spending seems appropriate, the board may reduce the discount rate. Chapter 11 will discuss in more detail how discount-rate manipulation is used as an instrument of monetary policy.

In addition to lending reserves to member banks, the Federal Reserve banks may also make advances to individuals, partnerships, and corporations when alternative lending sources are unable to do so. These advances have a maximum maturity of 90 days and must be secured by U.S. government securities. The rate charged for such loans depends on economic conditions in the various Federal Reserve districts. It cannot be less then $\frac{1}{2}$ percent higher and is now 2 percent higher than the discount rate on advances to member banks secured by U.S. government securities. Direct loans of this type are very rare in today's prosperity economy. As a matter of fact, Table 10–1 shows that, as of December 31, 1972, there were no loans of this type outstanding. When they are made, however, they tend to increase commercial bank reserves. As the borrowers use the proceeds of the loans, member banks acquire checks drawn on the Federal Reserve banks. When member banks present these checks for payment, the Federal Reserve banks increase member bank reserve deposit accounts. Conversely, loan repayments reduce member bank reserve deposits.

Acceptances

The purchase and sale of bankers' acceptances in the open market is one of the functions performed by the Federal Reserve Bank of New York for all the Reserve banks and for the FOMC. A bank or a business may draw up an order for a commercial bank to pay. The credit of the firm serves as collateral here. If the bank accepts the order to pay, the document becomes a *bankers' acceptance*. Since the bank has accepted the order, it is obligated to pay and the acceptance becomes fully negotiable. Bankers' acceptances are often created when importers want to facilitate their purchase of goods and services abroad. In foreign trade, the seller may know little about the credit of the buyer but be willing to accept the credit of a commercial bank. The importer, of course, will supply the bank with the necessary funds before maturity of the acceptance. An importer under these circumstances will have the foreign exporter draw a bill on the importer's bank. Once the bank accepts the bill, the bankers' acceptance that has been created can be sold by the exporter. This is how he receives payment for the goods and services he sold.

How do the purchase and sale of bankers' acceptances affect commercial bank reserves? When the Federal Reserve Bank of New York purchases these acceptances, it pays for them with checks drawn on itself. The checks are deposited by the recipients in their deposit accounts at commercial banks, and these banks present the checks for payment to the Federal Reserve Bank of New York. Payment is made on the checks by increasing the reserve accounts of the member banks. On the other hand, when the Federal Reserve Bank of New York sells bankers' acceptances, purchasers pay for them with checks written on commercial banks. The Federal Reserve Bank of New York collects on these checks by decreasing member bank reserve deposits.

Actual Federal Reserve purchases and sales of bankers' acceptances are minor. The volume of actual holdings was $107 million at the end of 1972.

U.S. Government Securities

Quantitatively, U.S. government securities are the most important asset held by the Federal Reserve banks. Of a total of $97.5 billion in assets held by the Reserve banks at the end of 1972, some $69.9 billion was in the form of U.S. government securities. These securities are purchased by the account manager at the Federal Reserve Bank of New York for all the Federal Reserve banks. Purchases are made either directly or on a repurchase agreement basis from government securities dealers. Under a repurchase agreement the securities dealer agrees to repurchase securities sold to the Federal Reserve within a specified period of time, normally 15 days or less. Purchases of this sort by the Fed are generally designed to provide banks with additional reserves in periods of temporary reserve shortages.

The securities issues bought and sold by the Federal Reserve are almost always old U.S. government securities. Rarely do the Federal Reserve banks acquire new security issues directly from the U.S. Treasury. In fact, the Federal Reserve Act provides that the Federal Reserve banks cannot hold more than $5 billion in securities purchased directly from the Treasury at any time. This stipulation presumably limits the ability of the Fed to assist the Treasury in inflationary financing of treasury deficits. Actually, when such purchases are made, they are usually for the purpose of helping the Treasury adjust to a lack of synchronization between its tax receipts and payments. As Chapter 12 will show, the purchase of old securities can also lead to inflationary pressures.

The securities purchased today by the Federal Reserve System are of varying maturities. From 1951 to 1961, Federal Reserve purchases were concentrated in short-term securities. But since February 1961 the Federal Reserve banks have acquired some long- in addition to some short-term government securities. These purchases of longer-term securities are designed to achieve two policy ends: a stable domestic economy and a favorable balance of payments. In a less than full employment economy, Federal Reserve open market operations, if concentrated in securities with short maturities, only tend to satisfy the requirements of policies designed to achieve economic stability. Purchases of short-term securities at this time usually increase reserves (as we shall demonstrate in succeeding paragraphs), lower short-term interest rates, and induce an outflow of dollars from the U.S. economy (see Chapters 23 and 24). To compensate for this maladjustment in policy, the Board of Governors decided in 1961 that the Federal Reserve banks should buy and sell throughout the maturity range of U.S. government securities. By expanding long-term instead of short-term holdings, bank lending ability should expand and short-term interest rates should be maintained, thus presumably reducing a possible flow of funds abroad.

How do Federal Reserve operations in U.S. government securities affect member bank reserve positions? In precisely the same manner as the purchase and sale of bankers' acceptances by the Federal Reserve. The Fed buys U.S. government securities from dealers who specialize in the trading of these securities, paying for them with checks written on itself. When a government securities dealer deposits this Federal Reserve check in his deposit account at a commercial bank, his deposits are increased. When his bank presents the check to the Fed for collection, that bank receives an increase in its reserve deposits. The following balance sheets show the effects of a purchase of $1 million in securities:

BALANCE-SHEET CHANGES FOR THE FEDERAL RESERVE BANKS

ASSETS		LIABILITIES + CAPITAL ACCOUNTS	
U.S. government securities	+$1,000,000	Deposits Member bank reserves	+$1,000,000

BALANCE-SHEET CHANGES FOR THE COMMERCIAL BANKING SYSTEM

ASSETS		LIABILITIES + CAPITAL ACCOUNTS	
Reserves	+$1,000,000	Demand deposits	+$1,000,000

The increase in the demand deposits of the securities dealer are only temporary, however, since he in turn must pay whoever sold him the securities purchased by the Federal Reserve System.

When the Federal Reserve sells government securities, just the reverse of this procedure takes place. The account manager tells the securities dealers that he wishes to sell. Buyers of the securities pay their brokers with checks written on their demand-deposit accounts at commercial banks. The securities dealers deliver the securities to the buyers and pay the Federal Reserve System with checks drawn on their accounts at commercial banks. The Fed then collects on the checks by lowering the reserve deposits of the commercial banks.

Thus, a sale of securities by the Federal Reserve means a decrease in commercial bank reserves; a purchase means an increase in reserves. As we shall see later, the Federal Reserve is continually buying and selling securities. What is important for commercial banks and economic policy is the net effect of these transactions on commercial bank reserves and lending.

In addition to U.S. government securities, the Fed also buys and sells various Federal agency obligations in the open market. The effects of these transactions on bank reserve positions are identical to those described in the preceding paragraphs with respect to U.S. government securities.

Float

Federal Reserve "float" is not an asset. It is simply the difference between an asset (cash items in process of collection) and a liability (deferred availability cash items). Cash items in process of collection are checks that the Federal Reserve banks have received but have not as yet collected on by decreasing member bank reserves. Deferred-availability cash items are checks that the Federal Reserve banks have received but have not as yet paid by increasing member bank reserves. Theoretically, these two items should equal one another. In point of fact, however, they do not, since the Federal Reserve banks generally increase the accounts of depositing banks prior to collecting from the banks on which the checks were drawn. As a result, there is a time gap during which cash items in process of collection are larger than deferred-availability cash items. This difference is termed the *float*. Variations in the float can significantly affect member bank reserve positions.

Some 85 percent of deferred-availability cash items are paid within one day if the checks are drawn on local banks and the remaining 15 percent within two days if they are drawn on distant banks. This is done almost automatically. It usually takes longer than this to collect on checks, however, since the checks received may have been written on banks in another Federal Reserve district. If so, such a check must be mailed to that district's Federal Reserve bank and then to the bank on which it was drawn, and this takes time. If for some reason the mails are delayed, the accounts of the depositing banks will still be increased within two days, even though the collection of the cash items has been delayed. The result is an increase in member bank reserves.

An increase in the volume of checks being written, and hence being cleared, will also increase float and reserves. A larger volume of checks being cleared strains the check-clearing mechanism of the Federal Reserve banks and slows up the collection process. Such increases in check payments occur regularly at the end of each week, at mid-month, and at the end of the year. Increased collection of checks, on the other hand, will reduce float and, accordingly, member bank reserves.

Other Assets

Other Federal Reserve bank assets consist primarily of the physical property comprising bank premises, holdings of foreign currencies, and accrued interest. The value of bank premises changes slowly. Any increase in these assets involves an increase in member bank reserves, since the assets are paid for by checks drawn on the Federal Reserve banks. When these checks are deposited in commercial bank deposit accounts, they are forwarded to the Federal Reserve for payment in the form of increased reserve deposits.

Federal Reserve holdings of foreign currencies increase and decrease in response to purchases and sales by the account manager at the Federal Reserve Bank of New York. These purchases and sales generally result in a corresponding increase or decrease in foreign deposits with the Fed. Member bank reserves are affected only when foreigners use these accounts in their dealings with domestic commercial banks and the nonbank public.

Accrued interest is a somewhat different matter. This item consists principally of interest accrued on Federal Reserve holdings of U.S. government securities. Changes in this asset do not normally affect commercial bank reserve positions. As accrued interest increases, Federal Reserve surplus accounts increase. When the interest is paid, Treasury deposit accounts and accrued interest decrease. Commercial bank reserves are unaffected by these transactions. To the extent, however, that the Treasury has to transfer funds from its tax and loan accounts at commercial banks in order to meet the interest payments, commercial bank reserves decrease.

FEDERAL RESERVE BANK LIABILITIES

Federal Reserve Notes

Federal Reserve notes were described in Chapter 2. They are the principal liability of the Federal Reserve banks that issue them. What are the effects of note increases on member bank reserves? There is no direct effect until member banks distribute them to the nonbank public. Member banks purchase currency (both treasury and Federal Reserve currency) by drawing down their reserve deposit accounts. At this point, they have merely switched reserves from one form (reserve deposits) to another (vault cash). However, as soon as the nonbank public demands the currency, commercial bank vault cash reserves will be reduced. Conversely, return of currency to the banks will lead to an increase in reserves. Chapter 6 explained the effects of cash drains and inflows on bank lending capacity; this topic will be raised again in Chapter 14, where the various factors that determine bank reserves and the money supply are summarized.

Deposits

Member bank reserves. Member bank reserve deposits are the second largest liability of the Federal Reserve banks. At the end of 1972, these reserves amounted to $25.5 billion and supported $482.1 billion in various member bank deposit liabilities.

Movements in member bank reserve deposits do not occur independently of changes in other items on the balance sheet of the Federal Reserve banks. On the contrary, member bank reserves increase and decrease *in response to* changes in other balance-sheet assets, liabilities, and capital accounts. Thus, they are the residual item that the Federal Reserve System attempts to regulate in order to promote domestic economic stability.

U.S. Treasurer general account. Earlier chapters have discussed the meaning of the general account of the U.S. Treasurer. It is principally through these deposit accounts that the federal government makes expenditures. Variation in the size of these treasury accounts at Federal Reserve banks will usually affect member bank reserve positions.

Whenever the Treasury uses its balances at the Federal Reserve banks to make payments to the nonbank public or to the commercial banking system, there is an increase in member bank reserves. Assume, for example, that the Treasury uses $1 million of its deposits at Federal Reserve banks to retire U.S. government securities held by members of the nonbank public. The Treasury retires the securities with checks drawn on its accounts at the Federal Reserve banks. When the nonbank public deposits these checks in its checking accounts, the demand-deposit liabilities of the commercial banking system increase by $1 million. Assuming a 15 percent reserve requirement, required reserves increase by $150,000. Excess reserves also increase, however. When the treasury checks deposited by the nonbank public are presented to the Federal Reserve banks for collection, member bank reserves are increased by $1 million. Since required reserves amount to only $150,000, excess reserves have increased by $850,000. This permits a substantial increase in the lending activity of commercial banks. The changes resulting from such a debt retirement operation are summarized in the following balance sheets:

BALANCE-SHEET CHANGES FOR THE FEDERAL RESERVE BANKS

ASSETS	LIABILITIES + CAPITAL ACCOUNTS	
	Deposits	
	Member bank reserves	+$1,000,000
	U.S. Treasurer	−$1,000,000

BALANCE-SHEET CHANGES FOR THE COMMERCIAL BANKING SYSTEM

ASSETS		LIABILITIES + CAPITAL ACCOUNTS	
Reserves	+$1,000,000	Demand deposits of the nonbank public	+$1,000,000

Precisely the same balance-sheet changes occur when goods and services are purchased by the U.S. government from the nonbank public. There would be some difference, however, if the Treasury used its balances with the Federal Reserve banks to retire government securities held by commercial banks or to make other types of payments to commercial banks—the demand-deposit liabilities of the commercial banking system would not be directly affected. Commercial bank reserves would increase, however, because when treasury checks are presented to the Federal Reserve for collection, payment is made by increasing member bank reserves.

On the other hand, not all decreases in treasury deposits with the Fed will affect commercial bank reserves. Transactions between the Federal Reserve banks and the Treasury may not initially involve either the commercial banks or the nonbank public. For example, if the Treasury uses its deposit balances to retire public debt held by the Federal Reserve banks, Reserve bank assets in the form of U.S. government securities are reduced, as are liabilities in the form of U.S. government deposits. The commercial banking system is in no way involved.

How do increases in treasury deposits at the Fed affect member bank reserves? If the transaction involves only the Federal Reserve banks and the Treasury, there is no direct effect. For example, as previously mentioned, an issuance of SDR certificates by the Treasury will increase both the holdings of these certificates and treasury demand deposits at the Federal Reserve banks. However, if an increase in treasury deposits with the Fed involves the commercial banking system, a decrease in member bank reserves takes place. If, for example, the Treasury decides to transfer $1 million from its tax and loan accounts at commercial banks to its general accounts with the Federal Reserve banks, the reserves of the banks decrease by $1 million and so do their deposit liabilities. The reduction in deposit liabilities means a decrease in required reserves, but since actual reserves have decreased by an equal amount, the net effect is a reduction of some magnitude in member bank excess reserves. Assuming a 15 percent reserve requirement, a $1 million decline in member bank demand deposits and reserves means an $850,000 decrease in excess reserves.

As noted in Chapter 9, treasury deposits are very active. The Treasury is continually meeting government obligations and is also making transfers out of tax and loan accounts at commercial banks and into its general account several times each week.

Foreign deposits. Foreign governments and foreign central banks maintain deposit accounts with our Federal Reserve banks and with commercial banks. (Some mention of this was made in Chapter 9.) When foreigners need money to purchase goods and services in the United States, funds are transferred from foreign dollar holdings at the Federal Reserve banks to commercial banks. This results in an increase in member bank deposit liabilities and a simultaneous increase in reserves. A reverse flow—from checking-deposit accounts at member banks to Federal Reserve foreign accounts—means a reduction in commercial bank deposit liabilities and reserve deposits.

Other deposits. "Other deposits" consist principally of nonmember bank clearing accounts, deposits of businesses engaged in foreign banking, deposits of various international organizations, and deposits of some government agencies. An increase in the total of "other deposits" usually decreases member bank reserves.

Nonmember banks that remit at par may maintain checking-deposit accounts with the Federal Reserve banks, primarily to facilitate the clearing of their checks. It is not necessary for a nonmember bank to have such an account to have access to the Federal Reserve clearing process, however. Large city correspondent banks will handle the clearing of checks for the nonmember banks.

An increase in nonmember bank deposits with the Federal Reserve banks will tend to decrease member bank reserves, but not necessarily all commercial bank reserves. In Connecticut, for example, nonmember banks may keep part of their reserves with Federal Reserve banks and part with commercial banks. If a Connecticut nonmember bank transferred some of its reserve deposits from member banks to Federal Reserve banks, a decrease in the reserves of the member banks would occur, but there would be no change in nonmember bank reserves. However, if the same bank transferred to a Federal Reserve bank its deposits in a member bank that was not authorized by the state's commissioner to hold nonmember bank reserves, there would be an increase in nonmember bank reserves and a decrease in member bank reserves. The precise effects on all bank reserves of changes in the location of nonmember bank reserves and deposits with other banks depend on the various state statutes governing the reserves of nonmember banks.

It is also difficult to know precisely how the remaining components of "other deposits" will affect bank reserve positions. Nor are the changes that take place in these deposits subject to direct control by the Fed. Fortunately, the relative importance and activity of these accounts is not great. Changes affecting commercial bank reserves in an undesired manner can usually be offset by open market operations undertaken by the Federal Reserve.

CAPITAL ACCOUNTS

Capital Paid In

Capital paid in refers to the par value of the stock of the Federal Reserve banks that has been purchased by the member banks. When banks become members of the Federal Reserve System, or as members become larger, they must purchase stock in their district Federal Reserve bank. To the extent that member banks use reserve deposits to purchase Federal Reserve bank stock, their reserves decrease. A retirement of stock, on the other hand, means an increase in member bank reserves.

TABLE 10–2 EARNINGS AND EXPENSES OF FEDERAL RESERVE BANKS DURING 1972
(IN DOLLARS)

ITEM	TOTAL
Current earnings	
Discounts and advances	14,376,315
Acceptances	4,095,809
U.S. government securities	3,771,209,607
Foreign currencies	1,117,244
All other	1,535,548
Total	3,792,334,523
Current expenses	
Salaries:	
Officers	15,596,648
Employees	186,278,708
Retirement and other benefits	33,728,876
Fees – Directors and others	3,291,136
Traveling expenses	4,873,832
Postage and expressage	46,048,583
Telephone and telegraph	5,049,075
Printing and supplies	15,397,840
Insurance	702,230
Taxes on real estate	8,705,367
Depreciation (buildings)	5,091,938
Light, heat, power, and water	3,879,733
Repairs and alterations	2,761,013
Rent	3,254,400
Furniture and equipment:	
Purchases	11,414,870
Rentals	22,480,935
All other	7,173,338
Inter-Bank expenses	−2,451
Subtotal	375,728,542
Federal Reserve currency	31,454,740
Assessment for expenses of Board of Governors	35,234,499
Total	442,417,781
Less reimbursemnt for certain fiscal agency and other expenses	27,811,430
Net expenses	414,606,351
Profit and loss	
Current net earnings	3,377,728,169
Additions to current net earnings:	
Profits on sales of U.S. government securities	3,009,111
All other	2,002,096
Total additions	5,011,207
Deductions from current net earnings:	
Losses on foreign exchange transactions	51,897,303
All other	2,729,691
Total deductions	54,626,994
Net deduction from (−1) current net earnings	−49,615,787
Net earnings before payments to U.S. Treasury	3,328,112,382
Dividends paid	46,183,719
Payments to U.S. Treasury (interest on Federal Reserve notes)	3,231,267,663
Transferred to surplus	50,661,000
Surplus, January 1	742,184,050
Surplus, December 31	792,845,050

Note: Details may not add to totals because of rounding.
SOURCE: Board of Governors of the Federal Reserve System. *Annual Report* (1972), pp. 238–39.

Surplus

Surplus changes as Federal Reserve bank earnings change. These earnings are substantial because receipts from the interest on Federal Reserve bank U.S. government security holdings and discounts and advances are far in excess of their operating expenses. Table 10–2 shows the earnings and expenses of the Federal Reserve banks in 1972. Current net earnings in that year were $3.4 billion. However, most of this amount was paid to the Treasury instead of being transferred to surplus. The Federal Reserve banks, at present, pay a 6 percent statutory dividend to member banks and increase the surplus by enough to keep the surplus account approximately equal to the value of the capital stock paid in. All remaining earnings are paid to the Treasury, technically in the form of interest on Federal Reserve notes. Thus, most of the interest earned on U.S. government securities is turned back to the Treasury. In 1972, the Treasury paid almost $3.8 billion in interest to the Federal Reserve banks, and received almost $3.2 billion back.

The net effect of this Federal Reserve policy is that there are only small yearly changes in surplus. Nevertheless, any increase in surplus means a decrease in member bank reserves, since it reflects an excess of receipts over payments. Payments by the Federal Reserve banks to employees, the U.S. Treasury, and member banks increase reserves, but the receipts remaining after these payments have been made tend to decrease reserves.

SUMMARY

In this chapter we have studied the components of the balance sheet of the Federal Reserve banks. The focus has been upon the effect of changes in these items on the reserves of commercial banks. Although our discussion has been almost exclusively in terms of member banks, it should be remembered that the reserves of nonmember banks will be affected in a manner similar to those of member banks.

In general, when Federal Reserve assets increase and there is no offsetting increase in other liabilities (defined as total liabilities less member bank reserve deposits) or capital accounts, member bank reserves increase; when Federal Reserve assets decrease and there is no corresponding decrease in other liabilities or capital accounts, member bank reserves decrease. If, on the other hand, Federal Reserve bank assets remain constant and the total of other liabilities and capital accounts increases, there is a decrease in member bank reserves. Conversely, a decrease in other liabilities and capital accounts means an increase in member bank reserves.

But this summary merely reflects the truisms inherent in the construction of the balance sheet. What is more relevant is the impact on reserves of a change in a specific balance-sheet item. As the preceding analysis has shown, it cannot be predicted precisely that a change in a specific asset, another liability, or a capital account will necessarily affect member bank reserves; possibly some other balance-sheet asset, liability, or capital account will change instead. In spite of these difficulties, however, some specific conclusions can be derived:

First, an increase in loans to member banks will increase member bank reserves; a decrease in loans by member banks will decrease member bank reserves.

Second, a purchase of bankers' acceptances in the open market by the Fed will increase member bank reserves; a sale of bankers' acceptances in the open market will decrease member bank reserves.

Third, a purchase of U.S. government securities in the open market by the Fed will increase member bank reserves; a sale of these securities will reduce member bank reserves.

Fourth, an increase in float will increase member bank reserves; a decrease in float will decrease member bank reserves.

Concerning any other changes, the most we can say is that changes in assets, other liabilities, and capital accounts will be associated with certain types of changes in member bank reserves. The more important changes are summarized as follows: (1) increases and decreases in gold certificate holdings and SDR certificates tend to be associated with increases and decreases in member bank reserves, (2) increases and decreases in Federal Reserve notes (a Reserve bank liability) result in equivalent decreases and increases, respectively, in member bank reserve deposits, without changing the total of member bank reserves, and (3) increases and decreases in U.S. Treasurer general account deposits (also a Federal Reserve liability) tend to cause decreases and increases, respectively, in member bank reserve deposits.

Supplementary Readings

Board of Governors of the Federal Reserve System. *The Federal Reserve System: Purposes and Functions* (Washinton, D.C., 1963), Chapter 11.

Federal Reserve Bank of Chicago. *Modern Money Mechanics: A Workbook* (Chicago, 1971).

11 Federal Reserve Instruments of Monetary Control, Part I

At present the Federal Reserve has six broad tools at its disposal to implement monetary, fiscal, and international economic policy. These instruments of control are (1) the reserve requirement, (2) the discount rate, (3) open market operations, (4) Regulation Q, (5) the margin requirement, and (6) voluntary foreign credit restraint guidelines. The first three are *general monetary controls* which do not directly affect the specific types of credit extension engaged in by commercial banks. The last three are *selective credit controls*.

Chapters 11 and 12 examine these Federal Reserve instruments of monetary control in some detail. *First*, we shall consider how the Board of Governors may use these instruments of policy in alternative economic situations. *Second*, we shall examine the recent history of each policy instrument to see how it has actually been employed; some attempt will be made to assess whether or not the uses of each instrument have been appropriate. The purpose here is to master a basic understanding of each instrument and the difficulties inherent in its use. *Finally*, we shall attempt an overall assessment of monetary policy. Clearly it is dangerous to consider each tool in isolation from every other instrument of monetary and fiscal policy. To reach a judgment concerning the merits of Federal Reserve monetary action, we must consider the net effect of all instruments of policy upon commercial bank credit and money creation.[1]

APPROPRIATE USE OF FEDERAL RESERVE MONETARY CONTROLS

Recession Policy

A period of recession—when human and nonhuman resources are less than fully employed—calls for increased spending. An increase in spending in either the public or private sector of the economy will expand the

[1] Some instructors may prefer to postpone a study of the actual use of Federal Reserve policy instruments until Part V, where alternative economic policies are treated. This is certainly an acceptable pedagogical procedure. However, the present outline (1) avoids a mechanical ticking off of the policy instruments divorced from the historical world in which we live, and (2) provides some introduction to the theoretical apparatus considered in Part IV—a particularly important factor in courses where time prohibits an extensive elaboration of Parts IV and V.

demand for goods and services, raise incomes, and stimulate employment of resources. However, before any additional spending can take place, funds are needed. A desire to spend will affect the economy only to the extent that it is financed, either by (1) an increase in the supply of money, or (2) a more intensive utilization of the present supply of money—that is, an increase in the velocity of circulation. In the absence of these two conditions, an increase in the desire to spend cannot be implemented and hence will not lead to higher employment levels.

Encouraging an increase in total spending can be difficult; increased spending depends in part on how the increase is financed. For example, an increase in federal government expenditures will be financed through increased taxes or through borrowing. If increased government spending is financed through taxation, its effects may be canceled out, at least in part, by reductions in spending by taxpayers. If increased expenditures are financed by the sale of government securities, the effects of the increased spending will depend on who purchases the securities. If the nonbank public buys them, using idle funds, total spending will actually rise in the economy. However, if the nonbank public makes the purchase with funds that would otherwise have been spent on goods and services, the impact of the increased government spending will be lessened. If Federal Reserve banks buy the securities, public spending will be strongly stimulated, since the use of funds provided by the Federal Reserve will lead to an increase both in the total money supply and in commercial bank reserves.[2]

An increase in private spending can be induced only by manipulating the determinants of private spending (these determinants will be examined in detail in Chapter 19). In general, however, a drop in the interest rates charged to borrowing consumers and businesses tends to lead to increased borrowing and spending. A general increase in income brought about by increased government spending tends to induce an increase in private spending, and improved profit expectations by businesses often lead to greater investment spendings. Finally (a tricky thing to establish empirically, but important analytically), increased liquid wealth holdings, particularly in the form of money and near monies, tend to induce people to spend more liberally.

The Federal Reserve plays a significant role in the process of economic stimulation. Appropriate use of Federal Reserve instruments of monetary control can directly increase commercial bank lending ability and the supply of money. With increased borrowings from commercial banks by business firms and consumers, more funds are made available to the economy, thereby providing a base for additional spending.

Some economists argue that Federal Reserve action in periods of reces-

[2] The potential effects of federal government spending on the stock of money and commercial bank reserve positions are discussed in Chapter 14. The theory behind this analysis of how effective demand increases by the federal government affect the economy is outlined in the model of economic activity developed in Part IV.

sion is inadequate to actually reverse an economic decline. This may be true in many instances, but appropriate monetary policies during a recession will at least ease the path taken in recovery. Although expansionary policies may not reverse a downward trend in the economy, they can intensify the speed of recovery once an upward trend is underway. On the other hand, inadequate creation of reserves by the Federal Reserve banks during recession and economic upturn can slow down the process of economic recovery.

What, then, are some of the possible uses of the instruments of central bank policy during recession?

First, reserve requirements may be lowered. A reduction of reserve requirements will increase excess reserves and hence the lending ability of the commercial banking system.

Second, discount rates may be reduced. A drop in discount rates will make it easier for commercial banks to borrow reserves for the purpose of expanding lending operations.

Third, the Federal Reserve Bank of New York may purchase U.S. government securities and banker's acceptances in the open market. Purchases of securities and acceptances will directly increase the volume of commercial bank reserves. More important, they will also increase the excess reserves of the commercial banking system. To the extent that the securities purchased were originally held by the nonbank public, the money stock will be increased.

Fourth, no action need be taken to adjust the maximum interest rate payable on time deposits by member commercial banks under Regulation Q. During recession, the rates actually paid by commercial banks are already likely to be below the permissible maximum.

Fifth, the Federal Reserve can lower margin requirements for the purchase and carrying of securities. Most economists today, however, do not consider margin requirement changes an effective means of inducing increased spending in the economy. Instead, the consensus is that this instrument should be used primarily to minimize the use of borrowed funds to finance speculation in stock.

All these actions make it easier for banks and other financial institutions to lend. Given the funds to do so, people will spend more. Interest rates, too, will ease because of abundant reserves and a plentiful money stock, and this will further stimulate borrowing and spending. True, the interest rate structure of the economy during a recession will probably be low already, but monetary policy can keep it low during an economic upturn as well, thus accelerating the recovery process.

Neither the effectiveness nor even the advisability of monetary controls can be taken for granted in every situation, however. As we shall see later, these controls are subject to a number of limitations. Also, some instruments are more difficult to employ than others; in fact, only open market operations can be regulated with some degree of precision, and these operations may be necessary to compensate for errors of judgment if caution is not exercised in applying the other tools of monetary policy.

Different types of recession call for different types of monetary action. A deep depression clearly calls for an aggressive use of all policy tools. A very mild recession, on the other hand, may necessitate only a very small increase in Federal Reserve bank holdings of U.S. government securities and bankers' acceptances. It is even possible that *no* acquisition of securities and acceptances may be needed in a mild recession, since a recovery may be underway by the time the effects of a purchase are felt in the economy and that purchase may serve only to intensify inflationary tendencies in the next economic boom.

Qualifications such as these raise serious questions concerning the effectiveness of our policy instruments. Some economists even go as far as to argue that the Federal Reserve should engage in no discretionary use of monetary controls at all. Instead, they believe that some type of automatic policy may be needed, one that would eliminate perverse variations in the stock of money as a source of economic instability. Such a policy might include the automatic use of monetary tools to maintain price stability or the use of open market operations only to maintain a steady increase in the money stock at some low, predetermined rate. Several alternative policy proposals are evaluated in the discussion of the relationship between money and financial policy in Part V.

The instruments recommended to implement monetary policy during recession — the lowering of reserve requirements, the reduction of discount rates, and the purchase of U.S. government securities and bankers' acceptances — should not, therefore, be advocated without qualification. We mention them here simply to indicate the nature of the policies that might serve to mitigate a recession.

Economic Boom Policy

As long as there are unemployed resources available in the economy, increases in the money stock, and thus in the demand for goods and services, should not normally lead to substantial price-level increases. Once productive resources are fully utilized, however, in the absence of countermeasures, money stock increases and excess demand will lead to rising prices. The rise in output that occurs during the early part of a boom — before resources are fully employed — is usually desirable. However, the increased price level and the consequent deterioration in the purchasing power of most liquid wealth, which are apt to result from a further extension of the boom, are in themselves undesirable. If the inflationary problem becomes sufficiently serious, countermeasures should be taken. These measures may take several forms. Wage or price controls may be imposed, for example, although such measures deal only with the symptoms — not the causes — of inflation. Prices have risen because of excess spending and increased costs. The full employment output of goods and services has produced a low supply relative to the effective demand. To halt a serious inflation, either the source of the excessive spending must be eliminated or ultimately, the price controls must be supplemented by a second pricing mechanism — a rationing system.

If the inflationary period occurs during wartime, when the increased spending that produces the inflationary pressures is made up of government military outlays that cannot be reduced, taxes may have to be increased — an unpopular measure at any time — in order to decrease demand in the private sector of the economy. In the absence of increased taxation, the only alternative is to enforce controls that will prevent the increased wartime incomes from being spent.

In peacetime, economic controls are usually politically unacceptable in a democracy like the United States, and different ways must be found to reduce spending. Public pressure can force the government to reduce its expenditures. Pressure may also be brought against businesses and consumers to decrease expenditures. Labor unions may be persuaded to postpone demands for wage increases. If these pressures do not work, then economic controls may indeed be set up, as they were in the United States in 1971.

Generally, however, aside from increased taxation, the most frequently employed restrictive policy during inflation is some form of monetary control. To succeed in reducing the effective demand for goods and services, either the money stock or its velocity must be decreased.[3]

There are five basic ways in which monetary policy can attack this problem:

First, reserve requirements may be raised, thereby reducing commercial bank excess reserves and lending ability.

Second, discount rates may be increased, making it more difficult for commercial banks to borrow additional reserves and reducing the difference between the interest rate that commercial banks earn on loans and the amount they pay on borrowed reserves.

Third, the Federal Reserve Bank of New York may sell bankers' acceptances and U.S. government securities in the open market, thereby reducing the money stock and commercial bank reserves directly.

Fourth, when nonbank financial institution lending has expanded during the boom, *the Federal Reserve may raise the maximum rate of interest payable on time deposits by member commercial banks under Regulation Q* to woo funds away from these institutions and decrease their lending ability.

Fifth, the Federal Reserve may raise margin requirements, thereby

---

[3] Keep in mind that an economic boom must be financed in some manner. Thus, increased spending may well have resulted from a too liberal use of expansionary policy instruments during the preceding economic recovery.

halting any speculation in stocks that is taking place on the basis of borrowed funds.

These policy actions collectively raise interest rates, making it more difficult for businesses and individuals to borrow. In addition, they may decrease the rate of increase in the stock of money and the volume of near monies. These measures should reduce spending in the economy.

The preceding section presented the argument that a policy of monetary ease cannot actually bring about an economic recovery by itself. The converse of this statement is not true, however. A policy of monetary restriction *can* generally bring inflation to an end. The tools of monetary policy *are* strong enough to reverse almost any type of boom except one caused by excessive federal budget deficits accompanied by sharp money stock increases. In fact, the danger in applying monetary instruments to curb inflation is not that these instruments will be unsuccessful in halting the inflation, but rather that they may throw the economy into a sharp recession if used improperly. Whereas an increase in excess reserves *may* cause banks to expand credit, a deficiency of reserves *must* cause them to curtail credit and even to contract loans, investments, and demand-deposit liabilities. Too sharp a reduction in reserves, therefore, may curtail spending drastically. For this reason, just as caution must be used in employing monetary techniques to ease credit, even more care must be taken in using devices to restrict credit.

The sixth policy instrument, foreign credit guidelines, has not been discussed here, since it is geared to helping correct U.S. balance of payments problems, rather than to correcting inflation and/or recession. Foreign credit guidelines will be discussed in Chapter 24 in conjunction with the consideration of recent U.S. balance of payments difficulties.

GENERAL MONETARY CONTROLS

The tools of monetary policy are all designed to regulate the lending ability of the financial sector of the economy. Three of these policy instruments—the reserve requirement, the discount rate, and open market operations—are principally aimed at manipulating the reserve position of the commercial banking system. A consideration of the first two of these instruments follows. (For a discussion of open market operations, see Chapter 12.)

The Reserve Requirement

An increase in member bank excess reserves expands the lending and investment capacity of the banking system. In the process, the ability of the system to create demand-deposit money is increased. Conversely, a decrease in commercial bank excess reserves diminishes the ability of banks to lend, invest, and create money. A substantial deficiency of reserves will force a contraction in the economy.

Changes in the reserve requirement can be used to affect commercial bank reserve positions by altering the composition of commercial bank reserves. An increase in the reserve requirement means that some reserves formerly classified as excess become required reserves. A decrease in the reserve requirement, on the other hand, reduces required and raises excess reserves.

Table 11-1 lists the changes that have taken place in the reserve requirements of member banks since 1917. Reserve requirements were fixed by statute until the passage of the Banking Act of 1935, which gave the Board of Governors the authority to vary them within legally prescribed limits. From 1935 to 1959, those limits for demand deposits were from 7 to 14 percent for country banks, from 10 to 20 percent for reserve city banks, and from 13 to 26 percent for central reserve city banks. The designation "central reserve city bank" was eliminated in 1962. As the commercial banking system developed, financial centers other than the former central reserve cities assumed greater responsibility for the finances of the nation. Today, member banks are now either reserve city or country banks. A country bank has net demand deposits up to $400 million; a reserve city bank has net demand deposits in excess of $400 million. The legally prescribed limits for the reserve requirements on demand deposits at country banks are 7 to 14 percent; for reserve city banks, these limits are 10 to 22 percent. The reserve requirement limits for time deposits are 3 to 10 percent for all classes of banks. The labels "country" and "reserve city" banks have had no actual meaning since 1972, however. As Table 11–1 shows, reserve requirements are now based solely on the size of a bank's net demand deposits.

Increases in reserve requirements. The first discretionary increase in reserve requirements occurred in 1936–37. From August 1936 to May 1937, all reserve requirements were raised to their legally permissible maximum. This amounted to a doubling of the requirements existing on August 15, 1936, and the move evoked considerable controversy. Many economists today regard it as an example of the inappropriate exercise of monetary policy by the board. The economy had improved relative to the severe depression years of 1932 and 1933, when over 12 million persons were unemployed. We still did not have a full employment economy, however. There were nine and one-half million people unemployed in 1936, close to eight million in 1937, and more than ten million in 1938.[4] It is entirely possible, therefore, that these increases in the reserve requirements in 1936 and 1937 aggravated, if they did not cause, the recession that followed in 1937 and 1938.

The official justification for the reserve requirement increases in 1936 and 1937 was that the "Board's action was in the nature of a precautionary

[4] U.S. Department of Commerce. *Statistical Abstract of the United States* (Washington, D.C., 1953), p. 186.

TABLE 11–1 MEMBER BANK RESERVE REQUIREMENTS, PERCENT OF DEPOSITS
[DEPOSIT INTERVALS ARE IN MILLIONS OF DOLLARS]

THROUGH JULY 13, 1966

EFFECTIVE DATE*	NET DEMAND DEPOSITS†			TIME DEPOSITS	
	Central Reserve City Banks‡	*Reserve City Banks*	*Country Banks*	*Central Reserve and Reserve City Banks*‡	*Country Banks*
1917 – June 21	13	10	7	3	3
1936 – August 16	19½	15	10½	4½	4½
1937 – March 1	22¾	17½	12¼	5¼	5¼
May 1	26	20	14	6	6
1938 – April 16	22¾	17½	12	5	5
1941 – November 1	26	20	14	6	6
1942 – August 20	24				
September 14	22				
October 3	20				
1948 – February 27	22				
June 11	24				
September 24, 16	26	22	16	7½	7½
1949 – May 5, 1	24	21	15	7	7
June 30, July 1		20	14	6	6
August 1			13		
August 11, 16	23½	19½	12	5	5
August 18	23	19			
August 25	22½	18½			
September 1	22	18			
1951 – January 11, 16	23	19	13	6	6
January 25, February 1	24	20	14		
1953 – July 9, 1	22	19	13		
1954 – June 24, 16	21			5	5
July 29, August 1	20	18	12		
1958 – February 27, March 1	19½	17½	11½		
March 20, April 1	19	17	11		
April 17	18½				
April 24	18	16½			
1960 – September 1	17½				
November 24			12		
December 1	16½				
1962 – July 28	(‡)			(‡)	
October 25, November 1				4	4

BEGINNING JULY 14, 1966

EFFECTIVE DATE*	NET DEMAND DEPOSITS§				TIME DEPOSITS‖ (ALL CLASSES OF BANKS)		
	Reserve City Banks		*Country Banks*			*Other Time Deposits*	
	Under 5	*Over 5*	*Under 5*	*Over 5*	*Savings Deposits*	*Under 5*	*Over 5*
1966 – July 14, 21	16½		12		4	4	5
September 8, 15							6
1967 – March 2					3½	3½	
March 16					3	3	
1968 – January 11, 18	16½	17	12	12½			
1969 – April 17	17	17½	12½	13			
1970 – October 1							5

TABLE 11–1   (*Continued*)

BEGINNING NOVEMBER 9, 1972

EFFECTIVE DATE*	NET DEMAND DEPOSITS§,#					TIME DEPOSITS‖		
							Other Time Deposits	
	0–2	2–10	10–100	100–400	Over 400**	Savings Deposits	0–5	Over 5
1972 – November 9	8	10	12	16½††	17½	3	3	5
November 16				13				
In effect July 2, 1973	8	10½	12½	13½	18	3	3	5

Present legal requirement:	Minimum	Maximum
Net demand deposits, reserve city banks	10	22
Net demand deposits, other banks	7	14
Time deposits	3	10

* When two dates are shown, the first applies to the change at central reserve or reserve city banks and the second to the change at country banks.

† Demand deposits subject to reserve requirements which, beginning with August 23, 1935, have been total demand deposits minus cash items in process of collection and demand balances due from domestic banks (also minus war loan and Series E bond accounts during the period April 13, 1943 to June 30, 1947).

‡ Authority of the Board of Governors to classify or reclassify cities as central reserve cities was terminated effective July 28, 1962.

§ (a) Demand deposits subject to reserve requirements are gross demand deposits minus cash items in process of collection and demand balances due from domestic banks. (b) Requirement schedules are graduated, and each deposit interval applies to that part of the deposits of each bank. (c) Since October 16, 1969, member banks have been required under Regulation M to maintain reserves against balances above a specified base due from domestic offices to their foreign branches. Effective January 7, 1971, the applicable reserve percentage was increased from the original 10 percent to 20 percent. Regulation D imposes a similar reserve requirement on borrowings above a specified base from foreign banks by domestic offices of a member bank.

‖ Effective January 5, 1967, time deposits such as Christmas and vacation club accounts became subject to the same requirements as savings deposits.

Effective November 9, 1972, a new criterion was adopted to designate reserve cities, and on the same date requirements for reserves against net demand deposits of member banks were restructured to provide that each member bank will maintain reserves related to the size of its net demand deposits. The new reserve city designations are as follows: a bank having net demand deposits of more than $400 million is considered to have the character of business of a reserve city bank, and the presence of the head office of such a bank constitutes designation of that place as a reserve city. Cities in which there are Federal Reserve banks or branches are also reserve cities. Any banks having net demand deposits of $400 million or less are considered to have the character of business of banks outside of reserve cities and are permitted to maintain reserves at ratios set for banks not in reserve cities.

** Reserve city banks.

†† The 16½ percent requirement applied for one week only to former reserve city banks. For other banks, the 13 percent requirement was continued in this deposit interval.

Note: All required reserves were held on deposit with Federal Reserve banks from June 21, 1917 until December 1959. From December 1959 to November 1960, member banks were allowed to count part of their currency and coin as reserves; effective November 24, 1960, they were allowed to count all as reserves.

SOURCE: Board of Governors of the Federal Reserve System. *Annual Report* (1968), pp. 382–83, and *Federal Reserve Bulletin* (July 1973), pp. 548 and A-9.

measure to prevent an uncontrollable expansion of credit in the future."[5] Commercial banks had accumulated $3 billion in excess reserves by the mid-thirties, and the Board of Governors feared that use of these excess reserves to expand credit in the economic upswing then underway might cause a price inflation. Hence, it took restrictive action, which was soon followed by a substantial decline in the stock of money.

[5] Board of Governors of the Federal Reserve System. *Annual Report* (1936), p. 2.

It is difficult to appraise the wisdom of the board's decision. If the large volume of excess reserves existed because of lack of demand for bank loans, the restrictive action could have had little direct effect on bank money creation and the 1937–38 recession. Thus the Federal Reserve may have been correct in moving to reduce the inflationary potential of these unused reserves. Proponents of this view at most concede that "the timing of the increase in requirements proved unfortunate. For various extraneous reasons, there followed a sharp decline in business and prices."[6]

On the other hand, if one accepts the view that the banking system did not regard these reserves as excess reserves available for credit expansion, then the restrictive action *was* a significant factor in the 1937–38 contraction. It has been argued, for example, that

. . . experience during the years from 1929 to 1933 had taught banks that it was not enough to keep in the form of high-powered money only the minimum amount required by law; legally required reserves could not be drawn on to meet emergency demands without the banks being liable to closure. . . . Doubling of required reserves . . . reduced drastically the cushion of effective reserves, as the banks viewed them, available against liabilities needing protection . . . the result was to induce banks to seek to rebuild their so-called excess reserves, thereby producing downward pressure on the money supply.[7]

The years 1936 and 1937 gave us our first experience with increases in the reserve requirement. Other increases occurred in 1941, 1948, and 1951. The increases in 1941 and 1951 were designed to help restrict credit extension in the private sector—during a period of impending war in the first instance and during a period of actual war in the second. The 1948 increase was a move to help restrain inflationary forces already at work in the economy. The effects of the 1948 and 1951 actions, however, were in part offset by another Federal Reserve policy—support of the government securities market. During this same period, commercial banks were selling securities to the Federal Reserve banks, thereby adding to member bank reserves. It will be recalled that the sale of government securities by the Federal Reserve causes member bank reserves to decline. Aside from the conflicting effects of other Federal Reserve actions, however, these three reserve requirement increases were economically appropriate and timely.

Since 1951, the Fed has used reserve requirement increases sparingly, and in only four instances have these increases been contracyclical measures. In November of 1960, the reserve requirement for the demand-deposit liabilities of country banks was increased from 11 to 12 percent. Simultaneously, it was announced that all member banks would be per-

---

[6] E. A. Goldenweiser. *American Monetary Policy* (McGraw-Hill, 1951), p. 180.
[7] Milton Friedman. *A Program for Monetary Stability* (Fordham University Press, 1960), p. 46.

mitted to count vault cash as part of their legal reserves. Since country banks had substantial volumes of vault cash, the increase in reserve requirements for these banks was necessary to avoid a sharp increase in their excess reserves. These actions were not contracyclical in nature.

The year 1966 saw the Federal Reserve raise reserve requirements from 4 to 5 percent for member bank holdings of time deposits (other than savings deposits) in excess of $5 million. Large banks that sold CDs aggressively, paying the maximum interest allowable, had attracted deposits and hence reserves away from other commercial banks in the system. This increase in the reserve requirement caused a deterioration in the reserve position of member banks, particularly reserve city banks. At the same time the Federal Reserve reduced the rate payable by member banks on CDs. This helped reduce the flow of funds to large reserve city banks, since other interest rates in the economy were climbing. Banks sold investments in order to find funds to enable them to expand loans. Overall lending activity, as a result of this aggressive contracyclical policy, was restricted. Whether all these actions, in particular the rise in the reserve requirement, were economically appropriate is highly problematical. As we shall see in Chapter 12, the restrictive policies of late 1965 and the first three quarters of 1966, though in the right direction, may well have been too harsh. Evidence of this can be found in the leveling off of construction activity in 1966.

In January 1968, the Federal Reserve increased the reserves member banks are required to maintain against demand deposits in excess of $5 million. This was the first increase made in reserve requirements for demand deposits since the readjustment of 1960. The action markedly increased total required reserves, particularly for reserve city banks. In view of the very high employment levels prevailing, rising prices, and rising Vietnam war expenditures, it would appear that this action was appropriate.

In April 1969, the Fed raised all reserve requirements against demand deposits by $\frac{1}{2}$ percent. This action was designed to restrict bank lending and private spending, which had not yet responded to the surtax of July 1968. With rising prices, the Fed felt it necessary to restrict further credit in a wartime, high employment economy.

In addition to the aforementioned reserve requirement increases, the Fed has also imposed reserve requirements on some nondeposit sources of funds. Reserve requirements were imposed upon Euro-dollar borrowings in late 1969 and upon commercial paper sold by nonbank affiliates of one-bank holding companies in 1970. These requirements were not designed to correct an economic boom, for the U.S. economy was in a recession from late 1969 through 1970. Instead, the requirements were intended to (1) help alleviate U.S. balance of payments difficulties in the case of Euro-dollars, and (2) reduce the expanding abilities of one-bank holding companies to acquire additional reserves from other commercial banks through the sale of commercial paper.

Finally, in 1973 the Fed raised reserve requirements by $\frac{1}{2}$ percent on all net demand deposits in excess of $2 million at each member bank. This action, given a decreasing unemployment level, rising prices, and an economic boom, appeared to be an appropriate monetary action.

Overall, aside from periods of war, the Fed has been reluctant to use increases in reserve requirements to combat expansionary forces in the economy. There are several reasons for this attitude.

First, commercial bankers feel the direct impact of reserve requirement increases, since these increases force them to readjust loan and investment activities. Other tools of Federal Reserve policy like open market operations do not have such a direct impact. A sale of securities by the Federal Reserve banks reduces total and excess reserves, but no one commercial bank can directly blame the Federal Reserve for the stringency of its reserve position. It is the purchase of securities by bank customers that affects the reserve position of the bank directly, not the sale of these securities by the Federal Reserve. A bank adjusts to customer actions of this sort in the course of everyday business. Furthermore, reserve requirement increases may encounter substantial resistance from bankers. Political pressure may be exerted on the board to reverse itself, particularly if member bank profit positions are threatened.

Second, frequent reserve requirement changes can create difficulties for the managers of small banks. These banks are not equipped to make the rapid alterations in the composition of their portfolios that such changes necessitate. In addition, the fact that changes in reserve requirements usually are announced in advance of the date on which they are to become effective causes a simultaneous attempt by all the affected banks to adapt in advance, further complicating the adjustment process. For example, an announced increase in reserve requirements may induce many banks to sell U.S. government securities immediately to obtain additional reserves before the increase becomes effective. This may cause a sharp drop in the price of those securities and substantial capital losses for the selling banks. The adjustment process is difficult for banks whether the reserve requirement increases or decreases, but increases cause more difficulty. Decreases are favorably received by banks.

Third, the most important reason that reserve requirement increases are used infrequently is that they have an extraordinarily strong contractionary effect. The Federal Reserve has never raised reserve requirements less than $\frac{1}{2}$ percent. Offhand, this amount may seem minimal, but even this small an increase has a significant impact on the commercial banks' money-creating potential.

Effects of a $\frac{1}{2}$ percent change in reserve requirements. Assume, for example, that a $\frac{1}{2}$ percent increase in the reserve requirement for demand deposits is contemplated. By how much would this reduce the money-creating ability of the member banks? To solve this problem we can use the following equation, developed in Chapter 6:

$$D = \frac{R - r'(TD)}{r + i'} \qquad [6-5]$$

The factors included in equation 6–5 are D, the amount of demand deposits the member banks are capable of supporting, given the other factors; R, the volume of member bank reserves; r, the reserve requirement for demand deposits; r', the reserve requirement for time deposits; TD, the volume of member bank time deposits; and i', the ratio of excess reserves to demand deposits that member banks wish to maintain.

Assume that prior to any change in the reserve requirements, the following situation prevails:

If:
$$R = \$32.908 \text{ billion}$$
$$r' = 0.04$$
$$TD = \$243.42 \text{ billion}$$
$$r = 0.13558$$
Then:
$$i' = 0.00147$$
$$D = \$169.062 \text{ billion}$$

If the actual volume of commercial bank demand-deposit liabilities is equal to D — the volume that commercial banks can support — then the member banks cannot further expand loans, investments, and demand-deposit money. However, this does not mean they have no excess reserves. The fact that i' is greater than zero indicates they do — under our assumptions above, member banks have $249 million in desired excess reserves. However, they cannot expand operations without converting some of their excess reserves to required reserves to cover c (the desired ratio of currency to demand deposits discussed in Chapter 6) and i'.

Now suppose there is a $\frac{1}{2}$ percent increase in required reserves and r becomes 0.14058. Assuming there is no cash drain or inflow, this results in a decreased D of $164.824 billion. In other words, an increase of $\frac{1}{2}$ percent in the reserve requirement for demand deposits leads to a $4.238 billion reduction in the money supply. In percentage terms, the forced contraction is equal to more than 2 percent of the original volume of demand deposits. Thus, only a small change in the reserve requirement has induced a rather sharp contraction in the money supply.

Equation 6–5 is useful largely for pedagogical purposes, but it does bear a strong relationship to reality. The values chosen here for r, r', and TD are close to the actual values of these factors for member banks during the four-week period ending January 24, 1973. Since a single value was necessary for r', it was assumed to be 0.04, rather than the actual differential requirements of 0.03 and 0.05. Similarly, we assumed that demand-deposit liabilities for *all* banks were subject to a fixed 0.13558 requirement rather than a differential requirement based on bank size. The value of r was calculated as the ratio of required reserves for demand-deposit liabilities to the sum of net demand-deposit liabilities for all member banks. Thus, 0.13558 represents the actual average reserve requirement for the demand-deposit liabilities of all member banks during this period, as limited by the foregoing assumptions. On the other hand, assuming a fixed value of 0.00147 for i' is unrealistic, since i' is unlikely to remain fixed. For our purposes, however, a fixed value for i' simplifies the example without invalidating the results.

Whether conditions in the period on which these figures were based actually called for an increase in r is another matter. Most economists agree that a tightening of credit in early 1973 would have been desirable, but a $\frac{1}{2}$ percent rise in reserve requirements, which would have resulted in a $4.238 billion reduction in member bank demand-deposit liabilities, would have been undesirable. Smaller increases are feasible, but the Federal Reserve System does not normally change reserve requirements by less than $\frac{1}{2}$ percent. Apparently small increases in the reserve requirement can exert a strong contractive force on the economy. If excess reserves are not large, a small increase can lead to a sharp contraction of loans and investments and, consequently (as Chapter 6 demonstrated), to a sharp reduction in the volume of demand-deposit money.

We can also illustrate that small decreases in reserve requirements lead to large increases in the ability of banks to expand deposit money by simply reversing the figures used in the preceding example. If r were initially 0.14058, then D could not exceed $164.824 billion. If r were subsequently reduced to 0.13558, then D could expand to $169.062 billion. Thus, if banks utilized all their increased lending capacity, a $4.238 billion *increase* in the money stock—a substantial increase in any economic situation—would take place.

It is for the reasons given here—(1) the disproportionately heavy impact upon banks, (2) the portfolio adjustment difficulties banks experience, and (3) the severity of the resultant contractionary forces—that the Board of Governors makes infrequent use of reserve requirement increases. The board can soften the overall impact of this device by simultaneously purchasing U.S. government securities, however, a fact which suggests that open market operations are a superior anti-inflationary measure in the first place.

Decreases in reserve requirements. Decreases in reserve requirements have been more frequent than increases. The first decrease, which occurred in 1938, was clearly appropriate in light of the depressed condition of the economy at the time. The next decrease, during a war year—1942, was limited to central reserve city banks. This action was not contracyclical. Rather, it was intended to lessen the effect of large government security issues on bank reserves. The New York and Chicago banks had been experiencing reserve drains as large volumes of government securities issued to finance government defense expenditures were sold by the Treasury in Chicago and New York. As depositors drew down their accounts to buy these securities, reserves were lost. To compensate for this drain, the government reduced the reserve requirements for central reserve city banks.

Since the end of World War II, reserve requirements have generally been reduced in periods of recession or less than full employment. Thus, reductions were made in the 1949, 1953–54, 1957–58, and 1969–70 recessions. During the 1960–61 recession, however, reserve requirements were not lowered; instead, each bank's lending capacity was increased by allowing all banks to count vault cash as part of their reserves. The reserve requirement for time deposits was decreased in the fall of 1962, however. The economy was expanding at this time, but there was still a substantial amount of unemployment, and the purpose of the reduction was to provide reserves for long-term deposit growth. Another reduction, this time in the reserve requirement for savings deposits, occurred in March 1967. Again, the stated purpose of the reduction was to provide for long-term growth in deposits.

How effective have reductions in reserve requirements been as a contracyclical monetary technique? The actions cited in the previous paragraph appear to have been theoretically in the right direction. Periods of less than full employment and recessions do call for increased lending capacity. However, these decreases in reserve requirements were frequently accompanied by Federal Reserve bank sales of U.S. government securities, which tended to offset the expansive effects of the decreases. Apparently the Board of Governors felt that the increases in excess reserves caused by the reserve requirement decreases were too great. Subsequently, as the economy gained strength, the board made open market purchases of U.S. government securities so that additional reserves could be released gradually to the banking system. Again, the point can be made that open market operations might have been a superior policy instrument in the first place.

The March 1967 decrease in reserve requirements against time deposits was not accompanied by a sale of securities. Despite low unemployment, the Federal Reserve followed a policy of aggressive ease, motivated perhaps by the slowdown in construction activity that began in 1966 and by a continuing decrease in automobile sales. In a further move the board lowered the discount rate in April 1967. These actions led to rapid increments in the money stock. If the Federal Reserve's judgment was correct, its policy of monetary ease in late 1966 and much of 1967 may well have stopped a slowdown in economic activity from becoming a recession. On the other hand, as will be noted later, by maintaining a policy of monetary ease for an excessive length of time in 1967, the Federal Reserve may have aggravated the inflationary pressures of late 1967 and 1968.

The decrease in reserve requirements that occurred in the 1969–70 recession was small. The reserve requirement on time deposits in excess of

$5 million at each member bank was dropped from 6 to 5 percent on August 17, 1970. This decrease, like the one in 1967, was not accompanied by open market sales of government securities. At the same time the Federal Reserve announced that reserve requirements would be imposed on commercial paper issued by affiliates of commercial banks—an action equivalent to an increase in reserve requirements. These two policy actions considered together released some additional reserves to the banking system—an appropriate contracyclical economic policy.

Evaluation of the reserve requirement as a policy instrument. There is considerable doubt as to the merits of using variable reserve requirements as an instrument of economic policy. Contracyclical increases are unpopular in that they create management difficulties for bankers and force banks to contract sharply in the absence of offsetting open market operations. And contracyclical reductions may prove to be undependable in economic crises. For example, it is often argued that banks cannot be forced to expand loans and investments; hence, almost any type of central bank action designed to expand reserves, and thereby economic activity, will be ineffectual. The adage that you can bring a horse to water but can't make him drink is often cited at this point as evidence of the weakness of all forms of monetary action. The economic history of the postwar period seems to belie this adage, however. The cold war situation and an awareness of the economic and human loss associated with depression have helped to sustain comparatively high levels of employment and output. Postwar recessions have been mild. Banks have typically operated with small margins of excess reserves. Thus, it is reasonable to assume that, at least in mild recessions, banks will shortly make use of an increase in their money-creating abilities.

A change in reverse requirements is a blunt instrument of policy. Full utilization of a $4.2 billion increase in the loan and investment potential of the banking system—the figure given in the preceding example—over a short period of time could create undesired inflationary pressures and make offsetting open market operations necessary; a full $4.2 billion decrease in demand deposits pursuant to a $\frac{1}{2}$ percent rise in reserve requirements could cause a recession. Only if variations in reserve requirements are substantially less than $\frac{1}{2}$ percent can they be used without offsetting open market operations.

Is there then no justification for using reserve requirements as an instrument of economic policy? Some time ago, the Board of Governors recognized the difficulties inherent in the use of this policy instrument when it argued that "As an instrument of monetary management, changes in required reserve percentages are less flexible and continuously adaptable than the open market and discount instruments."[8] Nevertheless, the board

[8] Board of Governors of the Federal Reserve System. *The Federal Reserve System: Purposes and Functions* (Washington, D.C., 1961), p. 54.

believes that reserve requirement changes still have a place among monetary management techniques today. These changes immediately affect the excess reserves of *all* member banks, whereas open market operations first affect the reserve position of banks in New York City where the U.S. government securities market is concentrated. Thus, the board believes that the effects of a change in reserve requirements will be felt throughout the country more quickly than the effects of security purchases and sales by the Federal Reserve Bank of New York will be. The fact that the Federal Reserve often sells securities at the same time it lowers reserve requirements (or buys securities when it raises requirements) seems to cast suspicion on this line of reasoning, however. If the immediate effects of open market operations are in fact concentrated in New York City, how can this action effectively offset a change in reserve requirements? Nothing has been done to change the full-expansion capabilities of banks outside New York. Only if banks in other areas adjusted to their changed excess reserves much more slowly than the New York banks would a countermeasure directed toward the New York banks alone be acceptable.

There is considerable evidence that banks outside New York are only slightly slower in responding to open market induced changes in excess reserves than New York banks. One study concluded that

. . . the relative impact of open market operations on reserve city banks is close to unity, meaning that reserve city banks participate in open market sales or purchases according to their average share in total reserves. . . . the relative short-run impact of open market operations on country banks indicates that 67 percent of the total impact will take place on such banks within one month. Thus, although country banks receive less than their share, the short-run impact is substantial.[9]

Thus, it would seem that open market operations are a flexible instrument of monetary policy. Although reserve requirement changes do have some edge in this respect, since they affect the excess reserve positions of all member banks immediately, open market operations also transmit their effects rapidly.

The Discount Rate

The discount rate is the "price" that a district Federal Reserve bank charges member banks who borrow reserves.[10] Such borrowing is generally for a short period of time, usually from 15 to 90 days. Each district Reserve bank sets its own discount rate, but the decision is subject to review by the Board of Governors. Although rate changes do not occur frequently, rates are reviewed by the Federal Reserve every 14 days.

[9] Roy J. Ruffin. "An Econometric Model of the Impact of Open Market Operations on Various Bank Classes." *Journal of Finance* (September 1968), p. 636.
[10] The term "discount rate" includes all three rates described in Chapter 10.

Figure 11–1. Short-term interest rates, 1919–73.

When changes are announced, the new rates are usually the same among the various Federal Reserve banks. This tendency has become more pronounced in recent decades as various sections of the nation have lost their regional character and, in financial matters, have become part of the national money market.

As pointed out earlier, member banks borrow to meet temporary shortages of reserves or to build up reserves prior to increasing their lending activity. The Federal Reserve banks and the Board of Governors change discount rates in order to affect member bank lending. Theoretically, increases in the rate restrict member bank borrowing of reserves and hence bank lending activity; conversely, decreases in the rate are believed to encourage borrowing of reserves and lending activity.

Unfortunately, matters are not quite that simple. The data show that Federal Reserve bank discounts and advances move in the same direction as the discount rate. Logically one might expect them to move in opposite directions if discount rate manipulations are to have their intended contracyclical effects. Banks, however, tend to borrow additional reserves on the upward part of the cycle, even with high discount rates — partly because of increased business and consumer demand for funds and partly because the earnings possible on loans exceed the discount costs. On the downward side of the cycle, the situation is reversed.

The behavior of discount rates and discounts and advances through 1973. Figure 11–1 shows the movement in the discount rate of the Federal Reserve Bank of New York and the prime commercial paper interest rate from 1919 to 1973. The discount rate depicted on the graph represents ad-

Figure 11–1.   (Continued)

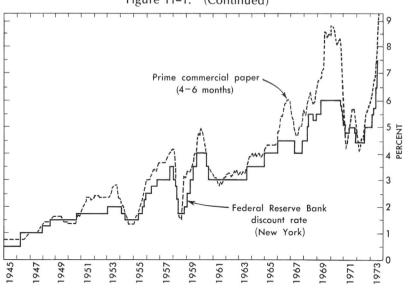

SOURCE: Board of Governors or the Federal Reserve System. *Federal Reserve Historical Chart Book* (1972), pp. 26–27; and *Federal Reserve Bulletin* (1973), p. A-34.

vances secured by U.S. government securities and discounts and advances secured by eligible paper. Table 11–2 shows the present structure of discount rates, and Table 11–3 gives the volume of Federal Reserve bank discounts and advances from 1917 to 1973. These figures support the contention that the volume of discounts and advances fluctuates in the same direction as the discount rate.

1917–32. In general, from 1917 to 1932, the Federal Reserve banks moved discount rates contracyclically. Principal exceptions were the low rates of World War I, the high rates prevailing through much of the 1921 recession, and the depression increases of 1929 and 1931. However, despite discount rate increases at both appropriate and inappropriate times, this was a period of easy money: Figure 11–1 shows that discount rates were typically below what commercial banks could earn on commercial paper from 1919 to 1932.

Although in terms of the national economy the manipulation of discount rates was generally appropriate during this period, the movement of discounts and advances was not in the same direction. In every year when discount rates increased, discounts and advances to member banks increased. In every year (except 1932), when discount rates decreased, discounts and advances to member banks decreased. This is exactly the opposite of what might be expected to happen.

1933–51. Member bank borrowing of reserves declined to insignificant levels in the 1930s. Member banks had substantial volumes of excess

TABLE 11-2 FEDERAL RESERVE BANK DISCOUNT RATES

(PERCENT PER ANNUM)

FEDERAL RESERVE BANK	LOANS TO MEMBER BANKS				LOANS TO ALL OTHERS UNDER LAST PAR. SEC. 13A‡	
	Under Secs. 13 and 13a*		*Under Sec. 10b†*			
	Rate on Aug. 15, 1973	*Previous Rate*	*Rate on Aug. 15, 1973*	*Previous Rate*	*Rate on Aug. 15, 1973*	*Previous Rate*
Boston	7½	7	8	7½	9½	9
New York	7½	7	8	7½	9½	9
Philadelphia	7½	7	8	7½	9½	9
Cleveland	7½	7	8	7½	9½	9
Richmond	7½	7	8	7½	9½	9
Atlanta	7½	7	8	7½	9½	9
Chicago	7½	7	8	7½	9½	9
St. Louis	7½	7	8	7½	9½	9
Minneapolis	7½	7	8	7½	9½	9
Kansas City	7½	7	8	7½	9½	9
Dallas	7½	7	8	7½	9½	9
San Francisco	7½	7	8	7½	9½	9

* Discounts of eligible paper and advances secured by such paper or by U.S. government obligations or any other obligations eligible for Federal Reserve bank purchase. Maximum maturity: 90 days, except that discounts of certain bankers' acceptances and of argicultural paper may have maturities not over six months and nine months, respectively.

† Advances secured to the satisfaction of the Federal Reserve bank. Maximum maturity: four months.

‡ Advances to individuals, partnerships, or corporations other than member banks secured by direct obligations of, or obligations fully guaranteed as to principal and interest by, the U.S. government or any agency thereof. Maximum maturity: 90 days.

SOURCE: Board of Governors of the Federal Reserve System.

TABLE 11-3   FEDERAL RESERVE LOANS (DISCOUNTS AND ADVANCES),
ANNUAL AVERAGES OF DAILY FIGURES, 1917-73
(IN MILLIONS OF DOLLARS)

YEAR	AMOUNT	YEAR	AMOUNT	YEAR	AMOUNT
1917	376*	1936	6	1955	666
1918	1,134	1937	14	1956	833
1919	1,906	1938	9	1957	850
1920	2,523	1939	5	1958	295
1921	1,797	1940	4	1959	812
1922	571	1941	5	1960	436
1923	736	1942	7	1961	83
1924	373	1943	25	1962	136
1925	490	1944	135	1963	269
1926	572	1945	376	1964	300
1927	442	1946	310	1965	474
1928	840	1947	219	1966	637
1929	952	1948	331	1967	209
1930	272	1949	231	1968	569
1931	327	1950	129	1969	1,101†
1932	521	1951	293	1970	835
1933	283	1952	801	1971	412
1934	36	1953	777	1972	321
1935	7	1954	217	1973	1,631†

* Based on data for August–December.
† Based on data for January–June.
SOURCE: 1917–60, Board of Governors of the Federal Reserve System. *Supplement to Banking and Monetary Statistics*, Section 10 (Washington, D.C., 1962), p. 14; 1961–73, computed from *Federal Reserve Bulletin*, various issues, 1961–73.

reserves throughout this period and as a result had no need to borrow reserves. Discount rates, as Figure 11–1 shows, were low.

Although discount rates were very low in the 1930s, it does not necessarily follow that the period was one of easy money. Since banks had substantial volumes of excess reserves and few lending and investment opportunities, there was no serious need for trips to the discount window. The criterion of ease or restrictiveness in central bank policy should not be the absolute level of discount rates; rather, it should be the level of discount rates relative to what banks can earn through their investment and lending opportunities. "The New York discount rate was never below the average four- to six-month commercial paper rate in any week in the eight years from 1934 through 1941. The result, of course, was negligible use of rediscounting facilities."[11] As Table 11–3 shows, Federal Reserve bank discounts and advances reached a low of $4 million in 1940. From this perspective a policy of apparent monetary ease may actually be viewed as restrictive. Many economists would disagree with this view, but it merits some thought, nevertheless.

Discount rates remained stable during World War II and the early

[11] Milton Friedman and Anna Schwartz. *A Monetary History of the United States, 1867–1960* (Princeton University Press, 1963), p. 514.

postwar years. This stability of discount rates at low levels was inappropriate from a contracyclical point of view, since it encouraged borrowing of reserves and credit expansion during a period of full employment, causing inflation.

The volume of discounts and advances made by the Federal Reserve banks increased during the war. From a prewar low of $4 million in 1940, they increased to an average of $376 million in 1945. Following World War II, commercial banks used the discount window with substantially greater frequency than they had during the depressed thirties, but the volume of discounts and advances never approached that of the 1920s. A tendency on the part of banks to avoid borrowing reserves has always been part of our banking heritage. The 1930s merely reinforced this tradition—a tendency that has remained somewhat evident to the present day. Another factor contributing to the small volume of discounting in the years 1933–51 was the open market policy of the Federal Reserve System. The Federal Reserve had committed itself to supporting the government bond market during World War II, and it continued this policy of support through early 1951. One way in which commercial banks may provide themselves with additional reserves to expand loans is sell some of their holdings of U.S. government securities. Normally, widespread security sales would lead to a capital loss for the selling banks, since the increased supply of bonds would depress bond prices. With the Federal Reserve committed to maintaining bond prices, however, commercial banks were able to obtain reserves in this manner and thus had little need for additional reserves from discounts and advances. To the extent that banks refrained from borrowing because of the Federal Reserve's open market policy, the effectiveness of contracyclical discount rate changes was reduced.

1951–73. Support of the government bond market by the Federal Reserve System ended with the Treasury–Federal Reserve Accord in March of 1951. Since that time, discount rate changes have been used frequently to promote economic stability. Discount rates were lowered in the contractions of 1953–54, 1957–58, 1960–61, and 1970, and raised in the expansions of 1950–53, 1954–57, 1958–60, 1961–69, and 1971–73. On occasion, during expansions the Fed did not change discount rates in the expected direction, and yet its actions were not inappropriate. There are three recent examples. In 1967—a year of economic expansion—rates were lowered in April. As we mentioned in discussing the reserve requirement, this decrease was apparently motivated by slack conditions in the automobile and construction industries. Rates were subsequently increased in November 1967. In addition, discount rates were temporarily lowered in the fall of 1968 as the Federal Reserve attempted to anticipate a possible drop in economic activity attributable to the 1968 surtax. These decreases were rescinded as soon as it became apparent that economic activity was continuing to move upward. Finally, discount rates were lowered or stabilized in the early part of the 1971–73 expansion, primarily because of continued high levels of unemployment. However, in 1973 discount rates were raised sharply as the U.S. economy experienced a boom and reduced unemployment rates.

For the most part, contracyclical adjustments since 1951 appear to have been in the right direction. Nevertheless, discount rates and the volume of discounts and advances almost never moved in opposite directions. Furthermore, as Figure 11–1 shows, in periods of upswing, the discount rate was always below the rate for four- to six-month commercial paper, even when discount rates were being increased; at the bottom of each contraction, the rate for four- to six-month commercial paper was less than the discount rate, even after discount rate decreases. Thus it appears that, despite the correct direction of discount rate changes, these changes in themselves have not been great enough to produce the desired economic effect. They probably decreased the volume of increased borrowings in economic expansion and minimized the decrease in borrowings in contraction to some degree. This, of course, is a contribution to maintaining economic stability, but it is very difficult to establish quantitatively how large a role discount rate changes actually play in regulating the economy.

Evaluation of the discount rate as a policy instrument. In general, discount rate manipulation does not appear to have been a particularly successful tool of economic policy. The contracyclical uses made of this instrument in the 1920s and since 1951 have, for the most part, been in the right direction. The ameliorative effects of these discount rate changes have not been quantitatively observable, however: discounts and advances have usually moved in the same direction as discount rates, largely because the rate on four- and six-month commercial paper has remained above discount rates in periods of economic expansion and below them in recession. Whenever discount rates are below market yields on assets, such as commercial paper, on which commercial banks are able to make substantial earnings, the banks are encouraged to borrow reserves to expand their investment in these assets. Thus, in economic upswing, when this type of differential has tended to exist, Federal Reserve discounts and advances have increased. One way in which the Fed could avoid this contradictory effect, of course, would be to make larger increases in the discount rate.

On the other hand, when discount rates are above market yields on assets such as commercial paper, banks are discouraged from borrowing reserves and expanding loans and investments. This type of differential has existed in recessions, and thus Federal Reserve discounts and advances have decreased. While it is true that some decrease may well be inevitable in recession because of a lack of demand for loans, it is legitimate to question whether the fact that discount rates exceed market rates aggravates a cyclical decline. Although discount rates are lowered at such times, shouldn't they be reduced still further to bring them beneath market rates? The answer to both questions is probably yes.

Thus, previous experience indicates that *discount rate changes, by them-*

selves, have not been an effective instrument of monetary policy. This conclusion is based primarily upon the movement of market rates of interest, discount rates, and the volume of discounts and advances.

It is usually argued by the Fed, however, that discount rate increases and decreases are not intended to bring about absolute decreases and increases, respectively, in member bank borrowing of reserves. For example, interest rates generally rise in periods of expansion, and the Fed argues that it raises discount rates merely to keep them in line with rising private rates. Raising the cost of borrowing reserves during economic expansion is thus intended to hold down the increase in reserve borrowing that would take place in the absence of a rate increase. There is a strong demand for funds by the nonbank public in periods of expansion. Banks, as profit-seeking business enterprises, are anxious to satisfy that demand by expanding loans and investments. They tend to utilize their existing reserves more intensively at such times, as well as to expand their reserve base by borrowing from the Federal Reserve banks. Thus, discount rate increases have little apparent effect on borrowings because the high return on commercial bank alternative investment opportunities relative to discount rates tends to sustain member bank borrowing. In such situations, discount rate increases at best only hold down the rate of increase of member bank borrowing.

Other factors, largely nonquantitative, also tend to work against the success of discount rate policy:

1. The volume of discounts and advances is directly determined by member bank demands, not by Federal Reserve bank control.
2. Many member banks are reluctant to borrow reserves.
3. Announced discount rate changes may have adverse effects on member bank borrowing.
4. A change in the discount rate may not be a signal for a change in Federal Reserve policy.
5. No change in discount rates may itself become a policy tending to restrict or encourage credit changes.

First, the Federal Reserve banks have no direct control over the volume of discounts and advances. If banks meet the prescribed qualifications, they can almost always borrow reserves from their district Federal Reserve bank. This provides an escape for banks that wish to expand loans and investments in periods of full employment, rising prices, and a restrictive monetary policy. Even with large discount rate increases, banks that choose to pay the price for additional reserves can usually obtain them, thereby circumventing Federal Reserve policy.

The Federal Reserve banks cannot directly change member bank reserves through discount rate policy. The most they can do is encourage or discourage borrowing of reserves. Commercial banks may decide for themselves how much in reserves they wish to have. Thus, discount rate changes have the desired effect upon member bank reserve positions only when the Fed has correctly guessed member bank reserve borrowing intentions. When it predicts incorrectly, it must use other instruments of policy to offset undesirable movements in member bank borrowings. Typically, in such a situation, the Federal Reserve resorts to open market operations — another instance that makes one wonder why open market operations are not used in the first place to bring about desired changes in member bank reserve positions.

This does not mean there is no need for the discounting mechanism. Open market operations alone cannot take care of short-term needs for additional reserves for specific banks in specific communities:

First among the basic principles governing the use of Federal Reserve credit is that Federal Reserve System lending is to accommodate bank asset and liability adjustments over limited time periods and to meet essentially short-term fluctuations in member bank needs for funds. . . .

Federal Reserve Banks always stand ready to lend to any of their member banks caught in special regional or local adversities — such as droughts, drastic deposit drains, or other emergencies — for as long as reasonably needed for the bank to work out of these circumstances.[12]

Second, some member banks are apparently reluctant to borrow reserves. These banks usually maintain large volumes of excess reserves. Thus, if they wish to increase their credit holdings, they can do so even if the Federal Reserve raises discount rates above market rates in an economic upswing. Changes in the discount rate cannot restrict the lending operations of these banks; other tools in monetary policy must be used.

On the other hand, banks that typically operate with a narrow margin of excess reserves may be seriously affected by discount rate increases. To the extent that discount rates are raised sharply because of increasing bank loans (made by the banks with large excess reserves and a reluctance to borrow), the brunt of the contractionary policy is borne by those banks operating with a narrow margin of excess reserves. A discount rate increase, therefore, can be discriminatory and may unwittingly enhance the competitive position of one group of banks at the expense of another. Eventually, of course, a contractionary discount rate policy will affect all banks; as the banks with excess reserves expand their loans and investments, their excess reserves will dwindle. Open market operations could bring this about considerably sooner, however.

Generally, the smaller banks are more reluctant to borrow reserves and

---

[12] Board of Governors of the Federal Reserve System. *Reappraisal of the Federal Reserve Discount Mechanism* (July 1968), p. 1.

the large banks go most often to the discount window. In May 1973, 178 large banks had an $84 million deficiency in reserves, whereas 5,517 small banks had $27 million in excess reserves. The small banks had borrowings of $781 million. The large banks, on the other hand, had $1,006 million in borrowings.[13]

To some extent small banks may not be reluctant to borrow, but may lack investment opportunities. Large city banks are usually located in important financial centers which provide opportunities for investment not available to country banks. Furthermore, the smaller average size of the small bank precludes loan extensions to large businesses. Finally, the large city banks operate on a bigger scale than the small banks, with large staffs specialized in each of the many different facets of banking activity. This enables them to gauge their reserve positions more accurately and so to be more economical in their use of reserves. All this suggests that the small bank's reluctance to borrow reserves is not built in; rather, its smaller size and less efficient operations force it to maintain a relatively large volume of excess reserves as a safeguard. The fact that small bank borrowing of reserves increases during periods of strong cyclical upturn also supports this theory. In addition, small banks are encouraged to keep excess reserves because of the return they can earn on them in the federal funds market.

Whether small bank reluctance to borrow is built in or forced in no way alters the conclusion that this reluctance weakens discount rate manipulation as an instrument of contracyclical economic policy. Increased discount rates cannot force banks that already have excess reserves to reduce loans and investments.

Third, announced discount rate changes may have undesired effects on member bank borrowing. For example, an increase in rates should normally discourage borrowing of reserves. However, if expectations concerning future economic trends are such that the announcement of a rate increase leads to public anticipation of further interest rate increases, there may well be an increased demand for loans by borrowers eager to obtain funds before subsequent increases occur. Commercial bankers may then have to expand their borrowings in order to meet the increased demands for credit.

Similarly, a decrease in rates should encourage bank borrowing of reserves; but if expectations are such that future rate decreases are anticipated, the demand for bank loans may decrease and bank borrowing of reserves may decline.

Fourth, a change in the discount rate may not be a signal for a change in Federal Reserve policy. For example, "when market rates of interest have moved away from close relationship with the existing discount rate, a change in the level of rates may represent merely a technical adjustment of

---

[13] *Federal Reserve Bulletin* (June 1973), pp. A-6, A-7, A-18, and A-19.

discount rates to market rates so that the system's discount mechanism will function effectively in line with current policy."[14] If technical adjustments in discount rates are mistaken for signs of a change in Federal Reserve policy, this misinterpretation may cause some degree of economic uncertainty. Suppose, for example, that a firm contemplating expansion considers a decrease in the discount rate as a signal that the Fed believes an economic slump is imminent. The company may decide to postpone its expansion until the economic outlook is more favorable. A decrease in expenditures for expansion may then contribute to an actual economic downturn never anticipated by the Federal Reserve.

Fifth, failure to change existing discount rates may itself become a policy tending to discourage or encourage credit changes. It is the *difference* between market and discount rates that influences bank lending activity. If discount rates remain unchanged while market rates change, then, depending on the nature of the change in market rates, member bank borrowing and lending activity will either increase or decrease. This implies that if discount rate changes are to be effective as an instrument of contracyclical economic policy, they must frequently be made in response to changing market rates of interest and the current economic situation.

Proposals to revise the Federal Reserve discount mechanism. The Federal Reserve completed a reappraisal of its discount mechanism in 1968. This study reaffirmed the principle that member banks should have access to the discount window (1) to meet short-term fluctuations in the need for funds, and (2) to meet special regional and local adversities. At the same time the Fed argued, as it always has, that member banks should not be continually in debt to the Federal Reserve banks.

The most important proposal by the Fed was to give each member bank a *basic borrowing privilege,* on a virtual "no questions asked" basis, that would be equal to a proportion of its capital stock and surplus. If followed by the Federal Reserve, the new procedure would be a marked departure from earlier lending practices. You may recall from the preceding section that qualifying banks "can generally" borrow reserves from their district bank. This borrowing privilege has never been unlimited. Obviously, loan officers at the Fed consider the size of the bank, its previous borrowing and repayment practices, etc., in determining the size of loans to individual member banks. Practice varies from one district to another and from one loan officer to another, however. As a result, commercial banks are sometimes uncertain about their ability to borrow from the Fed — another reason why some banks hesitate to use the discount window. Nevertheless, loan officers as a rule will try to accommodate what they consider to be "reasonable" requests from member banks. There generally has been no at-

[14] Board of Governors of the Federal Reserve System. *The Federal Reserve System: Purposes and Functions,* (Washington, D.C., 1961), p. 47.

tempt by the Federal Reserve to withhold funds from member banks.[15]

The Federal Reserve justified its proposed redesign of the discount mechanism by stating that

. . . its chief objective is increased use of the discount window for the purpose of facilitating short-term adjustments in bank reserve positions. A more liberal and convenient mechanism should enable individual member banks to adjust to changes in fund availability in a more orderly fashion and, in so doing, should lessen some of the causes of instability in financial markets without hampering overall monetary control.[16]

The Fed further argued that open market operations

. . . in Government securities by the central bank serve effectively as the preponderant means of secular reserve provision and the leading edge of monetary policy implementation. The role of the discount mechanism, on the other hand, is to cushion the strains of reserve adjustment for individual member banks and, thereby, for financial markets.[17]

This line of reasoning may be contradictory, however. The evidence presented in Table 11–3 shows the procyclical character of Federal Reserve discounts and advances. Discounting actually runs counter to open market operations, providing an escape for banks wishing to expand loans and investments. Giving commercial banks an automatic right to borrow reserves, even though in limited amounts as proposed, would further enable them to avoid the effects of restrictive monetary policy. It is exceedingly difficult to determine what portion of reserve borrowing is to cushion the strains of reserve adjustment for individual banks and what portion is to help finance expansion of loans to meet a strong demand for funds.

If banks individually increase their borrowings, their reserves increase and the Fed must sell still more government securities. Since the effects of open market operations are felt relatively quickly throughout the banking system, before long many banks would again be short of reserves and would again be induced to borrow more at the Fed.

The real bills doctrine once again. The discount mechanism was originally set up to meet the real and legitimate needs of trade, "to facilitate the production and orderly marketing of goods and not to finance the specula-

---

[15] During late 1966 it appeared that banks were borrowing reserves principally to meet sharp increases in the demand for funds by borrowers. Hence, the Federal Reserve argued that ". . . the System believes that a greater share of member bank adjustments should take the form of moderation in the rate of expansion of loans, and particularly business loans. Accordingly, this objective will be kept in mind by the Federal Reserve Banks in their extensions of credit to member banks through the discount window. Member banks will be expected to cooperate in the System's efforts to hold down the rate of business loan expansion—apart from normal seasonal needs—and to use the discount facilities of the Reserve Banks in a manner consistent with these efforts." *Federal Reserve Bulletin* (September 1966), p. 1339.

[16] Board of Governors of the Federal Reserve System. "Report of the System Committee." *Reappraisal of the Federal Reserve Discount Mechanism* (July 1968), p. 1.

[17] *Ibid.*

tive holding of excess stocks of materials and merchandise."[18] This amounted to an acceptance by the Federal Reserve of the real bills doctrine discussed in Chapters 3 and 8. One wonders if the suggested revision of the discount mechanism is not a return to this doctrine. A basic borrowing privilege, even though proportionately related to a bank's capital stock and surplus, theoretically could lead to a continual expansion of bank reserves. Commercial banks could decide to sell additional stock, thereby raising capital accounts. This would increase the amount of reserves they could borrow automatically and could lead to an increase in bank flows, money balances, and the demand for goods. In a full employment economy this would mean rising prices, a greater demand for loans by the nonbank public, still more bank borrowing of reserves, etc. The Fed, of course, could stop this via open market sales of U.S. government securities, but (at least theoretically) the Fed could ultimately run out of government securities. Or the Fed could raise the reserve requirement—a move which might be viewed as a politically unpopular refusal to give banks additional reserves at the discount window. Admittedly, it is highly unlikely that this sequence of events would occur in the real world. Nevertheless, it is interesting to speculate on what could happen if the basis of Federal Reserve reasoning on the discount mechanism were carried to what some economists consider to be its logical conclusion.

The Federal Reserve counters these speculations by arguing that it could limit borrowing by linking the discount rate more closely to market rates of interest. "The closer linkage of the discount rate to market rates will probably call for more frequent changes in the discount rate than have been made in recent years."[19] Still it is hard to see how this would strongly limit borrowing. The Federal Reserve itself acknowledges that "market rates are likely to be somewhat above the discount rates so long as reserves are in scarce supply and rate relationships are allowed to seek their own levels."[20] *This is the way it has always been. The Federal Reserve discount rate has normally been above market rates of interest at the trough of a recession and below market rates of interest on the upward part of the cycle.* Thus it is difficult to see how the Fed's proposed revision of the discount mechanism would have an ameliorative economic effect.

Although the Fed had not implemented its proposed changes as this was being written (1973), the discussion of these policies was very much alive among the Board of Governors. In late 1972, Governor Andrew Brimmer publicly advocated the basic borrowing privilege, coupling it with converting the discount rate into a "penalty rate" which would be above private market interest rates.

Supplementary Readings

See end of Chapter 12.

[18] Federal Reserve Board. *Annual Report* (1923), p. 5.
[19] "Report of the System Committee," *op. cit.,* p. 20.
[20] *Ibid.*

12 Federal Reserve Instruments of Monetary Control, Part II

GENERAL MONETARY CONTROLS (CONTINUED)

Open Market Operations

The most potent instrument of monetary policy the Federal Reserve has at its disposal is its ability to engage in open market operations. By purchasing U.S. government securities and bankers' acceptances from the nonbank public, it can directly increase both commercial bank reserves and the volume of demand-deposit money. By selling U.S. government securities and bankers' acceptances to the nonbank public, it can directly decrease both commercial bank reserves and the volume of demand-deposit money.

When properly used, open market operations can be of great help in stabilizing the economy. Since the purchase and sale of securities can be done in small or in large amounts, it is possible to change the excess reserve position of the commercial banking system quickly or gradually and in limited amounts. As noted earlier, this is not the case with reserve requirement changes.

Open market operations are not subject to the shortcomings of discount rate changes, either. Since they change reserve positions directly, their effectiveness does not depend on the demands of the commercial banking system for reserves. In addition, open market operations do not generally suffer from the "announcement" shortcomings of the discount mechanism. As the FOMC continually engages in open market operations, commercial banks find it difficult to tell whether an increase in Federal Reserve holdings of securities is an actual change in policy or a normal adjustment in response to a seasonal need for additional bank reserves. Although the absence of a clear-cut announcement of change in Federal Reserve open market policy may cause some difficulty with respect to the use of this instrument, it does lessen the probability of the adverse bank borrowing action that sometimes occurs when discount rate changes are announced.

The Use of the Open Market Tool

1917–35. The use of open market operations as an instrument of economic policy is comparatively recent. When the Federal Reserve System was set up in 1913, it was expected that holdings of U.S. government securities would simply be a source of earnings for the Federal Reserve banks. In addition, some open market operations in bankers' acceptances were envisioned; the initial purpose of these operations was to facilitate the role of the United States in international trade through the development of a bankers' acceptance market. In practice, however, open market operations in bankers' acceptances have never played a significant role in the implementation of monetary policy, whereas operations in government securities have assumed ever-increasing importance.

Initially, each district bank was permitted to carry on its own open market operations, in accordance with the congressional intention that each Federal Reserve bank should have a substantial amount of local autonomy in regulating banking in its particular district. It was soon discovered, however, that independent operations in government securities tended to have destabilizing effects on the economy. For example, if a Federal Reserve bank in one district sold securities that were purchased in another district, the result would be a loss of reserves by banks in the district where the securities were purchased, thereby leading to an unanticipated and frequently undesirable tightening of credit conditions in that district.

In addition, it was soon recognized that if open market operations were undertaken by the Federal Reserve purely for the purpose of making a profit, this could have a destabilizing effect not only on regional economies but on the national economy as well. In the early 1920s, for example, it was discovered that Federal Reserve bank purchases of U.S. government securities reduced the borrowing of reserves by member banks and that sales of securities increased borrowing. Hence, a contracyclical discount rate policy could be undermined by individual Federal Reserve banks as they purchased and sold government securities to increase earnings. Thus, even as early as the 1920s, the need for coordination between the discount mechanism — the principal instrument of monetary management at that time — and open market operations was obvious.

In 1922, a committee composed of men from various Federal Reserve banks was set up to coordinate purchases and sales of U.S. government securities by the district banks. The following year, this committee was replaced by the Open Market Investment Committee, which was to buy and sell securities for all Federal Reserve banks. Technically, individual district banks still had the power to buy and sell securities, but they did so in very limited amounts.

One shortcoming of the Open Market Investment Committee was that its membership did not include representatives from all the Federal Reserve banks. Accordingly, in 1930, membership in the committee was broadened to include a representative from each bank. At the same time, it was renamed the Open Market Policy Conference. The Banking Act of 1933 formalized this arrangement and renamed the conference the Federal Open Market Committee. It also denied each Federal Reserve bank the right to engage in open market operations independently, although an individual bank could still refrain from participation in FOMC operations if it wished. The Banking Act of 1935 removed this last right of individual Federal Reserve banks and established the FOMC in its present form.

Thus, only since 1935, have open market operations as we know them been effective. Throughout most of the 1920s and early 1930s, however, some attempt was made to coordinate the administration of policy instruments, and the various committees in charge of security purchases and sales did make an effort to avoid conflict with discounting policy.

How effective were open market operations as a contracyclical device prior to 1935? This is a difficult question. We tend to judge the use of this policy instrument in terms of our current policy that security purchases and sales should be used to influence the expansion and contraction of the economy. During the period being considered, however, this was not an established objective of open market operations. Instead, the policy was simply to coordinate discounting and open market operations. In addition, most of the security sales and purchases during this period were primarily aimed at adjusting bank reserve positions to seasonal and temporary reserve needs. This is true even today; it is the main reason why the account manager buys and sells securities on a daily basis. Contracyclical purchases and sales of securities are only a small part of overall market operations. In the 1920s and early 1930s they were even less significant.

Nevertheless, small variations in Federal Reserve security purchases and sales can have a contracyclical effect, even though the bulk of the operations have no contracyclical purpose. Table 12–1 shows the annual average amount of U.S. government security and bankers' acceptance holdings of the Federal Reserve banks from 1917 through mid 1973. From the beginning of the period through 1935, there was a marked increase in Federal Reserve security holdings (U.S. government securities plus acceptances). From a contracyclical point of view, the security purchases from 1930 to 1934 were quite impressive. These were depression years and the increased holdings from $449 million in 1929 to $2.457 billion in 1934 were clearly appropriate contracyclical action. Unfortunately, other actions by the monetary authorities during this period offset the effects of these vigorous and appropriate purchases.

1935–45. Federal Reserve open market operations had developed into an important instrument of contracyclical monetary policy by the early 1930s. Starting in 1935, however, with a slight decrease in Federal Reserve bank security holdings, this use of open market operations was abandoned, and from 1935 through 1940 the level of securities held by the System stabilized. There were some year-to-year variations, but they were relatively insignificant compared with the substantial increases of the early 1930s. The apparent policy objective during this time was to maintain an orderly market for government securities.

Beginning in 1937, the maintenance of an orderly government securities

TABLE 12-1 FEDERAL RESERVE HOLDINGS OF U.S. GOVERNMENT SECURITIES
AND ACCEPTANCES, 1917-73
ANNUAL AVERAGES OF DAILY FIGURES
(IN MILLIONS OF DOLLARS)

YEAR	U.S. GOVERNMENT SECURITIES	ACCEPTANCES	YEAR	U.S. GOVERNMENT SECURITIES	ACCEPTANCES
1917*	100	188	1946	23,250	8
1918	134	287	1947	22,330	—
1919	254	324	1948	21,511	—
1920	324	385	1949	19,560	—
1921	254	91	1950	18,410	—
1922	455	159	1951	22,756	—
1923	186	227	1952	23,066	—
1924	402	172	1953	24,661	—
1925	359	287	1954	24,646	—
1926	350	281	1955	23,891	13
1927	417	263	1956	23,709	23
1928	297	328	1957	23,345	27
1929	208	241	1958	24,654	40
1930	564	213	1959	26,194	35
1931	669	245	1960	26,373	39
1932	1,461	71	1961	27,393	—†
1933	2,052	83	1962	29,522	—†
1934	2,432	25	1963	31,764	—†
1935	2,431	5	1964	34,618	—†
1936	2,431	4	1965	38,661	—†
1937	2,504	3	1966	41,856	—†
1938	2,565	1	1967	46,134	—†
1939	2,584	—	1968	51,303	—†
1940	2,417	—	1969	54,031	—†
1941	2,187	—	1970	58,180	—†
1942	3,191	—	1971	65,350	—†
1943	7,724	—	1972	70,141	—†
1944	14,772	—	1973	74,330‡	—†
1945	21,363	—			

* Based on data for August–December.
† Not shown separately in data source.
‡ Based on data for January–June.
SOURCE: 1917–60, Board of Governors of the Federal Reserve System. *Supplement to Banking and Monetary Statistics,* Section 10 (Washington, D.C., 1962), p. 14; 1961–73, computed from *Federal Reserve Bulletin,* various issues, 1961–73.

market became an increasingly important goal of open market operations. This meant stabilizing U.S. government security prices. The first direct action came in 1937, when the Federal Reserve began buying long-term securities to prop up their declining prices. Short-term securities were sold at the same time so that member bank reserve positions would not be increased by the purchase of the long-term issues. The Federal Reserve again entered the market with a view to propping up government bond prices in September of 1939, with the beginning of World War II. Subsequent entries were made in early 1940 and immediately after Pearl Harbor in 1941.

With the start of World War II, the Federal Reserve firmly committed itself to supporting the government bond market. The *Annual Report* of the Board of Governors for 1941 stated:

The System is prepared to use its powers to assure that an ample supply of funds is available at all times for financing the war effort and to exert its influence toward maintaining conditions in the United States government security market that are satisfactory from the standpoint of the government's requirements.[1]

To implement this policy, the Fed stood ready to buy any amount of government securities that commercial banks and the nonbank public wished to sell. Since the government was issuing large volumes of securities to finance the deficit created by our huge armament expenditures, bond prices would have declined without Federal Reserve support. The increased supply would have forced the Treasury to offer higher interest rates in order to sell additional securities. This, in turn, would have meant increased government expenditures in the form of interest payments —funds for which would have had to come either from taxes or additional bond sales. Money would have had to be diverted from armament expenditures to pay the increased interest. Federal Reserve support of the government bond market, in effect, increased the demand for the securities and thereby helped to maintain their price and hold down the interest burden of the Treasury. The effects of this policy on Federal Reserve holdings may readily be seen in Table 12.1. U.S. government security holdings increased from $2.187 billion in 1941 to $21.363 billion in 1945.

The money stock also increased substantially—from $45.5 to $94.2 billion in the same period—as a result of this policy.[2] This happened as the U.S. government sold securities to the nonbank public and the commercial banking system. To the extent that the nonbank public purchased the securities, no new money was created. The Treasury simply received the money balances of the nonbank public and then spent those funds for wartime armaments, thereby returning the money to circulation. When members of the nonbank public sold their security holdings to the Federal Reserve or to commercial banks, however, there was an increase in demand-deposit money. Furthermore, to the extent that securities sold by the Treasury were purchased by the commercial banking system, there was also an increase in the money supply. Initially treasury demand deposits increased; as the proceeds of the security sales were spent by the Treasury, the funds were received by the nonbank public, thereby increasing the money supply.

The commercial banking system was an important cog in this process. Whenever it purchased securities, deposit liabilities increased. As deposit

[1] Board of Governors of the Federal Reserve System. *Annual Report* (1941), p. 1.
[2] The data are for June 30, 1941, and June 30, 1945. Data source: Board of Governors of the Federal Reserve System. *Supplement to Banking and Monetary Statistics,* Section 1 (Washington, D.C., 1962), p. 15.

liabilities increased, however, excess reserves decreased and so did the lending ability of the banking system. The FOMC, by buying securities, created the reserves needed for expansion.

1946–51. The Federal Reserve continued to support the government bond market during the early postwar years. The Treasury was no longer confronted with finding a market for an expanding government debt; the war was over and government expenditures had decreased. However, it was confronted with the problem of refunding the large national debt built up during the war. Large volumes of new securities had to be sold in order to obtain the needed funds to retire old securities as they reached maturity. After the war, people demanded the goods and services they had been denied during the war. They neither wanted nor demanded government bonds. Without continued Federal Reserve support, bond prices would have dipped and interest costs increased.

The economy showed inflationary tendencies from 1946 through mid-1948. The commercial banking system tended to abet the price rises during this period by actively expanding loans, although deposit money increased only in 1946 and 1947. It was the security price support program of the Federal Reserve that enabled commercial banks to switch from U.S. government securities to loans without incurring capital losses.

One would imagine, given this set of circumstances, that the Federal Reserve would have sharply increased its security holdings from 1946 to 1948. Actually, these holdings increased only in 1946; decreases occurred in 1947 and 1948, due in large part to treasury debt retirement practices. Federal government tax receipts exceeded expenditures in these years and yielded a large cash surplus. This surplus was used by the Treasury to retire federal debt, much of which was held by the Federal Reserve banks. Thus, although actual Federal Reserve open market policy during these years of inflation was basically expansive, debt retirement in 1947 and 1948 induced a decrease in Reserve bank security holdings — the right direction for Federal Reserve security holdings to move in periods of full employment and inflation. Had the Fed followed an aggressive, contracyclical monetary policy, there would have been significant additional decreases in Federal Reserve bank security holdings. In practice, however, the treasury surplus was the principal deflationary force at work in the economy; Federal Reserve policy was expansive, and the result was inflation. From 1946 to 1948, commercial bank reserves rose from $16 to $18 billion; excess reserves, despite a reserve requirement increase in 1948, were never less than $740 million in any month of the three-year period.[3]

In 1949, the situation was substantially different. Businesses found themselves with excessive inventories and proceeded to reduce them. This helped set contractionary forces in motion and a recession developed.

[3] *Supplement to Banking and Monetary Statistics, op. cit.,* Section 10, p. 16.

Open market operations at this time were again perverse. Instead of buying more government securities, the Federal Reserve sold them. Its holdings of government securities decreased by $4 billion in 1949, causing member bank reserves to fall by $2.6 billion.[4] In a recession, there is generally a strong demand by commercial banks and financial investors for government securities because they represent a safe investment. This increased demand usually causes bond prices to rise. Federal Reserve sales of securities in 1949 prevented these price rises from taking place.

The beginning of the Korean conflict in June 1950 triggered a sharp economic expansion. The Fed attempted to restrain inflationary forces by raising reserve requirements and discount rates. The commitment to support government bond prices interfered with these contracyclical moves, however. From June 1950 to March 1951, Federal Reserve holdings of government securities actually expanded by $4.5 billion; member bank reserves and the money stock each rose by $3 billion.[5]

Throughout most of the 1940s, the members of the FOMC had generally agreed with the policy of supporting the price of government bonds, but by 1950 many of them had become quite dissatisfied with the policy. This produced some dissension between the Federal Reserve System and the U.S. Treasury. The FOMC felt that it was unwise to continue to support government bond prices; the Treasury, on the other hand, wanted this easy money policy continued to keep the interest burden of the national debt low. After considerable controversy, which even involved President Truman, the Federal Reserve and the Treasury reached an accord in March of 1951. The issue was resolved in favor of the Federal Reserve and, for the first time in almost ten years, the Fed was allowed to follow a restrictive monetary policy without having to undercut that policy by buying government securities at fixed prices whenever commercial banks were short of reserves.

March 1951–64. Following the Treasury–Federal Reserve Accord of 1951, the Fed's use of open market operations was for the most part in an appropriate contracyclical direction. For example, Federal Reserve holdings of government securities expanded in the recessions of 1953–54, 1957–58, and 1960–61. During the upswing of 1955–57, policy changed to one of increasing restraint, and security holdings decreased somewhat through 1957. During the 1959–60 upswing, on the other hand, security sales did not occur until late in the expansion, primarily as a result of unemployment levels continuing in excess of 5.5 percent.

The recession of 1960–61 ended in February 1961. Logically, it would seem that a decrease in Federal Reserve holdings of securities should then have occurred. The economy seemed to be improving rapidly throughout

---

[4] *Ibid.*, p. 17.
[5] *Ibid.*, pp. 15, 17.

the period 1961–64. Gross national product increases were substantial and there were significant increases in the stock of money as a result of the Fed's easy money policies. Unemployment was persistent, however. Although the number of people employed was at a record level, the civilian work force was growing so rapidly that the unemployment rate during this period was usually close to 6 percent. Unemployment did not begin to approach 5 percent until mid-1964. Apparently the Board of Governors and the FOMC considered this statistic important enough to warrant the continuation of a policy of moderate ease.

"Bills Only." Shortly after the Treasury–Federal Reserve Accord of March 1951, the board decided that the FOMC should minimize its intervention in the securities market—that it was preferable to allow the forces of a free competitive market to set the price and interest rates for both private and government securities. Nevertheless, the board emphasized that some intervention would be necessary since open market operations were our most flexible policy instrument. Thus, the question was how best to minimize intervention in free market forces and simultaneously stabilize the economy by manipulating bank reserves. The solution decided upon was to confine open market operations to the short-term portion of the government securities market. As a result, starting in 1952 and 1953, open market operations were restricted principally to Treasury bills.

Treasury bills are obligations of the U.S. Treasury that have maturities from three months to a year. Most issues consist of 91- and 182-day bills, however. Because of their short maturities, there is a continual market for these securities and trading in treasury bills is more active than in any other type of securities. For this reason the FOMC believed that open market operations would have the "least impact" in this part of the government securities market.

The board's decision to confine open market operations principally to treasury bills was known as the "bills only" policy. Actually, the FOMC did not limit itself entirely to treasury bills. Other government securities with maturities of less than 15 months were also bought and sold, and on a few occasions the Federal Reserve was again called upon to support other sectors of the government securities market—briefly in December 1955 and in July 1958.

Apparently, the Fed felt that restricting security purchases to short-term government securities would be an important step toward simplifying the decision-making process. The FOMC had to be concerned only with the volume of open market operations and their influence on bank reserve positions, and no longer had to worry about choosing among a variety of maturities. Staying out of the longer-term securities market would permit private demands for government securities to determine their prices and interest yields. Federal Reserve purchases and sales of short-term securities would not have a particularly destabilizing effect on security prices because of the large volume of private dealings in this market. In addition, much was made of the point that if

. . . Federal Reserve operations were regularly conducted in all maturity sectors of the government securities market, the portfolio managers of financial institutions, other investors, and professional traders might well become unduly sensitized to possible changes in monetary policy. A particular hazard, for instance, would be that the trading in the longer-term area of the market, which normally experiences the widest price swings, might become overly influenced by guesses about the maturities that might be involved in System operations.[6]

There was considerable opposition to this "bills only" policy. Many within the Federal Reserve System and the U.S. Treasury felt that the FOMC should not manipulate the economy only by influencing member bank reserve positions, but that it should also help to set short-term and long-term rates of interest. This could only be done, it was thought, if the FOMC dealt in issues of all maturities. Was it not desirable on occasion to reduce long-term interest rates, for example? Would this not induce decreases in private long-term rates and thereby serve to stimulate business investment in plant and equipment?

"Operation Twist." Changes in economic conditions have a way of forcing changes in the way policy instruments are used! An adverse U.S. balance of payments developed in the late 1950s and early 1960s. This led to a reduction of U.S. gold reserves as foreigners chose to take gold instead of building up their claims to American dollars. Under the "bills only" policy, Federal Reserve security purchases in the 1960–61 recession were heavily concentrated in short-term issues. With increased demand, short-term interest rates tended to go down. Part of the adverse balance of payments of this period was due to the difference between U.S. and foreign short-term rates of interest. Higher short-term yields abroad induced individuals, businesses, and financial institutions in the United States to invest idle funds in foreign short-term securities rather than in domestic issues. Foreigners were also induced to restrict their purchases of U.S. securities. As a result, there was an increased short-term capital outflow from the United States, and foreign claims to American dollars and gold rose. It was decided that heavy Federal Reserve purchases of short-term government securities aggravated this situation, inasmuch as they tended to hold down our short-term interest rates.

As a consequence, the "bills only" policy was abandoned in favor of a new policy that, while inducing easy credit conditions in the United States by providing banks with ample lending capacity, might at the same time lead to short-term interest rate increases and thereby reduce the gold

[6] Board of Governors of the Federal Reserve System. *The Federal Reserve System: Purposes and Functions* (Washington, D.C., 1961), pp. 40–41.

outflow. Under this new policy, called "Operation Twist," the Federal Reserve would sell some short-term government securities to raise the yields and thus eliminate short-term capital outflows; simultaneously, the Fed would buy long-term government securities to provide banks with greater lending ability. The purchase of long-term securities would also depress long-term interest rates; this could lead to investment demand increases and thereby sustain domestic employment levels.

The "bills only" policy was officially abandoned in February 1961, and the decisions of the account manager again became complicated by a choice of maturities. The policy did not change the structure of interest rates, primarily because the Fed was buying some intermediate and long-term securities while the Treasury was aggressively selling them. Thus, treasury and Federal Reserve actions merely offset one another.

Today the Fed continues to operate in both long- and short-term government securities, but the bulk of open market operations are concentrated in short-term securities. "Operation Twist" is no longer the official policy of Federal Reserve government debt operations, however.

1965–73. On the basis of the raw data on the movement of Federal Reserve holdings of government securities, one might conclude that open market operations were often inappropriate from 1965 through 1973. *However, as must now be evident from the analysis of preceding periods, it is exceedingly difficult to interpret the net expansive or contractive effects of open market operations.* Increases in Federal Reserve security holdings are not necessarily indicative of a policy of monetary ease, and decreases do not always imply a policy of restraint. Open market operations are often used to make adjustments for seasonal or unanticipated changes in commercial bank reserves. They are also used as a contracyclical instrument of economic policy, in part to cushion the contracyclical effects of other policy instruments. The data for 1965–73 reflect such diverse ends.

The unemployment rate steadily decreased to less than 5 percent of the civilian labor force in 1965, and in 1966 to less than 4 percent—the level at which it remained throughout 1967 and 1968. On this basis, possibly some expansion of Federal Reserve government security holdings was called for, at least in 1965. Aside from seasonal decreases in January and September of 1965, such expansion did take place. The system's holdings of government securities rose by $4 billion. Only about $1 billion of this became additional commercial bank reserves, however; the remaining $3 billion served to offset decreases in reserves generated by our dwindling gold stock and the expansion in the demand for currency.

Although the unemployment rate in 1965 seemed to justify an expansive policy, there is no such justification for the expansion of Federal Reserve holdings of government securities by more than $3 billion in 1966, when unemployment was less than 4 percent. Are there other justifications? Due to gold flows and an increased demand for currency, the net increase in member bank reserves in 1966 was only about $1 billion, and the Federal Reserve itself argues that it followed a policy of restraint through most of the year.[7] Some of the data bears out this contention. Federal Reserve holdings of government securities declined in January, February, and March of 1966, and the overall increase in security holdings by the Fed was less than it was in the preceding year. In addition, in December 1965, discount rates had been increased and Regulation Q invoked; various classes of reserve requirements were raised in June and August of 1966, and in September the Federal Reserve requested that member banks voluntarily restrain their expansion of business loans.

Mid-1966 saw an apparent contradiction in this asserted policy of restraint. In July and September, the Fed exercised its power under Regulation Q to lower the maximum rates of interest payable on various classes of time deposits. The purpose of these decreases was to offset some of the competitive edge that commercial banks had gained over nonbank financial intermediaries following the use of Regulation Q in December of 1965. Savings and loan associations, finding it difficult to attract funds as a result of this action, had been forced to restrict mortgage loans. A sharp decrease in new construction contracts followed. The decrease in construction activity continued into late 1966. There was also some slack in automobile demand. Because of this the Federal Reserve changed direction, instituting a policy of monetary ease in the last quarter of 1966. Open market operations became decidedly expansive at that time.

On balance, it appears that the expansion of government security holdings by the Federal Reserve was justified by current economic conditions during 1966. However, as we shall see later in the chapter, this does not mean that overall Federal Reserve policy was correct.

Federal Reserve holdings of U.S. government securities expanded by approximately $4½ billion during 1967—until then the biggest increment since World War II. About $3 billion of the increase covered reserve losses attributable to gold flows and increased currency in circulation. The remainder represented an increase in member bank reserve deposits. At the same time, the consumer price index rose 3.2 percent, unemployment rates remained low, and the stock of money increased by 4 percent. Construction activity recovered early in the year. The Federal Reserve took no restrictive economic action until late 1967, when it raised discount rates. Even then there was no contraction of government securities holdings. The only curtailment in a continual expansion of Federal Reserve holdings of government securities occurred in the months of August and September, and represented principally a seasonal decrease. Open market operations in 1967 thus appear to have been procyclical and inappropriate.

Economically, 1968 was much the same as 1967. Unemployment remained low, while the consumer price index went up 5 percent. Again the

---

[7] Board of Governors of the Federal Reserve System. *Annual Report* (1966).

Federal Reserve banks expanded their holdings of U.S. government securities, this time in excess of $5 billion, with almost all the expansion designed to compensate for member bank reserve decreases resulting from gold and currency drains. On the surface, it appears that central bank policy was contracyclical and therefore appropriate. The increased reserve requirements, increased discount rates, and an increase in the income tax rate in 1968 indicate an overall governmental policy of restriction. On the other hand, these moves were more than offset by the expansionary effects of government military spending, float increases, discount and advance increases, and drops in Treasury cash holdings and other federal reserve accounts. (Chapter 14 will show how the forces cited combine to expand money and reserves.)

Federal Reserve holdings of government securities increased $2.7 billion in 1969, barely enough to cover the increased currency holdings of the nonbank public, part of an economic policy of restriction designed to cope with rising prices. As such, it appears to have been appropriate, but by August 1969, some economists were voicing fears that the policy was overly restrictive and would "overkill" the inflation by creating too much unemployment.

Beginning in late 1969 and continuing through 1970, the U.S. economy experienced a recession. While recovery began in late 1970, high unemployment levels (as had occurred in the early 1960s) continued well into 1973. The unemployment rate for 1971 (5.9 percent) was actually higher than for 1970 (4.9 percent), and did not dip to less than 5.0 percent again until mid 1973. Appropriately, the Fed instituted a policy of monetary ease in 1970—a policy that did not begin to moderate until late in 1972 and still continued until May 1973 when a contractive policy began. Open market operations contributed to this expansion when Federal Reserve holdings of government securities increased annually, starting from $54 billion in 1969 and rising to $77 billion by May of 1973.

In addition to persistent unemployment (halting in mid 1973), price inflation continued throughout the period 1970–73. While the rate of price increase dropped from 6 percent in 1969 to 3 percent in 1972, it rose again in 1973, and it was feared that, unlike the early 1960s, the economy would be plagued by both persistent unemployment and inflation in the mid-1970s. Were economic conditions such that to reduce unemployment to a 4 percent level, demand would have to be stimulated so much that inflation reached a level of 6 percent?[8] How could open market operations function satisfactorily in such a complex economic environment?

Evaluation of the open market policy instrument. There are four principal advantages to the open market instrument. Increases or decreases in Fed-

---

[8] See Chapter 21 for a theoretical discussion of the trade-off between unemployment and price change.

eral Reserve bank security holdings may be made (1) slowly or rapidly and (2) in limited or in large amounts. In addition, open market operations (3) enable the FOMC to directly manipulate the reserve positions of member banks, and (4) when they involve the nonbank public, directly affect the stock of money. These four factors make open market operations a swift and flexible corrective for economic instability. They also permit the Federal Reserve to compensate for inappropriate uses of monetary tools, including the open market instrument itself.

This does not mean that it is easy to use open market operations as an instrument of monetary policy. Just as reserve requirement changes and discount rate manipulation pose problems for the monetary authorities, so does the purchase and sale of securities. Fortunately, however, the problems created by the open market instrument are not as great as those created by the other policy instruments.

Problems posed by the use of open market operations. *First,* we may be attempting to accomplish too much by using open market operations in both a dynamic and a defensive manner. Open market operations are used "defensively" to make adjustments for seasonal or unanticipated changes in commercial bank reserves. "Dynamically" they are an instrument of contracyclical economic policy. These dual objectives often complicate the account manager's job. For example, an influx of currency into the banking system from the nonbank public normally occurs around the first of the year. Since this tends to increase bank reserves and lending ability, and since such large increases in lending capacity are considered undesirable by the FOMC, the account manager sells securities.

The problem at first appears simple enough. The sale of securities must be sufficiently high to offset the undesirable increase in reserves, thereby neutralizing its effect on the economy. It is very easy to miscalculate in such matters, however. The account manager may overestimate the extent of the expected cash inflow and sell too many securities. The result will be an unintended tightening of credit conditions. Banks, in turn, may interpret the tightness of their reserve positions as a sign of a change in Federal Reserve policy, and accordingly reexamine their lending and investment policies.

To help him avoid such miscalculations, the account manager has a great deal of statistical information available—detailed records of how the forces over which the Federal Reserve usually has no direct control (e.g., changes in vault cash, foreign accounts, or the balance of payments) have behaved in the past. He has been informed by the Treasury of impending security sales, tax receipts, and the expected future rate of government expenditures. He knows the extent to which banks have been borrowing reserves, either from the Federal Reserve banks or in the federal funds market. All this information helps him reach his daily decision on security purchases and sales for defensive purposes. Various statistical indicators, such as changes in the stock of money, the unemployment rate, or the gross national product, also help the account manager decide how much dynamic action is required to carry out the current FOMC directive. In addition, of course, his long experience in the securities market gives him a "feel" for market conditions. Thus, he combines the quantitative and qualitative information available to him and makes his overall decision—whether to buy or sell.[9]

Nevertheless, miscalculations can occur. The data may have been interpreted incorrectly. Knowledge of the past is usually a reliable basis for prognostication, but each new statistic has a way of altering past performance records. All this suggests that it might be simpler to use open market operations for dynamic purposes alone. Commercial banks would then be forced to resort to the discount window and the federal funds market to obtain the needed reserves to meet seasonal and unanticipated shortages. These borrowings could be repaid when seasonal and unanticipated reserve increases occurred. This is not a specific policy recommendation; it is merely one of a number of alternative ways of handling monetary problems that should be considered if the Federal Reserve is to be the viable and adaptive institution it has striven to be since the Accord of 1951.

Second, the variety of purposes for which we use open market operations makes it difficult to interpret the significance of these transactions. The defensive measures just mentioned, for example, could lead to decreases in the quantity of securities held by the Federal Reserve in a period when a dynamic approach calls for an increase in security holdings. The actual movement of total security holdings may be quantitatively correct, but imply, from a reading of the data change, a modification in policy that has not actually taken place. This, in turn, may set off a change in bank expectations. *Changes in the absolute level of reserves and Federal Reserve security holdings, therefore, are difficult to interpret and should not always be regarded as indicative of the degree of tightness in monetary policy.*

In addition, since the Accord of 1951, Federal Reserve use of open market operations has been coordinated, for the most part, with discount rate and reserve requirement changes. This further complicates the task of interpreting Federal Reserve open market operations policy alone. It is impossible to isolate these operations and determine whether or not they have been appropriate. A purchase or sale of securities may have been made to compensate for undesired changes in commercial bank reserves resulting from incorrect applications of other instruments of policy. Reserve requirement changes, for example, can lead to extreme changes in member bank reserve positions; open market operations may be used to correct this situation. Thus, to evaluate the open market instrument properly, we must consider it within the context of overall Federal Reserve policy.

---

[9] For a detailed account of just how the account manager conducts open market operations, see Alan R. Holmes. "A Day at the Trading Desk." Federal Reserve Bank of New York. *Monthly Review* (October 1970), pp. 234–38.

SELECTIVE CREDIT CONTROLS

General monetary controls—the reserve requirement, the discount rate, and open market operations—are designed to affect the reserve position of member banks. *Selective credit controls* affect the flow of funds between financial institutions, nonfinancial businesses, and individuals. Some selective credit controls regulate the interest rates payable on various types of time deposits; others regulate the terms on which funds may be borrowed for specific spending purposes. These controls are based on the presumption that certain types of spending are more important sources of economic instability than others. By regulating the relative ease of borrowing for spending purposes in recession or inflation, monetary authorities hope to dampen undesired cyclical instability. Only what are essentially domestic selective credit controls are considered here. Foreign credit restraint guidelines will be discussed in Chapter 24.

The Use of Regulation Q

Regulation Q enables the Federal Reserve to set the maximum rate of interest payable by member banks on various classes of time deposits. The Fed argues that it uses this monetary control to keep the rates paid by member banks in line with yields on other types of near monies, in order to "forestall excessive interest rate competition among financial institutions for consumer-type time deposits."[10]

Theoretically, the yield on one type of liquid asset relative to yields on other types influences the demand for that asset. For example, should the yield on time deposits rise relative to yields on competing financial assets, the volume of time deposits demanded will rise and the demand for other liquid assets will decline. Because the higher yield on time deposits makes them a more attractive savings form, more of these deposits will be demanded and fewer other liquid assets will be purchased. Conversely, a relative decline in yield on a financial asset will decrease the demand for that asset. *Hence it can be argued that the demand for a liquid asset is an increasing function of its own yield and a decreasing function of other yields.* Should the yield on competing liquid assets remain the same relative to the yield on time deposits, we would expect little substitution to occur. The presumed objective of the Federal Reserve's use of Regulation Q has been just this—namely, to allow time deposit rates to keep pace with yields on other liquid assets. Had this policy been successful, we would have had to find other explanations for changes in the composition of near monies in the economy. As Chapter 5 demonstrated, however, the Federal Reserve has not managed to keep the yield on time deposit liabilities of member banks the same relative to yields on competing financial assets.

---

[10] Board of Governors of the Federal Reserve System. *Annual Report* (1966), p. 10.

1936–73. Let us examine the actual use made of Regulation Q by the Fed. Table 12–2 shows the maximum interest rates payable on time and savings deposits from 1936 into 1973. The rates apply to all insured commercial banks. (The Federal Reserve sets the rates for member banks, and the FDIC has established identical rates for nonmember insured commercial banks.) The rates payable remained the same from 1936 until 1957, when all classes of rates, except those on time deposits payable in less than 90 days, were raised by $\frac{1}{2}$ percent. Following the 1957 increase, rates again remained constant—this time for five years. During the mid-1960s, rate changes occurred more frequently—in 1962, 1963, 1964, 1965, and 1966.

Not until 1964, did the growth rate of commercial bank assets first equal and then exceed that of the banks' principal rivals for consumer-type time deposits, the savings and loan associations. The inability of the commercial banking system to compete for time deposits, particularly in the 1950s and early 1960s, was one result of the Fed's failure to make more frequent adjustments in the maximum rates payable under Regulation Q. This in turn contributed to increases in the velocity of money and in spending. It was in 1964 that the Federal Reserve first increased the yield payable on time deposits with a maturity of less than 90 days from its traditional 1 percent to 4 percent.

Prior to 1964, most of the activity in nonsavings types of time deposits was conducted by the large money market banks in New York, which sold CDs to business enterprises having temporarily idle funds. This, of course, increased the reserves of these banks. Thus, activity in the CD market was and still is one way for individual commercial banks to acquire additional reserves. Following the Federal Reserve action of 1964 which raised maximum rates of interest payable on commercial bank time deposits, consumer-type time deposits (other than savings deposits) began a marked rate of growth. This contributed to the relative decline of nonbank financial-institution growth rates. Subsequently, in December 1965, the Federal Reserve again increased the maximum rates payable by commercial banks on time deposits. This increase was particularly marked and drew funds from other savings institutions. As mentioned in Chapter 5, the funds drawn from savings institutions are their deposits at commercial banks. These are cash reserves of savings institutions, and any reduction constitutes a decrease in their reserves and lending ability. The result, therefore, of the 1965 action by the Fed was a reduction in the lending ability of nonbank financial institutions, particularly savings and loan associations. Since savings and loan associations are a major source of funds for the construction industry, mortgage funds became very limited in 1966 and there was a slump in the housing industry. Increased Vietnam war expenditures, no federal tax increases, and high employment levels in 1966 justified some monetary restraint. The Fed's action was officially intended to keep commercial bank rates in line with other yields and "to enable banks to attract and retain time deposits of businesses and individuals and thus to assure an

TABLE 12-2 MAXIMUM INTEREST RATES PAYABLE ON TIME AND SAVINGS DEPOSITS, 1933–73
(PERCENT PER ANNUM)

NOVEMBER 1, 1933–JULY 19, 1966

TYPE OF DEPOSIT	Nov. 1, 1933	Feb. 1, 1935	Jan. 1, 1936	Jan. 1, 1957	Jan. 1, 1962	July 17, 1963	Nov. 24, 1964	Dec. 6, 1965
Savings deposits:								
12 months or more	3	2½	2½	3	4	4	4	4
Less than 12 months	3	2½	2½	3	3½	3½	4	4
Postal savings deposits:*								
12 months or more	3	2½	2½	3	4	4	4	4
Less than 12 months	3	2½	2½	3	3½	3½	4	4
Other time deposits:†								
12 months or more	3	2½	2½	3	4	4	4½	5½
6 months to 12 months	3	2½	2½	3	3½	4	4½	5½
90 days to 6 months	3	2½	2	2½	2½	4	4½	5½
Less than 90 days (30–89 days)	3	2½	1	1	1	1	4	5½

RATES BEGINNING JULY 20, 1966

TYPE OF DEPOSIT	July 20, 1966	Sept. 26, 1966	April 19, 1968	Jan. 21, 1970
Savings deposits	4	4	4	4½
Other time deposits:†				
Multiple maturity:‡				
30–89 days	4	4	4	4½
90 days–1 year	5	5	5	5
1 year to 2 years	5	5	5½	5½
2 years and over	5	5	5¾	5¾
Single-maturity:				
Less than $100,000:				
30 days to 1 year	5½	5½	5	5
1 year to 2 years	5½	5½	5½	5½
2 years and over	5½	5½	5¾	5¾
$100,000 and over:				
30–59 days	5½	5½	6	§
60–89 days	5½	5½	6	§
90–179 days	5½	5½	6¼	6¾‖
180 days to 1 year	5½	5½	6¼	7‖
1 year or more	5½	5½	6¼	7½‖

RATES BEGINNING JULY 1, 1973

TYPE OF DEPOSIT	
Savings deposits	5
Other time deposits	
Multiple maturity	
30–89 days	5
90 days–1 year	5½
1 year–30 months	6
30 months or more	6½
Single maturity	
Less than $100,000	
30–89 days	5
90 days–1 year	5½
1 year–30 months	6
30 months or more	6½
More than 1,000	
4 years or more	#
More than $100,000	#

* Closing date for the Postal Savings System was March 28, 1966.

† For exceptions with respect to foreign time deposits, see *Annual Reports* for 1962, p. 129; 1965, p. 233; and 1968, p. 69.

‡ Multiple-maturity time deposits include deposits that are automatically renewable at maturity without action by the depositor and deposits that are payable after written notice of withdrawal.

§ The rates in effect beginning January 21 through June 23, 1970, were 6¼ per cent on maturities of 30–59 days and 6½ per cent on maturities of 60–89 days. Effective June 24, 1970, maximum interest rates on these maturities were suspended until further notice.

‖ Rates suspended May 16, 1973.

\# No maximum rate of interest.

NOTE: Maximum rates that may be paid by member banks as established by the Board of Governors under provisions of Regulation Q; however, a member bank may not pay a rate in excess of the maximum rate payable by State banks or trust companies on like deposits under the laws of the State in which the member bank is located. Beginning February 1, 1936, maximum rates that may be paid by nonmember insured commercial banks, as established by the FDIC, have been the same as those in effect for member banks.

SOURCE: Board of Governors of the Federal Reserve System, *Annual Report* (1972), p. 246; and *Federal Reserve Bulletin* (July 1973), p. 522.

adequate flow of funds."[11] In actuality, the action turned out to be contracyclical.

Why did the savings institutions choose not to retaliate by raising their rates? After all, savings and loan association dividend rates at that time were directly determined by the individual associations, not by monetary authorities. They did not raise their rates principally because the Federal Home Loan Bank Board, for almost the first time in its history, began to exercise some contracyclical monetary power. The FHLB Board exercised indirect control over savings rates paid by federal savings and loan associations in 1966 by restricting the volume of advances its regional banks could make to savings and loan associations that had increased their dividend rate excessively. This policy was enforced from 1965 through mid-1966.

The contracyclical use of Regulation Q in December 1965 proved so effective that the Federal Reserve had to take action in mid-1966 to reduce the strong competitive edge that the commercial banks had gained. The Fed raised reserve requirements against time deposits and reduced the maximum rates payable on new multiple-maturity time deposits of 90 days or more from $5\frac{1}{2}$ to 5 percent and from $5\frac{1}{2}$ to 4 percent on similar deposits with maturities of less than 90 days. At the same time, the FHLB Board ended its advance restriction policy, and savings and loan associations began to increase their dividend rates. These actions of monetary ease may have been appropriate because one industry—housing—was being so sharply affected by contracyclical monetary policy.

Regulation Q was not used in 1967. Overall policy in that year, as noted in earlier portions of this chapter, was one of monetary ease. During April 1968, the maximum rates of interest payable by member banks on large denomination, single-maturity time deposits were increased. Consumer-type time deposits were not involved. This action was clearly aimed at keeping commercial bank rates competitive with other short-term rates.

Regulation Q was not used in 1969. In January of 1970, the interest ceiling on all time deposits was raised, an action primarily intended to "bring about greater equity in the rates payable on smaller savings balances. . . ."[12] And in June of 1970, the Fed removed the ceiling on the large denomination CDs with maturities less than 90 days principally purchased by large businesses with temporarily idle funds. Apparently the Fed's motive here was to permit commercial banks to compete with nonbank sellers of commercial paper in seeking short-term idle business funds.

Following 1970, there were no changes in the legal interest rate ceilings on time deposits at member banks, nonmember banks, mutual savings banks, or savings and loan associations until 1973. It appears that the slack in the economy that persisted from 1970 into early 1973 lowered the level

---

[11] Board of Governors of the Federal Reserve System. *Annual Report* (1965), p. 13.
[12] Board of Governors of the Federal Reserve System. *Annual Report* (1970), p. 8-II.

of interest rates on securities to the point that they no longer competed with the interest ceilings on time deposits; thus, the ability of banks to attract savings funds was not restricted.

By mid 1973, the U.S. economy was in a boom. The unemployment rate was down to 4.7 percent; prices were rising sharply; interest rates were at record levels. The prime rate on commercial paper reached 10 percent in September and the discount rate increased to $7\frac{1}{2}$ percent in August. In this economic climate, the government feared that commercial banks, savings and loan associations, and mutual savings banks would have difficulty in competing for funds with nonbank and nonsavings-institution suppliers of securities. Accordingly, the Fed, FDIC, and FHLB Board simultaneously raised the ceilings on interest payable on the time-deposit liabilities of all insured commercial banks, mutual savings banks, and savings and loan associations. The ceiling rates were raised more for commercial banks than for other financial institutions, possibly because commercial bank growth had dropped so markedly relative to savings institution growth in 1971 and 1972 (see Table 5–6). These measures proved unsuccessful in preventing the withdrawal of funds from these financial insitutions and their use in the purchase of high-yield securities issued by other classes of business. The net effect was contraction, primarily by savings institutions—a desirable occurrence from a contracyclical point of view, but an undesirable one for those institutions and their customers such as the housing industry. Raising the interest rate did not prevent disintermediation and a diversion of funds from one industry to another even though all industries competed more freely for funds.

Evaluation of Regulation Q. This is a comparatively new instrument of policy. If the Fed were to raise yields paid on time deposits by commercial banks relative to those paid by nonbank financial institutions and other borrowers, then nonbank lending activity could be restricted on the upward part of the cycle. Any potential expansion of the lending capacity of commercial banks could be eliminated at the same time via open maket operations.

This line of analysis assumes that other regulatory agencies such as the FDIC and FHLB Board would cooperate with the Federal Reserve in allowing relative yields on time deposits to change. Today the official policy of these agencies is one of cooperation to eliminate rate competition among various types of financial institutions. Since this means keeping relative yields on all time deposits approximately the same, a contracyclical use of Regulation Q to manipulate relative yields seems highly unlikely. A policy of maintaining relative yield levels may have some virtue, however, since it would tend to eliminate, at least in part, such undesired increases in the velocity of money as occurred in the 1950s and early 1960s. (See Chapter 5.)

On the other hand it can be argued that competition is the distinguishing characteristic of a free enterprise economy. Why set any legal ceilings on interest rates payable by financial institutions on their time deposits? Perhaps these institutions should be permitted to compete freely with each other and with nonfinancial business seekers of funds. Does not our present system result in a malallocation of financial resources? In competitive markets, the demand for and supply of funds determines interest rates and the distribution of available funds. Interest ceilings on the monies provided by small savers, who typically hold savings accounts and purchase small-denomination CDs, prevent these people from competing for the securities sold in high denominations to businesses. The small saver therefore channels his funds to banks and savings and loan associations. As Chapter 7 demonstrated, a high proportion of these funds find their way into the residential construction industry. In effect, interest ceilings on savings accounts and CDs for small savers result in an increased flow of low cost funds to the housing industry, and thereby constitute a subsidy to that industry. This line of analysis suggests that our monetary authority needs to reexamine its objectives—should it counter the cycle or give support to selected industries?

In addition, as we have already seen, a failure to lift the interest ceilings during periods of high interest rates diverts funds from financial institutions and their borrowers. These funds then move to less regulated financial institutions and borrowers. Again the question can be raised: Does our present system result in a malallocation of financial resources? Apparently the current administration in Washington, D.C., is now considering this question, since it was proposed in August 1973 that the ceilings on interest rates paid by banks and other savings institutions be phased out over a $5\frac{1}{2}$-year period.

Other Selective Credit Controls

Real-estate credit controls. Borrowing for residential construction can be controlled in a number of ways. The required down payment may be varied, the interest rates charged for mortgage loans may be manipulated, and the time allowed for repayment may be shortened or extended. For example, if monetary authorities believe that increased expenditures on residential construction during a period of full employment represent a primary source of rising prices, repayment periods can be shortened for new construction loans and interest rates and required down payments increased. This should cause spending on residential construction to decrease and the inflationary forces extant in the economy to diminish.

Real-estate credit controls were imposed for the first time during the Korean conflict. While in effect, they fixed minimum down payments and the maximum maturities for mortgage loans. It was hoped that higher down payments and shorter maturities would restrict the expansion of real-estate credit that had been taking place in 1950. However, the effectiveness of these controls was hampered by the backlog of construction orders that had been placed before the controls were scheduled to take effect. They also encountered considerable resistance from builders, the public, and veterans' groups. Real-estate credit controls expired in 1953.

Consumer credit controls. Controls over borrowing for residential construction purposes are only one set of selective credit controls that have been designed to regulate specific forms of spending. In addition to real-estate credit controls, we have also had experience with consumer credit controls. These controls are usually designed to regulate spending on consumer durable goods because consumer spending tends to fluctuate with the business cycle. Normally the purchase of such consumer durables as refrigerators and washing machines increases during the upward part of the cycle and decreases during the downward part. This type of spending behavior in itself tends to intensify whichever economic fluctuation is current. To the extent that consumers borrow to make these purchases and are sensitive to changes in the terms on which they may borrow, the use of consumer credit controls may lessen economic instability.

Consumer credit controls were imposed in World War II, from 1948 to 1949, and during the Korean conflict to relieve the inflationary pressure of increased expenditures on consumer durables. Minimum down payments were fixed and the terms of installment contracts limited. During World War II, the volume of consumer credit decreased, but this might have occurred even without credit controls. Increased incomes during the war encouraged debt repayment, and the lack of available consumer durables naturally restricted the total volume of expenditures for these items. One of the principal difficulties with consumer credit controls was the enforcement problem; the number of business establishments and the variety of goods covered was enormous.

Many economists in the past felt that consumers were not sensitive to interest rate changes but were responsive to the other terms upon which consumer goods were purchased. Hence they argued that general credit controls, which tended to affect interest rates, were ineffective as a means of regulating consumer spending. If this argument is correct, then direct control of consumption expenditures is a logical alternative. A more recent view "is that monetary variables have a significant effect on consumer purchases of durable goods and that the most appropriate measures of these variables are interest rates."[13] If this view is correct, and if consumer demand does respond to interest rate changes without too great a lag, then there should be no need for consumer credit controls. General credit controls, by affecting interest rates, would soon lead to changes in the amount

[13] Michael J. Hamburger. "Interest Rates and the Demand for Consumer Durable Goods." *American Economic Review* (1967), p. 1131.

of consumer durables demanded. The recently enacted "truth in lending" bill is designed to make consumers more aware of the true interest cost of borrowing.

Margin requirements. Unlike consumer and real-estate credit controls, regulations over stock market credit do not affect the volume of spending on real economic goods. Instead, selective credit controls over the purchase and sale of stock are designed to lessen speculation in stocks. For example, a margin requirement of 80 percent means that a lender may lend an amount up to 20 percent of the current market value of the stock that the proceeds of the loan will be used to purchase. Therefore, an increase in the margin requirement will decrease the amount that may be loaned for the purchase of stock. Theoretically, this should reduce the amount of borrowing for the purpose of purchasing stock and, at the same time, reduce speculation in securities. Furthermore, a reduction in borrowing to acquire stock should tend to reduce the demand for stocks and, consequently, to reduce upward pressures on stock prices. This is regarded as a significant move in a period of high stock speculation such as in an inflation, since rising stock prices increase the amount that can be borrowed for stock purchase purposes, given a fixed margin requirement. Increased borrowing can then lead to additional increases in the price of stock and a "pyramiding" of borrowing can take place.

Stock speculation in itself has little direct effect on spending for real goods and services in the economy. The danger of stock speculation lies in its influence on expectations. Rising stock prices may lead to a favorable economic outlook that is wholly unwarranted. Those whose stock holdings have sharply increased in value on paper may be induced by this to increase their borrowings and spendings on real goods and services. In a period of full employment, this can contribute to price inflation. In addition, if many stockholders then decide to collect their profits, this could cause a collapse of stock prices. Those who borrowed to purchase stocks or goods and services would be forced to liquidate asset holdings to repay their loans as they came due, causing stock prices to fall even further; lower stock prices and credit reduction might then lead to the expectation of an economic decline. If this occurs, spending plans would be reexamined and actual spending, income, and output would decline. Hence, it is often contended, there is a need for controls designed to lessen stock speculation.

Margin requirements are set by the Board of Governors in accordance with the Securities Exchange Act of 1934. Their purpose is to limit the amount of credit that may be extended on a security by prescribing its maximum loan value, which is calculated as a specified percentage of its market value at the time of credit extension. The *margin requirement* is thus the difference between the market value of the security and its maximum loan value. For example, if a security has a market value of $100 and if the margin requirement is 70 percent, then the maximum amount that may be loaned for the purchase of the security is $30.

Margin requirement control is regulated by the Federal Reserve to avoid a recurrence of the stock market speculation that occurred in the late 1920s. It was common practice during this period to purchase stocks almost entirely with borrowed funds. This created a strong demand for stocks and buoyed up their prices. Once stock prices broke, however, those who had borrowed were unable to cover their debts. When the value of stock fell beneath the volume of borrowings, borrowers could no longer obtain enough funds from the sale of stock to cover their debts. With the stock market crash of 1929, stock values declined so markedly that hundreds of thousands of people were financially ruined. Borrowers could not repay their loans; lenders were unable to collect. The outcome of this financial chaos was a complete revamping of our laws governing the sale of stocks, the establishment of the Securities and Exchange Commission, and the granting of margin requirement control to the Federal Reserve.

TABLE 12-3 MARGIN REQUIREMENTS, 1937–73
(PERCENT OF MARKET VALUE)

PERIOD		FOR CREDIT EXTENDED UNDER REGULATIONS T (BROKERS AND DEALERS), U (BANKS), AND G (OTHERS THAN BROKERS, DEALERS, OR BANKS)						
		On margin stocks			On convertible bonds			On short sales
Beginning date	Ending date	T	U	G	T	U	G	(T)
1937 – Nov. 1	1945 – Feb. 4	40						50
1945 – Feb. 5	July 4	50						50
July 5	1946 – Jan. 20	75						75
1946 – Jan. 21	1947 – Jan. 31	100						100
1947 – Feb. 1	1949 – Mar. 29	75						75
1949 – Mar. 30	1951 – Jan. 16	50						50
1951 – Jan. 17	1953 – Feb. 19	75						75
1953 – Feb. 20	1955 – Jan. 3	50						50
1955 – Jan. 4	Apr. 22	60						60
Apr. 23	1958 – Jan. 15	70						70
1958 – Jan. 16	Aug. 4	50						50
Aug. 5	Oct. 15	70						70
Oct. 16	1960 – July 27	90						90
1960 – July 28	1962 – July 9	70						70
1962 – July 10	1963 – Nov. 5	50						50
1963 – Nov. 6	1968 – Mar. 10	70						70
1968 – Mar. 11	June 7	70			50			70
June 8	1970 – May 5	80			60			80
1970 – May 6	1971 – Dec. 3	65			50			65
1971 – Dec. 6	1972 – Nov. 22	55			50			55
Effective Nov. 24, 1972		65			50			65

Note: Regulations G, T, and U, prescribed in accordance with the Securities Exchange Act of 1934, limit the amount of credit to purchase and carry margin stocks that may be extended on securities as collateral by prescribing a maximum loan value, which is a specified percentage of the market value of the collateral at the time the credit is extended; margin requirements are the difference between the market value (100 percent) and the maximum loan value. Regulation G and special margin requirements for bonds convertible into stocks were adopted by the Board of Governors effective March 11, 1968.
SOURCE: *Federal Reserve Bulletin* (July 1973), A-10.

Three specific regulations of the Fed — Regulations T, U, and G — cover the extension of credit for the purchase and carrying of securities. Regulation T applies to lending by brokers and dealers in corporate securities; Regulation U applies to lending by commercial banks on stocks listed on national stock exchanges; and Regulation G applies to lending by persons other than banks, brokers, or dealers for purposes of purchasing registered stocks. The margin requirements for all three types of lenders are the same.

The Federal Reserve frequently employs margin requirements as an instrument of contracyclical economic policy, as shown in Table 12–3. Margin requirements have been increased 12 times, in each case during a period of economic upturn. They have been decreased eight times, all decreases except those of 1947 and 1962 coinciding approximately with an economic downturn. The 1947 decrease followed an earlier 1946 increase to 100 percent; the 1962 decrease followed a sharp break in the price of stocks on the various U.S. stock exchanges in May 1962.

Evaluation of other selective credit controls. All forms of selective credit controls suffer from one main defect: *In the absence of direct controls on the manner in which individuals may spend their funds, there is almost no way in which credit controls can be made to produce the desired type of spending restriction.* It is always possible to borrow for one purpose and use the proceeds of the loan for some other purpose. When an individual borrows, the funds are simply placed in his checking account. No distinction is made between the borrowed funds and the other funds in that account. Thus, it would be possible to use the entire proceeds from an unsecured consumer loan for the purchase of stock. Even if the proceeds are actually used for some specified purpose, such as debt consolidation, the loan may still result in the freeing of other funds for speculation in real estate or stock.

This shortcoming inhibits the effectiveness of most selective credit controls. Although they are still used to some extent, they function at present as a minor tool of general monetary policy. Manipulation of the margin requirements for the purchase of stock and Regulation Q are the only forms of domestic selective credit control currently used by the Board of Governors. However, it should be noted that since 1969 the president has had the power to authorize the Fed to regulate and control all forms of credit extension. As of 1973, this power had not been used; yet these are latent tools and must be considered when evaluating the arsenal of our monetary instruments.

Finally, direct controls over real-estate, consumer, and stock credit extensions suffer from the same deficiency as the control over interest rate ceilings on time deposits — namely, they interfere with the competitive process. Controls prevent demand and supply forces from setting market interest rates and change the distribution of financial resources among businesses and individuals.

EVALUATION OF MONETARY CONTROLS

Have monetary controls been used in a contracyclical manner? The preceding discussion has reached the following broad conclusions, based on the historical effectiveness of each of the instruments of monetary policy.

First, the Federal Reserve has had the power to change reserve requirements only since 1935. From 1935 through 1973, the only move the Fed made in the wrong direction was the doubling of reserve requirements from 1936 to 1937. Other changes in the reserve requirement seem to have been correct in light of prevailing economic conditions.

Second, discount rate changes have generally been in the right contracyclical direction, particularly since 1951. However, the movement of discounts and advances, and the relation between the discount rate set by the Federal Reserve Bank of New York and the interest rate on four- to six-month commercial paper, seem to indicate that the changes made were frequently too mild. The increase in discount rates in August 1957 were probably a miscalculation. The decreases in rates in April 1967 and September 1968 were likewise inappropriate.

Third, open market operations have been a formal instrument of policy only since 1935, although they were used to some extent in the 1920s and early 1930s. Movements in security holdings of the Federal Reserve banks, although often inappropriate in the 1920s, were definitely used in an appropriate contracyclical manner in the early 1930s. The commitment to support prices in the government bond market eliminated open market operations as an instrument of contracyclical policy from 1935 until March 1951. Since that time, open market operations have generally resulted in correct contracyclical movements of Federal Reserve bank holdings of securities.

Fourth, the Federal Reserve does not regard Regulation Q as an instrument of contracyclical monetary policy. Yet the use of this instrument, for example, in December 1965 to raise the maximum interest rates payable on time and savings deposits, was so strong that it caused some slack in the residential construction industry, which in turn brought about compensatory action by the Fed in 1966. In addition, the use of Regulation Q did not prevent disintermediation from occurring in 1973.

Fifth, margin requirement changes have been appropriate since the end of World War II.

The preceding summary is based on the effectiveness of each policy instrument used separately. How well do these controls work together, however? Table 12–4 lists the various uses made of the major policy instruments in recent years and the effect of this combination of forces on the money stock. The last column shows the overall ease or tightness of Federal Reserve policy during each of the economic expansions and contractions since October 1949. Table 12–5 shows the movements in both the stock of money and in free reserves, which are also regarded as impor-

TABLE 12–4 THE USE MADE OF MONETARY INSTRUMENTS OF POLICY, 1949–73

REFERENCE DATES FOR U.S. BUSINESS CYCLES	USE OF RESERVE REQUIREMENTS	USE OF DISCOUNT RATES	DISCOUNTS AND ADVANCES	FEDERAL RESERVE BANK SECURITY HOLDINGS	GROWTH IN STOCK OF MONEY	OVERALL POLICY
Expansion following October 1949 trough, through July 1953 peak	+January, February 1951	+August 1950, January 1953	−1950 +1951 through July 1953 peak	+through whole expansion	+through whole expansion	Ease
Contraction through August 1954 trough	−July 1953; June, July, August 1954	−February, April, May 1954	−through whole contraction	−gradual decline in contraction	Slower than required growth	Ease
Expansion through July 1957 peak		+April, May, August, September, November 1955; April, August 1956	−remainder 1954 +1955–56	−1955; February–June 1957	Slower than required growth	Increasing tightness
Contraction through April 1958 trough	−February, March, April 1958	+August 1957 −November, December, 1957; January, March, April 1958	−through whole contraction	+March–April 1958	Almost no change	Tight in early part; ease in latter part
Expansion through May 1960 peak	−December 1959	+September, October, November 1958; March, May, June, September 1959	−remainder 1958 +1959 −March to May 1960	+May 1958– December 1959 −January 1960	At required growth in early part; decrease in latter part	Tight

		September 1960	contraction	contraction		
February 1961 trough	November, December 1960					Ease
Expansion through 1964	−October, November 1962	+July 1963; November 1964	−remainder 1961 +1963	+through 1964	Slow in early part; at required growth in latter part	Ease
Expansion through November 1969 peak	+July, September 1966 −March 1967 +January 1968; April 1969	+December 1965 −April 1967 +November 1967 +March, April 1968 −August 1968 +December 1968 +April 1969	+1965–66 −1967 +1968–69	+through 1969	Greater than required growth through 1968; slow growth in mid–1969	Ease through 1968; tight in 1969
Contraction through November 1970 trough	−October 1970	−November 1970	−1970	+through 1970	Steady growth	Tight
Expansion through 1973	+June 1973	−December 1970, January, February 1971 +July 1971 −November, December 1971 +January, February, April, May, June, July, August 1973	−1971–72 +1973	+through 1973	Greater than required growth through early 1973	Ease to mid 1973; increasing tightness in mid 1973

TABLE 12-5 ANNUAL PERCENTAGE CHANGE IN THE STOCK OF MONEY
AND DOLLAR CHANGE IN FREE RESERVES, 1949-73

YEAR	ANNUAL PERCENTAGE CHANGE IN THE STOCK OF MONEY	FREE RESERVES (IN MILLIONS OF DOLLARS)
1949	−1.0	706
1950	2.6	675
1951	4.5	467
1952	5.0	−66
1953	2.5	−91
1954	1.6	627
1955	3.1	−20
1956	1.2	−270
1957	0.6	−323
1958	1.2	297
1959	3.5	−353
1960	−1.2	116
1961	1.6	520
1962	2.2	421
1963	2.9	197
1964	3.9	107
1965	4.2	−90
1966	4.5	−276
1967	3.9	194
1968	7.1	−206
1969	6.0	−871
1970	4.1	−616
1971	6.8	−207
1972	8.3	−128
1973*	8.0†	−1,456

* Based on January–June 1973.
† Estimated by author.
SOURCE: Board of Governors of the Federal Reserve System. *Supplement to Banking and Monetary Statistics* (Washington, D.C., 1962), Section 1, p. 20, and Section 10, p. 56; various issues of the *Federal Reserve Bulletin*; and the Federal Reserve Bank of St. Louis' *Rates of Change in Economic Data for Ten Industrial Countries*, various issues.

tant indications of the ease or restrictiveness of Federal Reserve policy. Finally, Figure 12–1 shows movements in the money stock since 1962.

An Evaluation of Federal Reserve Policy Since 1951

Before evaluating the general implementation of monetary policy, some comment on the stock of money and free reserves as indicators of the ease or restrictiveness of policy is in order. It is the result of monetary policy that counts, not whether individual policy instruments were used appropriately. Some economists, in particular the quantity theorists (discussed in Parts IV and V), contend that changes in the money stock and economic activity are closely related. They judge the effectiveness of Federal Reserve policy by observing the rate of change in the stock of money. To them, a greater than normal increase in the money stock indicates a policy of ease; a less than normal increase indicates restriction. On the other hand, Federal Reserve action affects member bank reserve positions more

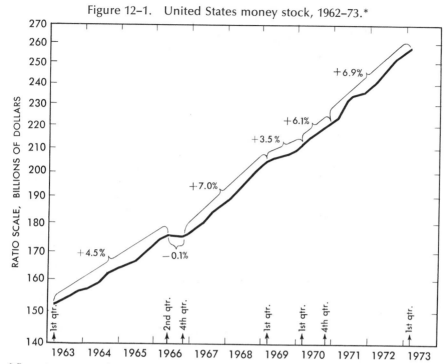

Figure 12–1.   United States money stock, 1962–73.*

* Percentages are annual rates of change for periods indicated.

SOURCE: Federal Reserve Bank of St. Louis. *Rates of Change in Economic Data for Ten Industrial Countries* (June 6, 1973), p. J-1.

directly than it does the stock of money. Thus, it can be reasoned that changes in member bank free reserve positions should be interpreted as indicative of policy change.

Free reserves are defined as member bank excess reserves less member bank borrowed reserves. A large volume of free reserves is interpreted as indicative of an easy money policy. As was shown earlier, a purchase of securities by the Fed raises bank excess reserves. This should induce banks to reduce their borrowed reserves, make it easier for them to lend, and hence cause interest rates to drop and the money stock to rise. Net borrowed reserves (*negative* free reserves) are considered to be a sign of a tight money policy. A sale of securities by the Fed should lower excess reserves, raise interest rates, discourage borrowing, and reduce the growth of the money stock. Actually, a given level of free reserves can produce either easy or tight money conditions, depending on the relationship between commercial bank desired free reserves and the free reserve level deemed appropriate by the Fed.[14]

[14] See William G. Dewald. "Free Reserves, Total Reserves, and Monetary Control." *Journal of Political Economy* (1963), pp. 141–53; and A. P. Meigs. *Free Reserves in the Money Supply* (University of Chicago Press, 1962).

Following the Treasury–Federal Reserve Accord of 1951, the FOMC used free reserves as a guide to open market operations. However, theoretical arguments and empirical evidence demonstrated deficiencies in using the level of free reserves as a monetary policy guide. By 1968, one Federal Reserve economist had already argued

. . . the Committee has come to rely less than in the 1950s on any single measure, such as free reserves. It tries instead, with the aid of its staff, to specify for a constellation of variables the ranges of short-term variation that are believed to be consistent with a projected rate of growth in total bank deposits over the next month or so.[15]

Since 1970, the directives of the FOMC to the account manager have expanded the targets to be considered in the implementation of open market operations as a contracyclical instrument of economic policy. In addition to free reserves, and interest rates (especially the Federal Funds rate – the rate at which member banks lend each other excess reserves), the Fed now considers such aggregate targets of monetary policy as the growth of the money stock and bank credit. In the analysis that follows, we shall use both the rate of change in the money stock and the level of free reserves as indicators of the actual course of Federal Reserve policy.

1951–65. Our previous analysis of the use of each policy instrument indicated that since 1951 the Federal Reserve has frequently followed a correct contracyclical policy. Since the Accord of March 1951 occurred in the midst of an economic expansion, we shall start our discussion with an earlier reference point – the beginning of this expansionary period in October 1949.

Normally, economic expansion during periods of high employment calls for a restrictive monetary policy, and economic contraction calls for monetary ease. In terms of the reference dates for United States business cycles listed in Table 12–4, this means that there should have been a policy of ease in the contractions of 1953–54, 1957–58, 1960–61, and 1969–70. The expansions of 1949–53 and 1955–57 called for some tightening of money and credit conditions, whereas those of 1958–60, 1961–64, and 1970–72 called for some ease in money and credit conditions, since the unemployment rate continued to be high after both the 1957–58 and 1969–70 recessions. The expansion of 1965–68 called for restraint, since the period was one of rising prices, high employment, and increased military expenditures.

Tables 12–4 and 12–5 and Figure 12–1 show that our experience with Federal Reserve policy has been mixed. *During the expansion following the October 1949 trough through the cyclical peak reached in July 1953,*

[15] Paul Meek. "Discount Policy and Open Market Operations." Prepared for the Steering Committee for the Fundamental Reappraisal of the Discount Mechanism Appointed by the Board of Governors of the Federal Reserve System (February 26, 1968), p. 9.

the Fed generally followed a policy of monetary ease. While discount rates were increased in August 1950 and reserve requirements were raised in early 1951, these movements were offset by Federal Reserve security purchases. The year 1952 was also one of monetary ease—witness the 5 percent increase in the stock of money. Nevertheless, member bank borrowings increased substantially in 1952, with the result that free reserves had became negative for the first time in 20 years. This may be considered a sign that the Fed moved toward a policy of some restraint late in the period as the threat of inflation became apparent.

Expansion during this period was unique until early in 1953. Employment levels were extremely high and prices were very stable. Prices had not yet increased, but fearing they would, the Fed sought to halt the incipient price inflation that might have started from bank credit expansion in a period when industry was operating close to capacity. As noted, free reserves became negative in 1952. Action was taken in January 1953 to raise discount rates in order to pressure banks into reducing their borrowings. Interest rates increased, and member banks attempted to improve their reserve position by reducing investments. This reaction of the banking system led the Federal Reserve to concur that its restrictive action had been too severe. A quick reversal of policy was made in May 1953, when the Fed increased its holdings of government securities. This action did not immediately result in a substantial easing of credit conditions, but the member banks' borrowed reserve position did decrease from −$631 to −$303 million from April to May 1953.[16]

How effective was Federal Reserve policy in controlling the expansion just discussed? In isolation, the use made of the reserve requirement and discount rate mechanisms was appropriate throughout the entire period; the actions taken were in the right direction. However, the movement of the stock of money and member bank free reserves indicates a policy of monetary ease through most of the period. This was clearly inappropriate in view of the prevailing high employment levels, and it is surprising that we did not have a price inflation in 1952. Restrictive action in early 1953, late in the expansion, was also inappropriate. On the other hand, the rapid change in policy from restriction to ease in May 1953 was clearly correct because it preceded the cyclical peak in July 1953 and the subsequent economic contraction.

The Federal Reserve tried to follow a policy of monetary ease throughout the *1953–54 contraction*. Reserve requirements and discount rates were lowered. There was a very small contraction in Federal Reserve bank security holdings, but it was not restrictive in character; the decrease in credit coincided primarily with the 1954 rather than the 1953 reserve requirement decreases. Thus, the impact of the July 1953 reserve require-

---

[16] Board of Governors of the Federal Reserve System. *Supplement to Banking and Monetary Statistics* (1962), Section 10, p. 14.

ment decrease was not undermined by offsetting reserve credit decreases. As a consequence, credit conditions remained relatively easy through much of the 1953–54 contraction. Member bank free reserves changed from a net borrowed position early in the contraction to a large free reserve position in the latter part of the contraction. The stock of money grew at a much slower rate than it had in the preceding expansion, however.

Federal Reserve policy became increasingly restrictive during the *1954–57 economic expansion*. Discount rates were increased and Federal Reserve security holdings decreased. Except in 1955, the money supply grew very slowly. For example, it increased only 1 percent in 1956, too small an amount to provide for the needs of a growing economy.

In economic expansion and boom, commercial banks need additional reserves to support increased lending. When those reserves are not provided by the Fed, member banks are forced to borrow at the discount windows. Beginning in early 1955, member bank borrowings increased sharply. Free reserves dropped, becoming negative in August 1955 and remaining that way through the remainder of the boom except for one month—January 1957. Member bank reserves, of course, did not increase. The borrowed reserves and some increase in float simply offset the decrease in member bank reserves that would otherwise have occurred as a result of the open market sales that were taking place. Member bank reserves, therefore, were not permitted to increase.

Without additional reserves to meet the demand for funds, banks had to reduce their investments to increase their lending activity. The net result of this action, as explained in Chapter 5, was a transfer of money balances from the less active portion of the nonbank public to the more active borrowing and spending portion. At the same time, the banking activity of nonbank financial institutions increased. Increased inflationary pressures were therefore at work in the economy.

The period of the 1954–57 expansion was one of high employment levels, rising prices, increasing private investment outlays, and rapidly increasing gross national product; monetary policy at the time was, appropriately, one of restraint. Ironically, however, prices increased in this period, since increased lending, together with price and cost increases in the automobile and investment goods industries, helped offset the effects of the restrictive monetary policy.

The *contraction* that followed the 1954–57 expansion was short but sharp. Unemployment increased substantially. Our monetary authorities were slow to respond to the downturn in the economy. Discount rates were increased in August 1957 and were not reduced until November. Reserve requirements were reduced in early 1958, and some open market purchases were made in March. Free reserves did increase as reserve requirements were lowered, but by this time we were already in the latter stages of a recession. The stock of money actually dropped during the 1957–58 contraction. Monetary policy for this period, therefore, does not appear to have been appropriate.

Federal Reserve monetary action during the *1958–60 expansion* is more difficult to interpret. Discount rates were increased three times in 1958 and four times in 1959. Such restrictive action is often appropriate in a period of business expansion. In all but four months of this period, however, the unemployment rate was in excess of 5 percent. The lowest average unemployment rate for any full year, $5\frac{1}{2}$ percent, was in 1959.[17] On the basis of the unemployment statistics, a policy of monetary ease would probably have been preferable.[18] Instead, the discount rate increases were so prompt and strong that, at the time of each increase, the discount rate for the Federal Reserve Bank of New York almost equaled the prime rate on four- to six-month commercial paper. This was as close as the Federal Reserve System came in the post-Accord period to pushing the discount rate above the commercial paper rate in economic expansion. This action came, however, when we still had a large volume of unemployment! To make matters worse, the high discount rate set in September 1959 was maintained for nine months; it was not lowered until six months after the commercial paper rate had begun to decrease.

Federal Reserve open market policy was significantly different from its discount rate policy during this period of expansion. Security purchases began in May 1958 and continued through December 1959. This would seem to indicate a policy of monetary ease, but such was not the case. Free reserves became negative in 1959. Most of the large increases in Federal Reserve security holdings were designed merely to offset other forces that were tending to decrease member bank reserves — namely, increases in currency in circulation and decreases in the gold stock. Federal Reserve security holdings from May 1958 through December 1959 increased by $3 billion, whereas the increase in currency in circulation and the decrease in gold stock were $2 billion and $2.3 billion, respectively. Since discounts and advances and float had increased, member banks reserves in the same period increased by $0.7 billion.[19] The one contradiction in this picture of monetary restriction was an increase in the money stock of 3.5 percent in 1959. It can be argued, however, that this increase represented merely a moderate "catching up" of the money stock to the legitimate needs of the economy. The average yearly increase in this economic indicator had been only 1.6 percent during the period 1953–58.

With economic growth, a larger population, and increased real output in the economy, some expansion of commercial bank reserves and the stock of money was surely needed. Federal Reserve policy, however, apparently called for limiting the availability of new reserves to member banks and

---

[17] *Federal Reserve Bulletins* (January 1960), p. 78, and (January 1961), p. 88.

[18] It must be recognized, however, that if an easy money policy leads to demand increases in those sectors of the economy that have full employment, price inflation will follow. It is important that spending increase where unemployment exists. If many people are permanently unemployed due to a lack of proper job skills, then inflation and less than full employment may exist simultaneously.

[19] *Supplement to Banking and Monetary Statistics, op. cit.,* Section 10, p. 19.

severely limiting the increment in the stock of money. *This policy was apparently based on the assumption that the expansion of 1958–60 was much like earlier expansions, with comparatively high employment levels and potential price level increases.* It is because this assumption was questionable that the policies of this period are difficult to interpret. First, the period was one of expansion, which theoretically calls for monetary restriction if inflation is to be avoided. Second, discount rates were increased — an appropriate action in light of the first point. Third, the Federal Reserve purchased securities, normally an expansionary action; but in this case the increase in security holdings merely served to offset other forces tending to decrease member bank reserves and open market policy remained basically restrictive, also an appropriate action in terms of the first point. Fourth, unemployment in this period was usually in excess of $5\frac{1}{2}$ percent, a level that theoretically calls for credit expansion and monetary ease. Hence, restrictive policies were inappropriate in light of the employment situation.

The *contraction* from *June 1960* through *February 1961* and the subsequent *expansion* as it continued into 1965 are generally believed to have been periods of monetary ease. Reserve requirements were lowered in the contraction. Discount rates were also lowered in the contraction, but were raised slightly in the expansion to reduce the gold outflow. Federal Reserve bank security holdings and free reserves both increased during the contraction and the early part of the expansion. Again, security purchases were greater than the increase in member bank reserves. As in preceding periods, the decreases in gold stock and increases in currency in circulation tended to absorb some of the reserve-creating potential of Federal Reserve open market purchases. At no time, however, did it appear that member banks were deficient in reserves. From June 1960 through December 1964, member bank free reserves were positive, although they became comparatively low at the end of 1963 and finally negative in 1965. All these forces indicate that monetary policy was expansive through both the contraction and the expansion in the first half of the 1960s.

In light of continued high unemployment levels, expansionary policy was appropriate. Unemployment did not drop below 4 percent until 1966. However, the data in Table 12–5 belie the preceding conclusion concerning the ease of monetary policy during the early 1960s. The stock of money had begun to decline in the fourth quarter of 1959. This may well have been a source of the 1960–61 contraction. The money stock continued to decline through the second quarter of 1960; not until the fourth quarter of 1961 did it again reach and finally exceed the 1959 high of $144 billion. Overall, the money stock decreased 1.2 percent in 1960 and increased only 1.6 percent in 1961. These figures show that policy actions during 1960–61 resulted in monetary restriction rather than the intended monetary ease. The following four years, 1962–65, brought average annual increases in the money stock of 3.2 percent — a figure more nearly in accord with the long-run need of the economy for an annual increase in the supply of money equal to the rise of productivity.

1965–69. Expansion in the economy continued *through November 1969*. Until September 1969, unemployment levels were always less than 4 percent.[20] The Fed switched to a policy of monetary restraint in 1965. Discount rates were increased in December, as were the rates payable on time deposits; free reserves declined to a net borrowed position early in the year. The stock of money continued to grow, however. The rate of increase in the money stock was 6.3 percent for the second quarter of 1965 through the first quarter of 1966, the largest rate of increase in any four-quarter period since the Korean conflict.

Stock of money and free reserve figures both attest to a policy of restraint through most of 1966. The money stock increased at a rate of −0.1 percent from the second through the fourth quarters of 1966. Net borrowed reserves increased to −$431 million in October and then sharply declined.

Late 1966 gave rise to a policy of monetary ease which continued through 1967. Unemployment rates, as we noted in earlier sections of the chapter, continued to be low. However, the use of Regulation Q in late 1965 had caused a slack in the construction industry through much of 1966. We find that free reserves became positive in March 1967 and remained so throughout the year. From the fourth quarter of 1966 through the third quarter of 1967 the stock of money increased 6.4 percent. Overall, in 1967, the stock of money increased only 3.9 percent, however. Discount rates were lowered slightly in April, and reserve requirements against time deposits were lowered slightly in March. Although the consumer price index rose 3.2 percent, no restrictive action was taken until the discount rate was increased in November. This policy of monetary ease hardly seems justified in view of the economic situation during 1967. The strongest expansionary force in the economy—the Vietnam war effort—had already been sharply expanded in 1965. In addition, ever increasing federal deficits and the failure of Congress to enact a tax increase contributed to rising interest rates and made it increasingly difficult for the Treasury to both finance the deficit and refinance old debt as it came due. Thus the Federal Reserve may have been forced into a policy of monetary ease in order to assist the Treasury in financing government expenditures. More and more frequently, FOMC policy directives to the account manager at the Federal Reserve Bank of New York included the provisional clause "taking account of expected treasury financing activity."[21]

More of the same was in store for the economy in 1968. Officially, the Federal Reserve followed a policy of monetary restraint. Free reserves

[20] This does not mean that all segments of the work force were prosperous. Unemployment rates for black Americans were substantially higher than those for whites. Teen-age unemployment rates were particularly high—often reaching 25 percent—among Negroes and other minority groups. Generally, high levels of employment bring into sharper focus continuing pockets of poverty; this gives rise to social and economic disruption as people in these areas realize their plight and begin to demand a greater share in the economy's wealth.

[21] See, for example, *Federal Reserve Bulletin* (October 1967), p. 1720.

finally moved into a net borrowed position in March. Increases occurred in reserve requirements in January, discount rates in March and April, interest rates on certain classes of time deposits in April, and margin requirements in June. Yet the percentage growth in the stock of money for the first two quarters of the year was $4\frac{1}{2}$ percent, with the overall annual rate of change having been $5\frac{1}{2}$ percent since the third quarter of 1967. This was a rate of change hardly consonant with restraining a booming economy.

Congress finally passed an increase in the income tax rate in July 1968. Anticipating some slack in the economy following this increase, the Federal Reserve lowered discount rates slightly in August and made it easier for commercial banks to meet their reserve requirements by instituting a change in the reserve accounting period. In addition, continued high military expenditures no doubt placed considerable pressure on the Federal Reserve to help in treasury financing activities.

What was happening to economic indicators during this time? Unemployment rates continued low, the consumer price index continued to increase, and anticipated decreases in demand failed to materialize. Business demands for investment goods and services continued strong, residential construction actually increased, and consumer demand continued high. It may well be that the private sector of the economy anticipated continuing price increases, and thereby offset some of the restraining effects of the tax surcharge.

In view of these facts, a policy of monetary ease was hardly appropriate during 1968. Only if demand had actually leveled off following the tax increase in July, would the move toward additional ease in the third quarter of 1968 have been warranted.

As noted earlier in our discussion of open market operations, economic policy became very restrictive early in 1969. Discount rates and reserve requirements were increased, government security purchases by the Fed for a time were negligible, net borrowed reserves increased markedly, and the stock of money grew very slowly. These were all signs of an appropriately restrictive monetary policy. On the other hand, the real rate of growth of the economy had slowed by mid-year, and some monetary economists were predicting an economic decline. It was felt that both the decrease in the growth rate of the money stock and the large increase in net borrowed reserves were too sharp—that the monetary authority had turned to a restrictive policy too late and too sharply. The federal budget moved toward a surplus—from a $25 billion deficit in fiscal 1968, to a $3 billion deficit in 1969, and a $3 billion surplus in 1970.[22]

1969–73. The growth of the economy which, aside from a short pause in 1966 had been continual since 1961, halted with the *peak of November 1969.* That the U.S. economy had entered its first recession in almost a

[22] *Federal Reserve Bulletins* (January 1971), p. A-41, and (September 1972), p. A-43.

decade was not at first generally apparent. But by early 1970, a recession was clear — a decline that would be accompanied by rising prices, as sometimes occurs when a recession follows an inflationary boom. The economic decline continued through November 1970.

The response of the monetary authority to the 1969–70 recession was sluggish. The growth rate of the money stock did not increase until the second quarter of 1970. The overall increase in the money stock in 1970 was 4.1 percent, what would have been considered a normal growth figure in other periods, but was now too low. With inflation persisting at a rate of 6 percent in 1970, the real stock of money actually decreased. Net borrowed reserves dropped in 1970, but not markedly until the latter part of the year when it was widely accepted that the economy was in a recession.

Federal Reserve holdings of government securities expanded, but by barely enough to cover the loss of reserves banks incurred as the amount of currency held by the public expanded. There was a small decrease in reserve requirements, and a drop in discount rates came late in the year. Unemployment grew from 3.5 percent in December 1969, to 5.0 percent in May 1970, and finally to 6.0 percent in December 1970.[23] In retrospect, it appears that the Federal Reserve and the administration may have worried more about inflation than the growing unemployment rate, feeling that rising unemployment would be temporary as the country moved from its heavy Vietnam war commitment to an economy more oriented toward peace. Overall, 1970 was a year of recession, mounting unemployment, rising prices, and a restrictive monetary policy. In view of the unemployment rate, monetary policy was inappropriate throughout 1970; in view of continued inflation during this period, it was appropriate.

A situation of simultaneous unemployment and inflation poses an enigma for a discretionary monetary authority. Economic theory tells us that most inflations are initially demand-induced and that, as full employment is approached, excess demand financed by a growing money stock and federal deficits leads to wage and cost increases. This was our situation in the late 1960s. The typical cure for inflation is to check demand expansion by cutting down the size of federal deficits and the growth rate of the money stock. But when demand is reduced in this manner, unemployment is bound to rise — particularly when money stock growth, increased taxes, and peacetime reconversion occur simultaneously. Can the monetary authority check inflation without raising unemployment? If not, should it check inflation at all? Questions of this sort continually plague the monetary authority. We shall return to them in Parts IV and V, where alternative economic policies and the possible trade-off between inflation and unemployment will be considered.

Officially the *trough* of the recession came in *November 1970,* and the ensuing expansion in national output continued *through 1973.* This expan-

---

[23] *Federal Reserve Bulletin* (January 1971), p. A-64.

sion was marked by continued high levels of unemployment. The unemployment rate hovered around 6 percent through all of 1971 and the first half of 1972, first dipping to 5.5 percent in June of 1972, then down to 5.0 percent in January 1973, and 4.7 percent in July 1973. It appears that the high unemployment rate decreased as slowly as it had in the last somewhat comparable expansion of 1962–64. Because of this, the monetary authority switched to a policy of ease in 1971 and, aside from a brief miscalculation late in 1971, the money stock grew at a rate well in excess of 6 percent through 1972. Discount rates were aggressively lowered in 1971, and Federal Reserve holdings of government securities expanded sufficiently to permit member bank reserves to rise by more than $2 billion in 1971. The federal budget swung from a $3 billion deficit in fiscal 1970 to $23 billion deficits in 1971 and 1972.

To combat inflation, the administration imposed selective wage and price controls in August of 1971. Whether these controls were appropriate is still a subject of debate among economists. True, the inflation rate declined following the imposition of controls. Yet if one accepts the "monetarist" view[24] that discretionary monetary policy affects the economy very slowly, it would follow that the decreased rate of inflation was attributable to the monetary restraints of 1969 and 1970. In any event, it appears that the administration tried to foster expansion in output and employment with money growth and federal deficits and to check inflation with economic controls on prices and wages.

As noted earlier, 1973 was proving to be a year of marked expansion. With decreasing unemployment, record high interest rates, and record advances in retail food prices, a restrictive monetary policy was needed. The Fed responded with increases in the discount rate and in the reserve requirement. In addition, for the first time since 1970, the federal budget seemed closer to being in balance by 1974. Since there was no desire for a repetition of the 1966 slack in the housing industry, ceilings on interest payable on time deposits at financial institutions were raised. Liquidity reserve requirements for savings and loan associations were lowered. These last two actions may have been designed to forestall an overall policy of monetary-fiscal restraint from causing an economic contraction.

Yet it increasingly appeared to many economists, including the author, that a sharp economic contraction was a strong possibility in 1974. The rate of money stock increase appeared to be dropping too sharply. Too many contractionary monetary instruments were being utilized simultaneously. These actions might have been taken as signs of an administration determined to combat inflation with traditional monetary-fiscal measures. If interpreted this way, they might have helped to stabilize price inflation at a high level of employment. There were too many uncertainties extant in the country, however. Was the monetary-fiscal restraint a mere expediency to

---

[24] Alternative monetary policies will be discussed in Chapter 26.

obscure the failure of direct wage and price controls—a policy that many economists had opposed all along? The Watergate investigations and the uncovering of possible mendacity by members of the administration in Washington, D.C., seemed to contribute to the weakness of the dollar abroad and adverse expectations concerning the economic future at home. All in all, 1973 was an economically and politically troubled year—one which did not lend itself to a favorable prescience about the economic future.

In general, an assessment of the appropriateness of Federal Reserve monetary policy since the Treasury–Federal Reserve Accord yields mixed results. Federal Reserve policy was appropriate *for the most part* in five periods: the contraction of 1953–54, the expansion of 1954–57, the contraction of 1960–61, the 1961–65 portion of the expansion of 1961–69, and the expansion of 1971–73. In the remaining periods, basic policy appears to have been incorrect. A number of specific monetary actions taken during these periods were correct, however, either on the basis of prevalent national economic trends or in light of what the monetary authorities considered to be the major economic problems of the period. *Our use of general monetary instruments will continue to be imperfect as long as our knowledge of the present status of the economy, of the probable course of economic events, and of the effect our use of monetary policy instruments will have on the behavior of the economy is imperfect. In addition, our use of monetary instruments will continue to be defective as long as monetary and fiscal policies are not coordinated. When wars are financed by federal deficits, almost inevitably the monetary authority supports Treasury financing operations with an ensuing abnormally high growth in the stock of money and prices.*

Additional Problems in the Use of Monetary Controls

Most economists agree that *general monetary controls can break the back of almost any inflation,* provided it is not stimulated by increases in bank reserves and the money supply due to conflicting expansionary policy actions. An increase in reserve requirements or a sufficiently large sale of government securities by the Federal Reserve banks can wipe out member bank excess reserves as quickly as they are created through discounts and advances. These techniques must be used in moderation, however, since there is always the danger of causing a sharp economic contraction rather than merely stemming rising prices.

On the other hand, as noted earlier, economists are by no means in agreement that an easing of credit and money conditions will produce economic recovery. The consensus is that, at best, monetary ease may encourage an economic upturn, but that the true source of a recovery is an increased desire to spend. We shall examine this thesis further in Parts IV and V, where monetary theory and alternative economic policies are considered. Some economists regard the presumed inability of monetary instruments to cause an economic upturn as the *principal shortcoming* of contemporary monetary policy.

There are other problems connected with the use of general monetary controls, too. An appropriate policy may be offset by other forces. For example, increased cold war pressures during a period of full employment may lead to an increase in government expenditures, a deficit, and rising prices — thereby offsetting a contractionary monetary policy. There may be little that can be done about such a situation in the absence of Congressional approval of needed tax increases — witness the situation caused by the delay in passing the 1968 surtax increase.

Also unfortunate is the fact that an appropriate policy may be partly offset by *forces touched off by the use of the instruments themselves*. There are basically three such forces: (1) velocity increases due to commercial bank asset and liability management, (2) velocity increases due to the lending activity of nonbank financial institutions, and (3) velocity increases attributable to nonmember bank lending and investing activity.

First, commercial bank asset and liability management may induce undesired changes in the velocity of money that would tend to offset an appropriate use of the instruments of monetary policy. For example, in periods of economic expansion, banks try to compensate for the restrictions placed on their lending abilities by selling investments. The purchase of these securities then draws down the comparatively idle demand deposits of the nonbank public. The banking system is then able to expand loans and create deposits in an amount equal to the reduction of its investments. The funds received by borrowers are active money balances and will be spent. Thus if there is no change in the money supply, its utilization will have increased. This velocity increase adds to the demand for goods and services and, in a full-employment economy, may lead to price inflation. The monetary authorities could then follow a more restrictive policy, but if applied too rigorously this might lead to an economic reverse. Furthermore, a tighter money policy might enhance the competitive position of nonbank financial institutions and, as some argue, further weaken the controls of the Federal Reserve system over the economy.

Banks are limited in their ability to transfer assets from investments to loans for the purpose of maximizing their earnings during an economic expansion. For liquidity purposes, the Federal Reserve insists that, in addition to required reserves, member banks maintain at least a certain amount of their assets in safe U.S. government securities. This restricts the shiftability of member bank assets. However, as noted in earlier chapters, banks have other forms of asset and liability management available to them. By competing for reserves in the Euro-dollar market, by selling certificates of deposit, or by having nonbank affiliates of one-bank holding companies sell commercial paper, the ownership of bank reserves can be transferred from less active to more actively lending banks. The result is again a change in demand-deposit ownership from less active to more active spenders, a rise in velocity, and an expanded demand for goods and services.

Second, velocity increases attributable to the increased lending activity of nonbank financial institutions may also occur thereby further weakening the effects of a restrictive monetary policy. Briefly, the funds that nonbank financial institutions attract come to them in the form of commercial bank demand deposits. When these funds are switched from inactive deposits at commercial banks to the accounts of nonbank financial institutions, these institutions will activate the money. The funds will be used to expand mortgage loans and corporate security holdings. Increased spending of a given volume of money will increase inflationary pressures. As long as nonbank financial institutions are able to attract deposits from commercial bank depositors and, at the same time, satisfy their own comparatively low reserve requirements, these institutions will continue to expand the velocity of the money supply and thereby to counteract a restrictive monetary policy.

Third, the regulations of the Federal Reserve System extend only to member banks. Although member bank deposit liabilities constitute better than 79 percent of the deposits of all commercial banks, in terms of total bank numbers, nonmember banks are in the majority. Nonmember banks are subject to state banking laws rather than to the Federal Reserve Act. The banking laws and regulations of many states are less stringent than the requirements of the Federal Reserve Act. As a result, the ratio of cash assets to deposits is frequently lower for state nonmember banks than for small member banks. Thus, nonmember bank loans increase proportionately more than those of small member banks during periods of monetary restriction. During periods of monetary ease, however, nonmember banks expand loans less than do member banks. This behavior pattern means that nonmember banks may be less responsive than member banks to changes in monetary policy.

Less stringent regulations make it possible for nonmember banks to offset the desired effects expected from a particular type of Federal Reserve monetary policy. If member bank lending activity is being restricted by the Federal Reserve, borrowers may be able to obtain loans from nonmember banks. Increased loans lead to an increased money stock and thus cause increased spending. To offset this trend, the Federal Reserve may have to tighten credit conditions even further for member banks. This situation has not yet occurred to any considerable extent because the size of nonmember relative to member banks is still small. This situation is changing, however. Nonmember bank demand deposits as a percentage of all bank demand deposits increased from 13.1 percent in 1947 to 25 percent in 1972.[25] Much of nonmember relative to member bank growth has been concentrated in periods of monetary restriction—one of the reasons why

---

[25] *Federal Reserve Bulletin* (August 1973), p. A-23.

economists and the government contend that all commercial banks should be required to become member banks.[26]

Conclusion

Our discussion of the instruments of general monetary control has emphasized the difficulties inherent in policy implementation. The basic tools have sometimes been used correctly; at other times, there have been miscalculations. Rapid changes sometimes occur in the economy, and it is difficult to predict both the course of economic fluctuations and the response of consumers and business to policy changes. The Vietnam war—like World War I, World War II, and the Korean conflict—reduced the Federal Reserve's freedom of action and forced it to follow a program of monetary ease. Nevertheless, the monetary instruments of policy discussed in Chapters 11 and 12 have been our principal weapons in combating cyclical movements in the economy since 1951. The Federal Reserve is constantly seeking to develop measures superior to those presently used in forecasting the future performance of the economy and its reaction to the discretionary instruments of monetary management. Perhaps entirely new techniques of monetary management will be necessary in the future. We shall consider some possible alternatives to the present policy instruments in Part V.

Supplementary Readings for Chapters 11 and 12

Board of Governors of the Federal Reserve System. "Research Studies Prepared for the Steering Committee." *Reappraisal of the Federal Reserve Discount Mechanism* (Washington, D.C., 1968).

Board of Governors of the Federal Reserve System. *The Federal Reserve System: Purposes and Functions* (Washington, D.C., 1963), Chapter 3.

Friedman, Milton. *A Program for Monetary Stability* (Fordham University Press, 1960), Chapter 2.

Friedman, Milton, and Anna Schwartz. *A Monetary History of the United States, 1867–1960* (National Bureau of Economic Research, 1963), Chapters 6, 7, and 11.

Goldenweiser, E.A. *American Monetary Policy* (McGraw-Hill, 1951), Chapters 8, 9, 10, and 11.

Hodgman, Donald R. "Selective Credit Controls." *Journal of Money, Credit and Banking* (1972), pp. 342–59.

Klein, John J. "Commercial Bank Behavior: Nonmember Bank Operations Relative to Reserve City and Country Member Banks." *A Report to the Bureau of Business and Economic Research*, Georgia State University (1972).

---

[26] See: Commission on Financial Structure and Regulation. *The Report of the President's Commission on Financial Structure and Regulation* (Washington, D.C., December 1971).

Mann, Maurice. "How Does Monetary Policy Affect the Economy?" *Journal of Money, Credit and Banking* (1969), pp. 538–48.

Mayer, Thomas. "Financial Guidelines and Credit Controls." *Journal of Money, Credit and Banking* (1972), pp. 360–74.

Saving, Thomas R. "Monetary-Policy Targets and Indicators." *Supplement to the Journal of Political Economy* (1967), pp. 446–56.

Smith, Warren L. "The Instruments of General Monetary Control." *National Banking Review* (1963), pp. 47–76.

13 Monetary Powers of Other Government Agencies

The Federal Reserve is the only government agency that has both the responsibility of promoting general economic stability and the power to do so. Other federal agencies possess monetary powers, but none have as their primary function the regulation of the entire economy. The Treasury, for example, implements the fiscal policies articulated by Congress and the president, but the extent to which it can operate independently of Congress and the president is very limited. The Treasury cannot increase spending or reduce tax rates in order to stimulate the economy in the same way that the Board of Governors can manipulate discount rates, reserve requirements, and open market operations. Other government agencies, like the Federal Housing Administration or the Federal Intermediate Credit Banks, have the power to affect specific types of credit extension, but they do not operate to promote general economic stability and growth. Only to the extent that their operations in one specific area of credit extension are contracyclical do these agencies contribute to overall economic stability. The Council of Economic Advisers, like the Federal Reserve, is concerned with general economic stability, but the Council's powers are principally advisory. It attempts to set up wage-price guidelines, makes projections about the future course of the economy, and recommends economic policy actions to the president.

In this chapter we shall briefly examine the monetary powers of various federal agencies and how, potentially, they can affect money and the economy.

THE U.S. TREASURY

The Treasury may influence commercial bank reserves and the money stock (1) by buying and selling gold and issuing SDR certificates, (2) by issuing coin and currency, (3) by movements in its balances at commercial banks, and (4) by various debt management techniques. It must be emphasized, however, that the Treasury does *not* have the power to create government deficits or surpluses. Congress and the president determine deficits and surpluses. The Treasury, through its debt management operations, merely determines how deficits will be financed, how tax surpluses will be used in debt retirement, and how debt will be refunded.

The Purchase and Sale of Gold and SDRs

The influence of gold and SDRs on bank reserve positions was briefly discussed in Chapter 10. It will be recalled that when the Treasury uses its funds at the Federal Reserve banks to purchase gold and monetize SDRs, there is generally an increase in member bank reserves and demand-deposit liabilities. Conversely, the sale of gold and the withdrawal of SDR certificates by the Treasury would tend to decrease member bank reserves and demand-deposit liabilities.

Since March 1968, treasury transactions in gold have virtually ceased. Until then, the Treasury bought and sold gold from foreign governments and in foreign private markets. In addition, it bought gold from domestic mines and sold it to domestic industrial users. Of these actions, only gold transactions with foreign governments continue today, and even these are so negligible that the U.S. gold stock has been almost constant since March 1968. The overall level of gold in major world treasuries has been frozen, with almost all new output being sold in the private gold market.

Treasury operations in monetizing Special Drawing Rights are negligible. For example, the volume of SDR certificates held by the Federal Reserve banks in 1973 was $400 million. Today, the activity of the Treasury in both gold and SDRs has little influence on the stock of money and bank reserve positions.

The Issue of Coin and Currency

When the Treasury issues coin and currency, Federal Reserve holdings of treasury coin and currency increase, as do the treasury deposit accounts at the Federal Reserve banks. As the Treasury uses its increased balances to purchase goods and services from the nonbank public, commercial bank reserves and the demand-deposit component of the money supply increase. As the Federal Reserve banks put the currency into circulation, demand-deposit money is reduced. Thus, only when the Treasury spends the proceeds from the sale of coin and currency to the Federal Reserve banks is there a direct effect upon the stock of money.

The Treasury puts additional coin and currency into circulation as it is needed by the public. In recent years, the demand for coins in particular has been greater than the ability of the Treasury to mint them. A reduction of the total volume of treasury coin and currency in circulation rarely occurs, although, as noted in Chapter 8, the Treasury did begin to withdraw its silver certificates in 1963. Federal Reserve notes are now used in place of low-denomination treasury notes.

As in the case of gold and SDRs, the Treasury does not manipulate the volume of outstanding treasury coin and currency in order to affect the volume of bank reserves and the money stock.

Location of Treasury Balances

The Treasury fully controls the location of its funds. They may be held in tax and loan accounts at commercial banks, in the general account with Federal Reserve banks, or in the Treasury's own vaults. As noted in Chapters 5 and 10, the Treasury usually makes payments out of its general account, places payments received into tax and loan accounts, and transfers funds from tax and loan accounts to the general account as expenditures come due.

The purpose of the tax and loan accounts is to soften the economic repercussions of treasury tax collections and bond sales. Were such receipts to be placed immediately in the general account and held idle until such time as the Treasury needed them, serious deflationary forces would be set into motion. By keeping tax and bond sale receipts in tax and loan accounts, bank reserve positions and total commercial bank demand-deposit liabilities remain unaffected. The deposits are merely redistributed from the taxpaying public to the Treasury.

Although it is evident that the Treasury manipulates its balances to avoid affecting commercial bank money-creating abilities adversely, the location of these balances is still a potential tool of monetary control. In the past, the Treasury has usually left adjustment of commercial bank reserve positions to the Federal Reserve. However, if the Treasury decided to, it could exert a powerful force on bank reserves by changing the location of its funds. By transferring $1 million from its general account to tax and loan accounts, for example, it could increase commercial bank reserves by $1 million. Assuming a 12 percent reserve requirement, commercial bank required reserves would increase by $120,000 (because of the increase in demand-deposit liabilities owed to the Treasury). Excess reserves, however, would increase by $880,000. In terms of the simple money-expansion formula introduced in Chapter 6,

$$D = \frac{R}{r} \qquad\qquad [6\text{--}1]$$

we have

$$D = \frac{\$880,000}{0.12} = \$7,333,333$$

Thus, in the event of a $1 million transfer of treasury deposits to commercial banks, the lending and money-creating abilities of the commercial banking system would increase by $7,333,333.

A transfer of deposits in the opposite direction—from tax and loan accounts to the general account—would have a strong contractionary effect. Total reserves, required reserves, and excess reserves would decrease by

$1 million, $120,000, and $880,000, respectively. The ability of the banking system to support demand deposits would thus be reduced by $7,333,333.

Similarly, if the Treasury decreased the amount of cash in its own vaults by $1 million and placed these funds in tax and loan accounts, there would be an increase in commercial bank reserves of $1 million, which again would result in a multiple increase in the lending ability of the banking system. On the other hand, if the Treasury demanded cash in exchange for balances in its tax and loan accounts, a correspondingly large contraction would take place.

Debt Management

Manipulation of the composition of the national debt is termed *debt management*. Our present federal debt is nearly $450 billion. Some 42 percent of this amount was held by various federal agencies, $72.0 billion by the Federal Reserve banks alone in early 1973. Some $262 billion in securities, however, is owned by the public. Table 13–1 gives a more complete picture of the ownership of the federal debt.

Important decisions must be made periodically by the Treasury with respect to the handling of this enormous debt. Refunding decisions have to be made. If there is a budget surplus, the Treasury must decide how to handle it. If there is a deficit, its financing will need treasury attention. These decisions have a significant effect on the banking system and on economic activity.

TABLE 13–1   OWNERSHIP OF PUBLIC DEBT
(PAR VALUE IN BILLIONS OF DOLLARS)

HOLDER	AMOUNT AT THE END OF JANUARY 1973
U.S. government agencies and trust funds	116.2
Federal Reserve banks	72.0
Commercial banks	66.0
Mutual savings banks	2.6
Insurance companies	6.1
Other corporations	12.3
State and local governments	29.5
Individuals	
Savings bonds	58.0
Other securities	16.8
Foreign and international investors	54.3*
Other miscellaneous investors	16.3†
Total gross debt	450.1

* Includes investments of foreign balances and international accounts in the United States.
† Includes savings and loan associations, dealers and brokers, nonprofit institutions, and corporate pension funds.
SOURCE: *Federal Reserve Bulletin* (March 1973), p. A-44.

Refunding. The term *refunding* is used to describe the issuance of new debt and the use of the proceeds to retire old debt. Almost 50 percent of all marketable U.S. government securities have a maturity of less than one year.[1] As a consequence, a large volume of debt is refunded annually. The Treasury must decide what type of security is to be used to replace old debt as it comes due. Since the ownership distribution of securities may be affected by the refunding decision, bank reserve positions may also be affected. For instance, if new issues are sold to the commercial banks, and the proceeds used to retire securities held by the Federal Reserve banks, commercial bank reserves will decrease. The balance-sheet changes for such a transaction are:

BALANCE-SHEET CHANGES FOR THE COMMERCIAL BANKING SYSTEM

ASSETS	LIABILITIES + CAPITAL ACCOUNTS
U.S. government securities +$1,000,000 (a)	U.S. government demand deposits +$1,000,000 (a)
Reserves −$1,000,000 (b)	U.S. government demand deposits −$1,000,000 (b)

BALANCE-SHEET CHANGES FOR THE FEDERAL RESERVE SYSTEM

ASSETS	LIABILITIES + CAPITAL ACCOUNTS
U.S. government securities −$1,000,000 (b)	Member bank reserves −$1,000,000 (b)

Entries labeled (a) show the effects of the sale of the securities; entries labeled (b) show the effects of the retirement of securities held by the Federal Reserve banks.

On the other hand, had the new securities been sold to the Federal Reserve System and the proceeds used to retire old securities held by the commercial banking system, the situation would have been reversed. Commercial bank reserves would have increased and their ability to lend and create money would have been expanded.

In general, if new securities are sold to the commercial banking system or the nonbank public and the proceeds are used to retire debt held by government agencies, the result will be a decrease in commercial bank lending ability. If, however, new securities are sold to the Federal Reserve banks (this can be done only in very limited quantities) and the proceeds used to retire debt held by the nonbank public or the commercial banking system, then commercial bank reserve positions will be improved.

Surpluses. When the federal government collects more in taxes than it spends, a surplus is created. It is up to the Treasury to decide whether to

[1] *Federal Reserve Bulletin* (March 1973), p. A-45.

hold the surplus idle or to use it to retire part of our debt. If the Treasury decides to retire debt, then commercial bank reserves will be affected, depending on whose debt holdings are retired.

The surplus itself represents a decrease in nonbank public demand-deposit holdings and an increase in treasury accounts. If the debt retired is held by the nonbank public, then the surplus and debt retirement have no effect on bank lending positions; demand deposits are simply redistributed from one part of the nonbank public (taxpayers) to another (bondholders). If the debt retired is held by the Federal Reserve banks, commercial bank reserves are reduced. If the debt is held by commercial banks, there is no change in total bank reserves; excess reserves are increased, however, because of an overall decrease in commercial bank demand-deposit liabilities:

BALANCE-SHEET CHANGES FOR THE COMMERCIAL BANKING SYSTEM

ASSETS	LIABILITIES + CAPITAL ACCOUNTS
	Nonbank public demand deposits −$1,000,000 (a)
	U.S. government demand deposits +$1,000,000 (a)
U.S. government securities −$1,000,000 (b)	U.S. government demand deposits −$1,000,000 (b)

Entries labeled (a) show the effects of the tax surplus; entries labeled (b) show the effects of the security retirement on commercial banks.

Deficits. When the federal government spends more than it collects in taxes, funds must be found to meet the excess expenditures. Two alternatives exist: (1) the Treasury may print more currency and use it to meet the deficit, or (2) it may borrow the funds. In the United States the first alternative is not considered acceptable. Therefore, the Treasury resorts to borrowing: it issues new government securities. The principal purchasers of new securities are the nonbank public and the commercial banking system.

When funds are borrowed from the commercial banking system, there is an initial increase in commercial bank holdings of U.S. government securities and an equal increase in treasury tax and loan accounts. Since the banks have used some of their capacity for loan and investment expansion to buy government securities, their ability to make loans to the nonbank public is decreased. Subsequently, as the Treasury spends the proceeds of the loan, money balances will be transferred to the nonbank public. The net effect of financing a deficit in this manner is an increase in the demand-deposit holdings of the nonbank public and thus in the stock of money.

A deficit need not always result in an increase in the stock of money, however. If the Treasury were to sell securities to the nonbank public, for example, there would be no change in the money stock. Instead, demand deposits would be transferred from one part of the nonbank public—those who bought bonds—to the U.S. Treasury, and then in turn to another part of the nonbank public—those who sell goods and services to the Treasury. Thus, money balances would simply be redistributed among the members of the nonbank public. The impact of this redistribution of deposit ownership, however, is not likely to be neutral. Those who produce goods and services for sale to the Treasury generally utilize their money balances more intensively than those who purchase securities. As a result, the velocity of the money supply increases, thereby leading to increased expenditures in the economy.

It is very dangerous to finance a deficit in an inflationary period by selling new securities to the central bank. If the Treasury were to sell securities to the Federal Reserve banks and then spend the proceeds, commercial bank reserves and demand deposits would initially increase by an equal amount. Without any offsetting action by the central bank, the banking system could then create deposits by a multiple of the volume of excess reserves created by the rise in total reserves. This would set more inflationary forces in motion. It is equally dangerous to finance a deficit by having the central bank support the government bond market by purchasing securities previously purchased by the nonbank public and the commercial banking system. The results are the same as if the central banking system had bought the securities in the first place—commercial bank reserves increase. A large part of our World War II and Vietnam deficits were financed in precisely this manner, and the result was continued inflationary pressures in the economy.

Debt management and economic fluctuations. As we have seen, treasury debt management techniques can affect commercial bank reserve positions and money-creating abilities in a variety of ways. Refunding may expand or contract reserves, depending on whose securities are retired and who purchases the new securities. To the extent that the central banking system buys new securities, commercial bank reserves will probably increase. To the extent that the central banking system has its security holdings retired by the Treasury, commercial bank reserves will probably decrease, unless the Federal Reserve also buys new securities. In addition, a treasury surplus reduces bank reserves when it is used to retire securities held by the Federal Reserve. A deficit expands reserves when the Federal Reserve banks buy newly issued government securities.

Normally, however, the Treasury does not make debt management decisions for the specific purpose of regulating the economy through the banking system. It uses debt management to complement the activities of the Federal Reserve, not to interfere with them. *The principal job of regulation is left to the Board of Governors of the Federal Reserve System.* Not that there is never any treasury interference with Federal Reserve policy actions. The support of the government bond market by the Federal

Reserve during and after World War II is an excellent example of how a decision to manage the debt in a particular way—in this case to keep the interest burden low—can interfere with the monetary authorities' control of the banking system.

From the point of view of economic stability, it is advisable for the Treasury to avoid changes in the maturity, ownership, and interest yields of the federal debt that provoke procyclical reactions in the economy. Whenever possible, debt management decisions should be contracyclical.

What would be appropriate contracyclical treasury debt management policy? In a *recession,* the following guidelines might be used: *First,* if there is a deficit and the recession is severe, then the debt should be financed through the sale of securities to the central banking system.[2] However, if the recession is mild, the securities should be sold either to the commercial banks or to the nonbank public. In a mild recession, the economy may be overstimulated by the sharp increase in reserves that arises from central bank security purchases. *Second,* if there is a tax surplus (which is unlikely in a recession), it should not be used to retire securities held by the central banking system, since this would reduce commercial bank reserves. Instead, it should be used to retire securities held by either commercial banks or the nonbank public. This would help somewhat in reducing the deflationary effects of the surplus itself. *Third,* new security issues and debt retirement should be manipulated in such a way that the *maturity structure of the debt is shortened.* The growth and prosperity of the economy are in large part dependent upon business investment expenditures. If the Treasury were to lengthen the maturity of the debt by selling long-term securities in a recession, a reduction of funds available for business investment might occur. Government debt is virtually without risk in terms of the ability of the borrower to repay it. Since private securities, on the other hand, generally involve some element of risk, in a recession lenders may be more inclined to purchase long-term government securities than corporate bonds. It is therefore advisable for the Treasury to shorten the maturity of the debt, permitting long-term funds to be channeled into business investment.

In an inflation, these policies should be reversed. *First,* if there is a deficit, it should not be financed by selling securities to the central bank. Such a move would be extremely inflationary. *Second,* if there is a surplus, it should be used to retire securities held primarily by the central bank. This will draw down the reserves of commercial banks and thus reduce their

[2] An even more efficient way of financing increased government expenditures during a severe recession would be pure money creation. Were the central bank able to finance the increased expenditures by creating money without simultaneously purchasing new treasury securities, there would be no increased interest burden on taxpayers and no accompanying problem of the deflationary aspects of possible future debt retirement. So drastic a measure would be advisable only for depressions of the magnitude experienced in the 1930s, however. Given an irresponsible legislature and executive, this policy could be disastrous in periods of full employment.

money-creating potential. *Third,* the maturity structure of the debt should be lengthened. If the Treasury concentrates on the sale of long-term securities, long-term funds may be drawn away from business investment, thereby reducing inflationary pressures. Unfortunately, this is precisely the period in which the Treasury may find it difficult to market long-term issues. During periods of full employment and inflation, interest rates are bid up by competitors for funds. Until 1973, the Treasury was prohibited by law from marketing issues maturing in five or more years at interest yields in excess of $4\frac{1}{4}$ percent, making it difficult for government securities to compete with private enterprise for long-term funds.

The Treasury made some effort to lengthen the maturity structure of the debt during the 1960s. From the latter months of the 1960–61 recession to September 1964, the average maturity of marketable U.S. government securities held by the public increased from 54 months to 66 months.[3] Much of this change in the composition of the debt was accomplished through the use of *advanced refunding.* Under this system, the Treasury offered owners of government securities new, longer-term issues in exchange for their old securities prior to the time they were due to mature. To induce bondholders to make the exchange, the new securities had a higher yield. However, starting in 1965 the Treasury found it increasingly difficult to use the advanced refunding technique. The expanded Vietnam war effort and inflation required increased treasury financing; competing domestic interest rates also increased. The net effect was to again reduce maturity structure of the federal debt. From the middle of 1965 to the end of 1972, the average maturity of marketable securities decreased from five years four months to three years one month.[4]

OTHER FINANCIAL PROGRAMS

The list of government agencies engaged in lending and insuring debt is almost too long to enumerate. We have noted in earlier chapters that the FDIC insures the deposit liabilities of commercial banks and mutual savings banks up to a maximum of $20,000 per account; the Federal Savings and Loan Insurance Corporation insures savings and loan share accounts up to the same amount; and the National Credit Union Association insures the accounts of credit union members. In addition, Federal lending and insurance programs are concentrated principally in three fields: agriculture, business, and housing. Federal activity in these fields involves both direct loans and participation in, or insurance of, private loans.

The Small Business Administration is the federal agency presently engaged in small business lending. Various types of agricultural loans are made by the Rural Electrification Administration, the Farmers Home Ad-

---

[3] Thomas R. Beard. *U.S. Treasury Advanced Refunding* (Washington, D.C.: 1966), p. 12.
[4] *Economic Report of the President* (1973), p. 274.

ministration, Banks for Cooperatives, and the Federal Land Banks. In addition, the Federal Intermediate Credit Banks are a source of funds for other agencies that lend to agriculture. Finally, various federal agencies are extensively engaged in extending or insuring real-estate credit. There was $335.1 billion in mortgaged debt outstanding on nonfarm family-unit dwellings in 1972. One-third of this debt was either insured by the Federal Housing Administration or guaranteed by the Veterans Administration.[5] The Federal Home Loan Bank Board and the Federal National Mortgage Association also have a significant impact on real-estate credit. (These two agencies will be discussed separately in the following section.)

How important are these extensive federal loan and insurance programs to monetary stability? Because they are designed to help particular industries, individual home purchasers, and specific firms, they may have procyclical effects. For example, in periods of full employment and rising prices, it frequently becomes difficult for small businesses to borrow for purposes of expansion. As the Federal Reserve makes it increasingly difficult for commercial banks—an important source of funds for small businesses—to lend, they will lend only to their larger and presumably more credit worthy customers. Small businesses then turn to the Small Business Administration for funds, and as the lending activity of the SBA expands, total lending in the economy increases. Thus, by providing additional funds in a period of inflation, a federal agency may make it more difficult for the Federal Reserve to regulate economic activity.

On the average, it appears that the various federal credit programs behave perversely relative to economic activity. One study of these programs in the 1950s argued that "Since World War II, they have created inflationary pressures in every year."[6] During the 1950s, the net change in total credit extended by federal agencies was positive in each year. Except for the recessions of 1953–54 and 1957–58, however, at least some *decrease* in credit extension was called for on contracyclical grounds. Thus, for the period through 1958, it seems reasonable to conclude that federal credit programs frequently had a procyclical effect.

Their record for the 1960s and early 1970s was not much better. Table 13–2 summarizes the lending and insurance activities of various federal credit agencies since 1959. Agricultural loans by Banks for Cooperatives, a federal program, increased in 1959 but remained steady during the recession of 1960–61. Subsequently, their loans increased every year through 1970, but remained stable in the relatively slack employment years of 1970–71. Federal Intermediate Credit Bank loans and discounts expanded in every year from 1959 through 1972. Likewise, Federal Land Bank mortgage loans increased each year during the same period. Thus, the last two agencies—the Federal Land Banks and Federal Intermediate Credit

---

[5] *Federal Reserve Bulletin* (March 1973), p. A-51.
[6] Warren A. Law. "The Aggregate Impact of Federal Credit Programs on the Economy," in Commission on Money and Credit. *Federal Credit Programs* (Prentice-Hall, 1963), p. 310.

TABLE 13-2 BALANCE-SHEET ITEMS FOR VARIOUS FEDERAL CREDIT AGENCIES, 1959–72
(IN MILLIONS OF DOLLARS)

YEAR	FEDERAL HOME LOAN BANK ADVANCES (END OF PERIOD)	FEDERAL HOME LOAN BANK ADVANCES (DURING PERIOD)	FEDERAL NATIONAL MORTGAGE ASSOCIATION MORTGAGE HOLDINGS (END OF PERIOD)	BANKS FOR COOPERATIVES LOANS TO COOPERATIVES (END OF PERIOD)	FEDERAL INTERMEDIATE CREDIT BANKS LOANS AND DISCOUNTS (END OF PERIOD)	FEDERAL LAND BANKS MORTGAGE LOANS (END OF PERIOD)	FHA INSURED RESIDENTIAL LOANS MADE	VA GUARANTEED RESIDENTIAL LOANS MADE
1959	2,134	2,067	5,531	622	1,397	2,360	7,694	2,787
1960	1,981	1,943	6,159	649	1,501	2,564	6,293	1,985
1961	2,662	2,882	6,093	697	1,650	2,828	6,546	1,829
1962	3,479	4,111	5,923	735	1,840	3,052	7,184	2,652
1963	4,784	5,601	4,650	840	2,099	3,310	7,216	3,045
1964	5,325	5,565	4,412	958	2,247	3,718	8,130	2,846
1965	5,997	5,007	4,731	1,055	2,516	4,281	8,689	2,652
1966	6,935	3,804	7,063	1,290	2,924	4,958	7,320	2,600
1967	4,386	1,527	8,870	1,506	3,411	5,609	7,150	3,405
1968	5,259	2,734	11,387*	1,577	3,654	6,126	8,275	3,774
1969	9,289	5,531	15,770*	1,732	4,275	6,714	9,129	4,072
1970	10,615	3,256	20,686*	2,030	4,974	7,186	11,982	3,440
1971	7,936	2,714	23,085*	2,076	5,669	7,917	14,689	5,961
1972	7,979	4,790	24,904*	2,298	6,094	9,107	12,320	8,293

* Includes mortgage holdings of Goverment National Mortgage Association and Federal National Mortgage Association. Since 1968, GNMA has carried on the former special assistance and liquidity and management functions of FNMA.

SOURCE: *Federal Reserve Bulletins* (September 1965), pp. 1314, 1321; (April 1969), pp. A-37, A-49, A-50; (July 1973), pp. A-38, A-51, A-52, and A-53.

Banks—acted procyclically except in the 1960–61 and 1970 recessions. The operations of Banks for Cooperatives were always procyclical.

FHA insured mortgages also behaved procyclically in the early 1960s, increasing prior to the 1960–61 recession, decreasing during the recession, and increasing again from 1962 through 1965. The FHA made fewer loans in 1966 and 1967, not out of concern for contracyclical policy but because interest yields on FHA insured mortgages were significantly lower than those on conventional mortgages and lenders were reluctant to purchase the FHA insured mortgages. This is reflected in the activity of the Federal National Mortgage Association, which sharply increased its holdings of FHA insured mortgages in 1966 and 1967. Subsequently, FHA insured loans expanded through 1972, apparently acting procyclically in 1968 and contracyclically in succeeding years. VA guaranteed mortgages behaved procyclically until 1964. The GI Bills of Rights, as well as the buildup of the armed forces and their subsequent decrease during the Vietnam conflict make it difficult to interpret the data concerning VA guaranteed mortgages from 1964 through 1972.

Apparently most federal lending and insuring agencies respond to demands for their services instead of taking aggressive contracyclical actions. The demand for funds behaves procyclically; accordingly, so do the activities of the majority of federal financial agencies.

The Federal Home Loan Bank Board

The Federal Home Loan Bank System is composed of four groups: the Federal Home Loan Bank Board, eleven Federal Home Loan Banks, the member institutions, and the Federal Savings and Loan Insurance Corporation. The board, which consists of three members appointed by the president for four-year terms, is the principal regulatory authority and controls the entire system. The Federal Home Loan Banks extend credit to member institutions. These are principally state-chartered and federal savings and loan associations, although a few savings banks are members and membership in the system is also open to insurance companies. The functions of the Federal Savings and Loan Insurance Corporation are similar to those of the FDIC.

Savings and loan associations are an important source of real-estate credit. As we noted in Chapters 7 and 12, mortgage loans are their principal asset. Increases in savings and loan share accounts provide most of the funds available to the associations for investment. However, borrowings from regional Federal Home Loan Banks are another source of funds. These borrowings can be used for emergencies, for balancing seasonal flows of funds, and for meeting the demand for mortgage funds when local increments in savings and loan share accounts are not sufficient to do so.

The maximum amount any member can borrow from the Federal Home

Loan Banks is set by statute at 50 percent of its liability for shares and deposits. Within this limitation, regional banks establish lines of credit for each member in the district. In addition to the statutory limitation, the Federal Home Loan Bank Board has established a basic limitation on borrowing for expansion purposes. Such borrowing cannot exceed $17\frac{1}{2}$ percent of a member's withdrawable accounts. Rates charged for new advances and existing loans are determined by the regional bank's cost of borrowing. A borrowing member must hold stock in its Federal Home Loan Bank equal to $\frac{1}{12}$ of 1 percent of its indebtedness to the bank, and all members must hold stock in the system equal in value to not less than 1 percent of the net balance of their mortgage loans.

One of the original objectives of the Federal Home Loan Bank System was to provide funds to member associations for expansion. Funds were to be made available to members where local savings were inadequate for such purposes. As Chapter 12 pointed out, this objective was temporarily modified in both 1965 and 1966. For example, in September 1965, the board issued a policy statement to regional banks forbidding advances for participation loans involving associations outside the borrowing member's normal lending area. In November 1965, the board advised regional banks that member borrowing in anticipation of future needs violated the System's general policy on advances. In April 1965, the board had recommended to the regional banks that the borrowing privileges of members that had raised dividend rates at the end of the preceding year be restricted. As a result of this policy, and the use of Regulation Q by the Federal Reserve in late 1965, the ability of savings and loan associations to compete for funds was severely diminished. The growth rate of these associations began to decline, and lending for construction purposes was curtailed. The subsequent drop in construction activity, as we noted in Chapter 12, helped restrict spending. Thus, for the first time in its history, the Federal Home Loan Bank Board was following a contracyclical economic policy. For reasons discussed earlier, the board abandoned this policy in July 1966. Since that time, the Federal Reserve and the Federal Home Loan Bank Board have cooperated to reduce the competition among savings and loan associations and commercial banks for individual-type time deposits.

Today regulation of the economy is left to the Federal Reserve, and the Federal Home Loan Bank Board is again concentrating on its early objectives. It feels that "The primary role of the Federal Home Loan Bank System is to provide members with the maximum amount of funds economically feasible to meet withdrawals and to make home mortgage loans."[7] Table 13–2 shows that Federal Home Loan Bank advances are generally procyclical. The Federal Home Loan Bank Board, like other federal credit agencies, responds to the demand for advances when providing funds for savings and loan associations. However, because its ac-

[7] Federal Home Loan Bank Board. *Annual Report* (1970), p. 43.

tions affect credit conditions and the ability of savings and loan associations to lend, it is prudent for the board to coordinate its policies with those
of the Federal Reserve. It does attempt to do this.

The Federal National Mortgage Association

The Federal National Mortgage Association received its charter in 1938
with the passage of the National Housing Act. This act was intended to assist the home-construction industry at that time and to provide financing
for mortgages. Until 1968, the FNMA operated as a quasi-governmental
agency, but it now acts as a public stock company. Congress passed legislation in 1968 enabling the FNMA to operate as a private enterprise.

The principal and best-known function of FNMA is its secondary
market operations. These operations provide assistance to the home-
mortgage market by increasing the liquidity of mortgages at times when the
normal buyers of mortgages are not active in the market. The FNMA does
not make mortgage loans directly, but offers to buy those held by other
institutions. It also stands ready to sell mortgages from its portfolio.

Any institution wishing to sell mortgages to the FNMA must purchase
common stock in the association in an amount equal to $\frac{1}{4}$ of 1 percent of the
funds to be committed by the FNMA. To be acceptable for purchase by
the FNMA under its secondary market operations, each mortgage must
cover residential property. These may be conventional mortgages, or they
may be mortgages insured by the FHA or guaranteed by the VA.

Numerous banks, mortgage companies, and realty firms are authorized
to do business with the FNMA. *It is the intention of the FNMA to act as a
temporary holder of mortgages. Theoretically, it buys at a time when there
are no other buyers and sells when the demand for mortgages is on the
increase.* The FNMA finances its operations through the sale of deben-
tures in the private market, the sale of common stock, and the liquidation
of holdings. The extent to which the association may borrow funds is set
by statute at 20 times its total capital, surplus, reserves, and undistributed
earnings.

When a mortgage is purchased and becomes part of its secondary market
portfolio, the FNMA can service the mortgage directly or pay the seller of
the paper to receive and transfer payments to it. The latter method is the
prevailing practice, and the servicing firm receives a fee of 0.5 percent of
the mortgage for handling this function. The homeowner is never aware
that his mortgage is owned by FNMA.

Table 13–2 shows how important FNMA operations have become since
the late 1960s. When its operations are combined with those of the Government National Mortgage Association, we see that mortgage holdings
doubled in the three years from 1968 through 1971. FNMA smooths the
flow of funds in the economy by purchasing mortgages from savings and

loan associations that need additional funds in order to finance new residential constructions, and at the same time selling the acquired mortgages to other savings and loan associations and financial institutions that have idle funds to invest. It should again be noted that this action is likely to be procyclical in character, however.

This chapter, together with Chapters 11 and 12, has concentrated on the monetary powers of the Federal Reserve and other governmental agencies. We have seen their potential influence on the money stock and its velocity. Subsequent chapters will develop the theory of money and its influence on the economy. First, however, it is appropriate to review the forces that directly determine the stock of money and bank reserves. This will be done in Chapter 14.

Supplementary Readings

Beard, Thomas R. *U.S. Treasury Advanced Refunding* (Board of Governors of the Federal Reserve System, 1966).

Commission on Money and Credit. *Fiscal and Debt Management Policies* (Prentice-Hall, 1963).

————. *Federal Credit Agencies* (Prentice-Hall, 1963).

Hand, John H. "Government Lending Agencies" in Polakoff, Murray (ed.), *Financial Institutions and Markets* (Houghton Mifflin Co., 1970).

14 Commercial Bank Reserves and the Money Supply

Although economists agree that variations in the money stock affect economic activity, there is some controversy as to the precise nature of the relationship. The following basic statement is generally considered axiomatic, however. *If an increase in the desire to spend is accompanied by either an increase in the stock of money or an increased turnover of a given money stock, then spending will rise and so will the level of general economic activity.* On the other hand, if a decreased desire to spend is accompanied by a decrease in the stock of money or its turnover, spending will decline and an economic recession will occur. Whether monetary changes *cause* spending changes or merely *accompany* them, variations in the money supply are clearly related to the level of economic activity. Because the volume of money is primarily dependent upon commercial bank reserve positions, the Federal Reserve seeks to stabilize the economy by regulating the level of reserves.

We shall examine the influence of the money supply on the economy in detail in Part IV. To understand this influence, however, certain basic points on the quantitative determination of the money stock must first be studied. Thus it is advisable to review briefly the factors determining the money stock covered in Part I. In this chapter we shall also examine the quantitative determination of member bank reserves by the forces covered in Chapters 10 to 13.

REVIEW

We have said that money is anything generally acceptable as a means of extinguishing debt. It facilitates the exchange of goods and services and acts as a store of value. In the United States, money consists of currency and demand deposits owned by the nonbank public. Other liquid assets perform *some* of the functions of money, but none are as convenient for use in transactions or as completely free from the possibility of default.

The volume of currency depends largely on the demands of the public, since our central bank—the Federal Reserve—will supply almost any amount of currency demanded. Changes in the volume of currency outstanding are usually accompanied by opposite changes in the volume of demand-deposit money. Because the U.S. government does not normally create currency to meet its own obligations, increases in the volume of currency occur only when individuals and businesses demand currency in exchange for demand-deposit money. When this happens, commercial banks use their reserve accounts at the Federal Reserve banks to acquire the additional currency. Conversely, the amount of currency in circulation decreases when currency is exchanged for demand deposits. Commercial banks then deposit their excess currency holdings with the Federal Reserve banks and their reserve accounts are increased.

Shifts in the volume of demand deposits are more significant than currency changes. The largest increases in demand-deposit money take place when commercial banks extend loans and make investments. In turn, demand deposits contract when loans and investments are retired.

The ability of an individual bank to create money (demand deposits) is limited by the volume of its excess reserves. The ability of the commercial banking system to create money also depends upon its excess reserve position. Because it operates under a fractional reserve requirement, however, the banking system can create a volume of deposits that is a multiple of its excess reserves. Similarly, when there is a deficiency of reserves, the banking system must contract deposits by a multiple of the reserve shortage.

Thus, the banking system's reserve position and its ability to create money depend upon (1) R, the volume of its reserves, (2) r, the reserve requirement for demand deposits, (3) TD, the volume of time deposits, (4) r', the reserve requirement for time deposits, (5) c, the ratio of currency to demand deposits that is currently desired by the public, and (6) i', the ratio of working balances of excess reserves to demand deposits desired by the banking system. Of these various factors, R, r, and r' depend principally upon Federal Reserve policies or, in the case of nonmember banks, upon state banking authorities. TD and c, on the other hand, depend upon the desires of the public. Only i' depends directly upon commercial bank policy. In Chapter 6 all these factors were combined into equations 6–4

$$\Delta D = \frac{\Delta A}{r + c + i'} \qquad\qquad [6\text{--}4]$$

and 6–5

$$D = \frac{R - r'(TD)}{r + i'} \qquad\qquad [6\text{--}5]$$

D is the volume of demand deposits the commercial banking system can support, given the other five factors; ΔD is the potential change in D given r, c, i', and some change in reserves, ΔA. Note that D refers to the volume of demand deposits the system *can* support, not the volume it will actually create.

To determine just how much money (currency and demand deposits) the economy has, however, we must consider more than just those factors that affect reserve positions. The amount of money in the economy depends on the interaction of the public's demand for money and the willingness and ability of the banking system to supply it.

THE QUANTITATIVE DETERMINATION
OF MEMBER BANK RESERVES

While bank reserve positions cannot be considered the sole element determining the volume of demand-deposit money in the economy, they are generally regarded as the most critical factor.

As noted in Chapters 9 through 12, the Federal Reserve is held responsible for promoting a stable and growing economy by manipulating member bank reserve positions. It does this by open market operations, reserve requirement changes, and discount rate manipulations. Of these techniques, open market operations are employed most frequently. They are used to augment or decrease member bank reserves for dynamic contracyclical purposes, and they are also used for defensive purposes — to meet seasonal needs or unanticipated reserve difficulties.

Many forces directly affect the volume of member bank reserves. This section summarizes *all* the forces that quantitatively determine the volume of reserves — forces the Federal Reserve must consider when engaging in open market operations. Although we shall focus here on member bank reserves, this does not mean that nonmember banks are unimportant; they are very important for the communities in which they are located. In the aggregate, however, the volume of demand deposits created by member banks is significantly larger. Member banks, as a group, also carry on a larger volume of banking activity. One note of caution applies to the following analysis: showing *how* member bank reserves change quantitatively in response to other factors does not explain *why* they change.

Factors Supplying Reserve Funds

Table 14–1 lists the various factors that tend to increase or decrease member bank reserves. Those that supply reserves are called *sources of funds*. When they increase, member bank reserves with Federal Reserve banks tend to increase; when they decrease, member bank reserves tend to decrease. This does not mean, however, that an increase or decrease in a source of funds *must* increase or decrease reserves. Other factors may offset its effect. For example, a float increase should lead to an increase in reserves, but if the increased reserves are not desirable from a contracyclical standpoint, the Federal Reserve may decide to sell government securities to depress reserves. *In itself,* therefore, an increase in a source of funds tends to increase reserves, but reserves may not increase if there is an offsetting decrease in some other source of funds. Thus it is the *total*

TABLE 14–1   FACTORS SUPPLYING RESERVE FUNDS, FEBRUARY 1972
AND FEBRUARY 1973

(IN MILLIONS OF DOLLARS)

AVERAGES OF DAILY FIGURES— RESERVES AND RELATED ITEMS	FEBRUARY 1972	FEBRUARY 1973	CHANGES IN FACTORS FROM FEBRUARY 1972 TO FEBRUARY 1973
Factors supplying reserve funds (*sources of funds*)			
Federal Reserve credit			
U.S. government securities	69,966	72,307	+2,341
Member bank borrowings	33	1,593	+1,560
Float	2,959	2,525	− 434
Other	957	1,004	+ 47
Total	73,915	77,429	+3,514
Gold stock	9,851	10,410	+ 559
Special Drawing Rights certificate account	400	400	0
Treasury currency outstanding	7,795	8,353	+ 558
Total	91,961	96,592	+4,631
Factors absorbing reserve funds (*uses of funds*)			
Currency in circulation	59,681	64,564	+4,883
Treasury cash holdings	436	382	− 54
Treasury, foreign, and other deposits with Federal Reserve banks	3,276	3,903	+ 627
Other Federal Reserve liabilities and capital	2,194	2,342	+ 148
Total	65,587	71,191	+5,604
Member bank reserves with Federal Reserve banks	26,374	25,401	− 973
Total	91,961	96,592	+4,631
Addendum			
Member bank reserves with Federal Reserve banks	26,374	25,401	− 973
Currency and coin	5,548	6,032	+ 484
Total	31,922	31,433	− 489

SOURCE: *Federal Reserve Bulletin* (March 1973), pp. A-4 and A-5.

change in bank sources of funds that is important for the purpose of member bank reserve determination.

Uses of funds compete with sources of funds in that they tend to absorb and thereby reduce reserves. When uses of funds increase, member bank reserves with the Federal Reserve banks tend to decrease; when uses of funds decrease, member bank reserves with the Federal Reserve banks tend to increase.

As Table 14–1 shows, sources of funds increased by $4,631 billion from February 1972 through February 1973. Uses of funds, other than member bank reserves with Federal Reserve banks, increased by $5,604 billion in the same period, however. Subtracting the increase in the factors absorbing reserves from the increase in the sources of funds leaves a $973 million decrease in member bank reserves with the Federal Reserve banks.

The relationship between member bank reserves held with the Federal Reserve banks and the sources and uses of funds can be conveniently summarized as follows:

Member bank reserves
with Federal Reserve = sources of funds − uses of funds   [14–1]
banks

Breaking this simple formula down into its components, we have:

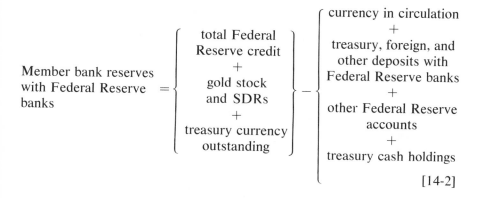

$$[14\text{-}2]$$

Almost all of these factors were discussed in Chapter 10 in examining the influences of various Federal Reserve balance-sheet items on member bank reserves. Here, however, U.S. Treasury balance-sheet items are also considered.

Federal Reserve credit. The major source of funds is Federal Reserve credit. When the Federal Reserve purchases bankers' acceptances, lends reserves to member banks, buys U.S. government securities, and finds that float is expanding, there is a direct increase in member bank reserves. Conversely, when these sources of funds decrease, member bank reserves decrease.

Gold stock and SDRs. The second most important source of funds until 1968 was our gold stock. As the Treasury buys gold using its accounts at Federal Reserve banks, member bank reserves are increased; as it sells gold, reserves are diminished. The value of our gold stock differs somewhat from the total value of the gold certificate reserves of the Federal Reserve banks. When the Treasury buys or sells gold, it almost always issues or retires an equal amount of gold certificates. However, not all treasury gold holdings are used as the basis for gold certificate issues; the Treasury retains a small volume of idle gold balances. For example, the gold stock at the end of February 1973 was $10,410 billion, but total gold certificates held by the Fed amounted to only $10,303.[1] SDR certificate holdings did not change from 1972 to 1973 (as indicated earlier, SDRs are a minor source of reserves).

Treasury currency outstanding. The third principal source of funds is treasury currency outstanding—the total value of currency issued by the Treasury. As noted in Chapter 10, when the Treasury issues additional currency, the Federal Reserve banks purchase it by increasing the Treasury's general account. Member bank reserves then increase as the Treasury spends its increased deposit balances. Although this factor accounts for approximately 8 percent of all sources of funds, changes in treasury currency have been less dramatic than changes in Federal Reserve credit. Only $558 million out of the total $4,631 billion change in sources of funds from February 1972 to February 1973 was attributable to changes in treasury currency outstanding.

Factors Absorbing Reserve Funds

Currency in circulation. The most important use of funds is currency in circulation outside the Treasury and the Federal Reserve banks—that is, currency held by the nonbank public or the commercial banking system. Although commercial bank reserves move in the opposite direction from public currency holdings, they need not vary in the opposite direction from currency in circulation. The part of currency in circulation held by commercial banks is actually part of their total reserves. Hence, only member bank reserves held with the Federal Reserve banks vary with currency in circulation. Other things being equal, if the public wants additional currency or if commercial banks choose to hold a greater portion of their reserves in the form of vault cash, then member bank reserves with the Federal Reserve banks must decline. On the other hand, a return of cash by the public to the banks or a decrease in the fraction of reserves that banks wish to hold in the form of vault cash will increase member bank reserves with the Federal Reserve banks.

As can be seen in Table 14–1, currency in circulation is by far the principal competing use for funds. From February 1972 to February 1973, currency in circulation expanded by $4,883 billion; banks picked up $484 million of this increase as vault cash. This means that the currency holdings of the nonbank public increased by $4,399 billion during the period. In the absence of preventative steps by the Federal Reserve, total member bank reserves would have been reduced by the same amount.

---

[1] *Federal Reserve Bulletin* (March 1973), p. A-12. Since 1968, treasury gold holdings have been almost constant.

Treasury, foreign, and other deposits with Federal Reserve banks; other Federal Reserve accounts. The second most important use of funds competing with reserves is a composite of various Federal Reserve liabilities and capital accounts—Treasury, foreign, and other deposits with Federal Reserve banks and other Federal Reserve accounts. These factors and their effects on bank reserves were described in some detail in Chapter 10.

Treasury cash holdings. The final competing use of funds is Treasury cash holdings—the cash held by the Treasury in its own vaults. If the Treasury draws down its cash holdings by increasing its cash payments, the nonbank public will receive the funds; part of these funds will find their way into the banking system, thereby building up commercial bank reserves. If the commercial banks do not wish to hold an increased amount of vault cash, they can send the cash to the Federal Reserve banks and have their reserve deposit accounts increased. In a similar manner, the increase of Treasury cash holdings will draw down member bank reserves with Federal Reserve banks.

THE QUANTITATIVE DETERMINATION OF THE STOCK OF MONEY

Just as we can describe the quantitative determination of member bank reserves, we can also describe the quantitative determination of the stock of money. The same note of caution, however, applies: showing *how* money stock changes quantitatively in response to various factors does not explain *why* it changes.

Three institutions have the power to vary the money supply: the commercial banking system, the Federal Reserve, and the U.S. Treasury. The components of our money supply—demand deposits, Federal Reserve notes, and Treasury currency—are liabilities of these three institutions.

It will be recalled that assets must equal liabilities plus capital accounts. Those liabilities that are part of the money stock are called *monetary liabilities*. If monetary and nonmonetary liabilities are separated, we have:

$$\text{Assets} = \text{Monetary liabilities} + \text{nonmonetary liabilities} + \text{capital accounts} \qquad [14\text{--}3]$$

and

$$\text{Monetary liabilities} = \text{Assets} - \text{nonmonetary liabilities} - \text{capital accounts} \qquad [14\text{--}4]$$

The quantity of the money stock is determined by subtracting the nonmonetary liabilities and capital accounts from the assets of the three institutions that create monetary liabilities. This is shown in Table 14–2.

From the relationships established in equation 14–4 and Table 14–2, it can be seen that the money stock will vary directly with changes in assets

TABLE 14–2 FACTORS TENDING TO INCREASE OR DECREASE THE STOCK OF MONEY FEBRUARY 29, 1973 AND FEBRUARY 28, 1973
(IN BILLIONS OF DOLLARS)

FACTORS	FEBRUARY 29, 1972	FEBRUARY 28, 1973	CHANGE IN FACTORS FROM FEBRUARY 29, 1972 TO FEBRUARY 28, 1973
Factors supplying money (*assets*)			
Gold stock and SDR certificates	10.0	10.8	+ 0.8
Treasury currency outstanding	7.8	8.4	+ 0.6
Commercial bank loans and investments	511.4	596.5	+85.1
Federal Reserve loans and investments	68.5	75.7	+ 7.2
Total	597.7	691.4	+93.7
Factors absorbing funds supplying money (*liabilities and capital accounts*)			
Nonmonetary liabilities			
Time deposits of commercial banks	278.9	323.9	+45.0
Treasury cash holdings	0.4	0.4	-0-
Treasury deposits at Federal Reserve banks	1.1	2.1	+ 1.0
Treasury deposits at commercial banks	7.3	11.2	+ 3.9
Net foreign deposits	2.6	3.5	+ 0.9
Other nonmonetary liabilities and capital accounts*	88.1	104.9	+16.8
Total	378.4	446.0	+67.6
Monetary liabilities			
Currency outside banks	51.5	55.7	+ 4.2
Demand deposits	167.8	189.7	+21.9
Total	219.3	245.4	+26.1
Assets less liabilities and capital accounts	0	0	0

* Computed as the difference between assets and the sum of all other nonmonetary liabilities and monetary liabilities.
SOURCE: *Federal Reserve Bulletin* (March 1973), pp. A-12, A-19, A-20.

and inversely with changes in nonmonetary liabilities and capital accounts. All the factors that tend to increase or decrease the stock of money have already been discussed in some other context, principally with respect to commercial bank reserve positions. As a result, the discussion at this point can be relatively brief.

Factors Tending to Supply Money

Commercial bank loans and investments are the greatest source of money. When commercial banks grant loans or make investments, they either create deposits or put currency into circulation. Conversely, as loans are retired or holdings of investments reduced, commercial bank deposit liabilities are reduced. In addition, since some people repay loans with currency, the currency of the nonbank public may also be reduced.

The second largest source of money is Federal Reserve bank loans and investments. When the Federal Reserve buys bankers' acceptances and U.S. government securities from the nonbank public, the stock of money is directly increased. Bank reserves move in the same direction as the stock of money. On the other hand, when the Federal Reserve buys bankers' acceptances and U.S. government securities directly from commercial banks, only bank reserves are initially increased. Similarly, the extension of discounts and advances to commercial banks will directly affect only bank reserves, not the currency and demand-deposit holdings of the nonbank public. This type of change in Federal Reserve loans and investments tends to affect "other nonmonetary liabilities and capital accounts" instead of monetary liabilities.

There is an indirect connection between Federal Reserve loans and investments and monetary liabilities even when the nonbank public is not directly involved in the loan and investment change. By purchasing securities from commercial banks or by making discounts and advances, the Federal Reserve banks may prevent commercial banks from contracting their assets and, accordingly, the stock of money.

Changes in the gold stock, SDRs, and treasury currency outstanding may also affect the stock of money. In the past, for example, when the buyers and sellers of gold to the Treasury were members of the nonbank public, the money supply varied in direct proportion to the gold stock. To the extent, however, that treasury currency is issued in response to the needs of the nonbank public, there is an increase in the currency in circulation but no change in the total money stock. Instead, treasury deposits at Federal Reserve banks will probably increase.

All the factors that tend to supply money expanded by $93.7 billion from February 1972 to February 1973, but the money stock rose by only $26.1 billion in the same period because of an increase in nonmonetary liabilities of $67.6 billion.

Factors Absorbing Funds Supplying Money; the Relationship between Assets and Nonmonetary Liabilities

The funds created when *assets supplying money increase* are not all assimilated by monetary liabilities. They may also be absorbed by nonmonetary liabilities and capital accounts. As commercial bank loans and investments expand, for example, some borrowers may choose to increase their time-deposit holdings instead of their currency or demand deposits. It is quite probable that many of those who receive payments from borrowing businesses will also build up time deposits. For instance, if commercial banks lend $10 million to businesses so that these firms may meet their payrolls, the employees, upon receiving the $10 million, may decide to put $8 million in demand deposits, $1 million in currency, and $1 million in time deposits. This would cause the stock of money to increase by $9 million instead of $10 million. The balance-sheet entries for this transaction would be:

BALANCE-SHEET CHANGES FOR THE COMMERCIAL BANKING SYSTEM

ASSETS		LIABILITIES + CAPITAL ACCOUNTS	
Loans and investments	+$10,000,000 (a)	Demand deposits of borrowing businesses	+$10,000,000 (a)
Vault cash	−$1,000,000 (b)	Demand deposits of borrowing businesses	−$10,000,000 (b)
		Demand deposits of payroll recipients	+$8,000,000 (b)
		Time deposits of payroll recipients	+$1,000,000 (b)

Entries labeled (a) show the effects of borrowing, and entries labeled (b) show what happens when the funds are spent by the borrowing firms.

Similarly, if commercial bank loans and investments expand as a result of the purchase of securities from the U.S. government, treasury demand deposits (rather than the demand deposits of the nonbank public) increase. Only when the Treasury spends the proceeds of the security sale will monetary liabilities increase.

Asset decreases may also be accompanied by nonmonetary liability decreases. For example, an individual may choose to repay a consumer loan by drawing down his time-deposit account rather than his checking account. Thus, changes in the factors supplying money may change either monetary or nonmonetary liabilities.

Changes in money-creating assets are not the only factors that can cause a shift in monetary and nonmonetary liabilities. Changes in one type of liability can affect another type of liability without any change occurring in assets. As a rule, in the absence of asset changes, monetary liability increases and decreases tend to accompany nonmonetary liability decreases and increases, respectively. For example, as noted in Chapter 2, there are frequent transfers between time and demand deposits. A rise in interest rates payable on time deposits will usually induce depositors to build up these accounts and to maintain lower demand-deposit balances. On the other hand, when consumers anticipate large capital expenditures, they will frequently transfer funds from time- to demand-deposit accounts.

As Table 14–2 illustrates, time deposits are the principal nonmonetary liability competing with monetary liabilities for funds. In the year from February 1972 to February 1973, time deposits expanded by $45.0 billion, whereas all other factors absorbing funds expanded by $22.6 billion.

SUMMARY AND EVALUATION

Reserve Fund Sources

As sources of funds increase, member bank reserves with Federal Reserve banks increase. As sources of funds decrease, member bank reserves with Federal Reserve banks decrease. In the absence of offsetting vault cash changes, when sources of funds change, total member bank reserves move in the same direction as member bank reserves with Federal Reserve banks.

As uses of funds increase, member bank reserves with Federal Reserve banks decrease. As uses of funds decrease, member bank reserves with Federal Reserve banks increase. Again, in the absence of offsetting vault cash changes, total member bank reserves move in the same direction as member bank reserves with Federal Reserve banks when uses of funds change.

The quantitative determination of member bank reserves should not be viewed mechanically. Actual bank reserve positions are determined by the influence of all the factors giving rise to or absorbing funds. In practice, a factor tending to increase reserves may well be offset by another factor tending to absorb reserves. Table 14–1 and equations 14–1 and 14–2 can be used to show the principal *quantitative reasons* for member bank reserve changes (movements in Federal Reserve credit and currency in circulation). Pinpointing the quantitative reasons for reserve changes, however, is not the same as explaining *why* these changes occur. To do this, we need to explain the behavior of our monetary authorities (who determine Federal Reserve credit), our balance of payments (which helps to determine the size of our gold stock and SDRs), and the actions of the nonbank public (which determine the nonbank public part of currency in circulation). For example, from February 1972 to February 1973, member bank reserves decreased by $0.5 billion, although Federal Reserve credit rose by $3.5 billion. How did this happen? An increase in currency in the hands of the nonbank public absorbed $4.4 billion.

Money Stock Sources

The money stock tends to increase as factors supplying money increase and decrease as these factors decrease. As factors absorbing funds supplying money increase, other things being given, the money stock decreases. As the same absorptive factors decrease, the money stock tends to increase.

Just as the quantitative determination of member bank reserves should not be viewed mechanically, neither should the quantitative determination of the stock of money. The actual stock of money is determined by all the supply and demand forces involved. A factor tending to increase the stock of money (such as increased loans and investments) can easily be offset by another factor (such as increased time deposits) that tends to decrease it. Table 14–2 and equations 14–3 and 14–4 merely list the forces that quantitatively determine the stock of money. As in the case of reserve base determination, we must examine *why* the forces that quantitatively determine the stock of money vary. To do this satisfactorily, a theory of the money supply is needed.

Evaluation and Preview

Equations 6–4 and 6–5

$$\Delta D = \frac{\Delta A}{r + c + i'} \qquad [6-4]$$

$$D = \frac{R - r'(TD)}{r + i'} \qquad [6-5]$$

are mathematical representations of the forces that determine reserves and the stock of money quantitatively, and, as such, have the same failings as other descriptive techniques. These equations merely state the relationships between these forces; they do not explain why the relationships exist. As previously noted, the actual amount of money in the economy depends on the interaction of the public's demand for money and the willingness and the ability of the banking system to supply it. In equations 6–4 and 6–5, R, r, and r' are principally supply forces determined by the Federal Reserve, TD and c are demand forces determined directly by the nonbank public, and i' is a supply force dependent upon commercial bank policy.

Surprisingly, for a long time the determination of the money stock has been taught simply in terms of such equations as 6–4 and 6–5 and Tables 14–1 and 14–2. In capsule form, most past explanations of money stock determination may be stated as follows: money consists of currency outside banks and demand deposits. Since variations in currency can occur only at the expense of demand deposits, the total volume of money depends primarily on demand-deposit variations. The ability of the banking system to create demand deposits depends on its reserve base, which in turn is controlled by the Federal Reserve. Contingent upon the required reserve ratios, the volume of demand deposits will be some multiple of the reserve base. Hence, it is argued, the volume of money is dependent upon central bank policy.

This line of analysis makes two rather untenable assumptions, however: (1) that the commercial banking system reacts passively to changes in its reserve base, and (2) that the Federal Reserve selects a specific amount of money that it considers suitable for the economy and counters any move by commercial banks to vary that amount.

The discussions in Chapters 5, 11, and 12 show that these assumptions are not valid. First, commercial banks tend to economize on reserves during periods of economic upturn. They expand loans, the turnover of money, and the money stock in order to profit from rising interest rates. The growth of loans, the turnover of money, and the volume of demand deposits are reduced during economic contraction as interest yields to banks on loans and investments drift downward. Thus, banks react quite vigorously to changes in reserve positions. Furthermore, as shown in Chapter 12, the Federal Reserve sometimes uses free reserves, not the stock of money, as its target variable. In addition, the Federal Reserve makes policy changes slowly. These considerations allow commercial banks substantial latitude in money creation, which they exercise through varying i' in equation 6–4.

Thus far in Parts I and II we have been primarily concerned with the roles that private financial institutions and the government play in the quantitative determination of the money stock and other forms of liquid wealth. Part III, which follows, discusses the theory of how financial investment portfolios are determined. The liquid wealth forms we have been discussing are the assets that go into portfolios. The interaction of the supply and demand for money and liquid wealth will then be discussed in Part IV; there we will see how the principal economic variables determine income and output.

Part III FINANCIAL MARKETS AND PORTFOLIO DECISIONS

15 Financial Markets and Portfolio Decisions: Microeconomic Foundations

SURVEY AND REVIEW OF FINANCIAL MARKETS AND INSTRUMENTS

Flow of Funds Accounts
Financial Markets
  Financial market participants
  Financial market instruments

INTEREST RATES AND PORTFOLIO DECISIONS

Interest Rate Structure
  The meaning of the interest rate
  The general structure of interest rates
  The term structure of interest rates
Portfolio Selection

Financial markets are those institutional relationships that bring the demanders and the suppliers of money in the economy together. The private financial institutions that participate in financial markets were discussed in Chapters 2–7, and government participants were considered in Chapters 9–13. This chapter first briefly recapitulates the institutions and instruments involved in financial markets and then discusses some aspects of microeconomic financial theory. Specifically, the relationship between interest yields on differing financial assets is discussed, as is the determination of optimal financial investment portfoiios.

In some ways the chapter is a digression, albeit an important one, from the main theme of this book: that money is important for the economy—that money and the other forms of liquid wealth that compete for a place in wealth portfolios have a unique relationship to aggregate economic activity and welfare. Our focus to this point has been on both private and governmental financial institutions and on the creation of liquid assets and their relationship to the national economy. We shall return to this theme and focus upon it in subsequent chapters. Here, however, we will delve briefly into the microeconomic theory of how interest rate differentials and wealth portfolios are determined. After all, is not the economic well-being of each of us within the national economy determined by the decision-making processes of individuals and institutions?

SURVEY AND REVIEW OF FINANCIAL MARKETS AND INSTRUMENTS

Most of the financial institutions and instruments involved in financial markets have already been discussed in earlier chapters. Previously we have focused upon financial institutions and their sources and uses of funds in relation to their impact upon the economy as a whole. In this section, we will briefly examine these same institutions and instruments in another way—from a *flow of funds* point of view—so that the complexities and interrelationships of the various financial arrangements in the economy will become clearer.

Flow of Funds Accounts

The Flow of Funds Accounts are a means of organizing the data on sources and uses of funds in the U.S. economy. These accounts enable us to examine the relationships between financial markets and the markets for real goods and services in the economy. We typically measure economic progress by the growth path of real output and employment, but, as was mentioned in Chapter 3, contributions to the economy by *all* economic sectors cannot be measured solely through the use of income and employment statistics. For example, the financial sectors must be judged in terms of their functions. The smooth movement of money among the financial and nonfinancial sectors of the economy is essential for economic progress. The Flow of Funds Accounts show us this movement of funds.

Table 15–1 summarizes the Flow of Funds Accounts for the year 1971. Listed across the top of the table are nine sectors of the economy. Several of these will be broken down into various subsectors later in our discussions. Each sector has data showing both its uses (U) and sources (S) of funds during 1971. Conceptually, the total sources (line 1) and uses (line 4) should equal each other, but because of data collection problems there is frequently a discrepency between the two which is given at the end of the table (line 42).

Rows numbered 5–9 show the *real uses* to which the various sectors put their funds. All other uses are *financial* (line 11). Each sector has both financial uses and sources of funds. Some sectors are surplus and others are deficit. Surplus sectors purchase the liabilities of the deficit sectors.

The *household sector* is broken down into households, personal trusts, and nonprofit organizations. In 1971, this was a surplus sector, expanding its holdings of financial assets by $91.4 billion while only increasing its financial liabilities by $44.7 billion. Thus the household sector made a net financial investment of $46.6 billion. Its expansion of financial assets (uses of funds) was primarily in the liabilities of financial institutions, whereas its increased financial liabilities (sources of funds) were largely in home mortgages and consumer credit.

The *nonfinancial business sector* consists of nonfinancial corporate business, and noncorporate farm and nonfarm business. In contrast to households, nonfinancial business was a deficit sector. Outstanding stock and liabilities expanded by $47.8 billion more than holdings of financial assets. This difference was made up by selling new stocks, bonds, and mortgages, primarily to private nonbank financial institutions.

The *state and local governments sector* also had a deficit, albeit a small one. This sector added to its holdings of U.S. government securities and time-deposit accounts at commercial banks $6.9 and $7.2 billion, respectively. Those governments that were in deficit took care of the shortage by adding $20.2 billion to their outstanding obligations.

The *rest of the world sector* is taken from data on the U.S. balance of payments. Since a detailed examination of our balance of payments appears in Chapter 23, we shall postpone our discussion of this account until then.

The U.S. government sector covers all the agencies and trust funds except for federally sponsored credit agencies and the Federal Reserve System. The U.S. government was in deficit in 1971 and, correspondingly, used the sale of additional securities to secure the necessary funds to meet outstanding obligations.

The *financial sectors* are divided into four broad categories, the first of which consists of *federally sponsored credit agencies*. There are six types of agencies covered in this group: Federal Home Loan Banks, Federal Land Banks, Federal Intermediate Credit Banks, Banks for Cooperatives, the Federal National Mortgage Association, and mortgage pools which issue Government National Mortgage Association guaranteed securities. Most of the preceding agencies were briefly described in Chapter 13 and need no additional descriptions here. As can be seen in Table 15–1, their financial sources and uses of funds were approximately equal in 1971. Their principal source of funds is U.S. government securities and their principal use of funds is in the mortgage market. For example, federally sponsored credit agencies issued an additional $3.9 billion in securities and added $6.4 billion in mortgages to their portfolios in 1971.

The second financial sector consists of the *monetary authority*—that is, the Federal Reserve. In addition, a few Treasury currency accounts are included in this category. The sources and uses of funds for this sector are identical with those studied earlier in connection with Table 14–1. The third column of Table 14–1 reveals the detail behind the few figures shown for the Federal Reserve in Table 15–1. Table 14–1 lists U.S. government security holdings of the Federal Reserve banks as the principal *source* of reserve funds. However, Table 15–1 deals with the sources and uses of funds in the various financial sectors of the economy. Accordingly, in Table 15–1 the increase in U.S. government security holdings of the Federal Reserve banks is treated as a *use* of funds by the Fed. Similarly, currency and bank reserves—the principal factors absorbing reserve funds—were called uses of funds in Table 14–1, but are sources of funds for the monetary authority in Table 15–1.

The meaning of the *commercial banking sector* is obvious. Each of the sources and uses of funds of commercial banks were described in some detail in Chapter 5.

Finally, *the private nonbank financial institutions sector* is a broad category covering all of the financial institutions previously considered in Chapter 7: mutual savings banks, savings and loan associations, life insurance companies, credit unions, pension funds, nonlife insurance companies, finance companies, and investment companies.

Overall, Table 15–1 shows that households are the most important surplus sector—this sector saves. The business sector is the largest deficit

TABLE 15–1 SUMMARY OF FLOW OF FUNDS ACCOUNTS FOR YEAR 1971

(SEASONALLY ADJUSTED ANNUAL RATES; IN BILLIONS OF DOLLARS)

| | TRANSACTION CATEGORY | PRIVATE DOMESTIC NONFINANCIAL SECTORS | | | | | | | | REST OF THE WORLD | |
| | | HOUSE-HOLDS | | BUSINESSES | | STATE AND LOCAL GOVT. | | TOTAL | | | |
SECTOR		U	S	U	S	U	S	U	S	U	S
1	**Gross saving**		186.1		89.9		−2.1		274.0		2.8
2	Capital consumption		98.5		80.0				178.5		
3	Net saving (1 − 2)		87.6		9.8		−2.1		95.4		2.8
4	**Gross investment (5 + 10)**	181.6		70.1		−5.4		246.3		13.6	
5	Private capital expenditures	134.9		118.0				252.9			
6	Consumer durables	103.5						103.5			
7	Residential construction	25.8		16.7				42.6			
8	Plant and equipment	5.6		97.6				103.2			
9	Inventory change			3.6				3.6			
10	**Net financial investment (11 − 12)**	46.6		−47.8		−5.4		−6.6		13.6	
11	**Financial uses**	91.4		23.4		15.6		130.4		22.2	
12	**Financial sources**		44.7		71.3		21.0		137.0		8.6
13	Gold, SDRs, and official foreign exchange									1.3	−1.7
14	Treasury currency and SDR certificates										
15	Demand deposits and currency										
16	Private domestic	8.5		4.6		.5		13.5			
17	U.S. government										
18	Foreign										.2
19	Time and savings accounts	73.5						81.3			
20	At commercial banks	32.7		.6		7.2		40.5			.5
21	At savings institutions	40.8						40.8			
22	Life insurance reserves	6.6						6.6			
23	Pension fund reserves	20.2						20.2			
24	Interbank items										
25	Corporate shares	−5.2			13.4			−5.2	13.4	.9	*
26	Credit market instruments	−11.6	41.6	8.1	49.6	7.7	20.6	4.2	111.8	26.4	5.6
27	U.S. government securities	−22.6		2.7		6.9		−13.1		26.3	
28	State and local obligations	4.9		1.0		−.2	20.2	5.7	20.2		
29	Corporate and foreign bonds	7.6			19.4	1.0		8.6	19.4	.3	.9
30	Home mortgages	.2	24.5		1.5	*		.2	26.1		
31	Other mortgages	2.3	1.4		19.4			2.3	20.9		
32	Consumer credit		10.4	2.6				2.6	10.4		
33	Bank loans		3.9		6.4				10.3		2.7
34	Other loans	−3.9	1.3	1.8	2.7		.4	−2.1	4.4	−.2	2.1
35	Security credit	*	2.1					*	2.1	*	*
36	To brokers and dealers	*						*		*	
37	To others		2.1						2.1		*
38	Taxes payable				4.0	.3		.3	4.0		
39	Trade credit		.6	4.0	3.9		.5	4.0	4.9	*	−.4
40	Equity in noncorporate business	−3.2			−3.2			−3.2	−3.2		
41	Miscellaneous claims	2.4	.5	6.2	3.6			8.6	4.0	−7.1	5.0
42	Sector discrepancies (1 − 4)	4.6		19.8		3.4		27.7		−10.8	

* Less than 0.1.

SOURCE: *Federal Reserve Bulletin* (November 1972), p. A-72.

TABLE 15-1. (Continued)

		FINANCIAL SECTORS														
U.S. GOVT.		TOTAL		SPONSORED CREDIT AGENCIES		MONETARY AUTHORITY		COMMERCIAL BANKING		PRIVATE NONBANK FINANCE		ALL SECTORS		DISCREP-ANCY	NATIONAL SAVINGS AND INVEST-MENTS	
U	S	U	S	U	S	U	S	U	S	U	S	U	S	U		
	−24.6		7.8	.1			−.1	3.9		3.9		260.0			257.2	1
			2.5						1.2		1.3	181.1			181.1	2
	−24.6		5.3		.1		−.1		2.7		2.6	78.9			76.1	3
−25.3		8.1		.1			−.1	3.6		4.5		242.8		17.3	241.8	4
			2.6						1.1		1.4	255.4		4.6	255.4	5
												103.5			103.5	6
												42.6			42.6	7
			2.6						1.1		1.4	105.8			105.8	8
												3.6			3.6	9
−25.3		5.6		.1			−.1	2.5		3.0		−12.7		12.7	−13.6	10
3.8		149.6		3.4		8.3		57.6		80.3		306.1			8.6	11
	29.1		144.1		3.3		8.3		55.1		77.3		318.7		22.2	12
−2.2		−.8				−.8						−1.7	−1.7			13
	.5	.5				.5						.5	.5	*		14
			18.4				4.4		14.0			17.7	18.4			15
		.7	15.1	.1			3.4		11.7	.7		14.3	15.1	.8		16
3.2			3.1				.9		2.2			3.2	3.1	−.1		17
			.2				.1		.1				.2			18
		.2	82.2							.2			82.2			19
.1		.2	41.4						41.4	.2			41.4			20
		*	40.8							*	40.8		40.8			21
	.1		6.6								6.6		6.6			22
	2.8		17.4								17.4		20.2			23
		5.0	5.0					−.2	4.1	5.2	.9		5.0	5.0		24
		19.1	1.3					*	*			19.2	1.3		14.8	25
3.2	25.5	117.4	8.3	2.8	3.9	8.8		49.8	.2	56.0	4.3	151.2	151.2			26
*	25.6	16.2	3.9	−1.5	3.9	8.6		6.0		3.1		29.4				27
		14.5						12.7		1.8		20.2				28
		15.8	4.3					1.3	.5	14.5	3.8	24.6				29
−.3	−.1	28.1	2.0	4.8				5.7		17.7	2.0	28.0				30
.4		18.3		1.6				4.2		12.5		20.9				31
		7.8						4.8		3.0		10.4				32
		14.4	1.4					14.4			1.4	14.4				33
3.2		2.3	−3.3	−2.0		.2		.8	−.4	3.3	−2.9	3.3				34
		2.8	.6					.8		2.0	.6	2.7				35
		.7	.6					.7			.6	.6				36
		2.1						.1		2.0		2.1				37
1.1			−.2				*		*		−.1	1.4	3.8	2.4		38
−1.7	−.7	.5								.5		2.8	3.8	1.0		39
											−3.2		−3.2			40
.1	.8	4.3	4.5	.6	−.5		−.2	1.9	−1.3	1.8	6.5	5.8	14.3	8.5		41
.7		−.3		*		*		.3		−.6		17.3		17.3	15.4	42

sector, with both the U.S. government and state and local governments also being deficit sectors. The financial sectors are normally neither in deficit nor surplus. This is as expected since a function of private financial institutions is to collect idle funds from those with surpluses and to help transfer them to deficit sectors. Private financial institutions serve as intermediaries which bring ultimate borrowers (businesses and governments) and lenders (households) together. This process of *intermediation* is seen clearly in Table 15-1. Households use their savings and borrowings to purchase real goods and to acquire the liabilities of commercial banks and private nonbank financial institutions. The financial uses of funds by households are the principal sources of funds for banks and nonbank financial institutions. In turn, banks and nonbank financial institutions invest their funds in the credit market instruments issued by businesses and governments, in addition to the consumer credit and mortgages of households. Of course, as has already been discussed extensively, in the process of doing this, financial institutions create their own liabilities and thereby problems for the monetary authority. Government sponsored credit agencies try to expedite the flow of funds between the other sectors. The monetary authority, in addition to its prime function of regulating economic activity, also tries to expedite the flow of funds through the various financial markets.

Financial Markets

There are two types of financial markets: money and capital. *Money markets* refer to the short-term borrowing and lending of money and *capital markets* to the long-term borrowing and lending of money. These financial markets are not necessarily located in any particular place; they are *arrangements* for the purchase and sale of financial instruments. New York City is still the major financial center of the nation and, accordingly, the great majority of security transactions are ultimately channeled there.

Since the principal participants and instruments in financial markets have been described in preceding parts of the book, we can confine ourselves here to a brief summary of the materials already presented.

Financial market participants. Money markets generally relate to an arrangement involving the lending and borrowing of funds for less than a year, whereas capital markets involve funds lent for longer periods. The participants in these markets are all of the sectors (both deficit and surplus) previously described. Each sector is sometimes a demander and sometimes a supplier of funds.

The *household sector* is normally involved in the money markets as a demander of funds: it seeks consumer credit at finance companies and commercial banks. As a supplier of funds, the household sector has limited access to the principal money markets. For example, individuals normally do not have direct access to the short-term government securities market, and instead invest their idle funds in the various savings instruments offered by financial institutions. Individuals can purchase short-term government securities indirectly through their banks or brokers, but only for a fee. Prior to 1969, individuals could purchase government securities directly from the Federal Reserve banks, which acted as agents of the U.S. government. The minimum purchase was $1,000. Now the minimum direct purchase is $10,000, and this effectively prohibits most individuals from directly participating in the government securities market. It should be noted, however, that nonprofit organizations—a part of the household sector—do have more direct access to financial markets.

On the other hand, the household sector is involved in capital markets as both a demander and supplier of funds. It provides a demand for funds through home mortgages, and it supplies funds through the purchase of U.S. government savings bonds (either at banks or on a payroll savings plan) and through certificates of deposit at financial institutions. Households also purchase corporate stocks and bonds, but these are rarely purchases of new issues.

The *nonfinancial business sector* is both a demander and supplier of short-term funds. Businesses frequently take out short-term loans from commercial banks, for example. They also invest temporarily idle funds in treasury bills or in certificates of deposit. Large businesses sell large-denomination unsecured promissory notes called *commercial paper*.

The business sector enters the capital markets as a demander of long-term funds. It sells new issues of stocks and bonds in order to obtain additional funds for plant and equipment purchases.

The *state and local governments sector* is both a supplier and demander of funds. State and local governments invest idle tax monies (until expenditures come due) in short-term U.S. government securities and in time-deposit accounts at commercial banks. They sell *tax anticipation notes* when they need funds to meet expenditures prior to their scheduled tax collection dates. State and local governments also sell bonds, primarily to help finance the construction of public facilities and schools.

The *U.S. government* is a demander of funds in both money and capital markets. In the money market, it sells short-term government securities—in part to help finance deficits, but also to compensate for the lack of synchronization between receipts and expenditures. Treasury bills are the principal form of money market instrument sold. Savings bonds and various negotiable bonds are sold in the capital market for government securities.

Federally sponsored credit agencies are primarily involved in capital markets. They acquire funds through the sale of government securities and purchase home mortgages.

The *Federal Reserve* (the monetary authority sector) operates in financial markets primarily through its activities in government security markets. Through open market operations, it seeks to regulate the economy without interfering in the flow of funds within the various segments of the private sectors of the economy.

The *commercial bank sector* is both a demander and supplier of funds in the money markets, but is primarily a supplier of funds in capital markets. Banks are demanders of funds (borrowers) when they engage in liability management. They are suppliers of funds (lenders) in money markets when they make short-term loans to businesses, individuals, governments, and other financial institutions. Although short-term lending is their principal activity, they do affect capital markets by purchasing and selling some mortgages and long-term governmental securities. And while almost all commercial banks deal in short-term money market instruments, it should be recognized that very few banks are directly involved in money market operations. Those few—mainly the large banks located in the financial centers of the nation such as New York, Chicago, and San Francisco—participate for themselves and for hundreds of customer banks.

Private nonbank financial institutions operate in both money and capital markets, depending upon the type of financial institution. Mutual savings banks, life insurance companies, and savings and loan associations are suppliers of long-term funds in the capital markets, primarily when they purchase mortgages and various types of bonds. Investment companies are also involved in the capital markets when they purchase and sell stocks and bonds. Finance companies are short-term demanders and suppliers of funds, often borrowing on a short-term basis from banks to make short-term consumer loans. Credit unions make short-term loans. Table 7–7 can be used to develop a further breakdown of how nonbank financial institutions participate in financial markets.

Financial market instruments. The preceding discussion of the Flow of Funds Accounts and financial market participants already provides us with some idea of the multitude of financial instruments that are traded. Table 15–2 lists the principal money and capital market instruments in order of their quantitative importance. Only a brief general statement about these instruments is needed here, given our preceding analyses.

Obviously U.S. government securities dominate the money markets. Most of the activity in these securities is channeled through some 22 government securities dealers located in New York City. The ultimate participants are private financial institutions, businesses with idle funds, individuals, governments, and of course the Fed with its dynamic and defensive use of open market operations. The securities traded are primarily treasury bills issued weekly with a comparatively short maturity of 90 days. Activity in the other money market instruments depends in part upon activity in the government securities market. If, for example, the Fed chooses to follow a tight money policy by raising discount rates or restricting its purchase of treasury bills, then banks seek more funds in the federal funds market, sell certificates of deposit, or engage more actively in the Eurodollar market. Nonfinancial businesses may issue more commercial paper.

TABLE 15–2 FINANCIAL MARKET INSTRUMENTS OUTSTANDING, BY ISSUER, END OF DECEMBER 1971
(IN BILLIONS OF DOLLARS)

Money Market Instruments		
U.S. government short-term marketable securities		$130.4
Negotiable certificates of deposit (commercial bank)		34.0
Commercial and finance company paper		30.8
Federal funds		20.0
State and local government short-term obligations		19.2
Security credit to brokers and dealers		12.5
Bankers' acceptances		7.9
Total		254.8
Capital Market Instruments		
Mortgages		
Households	$318.0	
Nonfinancial businesses	175.4	
Savings and loan associations	5.1	
U.S. government	1.4	
Total		499.9
Corporate bonds		187.3
State and local government bonds		147.3
U.S. government direct debt (excluding savings bonds)		132.7
Federally sponsored credit agency securities		43.2
Finance company bonds		26.7
Commercial bank bonds and commercial paper		4.9
Total		1,042.0
Corporate stock (at market value)		1,085.5
Total Financial Market Instruments		2,382.3

SOURCE: *Federal Reserve Bulletin* (June 1972) pp. A-72–73.2.

Capital markets, dealing as they do with long-term funds, are more directly involved with real investment in the economy than money markets. Mortgages arising out of household demands for homes are continually being issued, and the various financial intermediaries are always actively purchasing them. There is also an active market for previously issued mortgages. For example, the mortgage purchases of the Federal National Mortgage Association help to provide the selling financial institution with money to be invested in new residential construction.

In addition to capital market activity related to the housing industry, there are the real investment activities of those corporate businesses that sell new mortgages and issue new stocks and bonds to acquire funds for plant and equipment construction. Similarly, all levels of government sell new securities to help finance the construction of highways, schools, and public buildings—real capital goods that will provide the public with services for many years.

The new long-term securities sold by businesses are often sold directly to financial investors such as life insurance companies. These are called *direct placements* and the public as a whole does not have an opportunity to bid on them. Other new long-term securities are frequently underwritten by investment houses which then market them to the general public. These activities in new securities are in the *primary securities market*. Most of us, however, are more familiar with the *secondary securities market*—the market for previously issued stocks and bonds (both corporate and government). This market consists of the organized exchanges like the New York Stock Exchange and the American Stock Exchange, and the "over the counter market" (which encompasses the stocks and bonds not listed on the organized exchanges). Transactions in the secondary securities markets do not directly assist the issuers of the securities, but a ready secondary market makes it easier for them to acquire new funds in the future. Purchasers of new issues need a market in which to trade their holdings.

INTEREST RATES AND PORTFOLIO DECISIONS

Financial markets are complex—there are thousands of participants demanding and supplying securities of varying yields. How are these alternative securities and their yields related? Or are they related at all? As an individual with surplus funds, how is one to choose between alternative financial assets? The answers to these questions are difficult and contradictory. The following discussion outlines some of the conflicting views of economists and financial theorists.

Interest Rate Structure

The meaning of the interest rate. Economic treatises frequently sound as if there is only one rate of interest. For example, Chapters 19 and 20 in this book discuss the influence of "the interest rate" in the money and commodity markets. That there are actually many interest rates is self-evident, yet one of the functions of theory is to abstract from reality for the sake of greater clarity. We talk about "the interest rate" to attain a better idea of economic relationships. It is important, however, that we be precise in our meaning. *In this book, the term* interest rate *is a weighted average cost of all the methods of financing available in the economy.* The cost of each source of funds is weighted according to its relative importance in financing. Thus for example, if there were only two sources of funds—4 percent and 6 percent bonds—and if the volume of bonds outstanding in each class were $1 million and $5 million, respectively, then the average cost of funds would be

$$\frac{\$40,000 + \$300,000 \text{ (annual interest costs)}}{\$1,000,000 + \$5,000,000 \text{ (total value of bonds)}}$$

or $5\frac{2}{3}$ percent.

As we have seen, there are many different ways to obtain funds in the economy, and each has a cost attached to it. There are short-term and long-term rates of interest on U.S. government securities; the interest costs on privately issued industrial, public utility, and railroad bonds; and the dividend costs to issuers of corporate stocks. In addition, there are the short-term costs of trade credit and of borrowing from commercial banks, consumer finance companies, and sales finance companies. To examine the effects of the interest rate on the economy, we should really study this whole spectrum of rates, but that would necessitate some extremely complex calculations. Thus, to simplify our explanation of this relationship, we use the average cost of all methods of financing on the assumption that there is some stable functional relationship between the yields of all types of financing instruments. Just what the nature of this functional relationship between yields is depends on what theory one accepts concerning the determination of the structure of interest rates.

The general structure of interest rates. In a broad sense, it is not too difficult to explain the relationships between the yields on varying securities. The demand for and supply of each security determines its yield and price. The demand for a security depends upon the credit worthiness of borrowers, the yield on the security, the yields on competing securities, the maturity of the security, the availability of a secondary securities market for resale of the security, the growth of national income, and expectations concerning future prices and interest rates. The supply of a security depends upon the needs of borrowers for funds, the interest cost of the security, the growth of national income, and expectations concerning future prices and interest rates. Evidently, both the demand for and supply of securities are influenced by many of the same forces. Let us discuss these forces in a general way.

First of all, it should be noted that the demand for and supply of securities behave very much like the demand for and supply of all goods and services. The greater the demand for a security relative to its supply, the higher the price of that security. The higher the price, the lower the interest yield. For example, say that a security paying 6 percent on a face value of $1,000 increases in price to $1,250. This means that anyone buying the security at $1,250 only receives a 5 percent yield on his financial investment. Contrarily, the lower the demand for a security relative to its supply, the lower its price and the higher its yield.

Obviously those securities supplied by *good credit risks* will be in stronger demand than securities issued by poor risks. Likewise, the higher the *interest rate on a security* the greater will be the amount demanded. After all, assuming other factors are fixed, will not a high yield be more attractive to a security purchaser than a low yield? Also, should the *yields on other securities* decline relative to the yield on a particular security, the amount demanded of that particular security can be expected to increase.

The more *readily a security can be resold* in the secondary securities market, the greater the demand for it. In addition, the shorter the *maturity* of a security, the greater might be the demand for it, since funds need not be tied up over an extended period of time. These last two forces might lead to the expectation that long-term securities in general have a higher interest return than short-term securities. Yet we find that the reverse is often true. Why? Because of credit risk! Often poor credit risks who cannot borrow on a long-term basis will borrow for a short period of time at a high cost. Better credit risks with excellent records of repayment can borrow for long periods at comparatively low yields.

In addition to the preceding forces, interest rates in general depend upon certain basic economic considerations. If the level of *income* is rising rapidly, one can anticipate a strong desire to spend, a growing demand for funds, and, accordingly, a large supply of securities. Interest rates, in general, should then rise. *Rising prices* mean a lower real yield on interest returns. (The discussion of Irving Fisher in Chapter 17 elaborates on this point.) Hence security purchasers may insist on higher market rates of interest to compensate for rising prices. Similarly, should financial investors anticipate *rising interest rates,* they might immediately demand a higher return in fear of incurring future losses on their security holdings. In general, with rising incomes, prices, and interest rates, more rapid growth in future interest yields on all types of securities can be anticipated.

The term structure of interest rates. The preceding analysis applies in general to all interest rates, and economic theorists are not in conflict with its broad outlines. Sharp differences are the rule when considering the term structure of interest rates, however. By term structure of interest rates, we are referring to the relationship between interest yield and the maturity of comparable securities. There are three widely held theories concerning this relationship.

First, the *expectations theory* holds that a long-term rate of interest constitutes an average of expected future short-term rates, and that a forward rate is an unbiased estimate of future short-term rates.[1] Assume, for example, that people expect interest rates to be higher in the future than they are now. Lenders will demand higher long-term rates of interest. If they do not receive higher rates, they can refrain from lending on a long-term basis and lend instead on a short-term basis. Thus their funds will not be tied up in the future, when interest rates will have increased. The result is an increase in current long-term rates of interest. On the other hand, should people expect interest rates to decline in the future, borrowers will refrain from borrowing on a long-term basis. If long-term lenders are to be able to lend, they must therefore lend at lower rates of interest. Thus the long-term rate declines, and it may even become less than current short-term rates. If the long-term rate is truly an average of future short-term rates, then the return of a long-term security should be the same as the return on a series of short-term securities purchased over a period of time.

---

[1] A forward rate is the interest rate on a contract to purchase short-term securities in the future.

There are a number of underlying assumptions to this theory. First, there is the assumption that financial investors will *only* purchase a long-term security if they can obtain a yield equivalent to that on a series of short-term security purchases over a comparable period of time. This line of reasoning applies only when the alternative short- and long-term securities are comparable in all respects except maturity. Another assumption is that financial investors have accurate expectations about future interest rates, and this is what has caused people actually involved in security purchases and sales to reject the "expectations hypothesis" in their work. They accept the idea that forecasts are made about interest rates in the very short run, but they feel that accurate forecasts of the distant future are simply not possible.

The second theory, the *liquidity preference theory,* rejects the idea that long- and short-term securities can be treated as comparable except for maturity. This theory assumes that risks associated with long-term securities are greater. Thus long-term rates tend to be higher than short-term rates, and the market demands a premium often called a *liquidity premium* to hold long-term securities, which are poorer near monies. If the liquidity preference theory is correct, long-term interest rates should be consistently higher than short-term rates. This was the case in the 1930s when the theory first became popular, but subsequent interest rate behavior has not shown such a consistent pattern.

The inconsistencies in interest rate data have led some economists to wed the expectations and liquidity preference theories. Reuben Kessel, for example, building upon the expectations theory of Friedrich Lutz and David Meiselman and the liquidity preference theory of John Maynard Keynes, argued that forward rates are the sum of future short-term rates plus a liquidity premium.[2]

Finally, according to the *segmented market theory,* what happens in the market for one type of security has little relationship to what happens in the market for other types. It is the demand for and supply of a particular security that determines its yield. Those who are active in the market for long-term securities are not likely to be significantly influenced by yields on short-term securities. Hence securities with different maturities are poor substitutes. This view is popular in the business world, but until recently did not have much acceptance among economists and financial theorists.

Empirical work on these theories is still conflicting. For example, a 1972 study rejects both the expectations hypothesis and Kessel's alliance of the expectations and liquidity preference theories.[3] However, another study in the same journal seems to accept the view that liquidity premiums influ-

---

[2] Reuben Kessel. *The Cyclical Behavior of the Term Structure of Interest Rates* (Columbia University Press, 1965).

[3] Thomas J. Sargent. "Rational Expectations and the Term Structure of Interest rates." *Journal of Money, Credit and Banking* (1972), pp. 74–97.

ence spot rates.[4] Still another study leans toward the market segmentation theory, concluding ". . . that most interest rate theorists should reconsider their views on the nature and effective weight of interest rate expectations and investor portfolio preferences. The impact of hedging behavior appears to be greater than commonly believed."[5] What seems to be developing is an eclectic outlook — one which uses portions of all the conflicting theoretical and empirical views. Thus one study supported both the expectations and the market segmentation theories when it ". . . suggested instead a partial and sometimes predominant role for expectations and adjustments in yields and prices that occur independently of supply-demand notions. . . . All of this occurs such that the yield structure undergoes significant changes independently of the quantities brought to or withdrawn from the market."[6]

Portfolio Selection

This section develops a relatively simple model of portfolio selection and its relation to interest rates. Chapter 26 will return to the discussion developed here and show how it is basic to much contemporary reasoning about the demand for money.

The essential problem is to determine the optimum portfolio, the one which gives the greatest return and satisfaction at the lowest possible risk. Certainly interest return is one important force in selecting financial assets for inclusion. Other things being equal, the higher the interest yield, the greater the desire to hold that particular asset. We have also previously emphasized income, price and interest rate expectations, security maturity, credit risk, and asset convertibility as forces having an impact upon the demand for securities and hence upon portfolio determination. In addition, contemporary finance theory formulates portfolio selection on the basis of risk and utility analysis. This type of analysis does not lend itself well to empirical forecasting and the determination of real world optimum portfolios. Still, the theories developed give insights which financial managers should consider when determining the mix of financial assets for businesses and individuals to hold.

Some elementary diagrams can help to explain portfolio determination. Assume that investors prefer more interest return to less return and less risk to more risk (we assume that investors get more utility from more return and less risk). Figure 15–1 illustrates this principle. Here we measure the return from a portfolio of assets on the horizontal axis and the risk of

[4] Dudley G. Luckett and Allen R. Soltow. "Determinants of Interest Rate Expectations." *Journal of Money, Credit and Banking* (1972), pp. 272–82.

[5] John A. Naylor. "The Relative Impact of Expectations and Investor Preferences on the Structure of Government Yields." *The Southern Economic Journal* (1971), p. 477.

[6] William T. Terrell and William J. Frazer, Jr. "Interest Rates, Portfolio Behavior, and Marketable Government Securities." *Journal of Finance* (1972), p. 32.

Figure 15–1. An investor's indifference map.

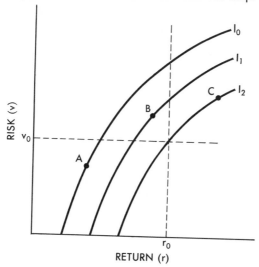

the portfolio on the vertical axis. The solid lines between the axes are *indifference curves,* and the given behind each curve is a particular level of satisfaction (utility). The lines labeled I_0, I_1, and I_2 represent successively higher levels of utility. Each curve shows the alternative combinations of risk and return that give the investor the same level of satisfaction. In other words, along a particular indifference curve, the investor is indifferent to the various combinations of risk and return. Each curve is drawn on the assumption that the investor is a risk averter. The slope of each curve becomes flatter as the amount of risk increases. This means that the investor requires successively more return on his portfolio each time he assumes more risk. Finally, we see that at a given return such as r_0, the higher the risk, the less the satisfaction. Similarly, at a given degree of risk such as v_0, the higher the return, the greater the level of utility achieved.

Each portfolio of financial and real assets has a particular return and degree of risk connected with it. Which portfolio will be chosen? In Figure 15–1, for example, will it be the portfolio that yields point A, B, or C? To answer this question we need more information than just the investor's indifference map. It is true that portfolio C yields more satisfaction than B, which, in turn, is superior to A. This is because A, B, and C are each on a successively higher utility yielding indifference curve. C will not necessarily be chosen, however.

What is missing from the preceding analysis is information about the risk and return associated with each portfolio. This problem can be resolved with the introduction of another line called the *efficient frontier* (or occasionally a *risk-earnings possibility curve*), shown in Figure 15–2 as line *EF*. Each point on this curve shows the minimum degree of risk that an in-

Figure 15–2. The efficiency frontier.

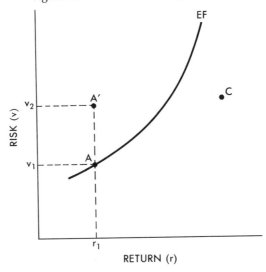

vestor can expect from a portfolio yielding some expected rate of return. For example, portfolio A yields a return of r_1 and has a minimum risk of v_1. The same portfolio could have a higher degree of risk, say v_2, and be labeled A'. This could occur if the investor had incorrectly estimated the risk connected with portfolio A.

Presumably, however, an investor has had long experience with the return and risk performance of various types of portfolios. This past experience should enable him to estimate the maximum return at minimum risk of the portfolio with some element of certainty. If he does this for a number of portfolios, we can derive the EF line (see Figure 15–2). Any point on or above this curve can be attained. It is best, of course, to be on the efficiency frontier. Any point beneath the EF curve, such as portfolio C, is unattainable and hence, even if it were to give greater utility, cannot be considered. The EF line gets steeper as we move along it to the right because of the underlying assumption that as one changes a portfolio to increase earnings by a given amount, risk increases more than in proportion to the increment in earnings.

We are now in a position to determine the *optimum portfolio,* the one that maximizes return, minimizes risk, and maximizes satisfaction. Figure 15–3 combines Figures 15–1 and 15–2, and determines that the optimum portfolio is B where the EF line is just tangent to an indifference curve. At this point, risk, return, and level of indifference are v_1, r_1, and I_1, respectively. Any portfolio above EF is inefficient and not to be sought; any portfolio below EF cannot be attained. Only points *on* EF should be considered. Point A, for example, is on EF and is attainable, but our investor's indifference map shows that point B is preferable. Apparently our investor at B relative to A gains more utility from more return than he loses from

Figure 15-3. Optimum portfolio determination.

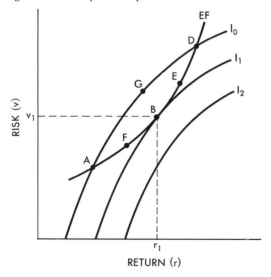

greater risk. Similarly, *D* is on *EF*, but the risk connected with this portfolio is high and the investor would gain more utility from a drop in risk than he would lose from a drop in return if he changed his portfolio from *D* to *B*.

The optimum portfolio we have been discussing is not absolute. Changes occur in the real world. For example, investor attitudes change. One may be willing to assume greater risk for a given level of earnings. In this case, the family of indifference curves might move upward and to the left. Some portfolio other than *B* would be chosen—one that assumed more risk, such as *E*. Or one might become more cautious, in which case the indifference map would move downward. One's new portfolio might now have less risk, say at *F*, or the efficiency frontier might change. If calculations about risk and return prove inaccurate due to excess optimism, then *EF* should move upward and to the left. The result might be a new portfolio such as *G* with more risk, less return, and less utility.

There are practical limitations to the preceding type of analysis. It is very difficult to estimate risk, return, and investor indifference maps. Portfolio managers in the real world must render independent judgments, and they can easily be wrong. But models of portfolio determination, at least, can improve investor judgments.

Supplementary Readings

Board of Governors of the Federal Reserve System. *Flow of Funds Accounts: 1945–1968* (Washington D.C., 1970), pp. I.7–I.45.

Lerner, Eugene M. *Managerial Finance: A Systems Approach* (Harcourt Brace Jovanovich, 1971), Chapters 15 and 20.

Advanced Readings:

Culbertson, J. M. "The Term Structure of Interest Rates." *Quarterly Journal of Economics* (1957), pp. 485–517.

Hicks, John R. *Value and Capital,* 2nd ed. (Clarendon Press, 1942).

Lutz, Friedrich. "The Term Structure of Interest Rates." *Quarterly Journal of Economics* (1940), pp. 36–63.

Markowitz, Harry. *Portfolio Selection: Efficient Diversification of Investments* (John Wiley, 1959).

Meiselman, David. *The Term Structure of Interest Rates* (Prentice-Hall, 1962).

Modigliani, Franco, and Richard Sutch. "Innovations in Interest Rate Policy." *American Economic Review* (May 1966), pp. 178–97.

See also footnotes 2–6.

Part IV   MONEY AND AGGREGATE ECONOMIC ACTIVITY

16 An Introduction
to Monetary Theory

OBSERVATIONS ON THEORY

MONETARY THEORY

PREVIEW OF PARTS IV AND V

OBSERVATIONS ON THEORY

Like most scientific theory, economic theory may function as a framework of analysis or simply as a series of hypotheses subject to empirical verification. As an analytical framework, economic theory provides a *measure* against which to observe the real world—a framework that may or may not correspond to the actual functioning of the economy. A set of economic hypotheses, on the other hand, attempts to *explain* how the world in which we live and work actually operates.

These two views of economic theory are obviously not completely distinct from one another. A set of hypotheses often leads to the formulation of a framework of analysis. Thus, in monetary theory, for example, what we now call the "Keynesian theory" led to the "Keynesian income-expenditure analytical framework," which any economist can use to help explain reality, no matter what set of hypotheses he tentatively accepts.

Most economists strive to make their framework of analysis correspond as closely as possible to reality. Thus, to some extent both aspects of economic theory have the same ultimate goal. It could be argued that it makes little difference whether economic theory bears a close relation to the real world, as long as it is useful in explaining and predicting the behavior of economic variables. This line of reasoning may be specious, however. It is somewhat like saying that we should continue to use the Ptolemaic system to explain the movements of the planets and stars because that system does a fairly good job of predicting the motions of some heavenly bodies. We have long since put aside the Egyptian astronomer's method because other systems seem to be closer to the reality of cause and effect and give even better results. Similarly, a particular economic theory may adequately predict behavior, but it may be completely misleading about the causal forces behind the economic events it forecasts.

To have value, economics must improve our understanding of the real world. All science is dedicated to this end. Since economics is specifically concerned with the study of our economic and social environment, its analytical framework and its hypotheses must come closer and closer to an approximately correct interpretation of economic causes, effects, and interrelationships. This can be accomplished only by the continual quantitative testing of hypotheses — testing designed not to prove hypotheses, but to disprove them. If a proposition is not disproved, it is tentatively accepted until a better explanation is offered. This scientific method of testing theories, sometimes called the *falsification method*,[1] involves the following steps: (1) formulation of a theory, (2) deduction of conclusions from the theory, (3) comparison of the theory with other theories, (4) quantitative testing of the theory's conclusions, and (5) tentative acceptance of the theory if it has not been proven false.

MONETARY THEORY

Monetary theory may be approached in the manner just described. Contemporary economists, when handling problems of income determination, economic fluctuations, and economic growth, treat these problems almost exclusively within the Keynesian income-expenditure analytical framework. Even those economists who reject many of the Keynesian hypotheses concerning money and income use the general Keynesian framework as a tool of analysis.

Monetary theory studies the influence of the demand for and supply of money upon prices, interest, output, and employment. Actually, monetary theory is part of a broader area of study — the theory of output and employment determination, sometimes called *macroeconomic theory*. The purpose here is to place money in its proper perspective within the broader study of macroeconomic analysis. In so doing, some time will have to be spent developing that framework of analysis, but the emphasis will be on money and the demand for it within that framework. A thorough treatment of aggregate economic activity may be found in books on output and employment theory.[2]

The role money plays in the economy is a subject of great controversy among contemporary economists. The areas of dispute are theoretical and empirical in nature. Most economists would agree that changes in the supply and in the demand for money play a significant role in determining the level of economic activity. The disagreement centers on the mechanism by which these changes influence the economy. Briefly, one position is that interest rates affect the demand for investment goods and that this demand, in turn, helps determine income and employment; variations in the stock of money and the demand for money change interest rates and hence affect income and employment. This is the view of many *Keynesian theorists*. Other economists, although they accept the view that money supply and demand determine the interest rate, believe in addition that a change in the money supply and in the demand for money may directly affect the demand

---

[1] Karl Popper. *The Logic of Scientific Discovery* (Basic Books, 1959), Chapter 4.
[2] See Robert L. Crouch. *Macroeconomics* (Harcourt Brace Jovanovich, 1972); and Edward Shapiro. *Macroeconomic Analysis*, 3rd ed. (Harcourt Brace Jovanovich, 1974).

for various forms of liquid and real wealth, and hence aggregate economic activity. This is the view of many contemporary *quantity theorists*. Ultimately, the differences between these two points of view may be resolved by empirical work.[3]

PREVIEW OF PARTS IV AND V

In Part IV we shall first be concerned with the historical development of monetary theory, referring briefly to several economists who have made significant contributions to the development of contemporary theories and our framework of analysis. After placing our current state of knowledge in historical perspective, we shall then study the Keynesian framework of analysis and use it to examine various contemporary hypotheses concerning the role that money plays in the economy. With this background in theory and analysis we will be better able to discuss the economic policy issues in Part V.

Supplementary Readings

DeAlessi, Louis. "Reversals of Assumptions and Implications." *Journal of Political Economy* (1971), pp. 867–77.
Friedman, Milton. "The Methodology of Positive Economics." In *Essays in Positive Economics* (University of Chicago Press, 1953).
Popper, Karl. *The Logic of Scientific Discovery* (Basic Books, 1959).

[3] A fuller exposition of these alternative theoretical positions will appear in Chapter 26.

17   The Historical Development of Monetary Theory

INTRODUCTION

THE SIXTEENTH CENTURY

Jean Bodin (1530–1596)

THE SEVENTEENTH AND EIGHTEENTH CENTURIES

John Locke (1632–1704)
John Law (1671–1729)
Richard Cantillon (1680–1734)

THE NINETEENTH CENTURY

Henry Thornton (1760–1815)
David Ricardo (1772–1823)
John Stuart Mill (1806–1873)
Definition of money
Value of money
Credit

THE EARLY TWENTIETH CENTURY

Irving Fisher (1867–1947)
The equation of exchange
Contemporary versions of the equation of exchange
Fisher's use of the equation of exchange
Fisher's theory of the cycle
Fisher on interest and inflation
Knut Wicksell (1851–1926)
The Cambridge School
The cash-balance equation
The cash-balance equation as a tool of analysis

SUMMARY AND EVALUATION

INTRODUCTION

In this chapter we shall attempt to summarize the historical development of monetary theory. Because any brief survey is necessarily incomplete, we shall emphasize a selected group of philosophers and economists whose work in some way constituted an advance in economic knowledge or synthesized a stream of analysis. By showing how earlier theorists visualized the relationship between monetary phenomena and the state of economic activity, we can view our contemporary framework of analysis in perspective.

The philosophers of the sixteenth, seventeenth, and eighteenth centuries were concerned with economic problems much like ours today — less than full employment, inflation, and a need for growth in the level of aggregate economic activity. The policy recommendations made then (to expand bank credit and the money stock during periods of depression and restrict the expansion of the money stock during periods of full employment and rising prices) were ones we still hear made today.

On the other hand, most economists of the nineteenth and early twentieth centuries concentrated on problems of the pricing process. They wanted to know how best to allocate productive resources among competing uses, and were concerned with how the prices of productive resources and final products were determined. These economists tended to neglect problems of the economy as a whole, largely because they assumed full employment of resources. Although they were aware that less than full employment situations existed, they accepted the view that production creates its own demand. Under this assumption, depression simply becomes a temporary departure from normal full employment. In the long run, money supply and demand changes lead to price changes, but not to output and employment changes.

During the early part of the twentieth century, there was a revival of interest in monetary economics and a renewed concern with crises affecting the level of economic activity. Economists sought to develop a framework of analysis that could explain both price behavior and cyclical movements in the economy. Thus, Irving Fisher developed the equation of exchange. Alfred Marshall, John Maynard Keynes, Dennis H. Robertson,

Leon Walras, and A. C. Pigou formulated alternative cash-balance equations. These equations, as we shall see, are still often used by economists to explain not only price-level behavior but also output and demand for money changes. Other economists placed greater emphasis on explaining the volatile nature of the economy — its cyclical ups and downs. Irving Fisher wrote on this problem, as did Knut Wicksell, Ralph Hawtrey, and others. They sought a complete theory of the cycle, focusing for the most part on the interest rate as the prime cyclical mover. As an economic policy, they advocated central bank control over the interest rate in order to eliminate recurrent inflations and recessions.

The depression of the 1930s demonstrated the inadequacies of these theories, however. The economic models of the early twentieth century were too elementary to handle the complex problems of our technically advanced society. The old theories reasoned too simply from cause to effect, neglecting the manifold interrelationships between variables. As a result, we were ready for the "Keynesian Revolution" which completely changed our notions about the determination of overall economic activity. (We shall analyze these developments at length in Chapters 18–21. Alternative current monetary theories will be examined in Chapter 26.)

THE SIXTEENTH CENTURY

Jean Bodin (1530–1596)

Those who write on economic subjects tend to do so within the context of the problems of their age. The fifteenth, sixteenth, and seventeenth centuries were periods of price revolution. Thus, many economic philosophers of the time were concerned largely with explaining why prices had risen.

In his "Reply to the Paradoxes of Malestroit Concerning the Dearness of All Things and the Remedy Therefor," for example, Jean Bodin argued that there were a number of reasons for the rise in French prices during the sixteenth century, the principal five being the abundance of gold and silver, monopolies, scarcity, the pleasure of princes, and the debasement of the coinage.

Bodin's "Reply" was a rebuttal of Malestroit's contention that prices in France were no higher than in the past since goods cost no more gold and silver than formerly. Bodin countered this by citing evidence that wine and wheat cost 20 times what they had a hundred years before, and that the price of land — which he assumed to be fixed in quantity and quality — was three times what it had been 50 years earlier. However, Bodin was not content merely to cite statistics to prove that prices had risen; he was fundamentally concerned with the *causes* of the rise in prices. He listed the five causes just cited, the most important of which was the first — the abundance of gold and silver.

I find that the high prices we see today are due to some four or five causes. The principal and almost the only one (which no one has referred to until now) is the abundance of gold and silver, which is today much greater in this Kingdom than it was four hundred years ago, to go no further back.[1]

Bodin went on to state that the amount of gold and silver, both used as currency in his time, had increased substantially and that, as a consequence, prices had risen. Here we have one of the first statements linking price movements to movements in the money stock. Bodin also raised this question: if it is the abundance of gold and silver that causes high prices, where does the increase in gold and silver come from? It arises, he explained, from trade with foreigners who have mines of gold and silver at their disposal. Spain, for example, with gold and silver obtained from the mines of Peru, was able to demand increased quantities of goods and services produced in France—wheat, cloth, dyes, paper, and books. England had mines also and, since she could not produce wine, prunes, and dye, she bought them from France with her gold and silver. Thus, as we would say today, the increased supply of money caused an increased demand for French goods. Prices responded by increasing both at home and abroad.

THE SEVENTEENTH AND EIGHTEENTH CENTURIES

The economic problems of the late seventeenth and much of the eighteenth century were quite different from those of the preceding period in which Bodin wrote. Now the problems were boom and bust, economic distress, and less than full employment—in many ways problems much like those of the depression years of this century. Writers of the seventeenth and eighteenth centuries argued that economic activity and trade depended on money and its circulation. They concentrated on the interaction of the demand for goods and services, the stock of money, the quickness of circulation, the volume of employment, and the price level.

John Locke (1632–1704)

John Locke, writing in the 1690s, advanced monetary theory considerably beyond Bodin.[2] Whereas Bodin had been primarily concerned with the effects of money on prices, Locke expanded Bodin's discussion by study-

---

[1] Jean Bodin. "La Réponse de Jean Bodin aux paradoxes de Malestroit touchant l'encherissement de toutes choses et le moyen d'y remedier." Reprinted in Arthur E. Monroe (ed.), *Early Economic Thought* (Harvard University Press, 1924), p. 127.
[2] See John Locke. *Consequences of the Lowering of Interest and Raising the Value of Money* (1692); and *Further Considerations Concerning Raising the Value of Money* (1696). For an excellent discussion of Locke and other writers of the eighteenth century, see Douglas Vickers' *Studies in the Theory of Money 1690–1776* (Chilton Company, 1959).

ing the effects of money on trade, the role of the demand for money, and the importance of interest rates in the economy. Locke held, for example, that money was necessary to carry on trade. If money were not generally available and in circulation, then it would be difficult to purchase goods and services and a stoppage of trade would result. Thus he posited a relationship between money and economic activity, although he did not explain precisely how this relationship operated.

To Locke, money was important in another respect: a certain amount of money was needed to carry on a specific amount of trade. The amount needed depended upon the "quickness of circulation" of money. Today we would say *velocity* of circulation, rather than "quickness." Both terms refer to the number of times that the money in the economy is spent or "turned over" during a given period. The more often money is spent, the more economic activity takes place. The less often it is spent, the lower is the volume of trade. To put it another way, the greater the amount of money people want to hold, the smaller its turnover (velocity) and the greater the amount of money that will be needed to carry on a specific volume of trade. The relative needs of the community for the necessities of life and the extent of its commerce thus determine how much money is demanded and, consequently, its "quickness of circulation." Here, Locke made a significant advance in monetary analysis; this is one of the first formulations of the velocity and the demand for money concepts.

Locke also had a relatively advanced notion of *interest*. He defined "interest" as the price for the hire of money, and the level of interest as determined by the relationship between the amount of money needed and the amount available. Thus, if the amount needed for trade were great relative to the supply, the interest rate would be high. Furthermore, if the rate of interest were legally to be forced beneath this high level, no additional borrowing could take place because lenders would be unwilling to lend.

John Law (1671–1729)

John Law, aside from his reputation as a romantic adventurer, financier, and organizer of the Banque Royale in France, is best known as the author of *Money and Trade Considered* (1705). Writing in a period of high unemployment, Law argued that trade depends upon money. Hence, the more money there is in the economy, the more likely we are to have full employment.

In Law's time, money consisted largely of gold and silver coin. Thus, according to his theory, the more coin there was in circulation, the greater the employment. Law went further than this, however, and extended the argument to bank notes. The more "credit money" in circulation, he said, the more people employed. In a period of less than full employment, the monetary authority could put more money into circulation and hence induce a higher level of employment by allowing banks to issue paper currency.

Law did not propose an unlimited issue of paper currency, but a limited one suited to the needs of trade so that there would be no danger of overextending currency. This argument is similar to the "commercial loan theory of banking," also called the "real bills doctrine,"[3] discussed in Chapter 3. Law proposed that the notes issued be secured by the value of land. Thus, the maximum amount of notes that could be issued would be limited by the total value of land. The actual amount of notes in circulation, as long as it was less than the value of land, would depend on the need for money in trade. Hence there would be little change in the value of money, and the amount of money would always be adequate to keep trade and employment active.

The flaw in this argument is that the system depends entirely on a permanent valuation of land. If the price of land were to increase, then more currency could be issued. This would drive up the price of other goods and increase the need for additional money balances. Cumulative price inflation would follow. If, on the other hand, the value of land were to decrease, a reduction in the amount of money in circulation would be necessary. This, in turn, would reduce trade, the price of other goods, and the need for money. Cumulative price deflation would ensue.

Law's principal contribution to monetary analysis was his attempt to establish a positive relationship between employment, trade, and the amount of metallic and bank money in the economy.

Richard Cantillon (1680–1734)

Richard Cantillon, in his essay "On the Nature of Commerce in General" (written in 1734 and published in 1755), went far beyond Bodin, Locke, or Law in his examination of monetary principles. He did not argue as directly as had his predecessors from money changes to either price or employment changes, however. Instead he was concerned with the process by which money stock changes affect price. Cantillon was apparently one of the first to argue that an increase in the quantity of money raises prices through its effect on demand. His contributions, however, valuable as they were, did not directly affect economic thought until the latter half of the nineteenth century when Stanley Jevons rediscovered Cantillon's work.

Cantillon's theory of money was principally concerned with the relation between money and prices, although he did discuss employment changes to some degree. He wanted to discover how the money-price relation operates. "The great difficulty of this analysis consists in discovering by what path and in what proportion the increase of money raises the price of things,"[4] The solution he arrived at was ". . . that in general an increase in

---

[3] See Lloyd W. Mints' *A History of Banking Theory* (University of Chicago Press, 1945), pp. 30–32, for the classic refutation of this doctrine.
[4] Richard Cantillon. "On the Nature of Commerce in General." Reprinted in Arthur E. Monroe, *op. cit.,* p. 264.

the monetary stock causes in a State a proportional increase in consumption, which by degrees produces the rise of prices."[5] Thus, an increase in the money stock stimulates demand, which eventually leads to price increases.

How does this occur? Cantillon presented several examples, two of which are considered here. First, if the increase in money comes from mining, then the mine owners and those who work the mines will increase their expenditures on food, clothing, and other goods. This gives added employment to artisans, who, in turn, will increase their expenditures. Thus, there will be a multiple round of expenditure and employment increases. In the process, however, prices begin to rise, and those people who did not participate in the initial round of expenditure and employment increases will suffer from the higher prices. Cantillon regards these people as fixed-income recipients with only two alternatives — they can reduce their consumption or leave the country. "This, roughly, is how a considerable increase of money from Mines increases consumption; and while diminishing the number of inhabitants, brings about a greater expenditure among those who remain."[6] The increased domestic price level would then induce people to make more purchases abroad, where goods are cheaper. This would cause money to leave the economy, and a reverse cycle of lower money circulation, poverty, and misery would follow.

Cantillon's second case imagines an increased money stock resulting from a country selling more abroad than it purchases — what we now term a favorable balance of trade. With more money coming into the country than is leaving, there will be a gradual increase in expenditures, consumption, and prices. This time, however, the process will not reverse itself unless the favorable balance of trade is upset.

Thus Cantillon developed a relatively sophisticated theory of how money affects the economy. He did not limit himself to a discussion of the supply of money; he also examined its velocity: ". . . an acceleration, or a greater speed, in the circulation of money in trade amounts to the same thing as an increase in standard money."[7] Cantillon showed that an increase in the velocity of money, given the money supply, would increase trade, just as an increase in the money supply, given constant velocity, would increase trade.

THE NINETEENTH CENTURY

There were relatively few developments in monetary theory in the nineteenth century. Economists turned away from the study of the economy as a whole to the study of commodity pricing and resource allocation. When discussing monetary phenomena, they generally assumed a full employ-

---

[5] *Ibid.*
[6] *Ibid.*, p. 265.
[7] *Ibid.*, p. 264.

ment economy, which led them to consider money changes in terms of price-level effects. As a consequence, many of these economists developed what today we would call a "crude quantity theory of money." In essence, they maintained that money stock changes led to proportionate price-level changes. Although they knew of the velocity concept, they usually assumed velocity to be constant.

Since they were primarily concerned with resource analysis, nineteenth-century economists did not consider short-run unemployment problems. They usually accepted *Say's law* that "production creates its own demand." According to this theory, when people work and create goods, they receive income—most of which is spent. What is not spent is saved, but this does not cause demand to fall since funds that are saved will eventually be channeled into investment demand for such goods as plant equipment. Thus the demand for new goods is created by the supply. Because demand is always sufficient to take goods off the market, less than full employment cannot persist long. Today, of course, we have only to point to the depression of the 1930s and subsequent recurring recessions to see the limitations of this concept.

Some nineteenth-century economists did write about money, however, and men like Thornton, Ricardo, and Mill made a number of contributions to monetary theory.

Henry Thornton (1760–1815)

Thornton wrote during the Napoleonic wars, when the Bank of England refused to convert paper currency into specie (metallic money). Prices rose because of "the restriction," as it was called, and a vigorous monetary debate followed. One group, the bullionists, argued that the value of paper currency had depreciated because it had been issued to excess. The other group, the antibullionists, did not believe that paper currency could be issued to excess if it were issued on the basis of the needs of trade. Here again is the real bills doctrine. Notice also how this debate centered on the relation between money and prices, not on the relation between money and employment.

Henry Thornton was a bullionist. Here is his view of how money stock changes lead to price changes:

Let us, now, trace carefully the steps by which an encrease of paper serves to lift up the price of articles. Let us suppose, for example, an encreased number of Bank of England notes [are] to be issued. In such case the traders in the metropolis discover that there is a more than usual facility of obtaining notes at the bank. . . . Every trader is encouraged by the knowledge of this facility of borrowing . . . is rendered, by the plenty of money, somewhat more ready to buy, and rather less eager to sell. . . . Thus an inclination to buy is created in all quarters, and an indisposition to sell. Now, since the cost of articles depends on the issue of that general conflict between buyers and sellers . . . it follows, that any circumstance which serves to communicate a greater degree of eagerness to the mind of one party than to that of the other, will have an influence on price.[8]

In Thornton's opinion, an increased money stock will lead to increased demand and consequently to higher prices. He does not say that price need rise proportionately to the increase in the money stock. Thornton was well aware that an increase in money may lead to the employment of idle factors of production and, hence, to more output but not necessarily higher prices. However, he argues that the number of unemployed persons is limited. Hence, once the idle are employed, prices will rise as long as the stock of money continues to increase:

An encreased quantity of articles can only arise from additional commodities either brought from abroad or produced at home through the exertion of new industry. . . .

When the Bank of England, enlarges its paper, it augments, in the same degree, as we must here suppose, its loans to individuals. These favoured persons immediately conceive, and not without reason, that they have obtained an additional though borrowed capital, by which they can push their own particular manufacture or branch of commerce. . . .

But, first, it is obvious, that the antecedently idle persons to whom we may suppose the new capital to give employ, are limited in number; and that, therefore, if the encreased issue is indefinite, it will set to work labourers, of whom a part will be drawn from other, and perhaps, no less useful occupations. . . .

. . . whatever view we take of the subject, we seem obliged to admit, that although additional industry will be one effect of an extraordinary emission of paper, a rise in the cost of articles will be another.[9]

Another of Thornton's contributions is the policy conclusion he draws from his analysis. He argues that the amount of paper money should be limited—that money should neither be issued to excess nor allowed to diminish sharply—in order to limit price variation. As the economy grows in productivity, however, some increase of money stock should be permitted.[10] Economists are still discussing proposals of this sort today.

David Ricardo (1772–1823)

Ricardo, like Thornton, was a bullionist. His writing, however, is by no means as succinct as Thornton's. If we were to judge Ricardo only on the basis of his work in *The Principles of Political Economy and Taxation* (1821), we would be forced to conclude that he was a crude quantity theorist. He argued that the value of paper money could be maintained by limiting its quantity.

[8] Henry Thornton. *An Enquiry into the Nature and Effects of the Paper Credit of Great Britain* (1802), pp. 195–96.
[9] *Ibid.*, pp. 257–61.
[10] *Ibid.*, p. 295.

In "On the High Price of Bullion," however, he introduced the idea of "rapidity of circulation":

The value of the circulating medium of every country bears some proportion to the value of the commodities which it circulates. In some countries, this proportion is much greater than in others, and varies, on some occasions, in the same country. It depends upon the rapidity of circulation, upon the degree of confidence and credit existing between traders, and above all, on the judicious operations of banking.[11]

In other words, given a constant stock of money and no change in productivity, an increase in the rapidity of circulation (velocity) of money will lead to a price-level increase. When velocity increases, the money supply is being used more often because people are demanding more goods and services. To obtain more goods, each individual draws down his money holdings, but collectively money holdings remain the same. This is how velocity increases. People, however, do not receive more goods because more are not available; hence the increased demand simply bids up the price of goods. Ricardo did not make this extension of the analysis, however. Like other bullionists, he assumed that velocity was as high as possible in Great Britain and hence was a constant. Because of this erroneous assumption, his statement that the value of money depends on the rapidity of circulation is rendered meaningless.

With respect to economic policy, Ricardo, too, felt that the amount of paper money issued should be limited because its overissue would lead to price increases.

John Stuart Mill (1806–1873)

The works of John Stuart Mill provide us with a synthesis of the classical economics of the nineteenth century. Although well aware of unemployment and business crises, Mill accepted Say's law. As a consequence, his monetary analysis, too, concentrated largely on the relation between money and prices.

Most of Mill's monetary theory is developed in Book III of his *Principles of Political Economy*. He begins with a definition of money that is actually very close to the definition many textbooks give today.

Definition of money. Mill defines money as a medium of exchange and common measure of value. Money is useful because of the inconveniences of barter and the necessity of having something durable in circulation. Mill thought gold and silver particularly well suited to these purposes; they are portable, imperishable, divisible, and acceptable to all people. "Of all com-

---

[11] David Ricardo. "On the High Price of Bullion," Reprinted in Piero Sraffa, *The Works and Correspondence of David Richardo,* Vol. 3, (London: Cambridge University Press, 1951), p. 90.

modities they are among the least influenced by any of the causes which produce fluctuations of value."[12] Furthermore, any change in their value would not be sudden, since their quantity could not readily be diminished or increased.

Value of money. Mill considered money a commodity, the value of which was determined like that of any other commodity—temporarily by supply and demand, and in the long run by the cost of production. Cantillon and Ricardo had held similar positions.

According to Mill, the value of money depends, other things being equal, upon its quantity and its rapidity of circulation. The purchasing power of money depends first on supply and demand.

The supply of money, then, is the quantity of it which people are wanting to lay out; that is, all the money they have in their possession, except what they are hoarding, or at least keeping by them as a reserve for future contingencies. The supply of money, in short, is all the money in circulation at the time.[13]

This concept of money supply differs from our current understanding of the term in that we include monetary hoards. The demand for money Mill defines as "all the goods offered for sale."[14] Our present definition of money includes demand deposits, but Mill considered only real commodities to be money.

How do demand and supply determine the value of money? "An increase of the quantity of money raises prices, and a diminution lowers them. . . ."[15] Thus, if other things remain unchanged, an increase in the supply of money would increase the demand for goods by an equal amount, and this would lead to a universal rise in prices.

The rapidity of circulation also helps determine the value of money. Mill defines it as "the average number of purchases made by each piece in order to effect a given pecuniary amount of transactions."[16] If the number of transactions and the amount of money is fixed, then the value of money varies inversely with the rapidity of circulation. That is, the higher the rapidity of circulation grows, the less the purchasing power of a particular amount of money will be and the higher the price of goods and services. This definition of velocity is very much like that later used by Irving Fisher. The basic concept is that the more often money changes hands in the purchase of goods and services, given the amount of goods available, the greater the demand for goods will be and the higher the prices of those goods.

[12] John Stuart Mill. *Principles of Political Economy,* Ashley Edition (Longmans Green, 1909), p. 485.
[13] *Ibid.,* 490.
[14] *Ibid.*
[15] *Ibid.,* p. 495.
[16] *Ibid.*

In general, Mill formulated what amounts to a relatively crude quantity theory of money. His other theory of the value of money—the cost of production theory—has been almost universally abandoned.

Credit. Mill did not ignore the importance of credit; on the contrary, he conceived of it as a major determinant of the price level. He felt that credit, no matter what form it took (bank notes, bills of exchange, promissory notes, or deposits and checks), had an influence on the price level. In fact, it would have the same influence on the price level as gold and silver money. An increase in the volume of credit extension would increase the demand for goods and, accordingly, raise prices. Similarly, an increase in the amount of inconvertible paper currency (paper money that is not convertible on demand into gold and silver coin) would cause price increases.[17]

THE EARLY TWENTIETH CENTURY

Economists of the early twentieth century continued in the tradition of nineteenth-century classical economics. They believed that the price level is determined by the volume of money, that relative prices are determined by the supply of and demand for commodities, and that full employment is the normal state of the economy. These scholars did advance monetary theory in two areas, however. First, they formulated alternative analytical approaches to explaining the economic role of money: the Fisher *transactions equation of exchange* and the various Cambridge *cash-balance equations* are examples of their development of monetary theory as a framework of analysis. Second, they made a renewed attempt to understand the role of money in short-term cyclical fluctuations, although they usually made little effort to verify their hypotheses empirically. The remainder of this chapter examines these early twentieth-century contributions to monetary theory.

Irving Fisher (1867–1947)

Irving Fisher, an American mathematician and economist, formulated the *equation of exchange,* attempted a statement of the quantity theory of money in the early twentieth century, developed a theory of the business cycle that was designed to explain economic fluctuations during periods of transition when prices are rising or falling, and related interest rates to inflation.

The equation of exchange. The equation of exchange formulated by Irving Fisher was

---

[17] *Ibid.,* Chapters 12 and 13.

$$MV + M'V' = \Sigma pQ \qquad [17\text{-}1]$$

where M is the amount of currency in the economy during a given year, V is the velocity of circulation (turnover) of this currency, M' is the volume of demand deposits in the economy during the year, V' is the velocity of circulation of these demand deposits, and ΣpQ is the sum of (1) the average price p of a commodity purchased in the economy during the given year multiplied by the quantity Q of it purchased, (2) the average price p' of another commodity purchased during the given year multiplied by the quantity Q' of it purchased, and (3) so forth for all other goods exchanged. In other words, equation 17–1 is a simplified way of expressing the following equation:

$$MV + M'V' = pQ + p'Q' \ . \ . \ . \qquad [17\text{-}2]$$

Fisher himself further simplified this equation to

$$MV + M'V' = PT \qquad [17\text{-}3]$$

where P is a weighted average of prices and T is the sum of all the Qs. Strictly speaking, this simplification is not legitimate, since it implies that one can add together such diverse commodities as eggs, guns, and oranges. If each of the symbols in equation 17–3 is expressed as an index number, however, this criticism no longer applies. P and T then become indices of prices and quantities, respectively, and the equation shows the relative change in each of their magnitudes rather than in their absolute values.

Contemporary versions of the equation of exchange. Today, many variants of equations 17–1, 17–2, and 17–3 are used by economists. One particularly popular version is

$$MV = PQ \qquad [17\text{-}4]$$

where M is the average amount of money in the economy during a specified period (such as a year), V is the number of times M is spent on PQ, and PQ is the sum of the values of a specified group of goods.[18]

There are two principal differences between Fisher's equation of exchange and this contemporary formulation. First, the contemporary definition of M includes both currency and demand-deposit money, whereas Fisher's M includes only currency. Second, Fisher's PQ includes all goods and services exchanged during a given period, whereas contemporary economists usually define PQ in terms of the specific problem they are considering. When the relation between money and gross national product is being considered, for example, PQ refers to gross national product — the value of newly produced final goods and services. V, in this instance, is an *income velocity* concept, showing the number of times that the volume of

---

[18] See Chapter 18 for a complementary discussion.

money M is spent on gross national product. When used in this manner, equation 17–4 is sometimes restated as

$$MV = Y \qquad [17\text{--}5]$$

where Y is gross national product.

On the other hand, when economists study the relation of the expenditure of money to all goods and services bought and sold, all transactions are considered—dealings in new goods and services, the resale of used goods, financial transactions, and so on. In this case, PQ is much larger than gross national product, and V represents *transactions velocity,* the number of times money is spent on *all* types of goods and services during a given period. This type of velocity figure, of course, is much larger than the income velocity figure in equation 17–5. Fisher's V and V' both represent transactions velocities. Sometimes, when economists wish to emphasize that they are concerned with transactions velocity, they will use the following type of Fisher equation:

$$MV = PT \qquad [17\text{--}6]$$

Here M is the average amount of money in circulation during a period, V is the number of times that M is used in the purchase of PT, and PT is the monetary value of all transactions in the economy during the period in question.

The difference between equations 17–5 and 17–6 can be illustrated as follows. Assume that the average amount of money in a given year t is $250 billion and that gross national product Y is $1,250 billion. Then, since $MV = Y$ and $250 billion $\times V =$ $1,250 billion, V (income velocity) must equal 5.0 in terms of equation 17–5. Thus, the money stock was used 5.0 times in the purchase of gross national product. If, in some subsequent time period $t + 1$, M rises to $300 billion and Y to $1,800 billion, then V must also increase to 6.0.

On the other hand, if M is $250 billion in time period t, and the value of all transactions is, say, $5,000 billion, then, since $MV = PT$, V must equal 20 in terms of equation 17–6. If M rises to $300 billion and PT to $5,700 billion, then V must decline to 19.

One factor that should be stressed concerning the equation of exchange is that the equation itself is a mere truism. No matter what variant of the equation is used, it merely summarizes what has occurred. The left-hand side—the money side—of the equation must always equal the right-hand side—the goods side. Thus, each side is simply a different way of describing the same phenomena—expenditures. The goods side expresses the value of expenditures; the money side expresses the volume of money multiplied by the number of times it is used in arriving at the value of expenditures.

The equation of exchange itself contains no statement of causality. Equation 17–4, for example, *does not explain why M, V, P,* and *Q* possess certain values, and it does not tell us how a change in one of the four magnitudes will cause a change in the others. This equation merely summarizes in convenient form the result of the values of $M, V, P,$ and Q. It is the task of theory, however, as hypothesis, to explain cause and effect. One of the functions of contemporary monetary theory, for example, as developed in Chapters 20 and 26, is to explain why velocity changes. Monetary theory seeks to define causality. Does a change in V lead to a change in PQ, or does the change in PQ determine the change in V? The equation of exchange alone cannot resolve these questions.

Fisher's use of the equation of exchange. An equation of this sort is merely a *tool* economists use to help explain economic changes. Thus Fisher, having formulated equation 17–3, proceeded to use it to explain economic relationships.

On the basis of the equation of exchange, he gave a precise statement of the *quantity theory of money:*

The price level varies (1) directly as the quantity of money in circulation (M), (2) directly as the velocity of its circulation (V), (3) inversely as the volume of trade done by it (T). The first of these three relations is the most important. It constitutes the "quantity theory of money."[19]

However, he carefully hedged this statement:

The quantity theory . . . does not claim that while money is increased in quantity, *other* causes may not affect $M', V, V',$ and the Q's, and thus aggravate or neutralize the effect of M on the p's. But these are not the effects of M on the p's. So far as M *by itself* is concerned, its effect on the p's is strictly proportional. . . .

We have emphasized the fact that the strictly proportional effect on prices of an increase in M is only the *normal* or *ultimate* effect after transition periods are over. The proposition that prices vary with money holds true only as between imaginary periods for each of which prices are stationary or are moving alike upward or downward and at the same rate.[20]

Thus, it would appear that the quantity theory of money, as formulated by Fisher, is valid only in the long run and when all quantities except M and P are constant.

As the preceding quotation shows, Fisher was well aware of how other causes could disturb the relation between money and prices. The factors that he felt would influence the volume of trade T are listed in Table 17–1. Fisher felt that historically these outside influences had usually tended to increase T and to decrease P. However, he looked upon them as long-run sources of change. Population, technical knowledge, and capital accumula-

[19] Irving Fisher. *The Purchasing Power of Money* (Macmillan, 1911), p. 29.
[20] *Ibid.,* pp. 158–59.

TABLE 17-1 FISHER'S OUTSIDE INFLUENCES ON THE VOLUME OF TRADE

Conditions affecting producers
 Geographical differences in natural resources
 The division of labor
 Knowledge of the technique of production
 The accumulation of capital
Conditions affecting consumers
 The extent and variety of human wants
Conditions connecting producers and consumers
 Facilities for transportation
 Relative freedom of trade
 Character of monetary and banking systems
 Business confidence

SOURCE: Irving Fisher. *The Purchasing Power of Money* (Macmillan, 1911), pp. 74–75.

tion changed slowly, but over time would lead to increased trade and possible price declines.

Fisher also examined the outside causes that affect the velocities of circulation of money and deposits. His classification of these factors is given in Table 17–2. He believed that three sets of forces—individual habits (thrift habits, the habit of charging, and the habit of using checks), the systems of payments in the community, and general causes (density of population and rapidity of transportation)—had tended historically to increase the velocity of circulation of money and hence to increase prices. As in the case of variations in T, Fisher saw these influences on velocity as long-run factors. In short-run periods of transition, he believed that there could be substantial variation in velocity.[21]

With respect to outside influences on the volume of deposits M', Fisher felt that the substitution of checks for cash payments had exerted a power-

TABLE 17-2 FISHER'S OUTSIDE INFLUENCES ON THE VELOCITIES
 OF CIRCULATION OF MONEY AND DEPOSITS

Habits of the individual
 As to thrift and hoarding
 As to book credit
 As to the use of checks
Systems of payments in the community
 As to frequency of receipts and disbursements
 As to regularity of receipts and disbursements
 As to correspondence between times and amounts of receipts and disbursements
General causes
 Density of population
 Rapidity of transportation

SOURCE: Irving Fisher. *The Purchasing Power of Money* (Macmillan, 1911), p. 79.

[21] Some of the sources of this short-run change in V are mentioned in our subsequent discussion of Fisher's transition period theory of the cycle. Some contemporary sources of velocity change have already been discussed: (1) commercial bank loan and investment behavior, (2) the development of nonbank financial intermediaries, and (3) the increased use of the credit card.

ful influence in the direction of raising prices. Since today we count demand deposits as part of the money stock, Fisher's argument, in modern terms, simply amounts to a statement that an increase in the money stock tends to increase prices—another way of stating the Fisher version of the quantity theory.

Fisher concluded that the long-run behavior of T tended to lower prices, but that the long-run effect of changes in V, V', and M' was to raise prices. The cumulative effects of these influences over time could well be significant for price-level variations, but in the short run their effects would tend to be negligible. This does not mean that Fisher believed that M and P must always move proportionately in the short run; as we have shown, he felt that M and P need not be proportional in periods of transition.

Fisher's theory of the cycle. Fisher recognized that the relation between money and prices was not rigid and that the economy is generally in a period of transition. He attempted to explain the behavior of prices and the state of economic activity during such periods, which we would term short-run cyclical fluctuations. His explanation is monetary, focusing on interest rate behavior as the source of economic instability: ". . . the peculiar behavior of the rate of interest during transition periods is largely responsible for the crises and depressions in which price movements end."[22]

Economic fluctuations, according to Fisher, occur because the rate of interest fails to respond quickly enough to price changes. In brief, his conception of the business cycle may be described as follows: assume that prices are rising. Because of rising prices and widening profit margins, businesses increase their borrowings at commercial banks. Hence deposit money M' expands. As these funds are spent, prices rise further, enabling profits to continue to increase and still more borrowing to take place. The cost of borrowing increases, but more slowly than prices increase. Disturbances in V, V', and the Qs also occur. Because of the apparent prosperity, increased spending occurs that is not financed solely by increased borrowing; hence, V and V' increase. Output also rises. Some unemployed workers are drawn into the productive process, but the size of population, the rate of invention, and the efficiency of labor "pretty definitely limit the amount of trade that can reasonably be carried on."[23] Thus the Qs can only increase to a limited extent, and the primary effects of the rising M', V, and V' will be on prices.

This type of expansion cannot continue indefinitely, however. As the boom continues, banks will begin to run short of reserves. As a result, the increase of deposit money will stop, although the cost of borrowing will continue to increase. Profits relative to the cost of borrowing will decrease and borrowing will diminish. In addition, firms that borrowed heavily will find themselves unable to renew their loans at former rates of interest.

[22] Fisher, *op. cit.*, p. 56.
[23] *Ibid.*, p. 62.

Some of these firms may fail and so precipitate a financial panic. Because of the loss of business confidence, the cycle then reverses itself: a continuing contraction of loans and deposits occurs, the velocity of money decreases, and people become sufficiently concerned with "solvency" to refrain from spending. All this leads to a decline in prices. Interest rate adjustments lag behind the decline of prices. Output tends to diminish somewhat, and a depression of trade occurs. Prices continue to fall until rates of interest diminish sufficiently but, by the time this happens, the weaker firms have been forced out of business. Once interest rates are low enough for borrowers to be in a position to resume borrowing, prices will stop falling and the previously described upward movement will begin anew.

From a present-day vantage point, the two greatest defects of Fisher's model of the business cycle are its overemphasis on the rate of interest as an economic determinant and the assumption that prices are flexible not only upward but downward. If the response of business borrowing to interest rate adjustments is negligible, as many contemporary economists contend, then the lag of interest rates behind price changes can no longer be considered the *modus operandi* of successive cyclical expansions and contractions. Furthermore, on the downward side of the cycle, businesses generally may refuse to accept lower prices in the face of decreased demand, preferring instead to reduce output (the Qs) and employment. In such a case, the decrease in output may not be temporary, as Fisher contended, and the cycle may therefore not be self-correcting.

Fisher on interest and inflation. The relationship between interest and inflation is another area in which Fisher made significant contributions to monetary economics. He developed a sophisticated theory of interest,[24] and part of his analysis has become important in current monetary theory—particularly the discussion that relates interest rates, anticipated rates of inflation, and aggregate demand.[25] These ideas will be developed further in succeeding chapters. For the present, we shall confine ourselves to some of the more rudimentary aspects of Fisher's discussion.

Fisher made an important distinction between the *market* rate of interest and the *real* rate of interest. The market rate is the actual rate of interest that borrowers pay and lenders receive; the real rate is the market rate of interest adjusted for inflation or deflation. If prices are stable, there is no difference between the two. If prices rise, then the real rate is the market rate minus the rate of inflation; if prices fall, the real rate is the market rate plus the rate of deflation. Thus,

$$r = i - \pi \qquad [17\text{--}7]$$

[24] See Irving Fisher. *The Rate of Interest* (Macmillan, 1907); and *The Theory of Interest* (Macmillan, 1930).
[25] See Jack Carr and Lawrence B. Smith. "Money Supply, Interest Rates, and the Yield Curve." *Journal of Money, Credit and Banking* (1972), pp. 582–94; and William E. Gibson. "Interest Rates and Monetary Policy." *Journal of Political Economy* (1970), pp. 431–55.

where r and i are the real and market rates of interest, respectively, and π is the rate of inflation. For example, if i is 10 percent and π is 10 percent, then the real rate is 0. That is, if an individual borrows $1,000 at 10 percent per annum and repays the principal and interest ($1,100) at the end of one year, and if prices have increased 10 percent in that year, the $1,100 repaid the lender will only purchase the same volume of real goods that $1,000 bought the preceding year. The borrower has, in effect, received the free use of $1,000 in real resources for one year and the lender has received a zero real return—that is, the lender has gained nothing in real terms. It would have been better for the lender to have invested in real goods than to have made a financial investment. On the other hand, if prices decline by 10 percent, then the real rate of interest is 20 percent, since the rate of inflation is a negative 10 percent. Borrowers repaying $1,100 are then giving up dollars that would have been worth $1,200 in real terms the year before.

Some lenders and borrowers may anticipate the rate of inflation, however. Suppose that they both correctly anticipate a 10 percent rate of inflation. Then the lenders would want a real return of 10 percent and might insist on a 20 percent market rate of interest so that they would be compensated for inflation. And the borrowers, knowing that they will gain from inflation, would be willing to pay a market rate of interest in excess of 10 percent.

The preceding line of analysis implicitly assumes that borrowers and lenders can correctly anticipate the rate of inflation or deflation. It will be recalled from the preceding section on Fisher's theory of the cycle, however, that economic fluctuations are in part induced by the failure of actual (market) rates of interest to keep pace with price-level changes. People often act as if they do not expect prices to change much in the short run. This means that if the price level rises, due to a money stock increase, for example, the market rate of interest will lag behind the price level and the real rate of interest will decline and give rise to economic expansion. Ultimately, the market rate of interest adjusts upward, helping to choke off the expansion and the rise in prices. This Fisherine type of analysis has become important in contemporary monetary theory and will be referred to several times in succeeding chapters.

Knut Wicksell (1851–1926)

Like Irving Fisher, Knut Wicksell was a quantity theorist concerned primarily with the relation between money stock, expenditure, price, and interest rate variations as sources of economic disturbance. He believed that changes in the quantity of money (which he defined as currency) would lead to variations in the demand for goods and services and, consequently, to changes in price and expenditures. Thus he argued that ". . . the result of the increase in the quantity of money is a rise in the demand for commodities, and a fall in their supply, with the consequence that all prices rise continuously—until cash balances stand once again in their normal relation to the level of prices."[26]

Changes in the quantity of money are not the sole cause of economic disturbances, however. Wicksell felt that the source of changes in money, output, expenditures, prices, and economic fluctuation lay in discrepancies between market and natural rates of interest. So long as these two rates are equal, he postulated, there will be no change in the price level. When the market rate of interest is less than the natural rate, however, then cumulative price inflation will occur until the two rates are equal. On the other hand, when the market rate is above the natural rate, a cumulative price deflation will take place until the two rates again coincide.

What is meant by the "natural" and "market" rates of interest? The *natural rate of interest* is much the same as what economists now call the marginal efficiency of capital or investment—*the expected yield on newly created capital*. The *market rate of interest is the rate charged by banks*. Should the natural rate be above the market rate, profit margins will be high, the demand for capital goods will be strong, and prices will increase. However, should the natural rate be less than the market rate, profit margins will be low, the demand for capital goods will be weak, and prices will decrease.

Wicksell thought that a discrepancy between these interest rates could set off cyclical distributions. Commercial bank behavior could be one cause of a variance between natural and market rates. For example, Wicksell indicated that banks

. . . raise the rate when their gold stocks are threatened with depletion or their current obligations are so great that their disparity in relation to their gold holdings is regarded as dangerous, or, still more, where both of these things occur together, as is often the case. They lower their rates of interest under the reverse conditions: increased gold holdings or diminished commitments, or both.[27]

Conversely, *a fall in the market rate of interest as banks lower their rates* might lead to the following sequence of events:

In the first place saving will be discouraged and for that reason there will be an increased demand for goods and services for present consumption. In the second place, the profit opportunities of entrepreneurs will be increased and the demand for goods and services, as well as for raw materials already in the market for future production, will evidently increase to the same extent as it had previously been held in check by the higher rate of interest. Owing to the increased income thus accruing to the workers, landowners, and the owners of raw materials, etc., the prices of consumption goods will begin to rise, the more so as the factors of production pre-

---

[26] Knut Wicksell. *Interest and Prices.* Translated by R. F. Kahn (Macmillan, 1936), p. 41.
[27] Knut Wicksell. *Lectures on Political Economy,* Vol. 2 (Macmillan, 1935), p. 204.

viously available are now withdrawn for the purposes of future production. Equilibrium in the market for goods and services will therefore be disturbed. As against an increased demand in two directions there will be an unchanged or even diminished supply, which must result in an increase in wages (rent) and, directly or indirectly, in prices.

. . . we are entitled to assume that all production forces are already fully employed, so that the increased monetary demand principally takes the form of rivalry between employers for labour, raw materials and natural facilities, etc., which consequently leads to an increase in their price, and indirectly, owing to the increased money income or labour and landlords and the increased demand for commodities, to a rise in the price of all consumption goods in addition to that which arises from diminished savings.[28]

Thus, according to Wicksell, an increased supply of money and decreased market rates of interest mean increased demand for consumption and capital goods, and, in a full employment economy, increased prices. This rise in prices will continue so long as banks can continue to lend and keep the market rate of interest beneath the natural rate. Wicksell did not believe, however, that this type of fluctuation would continue to be cumulative. Instead, he felt that the economic system contains self-corrective forces that tend to eliminate the differences between the natural and monetary rates of interest.

A rise in prices exerts its influence . . . on the demands of the monetary circulation. The quantity of coins and notes circulating in the hands of the public is usually much larger than the available reserves of the banks. It follows that quite a small rise in prices may bring about a very significant contraction of the banks' reserves.[29]

A loss of reserves, of course, would mean a reduction in the lending ability of the banking system. If bank solvency were threatened, banks would raise their lending rates. Once they approach the natural rate, the cumulative process of price inflation would stop.

On the other hand, a rise in the market rate above the natural rate, caused by a loss of bank reserves, for example, would reverse this process: consumption, the demand for capital goods, profit opportunities, and prices would all decrease. This process would continue until a return flow of reserves to the banking system occurred, permitting banks to reduce their lending rates. "It is thus confidently to be expected that the bank rate, or more generally the money rate of interest, will always coincide *eventually* with the natural capital rate, or rather that it is always *tending* to coincide with an ever-changing natural rate."[30]

Although Wicksell believed that changes in market rates could set off economic disturbances, he did not view them as the principal initiating

[28] *Ibid.,* pp. 194–95.
[29] Wicksell. *Interest and Prices, op. cit.,* pp. 113–14.
[30] *Ibid.,* p. 117.

force behind business fluctuations. Actually, he thought that the difference between the market and natural rates of interest was usually caused first by a change in the natural rate and then by the typical slowness of the banking system in adjusting its lending rates.

In other words, the difference between the actual loan and normal rates, which we have already designated as a major cause of fluctuations in commodity prices, arises less frequently because the loan rate changes spontaneously whilst the normal or real rate remains unchanged but on the contrary because the normal rate rises or falls whilst the loan rate remains unchanged or only tardily follows it.[31]

Anything tending to change the expected return on new capital would cause changes in this natural rate. If the prospects for production improved, possibly because of technological advances, then the natural rate would rise, and, with the lag of bank rates, a boom would take place. If, however, business expectations were to worsen or if few innovations occurred then the natural rate would fall and we would have "bad times."

Assuming this theory to be correct, is there some appropriate economic policy that would eliminate discrepancies between the market and natural rates of interest, and, accordingly, economic fluctuations? Wicksell thought that an appropriate central bank policy could do the job. "The only possibility of a rational control of the price level must lie in . . . the proper regulation of the interest policy of the banks."[32] Ideally, he argued, a "spontaneous raising or lowering of the discount rate should in the long run have a more powerful influence on prices than any other cause."[33]

The Cambridge School

While Irving Fisher in the United States was developing the equation of exchange, stressing the relation between M, V, p, and Q, various English economists were developing alternative equations. These economists are usually called members of the "Cambridge School," and the equations they developed are known as *cash-balance equations*.[34]

The main difference in approach between Fisher and the members of the Cambridge School is that Fisher related the money stock to total expenditures (ΣPQ) through the velocity of circulation, whereas the Cambridge School related the money stock to total expenditures through the demand for money. This alternative approach caused the Cambridge economists to stress the reasons for *holding* money, whereas Fisher had stressed the

---

[31] Wicksell. *Lectures on Political Economy,* Vol. 2, *op. cit.,* p. 205.

[32] *Ibid.,* p. 216.

[33] *Ibid.*

[34] Dennis H. Robertson, Alfred Marshall, A. C. Pigou, and John Maynard Keynes are usually identified with the Cambridge School. Leon Walras, on the Continent, also made significant contributions to the cash-balance approach.

reasons for *spending* it. Actually, as we shall see, the velocity of money and the demand for it are simply reciprocals of one another.

The cash-balance equation. There are many different formulations of the Cambridge equations. A frequently cited version is

$$M = KRP \qquad [17-8]$$

where M is the amount of money in circulation at a moment of time, R is the real national output of goods and services per unit of time, P is the price of R, and K is the proportion of RP that the community wishes to hold enough money to purchase.[35] The equation "can be read as follows: In a stable community the quantity of money in existence is also that which people wish to hold, having regard to the level of output, its price level, and their preferences as regards the form in which they hold their resources."[36]

This equation is closely related to the various equations discussed earlier. Consider equation 17–4, $MV = PQ$, in which PQ refers to gross national product. The PQ of this equation may be equated with RP in the Cambridge cash-balance equation 17–8. PQ and RP have the same meaning as long as the unit of time is a year. Thus, equation 17–8 may be rewritten as $M = KRQ$, and equation 17–4 may be restated as $M = PQ/V$. Then, since $PQ/V = KPQ$, it follows algebraically that $K = 1/V$. In other words, K and V are simply the reciprocals of one another; the demand for money to hold and the velocity of circulation of money are the inverse of each other. Assume for example, that the money supply M is used four times in the course of a year to purchase PQ. This is just another way of saying that in the course of a year people, on the average, held an amount of money equal to one-quarter of the value of their expenditures on PQ.

Stating the relationship between money and PQ in this manner enables us to focus on the motivations for demanding money to hold. Alfred Marshall, for example, stressed this when he reasoned:

The total value of a country's currency, multiplied into the average number of times of its changing hands for business purposes in a year, is of course equal to the total amount of business transacted in that country by direct payments of currency in that year. But this identical statement does not indicate the causes that govern the rapidity of circulation of currency: to discover them we must look to the amounts of purchasing power which the people of that country elect to keep in the form of currency . . . *changes in the rapidity of circulation of money are themselves incidental to changes in the amount of ready purchasing power which the people of a country find it advantageous to keep in their holding.*"[37]

[35] Dennis H. Robertson. *Lectures on Economic Principles,* Vol. 3 (Staples Press, 1959), Chapter 1.
[36] *Ibid.,* p. 18.
[37] Alfred Marshall. *Money, Credit and Commerce* (London: Macmillan, 1923), p. 43. (Emphasis added.)

What factors determine the relative demand for money K? They are actually much the same as the forces that determine Fisher's V. Dennis Robertson divides them into five groups:

1. Factors connected with business habits — the frequency and regularity with which payments are made, and so forth;

2. Factors connected with the structure of industry — in particular how far the production and sale of output are split up into stages in the hands of different firms between whom payments have to be made for the transfer of goods in process or in store;

3. The general conditions of social and business life, and hence the degree of certainty and confidence with which consumers and producers are making their plans . . . ;

4. The state of development of the markets for existing capital goods — land, houses, etc., and of paper titles thereto: this works both ways, — such things need money to exchange them with, but some of them are also partial substitutes for money;

5. The rate of return obtainable by employing resources otherwise than by tying them up in the form of money.[38]

The cash-balance equation as a tool of analysis. Given changes in any of the five groups of factors above, forces are set in motion that will lead to a change in the demand for money K and, consequently, to changes in any or all of the other three magnitudes in the cash-balance equation. For example, assume that adverse expectations concerning the business outlook lead to an increase in the demand for money relative to expenditures. In the absence of money stock increases, there will be a decrease in spending and hence a drop in gross national product RP. This occurs because the only way in which people can increase their money holdings in such a situation is to refrain from spending. Thus the demand for goods and services decreases. There are fewer sales, incomes decrease, and people discover that they are not really able to increase their money holdings. Some individuals will be able to increase their holdings, but only at the expense of others. It is impossible for the community as a whole to acquire additional money holdings unless the monetary authority is willing to supply more.

An almost identical description of events can be made using the Fisher velocity approach. Here, however, we start by saying that people reduce the velocity of money circulation because of adverse expectations concerning the business outlook. Reduced spending means less demand for goods and services, and hence less gross national product PQ.

While both the velocity and cash-balance approaches are equally valid, the latter is generally considered more satisfactory because, as the preceding quotation from Alfred Marshall implies, the cash-balance equation is

---

[38] Robertson, *op. cit.,* pp. 20–21.

more directly related to individual motivation and, in addition, fits the economists basic concepts of supply and demand more conveniently.

SUMMARY AND EVALUATION

Economists have long recognized a relation between money and economic activity. The relation between money and price was first stressed in the *sixteenth century*. In the *seventeenth and eighteenth centuries,* a fuller understanding of the relations between money, velocity, economic activity, and trade developed. It was argued that economic activity and trade depended on money and its circulation. Some distinction was made between the effects of money on trade (Locke) and on employment (Law).

In the *nineteenth century,* an era of comparatively high employment, there were few advances in monetary theory. Because economists tended to assume that full employment was the natural state of the economy, money stock changes were generally related to changes in the price level rather than to changes in employment and output.

The *early twentieth century* brought significant theoretical developments. Alternative analytical approaches were formulated, and comprehensive theories of the business cycle were developed. *Irving Fisher* was one of the most important monetary theorists of the period. His principal contribution was probably his statement of the equation of exchange—a tool of economic analysis that is used by economists of almost all theoretical leanings today. In addition, Fisher's statement of the quantity theory of money is succinct and carefully qualified. Rephrased to make money stock variations a principal cause of variations in gross national product rather than simply in prices, his statement of the quantity theory is viewed by some economists as a rough but relatively valid and current theory of income and output determination. Fisher was also one of the first economists to attempt to verify his hypotheses statistically. Close to one-quarter of his book *The Purchasing Power of Money* is devoted to an empirical verification of his views.

Fisher will also be remembered for his description of cyclical disturbances and his theory of interest. He seems to have overemphasized the importance of interest rate variations and to have been too concerned with the relation of money to prices rather than to aggregate real output. Although he stressed the fact that cycles differ markedly, his analysis of the causes of cyclical disturbances relied too much on a unidirectional sequence of events. In this, he did not differ substantially from other early twentieth-century economists like Ralph Hawtrey, who also developed theories of the business cycle. Economists today prefer to stress the interrelationship of these critical variables.

The monetary theory of the *Cambridge economists* was organized around the cash-balance equation. This equation, like Fisher's equation of exchange, provides us with a convenient framework for analyzing changes in macroeconomic behavior. By emphasizing the relation between K and RP, the Cambridge economists called attention to the motives for holding money. Their influence on contemporary thought has been substantial. The emphasis on the demand for money by the two current schools of economic thought — the "Keynesians" and the "Chicago School Quantity Theorists" — indicates the importance of the Cambridge contributions.

Knut Wicksell, like Fisher and the Cambridge economists, was a quantity theorist. While stressing the connection between money and prices, his analysis was not restricted to a mere treatment of a direct relation between the two. Instead, he developed a dynamic theory designed to explain price and business fluctuations which stressed interaction among many variables. Wicksell argued that the forces that determine the market and natural rates of interest could set off discrepancies between one another and, accordingly, induce a price-level change. A continued difference between these rates would mean either boom or bust, depending on whether the natural rate was higher or lower than the market rate. Pressures on bank reserve positions could bring cumulative price inflation or deflation to a halt. Wicksell advocated central bank action to regulate bank lending rates as a principle of economic policy.

The principal shortcomings of this analysis are fairly obvious. Wicksell assumed a full employment economy. As a result, cyclical changes necessarily meant price rather than output changes. He also assumed that prices were equally flexible upward and downward. In these respects, he made the typical early twentieth-century assumptions (see the earlier discussion of Irving Fisher). Also, like other monetary theorists of his period, Wicksell may have overemphasized the importance of the interest rate as a determinant of economic activity.

All the theories discussed so far could not adequately explain the depression of the 1930s. Economists in the third decade of the century were forced to meet the crises of those years. The theories they advanced are discussed in Chapters 18–21 and 26. As we study these theories, which form the basis for our contemporary framework of analysis, it will be helpful to bear in mind that they, too, are being improved by new approaches and hypotheses.

Supplementary Readings

PRE-TWENTIETH CENTURY

Hamilton, Earl J. "John Law at Lauriston: Banker, Gamester, Merchant, Chief." *American Economic Review* (May 1967), pp. 273–82.

Law, John. *Money and Trade Considered* (1705).

Locke, John. *Consequences of the Lowering of Interest and Raising the Value of Money* (1692).

_____. *Further Considerations Concerning Raising the Value of Money* (1696).

Mill, John Stuart. *Principles of Political Economy*. Ashley Edition. (Longmans Green, 1909), Book III, Chapters 7–13.

Mints, Lloyd W. *A History of Banking Theory* (University of Chicago Press, 1945), Chapter 4.

Monroe, Arthur E. *Early Economic Thought* (Harvard University Press, 1924), Selections 6 and 11.

Spengler, Joseph J. "Richard Cantillon: First of the Moderns." *Journal of Political Economy* (1954).

Sraffa, Piero. *The Works and Correspondence of David Ricardo* (Cambridge University Press, 1951), Volumes 1 and 3.

Thornton, Henry. *An Enquiry into the Nature and Effects of the Paper Credit of Great Britain* (1802), Chapters 8, 10, and 11.

Vickers, Douglas. *Studies in the Theory of Money, 1690–1776*. (Chilton Company, 1959).

Viner, Jacob. *Studies in the Theory of International Trade* (Harper, 1937), Chapters 3, 4, and 5.

EARLY TWENTIETH CENTURY

Fisher and the Transactions Approach

Fisher, Irving. *The Purchasing Power of Money* (Macmillan, 1911), Chapters 1–6, and 8.

_____. *The Theory of Interest* (Macmillan, 1930).

The Cambridge School and the Cash-Balances Approach

Hawtrey, Ralph. *Currency and Credit,* 3rd ed. (Longmans Green, 1923), pp. 1–63.

Keynes, John Maynard. *A Tract on Monetary Reform* (Harcourt Brace Jovanovich, 1923), Chapters 1–4.

Marshall, A. *Money, Credit, and Commerce* (London: Macmillan, 1923), pp. 38–50.

Pigou, A. C. "The Value of Money." In American Economic Association, *Readings in Monetary Theory*. (Irwin, 1951), pp. 162–83.

Robertson, Dennis H. *Lectures on Economic Principles*. (Staples Press, 1959), Volume 3, pp. 9–30.

The Swedish School

Wicksell, Knut. *Interest and Prices*. Translated by R. F. Kahn (Macmillan, 1936), Introduction, Preface, and Chapters 5–9.

_____. *Lectures on Political Economy* (Macmillan, 1935), Volume 2, pp. 127–228.

Myrdl, Gunnar. *Monetary Equilibrium* (Saunders, 1939).

Other

Walras, Leon. *Elements of Pure Economics* (Allen and Unwin, 1954).

18 A Model of Income Determination: Basic Concepts

INTRODUCTION

The monetary theories developed in the early part of the twentieth century could not adequately explain the continued depression in the 1930s, primarily because they rested on two assumptions no longer tenable in our economy by that time. Most economists of the 1920s and early 1930s accepted *Say's law* that "production creates its own demand." In addition, they assumed an upward and downward flexibility of wages and prices. Given these assumptions they deduced that conditions of less than full employment could not continue for long. When goods and services are produced, they create income equal to the value of production. According to Say's law, all this income must be spent. If consumers do not spend all their income immediately, the portion that they save will eventually be channeled to investors in plant and equipment. Thus the demand for and supply of goods always tend to be equal. Price and wage variations do not affect this conclusion. When prices rise, demand will be sufficient to remove goods from the market since wages are also rising. On the other hand, demand will be sufficient to remove all goods from the market when wages are falling because businesses will have decreasing costs and so will be able to lower prices; lower prices will stimulate demand and thereby eliminate any threat of a glut of goods on the market.

These arguments may have been plausible in the nineteenth century, but the depression of the 1930s clearly pointed to their inadequacy in a modern economy. The number of people unemployed in the 1930s and the overall duration of unemployment proved conclusively that the depression was anything but a temporary dislocation from long-run full employment.

In his *General Theory of Employment, Interest, and Money,* published in 1936, John Maynard Keynes flatly denied the validity of Say's law, arguing that "effective demand associated with full employment is a special case."[1] In addition, it was demonstrated that institutional rigidities (administered prices and labor unions) exist that often prevent downward movements in wages and prices. This disproved another fundamental assumption of earlier economists—that prices were fully flexible downward.

---

[1] John Maynard Keynes. *The General Theory of Employment, Interest, and Money* (Harcourt Brace Jovanovich, 1936), p. 28.

The abandonment of Say's law and early twentieth-century monetary theories was termed the "Keynesian Revolution." It caused economists to revise drastically both their *hypotheses* and their *framework of analysis.* We are going to study the developments at the second level of theory – the analytic level, what contemporary economists label the "Keynesian Income-Expenditure Framework." Although this approach is an outgrowth of Keynes' work, the theory presented here is actually a contemporary refinement developed by J. R. Hicks, Oscar Lange, Franco Modigliani, Don Patinkin, Lloyd Metzler, James Tobin, and many other economists.[2]

This contemporary income-expenditure framework of analysis, which emphasizes the role of money in the economy, will be studied in some detail in the following two chapters. In this chapter, we will lay the groundwork for that study. The income-expenditure framework of analysis is designed to explain the factors that determine the economic well-being of the nation and the measure that economists use to assess economic performance – gross national product. When gross national product indicates that output and employment are high and increasing, it is generally taken to mean that the economy is advancing, that standards of living are increasing, and that people are better off than they were before. In order to understand the principles governing economic performance, we must first understand the uses and limitations of this measure of performance, gross national product.

CONCEPTS OF NATIONAL INCOME ANALYSIS

GNP as the Market Value of All Goods and Services

By gross national product we mean the market value of all final goods and services produced in an economy within some specified period of time, usually a year. Gross national product (GNP) is not a measure of the total *number* of units of output, but only of their *value*. If the value of the production is increasing and the prices of the individual units of output remain constant, then we can say that the number of units of output produced has increased – that the economy is more productive and has more goods and services to distribute to the population than before.

This conception of gross national product as the total market value of goods and services produced in a year's time may also be expressed in symbols:

$$GNP = PQ$$
$$= p_1 q_1 + p_2 q_2 + p_3 q_3 + p_4 q_4 \ldots + p_n q_n \qquad [18\text{--}1]$$

Here p_1 represents the price of product number 1; q_1 is the number of units

---

[2] See the Supplementary Readings section at the end of Chapters 21 and 26 for specific references.

of product number 1 that were produced in the economy. Similarly, p_2, p_3, p_4, and p_n represent the prices of the second, third, fourth, and so on up to the nth product produced: q_2, q_3, q_4, and q_n are the respective quantities of these products produced. Gross national product is thus the sum of the price of each good or service multiplied by the amount produced. GNP has both a *price* and a *quantity* element, and may increase or decrease as a result of a change either in price or output. For this reason, we stated that when GNP increases, economic performance is thought to improve also — *barring a price increase*. GNP may be used as a measure of performance only if prices neither increase nor decrease. Prices change constantly, however. Column 1 of Table 18–1 shows that GNP was $208.5 billion in 1946 and $1,152.1 billion in 1972. This means that the *value* of all goods and services increased 5.5 times during this 26-year period. It does not mean, however, that *productivity* in the economy increased 5.5 times because, as column 3 in the table shows, prices increased 2.2 times. Thus

TABLE 18–1 UNITED STATES GROSS NATIONAL PRODUCT, REAL GROSS NATIONAL PRODUCT, AND IMPLICIT PRICE DEFLATOR, 1946–73

YEAR	GROSS NATIONAL PRODUCT (IN BILLIONS OF CURRENT DOLLARS)	REAL GROSS NATIONAL PRODUCT (IN BILLIONS OF 1958 CONSTANT DOLLARS)	IMPLICIT PRICE DEFLATOR (1958 = 100)
1946	208.5	312.6	66.7
1947	231.3	309.9	74.6
1948	257.6	323.7	79.6
1949	256.5	324.1	79.1
1950	284.8	355.3	80.2
1951	328.4	383.4	85.6
1952	345.5	395.1	87.5
1953	364.6	412.8	88.3
1954	364.8	407.0	89.6
1955	398.0	438.0	90.9
1956	419.2	446.1	94.0
1957	441.1	452.5	97.5
1958	447.3	447.3	100.0
1959	483.7	475.9	101.7
1960	503.7	487.8	103.3
1961	520.1	497.2	104.6
1962	560.3	529.8	105.8
1963	590.5	551.0	107.2
1964	632.4	581.1	108.9
1965	684.9	617.8	110.9
1966	749.9	658.1	114.0
1967	793.9	675.2	117.6
1968	864.2	706.6	122.3
1969	930.3	725.6	128.2
1970	976.4	722.1	135.2
1971	1,050.4	741.7	141.6
1972	1,152.1	789.7	145.9
1973	1,300.0*	850.0*	153.0*

* Estimated by the author.
SOURCE: *Economic Report of the President* (1973), pp. 193–96.

the economy was only about 2.5 times as productive in 1972 as it was in 1946. Hence, *GNP must be adjusted for price change to be valid as a measure of performance.*

To arrive at a value of gross national product that reflects only output change over time, we divide the dollar figures for GNP in a given year (often called *current dollars*) by the price index for that year (often called the *price deflator*).[3] The resultant figure tells us what the output for a given year would have cost had prices remained unchanged from some particular year in the past. This figure is termed the *real gross national product* or the *GNP in constant dollars*. Only when the real GNP figures for different years are compared, as in column 2 of Table 18–1, do we see the real output change.

The difference in the figures in columns 1 and 2 shows how price changes substantially alter the apparent performance record of our economy. For example, although output has increased almost continuously in the last three decades, it has not increased by as much as the GNP in current dollars indicates because prices have also increased.

GNP and the Time Period: Stock and Flow Concepts

GNP is what economists call a *flow* concept: it is a measure of the value of output *over a period of time.* Thus, when we say that the economy produced $1,152 billion worth of goods and services in the year 1972, for example, we are not saying that at any moment of time in 1972, $1,152 billion worth of goods and services were available in the economy, but rather than the *total value* of goods and services produced *during that year* amounted to $1,152 billion.

GNP is also used to express a *rate* rather than an *amount* of output. It could be said, for example, that in the second quarter of 1972 production was at the rate of $1,152 billion per year. This does not mean that $1,152 billion in goods and services were actually produced, but only that the economy might be expected to produce that amount of goods and services over the entire year if the pace of production during the second quarter were maintained. Thus, in 1972, only one-fourth of the $1,152 billion was actually produced in the time period measured. To arrive at the estimated annual rate, we must multiply the amount produced by four, the number of quarters in the year.

The concept of the rate of production is important in terms of economic policy considerations. Economic events move quickly. If the rate of output

---

[3] Division gives us this result because if GNP = PQ, then $Q = GNP/P$. Since GNP and P are known, Q can be determined. For a discussion of index number construction, *see* U.S. Department of Labor, Bureau of Labor Statistics. *BLS Handbook of Methods for Surveys and Studies* (1966). For a discussion of some of the limitations to the accuracy of real output measures based upon price indexes, see John J. Klein. "Price-Level and Money-Denomination Movements." *Journal of Political Economy* (1960), p. 369.

diminishes during one part of a year, it is important that appropriate offsetting action be taken without delay. Were the monetary authorities to permit a full year to pass in order to compare the different outputs for successive years before taking such action, the whole economic situation might worsen seriously. Shorter time periods are studied so that the future rate of production can be predicted more accurately.

We have said that GNP is a flow concept. As such, it may be contrasted with *stock* concepts. A stock of something is simply a quantity existing at a moment of time. Measures such as the stock of money, liquid wealth, and nonliquid wealth are stock measures.[4]

The importance of the distinction between stocks and flows cannot be overemphasized. Critical errors of analysis are often made because this distinction is not understood. For example, income and the amount of money on hand are often confused. An individual may receive money payments over the year totaling $12,000; his income, in other words, is $12,000. This is a flow concept. The amount of his money holdings at the end of one year compared with his holdings at the end of the next year is a stock concept, however, and depends only in part on the size of his income. Only if the income recipient makes no payments out of his income will his money *stock* increase by $12,000. On the other hand, if he purchases $12,000 in goods and services, there is no change in his money balances over the year. This illustrates an important relationship between stocks and flows: *a flow, other things being equal, will result in a stock change equal to the flow.*

This holds true for GNP also. If the economy produces $1,300 billion in final goods in a given year and only $1,000 billion are consumed, then the difference in the end-of-year stock of wealth figures for two consecutive years is equal to the value of the goods produced but not consumed during that year. This difference is termed *saving*. On the other hand, if an economy consumes more goods than it produces, there is a reduction of real wealth termed *dissaving*. These differences represent the connecting links between the flow (value of output) and the stock (real wealth) of goods in the economy.

The Identity of Income and Product

Equation 18–1 demonstrated that GNP has both a price and an output element. Thus:

$$\text{GNP} = PQ \qquad [18\text{–}1]$$

---

[4] Sometimes stock measures are stated as averages over time rather than as totals at a moment of time. Thus, if we were to add up the end-of-the-month liquid wealth holdings of the nonbank public for 13 consecutive months starting with December 31, 1972, and ending with December 31, 1973, and divide the sum by 13, we would have the average liquid wealth holdings of the nonbank public for the year 1973. This figure would be the amount of liquid wealth that people had, on the average, *at any moment of time during 1973.*

GNP may also be interpreted as a measure of the nation's expenditures on its total product or as a measure of its income. In the first instance, emphasis is placed on the expenditures that are made on particular types of goods and services. The U.S. Department of Commerce, for example, calculates GNP as the sum of expenditures on consumption, investment, and government goods and services. Also included is the difference between the value of our production for export and our imports of goods and services. All this may be expressed mathematically as

$$Y = C + I + G + (X - M) \qquad [18\text{--}2]$$

where Y is gross national product, C is expenditures by households on consumer goods and services, I is expenditures on investment goods, G is government expenditures on goods and services, X is exports of goods and services, and M is imports of goods and services.[5]

Gross national product may also be a measure of income. Incomes are earned in the process of producing the goods and services for which expenditures are made. Individuals receive wages and salaries in exchange for their productive efforts. After taxes and other adjustments, they are left with *disposable personal income,* the amount of income that each is actually able to spend or save over a year's time. Businesses have profits after selling their output, meeting their costs of production, and paying taxes. Government collects the taxes for its income. Thus, the total value of the output is distributed to producers in the form of personal income, profits, and taxes. This may be expressed in symbols as[6]

$$Y = Y_d + S_b + T \qquad [18\text{--}3]$$

where Y is gross national income or product, Y_d is disposable personal income, S_b is business saving, and T is federal, state, and local government tax receipts.

Since

$$Y = C + I + G + (X - M) \qquad [18\text{--}2]$$

and

$$Y = Y_d + S_b + T \qquad [18\text{--}3]$$

it follows that

$$C + I + G + (X - M) = Y_d + S_b + T \qquad [18\text{--}4]$$

This equation can be simplified still further when we consider how individuals use disposable income. They either spend it or save it. Thus

[5] From this point on, in accord with general practice, we shall refer to gross national product as Y.

[6] For the most part, the symbols in the following equations are drawn directly from the terms they represent: As examples, T stands for *t*axes and S_p for *p*ersonal *s*aving.

$$Y_d = C + S_p \qquad [18\text{--}5]$$

where S_p is personal saving. Substituting equation 18–5 for Y_d in equation 18–4, we have

$$C + I + G + (X - M) = C + S_p + S_b + T \qquad [18\text{--}6]$$

Since C is the same on both sides of the equation, then

$$I + G + (X - M) = S_p + S_b + T \qquad [18\text{--}7]$$

This equation must always hold true for the past performance of an economy because of the equality of income and product. When product is produced, its value is distributed as income to its producers. Tables 18–2, 18–3, and 18–4 demonstrate this by giving the components of gross national product and gross national income for a recent year, 1972. These tables relate the components of the preceding equations to actual income statistics.

TABLE 18-2 GROSS NATIONAL PRODUCT, 1972
(IN BILLIONS OF CURRENT DOLLARS)

Personal consumption expenditures (C)			
Durable goods		116.1	
Nondurable goods		299.5	
Services		305.4	
Total			721.0
Gross private domestic investments (I)			
Fixed investment			
Nonresidential			
Structure	42.2		
Producers' durable equipment	78.3		
Total		120.6*	
Residential structures			
Nonfarm	53.2		
Other	0.8		
Total		54.0	
Total		174.6	
Change in business inventories		5.9	
Total			180.4*
Net exports of goods and services ($X - M$)			
Exports	73.7		
Imports	−77.9		
Total			−4.2
Government purchases of goods and services (G)			
Federal			
National defense		75.9	
Other		29.9	
Total		105.8	
State and local		148.8	
Total			254.6
Gross national product			1,151.8

* Totals may differ due to rounding.
SOURCE: *Federal Reserve Bulletin* (March 1973), p. A-70.

TABLE 18-3   GROSS NATIONAL PRODUCT AS INCOME, 1972
(IN BILLIONS OF CURRENT DOLLARS)

Disposable personal income (Y_d)			
Personal outlays (C)			
Personal consumption expenditures	721.0		
Consumer interest payments	18.2		
Personal transfer payments to foreigners	1.1		
Total		740.3	
Personal saving (S_p)		54.8	
Total			795.1
Disposable business corporate income (S_b)			
Corporate profits and inventory valuation adjustment	87.3		
Dividends	−26.4		
Profit tax liability	−40.8		
Excess of wage accruals over disbursements	− 0.5		
Total		20.6	
Capital consumption allowances		103.7	
Total			124.3
Government taxes (T)			
Personal tax and nontax payments		140.8	
Indirect business tax and nontax liability		110.1	
Corporate profits tax liability		40.8	
Contributions for social insurance		74.0	
Government transfer payments		−99.1	
Net interest paid by government and consumer		−31.6	
Subsidies less current surplus of government enterprises		− 1.7	
Total			233.3
Statistical discrepancy			0.1
Gross national product as income			1,152.8

SOURCE: Adapted from *Federal Reserve Bulletin* (March 1973), p. A-71

TABLE 18-4   DISPOSABLE PERSONAL INCOME, 1972
(IN BILLIONS OF CURRENT DOLLARS)

Compensation of employees			
Wages and salaries			
Private	491.9		
Military	20.6		
Government civilian	114.0		
Total		626.5	
Supplements to wages and salaries		78.8	
Total			705.3
Proprietors' income			
Business and professional		55.6	
Farm		19.6	
Total			75.2
Rental income of persons			25.6
Net interest			41.3
Government transfer payments			99.1
Net interest paid by government and consumers			31.6
Dividends			26.4
Business transfer payments			4.9
Excess of wage accruals over disbursements			0.5
Personal tax and nontax payments			−140.8
Contributions for social insurance			− 74.0
Disposable personal income (Y_d)			795.1

SOURCE: Adapted from *Federal Reserve Bulletin* (March 1973), pp. A-70, A-71.

Money and GNP

In the preceding discussion we established that PQ, Y, $C + I + G + (X - M)$, and $Y_d + S_b + T$ are equivalent. No mention has been made of the financing of these magnitudes, however. Obviously, money is the medium used when Y is purchased. As we indicated in Chapter 17 (equation 17-5,), when the average amount of money in the economy during a specified period of time, such as a year M is multiplied by the number of times it is spent on final goods and services V, the product is a measure of the value of the expenditures on final goods and services produced. That product, of course, is Y.

Hence it follows that:

$$Y = C + I + G + (X - M) = Y_d + S_b + T = PQ = MV \quad [18\text{--}8]$$

Each section of this equation is simply a different way of looking at the same thing, Y. The significance of equations 18–1 through 18–8 for income determination will be developed more fully in the chapters that follow.

Supplementary Readings

Hawtrey, R. G. "Money and Index Numbers." Reprinted in F. A. Lutz and Lloyd W. Mints (eds.), *Readings in Monetary Theory* (Blakiston, 1951).

Data Sources

Council of Economic Advisors. *Annual Reports* (Washington D.C.).
U.S. Department of Commerce, Office of Business Economics. *The National Income and Product Accounts of the United States, 1929–1965 Statistical Tables* (Washington, D.C., 1966).
_____. *Survey of Current Business* (August 1973).

19 A Model of Income Determination: Demand for Product Forces

Monetary theory seeks to explain the role monetary supply and demand forces play in the determination of economic activity. However, many variables in addition to money help determine income and output. Monetary theory today is thus an integral part of macroeconomic theory: To appreciate the importance of money, we must understand how it works with and is affected by other economic variables.

This chapter and the next are concerned with contemporary macroeconomic theory. Specifically, the factors that cause changes in our measure of economic performance—gross national product—are examined. The most important sources of economic change will be isolated within two frameworks, one using *graphs* and one being *general functional equations*. These abstractions from reality constitute a type of economic model. Despite the fact that our economic model is an abstraction, however, it will be fairly rigorous so that the complexities of the economy can be realistically described. The model should help us interpret income determination by depicting the interaction of the most important sources of economic change both visually and in general behavior equations. The development of the model is divided into two sections. This chapter examines the determination of the factors in equation 18–6:

$$C + I + G + (X - M) = C + S_p + S_b + T$$

Chapter 20 will then add monetary supply and demand to the model, and Chapter 21 will show how this expanded model may be used to interpret the interaction of various economic forces.

INTRODUCTION TO THE MODEL

In essence, contemporary income theory argues that the interaction of demand and supply forces determines the level of economic activity. When demand is less than supply, stocks of goods accumulate and businesses are forced to reduce Y, aggregate output. If prices do not subsequently decline when supply exceeds demand, then all of the drop in gross national product is in real output. On the other hand, when the demand for goods and services exceeds the supply, the stock of goods declines, business expectations improve, and firms are induced to increase their output; hence, gross national product increases. Should the economy already be operating at full employment or capacity, however, all the increase in Y will be in prices; the value of output will grow, but not the amount. Thus, the only time that Y will not change is when there is neither a shortage nor an excess of demand relative to output – when demand equals supply.

These are the essentials of modern income analysis. The demand for goods relative to the supply is of crucial significance, and businesses respond to differences between demand and supply by adjusting aggregate output. This does not explain the fundamental sources of income and output change, however. For this we must examine the components of demand in more detail.

Equation 18–6 offers some insight into the sources of demand determination. We have said that this equation is always accurate for past performance. Thus, when we say that the sum of C, I, G, and $(X - M)$ must equal the sum of C, S_p, S_b, and T, we are speaking after the fact – we are discussing what has occurred. This is what economists call *ex post* analysis.

Since investment, saving, and expenditure *plans* are made independently and by different individuals, there is no reason why the *planned* magnitudes should be equivalent. Thus the two sides of our equation may differ when the magnitudes of the variables represent plans that look to the future. The total amount of planned expenditures of businesses, of governing bodies, and of exporters and importers may differ, therefore, from the total amount of planned personal saving, expected business profits, and expected government tax receipts. When we say that the sum of the *plans* for C, I, G, and $(X - M)$ may differ from the plans for C, S_p, S_b, and T, we are speaking before the fact – we are looking ahead to what has not yet occurred. This is what economists call *ex ante* analysis.

When the plans for the magnitudes on each side of equation 18–6 *are* equal, then the economy is said to be in *equilibrium*: There are no forces at work tending to change income and output. Aggregate demand and supply will be equal; businesses will produce just enough goods to meet anticipated demands.

Therefore, it is the plans for C, I, G, $(X - M)$, S_p, S_b, and T that are sources of income determination. The remainder of this chapter examines each of these magnitudes in some detail and then places them in our model of income determination.

METHODOLOGY AND SYMBOLS

As previously noted, we will employ both graphs and general behavior equations in constructing our model. In order to keep the pedagogical techniques as simple as possible, the graphical relationships will usually be shown as straight lines. This does not mean that real-world relationships are actually linear. In addition, some of the standard four-quadrant techniques used in national income analysis textbooks will not be used here since their applicability to a general model is limited.

The general behavior equations introduced in this chapter describe the behavior of various groups in the economy. For example, the following section develops an equation for saving that shows how saving by households is related to various factors, the most important of which is disposable personal income. Specific forms of these equations are not developed since we are concerned here with the general nature of the sources of economic change. Complex diagrams and specific equations can be found in the formal study of macroeconomic analysis.[1]

The symbols used in our model of income determination follow. They are presented here to provide a convenient listing of brief definitions to refer to throughout the coming chapters. Except for the symbols presented earlier, they are listed in order of their appearance in the book.

Y = gross national product
C = consumption expenditures
I = investment expenditures
G = government expenditures
F or $(X - M)$ = net foreign investment (the difference between exports and imports of goods and services)
Y_d = disposable personal income
S_b = business saving
T = tax receipts
S_p = personal saving
f = "a function of"
i = rate of interest
W_h = liquid wealth of households
X = all forces other than Y, i, and W_h that may influence C and S_p
U = any forces other than Y that may influence S_b
Z = all the forces other than Y that cause the legislature to change the tax rate or government spending
W_f = liquid wealth of firms
U' = all forces other than Y, i, and W_f that may help determine the marginal efficiency of investment
J = all of the forces that cause F to change
M_s = the supply of money
H = high-powered money: currency plus reserves for demand deposits
Z' = variables other than H and i that may influence the supply of money

---

[1] For an undergraduate approach to macroeconomic theory, see Edward Shapiro. *Macroeconomic Analysis*, 3rd ed. (Harcourt Brace Jovanovich, 1974). A graduate-level approach can be found in R. D. G. Allen. *Macroeconomics* (St. Martin's Press, 1965).

W' = total wealth (W + real wealth)
W = total liquid wealth
X' = variables other than Y, i, and W' that may influence the demand for money
M_d = the demand for money
P = the price level

One very important assumption that must be made explicit at this point is that we have put into real *terms all of the above variables generally expressed in* monetary *terms.* Thus, GNP, money supply, money demand, consumption demand, investment expenditures, liquid wealth, and so on, have all been *adjusted for price change.* Subsequent tables and references to data will usually be in monetary terms (unadjusted for the price level), but all of the analysis and theory (except where explicitly contrary assumptions are made) will be in real terms. As we learned in Chapter 18, the only way to gauge the true performance of an economy over time is to adjust GNP and other forces for price change. After all, do not many people look at their incomes and liquid wealth holdings and think in terms of their real purchasing power? In other words, except where explicitly stated otherwise, *we are assuming that people are free of what economists call "money illusion"*—that is, demanding or supplying real goods in response to changes in circumstances not adjusted for price change. *Along the same lines we are assuming that market and real rates of interest are equal.* (See Chapter 17.)

PERSONAL SAVING AND CONSUMPTION DEMAND

Individuals may either spend or save personal disposable income. Thus, a decision to save may also be looked upon as a decision not to make a consumption expenditure. Hence

$$Y_d = C + S_p \qquad [18\text{--}5]$$

where Y_d is disposable personal income, C is consumption demand, and S_p is personal saving. Changes in decisions to save and spend lead to changes in spending and therefore to changes in gross national product. Since consumption spending is, quantitatively, the single most important component of Y, we shall first examine those variables that economists consider most likely to influence behavior in this area.

Disposable Personal Income

The principal determinant of personal saving and consumption demand is generally believed to be the level of disposable personal income. The logic of this view is quite simple: Increased incomes enhance the spending ability of individuals; with more to spend, people tend to raise their standards of living and save just a portion of their increased incomes. Decreased incomes decrease the spending ability of individuals, but the reduction in actual spending will not usually equal the decrease in income because people typically attempt to maintain their prior living standards under such conditions. This analysis applies not only to the individual, but also to the aggregate of individuals. For example, income and output may increase without actually raising the income of anyone already working. This is what happens when more people are employed. As the unemployed are drawn into the work force, their disposable incomes rise and they increase their expenditures and saving. Whether the increased incomes are of those already working or of the newly employed, the economy still feels the impact of the consumption expenditure and saving increases.

TABLE 19-1 GROSS NATIONAL PRODUCT AND ITS COMPONENTS, 1946-73

	GNP AND ITS COMPONENTS (IN BILLIONS OF DOLLARS)					COMPONENTS OF GNP AS PERCENTAGES OF GNP*					
YEAR	GNP	C	I	G	$(X-M)$	Y_d	C	I	G	$(X-M)$	$\dfrac{C}{Y_d}$
1946	208.5	143.4	30.6	27.0	7.5	160.0	68.8	14.7	12.9	3.6	89.6
1947	231.3	160.7	34.0	25.1	11.5	169.8	69.5	14.7	10.9	5.0	94.6
1948	257.6	173.6	46.0	31.6	6.4	189.1	67.4	17.9	12.3	2.5	91.8
1949	256.5	176.8	35.7	37.8	6.1	188.6	68.9	13.9	14.7	2.4	93.7
1950	284.9	191.0	54.1	37.9	1.8	206.9	67.0	19.0	13.3	0.6	92.3
1951	328.4	206.3	59.3	59.1	3.7	226.6	62.8	18.1	18.0	1.1	91.0
1952	345.5	216.7	51.9	74.7	2.2	238.3	62.7	15.0	21.6	0.6	90.9
1953	364.6	230.0	52.6	81.6	0.4	252.6	63.1	14.4	22.4	0.1	91.1
1954	364.8	236.5	51.7	74.8	1.8	257.4	64.8	14.2	20.5	0.5	91.9
1955	398.0	254.4	67.4	74.2	2.0	275.3	63.9	16.9	18.6	0.5	92.4
1956	419.2	266.7	70.0	78.6	4.0	293.2	63.6	16.7	18.8	1.0	91.0
1957	441.1	281.4	67.8	86.1	5.7	308.5	63.8	15.4	19.5	1.3	91.2
1958	447.3	290.1	60.9	94.2	2.2	318.8	64.9	13.6	21.1	0.5	91.0
1959	483.6	311.2	75.3	97.0	0.1	337.3	64.4	15.6	20.1	0.0	92.3
1960	503.8	325.2	74.8	99.6	4.0	350.0	64.5	14.8	19.8	0.8	92.9
1961	520.1	335.2	71.7	107.6	5.6	364.4	64.4	13.8	20.7	1.1	92.0
1962	560.3	355.1	83.0	117.1	5.1	385.3	63.4	14.8	20.9	0.9	92.2
1963	590.5	375.0	87.1	122.5	5.9	404.6	63.5	14.8	20.7	1.0	92.7
1964	632.4	401.2	94.0	128.7	8.5	438.1	63.4	14.9	20.4	1.3	91.6
1965	684.9	432.8	108.1	137.0	6.9	473.2	63.2	15.8	20.0	1.0	91.5
1966	749.9	466.3	121.4	156.8	5.3	511.9	62.2	16.2	20.9	0.7	91.1
1967	793.9	492.1	116.6	180.1	5.2	546.3	62.0	14.7	22.7	0.6	90.1
1968	864.2	536.2	126.0	199.6	2.5	591.0	62.0	14.6	23.1	0.3	90.7
1969	930.3	579.5	139.0	210.0	1.9	634.4	62.3	14.9	22.6	0.2	91.3
1970	976.4	616.8	137.1	219.0	3.6	689.5	63.2	14.0	22.4	0.4	89.5
1971	1,050.4	664.9	152.0	232.8	0.7	744.4	63.3	14.5	22.1	0.0	89.3
1972	1,151.8	721.0	180.4	254.6	-4.2	795.1	62.6	15.7	22.1	-0.4	90.7
1973†	1,290.0	810.0	205.0	280.0	-5.0	900.0	62.8	16.0	21.7	-0.4	90.0

* Figures may not total 100.0 due to rounding.
† Estimated by author.
SOURCE: *Survey of Current Business.* August 1965, pp. 24, 25, 32, and 33; *Federal Reserve Bulletins.* December 1967, pp. 2136-37; April 1969, p. A-67; October 1970, p. A-68; October 1971, p. A-70; and April 1973, p. A-68.

Figure 19-1. Gross national product, consumption expenditures, and disposable personal income, 1946–73.

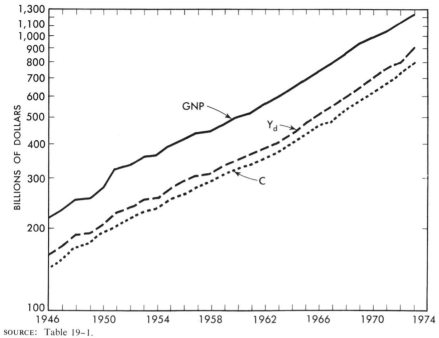

SOURCE: Table 19-1.

This contention seems to be supported by the data given in Table 19-1
and Figure 19-1, which show consumption to be closely related to changes
in Y and Y_d.[2] When gross national product and disposable personal income
rise, consumption also increases. When the growth rates of Y and Y_d
decline, the growth of consumption also decreases. The relationship
between Y, Y_d, and C has been fairly close historically. It should be noted,
however, that consumption is directly determined by Y_d rather than Y,
because the full amount of Y is not available to the spender. The chain of
causation, in other words, runs from Y to Y_d and then to C.

Wealth as a Source of Consumption and Saving Change

The volume of *liquid wealth* may also exert an influence on consumption
demand and personal saving. *Assume prices are constant.* Then, at any
given level of disposable personal income, the greater the volume of liquid
wealth, the greater the demand for consumption goods and services. The
logic on which this assertion is based is that more liquid wealth means
more command over goods and services and less need to save out of cur-

[2] The relationship between S_p and Y_d is not shown, since, according to equation 18–5, S_p is
simply the difference between C and Y_d.

rent income to meet contingencies. The lower the level of liquid wealth, the less ability individuals have to make high-level consumption expenditures and the greater the need to save.

The total volume of liquid wealth is influenced by saving. When a person saves and does not spend, his liquid wealth holdings increase. Initially, as disposable income exceeds consumption expenditures, money receipts will exceed money expenditures and liquid wealth holdings in the form of money balances will increase. Subsequently, however, the saver may decide to keep his increased liquid wealth holdings in another form—savings deposits, government securities, corporate stocks, privately-issued bonds, or insurance policies. As these forms of wealth increase in volume while holdings of physical wealth remain unchanged, it becomes more and more likely that the saver will increase his rate of expenditure on consumption goods and services and decrease his saving rate S_p. His ability to meet future expenditures, both foreseen and unforeseen, will have increased and, consequently, he will have less need to maintain the same saving rate he had at a lower level of liquid wealth.

The situation is different when consumption expenditures exceed disposable income and S_p is negative; dissaving occurs then. An excess of expenditures over income can only be financed by borrowing or drawing down liquid wealth holdings. Thus, the ability to make future expenditures and meet unforeseen contingencies is reduced, and to recoup these holdings, a reduction in expenditures is necessary. "As a general rule, the saving rate for individual households appears to vary inversely with the ratio of liquid assets to income, and the influence of liquid assets on saving tends to diminish as the level of income rises."[3]

Liquid wealth has been introduced as a possible influence on consumption demand and saving. *Real wealth* should also be considered. The amount of physical goods in the economy may help to determine expenditures on consumer durables. The more physical goods are owned, presumably, the less the need for additional units of them and hence the lower the expenditures on them.

This only applies if the average age of physical goods is constant over time, however. It is also true that the greater the average age of physical goods, the more likely there is to be an extensive demand for replacements, regardless of the total volume of real wealth then extant. For example, the increasing age of the stock of consumer durables during the depression and World War II underlay at least part of the strong postwar consumer demand for durables that occurred despite the fact that there was a large amount of physical goods in American households. Overall, the average age of real wealth owned by individuals in the United States tends to vary as consumer expenditures on durable goods fall off in recession and increase in more prosperous periods.

[3] Robert Ferber. "Research on Household Behavior." *American Economic Review* (1962), p. 37.

The Weath Effect and Price-Level Change

Thus far, we have assumed prices to be constant in our discussion of the influence of liquid wealth on expenditures and saving. What happens if prices vary? Assume, for example, that there is an increase in the price level. When this occurs, there is a corresponding decrease in the purchasing power of most forms of liquid wealth; about the only form of liquid wealth that will increase in value is stock, the price of which usually fluctuates along with the general price level. Other forms of liquid wealth generally have a fixed nominal value. Thus $1,000 in money or savings deposits continues to be $1,000, regardless of changes in the price level; a bond with a maturity value of $1,000 will continue to have that same maturity value, although its market price will probably decline. The decreased purchasing power of bonds and the availability of favorable alternative financial investments, such as corporate stocks, usually lead to a decline in the price of bonds that have already been issued.

On balance, the purchasing power of liquid wealth tends to decrease with a price-level increase. On the other hand, the real value of debt decreases with rises in the price level. Creditors lose with inflation, and debtors gain. What influence do these opposing forces have upon consumption demand and saving? In order to regain the ability to meet unanticipated expenditures and to recoup their lost liquid wealth position, creditors will increase saving out of income. Debtors may very well decrease saving and increase consumption out of income. If the propensity to spend out of income were the same for both creditors and debtors, then the effects of the price-level increase upon consumption and saving could well be zero. This would only be the case, however, if all forms of liquid wealth were owned and owed within the private sector of the economy.

Since liquid wealth includes wealth forms issued by the public as well as by the private sector of the economy, it follows that the liquid assets held by the nonbank public are greater than the debt it owes. The principal forms of public debt held by the private sector are currency and government bonds. To the extent, then, that the private sector does not view public debt as giving rise to future tax liabilities (aside from the taxes necessary to service interest on the public debt), a rise in the price level will affect consumption and personal saving primarily by reducing the real purchasing power of outstanding government debt and currency. Hence, a rise in the price level can be expected to cut the real value of the liquid wealth holdings of the private sector in the form of government obligations, reduce private consumption demand, and raise the saving rate. Contrariwise, a drop in the price level, by increasing the purchasing power of currency and government debt held by the private sector, can be expected to raise consumption demand and reduce the saving rate. The effect on demand attributable to a changed price level altering the real value of liquid wealth (in the form of currency and government debt) is called a *wealth effect*.

The preceding line of analysis is subject to some strong limiting assumptions, the first of which is that people will expect prices to remain constant. Once prices have risen, should people expect prices to continue to rise in the future, then it would pay to buy goods and to decrease saving in spite of continuing decreases in the purchasing power of liquid wealth. Similarly, should people expect prices to fall continually following some initial price-level decrease, it would pay to reduce spending and increase saving. After all, is it not better to purchase goods, particularly consumer durables, in the future when they are expected to be less expensive? This *price expectation effect* cancels out any change in demand resulting from the *wealth effect* just described.

Another assumption of the preceding analysis is that the propensity to spend out of income is the same for both creditors and debtors. For example, should the propensity of creditors to spend be greater than the propensity of debtors to spend, a rise in the price level, while affecting private liquid assets and debt equally, would cause creditors to reduce their spending by more than debtors would increase theirs.

While many economists do not believe that the wealth effect accompanying a price-level change is important empirically, it has been an important theoretical topic in monetary theory. The wealth effect that occurs when a changed price level alters the purchasing power of government-issued currency is known as the *real balance effect*. This form of wealth effect, in particular, has had a significant impact on monetary theory and will be discussed again in subsequent chapters.

The Rate of Interest

The rate of interest affects consumption demand in several ways. For example, an increase in the rate of interest usually may be expected to lead to an increase in the rate of saving and, other things being equal, to a decrease in consumption spending. Since interest is paid to savers to compensate for reductions in their current consumption, the higher the interest return, the more people are induced to save. Conversely, the lower the interest return, the less saving occurs.

The relationship between the rate of interest and consumption demand should also be considered from the borrower's point of view. The individual who finds that he may borrow a given amount of money at a reduced interest rate may be induced to borrow more and so increase his spending base. Similarly, when banks expand loans because of increased excess reserves and leave their lending rates unchanged, credit conditions are easier. Borrowers who previously did not qualify for loans may then be able to obtain them; when they do, their spendings will increase.

Changes in the interest rate and consumption demand may also occur in the same direction, however. Those people who only feel it necessary to obtain a specific dollar yield on their financial investments will save less if interest rates increase, since less savings will give the same total yield. Hence consumption demand may increase. For example, a person who wants $30 in interest income needs $1,000 in savings when the interest rate is 3 percent, but only $500 in savings when the rate is 6 percent.

There are still other possibilities. A rise in the rate of interest paid on newly issued securities relative to that paid on already existing securities will cause the market price on the old securities to decline. If a potential bond purchaser is to be induced to buy an old security instead of a new one, he must be offered an *effective yield* on the old security comparable to the yield on the new security. Assume, for example, that an old bond has a par value of $1,000 and a 3 percent rate of return, while a comparable new security yields 4 percent. The price of the old security must drop in order to meet this competition. To give the investor an effective 4 percent return on his investment when the dollar yield on the old bond is $30, the seller must ask himself: $30 is 4 percent of how large a financial investment?

$$(x)\,(0.04) = \$30$$

or

$$(\$750)\,(0.04) = \$30$$

Thus, the price of old bonds declines during periods of generally rising interest rates. This means that the volume of liquid wealth in the form of old securities declines and that, accordingly, an increase in saving and a decrease in consumption demand are induced.

In general, economists who accept the Keynesian hypotheses often tend to minimize the influence of interest on consumption and saving. Lawrence Klein is representative of this group when he states:

There is no empirical evidence, so far, that shows significant interest effects on total spending or saving by consumers after income effects are taken into account. That is not to say that wide movements of interest rates and relative prices, much wider in the short run than have been observed, will have no influence on the total spending or saving.[4]

On the other hand, economists schooled in the quantity theory tradition or the new "portfolio" approach more often emphasize the interest rate as an important economic variable. These two groups of economists believe that interest rate increases tend to increase saving and to lower consumption, and that interest rate decreases have the reverse effect. However, it is difficult to make a reasonably accurate quantitative prediction as to the potential effects of interest rate changes on the rate of saving and consumption expenditures. There are many variables at work here, and the effects of interest rate changes are difficult to disentangle from the effects of other

[4] Lawrence R. Klein. *The Keynesian Revolution,* 2nd ed. (Macmillan, 1966), p. 201.

forces affecting consumption and saving. Evidence seems to be more concrete that interest rates do affect the demand for one type of consumer good—consumer durables, really a form of investment goods. Michael Hamburger, as we noted in Chapter 12, has demonstrated "that monetary variables have a significant effect on consumer purchases of durable goods and that the most appropriate measures of these variables are interest rates."[5]

One force that can upset the relationship between consumption, saving, and the rate of interest is the relationship between the market rate and the real rate of interest received by creditors and paid by debtors. It will be recalled from our discussion of Irving Fisher in Chapter 17 that the real rate of interest is the market rate plus the rate of deflation or minus the rate of inflation. If the market rate is rising but is lagging behind the rate of inflation, then the real rate is decreasing. This may induce borrowers to increase their borrowing and their demand for consumption goods. If lenders adjust their market rates quickly enough, however, these results need not occur. For a positive relation between saving and interest (to put it another way, the inverse relation between consumption and interest) to occur, it must be assumed that the real and market rates of interest are quite close.

Additional Explanations of Personal Saving and Consumption

In addition to the factors mentioned earlier, age, education, distribution of income, and price expectations are often mentioned as determinants of consumption demand and saving. It is often argued, for example, that the older the population, the less the need for consumer durable goods. Furthermore, the less education people have, the less income they may be expected to earn and the lower their level of spending will be. In addition, the greater the proportion of income going to high-income groups, the less tendency there will be to spend on consumption overall. Because their standards of living are already high, those with large incomes tend to save more and spend a smaller fraction of additions to their income than those with lower incomes. Finally, the greater the expectation that prices will increase, the greater the apparent need to buy before prices actually rise and the purchasing power of income deteriorates.

These are just a few of the other factors economists take into consideration when explaining consumer spending and saving. The explanation of spending behavior is a complicated affair, and many of the problems are not even touched upon here. For example, consumption behavior seems to be affected differently by short-run income changes than it is by long-run

[5] Michael J. Hamburger. "Interest Rates and the Demand for Consumer Durable Goods." *American Economic Review* (December 1967), p. 1131.

changes. Economists have offered numerous explanations for this paradox, none of which are completely satisfactory.

An Equation for Personal Saving

Having separately examined a number of the determinants of saving and consumption, we must now attempt to describe the combined effect of these various factors on consumption and saving behavior. Selecting those factors that seem most relevant on the basis of empirical study and careful a priori reasoning, we have disposable personal income Y_d, the rate of interest i, liquid wealth holdings of consumers (households) W_h, and X, all the other factors that may influence C and S_p. Putting this into equation form, gives us

$$S_p = f(Y_d, i, W_h, X) \qquad [19\text{--}1]$$

and, since $Y_d = C + S_p$ (equation 18–5), then, substituting, we have

$$Y_d = C + f(Y_d, i, W_h, X); \quad C = Y_d - f(Y_d, i, W_h, X) \qquad [19\text{--}2]$$

These equations (all expressed in real terms) tell us that consumption demand and personal saving are a function f of, or are determined by, disposable personal income, the rate of interest, liquid wealth, and other relevant variables. If X remains constant, we may assume that the *saving* rate increases with a rise in disposable personal income, a rise in the rate of interest, and a drop in liquid wealth. Thus, the relationship between saving, disposable income, and the rate of interest is direct, whereas the relationship between saving and liquid wealth is inverse. On the other hand, *consumption* rises with an increase in disposable income, an increase in liquid wealth, and a drop in the rate of interest. Thus, the relationship between consumption, disposable income, and liquid wealth is direct, whereas the relationship between consumption and the rate of interest is inverse.

In developing a diagrammatic representation of changes in Y, we shall concentrate on the saving equation, 19–1, rather than the consumption equation, 19–2, in order to keep the analysis comparatively simple. In a sense, the analysis will illustrate consumption determinants too, however, for C and its determinants may be derived readily from equation 19–1. Once we determine S_p, we can easily compute C from $C = Y_d - S_p$. This also means that we can deal with equation 18–7, $I + G + (X - M) = S_p + S_b + T$, instead of equation 18–6, $C + I + G + (X - M) = C + S_p + S_b + T$, since C is identical on both sides of equation 18–6 and thus cancels out.

The relation between the variables of equation 19–1 is illustrated diagrammatically in Figure 19–2. Planned personal saving at any level of Y is measured along the vertical axis; Y is measured along the horizontal axis. Y rather than Y_d is used as the horizontal axis because, ultimately, a model

Figure 19–2. The relationship between S_p and Y.

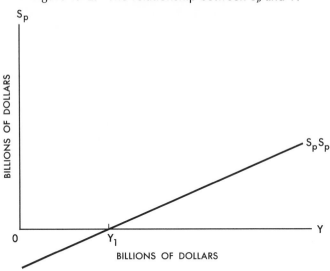

of income determination must be designed to explain changes in Y. Thus, in Figure 19–2 *the line* S_pS_p *shows the relationship between* S_p *and* Y. This line records the total amount of personal saving that people plan to do at various levels of Y. The greater the level of Y, the greater the volume of personal saving that people feel is necessary. Thus, at any point above an output of Y_1, people want to save. At any level of output below Y_1 there will be dissaving: People will tend to spend more on consumption goods than they receive in income.

The line S_pS_p also shows the relationship between changes in personal saving and changes in gross national product. Let the symbol Δ (delta), refer to a small change. By moving from any point on the line S_pS_p to another, we can observe the change in S_p that is induced by a change in Y. Thus, the ratio $\Delta S_p/\Delta Y$ is a measure of how changes in Y induce changes in S_p. In terms of the diagram, it is also a measure of the slope of the line S_pS_p (which is drawn as a straight line in Figure 19–2 to keep the analysis simple). The fact that the slope is less than one (since the angle made by S_pS_p and Y is less than 45°) reflects the desire of the public both to save and to spend when a change in Y occurs; thus, as Y increases, the amount of saving also increases, but by less than the increase in Y. The remainder of the change in Y is channeled into consumption expenditures, government tax collections, and business income.

This last point requires some further explanation. It will be recalled that Y_d, not Y, is the direct determinant of C and S_p. The ratio of a change in personal saving induced by a change in disposable personal income is $\Delta S_p/\Delta Y_d$; this is called the *marginal propensity to save*. The remainder of any change in Y_d is channeled into consumption change. The ratio of the change in consumption expenditures induced by the change in disposable personal income is $\Delta C/\Delta Y_d$, the *marginal propensity to consume*.

The marginal propensity to save $\Delta S_p/\Delta Y_d$ necessarily differs from $\Delta S_p/\Delta Y$. As gross national product increases, disposable personal income increases, but so do government tax collections and business saving. In our economy, the tax structure is geared to the level of income and output. The higher Y becomes, the greater the amount of taxes collected by the government becomes. For these reasons, the marginal propensity to save must differ from the ratio of the change in personal saving to a change in gross national product. The marginal propensity to save $\Delta S_p/\Delta Y_d$ must be *greater* than the ratio $\Delta S_p/\Delta Y$. Assume, for example, that 80 percent of the changes in Y is channeled into a change in Y_d, 10 percent into a change in business saving, and 10 percent into a change in government tax collections. Assume further that the marginal propensity to save is 0.20. Given these conditions, an increase of \$50 billion in Y will become a \$40 billion increase in Y_d, a \$5 billion increase in business saving, and a \$5 billion increase in government tax collections. In turn, the \$40 billion rise in Y_d will result in a \$32 billion increase in consumption expenditures and an \$8 billion rise in personal saving S_p. In other words, for every dollar change in Y, there will be a 16 percent change in S_p. Thus, the ratio of ΔS_p to ΔY is 0.16, in contrast to the marginal propensity to save of 0.20.

What about the other determinants of consumption and personal saving? How do they fit into this picture of the relation between S_p and Y? Since a two-dimensional diagram can only show the relationship between two variables along any one given line such as S_pS_p, the other variables must be assumed to be fixed. If other variables do change, however, then the position of the line S_pS_p must change to show the relationship between S_p and Y given the new values of the other variables. Thus, in terms of Figure 19–2, S_pS_p will move upward if, at any given level of Y, there is a decrease in liquid wealth or a rise in the rate of interest. In addition, anything that would cause X to change would also lead to a change in S_pS_p.

Business Saving and Taxes Added to Personal Saving

We have said that when the total of the plans for $S_p + S_b + T$ differs from the total of the plans for $I + G + (X - M)$, economic change occurs. What do the totals of the plans for S_p, S_b, and T look like at any given level of gross national product? This relationship is depicted in Figure 19–3.

The tax line TT shows the relationship between the tax receipts at all levels of government and the level of gross national product. This line is drawn sloping upward and to the right, since the various governmental bodies collect more taxes as incomes increase. For the sake of simplicity, we have assumed that government tax collections are a constant proportion of changes in Y. Because the position of line TT is determined by legislative action, it will not be directly influenced by economic variables such as

Figure 19–3. The relationship between S_p, S_b, T, and Y.

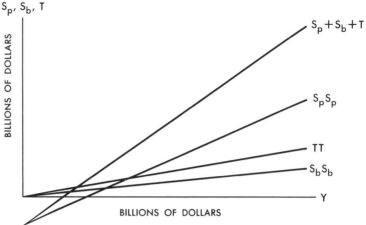

Y_d, i, and W_h. The legislatures are influenced by economic conditions indirectly, of course.

T may be defined as:

$$T = f(Y, Z) \qquad [19\text{–}3]$$

This equation tells us that T, total government tax collections, is a function of Y, the level of gross national product, and Z, a general variable standing for all those forces that cause legislatures to change tax rates. As already indicated, in Figure 19–3 the relationship between T and Y is assumed to be positive.

The business saving line $S_b S_b$ in the figure shows the relationship between the level of business saving S_b (consisting of disposable corporate income and capital consumption allowances) and gross national product.[6] This relationship is positive, for businesses expect to have higher earnings as the level of income in the economy rises. Again for the sake of simplicity, we have assumed that the relationship between changes in the amount of business saving and Y are always proportionate. Thus, the equation for S_b is

$$S_b = f(Y, U) \qquad [19\text{–}4]$$

where U stands for any forces tending to change S_b at any given level of Y, such as government taxes on business, corporate dividend policies, and capital consumption allowances. Decreases in business taxes, higher capital consumption allowances, and reduced dividend rates all will tend to

[6] The data published by the U.S. Department of Commerce for business saving covers only corporate enterprise. The earnings of unincorporated enterprises are included in disposable personal income.

raise $S_b S_b$. Hence, business saving may be increased at all levels of Y. As before, however, a given line such as $S_b S_b$ in Figure 19–3 assumes other factors to be fixed. Assuming that all determinants of S_p, S_b, and T other than Y are fixed, we may depict the combined impact on the three lines $S_p S_p$, $S_b S_b$, and TT. This is represented in the figure by line $S_p + S_b + T$, which shows the expected total of S_p, S_b, and T at various levels of Y. The relationship is positive, with a slope less than one but greater than zero.

Shifts in the $S_p + S_b + T$ Line

A shift in $S_p S_p$ attributable to changes in W_h and i will usually cause the entire line $S_p + S_b + T$ to shift by the same amount. Shifts in the combined $S_b S_b$ and TT line, however, may not move $S_p + S_b + T$ by the same amount, since these changes affect the level of disposable personal income. For example, if the distribution of gross national product changes as income rises so that a greater proportion of Y is channeled into business saving and taxes, the net effect will be a reduction in disposable personal income. Personal saving will also be affected: $S_p S_p$ will rotate down. As a result, the total line $S_p + S_b + T$ will rotate up somewhat, but the rotation in the total line will be less than the rotation in TT and $S_b S_b$. This is illustrated in Figure 19–4. We assume an increase in tax rates. $S_b S_b$ and TT are added together to simplify our analysis. The solid lines represent the original positions of $S_b S_b + TT$, $S_p S_p$, and $S_p + S_b + T$. The distance between the old $S_p + S_b + T$ and the new total line is equal to the difference between the rise in $S_b S_b + TT$ and the decrease in $S_p S_p$.

Figure 19–4. The relationship between $S_p S_p$, $S_b S_b + TT$ and changes in the tax rate.

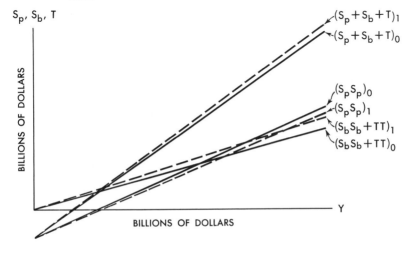

Summary of the Forces Affecting the $S_p + S_b + T$ Line

The $S_p + S_b + T$ line will shift whenever determinants of S_p, S_b, and T other than Y change. Thus:

1. S_pS_p, and hence $S_p + S_b + T$, fluctuate inversely with movements of liquid wealth.[7] S_pS_p and $S_p + S_b + T$ rise with a decrease in individual holdings of the components of liquid wealth—the stock of money, time deposits, savings and loan share accounts, U.S. government securities, corporate stocks, bonds, and life insurance policies. Conversely, S_pS_p, and hence $S_p + S_b + T$, fall with an increase in liquid wealth holdings.

2. S_pS_p, and hence $S_p + S_b + T$, vary directly with price-level changes because the purchasing power of liquid wealth changes. On the other hand, S_pS_p and $S_p + S_b + T$ vary inversely with price expectations.

3. S_pS_p, and hence $S_p + S_b + T$, vary directly with the interest rate.

4. S_pS_p falls whenever the tax rate is increased, but $S_p + S_b + T$ rises.The rise in $S_p + S_b + T$ is less than the increase in TT, however. Conversely, lower tax rates cause a downward turn in $S_p + S_b + T$, but by less than the decrease in TT.

5. S_pS_p varies inversely with changes in business saving, but $S_p + S_b + T$ moves in the same direction as business saving changes. Hence a change in $S_p + S_b + T$ is less than a change in S_bS_b.

6. TT changes with legislative actions that alter the tax rate. $S_p + S_b + T$ varies as described in point 4 above.

7. S_bS_b varies inversely with changes in the tax rates on business and corporate dividend payments, but directly with capital consumption allowances.

INVESTMENT BEHAVIOR

The Importance of Investment

A major role in bringing about economic prosperity is usually ascribed to investment expenditures. A high level of expenditure on plant and equipment, inventories, and residential construction is generally considered to be one sign of a healthy and growing economy. For instance, an increase in the amount of productive plant and equipment enhances the output capabilities of the work force and thus enables any given amount of labor to produce more goods for the economy. Higher output should lead to higher consumption levels and a higher standard of living. Even if there is no increase in the amount of plant and equipment, the maintenance of a given

---

[7] That is, at any given level of income, personal saving will increase with a drop in liquid wealth. This ignores the fact, discussed earlier, that liquid wealth increases as saving takes place. Liquid wealth accumulates as saving occurs, subsequently enabling S_pS_p, the *rate* of saving, to fall and consumption to increase at all levels of income.

amount by means of capital replacement may have similar beneficial effects on the economy since old plant and equipment are normally replaced by new, higher quality products.

Investment expenditures do not exhibit the same stability relative to gross national product that consumption expenditures do. Table 19–1 and Figure 19–5, for example, show that investment expenditure as a percentage of gross national product has varied in recent decades from a high of 19.0 percent in 1950 to a low of 13.6 percent in 1958. Year-to-year variations in *I* are substantial.

The data suggest that investment expenditure change may well be a source of income and output change, which in turn may induce a change in the amount of consumption expenditures. As can be seen in Table 19–2, a decline in investment spending is often accompanied by a small increase in consumption. From 1948 to 1949, *I* dropped by $10.3 billion and consumption rose by $3.2 billion; from 1953 to 1954, *I* fell $0.9 billion, while *C* increased $6.5 billion. From 1957 to 1958, *I* dropped by $6.9 billion, and from 1960 to 1961, by $3.1 billion; during those same years, *C* rose by $8.4 billion and $10.0 billion, respectively. More recently, *I* fell by $4.8 billion in 1967, principally because of a drop in business inventories; at the same time, *C* continued to expand sharply as a result of heavy Vietnam

Figure 19–5. Investment and government expenditures for the United States, 1946–73.

SOURCE: Table 19-1.

TABLE 19-2 INVESTMENT, CONSUMPTION, GOVERNMENT EXPENDITURE, AND GROSS NATIONAL PRODUCT CHANGES FROM THE PRECEDING YEAR, 1947–73
(IN BILLIONS OF DOLLARS)

YEAR	INVESTMENT CHANGE	CONSUMPTION CHANGE	GOVERNMENT EXPENDITURE CHANGE	$(X - M)$ CHANGE	GNP CHANGE
1947	+ 3.4	+17.3	− 1.9	+4.0	+ 22.8
1948	+12.0	+12.9	+ 6.5	−5.1	+ 26.3
1949	−10.3	+ 3.2	+ 6.2	−0.3	− 1.1
1950	+18.4	+14.2	+ 0.1	−4.3	+ 28.4
1951	+ 5.2	+15.3	+21.2	+1.9	+ 43.5
1952	− 7.4	+10.4	+15.6	−1.5	+ 17.1
1953	+ 0.7	+13.3	+ 6.9	−1.8	+ 19.1
1954	− 0.9	+ 6.5	− 6.8	+1.4	+ 0.2
1955	+15.7	+17.9	− 0.6	+0.2	+ 33.2
1956	+ 2.6	+12.3	+ 4.4	+2.0	+ 21.2
1957	− 2.2	+14.7	+ 7.5	+1.7	+ 21.9
1958	− 6.9	+ 8.4	+ 8.1	−3.5	+ 6.2
1959	+14.4	+21.1	+ 2.8	−2.1	+ 36.3
1960	− 0.5	+13.0	+ 2.6	+3.9	+ 20.2
1961	− 3.1	+10.0	+ 8.0	+1.6	+ 16.3
1962	+11.3	+19.9	+ 9.5	−0.5	+ 40.2
1963	+ 4.1	+19.9	+ 5.4	+0.8	+ 30.2
1964	+ 6.9	+26.2	+ 6.2	+2.6	+ 41.9
1965	+14.0	+31.6	+ 8.3	−1.6	+ 52.5
1966	+13.3	+33.5	+19.8	−1.6	+ 65.0
1967	− 4.8	+25.8	+23.3	−0.1	+ 44.0
1968	+ 9.4	+44.1	+19.5	−2.7	+ 70.3
1969	+13.0	+43.3	+10.4	−0.6	+ 66.1
1970	− 1.9	+37.3	+ 9.0	+1.7	+ 46.1
1971	+14.9	+48.1	+13.8	−2.9	+ 74.0
1972	+28.4	+56.1	+21.8	−4.9	+101.4
1973	+24.6	+89.0	+25.4	−0.8	+138.2

SOURCE: Table 19-1.

war expenditures. However, the increase in consumption in 1967 was less than in 1966 and 1968, when both investment and consumption moved upward sharply. During the 1970 recession, I fell and the growth of C slowed. On the other hand, when I increased markedly in 1950, 1955, 1959, 1962, 1965, 1966, 1968, and 1971–72, there were also very sharp rises in C.

Historically, the association between C and I is not clearly observable. Changes in C and I are not proportionate, and as a consequence the relationship between I and Y changes. The effects of changes in tax receipts and business saving must be considered. Changes in the other determinants of C and S_p may also occur. Thus, it is the overall effect of the interaction between $S_p + S_b + T$ and $I + G + (X - M)$ that must be examined.

At present, however, we are concerned with investment demand as a source of economic change. The *importance* of changes in I to economic progress and income change is clear, but how do economists explain the investment fluctuations themselves? This is the crucial question. From the perspective of economic policy, for instance, if *I* is the variable that should be manipulated, then our analysis must provide clues to the ultimate determinants of *I* so that they may be properly controlled to bring about the desired change in *I*.

The Determinants of Investment Expenditure

The following discussion describes the behavior of gross private domestic investment. We will not concern ourselves with the components of gross private domestic investment here, but rather with the determinants of total investment expenditures. A separate analysis could be made of the various types of investment expenditures, but in order to keep our economic model relatively simple and free of the complexities caused by a plethora of variables, we shall treat only the determinants of the aggregate *I*. Hence, for the most part, our analysis assumes that the behavior of most forms of investment is comparable to that of investment in capital assets, especially productive plant and equipment investments.

The investment criteria: the MEI and the rate of interest. Two forces are generally thought to determine investment: the marginal efficiency of investment and the rate of interest. *The marginal efficiency of investment (MEI) is that rate of return which will cause the present value of expected future yields from new investment to equal the actual outlay for new investment.* Suppose, for example, that a firm expects to increase its annual sales by $50,000 from the sale of a product it could make on a new machine. Then suppose that the annual increase in costs (principally labor and materials) of producing the additional sales is expected to be $25,000 and that the firm is in a 50 percent tax bracket. The average annual expected change in after-tax profits is thus $12,500. If the total cost of the new machine is $100,000 and it is expected to yield this income stream of $12,500 in perpetuity, we can calculate *r*, the marginal efficiency of investment, using the formula

$$r = \frac{R}{P} \qquad\qquad [19\text{--}5]$$

where *R* is the after-tax profit expected in perpetuity and *P* is the actual cost of investment. Thus:

$$r = \frac{12{,}500}{100{,}000} = 12\tfrac{1}{2}\%$$

This theory of investment expenditures assumes that entrepreneurs seek profit and are profit maximizers. The illustration above shows that, for a $100,000 investment in a machine, the firm can increase its annual profits by $12,500. But this does not mean that the firm will accept the project or will actually spend $100,000 on new investment. One important item has been omitted – the cost of funds. It is this cost that determines the cutoff point on new investments. Firms are continually considering alternative investments in plant and equipment, each of which is expected to yield a particular income stream. The profit-maximizing firm will rank alternative investment projects by rates of return and will accept new projects until a point is reached where the *marginal efficiency of investment is equal to the cost of obtaining the funds to finance the investment project.* This "cost of funds" is, of course, *the interest rate.* Thus, in our example, if the cost of the funds needed to buy the new machine were 10 percent, it would pay the firm to invest in the project, since total profits would increase by the $2\frac{1}{2}$ percent spread. It would not pay the firm to make investments yielding less than a 10 percent return, since interest costs would then exceed expected profits.

Let us modify equation 19–5 by substituting the current rate of interest i for the marginal efficiency of investment r, and V, the present value of the income stream expected from an investment project, for the actual cost of investment P. R is again the after-tax profit expected in perpetuity. We now have

$$V = \frac{R}{i} \qquad\qquad [19\text{--}6]$$

or

$$\frac{\$12,500}{10\%} = \$125,000$$

Here we see that the $12,500 income stream discounted at the interest cost of 10 percent gives rise to a present value of $125,000 for the machine. Since the actual cost of investment is only $100,000, there is a net gain of $25,000 and it clearly pays to invest in the machine. Thus the investment cutoff criterion can be stated in two ways, each of which is equivalent to the other. In order to maximize profits, a firm should

1. Accept investment projects for which the marginal efficiency of investment is greater than or equal to the interest cost, or
2. Accept investment projects for which the actual cost of investment is less than or equal to the discounted present value of the expected future yields.

Shortcomings of the analysis. The preceding analysis makes two assumptions that limit its applicability: (1) that an investment project yields a constant income stream, and (2) that this income stream is yielded in perpetuity. If the income stream is *not* constant, which is generally the case, then the firm must estimate the expected return for each year of the estimated life of the project. To do this, we must replace equations 19–5 and 19–6 with another equation:

$$V = \frac{R_1}{1 + i} + \frac{R_2}{(1 + i)^2} + \cdots + \frac{R_n}{(1 + i)^n} \qquad [19\text{-}7]$$

Here V and i are defined in the same way as in equation 19–6, R_i is the ith expected return, and R_n is the final return. Assume, for example, that a proposed investment is expected to yield \$10,000 (R_1), \$20,000 (R_2), and \$10,000 (R_3), respectively, for three years, at the end of which time the project will be scrapped. If the interest cost is 10 percent, then:

$$V = \frac{\$10,000}{1.10} + \frac{\$20,000}{(1.10)^2} + \frac{\$10,000}{(1.10)^3} = \$33,207$$

Unless the actual cost of investment is equal to or less than \$33,207, it will not pay the firm to invest in the project.

Another shortcoming of the preceding analysis is the treatment of the cost of funds (or capital) as constant interest cost. Firms have alternative sources of funds—retained earnings, depreciation, new stock sales, and new bond sales—each of which has a different annual cost. Some investment projects cost so much that they force firms to use all available sources of funds; others can be financed from just one source. Usually firms will use internally generated funds (retained earnings and depreciation) prior to selling new stocks and bonds. The cost of funds can be expected to increase as the amount of funds needed expands. Only in the simplest of circumstances can we assume a constant interest rate. Nevertheless, for the sake of simplicity, we will do just this. (It is actually more reasonable to assume a constant interest cost for the economy as a whole than for the individual firm, since different interest costs generally seem to be functionally related. See Chapter 15.)

The MEI for the economy. The preceding paragraphs have analyzed the MEI in terms of how a profit-seeking firm arrives at investment decisions. For the economy as a whole, the same line of reasoning applies. To arrive at an investment demand function, we simply add the investment demands of individual firms.

Conceptually, we may visualize the relationship between the marginal efficiency of investment and the amount of desired investment for the economy as an investment schedule like the one shown in Figure 19–6. Investment demand is measured along the horizontal axis, and the marginal efficiency of investment along the vertical axis. The investment demand schedule, line *II*, shows that the relationship is an inverse one; in mathematical terms, the slope of the demand schedule is negative. This is because alternative investment projects are ranked in order of their desirability—that is, in order of their marginal efficiency of investment. All projects to the left of I_1, for example, yield better than 8 percent returns. Projects between I_1 and I_2 yield between 8 and 4 percent. We assume that firms in

Figure 19-6. The investment demand schedule.

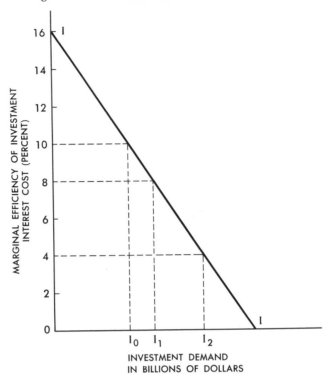

the economy prefer to invest in projects with high yields. It is unlikely that a firm would give priority to investment in a low-yield project unless it were somehow required for business survival (in which case its yield must, in an ultimate sense, be very high indeed). In the aggregate, however, this latter consideration is not likely to be particularly important in determining overall investment demand.

Now let us approach the topic in terms of the rate of interest on the vertical axis of the figure. If the interest cost is 8 percent, then businesses and individuals will plan to make investment expenditures of only I_1 billions of dollars. Additional investment expenditure is not likely because the interest cost of obtaining funds to invest in real plant and equipment would be greater than the expected return.

Given this investment schedule, changes in investment expenditure will take place only when there are variations in the rate of interest. If the interest rate should rise to 10 percent, for example, the level of planned investment expenditures would drop from I_1 to I_0. Many projects considered profitable when the interest cost was 8 percent would no longer be so and would have to be dropped. On the other hand, a decrease in interest costs to 4 percent should lead cause investment expenditures to rise to I_2. There would then be more projects yielding returns in excess of the interest cost, and hence a rise in investment.

On the basis of this line of reasoning, interest costs are clearly an important factor in determining the amount of investment in the economy. If this is true, then such determinants of interest rates as bank lending practices, central bank monetary policy, fiscal policy, the money supply, and money demand are also significant in determining the amount of investment demand and, hence, the overall level of expenditures and gross national product.

Some economists during the 1930s and 1940s argued that interest rates were not important determinants of investment. It was said, for example, that "remarks about the interest inelasticity of investment have been well substantiated by different types of empirical investigation,"[8] and that "since the late 1930s there has been a general tendency to suppose that investment is relatively insensitive to the interest rate."[9]

On the other hand, studies in the 1950s and 1960s tended to support the more traditional view presented here. Frank de Leeuw, for example, has demonstrated that the rate of interest and investment by manufacturers is inversely related.[10] Some economists who previously minimized the importance of interest rates even reversed their position:

Conclusions from [earlier studies] may have been premature, for results obtained since 1952 in samples that contain several observations at widely varying interest levels show that interest is a significant variable in equations of investment behavior. The new results show statistical significance for interest variables; they do not necessarily show high elasticity.[11]

And again:

In order of statistical significance, variations in yields on industrial funds, on treasury bills, and on government bonds appear to have an effect on manufacturers' fixed investment, but only with a one-year lag. The explanation offered for the relationship is that considerable time elapses between initial planning and carrying out of investment, and that interest rates serve as indices of credit availability.[12]

Thus, evidence concerning the influence of interest rates on investment is contradictory. For purposes of analysis, however, we shall treat investment as a function of the rate of interest. As subsequent chapters will demonstrate, the model of income determination we are developing can cope

---

[8] Klein, *op. cit.,* p. 65.
[9] J. S. Duesenberry. *Business Cycles and Economic Growth* (McGraw-Hill, 1958), p. 49.
[10] Frank de Leeuw. "The Demand for Capital Goods by Manufacturers: A Study of Quarterly Time Series." *Econometrica* (1962), pp. 407–23.
[11] Klein, *op. cit.,* p. 204.
[12] Franz Gehrels and Suzanne Wiggins. "Interest Rates and Manufacturers' Fixed Investment." *American Economic Review* (1957), p. 91.

with situations where investment is either responsive or completely nonresponsive to interest rate changes.

The MEI and other influences on investment demand. Influences on investment demand other than the interest rate are taken into account by the marginal efficiency of investment concept. Anything that can cause a change in MEI will lead to a change in the amount of investment at any given rate of interest. For example, if there is an increase in MEI, the expected rate of return for any given amount of investment will increase. Also, at any given interest cost, entrepreneurs will be willing to spend more on investment goods and services than formerly because more projects are profitable than formerly.

Figure 19–7 illustrates a shift of this sort. In it, line *II* is the original investment schedule and line *I'I'* represents the new investment schedule. In terms of investment I_1, this shift increases the return over cost from i_i to i_2. If the interest cost is originally i_1 and remains unchanged, then the differen-

Figure 19–7. Changes in the investment demand schedule.

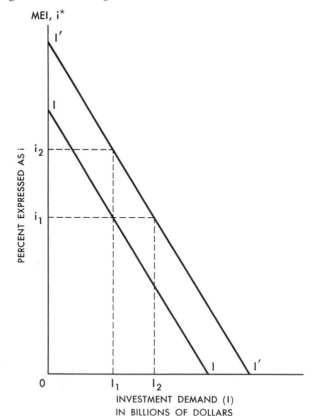

* MEI = marginal efficiency of investment; i = rate of interest.

tial between the rate of interest and the expected return permits an increase in investment expenditures from I_1 to I_2.

Some of the more important forces that influence the marginal efficiency of investment and, hence, the investment schedule are (1) income, (2) technology, (3) cost of labor and materials, (4) government tax policies, and (5) business expectations.

The *general level of income Y* is an important source of investment change. As income grows, demand for products also grows. Thus, it is likely that businesses will expand their demand for productive plant and equipment in order to tool up to meet the anticipated demand. The closer to capacity a business enterprise operates, the more likely it will be to increase investment expenditure as final product demand continues to exert a strong pull on the economy. When there is a decline in the economy, on the other hand, there is excess productive capacity, and anticipated final product demand and planned investment expenditures are low. For instance, Table 19–2 shows that the years of greatest investment increase were in periods of prosperity, whereas the largest investment decreases occurred in recessions. This would seem to indicate that investment is dependent on the level and rate of increase of income. The larger the growth of income, the greater the need for plant and equipment to meet the increasing consumption demand.

Technological change is another important factor that may be a source of change in the marginal efficiency of investment. When a cost-saving innovation occurs, the rate of return from investment increases. For instance, in our simple example on page 393, if a technological advance permits the firm to produce more product — say, $60,000 worth — at the same cost of labor and materials, and if the price of the machine is the same, then the marginal efficiency of investment is $17\frac{1}{2}$ percent. The cost per unit of output will be reduced, allowing greater production or the same production at a lower total cost. Either way the expected rate of return will increase.

Variations in the *cost of labor and materials* will also influence investment demand. If union pressures raise labor costs, for example, then expected costs on investment projects will also rise and the expected rate of return will diminish. An increase in raw material costs would have the same effect.

Government tax policies are also important. If taxes on business enterprise decrease, the after-tax profits accruing from any investment project increase, raising the expected rate of return. Similarly, government revision of depreciation schedules and depletion allowances also affects investment demand. If businesses are allowed to write off the cost of plant and equipment over a shorter period of time, during any given year while plant and equipment are being depreciated, for example, more funds are available to the firm for investment. Shorter depreciation periods and investment tax credits were allowed by the government from time to time in the

1960s and early 1970s, and these actions were generally followed by periods of markedly increased investment.

Business expectations of future trends in the economy are especially significant as a determinant of investment demand. In some ways, they are related to the current level of income and output. If Y is high and rising, expectations for investment spending will probably be favorable. On the other hand, a declining Y may generate adverse expectations and lead to a decline in investment expenditures. Expectations may be influenced by many considerations, however. The prospect of war may lead equipment producers to expect larger government orders and induce preparations for capacity expansion, for example. Legislative talk of a tax revision may cause businesses to postpone investment outlays until the precise nature of the reform is known. In this respect, uncertainty and anticipation concerning the future clearly influence investment. Expected increases in the cost of equipment will cause investment expenditures to be made prior to the time they would otherwise have occurred. Similarly, falling stock prices may cause concern about the future and induce investment decreases even in a healthy economy.

In general, the factors that increase expected receipts or reduce expected costs lead to an increase in the marginal efficiency of investment; they cause a shift of the investment demand schedule upward and to the right. The factors that decrease the marginal efficiency of investment cause a shift downward and to the left.

Additional restrictions on the analysis of investment. The preceding discussion covers most of the principal determinants of investment demand that are usually considered in macroeconomic analysis. Additional forces, which are of interest primarily because of their theoretical nature, can also be examined, however. These forces are very difficult to estimate empirically. Among them are the level of liquid wealth held by firms, the real purchasing power of firm liquid wealth holdings when prices change, and expectations concerning future prices and interest rates. Notice that these are also forces that influence the behavior of consumption demand. In fact, our analysis here will be virtually parallel to our earlier discussion on consumption.

Just as in households, the ability of firms to demand investment goods depends on their holdings of liquid wealth. The greater a firm's holding of liquid assets, the greater its ability to command new plant and equipment. Hence, there is a direct relation between investment demand I and the liquid wealth holdings of firms W_f. On the other hand, the greater the possession of real wealth by a firm, the greater its productive capacity and, hence, the less its need for additional plant and equipment.

Similarly, it can be reasoned that there is a wealth effect relating investment demand to price-level variations. For example, should the price level increase, the purchasing power of firm liquid asset holdings and, accordingly, firm ability to demand new plant and equipment would decrease. On the other hand, firms are generally net debtors in the economy—that is, their debt exceeds their liquid wealth holdings. Hence a rise in the price level might reduce real debt more than real liquid wealth holdings and, accordingly, an increase in the demand for investment goods might ensue.[13]

In addition, as previously noted, price expectations may also affect investment decisions. For example, should firms expect the price of new investment goods to rise in the future, then they might be induced to increase their plant and equipment purchases.

The relationship between interest rates and prices may also be important. Just as for consumers, should market rates of interest lag behind prices, so it is for producers. If prices are rising and market rates of interest are rising but lagging, real interest rates decrease and firms may increase their borrowing for capital expansion. Hence, investment expenditures expand.

Obviously, the study of investment demand is very complicated, and we can do no more than scratch the surface in a book devoted primarily to a study of the relationship between money and the economy. Detailed discussions of macroeconomic theory and capital budgeting treat investment theory in considerably more detail.

The Investment Demand Equation

We have said that investment is determined by the interaction of the rate of interest and the marginal efficiency of investment, and that the latter is determined primarily by income, wealth, technology, the cost of labor and materials, government tax policies, and business expectations. Of these six forces, two—income and wealth—are studied separately. Thus it can be said that investment is determined by i, the rate of interest, Y, gross national product, W_f, firm liquid wealth, and U', the forces other than Y and W_f that also help determine the marginal efficiency of investment. In equation form:

$$I = f(i, Y, W_f, U')$$

[19–8]

The relationship between interest and investment is inverse. The higher the level of interest costs, the smaller investment demand becomes; the lower the level of interest costs, the greater investment demand becomes. The relationship between investment and liquid wealth and income is positive, however. The higher the levels of income and liquid wealth, the greater the investment demand; the lower the levels of income and liquid wealth, the lower the investment demand. Similarly, when other forces U' increase the

---

[13] For a discussion of the effect of real money balances as a factor of production, *see* Allen Sinai and Houston H. Stokes. "Real Money Balances: An Omitted Variable from the Production Function." *Review of Economics and Statistics* (1972), pp. 290–96.

Figure 19–8. The relationship between investment and income.

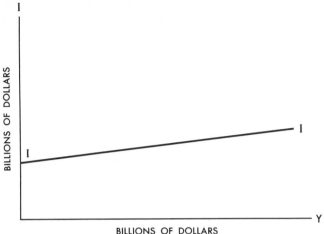

marginal efficiency of investment, investment demand increases; when they decrease the marginal efficiency of investment, investment demand decreases.

The relationship between income and investment is shown diagrammatically in Figure 19–8. Investment demand I is measured on the vertical axis and Y on the horizontal axis. Line II slopes upward and to the right, indicating that the higher the level of income and output, the greater the investment demand. Again, for simplicity, the investment demand schedule is shown as a straight line.

Line II in this figure differs from the investment demand lines in Figures 19–6 and 19–7, where we were concerned with the relationship between investment and the rate of interest. Here we are simply demonstrating the positive relationship between I and Y, and hence it is assumed that i, W_f, and U' are fixed. If i increases, then line II in Figure 19–8 must shift downward because of the inverse relationship between I and i. If either W_f or the marginal efficiency of investment decreases, line II must also shift downward.

ADDING GOVERNMENT EXPENDITURES AND THE BALANCE OF TRADE TO THE EQUATION

We have said that when the plans for $S_p + S_b + T$ differ from the plans for $I + G + (X - M)$, changes in income will take place. Earlier in this chapter, we discussed the relationship between $S_p + S_b + T$ and Y; to complete our discussion, we need to show the relationship between $I + G + (X - M)$ and Y.

Line GG parallel to the horizontal axis, in Figure 19–9, shows the relationship between government expenditures and Y. There is no change in G

Figure 19-9. The relationship between *I*, *G*, *F*, and *Y*.

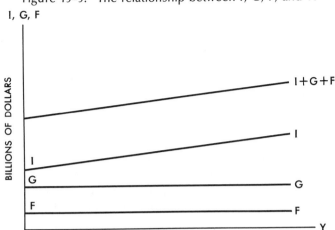

as *Y* increases along the horizontal axis because the level of government spending is assumed to be dependent on legislative action rather than on the level of income and output. An increase in government spending shifts the line upward; a decrease moves it downward.

Like tax receipts, government expenditures are determined by the legislature, which is influenced principally by considerations other than the current level of income and employment. During inflation, it is true, there is considerable talk of the need to hold down government expenditures, while in a recession expenditure increases are urged upon the legislature. For the most part, however, federal expenditures on final goods and services are influenced primarily by considerations of national defense, and state and local expenditures are influenced by the need for social goods and services such as highways and schools. Thus noneconomic factors are more crucial, in general, than economic ones.

Tables 19-1 and 19-2 and Figure 19-5 show the growth of government expenditures in recent decades. As might be expected, the greatest increases occurred in the Korean and Vietnam conflicts. During the first five years after World War II, government expenditures averaged 12.8 percent of GNP. With the advent of the Korean conflict, defense expenditures again rose and, in 1953, government expenditures as a percentage of GNP reached 22.4 percent. There was some reduction in defense spending following the Korean conflict, but not enough to bring government spending as a percentage of GNP back to the level of the 1930s and late 1940s. From 1954 through 1966, government spending as a percentage of GNP varied between 18.6 and 21.1 percent. Government expenditures increased to 23.1 percent of GNP in 1968, as the Vietnam war again raised defense outlays. Thus federal expenditures have been somewhat volatile, largely because of variations in our defense needs. In contrast, state and local expenditures in the post-World War II period have grown steadily in volume, year in and year out.

Putting these considerations in equation form, we have

$$G = f(Z) \qquad [19\text{--}9]$$

which tells us that G, total government expenditures, is a function of Z, a variable representing those forces that cause legislatures to change government spending. (This variable is the same as the Z variable in equation 19–3 that stood for all the forces that cause legislatures to change tax rates.)

The difference between exports and imports $X - M$ is also assumed to be independent of the level of income. Let F be $X - M$. Line FF in Figure 19–9 then represents F, the difference between exports and imports, and illustrates the independence of F and Y. FF shifts with changes in the forces that determine the volume of imports and exports. Line FF is above the horizontal axis when exports exceed imports, and beneath it when imports exceed exports.

The equation for the difference between exports and imports F is

$$F = f(J) \qquad [19\text{--}10]$$

where J is a variable representing the forces that cause F to change.

In some ways, the assumption that F is independent of the level of income is rather unrealistic; imports do depend on the level of income in one's own country. When income and output increase at home, people may be expected to increase their consumption of domestic goods and services *and* their consumption of imported goods. Likewise, if incomes decrease at home, the public will probably purchase less of both domestically produced and foreign goods and services. Thus, if exports remain constant and if the other determinants of imports remain unchanged, F should increase during recession and decrease in periods of prosperity and rising incomes.

The data available seem to support this line of reasoning. Table 19–3 lists the volume of exports and imports for the post-World War II period. Imports tended to decrease slightly or remain the same in the recessions of 1948–49, 1953–54, 1957–58, and 1960–61. The recession of 1970 was an exception to this general observation. Conversely, imports increased during the prosperous periods. The effects of these changes in imports on F, however, are barely discernible because exports did not remain constant. Just as U.S. imports depend on national income levels, so our exports depend on income levels abroad. If incomes increase abroad, foreigners will demand more of their own goods and also more U.S. goods. Thus, variations in foreign incomes may cause changes in U.S. exports and in F that cancel out any inverse relationship between F and Y in the United States arising from the positive relationship between imports and Y.

Furthermore, American imports and exports are also related. When imports increase because of income increases, exports eventually increase

TABLE 19–3 EXPORTS, IMPORTS, AND NET EXPORTS OF GOODS AND SERVICES
FOR THE UNITED STATES, 1946–73
(IN BILLIONS OF DOLLARS)

YEAR	EXPORTS	IMPORTS	NET EXPORTS*
1946	14.7	7.2	7.5
1947	19.7	8.2	11.5
1948	16.8	10.3	6.4
1949	15.8	9.6	6.1
1950	13.8	12.0	1.8
1951	18.7	15.1	3.7
1952	18.0	15.8	2.2
1953	16.9	16.6	0.4
1954	17.8	15.9	1.8
1955	19.8	17.8	2.0
1956	23.6	19.6	4.0
1957	26.5	20.8	5.7
1958	23.1	20.9	2.2
1959	23.5	23.3	0.1
1960	27.2	23.2	4.0
1961	28.6	23.0	5.6
1962	30.3	25.1	5.1
1963	32.3	26.4	5.9
1964	37.1	28.6	8.5
1965	39.2	32.3	6.9
1966	43.4	38.1	5.3
1967	46.2	41.0	5.2
1968	50.6	48.1	2.5
1969	55.5	53.6	1.9
1970	62.9	59.3	3.6
1971	66.1	65.4	0.7
1972	73.7	77.9	−4.2
1973†	84.0	89.0	−5.0

* Differences in net figures are due to rounding.
† Estimated by author.
SOURCE: Table 19–1.

also because an increased demand for foreign goods by U.S. citizens induces other nations to increase their production. As this happens, income
and output abroad increase, enabling foreigners to demand more American
goods. This leads to increased U.S. exports and incomes. Thus, the greater
the extent to which American purchases are concentrated in countries that
in turn make heavy purchases in the United States, the more likely that
increases in domestic output will lead to both import and export increases
for the United States. This makes it difficult to establish a definite relationship between F (the difference between exports and imports) and the
level of output. If exports change as discussed above, then either a direct
or an inverse relationship between F and Y is equally possible.

Relative prices between countries and official trade policies are two of
the other factors that affect the position of line FF in Figure 19–9. If prices
in the United States decline relative to those abroad, both U.S. citizens and
foreigners will demand more American goods. On the other hand, if prices

in the United States rise relative to those abroad, demand for the less expensive goods produced outside the United States will rise.

Changes in national trade policies will also affect the shape of the *FF* line. If the United States were to impose trade restrictions making it more difficult for Americans to buy abroad, imports would decline and, other things being equal, the *FF* line would rise. Of course, other things do not always remain the same. If it were more difficult for Americans to import, other nations would probably retaliate by restricting their imports from us. On the other hand, relaxing trade barriers can lead to a general increase in trade and a corresponding rise in both exports and imports.

The line $I + G + F$ in Figure 19–9 represents the sum of the three separate lines *II*, *GG*, and *FF*. The $I + G + F$ line runs parallel to the investment line *II*. the only variable that changes with income and output. $I + G + F$ will shift upward with upward movements in any of the lines that represent its components, and downward with downward movements in these lines. The component lines, in turn, will shift when changes occur in their determinants other than Y.

INCOME DETERMINATION

Figure 19–10 shows how the $S_p + S_b + T$ and $I + G + F$ lines interact to determine the income levels in the economy. In drawing these lines we are assuming, of course, that the determinants of each line (and consequently of Y) other than those listed are fixed.

Given lines $S_p + S_b + T$ and $(I + G + F)_0$, assume that the economy is initially producing at a rate of Y_1 billion dollars per year. At that rate of output, the planned expenditures on $I + G + F$ exceed $S_p + S_b + T$, the planned withdrawals from the income stream. Under these circumstances, a strong force for income change exists—excess demand. More goods and

Figure 19–10.   Income determination.

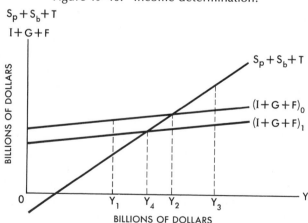

BILLIONS OF DOLLARS

services are wanted than are being produced, and inventories are being depleted. Businesses usually respond to this situation by increasing output, which in turn leads to increased incomes, consumption, personal saving, business saving, government tax takes, and investment. Thus C, S_p, S_b, T, and I all increase because each is partly determined by Y. These forces tend to increase income to Y_2, at which point demand equals supply and the economy is in a state of equilibrium.

On the other hand, if the rate of output is Y_3, then planned income withdrawals $S_p + S_b + T$ exceed expenditures on $I + G + F$. Again, a force for change exists—this time, excess supply. Not all that is produced by business will be sold, and a contraction will occur. Businesses will tend to cut back production until the excess supply is eliminated—again, until the equilibrium income Y_2 is reached.

The critical assumption for the preceding analysis is that other things remain the same. In the real world, however, other things are in almost continuous flux. Fortunately, our model of income determination enables us to predict the direction of economic change with some semblance of accuracy despite the almost continual variation in real-world conditions, since changes in these conditions usually occur slowly and in limited magnitudes.

Any of the forces that lead to a shift of either $S_p + S_b + T$ or $I + G + F$ may cause a change in Y. The nature of these possible changes was discussed earlier in this chapter and will be summarized briefly again at its conclusion. Let us examine one change in detail, however: a decrease in government expenditures. Assume that the economy is initially in equilibrium at Y_2. A decrease in G will then shift the $I + G + F$ line down to $(I + G + F)_1$ in Figure 19–10. Now there is excess supply at Y_2. Investment and consumption spending contract, and actual personal saving, business saving, and government tax receipts decrease until a new equilibrium income level is reached at Y_4.

Looking a little more closely at this situation, we see what happens when the government decreases its rate of expenditures. With a smaller demand for output, business must reduce its rate of production or face mounting inventories. With reduced output, employment declines, payments of wages and salaries drop, and disposable personal income decreases. With lower incomes, individuals must reduce their rate of consumption expenditures. People are reluctant to accept a drop in their standard of living, however, and therefore they will not reduce their consumption expenditures by as much as their disposable income has fallen. Consequently, their rate of personal saving also falls. Investment by businesses decreases because of reduced orders and lower Y. The induced consumption and investment expenditure decreases will cause income and output to fall even further. Business saving also decreases because of inadequate demand and the probability of falling profit margins as businesses produce at substantially less than optimum levels. Finally, government tax collections decrease because they are geared to the level of income. Ultimately, Y will have dropped by some *multiple* of the original reduction in government expenditures.

The overall drop in Y from Y_2 to Y_4 is greater than the drop in government expenditures because a drop in Y induces decreases in consumption demand and investment expenditures. Thus, there is a series of decreases in Y, C, and I. Each successive decrease, however, is smaller than the preceding one. The fact that people divide their falling incomes between consumption and saving decreases reduces the size of the successive income decreases arising out of the induced consumption expenditure decreases. Similarly, businesses drop their investment expenditures by only a small portion of their income decreases, since they are interested in maintaining their productive capacity.[14]

THE RELATIONSHIP BETWEEN Y AND i (THE *IS* CURVE)

The income determination process just described assumes one very important variable to be constant — the rate of interest. Because both personal saving and investment are a function of interest rate changes, different amounts of saving and investment take place at different rates of interest. Consequently, equilibrium income varies with the interest rate also.

Figures 19–11 and 19–12 illustrate this relationship. In Figure 19–11, i_1, i_2, i_3, and i_4 represent successively higher interest rates. Each higher rate of interest leads to a successively lower $I + G + F$ line. On the other hand, each higher rate of interest leads to a successively higher $S_p + S_b + T$ line and, as a consequence, equilibrium income levels become successively lower. If, for example, the rate of interest is initially i_1, equilibrium income is Y_1. If i is increased to i_3, other things being given, there is excess supply and income and output contract toward Y_3. For any level of Y to be one of stable equilibrium, the slope of the $I + G + F$ line must be less than the slope of the $S_p + S_b + T$ line.

---

[14] Economists frequently employ what is called *multiplier analysis* to predict changes in Y resulting from changes in government spending, changes in investment arising out of U' and W_f changes, or changes in consumption arising out of W_h and X changes. This multiplier analysis makes the assumption, however, that there are no interest rate changes. This very unrealistic assumption significantly impairs the usefulness of the comparatively simple multiplier analysis employed in the classroom.

The concept of the multiplier may be briefly described as follows. Assume that taxes and business saving are zero and are not geared to level of income. Further assume that there is no F, and that I and G are fixed. The marginal propensity to consume $\Delta C/\Delta Y_d$ is then equal to $\Delta C/\Delta Y$, and $\Delta S_p/\Delta Y_d$ equals $\Delta S_p/\Delta Y$. If this is the case, the ratio of the change in Y to a change in autonomous spending (ΔI or ΔG) will be equal to $1/1 - \Delta C/\Delta Y$. This is known as the *simple spendings multiplier* and can help predict Y changes from I and G changes. The difference between ΔY and ΔI or ΔG would be induced consumption expenditure change. For example, assume that the marginal propensity to consume is 0.8. Substituting into the multiplier formula, gives us $1/1 - 0.08$, or 5. This tells us that if government expenditures decrease by $1 billion, for example, the overall decrease in income induced will be $5 billion — $1 billion in the form of reduced government expenditures and $4 billion in reduced consumption spending. In terms of Figure 19–10, if the slope of the lines were drawn according to these assumptions, Y_4 would be $5 billion less than Y_2.

Figure 19–11. Income determination when the interest rate changes.

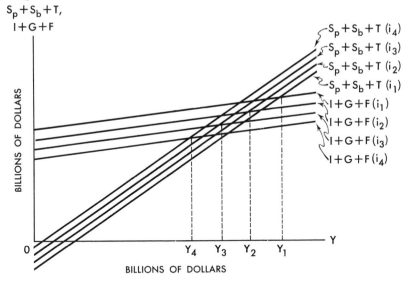

The relationship between these alternative rates of interest and their corresponding equilibrium income levels is plotted in Figure 19–12 as IS_0. The relationship is inverse; the higher the rate of interest rises, the lower the level of equilibrium income sinks. The line illustrating this relationship is called the *IS curve*. At every point on this line income is in equilibrium — that is, planned $I + G + F$ equals planned $S_p + S_b + T$. This type of

Figure 19–12. The relationship between the rate of interest and the equilibrium level of income.

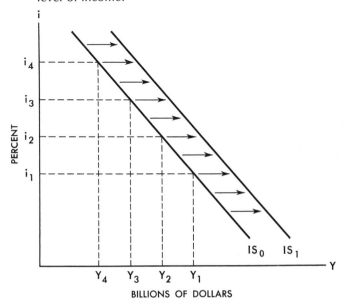

equilibrium is frequently called *commodity market equilibrium* because the demand for C, I, G, and F type commodities equals the supply of those products.

The *IS* curve is an important link in our model of income determination. Given the personal saving, business saving, tax, government spending, and net export functions, *the level of income is determined by the investment function.* Given the marginal efficiency of investment, *the rate of interest determines investment spending.* This further illustrates the economic importance of the rate of interest. Given the *IS* curve, there is a different possible level of equilibrium income for every different rate of interest. We cannot determine the actual equilibrium Y until we know the rate of interest and how it is determined, however. This will be taken up in Chapter 20.

SUMMARY OF THE FORCES AFFECTING *IS*

By bringing together the various functions described in this chapter, we are able to illustrate what happens to the *IS* curve given various changes in the economy. In general, anything other than i that causes $I + G + F$ to shift upward or $S_p + S_b + T$ to shift downward will move the position of the *IS* line to the right. For example, in Figure 19–11, all the $I + G + F$ lines will rise with an increase in government spending. Hence equilibrium income, as determined by the intersection of the $S_p + S_b + T$ and $I + G + F$ lines for a particular rate of interest, will be attained at a point farther to the right. This means that there is a new *IS* curve to the right of the old one. The line IS_1 in Figure 19–12 illustrates one possible new location for *IS*. The new position tells us that equilibrium income will now be higher at any given rate of interest. The new income and output will, of course, be some multiple of the government spending increase. Induced expansions of consumption and investment will have occured.

On the other hand, anything that lowers $I + G + F$ or raises $S_p + S_b + T$ shifts *IS* to the left, causing a contraction in Y at any given rate of interest.

More specifically:

1. $$S_p = f(Y_d, i, W_h, X) \qquad\qquad [19\text{-}1]$$

Given X, S_p varies directly with Y_d (disposable personal income) and i (rate of interest), and inversely with W_h (liquid wealth). When liquid wealth increases or decreases, *IS* shifts to the right or the left, respectively.

2. $$T = f(Y, Z) \qquad\qquad [19\text{-}3]$$

Government taxes are determined by legislative action (Z). Given Z, T (the government tax take) varies directly with Y. A change in Z leads to a change in tax rates. If tax rates increase, T increases at all income levels and *IS* shifts to the left. A decrease in tax rates moves the *IS* curve to the right.

3. $$S_b = f(Y, U) \qquad\qquad [19\text{-}4]$$

Given U, S_b varies directly with Y. A change in U (all those forces other than Y that affect business saving) leads to a change in S_b. If, because of changes in U, S_b increases at any given income level, IS moves to the left. If S_b decreases at any given income level, IS moves to the right.

4. $$I = f(i, Y, W_f, U') \qquad\qquad [19\text{-}8]$$

I (investment demand) varies inversely with i (rate of interest), and directly with Y (level of income) and W_f (firm liquid wealth). If U' (the other forces that change the marginal efficiency of investment) cause MEI to increase, the IS line moves to the right. Thus, a decrease in the costs of production or enhanced profit expectations lead to increases in IS. On the other hand, an increase in the costs of production or worsened profit expectations decrease IS.

5. $$G = f(Z) \qquad\qquad [19\text{-}9]$$

Government expenditures are determined by legislative action (Z). Increases or decreases in G will move IS to the right or the left, respectively.

6. $$F = f(J) \qquad\qquad [19\text{-}10]$$

IS moves to the right or left with respective increases or decreases in F (the difference between exports and imports) caused by changes in J (the forces that lead to import and export changes).

Supplementary Readings

See end of Chapter 21.

20 A Model of Income Determination: The Demand for and the Supply of Money

Chapter 19 demonstrated that given the commodity market equilibrium line *IS*, there is a different level of equilibrium income for each different rate of interest. Thus, to determine equilibrium income, an equilibrium rate of interest must be determined. This chapter adds monetary supply and demand to our contemporary model of income determination and demonstrates how they interact with the $I + G + F$ and $S_p + S_b + T$ lines to establish equilibrium income Y and equilibrium interest i. We shall see that to establish equilibrium income we must simultaneously establish a monetary equilibrium.

THE SUPPLY OF MONEY

Chapter 14 mentioned that until recently most theories of money supply determination assumed the supply of money to be fixed. Money consists of currency outside banks and demand deposits. Since variations in currency rency can occur only at the expense of demand deposits, the total volume of money depends primarily on demand-deposit variations. The ability of the banking system to create demand deposits depends on its reserve base, which in turn is controlled by the Federal Reserve. Depending on the required reserve ratios, the volume of demand deposits will be some multiple of the reserve base. Those who considered the money supply to be fixed argued that the Fed's powers are such that it can cause the reserve position of the commercial banks to be whatever it desires. It follows then that the volume of money depends on central-bank policy. Put another way, this means that the Federal Reserve can autonomously determine the stock of money independent of conditions endogenous to (produced from within) the economic system.

As noted earlier, this line of analysis makes two untenable assumptions: (1) that the commercial banking system reacts passively to changes in its reserve base, and (2) that the Federal Reserve selects a specific amount of money which it considers suitable for the economy, and counters any move by commercial banks to create a different amount. In fact, commercial banks react quite vigorously to changes in reserve positions. Furthermore, since the Federal Reserve makes policy changes slowly, commercial banks have substantial latitude in money supply creation. Our analysis of the effectiveness of various monetary controls shows that *the money stock actually tends to change procyclically, increasing on the upward part of the cycle and decreasing or increasing at a decreasing rate on the downward part of the cycle.* Thus, it cannot be argued that the Federal Reserve autonomously determines the stock of money.

A Theory of the Money Supply

Recently there have been numerous attempts to estimate money supply functions for the United States (see the references on money supply at the end of Chapter 21). Most of these studies work within what are roughly comparable conceptual frameworks. The formal theory usually assumes that the money supply M_s is the product of high-powered money H (currency plus bank reserves for demand deposits) and a money multiplier m. Expressed mathematically:

$$M_s = Hm \qquad [20\text{--}1]$$

This equation was derived formally in the appendix to Chapter 6. It will be recalled that high-powered money H is influenced by the Federal Reserve when it exogenously determines R, the reserve base of the banking system. The money multiplier in turn depends on the reserve requirement on demand deposits r, the reserve requirement on time deposits r', the non-bank public's desired ratio of currency to demand deposits c, the nonbank public's desired ratio of time to demand deposits t, and the commercial banking system's desired ratio of minimum excess reserves to demand deposits i'.

These factors are summarized in equation 20–2, which is part of equation 6–10 as developed on pages 115–16 in the appendix to Chapter 6.

$$m = \frac{1 + c}{r + r't + c + i'} \qquad [20\text{--}2]$$

Equations 20–1 and 20–2 are intended to predict the total money supply, inclusive of demand deposits and currency.

These two equations include both demand for and supply of money forces. The supply of money forces are H, r, r', and i'; t and c are demand for money forces. Assuming H, r, r', t, and c to be constants, there is an inverse relationship between i' and M_s. The desired ratio of excess reserves to deposits is assumed to depend on the earnings of commercial banks. Thus, i' is expected to vary inversely with the interest commercial banks can earn on loans and investments i. *The hypothesis is that commercial banks are willing to economize more and more on their reserves as the interest yields on loans and investments increase.* If this is so, then an increase in i will lead to an increase in the size of the money multiplier m, and thereby to an increase in the nominal stock of money. Ultimately i' will become zero, at which point the relationship between the money supply and the rate of interest becomes perfectly inelastic. At this point, commercial banks have no excess reserves and the money supply is at a maximum.

Figure 20–1 diagrammatically illustrates the relationship between i and M_s, given H and the forces behind m. The money supply line is called MM. High-powered money H is assumed to be fixed by the central bank. Quadrant I depicts the inverse relationship between the interest rate i and i'. Quadrant II shows how m varies inversely with i'. Quadrant III shows how M_s will then vary positively in response to m. Finally, Quadrant IV shows the results of variations in i on M_s. The chain of causation runs from i to i', to m, and then to M_s, thereby establishing a positive relationship between i and M_s. For example, if the rate of interest is i_1, then M_1 is the stock of money. When the rate of interest rises to i_2, i' becomes i'_2, m rises to m_2, and the money stock rises to M_2. When the rate of interest becomes i_3, m rises to its maximum m_3 and the money supply becomes M_3—the maximum amount that the economy can have since bank excess reserves are zero. From this point on, no matter how high the interest rate rises, the money stock cannot change as long as the other conditions given remain fixed.

Figure 20–1. The relationship between the money supply and the rate of interest.

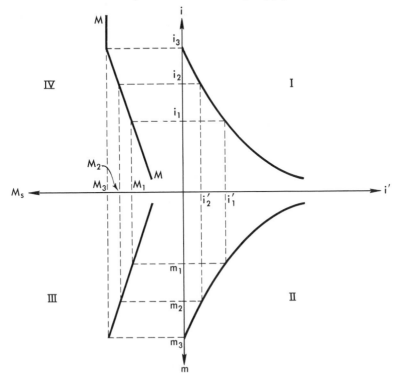

Putting all these forces together into one general behavior equation gives us

$$M_s = f(H, i, Z') \qquad [20-3]$$

where M_s is the money supply, H is the high-powered money determined primarily by the Fed, i is the rate of interest to which the banking system responds (by changing i' and hence m), and Z' represents all the other forces that affect m and thereby M_s.

Changes in *MM*

The line *MM* assumes a given high-powered money H. In addition, other factors controlled by the central bank, such as r and r', are assumed to be unchanged. These forces are included in Z'. What happens if the various forces controlled by the central bank are permitted to change? If bank reserves increase because of open market operations, for example, or if r and/or r' decrease, then, at any given rate of interest, commercial banks have more excess reserves and consequently can create additional money balances. The line *M'M'* in Figure 20-2 shows the effects of such changes. The money supply line has shifted to the right from *MM*. If H decreases, or r and r' rise, however, the banking system will no longer support as much money and the money supply schedule will shift to the left.

Changes in these forces will also affect the maximum amount of money in the economy. For example, a decrease in r and r' or an increase in H will expand the maximum amount of money. In Figure 20-2, this is demonstrated by the rise from M_3 to M_4 at i_3.

If the discount rate decreases, the spread between the return that can be

Figure 20-2. Changes in the supply of money schedule.

Figure 20–3. Changes in the supply of money schedule caused by discount rate changes.

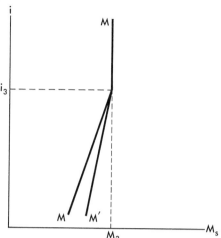

earned by commercial banks on loans and investments and the cost of borrowing reserves widens. This may induce banks to lend more money. Knowing that the cost of borrowing reserves is lower, banks may be more willing to take risks; accordingly, they may expand loans and thus the stock of money. The results of a discount rate drop are shown in Figure 20–3 as a movement from MM to MM'. Note that the amount of money that banks can create will expand only at interest rates beneath i_3. This is because the maximum amount of money that can be created under a given reserve base is not expanded. The discount rate has been permitted to change in this illustration, but the reserve base has not. Conversely, a rise in the discount rate would cause a movement to the left without changing the maximum money supply figure M_3. The interest rate at which we obtained this maximum amount of money, however, would still be i_3.

Two additional elements in equation 20–2 must be considered here—the ratio of currency to demand deposits c, and the ratio of time to demand deposits t. These forces are included in Z'. It will be recalled that as c increases, the ability of the banking system to create money decreases. In the absence of offsetting forces, the potential amount of money that banks can create is reduced by a multiple of the currency drain. Thus, an increase of c would lead to a reduction of the money multiplier m and shift the money supply line to the left, possibly from $M'M'$ to MM in Figure 20–2. Similarly, should t increase, more reserves would be needed to cover time deposits and less could be used to back demand deposits. Hence H would decrease and the money supply line would shift to the left. Of course the total volume of both demand and time deposits would increase, since r' is generally less than r.

Summary of the forces affecting *MM*. All these factors influence the *MM* line. An analysis of their combined impact will yield a theory of money supply determination:

1. The money supply schedule slopes upward and to the right with respect to the rate of interest; this means that the money supply and the rate of interest are directly related. The higher the rate of interest, the greater the potential supply of money; the lower the rate of interest, the lower the potential supply of money.

2. The money supply varies in direct proportion to *H*, high-powered money. As *H* increases and decreases, *MM* shifts to the right and to the left, respectively.

3. The money supply varies inversely with *r* (the reserve requirement for demand deposits), *r'* (the reserve requirement for time deposits), and the discount rate. Increases in these variables will cause *MM* to shift to the left; decreases in these variables cause *MM* to shift to the right.

4. The money supply varies inversely with *c* and *t*. Increases in *c* (the ratio of currency to demand deposits) and *t* (the ratio of time to demand deposits) cause *MM* to move to the left. Decreases in these forces cause *MM* to move to the right.

THE DEMAND FOR MONEY

The *MM* line shows how much money it is *possible* to have at varying rates of interest (other things being given), but how much money will there *actually* be at any given time? To determine the amount of money in the economy at any point in time, information about the demand for money as

Figure 20–4. The supply of money schedule.

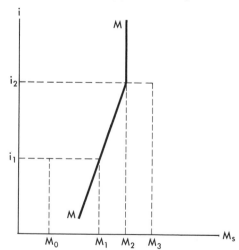

well as the money supply schedule is needed. For example, given *MM*, if at i_1 in Figure 20-4 people want only M_o and not M_1, there is an excess supply of money. If people want M_3 and not M_2 at i_2, there is an excess demand for money — that is, there is a shortage of money relative to individual and business demands. The following pages examine the demand for money in some depth. The position presented here is a synthesis of currently held views. Chapter 26 examines alternative contemporary theories on the demand for money in more detail.

The Demand for Money Equation

People want money for many reasons. Households demand money to purchase goods and services, to hold for future purchases, to meet unforeseen contingencies, to avoid the loss that is possible on other forms of liquid wealth, and to have funds available for financial investments when suitable profit opportunities arise. Businesses demand money for the same reasons, but are more likely to minimize cash balances in an effort to maximize profits. Governments also demand money, primarily to buy goods and services. It is customary to exclude federal government money holdings from the money stock, however.[1]

Liquid assets are not the only assets that can satisfy these motives for holding money. At any point in time, an individual may hold his wealth in the form of money, other liquid assets, or real wealth. Of course, only one of these assets — money itself — can serve directly as a medium of exchange in the purchase of goods and services. Thus a decision to hold money necessarily involves a decision not to hold that amount of wealth in other assets. When a householder or business enterprise decides to increase expenditures, wealth holdings are redistributed from money to goods. The composition of the wealth holdings of both the purchaser and the seller of goods changes.

Generally, other things being given, *the demand for money M_d,* and hence the asset composition of total wealth, *is determined by the rate of expenditures on gross national product* Y, *the rate of interest* i, *total wealth* W', *and other variables that may influence the demand for money* X'. Putting this in equation form, we have:

$$M_d = f(Y,i,W',X') \qquad [20\text{-}4]$$

This demand for money is a real demand; people holding money want to command real goods and services. Chapter 19 assumed that people are free of money illusion — that they adjust their holdings of various wealth forms and their income for the price level. In the following discussion, we con-

---

[1] It will be recalled that the money stock consists of currency and the demand-deposit holdings of the nonbank public. When the government taxes and spends, both the velocity and amount of money held by the nonbank public may vary.

tinue to make this assumption. We also continue to assume that market and real rates of interest are equal.

The Relationship Between the Demand for Money and Y

Other things being given, the relationship between the demand for money and the rate of expenditures is positive: the greater the expenditures, the more money needed to make them; the smaller the rate of spending, the less money needed. The demand for money, however, will always be a fraction of the rate of expenditures. Since expenditures and income receipts occur over time, the average amount of funds held during a period of time will usually be less than the total amount of expenditures.

If the rate at which funds are received and the rate at which expenditures are made remain unchanged, then the demand for money should remain the same. If expected expenditures increase, however, and the rate of income remains the same, then the amount of money demanded will increase; otherwise, the expected expenditure increases will not take place. The additional funds will be acquired by selling security holdings, converting time deposits into money, or borrowing from banks. Should expected expenditures decline, on the other hand, and the rate of income remain the same, there will be less need for money to carry out transactions. Money will grow idle, and the holders of idle balances may make efforts to lend to others, convert demand deposits into time deposits, or make profitable use of their excess funds in some other way.

Although M_d is directly related to transactions, it should be emphasized that the measure of transactions being used in our analysis is Y, gross national product. As was explained in Chapter 17, total transactions in the economy are greater than gross national product. Money is used to effectuate many types of transactions that do not involve the purchase of newly produced final goods, such as the purchase and sale of intermediate goods, the purchase and sale of goods produced in earlier income periods, and the purchase and sale of stocks and bonds.

The direct relationship between the demand for money and Y is frequently ascribed to the *transactions motive* for holding money. By this we mean "the need of cash for the current transactions of personal and business exchanges."[2] Another motive for holding money that is generally assumed to depend on the level of income and output is the *precautionary motive*. This refers to the "desire for security as to the future cash equivalent of a certain proportion of total resources."[3] These funds presumably are held to meet unforeseen contingencies. The greater the expected level of expenditures, the greater the demand for money to hold for precautionary purposes.

[2] John Maynard Keynes. *General Theory of Employment, Interest, and Money* (Harcourt Brace Jovanovich, 1936), p. 170.
[3] *Ibid.*

The model developed in this book does not make a distinction between the transactions, the precautionary, and the speculative (to be discussed later) motive. All people who demand money do so partly to satisfy all three motives, but as Milton Friedman has argued, "dollars of money are not distinguished according as they are said to be held for one or the other purpose."[4] Every dollar renders a variety of services and is not necessarily used to satisfy one motive for holding money rather than another.

The Relationship Between the Demand for Money and i

The relationship between the rate of interest i and the demand for money M_d, as we have defined them for the purposes of this analysis, is inverse. Other things being equal, the lower the rate of interest becomes, the greater the amount of money that is demanded. Conversely, the higher the rate of interest, the less money demanded.

There are a number of reasons why the amount of money demanded increases as interest rates decline.

First, business borrowers demand more funds since the widening spread between the expected return from the use of funds and the cost of borrowing the funds permits an increase in profitable investment expenditures.

Second, with easier credit, consumers also plan to increase their expenditures and borrowings.

Third, as interest rates decline, lenders become less willing to lend. Interest is regarded by many financial investors as a compensation for the risks of investment. Barring price inflation, there is no possibility of loss if funds are held in the form of money, other than the sacrifice resulting from not receiving an interest return on idle funds. Stocks and bonds, however, fluctuate in value. Government bonds and privately issued securities frequently sell beneath par. Thus, if bonds are not held to maturity, the holders may sustain capital losses. Some companies are unable to redeem their bonds. Similarly, in the event of liquidation, many stockholders do not receive the book value of their stock holdings. All these risks combine to inhibit lenders from purchasing stocks and bonds. As a consequence, borrowers offer an interest return on bonds and a dividend yield on equities as compensation to the lender for giving up his liquidity and a certain command over goods and services. *Therefore, when interest rates decline, the compensation for the risks of financial investment is reduced and the willingness of lenders to lend falls.*

Fourth, when interest rates have dropped below a certain point, some speculators may wish to hold more of their funds in the form of money because they expect interest rates to reverse themselves. By getting into money and out of bonds, for example, they may hope to avoid the capital losses bondholders incur as interest rates rise.

[4] Milton Friedman. "The Quantity Theory of Money: A Restatement." In *Studies in the Quantity Theory of Money,* Milton Friedman (ed.) (University of Chicago Press, 1956), p. 14.

On the other hand, as interest rates rise, the amount of money demanded decreases. Lenders become more willing to sacrifice the safety afforded by idle money balances for the chances of profit afforded by higher interest rates—that is, their willingness to lend increases. Borrowers, however, prefer to pay off debt rather than to incur the higher costs of further borrowing. Fewer consumers borrow, for this reason. Businesses find that the cost of funds has increased relative to the returns expected from investment, and business borrowing and investment expenditures both decrease as a consequence. Speculators reduce their demand for money and increase their demand for securities so that they may make capital gains if rates subsequently decline as they expect.

The inverse relationship between the demand for money and the rate of interest is frequently ascribed to the speculative motive. By this Keynes means "the object of securing profit from knowing better than the market what the future will bring forth."[5] The speculative motive is also called the *asset demand for money.* Basically, this motive arises out of uncertainty. Speculators assume, although no one can be sure it will happen, that interest rates will eventually reverse themselves. Thus they tend to demand more money as the interest rate decreases and less money as the interest rate increases, enabling them to move out of and into securities and to make speculative gains (as discussed in the preceding two paragraphs). Actually, ascribing the inverse relationship between the demand for money and the rate of interest to a speculative motive is a weak argument. It would be just as logical for investors to assume that the current trend in interest rates will continue indefinitely. This would mean a positive relationship between the demand for money and the rate of interest. Most economists now regard the "speculative" explanation of the relationship between the demand for money and the interest rate as weak. This statement should not be taken to mean that economists reject the inverse relationship between M_d and i, however. The other explanations, such as those discussed in the first three points above, are regarded as more important conceptually. *The inverse relationship between* M_d *and* i *is crucial to modern monetary theory.* This will be discussed extensively in Chapter 26 in conjunction with the neo-Keynesian and quantity portfolio theories on the demand for money. It is in Chapter 26 that the optimum portfolio theory introduced in Chapter 15 and the demand for money are brought together.

The demand for money schedule. The functional relationship between the demand for money and the rate of interest is depicted in Figure 20–5. The rate of interest i is measured along the vertical axis, and the demand for money M_d along the horizontal axis. Line LL represents the amount of money that is desired at varying rates of interest, other things being given. It slopes downward and to the right, showing the inverse relationship between the demand for money and the rate of interest. The position of LL,

---

[5] Keynes, *op. cit.*

Figure 20–5.   The demand for money schedule.

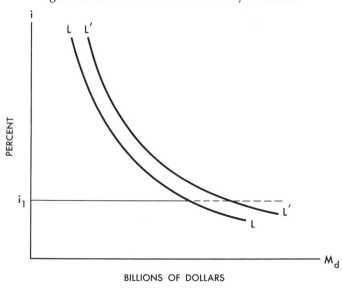

BILLIONS OF DOLLARS

as will be explained in a moment, depends on the value of the other determinants of the demand for money such as gross national product.

As drawn, line *LL* continues to slope downward and to the right as the rate of interest declines. Frequently, however, this line is shown as becoming parallel to the horizontal axis at some low minimum rate of interest. At this rate, the demand for money becomes perfectly elastic: The yield on securities is so low that it does not pay investors to incur the inconvenience and risk of converting money into securities; the yield may even be so low that it will not cover the broker's fees for the purchase of securities. When such a point is reached, the general expectation will be that interest rates must increase soon. As a consequence, no matter how much money is available in the economy, all of it will be demanded by the public at the low minimum rate of interest. This concept of a perfectly elastic segment of the demand for money curve is called the *liquidity trap*. It is depicted in Figure 20–5 as the dashed portion of the demand for money line starting at i_1. We have drawn the *LL* line downward and to the right beyond i_1 because we are building a general model of income determination. In many ways, the liquidity trap is a special case which some economists argue cannot be verified empirically. (More will be said of this in Chapter 26.)

The Relationship between the Demand for Money and Total Wealth

Total wealth consists of total liquid wealth ($W = W_h + W_f$) plus real wealth. The relationship between the demand for money and total wealth W' is positive. The greater the volume of wealth becomes, the more demand there is for money. Wealth increases as income and output increase. Thus the demand for all economic goods, including money, increases as income and output increase. In other words, if wealth rises, the demand for all components of wealth will rise also, provided that they are superior goods.[6] Assuming that individuals seek to maintain some optimum distribution among their different types of wealth holdings, it follows that if the amount of wealth held in one particular form increases, then this optimum distribution of wealth is disturbed. The situation may be corrected by increasing the amounts held in the other forms of wealth, and people usually attempt to do this by converting part of an increase in holdings of one form of wealth into other forms. In this manner, the optimum distribution of wealth can be reestablished. Similarly, the optimum distribution of wealth can be disturbed by a reduction in holdings of a particular wealth form. When this occurs, there is an increase in the demand for that particular wealth form and a decrease in the demand for other forms.

If the argument above is correct, the demand for money will increase when the desired ratio of money to total wealth is disturbed by an increase in total wealth that is unaccompanied by a proportionate increase in the stock of money. Similarly, the demand for money will decrease when the desired ratio of money to total wealth is disturbed by a decrease in total wealth that is unaccompanied by a proportionate decrease in the stock of money.

If it is the money stock that increases relative to other wealth forms,- then the demand for other wealth forms increases and the demand for money decreases—but not by as much as the total money stock increase. On the other hand, if there is a decrease in the money stock relative to other wealth forms, then the demand for other wealth forms decreases and the demand for money increases—but not by as much as the initial money stock decrease.

The significance of total wealth as a determinant of the demand for money should not be overemphasized, however. Economists generally regard i and Y as more important determinants of the demand for money since these variables can change quickly; the total volume of wealth in the economy is so large that percentage changes in the total are actually very small and occur only over sizable stretches of time. Thus wealth is regarded as a long-run determinant of the demand for money. Liquid wealth, however, does change comparatively quickly. Since the total of liquid wealth—at least that part that is in the form of near monies—is only a fraction of total wealth, percentage changes in liquid wealth are thought to be significant as a determinant of both the demand for money and the demand for consumer goods and services.[7]

[6] A "superior good" in this context may be defined as one for which there is an increase in demand as income and wealth increase. An "inferior good" is one for which there is a decrease in demand as income and wealth increase. Most goods are superior in this sense of the word. Some low-cost goods, such as potatoes and bread, will be inferior goods, however.
[7] It will be recalled from Chapter 19 that liquid wealth can be used as a determinant of consumption demand, personal saving, and investment demand.

The Relationship between the Demand for Money and Other Variables

X' is a variable representing all the other forces that can influence the demand for money, such as expectations regarding price and income movements, the desired distribution of the various wealth forms, and the various factors discussed by Irving Fisher and Dennis Robertson (see Table 17–2).

Saying that people expect *prices* to increase is another way of saying that people expect the purchasing power of money to decline. In such a situation, it pays for them to transfer their funds from money to other assets such as consumer durables or equities, which do not normally decrease in price as the price level rises. Thus, with expectations of rising prices, the demand for money decreases. Conversely, expectations of falling *prices* mean that people believe the purchasing power of money will increase. As a consequence they will demand more money, reduce their expenditures, and reduce their holdings of goods that decline in value.

The expectation that future *incomes* will rise simply means that people believe they will be getting more money receipts in the future and thus that their ability to buy goods and services will be enhanced. In anticipation of this, people may decrease their current demand for money and increase their current expenditures. The expectation of decreased incomes, however, means that people feel they will need additional money balances to cover future outlays. Therefore the current demand for money will increase, and the current rate of expenditures will drop.

If the desired *distribution* of wealth changes, then the demand for individual wealth components will also change. For example, in the United States, the number of alternative liquid wealth forms has increased in recent years. The comparatively recent development of such liquid wealth forms as savings and loan association share accounts, pension funds, and credit union share accounts has increased the number of wealth forms competing with money. Similarly, the number of new types of goods and services available each year creates additional uses to which money may be put. *The greater the number of goods (liquid and nonliquid) competing with money, the less demand there is for money as an asset.*

The various forces mentioned by Irving Fisher and Dennis Robertson also affect the demand for money. For example, the increased use of installment credit lengthens the period of payment on high-priced commodities and reduces the need to accumulate money balances. The more credit and credit cards used, the less money needed. Another closely related factor is the system of payments in the community. The more often and the more regularly people are paid, the less money they need to keep on hand. The more regularly disbursements can be made, the easier it becomes to match receipts and disbursements. Hence there is less need to hold money in reserve for unpredictable expenditures. The increasing use of credit—particularly that variety which involves monthly payments—regularizes expenditures. These are all primarily long-term factors, however; institutional changes are only made gradually.

The Demand for Money Schedule and Changes in GNP, Total Wealth, and Other Variables

The LL line in Figure 20–5 shows how the demand for money varies according to the interest rate, other things being equal. Obviously, however, other determinants of the demand for money such as Y, W', and X' do not remain unchanged. Suppose Y increases, for example. This causes the demand for money to increase, no matter what the rate of interest. Thus LL will shift to the right—to the position represented in Figure 20–5 by $L'L'$. Suppose, on the other hand, that there is a decrease in income and output. This will lead to a decrease in the demand for money and a shift in LL to the left. From this we deduce that a whole family of money demand lines exists relating the demand for money to the rate of interest, with each line representing the demand for money at a different level of income. Figure 20–6 describes this relationship. Successive LL lines represent the demand for money at successively higher levels of income Y_1, Y_2, Y_3, and Y_4. Each higher level of income leads, in turn, to a successively greater demand for money and, consequently, an LL line that is farther to the right. Lower income levels lead to successively lower demands for money and LL lines that are farther to the left.

Changes in W' also to changes in LL. Higher wealth levels will raise the demand for money and hence shift LL to the right. Lower wealth levels will lower the demand for money and shift LL to the left.

Figure 20–6. The relationship between the demand for money, the income level, and the supply of money.

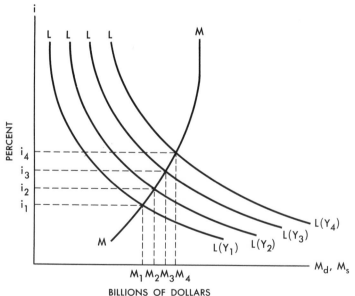

Similarly, to the extent that the forces included in X' operate to increase or decrease the demand for money, LL will shift its position also.

Gross national product, the rate of interest, and the demand for money are factors that can change rapidly. Total wealth and the forces represented by X', however, usually change gradually. Thus, it is relatively accurate to take the family of money demand lines as a hypothetical representation of the relationship between Y, i, and M_d in the short run. In other words, *given* W' *and* X', M_d *varies directly with* Y *and inversely with* i.

THE INTERACTION OF THE DEMAND FOR
MONEY AND THE SUPPLY OF MONEY

In addition to the demand for money lines, Figure 20–6 shows the supply of money schedule MM as developed in this chapter. Assuming that income is fixed at Y_1, there is one money demand line and the money supply line MM. The interaction between these two schedules determines the rate of interest and the actual money stock. Where the two schedules intersect, the demand for money and the supply of money are equal and we have equilibrium in the money market, as at i_1 and M_1 for Y_1. At any other rate of interest there can be no equilibrium since the demand for money and the supply are not equal.

At i_2, for example, given MM and $LL(Y_1)$, there is an *excess supply* of money. The amount of money that can be created exceeds the amount that is demanded. When this occurs, forces are set in motion that tend to reduce interest rates. For example, some lenders are willing to accept lower rates of interest in order to be able to invest their funds. As interest rates decline, the amount of money demanded increases because some borrowers become more willing to borrow. Similarly, some lenders who are unwilling to lend at these lower interest rates reduce their demand for securities and transfer their funds to money instead. The banking system also becomes less willing to make loans and create money at this lower rate of interest. Thus we move down and to the right along the demand schedule and down and to the left along the supply schedule until M_d and M_s are equal at an equilibrium rate of interest i_1.

On the other hand, at i_1, given MM and $LL(Y_2)$, there is an *excess demand* for money; the amount of money available is insufficient to meet the amount demanded. Forces are now set in motion that tend to raise interest rates. Many borrowers may be willing to borrow at interest rates higher than i_1. Thus, to ensure that they obtain the funds they feel they need, they will issue securities bearing yields higher than i_1. This, in turn, will induce some holders of funds to reduce their demand for money and to begin lending instead. Other borrowers, unable to pay the higher rates, will stop borrowing. Thus there will be a tendency for the economy to move up and to the left along the demand curve $LL(Y_2)$. At the same time, the higher rate of interest will induce banks to expand their loans and create additional money, causing the economy to move up the *MM* curve. The increase in the amount of money that banks are willing to create and the decrease in the amount demanded brings the demand and supply of money to equilibrium at i_2 and M_2.

THE RELATIONSHIP BETWEEN *Y* AND *i* (THE *LM* CURVE)

The preceding discussion assumed a given level of income. The forces that operate to change the rate of interest also operate to change the level of income, however. For example, a decline in the rate of interest, as we saw in Chapter 19, may expand investment and consumption demands and, consequently, *Y*. It is somewhat unlikely, therefore, that *Y* will remain stable as *i* changes. There is a different equilibrium rate of interest equating the demand for with the supply of money at every different level of income *Y*. Figure 20–7 shows this relationship between the rate of interest and the level of income. The left-hand portion of the figure is similar to Figure 20–6. Equilibrium is reached at interest rates i_1, i_2, i_3, and i_4 when income is at the successively higher income levels Y_1, Y_2, Y_3, and Y_4. The right-hand portion of Figure 20–7 plots the relationship between these alternative income levels and their various equilibrium rates of interest. The relationship is positive, showing that the higher the level of income becomes, the higher the rate of interest that equates the money supply and demand must be. The *LM* curve depicts this relationship; at every point on this line, the demand for is equal to the supply of money.

At any point to the right of *LM* the demand for money exceeds the supply. For example, if at income level Y_2 the rate of interest is i_1 instead

Figure 20–7.   The relationship between the rate of interest and the level of income.

of i_2, then the amount of money demanded is M_5, whereas the amount available is only M_1. This situation should set in motion forces that tend to raise i and reduce Y. Conversely, at any point to the left of LM the supply of money exceeds the demand. For example, if at income level Y_1 the rate of interest is i_2 instead of i_1, then the amount of money demanded is M_0, whereas the amount the banking system is willing to create is M_2. Now forces will tend to lower i and increase Y.

The same forces that determine the position of the money demand lines and the money supply schedule determine the position of the LM curve. Should W' increase or the X' forces operate to increase the demand for money, the family of LL lines will shift to the right. This will cause LM to shift to the left. A given rate of interest can now equate the demand for and supply of money only at a lower level of income and output. At a given rate of interest, assuming the relation between Y and M_d to be unchanged, an increase in the demand for money decreases the amount of money available for expenditures. It will be recalled from our earlier discussion that one of the ways in which money holdings of individuals may be increased is by reducing the demand for other goods and services.

On the other hand, a decrease in the demand for money caused by W' decreases or X' changes will shift the family of LL lines to the left. This will cause the LM curve to shift to the right. Since the demand for money to hold as an asset will have decreased, the amount of money available for expenditures will have increased. At any given rate of interest, therefore, expenditures should increase.

An increase in the money supply caused by a change in the forces that determine its position will cause the LM curve to shift to the right. Thus, at any given rate of interest and income level, the amount of money that can be created will have increased relative to the demand for it and, as a result, a higher level of expenditures can be maintained. On the other hand, a movement to the left of the money supply schedule will cause a shift to the left in LM.

THE INTERSECTION OF THE *IS* AND *LM* CURVES

The LM curve, like the IS curve, is an important element in our model of income determination. Chapter 19 established that, given the IS line, there is a different possible level of equilibrium income for every different rate of interest. At any level of Y and at any interest rate, planned $I + G + F$ will equal planned $S_p + S_b + T$. The relationship between Y and i under these conditions is inverse. We have established, however, that, given the LM curve, it is possible at any level of Y to select an interest rate that will equalize the demand for money and the supply of money. The relationship between Y and i under these money market conditions is positive. Given both the IS and LM curves, we are now in a position to determine how the total demand behind gross national product interacts with monetary supply

Figure 20–8.   The *IS* and *LM* curves.

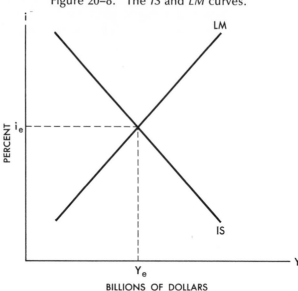

BILLIONS OF DOLLARS

and demand to determine equilibrium output and an equilibrium interest rate.

Figure 20–8 plots the intersection of the *IS* and *LM* curves, other things being given. These lines will intersect at only one point—(i_e, Y_e)—which is the only combination of *i* and *Y* capable of producing equilibrium in both the money and commodity markets. Only at point i_e, Y_e will the demand for money equal the supply of money and *ex ante* $I + G + F$ equal *ex ante* $S_p + S_b + T$. As explained earlier, at any point to the right of the *LM* curve the demand for money exceeds the supply. Conversely, at any point to the left of the *LM* curve the supply of money exceeds the demand. Either of these two situations will set in motion self-corrective forces that will tend to change both *Y* and *i* so that the demand for money will equal the supply.

Similarly, any points not lying on the *IS* curve are also points of disequilibrium. At any point to the right of *IS*, $S_p + S_b + T$ exceeds $I + G + F$; at any point to the left of *IS* the sum of *I*, *G*, and *F* exceeds the sum of S_p, S_b, and T.[8] Either of these situations will also set in motion self-corrective forces that will tend to bring $S_p + S_b + T$ into equality with $I + G + F$. In the first case, for example, these forces will tend to contract *Y*, whereas in the second they will tend to expand *Y*.

Chapter 19 examined the forces that cause changes in saving and spending, thereby inducing changes in *Y*. No mention was made of the

---

[8] From this point on, the adjectives *"ex ante,"* "planned," "intended," and so on will be omitted when referring to $I + G + F$ and $S_p + S_b + T$. When *"ex post"* is meant, it will be stated explicitly.

monetary sources of change until this chapter, however. The following chapter will explain some of the important interactions between the money market (LM) and the commodity market (IS) forces that tend to produce equilibrium in both markets, thereby determing Y_e and i_e. The model will be broadened to include price-level changes explicitly. Additional applications of the model can be found in Chapters 25 and 26, which deal with specific fiscal and monetary policy proposals.

Supplementary Readings

See end of Chapter 21.

21 Applications of the Model of Income Determination

This chapter shows how our macroeconomic model of income determination can be used to illustrate the interactions between money market and commodity market forces. We assume that the equations of the model developed in Chapters 19 and 20 determine an *IS* and an *LM* line.

THE MODEL IN EQUATION FORM

The following equations are used in this model:

1.	$M_s = f(H_0, i, Z_0')$	[20–3]
2.	$M_d = f(Y, i, W_0', X_0')$	[20–4]
3.	$S_p = f(Y_d, i, W_0^h, X_0)$	[19–1]
4.	$T = f(Y, Z_0)$	[19–3]
5.	$S_b = f(Y, U_0)$	[19–4]
6.	$I = f(i, Y, W_0^f, U_0')$	[19–8]
7.	$G = f(Z_0)$	[19–9]
8.	$F = f(J_0)$	[19–10]
9.	$M_d = M_s$	
10.	$I + G + F = S_p + S_b + T$	

Their original equation numbers are placed on the right to indicate the preceding location of each equation. However, there is one difference between the equations previously discussed in the book and the ones used here. Here, the subscript $_0$ is used to denote forces that are held constant, for purposes of simplicity. Two additional equations creating conditions necessary for equilibrium are 9 and 10.

Equations 1 and 2 determine the nature of the *LM* line. At any point on *LM*, the condition set up in equation 9 is satisfied. Equations 3–8 determine the nature of the *IS* line. At any point on *IS*, the condition set up in equation 10 is satisfied. There are ten variables in this system of equations: M_s, M_d, S_p, T, S_b, I, G, F, i, and Y. Everything else is fixed. All variables that have dollar values are expressed in real terms, since we assume no money illusion. Two of the variables, G and F, are known because we have arbitrarily assumed that their determinants, Z and J, are constant. Two other variables, Y and i, are fixed by the two equilibrium conditions in equations 9 and 10; Y and i are determined by the intersection of *LM* and *IS*. Y_d, of course, may be derived from Y, S_b, and T.

SHIFTS IN *IS* AND *LM*

Cases Involving a Shift in *IS*

Effects of an increase in government expenditures. Let $(LM)_0$ and $(IS)_0$ be the initial *LM* and *IS* lines in Figure 21–1. Accordingly, GNP and the rate of interest are in equilibrium at Y_e and i_e. Now assume that a change occurs. Suppose that as a result of an antipoverty program, federal expenditures increase and that they are financed through the sale of securities to the nonbank public. Thus *G* increases because *Z* has changed through legislative action. In terms of our diagrammatic analysis, the $I + G + F$ line is raised. As a consequence, the *IS* line shifts to the right by some multiple of the increase in government spending. This shift is represented in Figure 21–1 by the $(IS)_1$ line.[1]

Figure 21–1. A shift in *IS*.

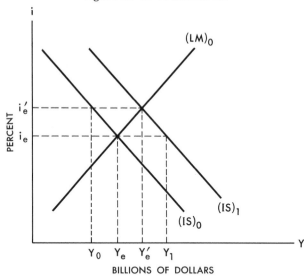

BILLIONS OF DOLLARS

[1] Something else has also occurred to change the position of the *LM* and *IS* lines. The method of financing the government expenditure increase has lead to an increase in total liquid wealth and a change in its composition. The nonbank public, after the government has spent the borrowed funds, will have as much money as before, but it will now have more government securities—another wealth form. Thus W', W, and X' will have changed and the *IS* line should shift to the right, indicating a positive wealth effect. The *LM* line would then shift to the left because the greater volume of government securities would cause people to increase their demand for money. If there were substitution effects, opposite results could occur (see Klein and Cebula in the supplementary reading section at the end of this chapter). These changes are not shown in Figure 21–1 since we have assumed that wealth changes do not affect the economy in the short run.

The shift of the *IS* curve to the right is a multiple of the change in government expenditures because, as we noted in Chapter 19, increased spending in one sector of the economy induces increased incomes, and hence higher levels of spending, in the other sectors. In this case, increased government expenditures should induce increased consumption and investment spending. As a result, the economy will no longer be in equilibrium at i_e and Y_e.

To what extent can the increased government expenditures induce an increase in Y? Were it not for money market forces, these expenditures could cause Y to increase to Y_1. Interest rates rise, however, choking off some investment and consumption expenditures that would have taken place had the rate of interest remained the same (since both investment and consumption are decreasing functions of the rate of interest).

Interest rates rise because the increased spending that is taking place causes an increase in the demand for money for transaction purposes. In Figure 20–7, this is illustrated by the higher demand for money lines that accompany higher levels of income. Again, at rate of interest i_e in Figure 21–1, the demand for money must exceed the supply. As the interest rate begins to rise, the amount of money supplied by the banking system also increases. This is represented by a movement up the *MM* line, not a shift in its position. The rate of interest will continue to rise as long as the demand for money increases because of rising incomes. In other words, *rising incomes induce an increased demand for money and a movement up and along the* LM *curve.* This movement continues until Y_e' and i_e' are reached; there both the money and commodity markets are again in equilibrium.

Thus, in general, increased government expenditures induce consumption and investment expenditure increases. As incomes rise, more money is needed for transactions. This induces a rise in the rate of interest which, in turn, restrains the potential growth of investment and consumption expenditure. It should also be noted that government tax collections and business saving, which are increasing functions of Y, increase during this expansionary process.

Effects of a decrease in government expenditures. If, on the other hand, we posit a tax surplus as a result of a decrease in government expenditures and assume that this surplus is being used to retire debt held by the nonbank public, then the process described in the preceding section would be reversed. The *IS* curve would shift to the left, and Y and i would decrease.

Let $(LM)_0$ and $(IS)_1$ be the initial *LM* and *IS* curves in Figure 21–1. Accordingly, income and the rate of interest are in equilibrium at Y_e' and i_e'. Suppose that as a result of the end of a conflict, such as the Vietnam war, federal expenditures decrease. The tax surplus that arises is used to retire debt held by the nonbank public. Initially, there is no change in the stock of money. Subsequently, as interest rates decline, there may be a change in the money stock. In terms of our diagrammatic analysis, the $I + G + F$ line is lowered because of the decrease in G. As a consequence, the IS curve shifts to the left by some multiple of the decrease in government spending. This shift is represented in Figure 21–1 by the $(IS)_0$ curve.

To what extent can the decreased government expenditures induce a decrease in Y? Were it not for money market forces, these expenditures would cause Y to decrease to Y_0. Interest rates decline, however, because the decreased spending taking place causes a decrease in the demand for money for transaction purposes. Lower interest rates, in turn, induce some investment and consumption expenditures that would not have taken place had the rate of interest remained the same. At rate of interest i'_e in Figure 21–1, the supply of money must exceed the demand. As the interest rate begins to decline, the amount of money supplied by the banking system also declines. The rate of interest will continue to decline as long as the demand for money decreases because of falling incomes. In other words, *falling incomes induce a decreased demand for money that is reflected in a movement down and along the* LM *curve.* This movement continues until Y_e and i_e are reached; there both the money and commodity markets are again in equilibirium.

Effects of an increase in the marginal efficiency of investment. Let $(LM)_0$ and $(IS)_0$ again be the initial LM and IS curve in Figure 21–1. Now suppose that a change occurs in business investment plans. In particular, assume that a technological advance has increased the rate but not the overall cost of production. This means an increase in the marginal efficiency of investment, and businesses will want to increase their rate of expenditures on capital goods permanently. As businesses carry out their plans to increase investments, the following changes occur in the economy: (1) the output of industry increases, (2) incomes rise because increasing output means increased employment of the various productive resources, (3) with rising incomes, people find that personal saving is greater than anticipated—hence there will probably be some increase in both consumption expenditures and personal saving, (4) the induced consumption expenditure increase will cause further rise in output and income, (5) rising income and output will induce additional increments in investment expenditure because investment is an increasing function of the level of income and output, and (6) as a result of all these forces, the IS curve will shift to the right by some multiple of the initial increment in investment expenditures. This shift, represented in Figure 21–1 by the $(IS)_1$ curve, represents the initial increment in investment, the induced increase in investment, the induced increase in consumption expenditure, and, incidentally, the increases in business saving and government tax collections that, in our model, are positively related to the level of income.

In the absence of changes in money market forces, these increments in expenditures would cause Y to increase to Y_1. However, just as in our earlier discussion of the effects of an increase in government spending, interest rates rise and choke off some investment and consumption expenditures that would have taken place had the rates of interest remained the same. Interest rates rise again because the increased spending taking place causes an increase in the demand for money for transaction purposes. At the old rate of interest i_e in Figure 21–1, the demand for money must exceed the supply. The rate of interest will continue to rise as long as the demand for money increases because of rising incomes. Again, *rising incomes have induced an increased demand for money and a movement up and along the LM curve*. This movement continues until Y'_e and i'_e, are reached; there both the money and commodity markets are again in equilibrium.

Other cases leading to shifts in the *IS* curve. We have discussed only three cases involving a shift in the *IS* curve. Many other cases are possible. For purposes of simplicity, we have used the subscript $_0$ in our model to denote forces that we have assumed to be constant. If there were changes in any of the forces behind S_p, T, S_b, I, or F, however, then appropriate *IS* shifts would occur. The process would be almost identical to the processes just described, but the initial source of the spending change would differ. Also, we have assumed in the preceding cases that money market forces involve movements only along the *LM* curve. Under different assumptions, the *LM* curve might also move.

Cases Involving a Shift in *LM*

Effects of a change in the money supply schedule. Assuming an economy at equilibrium at Y_e and i_e, suppose there is an open market purchase of U.S. government securities from the nonbank public by the Federal Reserve. This directly increases the money stock holdings of the nonbank public and H, high-powered money. The money supply schedule *MM* must, therefore, shift to the right. As a result, the *LM* curve in Figure 21–2 must shift from $(LM)_0$ to $(LM)_1$. Points i_e and Y_e are now to the left of $(LM)_1$: the supply of money exceeds the demand. Pressures are set in motion that, in the absence of income changes, will drive the rate of interest down to i_1.

Interest rate decreases affect the commodity market, however. Consumption expenditures increase and personal saving decreases. Investment expenditures rise because of the widening spread between the return expected from investment in plant and equipment and the cost of obtaining funds. As these expenditures increase, income increases and an additional rise in consumption and investment is induced. Business income and government tax collections rise accordingly.

As income rises due to these expenditure increases, the demand for money rises, thereby preventing a fall in the interest rate to i_1. Instead, i falls to some intermediate level, such as i'_e and equilibrium income rises to Y'_e.

Figure 21–2.   A shift in *LM*.

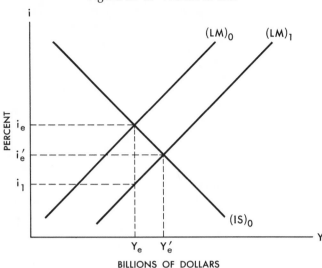

BILLIONS OF DOLLARS

Conversely, a sale of government securities to the nonbank public would result in a shift of the *LM* line to the left, with a corresponding decrease in *Y* and an increase in *i*. The process just described would be reversed.

An additional factor to be considered in a shift of the LM *line is that an increase in* MM *may cause a change in total wealth.* An open market purchase of securities from the nonbank public by the Fed increases the stock of money, but does not change total wealth. On the other hand, when the banking system expands money in response to an increase in reserves, the total wealth of the nonbank public rises.[2] This leads to an increase in the demand for consumption goods and shifts the *IS* curve to the right. However, the resultant increase in the demand for money will restrain forward movement along the *LM* curve beyond a certain point. These conclusions concerning the influence of wealth on *IS* and *LM* apply only if we assume that wealth has a short-run influence in addition to its acknowledged long-run influence on the economy.

Effects of changes in the money demand schedules. Changes in the family of *LL* curves will produce results similar to those produced by changes in the money stock. Shifts to the right in the *LL* schedules will cause *LM* shifts to the left, decreases in income, and increases in the interest rate. Shifts to the left in the *LL* schedule will cause *LM* shifts to the right, increases in *Y*, and decreases in *i*.

[2] Some economists would contend at this point that the relevant variable is *net worth*, rather than total or liquid wealth. Thus, when an increase in the money stock occurs as a result of borrowing at commercial banks, the net worth of the nonbank public remains unchanged, since both its assets and liabilities have increased.

Assume, for example, that X_0' changes due to institutional forces, such as the increased use of credit cards and check-credit plans. A decrease in the demand for money occurs. The *LL* schedules of Figure 20–7 shift to the left, causing an excess supply at the old rate of interest. In terms of Figure 21–2, $(LM)_0$ has shifted to $(LM)_1$. Competitive pressures will force the rate of interest down. Consumption and investment expenditures will increase. As expenditures increase, income increases, and this induces additional rises in consumption and investment spending. Ultimately, equilibrium income increases to Y_e'.

Shifts in *LM* and *IS*

Aside from the discussion of wealth effects, we have confined ourselves to cases in which either the *LM* or the *IS* schedule shifts. It is entirely possible, however, that both schedules may change simultaneously.

Consider the case of an increase in government spending. Assume that it is politically inexpedient to raise taxes and that the central bank supports the government bond market. A budget deficit is likely to follow an increase in government spending. The Treasury must find some means of paying for the increased expenditure commitments. It may borrow from commercial banks who then sell the securities to the Fed. When the Treasury borrows in this manner, its money balances are increased. As these funds are spent, members of the nonbank public who produce goods and services for the government receive money payments. Thus the money newly created by the central bank and the commercial banking system for the Treasury becomes part of the nonbank public's money holdings. The stock of money and government expenditures increase an equal amount. As a consequence, *IS* shifts to the right by some multiple of the increase in government spending, and *LM* also shifts to the right. These movements are represented in Figure 21–3 by the movement of *IS* from $(IS)_0$ to $(IS)_1$ and by the shift of *LM* from $(LM)_0$ to $(LM)_1$. The shift to the right in the *LM* curve is smaller than the shift to the right in the *IS* curve because the velocity of money is greater than 1. A \$1 increase in the stock of money will support more than a \$1 increase in the level of expenditures. For example, if the velocity of circulation of money is 4 (which is the same as saying that people want to hold on to \$1 for every \$4 they spend during the course of the year), then an increase of \$10 billion in Y can be supported by an increase of only \$$2\frac{1}{2}$ billion in the stock of money.

The fact that the increase in government spending was financed by an increase in the stock of money permits the equilibrium level of income and output to rise to Y_e'', rather than to Y_e' in Figure 21–3. As the level of income and output increase, the amount of money needed for transactions increases. This increase in M_d, in the absence of an increase in the stock of money, causes interest rates to rise to i_e'. However, with more money available to meet the increased demand for funds, the rate of interest rises

Figure 21–3.   Shifts in *LM* and *IS*.

BILLIONS OF DOLLARS

only to i_e'', thus helping to maintain consumption and investment expenditures that are related to the rate of interest and permitting Y to increase to Y_e''.

The preceding analysis indicates that the *LM* curve does not shift to the right by as much as the *IS* curve does. Over an extended period of time, *LM* could shift to the right more than *IS*, however. If government spending continues at the new high level and if the government also continues to run a deficit, then the stock of money must increase annually. This means that, other things being given, the *LM* curve must continually shift to the right as long as the deficit is financed by the sale of securities to the central bank. Interest rates will continue to fall and income levels to rise. Ultimately, as the economy approaches full employment and the demand for goods begins to exceed the rate of production, price inflation will occur.

The preceding examples of shifts in the *LM* and *IS* curves illustrate the many uses to which the model developed in Chapters 19 and 20 may be put. It is important to recognize that the commodity and money markets continually react upon one another. Changes in money market conditions are often related to changes on commodity market conditions, and vice versa. The supply of money is particularly important. *Given the demand for money, the model developed shows that the money supply schedule fixes the position of money market equilibrium* (LM) *and, through its influence on the rate of interest, helps determine the direction of change in income and output.* If we relax the assumptions made about the short-run influence of wealth, then the supply of money also affects saving and consumption directly, and thereby helps to determine the position of the *IS* line.

THE PRICE LEVEL

A Trade-off between Unemployment and Price Rise

Up to this point, we have made little mention of price change. Our analysis has been in real terms; implicitly we have usually assumed constant prices, which means that when equilibrium income changes as a result of shifts in *LM* or *IS*, all the change in *Y* is shown as a change in *Q* — real output. The assumption of constant prices is comparatively realistic under conditions of less than full employment. Individual prices may change, but the general price level tends to increase rather slowly as long as the economy has unemployed productive resources available. Once full employment is approached, however, prices are likely to rise sharply.

Figure 21-4 shows a hypothetical relationship between the unemployment rate and the average price rise — sometimes called a Phillips curve.[3] Notice along $(PC)_0$, that the price level can be expected to increase slowly as unemployment begins to decline, but as the economy nears full employment, the rate of increase in the price level becomes much higher. In other words, the curve in Figure 21-4 shows the trade-off in the economy between unemployment and price change.

Decreases in the unemployment rate occur as the demand forces we have been discussing expand — as government expenditures increase, as tax rates decrease, as the marginal efficiency of investment increases, as the stock of money increases, and so on. As these demand forces expand, the *LM* and *IS* curves move to the right. Their point of intersection also moves

Figure 21-4.   The trade-off between unemployment and price-level change.

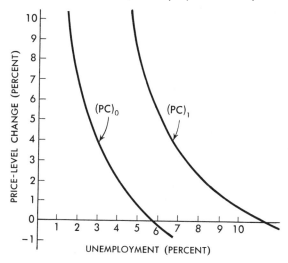

[3] See A. W. Phillips, "The Relationship Between Unemployment and the Rate of Change in Money Wage Rates in the United Kingdom, 1861–1957," *Economica* (November, 1958), pp. 283–99.

Figure 21–5. The relationship between *LM, IS,* the price level, and the productive capacity of the economy.

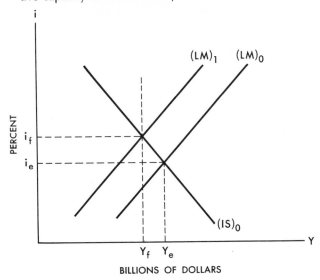

to the right and approaches the maximum amount of goods and services that the economy is capable of producing. This point is represented by Y_f in Figure 21–5. As Y_f is approached, the unemployment rate drops and, as Figure 21–4 demonstrates, the rate of increase in the price level becomes marked. Prices rise so sharply because the remaining unemployed resources are not specialized to the production of the products being demanded. The lack of proper job skills, education, inadequate health standards, and so on, almost precludes hard-core unemployables in the labor market.

Shifting the Phillips curve to the left. One means of making the trade-off between price rise and unemployment loss less marked at high levels of employment is to invest more in the human resource. A human being is, in many respects, comparable to plant and equipment capital. Man, too, is a productive resource; he creates a stream of services and output over an extensive period of time. The flow of goods and services produced by the human resource depends on the quantity and quality of the physical plant and equipment with which man works. It also depends upon his own capacities. Thus, given a constant amount of plant and equipment capital, man will produce more or less according to his innate capacities and the extent to which his abilities have been developed.

Increasing the education, health, and vocational training of the economy's human capital increases overall productivity and, thus, output and income. The improved efficiency of the human resource will shift a Phillips curve to the left (possibly from $(PC)_1$ to $(PC)_0$ in Figure 21–4), where aggregate demand can be more easily satisfied. An expansion of aggregate demand in order to reduce unemployment can now be achieved with a smaller price rise than it could before.[4]

Price expectations, economic controls, and the Phillips curve. Some economists contend that there is no tradeoff between inflation and unemployment, that the curve depicted in Figure 21–4 moves to the right as inflation in the economy comes to be expected. Assume, for example, that the unemployment rate is 2 percent and price-level change is 8 percent on $(PC)_0$ in Figure 21–4. According to the view being discussed here, the unemployment rate of 2 percent cannot be maintained if people are free of money illusion and adjust their money wage demands as the price level rises. If, in fact, people expected continuing price rises and were compensated with increased wages, then firm profit margins would decrease and there would be a decrease in the number of people employed. Possibly an inflation rate of 8 percent would then be associated with an unemployment rate of 5 percent instead of 2 percent. The Phillips curve would have shifted to the right, to $(PC)_1$ in Figure 21–4, making it harder to fight unemployment.

Traditional monetary-fiscal measures are designed to fight unemployment by stimulating demand which, in turn, creates some price inflation. But with a shifted Phillips curve, the inflation rate would have to be well above 8 percent to drive unemployment back down to 2 percent. Hence there is a conflict, sharper than that described in the preceding section, between the goals of stemming unemployment and inflation simultaneously. Only if expectations of future price rises were to stabilize could inflation be halted.

This was part of the logic behind the wage and price controls instituted in 1971. It was hoped by many that the rise in prices and wages would be stemmed, not so much from the direct effect of the controls themselves as from the psychological shock of the controls. A controls program should make the Phillips curve less steep. However, as these paragraphs were written in the late summer of 1973, controls were being removed and inflation was continuing. The two-year program of controls had apparently failed and may have impaired the allocative function of relative prices. Shortages of many goods had developed, in part due to the natural growth of demand in an expanding economy and in part due to the inhibiting of production by the controls program.

The Price Level and the *LM* Curve

How do price fluctuations fit into our macroeconomic model? People want real goods and services; they view their incomes and money holdings in terms of their ability to command real resources. They want a given

[4] The economist will recognize that I ascribed price inflation to *demand-pull* rather than *cost-push* forces. This does not mean that we cannot have cost-push inflation, but I do believe that cost-push (wage-induced) inflation cannot be sustained for long without the support of strong demand-pull forces such as continued federal deficits or an easy monetary policy.

amount of Q, not PQ. Assuming no wealth effects, this means that the position of the IS curve is not directly affected by price-level variations, even though it may be affected by changed price expectations.

The LM curve is affected by a change in the price level, however. The demand for money is a demand for real money balances—for a given amount of purchasing power. The supply of money schedule, however, merely records the nominal amount of money that the banking system is prepared to create; thus it is a real money supply schedule only when prices are constant. If prices increase, the real supply of money drops. For example, assume that the money supply at a given rate of i is $250 billion, given a price index of 100, and that, at this time, the real money supply equals the nominal supply—$250 billion. If all prices increase by 50 percent, however, so that the price index is now 150, then the real money supply amounts to only $166 billion, since $250 billion in nominal money can only buy $166 billion worth of the goods and services it could have purchased at a price index of 100. At any given interest rate, the smaller amount of real money balances ($166 billion) available can only support a smaller level of real income than formerly. This means that the LM curve has shifted to the left. Expressed differently, we find that for every different price level there is a different LM schedule, the schedule for consecutively lower price levels being successively farther to the right. For higher price levels, the LM schedules are successively farther to the left. For example, $(LM)_0$ in Figure 21–5 can be used to represent an LM curve with a low price level, and $(LM)_1$ can be used to represent an LM curve with a higher price level.

The preceding analysis means that, as prices rise and the relevant LM curve moves further to the left, pressures are set in motion that tend to raise the market rate of interest. As this occurs, consumption and investment demand decrease, thereby leading to income and output drops in real terms if the rise in prices pushes the LM curve, for example, to the left of $(LM)_1$ in Figure 21–5.

In sum, other things being equal, a rise in the price level is accompanied by a declining real money supply, rising interest rates, and possibly decreased output. On the other hand, a drop in the price level leads to an increase in the real money supply, and thus to a drop in interest rates and a rise in income and output in less than full employment situations. This may appear paradoxical in light of the fact that, in practice, output and prices tend to move in the same direction. It must be remembered, however, that we are concerned here only with the effects stemming from the price change. In the real world, prices generally begin rising as product demand increases because of IS shifts to the right.

The price level and the market and real rates of interest. Our model, to this point, has assumed that market and real rates of interest are equal. What happens if, as prices rise, lenders are slow to adjust market interest rates? Then real rates decline, as shown in our discussions of Irving Fisher in Chapter 17 and of consumption and investment in Chapter 19. Consumption and investment demand can then actually expand, contributing further to price inflation and reducing the real stock of money. If the interest rate axis in our diagrams is a measure of the market rate of interest, then, since there is a lower real rate of interest at any given market rate than formerly, the *IS* curve has actually shifted to the right: There is a greater demand for goods and services at any given market rate of interest. Eventually, the excess demand for goods, services, and money must force the market rate of interest to rise. Correspondingly, the real rate will rise, the *IS* curve will shift back to its original position, and the results outlined in the preceding section will follow.

THE PRODUCTIVE CAPACITY OF THE ECONOMY

Capacity and Stable Equilibrium

According to our model, the equilibrium Y_e will be the actual output Q the economy will tend to produce as long as we are at less than full employment. Once full employment is reached, however, any intersection of *LM* and *IS* to the right of maximum full employment output cannot be a position of stable equilibrium. In Figure 21–5, for example, Y_f is the maximum output of the economy. Y_e, therefore, where *IS* and *LM* intersect, cannot be produced. The demand for real goods Y_e exceeds the ability of the economy to produce them. Under these circumstances, entrepreneurs may raise prices, anticipating greater profits. In an attempt to meet the demand for goods and services, they will also bid labor and other productive resources away from one another. Costs of production will increase. Collectively, however, the most that can happen, since resources are already fully employed, is that the composition of output will be redistributed. A greater fraction of total output will be produced by those firms that have successfully lured productive resources away from other firms, but the production of the latter firms will have dropped. The rise in prices, wages, and costs decreases the real stock of money, causing the equilibrium money market schedule $(LM)_0$ to shift to the left until it reaches $(LM)_1$ and intersects $(IS)_0$ at full employment output Y_f.

It can also be argued that an intersection of *LM* and *IS* to the left of Y_f is unstable, but only if prices and wages are assumed to be flexible downward. If this situation exists, then the drop in prices caused by entrepreneurs' attempts to induce an increase in the demand for their products will shift *LM* to the right, and this will lead to lower interest rates and greater production. However, many economists consider the possibility of substantial downward price-wage flexibility in the contemporary American economy unrealistic.[5] On this basis, an intersection of *LM* and *IS* to the

---

[5] Downward as well as upward price flexibility is important to "theory as logic." This will be discussed later in this chapter.

left of Y_f may be regarded as a stable, less than full employment equilibrium point.

The Movement Toward Full Employment Equilibrium

Technological change, investment expenditures on new plant and equipment, and financial investment in the human resource all tend to increase the productive capacity of the economy. Until now, we have assumed that full employment equilibrium Y_f remains fixed. Actually, with a growing economy Y_f is always moving to the right. In Figure 21–5, for example, the ability of the economy to produce may shift from a maximum of Y_f to, let us say, Y_e. If the economy was originally in equilibrium at i_f and Y_f, with the relevant LM and IS curves $(LM)_1$ and $(IS)_0$, then, with the expansion of capacity, the economy is still in equilibrium but it is a *less than full employment* equilibrium. An expansion of demand is needed to bring the economy to a new and higher full employment equilibrium. This can be accomplished through an increase in the stock of money, an increase in government expenditures, a decrease in the tax rate, or an increase in investment expenditures. Other possibilities also exist. It is important that the expansion of demand be adequate to raise total demand for goods and services to a level equal to the output the economy is capable of producing. Nor will the new equilibrium necessarily continue to be a full employment equilibrium. As long as the productive capacity of the economy continues to expand—and it will do so as long as investment expenditures are positive—Y_f will move to the right. In order to achieve and maintain full employment, the many forces that determine the position of the LM and IS curves must continually change. Only in this way will the intersection of IS and LM move to the right with Y_f. On the other hand, these same forces need to be controlled so that they will not overshoot their mark and intersect to the right of Y_f, causing price inflation. We shall examine further the economic policies designed to avoid both unemployment and price inflation in Part V.

THE REAL BALANCE EFFECT AND ITS RELATION TO APPLICATIONS OF THE MODEL

The Real Balance Effect and Say's Law

Say's law, as noted in Chapters 17 and 18, was an important part of nineteenth and early twentieth century monetary theory. However, the protracted depression of the 1930s and subsequent developments in income-expenditure analysis caused economists to discard the notion that production creates its own demand. Keynes argued that a situation of satisfied effective demand and full employment production is not normal, but unusual. Nevertheless, despite the general abandonment of Say's law, certain theoretical aspects of the principle are still widely discussed in economic literature.

In terms of our income-expenditure model, effective demand and full employment production are equivalent only when the propensity to save and the inducement to invest are in a particular relationship — when planned $I + G + F$ equals planned $S_p + S_b + T$ at full employment output. Should *IS* intersect *LM* anywhere to the left of full employment output, a less than full employment equilibrium would exist. Figure 21-6 shows a less than full employment intersection of $(LM)_0$ and $(IS)_0$ at Y_e, which lies to the left of full employment output Y_f.

Some Keynesian theorists went even further and declared that a less than full employment equilibrium could be possible even with a downward flexibility of wages and prices. It is on this point that much monetary theory of the 1950s and 1960s focused. Most economists agreed that institutional rigidities exist that prevent downward movements in wages and prices. However, in theory, we may posit a situation where these institutional rigidities do not exist and, as a result, downward flexibility may be an equilibrator. It was on this theoretical level that the Keynesian argument was attacked.

We said earlier that there is a different *LM* curve for every different price level. As prices decline, the *LM* shifts to the right. Should the *IS* curve be sufficiently elastic so that at a positive rate of interest it can intersect *LM* at full employment output, then full employment can be reached via price-level declines. Such an intersection occurs at Y_f in Figure 21-6 when $(IS)_0$ and $(LM)_1$ meet. However, should *IS* not have sufficient elasticity, then it appears that declining prices and less than full employment equilibrium are

Figure 21-6. *IS, LM,* and the real balances effect.

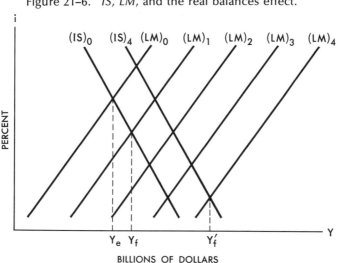

compatible. This would be reflected in Figure 21–6 if full employment output were at Y_f' instead of Y_f.

The above argument assumes, however, that the position of *IS* itself cannot be affected by price-level declines. A. C. Pigou and Don Patinkin have demonstrated that, given unlimited wage-price flexibility, full employment output *must* eventually be reached.[6] In their opinion, the *IS* schedule is affected by changes in *real balances* or in real wealth. Thus a drop in the price level increases the real purchasing power of money in the form of currency, and hence total real wealth. Given the desire of individuals to maintain some stable relationship between expenditures, real money balances, and real wealth, a drop in the price level will produce an increase in the demand for consumption goods and services. To the extent that businesses are similarly motivated, there will also be an increase in investment expenditures. These changes will cause an upward shift in the $I + G + F$ line and a downward shift in the $S_p + S_b + T$ line and, in turn, result in a movement of the *IS* line to the right. This process will continue as long as prices decline. At some point, therefore, the movement of the *IS* line to the right must lead to an intersection with the *LM* line at a point of full employment output. In Figure 21–6, *LM* and *IS* initially intersect at less than full employment output Y_e. With decreasing prices, both *LM* and *IS* will shift to the right, eventually reaching full employment Y_f' when the appropriate schedules are $(IS)_4$ and $(LM)_4$.

This phenomenon, already discussed in Chapter 19, is known as the *real balance effect*. Price-level decreases increase real balances and, hence, the demand for goods and services. On the other hand, price-level increases decrease real balances and hence reduce the demand for goods and services. Thus, if prices rise, the *IS* curve shifts to the left, creating the risk of less than full employment (assuming that prices do not drop as a result of general overproduction).

Pigou and Patinkin accept the real-world possibility of severe depression and less than full employment equilibrium, but they do not do so as completely as Keynes did. Given downward wage-price flexibility Pigou and Patinkin believe that full employment must be reached; given upward wage-price flexibility, less than full employment may also be reached.

How important is the real balance effect in practice? Although it is theoretically important as a framework of analysis, the real balance effect is likely to be offset in the real world by the effects of changing price expectations. As prices decline, expectations of continued price decreases tend to decrease spending—a time when the real balance effect calls for increased spending. Similarly, as prices rise, anticipation of further price rises leads to increased spending, rather than the decreased spending indicated by the changed real balances. Changes in real balances have an important eco-

[6] A. C. Pigou. "Economic Progress in a Stable Environment." *Economica* (1947); Don Patinkin. *Money, Interest, and Prices,* 2nd ed. (Harper & Row, 1965).

nomic effect only when people expect future prices to remain about the same as current prices.

An analogous discussion relating price-level changes, real government bonds, and the *IS* line could be developed here. Everything said earlier about real money balances in the form of currency would apply in this case as well. (This was discussed somewhat in Chapter 19 and in the first footnote to this chapter.)

Classical dichotomy. Another part of pre-Keynesian monetary economics, closely related to Say's law, was the *classical dichotomy*. According to this theory, the monetary sector of the economy determines the overall price level, whereas the demand for and supply of real goods and services determines relative prices. The price level thus has no effect on the demand for and supply of real goods and services. The real balance effect denies the existence of this dichotomy, for the change in real balances will affect the demand for and the supply of goods and services.

The interest-induced wealth effect. In terms of our model of income determination, by allowing for the real balance effect, we have now permitted the variable *wealth* to change. As real balances change due to price-level changes, real wealth and the demand for consumption and investment goods and services change. This is an appropriate point at which to mention other forces that also tend to change wealth. The real balance effect is a price-induced wealth effect. Boris Pesek and Thomas Saving, two contemporary economists, argue that we should also consider an interest-induced wealth effect.[7] They view wealth as simply the present value of the streams of income yielded by wealth discounted at the rate of interest. If the interest rate falls, given the same streams of income, wealth can be expected to increase. As individuals become wealthier, consumption and investment spending will increase. As the interest rate increases, given a constant income stream yielded by wealth, the value of wealth itself decreases and, consequently, the demand for consumption and investment goods and services decreases.

The Demand for Money and the Price Level

Another assumption of nineteenth- and early twentieth-century monetary economists was that changes in the price level and the demand for money are proportionate. For example, they believed that an increase of 10 percent in the price level should lead to a 10 percent increase in the demand for money, since people would want to maintain the same command over real goods and services. Similarly, a 10 percent decrease in the price level should lead to a 10 percent drop in the demand for money.

[7] Boris Pesek and Thomas Saving. *Money, Wealth, and Economic Theory* (Macmillan, 1967).

The real balance effect does not accept this postulate either. Assuming that all goods – including money – are superior goods, it follows that a rise in the price level decreases real balances. This, of course, decreases total real wealth and real money holdings relative to other wealth forms. If people want to maintain a given distribution among wealth forms, the demand for goods and services will decrease and the demand for real balances will increase. This demand is for an amount of real balances less than the volume held prior to the price-level increase, however. Decreasing their demand for goods and services enables people to recoup their real balances, but if these balances were completely recovered, the distribution among wealth forms would not be the same as before. Instead real balances would be a larger proportion of total wealth – that is, the demand for *nominal* money balances (real balances demanded, multiplied by the price level) increases, but not by enough to recoup all the real balances lost through price inflation. Thus, the demand for money (nominal balances) increases less than proportionately to the price level and has less than unitary elasticity.[8]

Supplementary Readings

THE COMMODITY MARKET

Baumol, William J. *Economic Theory and Operations Research,* 3rd ed. Prentice-Hall, 1972, Chapters 18 and 19.

Eisner, R., and R. H. Strotz. "Determinants of Business Investment." In Commission on Money and Credit, *Impacts of Monetary Policy,* 1963.

Ferber, Robert. "Research on Household Behavior." *American Economic Review* (1962), pp. 19–63.

Friedman, Milton. *A Theory of the Consumption Function.* Princeton University Press, 1957.

Jorgenson, Dale W. "Econometric Studies of Investment Behavior, A Survey." *Journal of Economic Literature* (1971), pp. 111–147.

Mayer, Thomas. "Tests of the Permanent Income Theory with Continuous Budgets." *Journal of Money, Credit and Banking* (1972), pp. 757–78.

Suits, D. B. "The Determinants of Consumer Expenditure." In Commission on Money and Credit, *Impacts of Monetary Policy,* 1963.

THE MONEY MARKET

Brunner, Karl. "A Schema for the Supply Theory of Money." *International Economic Review* (1961), pp. 79–109.

Cagan, Philip. *Determinants and Effects of Changes in the Stock of Money, 1875–1960.* Princeton University Press, 1965.

---

[8] This discussion is comparable to the analysis in Chapter 20 of the relationship between M_d and W'. A fuller exposition of these views can be found in Patinkin's *Money, Interest, and Prices, op. cit.*

Fand, D. I. "Some Implications of Money Supply Analysis." *American Economic Review* (May 1967), pp. 380–400.

Johnson, Harry. "Monetary Theory and Policy." *American Economic Review* (1962), pp. 335–84.

Klein, John J., and Richard Cebula, "More on the Analysis of Fiscal Policy and Bond Financing." *Economic Notes* (1972), pp 50–60.

Metzler, Lloyd A. "Wealth, Saving, and the Rate of Interest." *The Journal of Political Economy* (1951), pp. 93–116.

Teigen, Ronald. "Demand and Supply Functions for Money in the United States: Some Structural Estimates." *Econometrica* (1964), pp. 476–509.

Turner, Terry L. "A Multivariate Spectral Analysis of the Supply of Money and Credit." *Journal of Money, Credit and Banking* (1972), pp. 848–76.

Weintraub. Robert. "The Stock of Money, Interest Rates, and the Business Cycle, 1952–64." *Western Economic Journal* (1967), pp. 257–70.

Additional supplementary readings on money can be found at the end of Chapter 26.

GENERAL EQUILIBRIUM

Hicks, John R. "Mr. Keynes and the Classics: A Suggested Interpretation." Reprinted in American Economic Association, *Readings in the Theory of Income Distribution*. Blakiston, 1946, pp. 461–76.

Keynes, John Maynard. *The General Theory of Employment, Interest, and Money.* Harcourt Brace Jovanovich, 1936.

Lange, Oscar. *Price Flexibility and Employment*. Principia, 1944.

Modigliani, Franco. "Liquidity Preference and the Theory of Interest and Money. *Econometrica* (1944), pp. 45–88.

Patinkin, Don. *Money, Interest, and Prices,* 2nd ed. Harper & Row, 1965.

(See also the footnotes to Chapters 19, 20, and 26, and the Supplementary Readings at the end of Chapter 26.)

Part V MONEY AND ECONOMIC POLICY: INTERNATIONAL AND DOMESTIC POLICIES

22 The Meaning of Economic Policy

POLICY DEFINED

CHOOSING MEANS AND ENDS

SUMMARY AND PREVIEW

> I have become aware that anyone's sense of what
> is good and beautiful must have a somewhat
> narrow foundation, namely, his circumstances and
> his particular brand of human nature; and he
> should not expect the good or the beautiful after
> his own heart to be greatly prevalent or long main-
> tained in the world.
>
> —GEORGE SANTAYANA, *Dominations and Powers*

POLICY DEFINED

An economic policy is a governmental course of action designed to influence the future behavior of the economy. Basically, there are two types of
economic policies: microeconomic and macroeconomic. Those policies
designed to deal with the problems of specific industrial or regional areas of
the economy are called *microeconomic policies*. Farm, labor, business regulation, transportation, "pockets of poverty" policies are all microeconomic. *Macroeconomic policies,* on the other hand, deal with the problems
of the economy in the aggregate: unemployment, inflation, and growth. In
this final section of the book, we shall confine ourselves to the study of
macroeconomic policies.

Macroeconomic policy, or *aggregate economic policy,* as it is frequently
called, is *any* government course of action designed to attack national economic problems such as unemployment, inflation, and stalled economic
growth. Other matters such as exchange rate and international liquidity
problems may also enter the arena of macroeconomic policy when they affect the national economy.

Aggregate economic policy has three aspects. First, there is *monetary
policy:* any action taken by the Federal Reserve System to affect the
economy through its influence on the money stock and member bank
reserve positions. Second, there is *fiscal policy:* any action taken by the
Treasury or Congress to affect the economy through the spending, tax, and
debt operations of the federal government. Third, there is *international
financial policy:* any action taken by the Federal Reserve, the Treasury,

Congress, or the executive branch of the United States to affect the international monetary position of the United States.

Notice that the two words most frequently used in these definitions are *any action*. An *action* is merely a *means* to an *end*. Economic policy is also a *means* to an *end*—the elimination of basic national economic problems such as unemployment, inflation, and poor economic growth. To the extent that our policies help to correct these problems, they are considered effective. To the extent that they inhibit the correction of these deficiencies in the economy, they are deemed to retard economic welfare.

Yet, there are other goals that compete with the elimination of economic want and fear of economic collapse. For example, the freedom of individuals to do as they please so long as they do not harm others physically is usually viewed as a highly desirable political end. Are economic policy actions that restrict individual freedom of action and choice, then, to be regarded as bad, even if they eliminate pressing economic problems? Should economic policy be permitted to enhance the superior power position of the state—which, after all, is merely a collection of individuals—at the expense of the individual members of society?

CHOOSING MEANS AND ENDS

The preceding paragraph raises two basic questions: how are the ultimate goals of society determined, and how are the means to those ends selected?

Economists sometimes contend that it is not their function to deal with such broad social and philosophical questions. It is society's job, they say, to choose ends. It is the economist's job to indicate what means will best achieve the ends society selects. He uses economic theory as logic and as a set of substantive hypotheses to rank alternative economic policies according to their ability to satisfy society's ends. The choice between alternative policies and ends, however, is left to society.

This position of strict impartiality is illusory. Ethical principles are assumed in making a choice between alternative possibilities. Economics is a social science, dealing with our economic environment and its problems. The economist, like any other scientist, lives in the social and economic environment of his time—is influenced by the conditions surrounding him. To the extent that his circumstances differ from those of others in society, his thought and behavior patterns will differ. Furthermore, he lives and operates within the context of a given value system. His choice of study, the problems with which he is concerned, the very techniques he employs in scientific investigation, are partially influenced by "his circumstances and his particular brand of human nature."[1] Thus the scientist's so-called impartial statement of alternatives cannot be totally without bias. *The*

---

[1] George Santayana. *Dominations and Powers.* (Scribner's, 1951), p. 12.

economist, like other scientists, constantly makes normative judgments—hypotheses of what ought to be. Because of this, it is important that he makes his particular value system explicit.

The economist must also learn to shoulder some social responsibility. He should be willing to make a specific policy recommendation once he has made his set of values explicit. As a citizen, it is the scientist's duty to instruct his fellow citizens as well as to learn from them. In short, the economist should attempt to shape both the national ends and the means of achieving them.

How, then, is society to choose the criteria for evaluating economic policy? Several approaches are often used. All usually posit the value judgment that welfare maximization is the ultimate end of policy.

The *first approach* operating on the preceding premise argues that we should *choose that policy which provides more welfare for the members of society than it takes away.* The difficulty with this approach is that it assumes that welfare can be measured. In Part IV we said that per capita income is sometimes used as a measure of economic welfare. However, that measure provides us with only a rough idea of how a hypothetical "average" citizen is faring economically. The welfare maximization approach attempts to measure the gains and losses to individuals from particular policy actions—a far more difficult undertaking. Economists and psychologists are agreed that there is no way of exactly measuring human welfare and satisfaction and, consequently, no way of measuring gains and losses in individual satisfaction.

If welfare cannot be measured, is there some other way of evaluating alternative policies? Perhaps individuals themselves could rank various combinations of policies according to the amount of satisfaction produced. This technique is difficult to implement, however. People are reluctant to reveal their preferences. For example, it is frequently argued that taxes should be based on the benefits received from such social goods as education and highways. The individuals who receive little benefit would be taxed the least for the social good and those who most value the good would pay the most taxes. Social goods are generally available, however; they would not be removed by nonpayment of taxes. As a result, those who benefit from social goods would attempt to conceal their true preferences. Also, those who need social goods the most are frequently those least able to pay taxes.

A *second approach* argues that in order to maximize welfare we should *choose that policy which produces some gain and no harm.*[2] This approach is, in essence, a policy of inaction. It requires unanimous support for economic policy, and complete unanimity of opinion is, to all intents and purposes, unattainable in this world.

---

[2] This criterion for economic policy choice is called the *criterion of Pareto optimality* by economists.

Since society cannot reach a policy decision on the basis of the two previous approaches, it may do so by means of the *voting process*. Ideally, the voting process should reflect the values of the individual voting members of society and thereby permit society to arrive at a rational social consensus on policy. Unfortunately, even this approach has its difficulties. A democratic majority voting process will lead to a rational social decision only if (1) the values of the members of society are relatively homogeneous, and (2) the value systems of the members of society are single-peaked.

The implications of the first condition are obvious. If people have widely disparate views and if no majority shares the same views, then no consensus can be reached. Whatever decisions are made will be arrived at on the basis of temporary coalitions of competing groups. Thus whenever there is a realignment of groups within coalitions, previous decisions will be changed and political chaos will result. The Weimar government of Germany in the 1920s, the various French governments of the 1940s and 1950s, and the rapidly changing governments of present-day Africa all illustrate the political situation that exists when the members of a society have radically different value systems.

The second condition, a single-peaked value system, must also exist before social consensus can be achieved. Assume, for example, that voters are confronted with three policy choices: an extreme left-wing measure, a middle-of-the-road measure, and an extreme right-wing measure. A society that has a relatively homogeneous, single-peaked value system will choose only one of the three alternatives. On the other hand, if the second condition is missing and voters have a double-peaked value system, no consensus is possible. This would occur in the previous example if voters preferred either of the extremes to the more moderate middle-of-the-road measure.

Fortunately, both these conditions prevail in the United States. In countries where they do not, policy decisions can be reached by the voting process only on the basis of weak coalitions. If such a condition persists, it may so immobilize the government that the only solution may appear to be some form of dictatorship.

SUMMARY AND PREVIEW

One could say that this chapter has provided a glimpse of what welfare economics is all about and how it relates to economic policy. When viewed in conjunction with Chapter 16 on the meaning of economic theory, this chapter may give one some insight to the empirical, a priori, and intuitive approaches to the acquisition of human knowledge. To make policy recommendations, one should not only be versed in economics but also have made an effort to become an educated person — one who has read some of the great literature of the past and present in various fields and one who sees relationships between the condition of man and his intellectual heritage.

Ultimately, our decisions concerning policies and goals must be based on value judgments. In questions of economic and social policy, it is particularly important that we make explicit the *modus operandi* of a value judgment. Within much of western society, there is a single-peaked value system and relative homogeneity of values. A social consensus may thus be reached by means of the voting process.

When prescribing economic policy, the economist should make his value judgments explicit. To the extent that he can take as given such goals as full employment, stable prices, economic growth, and a favorable balance of payments, he should use the tools of his profession to outline the alternative means available for attaining these goals. In addition, he should take an active part in the decision-making process; he should clearly express his preferences in matters of economic policy.

Succeeding chapters outline alternative monetary, fiscal, and international financial policies. The focus is on the effectiveness of these policies in combating the basic national economic problems of unemployment, inflation, poor economic growth, and international financial instability. Where possible, the underlying political bases of these alternative policies are considered.

Supplementary Readings

Arrow, Kenneth J. *Social Choice and Individual Values*. Wiley, 1951.

Dewey, John. *The Quest for Certainty*. G. P. Putnam's Sons, 1960.

Musgrave, Richard A. *The Theory of Public Finance*. McGraw-Hill, 1959, Chapters 4–6.

Rader, Trout. *Theory of Microeconomics*. Academic Press, 1972, Chapter 1.

Rothenberg, Jerome. *The Measurement of Social Welfare*. Prentice-Hall, 1961, Chapters 1–2, 12–13.

23 Exchange Rates and the Balance of Payments Problem

GROSS NATIONAL PRODUCT AND THE
BALANCE OF TRADE

An economy does not function in isolation; the domestic economic policies of one nation influence economic behavior in other countries, and vice versa. Recession or inflation in one country may have international repercussions.

For example, rising incomes in one nation often lead to increases in the exports of other countries, for as disposable income increases, the demand for both domestic *and* foreign goods and services increases, inducing expansion of production abroad. On the other hand, a decline in disposable income at home causes a reduction in the demand for both domestic and foreign goods and can, in turn, lead to decreased incomes abroad.

The United States is a large nation, and most of its production is designed for the domestic market. Exports amount to only about 6 percent of the American gross national product. For this reason, the United States is not likely to be materially affected by economic conditions abroad, except insofar as changes in foreign economic conditions influence American expectations concerning the vigor of the domestic economy.

Imports also represent a small, but growing, percentage of our gross national product. Their dollar volume, however, is large; total imports for the year 1972 were valued at $78 billion.[1] Exports to the United States are a major source of the gross national products of many small countries, and the condition of the U.S. economy may well have an important direct effect on the prosperity of these countries.

Goods and services sold abroad are a part of gross national product. They also give rise to a flow of payments into the exporting country. Imports do not contribute directly to gross national product, but they do give rise to a flow of payments out of the importing country. The annual difference in value between a country's imports and exports is termed its *balance of trade*. If exports are greater than imports, the balance of trade is considered positive. If the value of exports is less than that of imports, the balance of trade is negative. The balance of trade for the United States has

[1] *Federal Reserve Bulletin* (February 1973), p. A–70.

almost always been positive. Until 1971, the payments owed the United States were usually greater than the payments it owed other nations for the purchase of goods and services. Presumably, this put the United States in a strong position in the international economy until 1971.

Generally this was the case, but beginning in the late 1950s and continuing into the 1970s, the United States experienced balance of payments difficulties. The balance of trade constitutes only a portion of the balance of payments. Other types of international financial transactions are included in this figure in addition to those involving real goods and services. These other transactions were the source of balance of payments difficulties for the United States until 1971.

THE BALANCE OF PAYMENTS

Definition

A nation's *balance of payments* is a record of the various payments it has made to foreigners and the payments it has received from them over a period of time. The record of the balance of payments is not to be confused with a balance sheet, however. The balance of payments records the *flow* of international payments and receipts. A balance sheet shows a financial position at a moment of time; it is a *stock* concept.

Actually, a country's record of international payments and receipts – its balance of payments – is always in balance over time. This is because the record is an *ex post* concept: it refers to what has already occurred. Actual receipts must always equal actual expenditures. This need not be true *ex ante* (regarding what has not yet occurred), however. Different groups make expenditure decisions at home and abroad. Investors at home decide to make financial investments abroad; foreign investors do the same. Consumers and businesses at home buy goods and services abroad; foreigners do also. Governments grant loans, make military payments abroad, and so on. Since expenditure plans are made independently by citizens of different countries, there is no reason why the planned foreign expenditures by the citizens of one country need equal the expenditures planned by foreign nationals to be made within the same country. Therefore the balance of payments need not be in equilibrium *ex ante*.

When planned expenditures abroad are greater than expected receipts (planned expenditures by foreigners), the result is a *balance of payments deficit* if the various expenditure plans are carried out. To make up the difference and achieve an *ex post* balance of payments, the debtor country can draw on its previously accumulated balances of foreign monies, borrow foreign monies, or reduce reserve assets such as gold and SDRs to meet the demands of creditor nations. A country that does not meet its obligations in gold or SDRs will cover its deficit by transferring to its creditors claims on some internationally accepted money, such as the American dollar.

On the other hand, a *balance of payments surplus* exists when expected receipts are in excess of planned payments and expenditure plans are carried out. To make up the difference, countries can follow the reverse policies: accumulate balances of foreign monies, lend to the deficit countries, or purchase reserve assets.

The preceding policies apply only for temporary surpluses or deficits. More permanent solutions must be found when a surplus or deficit is chronic. When a country has a continuing surplus, it means that other countries are short of funds with which to buy goods and services in the surplus country. Therefore, the surplus country must make adjustments to provide foreigners with additional funds, or the deficit countries will be forced to cut down on their expenditures in the surplus country. Thus, when the United States had a balance of payments surplus after World War II, it provided other nations with funds in the form of grants-in-aid. More recently, other countries with surpluses, such as Germany, have found different solutions to the problem. Germany, for example, revalued its currency upward. Deficit nations, on the other hand, must either cut back on payments or stimulate surplus nations to increase their expenditures. One common solution for the deficit nation is currency devaluation; Britain did this in 1949 and 1967, as did France in 1969, and the United States in 1972 and 1973. In other cases, a change in the interest rate structure can also help to achieve a balance of payments equilibrium.

Thus, in general, continual surpluses dictate the need for a permanent increase in payments or a decrease in receipts; continual deficits require a permanent decrease in payments or an increase in receipts. If the measures taken to achieve these goals are successful, a balance of payments equilibrium will be achieved and there will be only a minimal fluctuation in the balancing items of international reserves and short-term claims.

The U.S. Balance of Payments

Table 23–1 shows the United States' balance of payments for 1970–72. Most of the items listed are self-explanatory. Minus signs (−) indicate payments; all figures without minus signs represent receipts from abroad. The item in line 11, the *balance on goods and services,* corresponds to net exports of goods and services $(X - M)$ in our national income accounts shown earlier in Tables 18–2 and 19–1. This item includes our merchandise trade balance, net military transactions, net travel and transportation (principally tourism by foreign nationals in the United States less American travel abroad), and net investment income. The major item, the merchandise trade balance, was positive for several decades before becoming negative in 1971.

Line 12 shows *net remittances, pensions, and other transfers.* These consist primarily of emigrant remittances, which is the term used to describe the currency outflow arising when immigrants and their families in the United States send money to friends and relatives abroad. Historically, this item has always been negative.

TABLE 23-1 U.S. BALANCE OF PAYMENTS: 1970–72.
(IN MILLIONS OF DOLLARS)

LINE	CREDITS +, DEBITS –	1970	1971	1972
	SUMMARY – SEASONALLY ADJUSTED			
1	Merchandise trade balance*	2,176	–2,698	–6,912
2	Exports	41,964	42,768	48,769
3	Imports	–39,788	–45,466	–55,681
4	Military transactions, net	–3,374	–2,918	–3,558
5	Travel and transportation, net	–2,013	–2,288	–2,853
6	Investment income, net†	6,260	7,972	7,862
7	U.S. direct investments abroad	7,920	9,456	10,433
8	Other U.S. investments abroad	3,506	3,443	3,492
9	Foreign investments in the United States	–5,166	–4,927	–6,063
10	Other services, net	581	739	850
11	*Balance on goods and services** *	3,630	807	–4,609
12	Remittances, pensions, and other transfers	–1,481	–1,553	–1,570
13	*Balance on goods, services, and remittances*	2,150	–745	–6,179
14	U.S. government grants (excluding military)	–1,734	–2,045	–2,174
15	*Balance on current account*	416	–2,790	–8,353
16	U.S. government capital flows (excluding nonscheduled repayments), net††	–1,829	–2,117	–1,714
17	Nonscheduled repayments of U.S. government assets	244	225	137
18	U.S. government nonliquid liabilities to other than foreign official reserve agencies	–433	–467	238
19	Long-term private capital flows, net	–1,429	–4,401	–151
20	U.S. direct investments abroad	–4,410	–4,943	–3,404
21	Foreign direct investments in the United States	1,030	–115	160
22	Foreign securities	–942	–966	–614
23	U.S. securities other than treasury issues	2,190	2,269	4,335
24	Other, reported by U.S. banks	178	–862	–1,120
25	Other, reported by U.S. nonbanking concerns	526	216	492
26	*Balance on current account and long-term capital* ††	–3,031	–9,550	–9,842
27	Nonliquid short-term private capital flows, net	–482	–2,347	–1,637

28	Claims reported by U.S. banks		-1,023	-1,802	-1,495
29	Claims reported by U.S. nonbanking concerns		-361	-530	-315
30	Liabilities reported by U.S. nonbanking concerns		902	-15	173
31	Allocations of Special Drawing Rights (SDRs)		867	717	710
32	Errors and omissions, net		-1,205	-10,784	-3,112
33	*Net liquidity balance*		-3,851	-21,965	-13,882
34	Liquid private capital flows, net		-5,988	-7,788	3,542
35	Liquid claims		252	-1,097	-1,234
36	Reported by U.S. banks		-99	-566	-742
37	Reported by U.S. nonbanking concerns		351	-531	-492
38	Liquid liabilities		-6,240	-6,691	4,776
39	To foreign commercial banks		-6,508	-6,908	3,862
40	To international and regional organizations		181	682	104
41	To other foreigners		87	-465	810
42	*Official reserve transactions balance*		-9,839	-29,753	-10,340
	Financed by changes in:				
43	Liquid liabilities to foreign official agencies		7,637	27,615	9,720
44	Other readily marketable liabilities to foreign official agencies		-810	-551	399
45	Nonliquid liabilities to foreign official reserve agencies reported by U.S. government		535	341	189
46	U.S. official reserve assets, net		2,477	2,348	32
47	Gold		787	866	547
48	SDRs		-851	-249	-703
49	Convertible currencies		2,152	381	35
50	Gold tranche position in International Monetary Fund		389	1,350	153

BALANCES EXCLUDING ALLOCATIONS OF SDRs—SEASONALLY ADJUSTED

Net liquidity balance	-4,718	-22,682	-14,592
Official reserve transactions balance	-10,706	-30,470	-11,050

* Adjusted to balance of payments basis; excludes transfers under military grants, exports under U.S. military agency sales contracts, and imports of U.S. military agencies.

† Includes fees and royalties from U.S. direct investments abroad or from foreign direct investments in the United States.

** Equal to net exports of goods and services in national income and product accounts of the United States.

†† Includes some short-term U.S. government assets.

Note: Data are from U.S. Department of Commerce, Bureau of Economic Analysis. Details may not add to totals because of rounding.

SOURCE: *Federal Reserve Bulletin* (July 1973), pp. A-72-73.

Line 14, *U.S. government grants,* includes economic (nonmilitary) grants-in-aid to foreign governments and is another negative (outflow) item in our balance of payments.

The sum of lines 11, 12, and 14 equals our *balance on current account* (line 15) and represents almost all recorded transactions exclusive of long-term and short-term capital (financial) flows to and from the United States.

In addition to our balance on current account, financial flows and errors and omissions contribute to the balance of payments. Lines 16–18 primarily represent long-term loans by the U.S. government to foreign governments, less repayments. These lines are often negative and contribute to our balance of payments deficit. Line 19, *long-term private capital flows, net,* includes the purchase of plant and equipment abroad by American businesses (a negative item in the balance of payments), American purchases of foreign securities (a negative item), and the purchase of U.S. private securities by foreigners (a positive item).

The sum of line 15 (the balance on current account), lines 16–18, and line 19 equals line 26, *balance on current account and long-term capital*—a very large negative line.

Line 27 shows *nonliquid short-term private capital flows, net.* These are short-term loans by U.S. banks and U.S. nonbank businesses to foreigners (lines 28 and 29), and short-term loans by foreigners to U.S. nonbank businesses (line 30). Line 27 is generally negative.

Line 31 represents the *allocation of Special Drawing Rights* (SDRs) to the United States by the International Monetary Fund (IMF). SDRs are automatically allocated by the IMF to its members annually, enhancing their international reserve assets. These may, in turn, be used to settle international transactions, as described earlier in Chapter 10.

Finally, line 32, *errors and omissions, net,* covers statistical errors and unrecorded transactions. Usually a minor item, in 1971 it was extraordinarily large—some $11 billion. Much of this was attributable to unrecorded short-term capital outflows by people and businesses who anticipated an official change in the gold content of the dollar, an anticipation borne out in 1972 when Congress increased the dollar price of gold.

When lines 27, 31, and 32 are added to line 26, we arrive at line 33—the *net liquidity balance* or our *balance of payments.* This was −$13,882 million in 1972 (see Table 23–2), our second largest deficit in history. How was this deficit balanced? The first balancing item was an accumulation of private short-term claims against American money by foreigners, as reflected in line 34, *liquid private capital flows, net.* The principal receipt here was from the sale of short-term securities to foreign commercial banks (line 39). The second, and most important, balancing item was in large *official reserve transactions* (line 42), which were −$10,340 million in 1972. These U.S. reserve transactions were accomplished primarily by the increase in U.S. liabilities held by foreign governments and central banks (lines 43 and 44).

TABLE 23–2 U.S. BALANCE OF PAYMENTS AND NET MERCHANDISE
BALANCE, 1946–72
(IN MILLIONS OF DOLLARS)

YEAR	NET LIQUIDITY BALANCE* (THE BALANCE OF PAYMENTS)	NET MERCHANDISE BALANCE
1947	4,210	10,124
1948	817	5,708
1949	136	5,339
1950	−3,489	1,122
1951	−8	3,067
1952	−1,206	2,611
1953	−2,184	1,437
1954	−1,541	2,576
1955	−1,242	2,897
1956	−973	4,753
1957	578	6,271
1958	−3,365	3,462
1959	−3,870	1,148
1960	−3,676	4,906
1961	−2,251	5,588
1962	−2,864	4,561
1963	−2,713	5,241
1964	−2,696	6,831
1965	−2,477	4,942
1966	−2,151	3,824
1967	−4,683	3,817
1968	−1,610	612
1969	−6,122	621
1970	−3,851	2,164
1971	−21,965	−2,689
1972	−13,882	−6,964

* Data for 1960–72 are not comparable to data for 1947–59.
SOURCE: 1947–59: *Economic Report of the President* (1968), p. 307; 1960–72: *Economic Report of the President* (1973), p. 294; and *Federal Reserve Bulletin* (July 1973), p. A-72.

Table 23–2 places our current balance of payments deficit in perspective by presenting the record of U.S. balance of payments from 1946 through 1972. Here we see that the United States had a balance of payments surplus in the early post-World War II period. The productive facilities of Europe had been devastated by the war, and the United States was the only country large enough and sufficiently industrialized to meet European demands for new plant and equipment. European countries were faced with a "shortage" of dollars, however, because of the lack of U.S. demand for European goods. To solve this problem, the United States helped provide funds for needy countries through unilateral gifts. The Marshall Plan was an early example of such assistance. Economic aid played a very important role in reducing foreign balance of payments deficits in the early postwar years. In 1947, for example, the American merchandise balance was $10.1 billion. In the absence of offsetting forces, this would have led to a $10.1

billion balance of payments surplus. The actual surplus for that year amounted to only $4.2 billion, however. Government grants and capital outflows accounted for almost the entire difference between the balance of trade surplus and the balance of payments surplus. This government aid enabled other countries to buy goods and services in the United States.

As the rest of the world slowly recovered from the after effects of World War II, the dollar shortage gradually diminished. Foreign economies, aided by U.S. economic assistance, were able to resume the production of an ever wider variety of goods and services. As a consequence, people in the United States began to purchase more goods abroad. This occurred to such a degree that our imports grew more rapidly than our exports, cutting down the size of our merchandise surplus. At the same time, U.S. government grants began to increase, and both economic aid and military expenditures abroad rose. Most of these expenditures were directed toward less developed nations, as part of our cold war strategy. Britain, Germany, France, and other developed nations of the West we assisted immediately after World War II no longer need our economic aid. The United States continues to make military expenditures in many countries, however, because we have deemed it necessary to maintain a large military establishment overseas. These grants and military expenditures, combined with a decreased trade surplus, contributed to balance of payments deficits and a dollar surplus starting in the late 1950s and continuing into the 1970s.

An additional factor contributing to the deficits was the sharp increase in private direct investment and long-term security purchases abroad. Enlarged foreign markets and greater political stability abroad tended to expand these long-term financial outlays. Higher interest rates abroad on long-term securities also stimulated overseas investment. From time to time, higher foreign short-term interest rates also increased the outflow of short-term funds. Ultimately, of course, these outflows led to return flows in the form of *investment income, net* (line 6 of Table 23–1). In the absence of these return flows, our balance of payments deficits would have been even greater in the 1970s.

The balance of payments deficits confronting the United States in the 1970s were primarily a result of a continuing deterioration in the U.S. merchandise balance, which became negative in 1971. Military transactions, grants-in-aid to foreign countries, increased American tourism, and private capital flows out of the country had all increased gradually over the years and contributed to the deficit in the balance of payments, but it was our trade balance that forced speculation about devaluation of the dollar and, ultimately, devaluations in both 1972 and 1973. Clearly, the U.S. balance of payments has not been in equilibrium in recent years, principally because of domestic inflation. Rates of inflation are an underlying economic source of balance of payments disequilibrium. Whereas the U.S. dollar has usually been in a unique position relative to foreign monies in that it serves as international money, we can no longer rely on this uniqueness to avoid correcting our chronic deficit. Since transactions between countries all over the world are settled with dollar deposits, governments in the past *chose to accommodate* the United States when its balance of payments was in deficit by accumulating claims to dollars. Germany and Japan, for example, purchased billions of dollars that individuals and businesses sold in foreign exchange markets prior to the U.S. devaluation of 1973. By 1973, it was clearly apparent that international solutions were needed to help the United States correct its balance of payments deficit.

The following chapter examines some specific solutions to international balance of payments difficulties. First, however, some of the underlying economic determinants of the balance of payments need to be examined. To this point, we have generally provided a description of the balance of payments, not a framework of analysis. We will begin this discussion by explaining the connection between the balance of payments and the exchange rate. Previously, no mention was made of the fact that different countries employ different monetary units of account. This, as we shall see, creates important balance of payments problems.

THE EXCHANGE RATE

Introduction

Each country has its own monetary unit of account. Prices and money in the United States are measured in terms of the dollar; the unit of account in France is the franc; in Japan, the yen; and in Germany, the Deutsche mark. Within the boundaries of each nation, each currency circulates freely. In international trade, however, there is no single international unit of account. Although dollars are often used to settle international transactions, importers and exporters usually need specific currencies to carry on their transactions. For example, U.S. exporters receive claims against foreign money in payment for their goods, but they need American currency to meet their internal obligations; conversely, importers need foreign monies to buy goods abroad. Consequently these merchants make use of the foreign exchange market, where different types of currencies may be obtained. This market consists of the banks, brokers, and agents who deal in the purchase and sale of foreign exchange (foreign currency).

The principal suppliers of foreign currency in this market are exporters and those who sell securities abroad; the principal demanders of foreign currency are importers and buyers of foreign securities. *The exchange rate tells us the number of units of domestic currency necessary to purchase foreign currency.* In other words, *the exchange rate is the price of domestic currency in terms of foreign currency.* It records how much of one country's currency is needed in exchange for a given amount of another country's currency. For example, the exchange rate between the American dollar and the German Deutsche mark during 1973 was approximately 1

Deutsche mark = \$.358. From the American point of view, this means that \$1 = 2.8 Deutsche marks.[2]

The Relationship between the Exchange Rate and the Balance of Payments

We have said that the demand for a country's currency depends on the total value of its exports, the inflow of remittances and pensions, the inflow of foreign government capital, and the inflow of private foreign capital funds. On the other hand, the supply of a nation's currency depends on the total value of its imports, the outflow of remittances and pensions, the outflow of government funds, and the outflow of private capital funds.

Thus, at a given rate of exchange, should the demand for a nation's currency exceed its supply, there is a balance of payments surplus. On the other hand, at a given exchange rate, should the supply exceed the demand, there is a balance of payments deficit. Should the exchange rate change, however, the amounts of a nation's currency demanded and supplied will also change, and so will the balance of payments. Not only does the exchange rate give the price of one country's currency relative to foreign currency, it also indicates how much foreign goods and services cost in terms of one's own currency (assuming prices in the foreign country remain unchanged).

For example, if a German product costs 10 Deutsche marks, then, with an exchange rate of \$1 = 3.2 Deutsche marks, the cost in dollars of the German product is \$3.2. Should the exchange rate change to \$1 = 5 Deutsche marks, the dollar price of the German good will be reduced to \$2.00. This should lead to an increase in the amount of commodities demanded by U.S. citizens. In addition, it should cause an increase in the total amount of American money supplied as foreign exchange. This assumes, however, that the American demand for the German good is *price-elastic*—that the amount of the German product demanded expands more than proportionately to the decrease in the price of the product to Americans. For example, if ten units of product are demanded at a price of \$1, then at a price of \$.50 per unit the amount demanded would expand to more than twenty units, leading to expenditures in excess of \$10.

A drop in the exchange rate also works in the opposite direction. If the exchange rate falls to \$1 = 2.8 Deutsche marks, the price of German goods

---

[2] We use the term "exchange rate" here as if there were only one rate of exchange between two different national currencies. Actually, there are a number of different rates—among them, the spot and forward rates. The *spot exchange rate* covers transactions the next day; *forward exchange rates* cover transactions for longer periods, such as 30, 60, or 90 days, or even longer. Generally, the rate will be higher the sooner one wants foreign monies. If a government has established a fixed ratio between its currency and that of other countries, then the various exchange rates will be very close to the official rate.

Figure 23–1. A hypothetical supply and demand for dollars in the foreign exchange market.

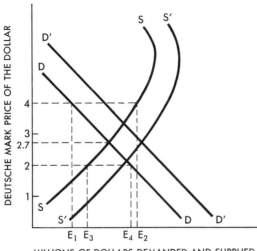

MILLIONS OF DOLLARS DEMANDED AND SUPPLIED

to Americans is increased.[3] This will cause a decrease in the amount of foreign goods demanded. If the American demand for a German product is price-elastic, total expenditures on the product will decrease and the amount of American currency supplied in the foreign exchange market will also decrease. Hence, *the quantity of a country's currency supplied in the foreign exchange market will tend to increase with increases in the exchange rate.* This statement, however, assumes (1) that the demand for foreign goods is elastic, and (2) that other things remain equal—that there is, for example, no change in capital flows or in the foreign prices of goods and services. This situation is illustrated in Figure 23–1 by the part of the *SS* curve that slopes upward and to the right.

Conversely, should the demand for foreign goods and services be price-inelastic, then, as the exchange rate rises, the total volume of currency supplied decreases. When the demand for a product is price-inelastic, the amount of the product demanded expands less than proportionately to a decrease in the price of that product. Hence there would be an increase in the number of units sold but a decrease in total expenditures. In the foreign exchange market, expenditures on imports are part of the supply of a nation's currency. When an import is price-inelastic, therefore, the supply of currency slopes upward and to the left as a result of decreased expendi-

---

[3] By a fall in the exchange rate, we mean a decrease in the amount of a foreign currency that a unit of another given currency can command. For the other country, however, this situation is viewed as a rise in the exchange rate because its currency can now command more units of the depreciated foreign currency.

tures on foreign goods and services. This decreased supply of currency is shown in the backward-bending part of the SS curve in Figure 23–1.

The demand schedule for a country's currency slopes downward and to the right, as shown by line DD in Figure 23–1. The demand for a country's currency is equal to the total payments other countries are willing to make. *Thus, other things being equal, the lower the exchange rate, the lower the price of a country's exports and the greater the amount of its currency demanded.* Assume, for example, that an American product costs \$1. When the exchange rate is \$1 = 3.2 Deutsche marks, the cost of the American product to a German buyer is 3.2 Deutsche marks. Should the exchange rate fall to \$1 = 2.8 Deutsche marks, then the price of the good to a German falls to 2.8 Deutsche marks. This lower price will probably induce Germans to purchase more of the American product. In order to do this, however, additional American money is needed, since the dollar price of the product remains unchanged. The change in the exchange rate simply reflects a change in the Deutsche mark price. For this reason, other things being equal, the demand for a country's currency will almost always slope downward and to the right in terms of the demand curve in Figure 23–1.[4]

The figure shows hypothetical demand and supply schedules for American dollars. For the sake of simplicity, we have assumed a two-country universe, consisting of Germany and the United States, in which Germany represents the rest of the world with which the United States trades. On the vertical axis we can measure the Deutsche mark price of the dollar. The number of dollars demanded and supplied at varying exchange rates is measured on the horizontal axis.

The balance of payments surplus or deficit is really the difference between the demand and supply schedules DD and SS. For example, in terms of our hypothetical supply and demand schedule, if the exchange rate is \$1 = 4.0 Deutsche marks, we know that the supply of American dollars exceeds the demand for American dollars in the foreign exchange market. American payments exceed receipts, causing a balance of payments deficit equal to $E_2 - E_1$ million dollars (Figure 23–1). This deficit can be sustained by accommodation only when the debtor country is able to borrow foreign currency, draw on previously accumulated balances of foreign monies, reduce its international reserves, or persuade foreign countries to permit a buildup of their claims against the currency of the debtor country.

On the other hand, when the exchange rate is \$1 = 2 Deutsche marks, the demand for American dollars exceeds the supply. American receipts exceed payments and there is a balance of trade surplus equal to $E_4 - E_3$

[4] If the German demand for American goods in this illustration had been price-inelastic, the demand curve for American dollars would still have sloped downward and to the right. For price-inelastic goods, Germans would be giving up less of their own currency for American dollars if the value of the mark were raised. The total number of dollars demanded would still increase with a decrease in the exchange rate because the dollar price of the American goods would be unchanged by the revaluation of the mark. Therefore, as they sought to purchase more American goods, Germans would need more American dollars.

million (Figure 23–1). For there to be no balance of payments deficit or surplus, the exchange rate must be $1 = 2.7 (see figure) Deutsche marks. This rate will bring equilibrium to the balance of payments, since it is at this point that the demand and supply schedules intersect.

The Position of the Foreign Exchange Demand and Supply Schedules

The position of *DD* and *SS* in Figure 23–1 depends on a series of given factors. The *first* is the *level of domestic income*. As incomes increase, the demand for home-produced *and* foreign goods and services increases also. Therefore, if income in the United States should increase, the demand for foreign goods would increase and the supply of American dollars in the foreign exchange market would grow accordingly. In terms of Figure 23–1, the *SS* curve would shift to the right, to *S'S'*. At any given exchange rate, this would mean that the supply of currency has increased relative to the demand. Thus any deficit existing prior to the income increase has widened, and any surplus existing prior to the income increase has narrowed. At the same time, the demand for American currency has decreased, possibly from *D'D'* to *DD* in the figure. American industry produces to meet both foreign and domestic demands. When domestic demand expands, there will be a shift of production to meet the increased demand. Hence, there will be fewer American goods available to foreigners, fewer American exports, and a decreased demand for American currency at any given exchange rate. The decreased demand for American currency will further aggravate any balance of payments deficit.

Conversely, a decrease in domestic income reduces the demand for foreign goods and services. The supply of the currency decreases, deficits narrow, and surpluses widen. In addition, the production of goods for foreign markets expands relative to that for domestic markets, and the demand for American currency expands—possibly from *DD* to *D'D'*. This helps to narrow a balance of payments deficit or to widen a surplus.

Second, incomes abroad affect the position of the demand for and supply of currency. Increased incomes abroad mean that other nations demand both more domestically-produced goods and more foreign goods. For example, an increase in German gross national product induces an increase in the demand for American goods. To obtain more American goods, however, the Germans need more American dollars. Thus the *DD* line shifts to the right, becoming *D'D'*. (If prior to the German income change there had been a deficit U.S. balance of payments, this deficit would now have narrowed.) At the same time, German producers increase domestic production at the expense of exports; this should shift the supply of U.S. currency to the left, possibly from *S'S'* to *SS*.

Third, prices at home relative to those abroad affect both the demand for and the supply of currency in the foreign exchange market. Suppose that prices in the United States decline relative to those in Germany, making American products more attractive than the comparable German products. Both Americans and Germans demand more American goods and fewer German goods. The result is a decrease in the supply of American currency entering the foreign exchange market (a shift to the left in SS) and an increase in the demand for American currency by Germans (a shift to the right in DD). This improves the American balance of payments situation, unless the elasticities are unfavorable. On the other hand, a rise in prices in the United States relative to those in Germany will increase the supply of American dollars in the foreign exchange market and decrease the demand for American dollars. More German products and fewer American products will be demanded, and the American balance of payments situation will worsen.

Fourth, interest rates at home relative to those abroad influence the demand for and supply of currency in the foreign exchange market. Should interest rates decline in the United States relative to those in Germany, the demand for dollars will decline and the supply will increase. The decline in U.S. interest rates makes German securities a more attractive financial investment. As a consequence, Germans demand fewer American securities and, hence, less U.S. money. Americans also purchase fewer of their own securities and increase their purchases of German securities, thereby further increasing the supply of American dollars on the foreign exchange market. Conversely, a rise in U.S. interest rates relative to those abroad will increase the demand for American dollars and decrease the supply.

Fifth, expectations are an important determinant of both the demand for and the supply of currency. Suppose that the domestic political stability of a country is threatened. As a rule, this situation will cause a capital flight: inhabitants of the unstable country will try to transfer their currency holdings into the currency of a more stable nation. At the same time, foreign demands for the goods, services, and securities of the troubled nation will diminish. This will cause DD to shift to the left and SS to the right, and the balance of payments situation to worsen.

Expectations concerning future exchange rates are also important. If, for example, it is probable that the exchange rate will increase, then it pays to postpone purchases abroad until one's own currency is actually able to command more foreign money. Such a delay causes a shift to the left in the SS curve. At the same time, foreign nations are trying to get into the currency that is soon to be appreciated; they prefer to buy goods, services, and securities prior to the change in the exchange rate. This causes a shift to the right in the DD line. Reverse movements will occur when a drop in the exchange rate is expected, as in the United States in 1971 and 1973.

And lastly, there are a series of exogenous forces at work affecting the demand for and supply of a country's currency internationally. For example, increased economic and military commitments to our foreign friends cause more U.S. military and economic aid payments, thereby shifting SS

to the right and increasing a balance of payments deficit. To the extent that U.S. grants to others are spent in the United States, however, the movement of *SS* would be reduced. These exogenous forces are largely noneconomic and, accordingly, difficult to forecast.

SUMMARY

This chapter has examined some of the monetary effects of a nation's international balance of payments. It has explained the relationship between the balance of payments and the exchange rate. A nation's balance of payments is in deficit when, at a given exchange rate, the demand for its currency is less than the supply in the foreign exchange market. Conversely, there is a balance of payments surplus when the demand for a country's currency is greater than its supply in the foreign exchange market. A major part of the following chapter will be devoted to various solutions to balance of payments difficulties.

Supplementary Readings

Haberler, Gottfried. *A Survey of International Trade Theory*. Princeton University Special Papers in International Economics, 1961.

Haberler, Gottfried, and Thomas D. Willett. *A Strategy for U.S. Balance of Payments Policy*. American Enterprise Institute, 1971.

24 Alternative International Economic Policies

FLEXIBLE EXCHANGE RATES

THE GOLD STANDARD

ADJUSTMENTS TO BALANCE OF PAYMENTS PROBLEMS UNDER RELATIVELY FIXED EXCHANGE RATES

Primarily Internal Policy Alternatives
  Depressing domestic income growth
  Reducing inflation
  Raising interest rates
  Reducing U.S. government expenditures and loans abroad
Direct Controls
  The interest equalization tax
  Voluntary foreign credit restraint guidelines
  Trade and exchange controls
Policy Alternatives Requiring International Cooperation
  Gold, the gold pool, and the development of a two-tier gold system
  The swap network
  Devaluation and floating exchanges
Fixed Rates, Controls, and Floating Exchange Rates

THE PROBLEM OF INTERNATIONAL LIQUIDITY

Strengthening the International Monetary Fund
Revaluation of Gold
The Triffin Plan

Chapter 23 examined the relationship between the balance of payments and the exchange rate. Chapter 24 considers some alternative solutions to balance of payments problems. In addition, it briefly examines the problem of international liquidity and international monetary organizations.

FLEXIBLE EXCHANGE RATES

One way to establish a balance of payments equilibrium is by means of a *flexible exchange rate*. When the exchange rate is above the equilibrium level, the supply of currency exceeds the demand and there is a balance of payments deficit. If the government permits its exchange rate to fluctuate freely in response to market forces, however, the exchange rate will decline in response to this deficit. The price of domestic goods will then drop relative to foreign goods and purchases of domestic goods and services will increase accordingly. Foreigners will increase their purchases of goods and services in the country experiencing the exchange rate decrease. This will cause the amount of currency demanded to increase. At the same time, imports will fall and the amount of currency supplied will decrease. Hence the balance of payments deficit will decrease.

On the other hand, should the exchange rate fall below the equilibrium level, the demand for money exceeds the supply in the foreign exchange market and there is a balance of payments surplus. Currency that is in relatively short supply can be expected to increase in value relative to other currencies. This will increase the price of domestic goods relative to foreign goods. Citizens of the surplus country, induced by the increased value of their currency abroad, will increase their foreign purchases and decrease their domestic purchases. Conversely, citizens of other countries will decrease their purchases abroad and increase their domestic purchases. Thus the amount of the surplus country's currency demanded will decrease and the amount of its currency supplied will increase. In this fashion, the balance of payments surplus will decrease.[1]

[1] Professional economists will recognize that the preceding analysis assumes the Marshall-Lerner condition to be satisfied. According to this condition, if the sum of the elasticities of demand for a country's exports and of its demand for imports is greater than one, a decrease in the exchange rate will improve the country's balance of payments and an increase in the exchange rate will worsen it.

If a country allows its exchange rates to fluctuate freely, payments equilibrium will be quickly established and chronic balance of payments deficits and surpluses will be eliminated. Proponents of this type of international policy believe that it would permit a nation to design its monetary and fiscal policies with purely internal problems in mind. There would no longer be a conflict between policies for internal and external economic stability. For example, interest rates are often decreased by the monetary authorities as a means of stimulating the economy during a recession. This domestic policy frequently endangers balance of payments stability, however. As Chapter 23 showed, a decline in domestic rates relative to those abroad will tend to expand a balance of payments deficit. Thus the monetary authority is forced to choose between continuing to keep interest rates low to stimulate economic recovery and raising them to eliminate the balance of payments deficit.

Fiscal stabilization policies face the same dilemma. Anti-recessionary fiscal policies could well involve both a decrease in taxes and an increase in government spending. This would lead to much needed increases in income and output, but it would also conflict with balance of payments stability. Rising incomes lead to increased purchase of goods and services abroad, and, as previously noted, the supply of currency widens relative to the demand for it in the foreign exchange market. Thus, the balance of payments deficit would be increased.

Permitting exchange rates to fluctuate freely could eliminate this conflict between internal and external objectives. No surplus or deficit in the balance of payments could long continue because changes in the exchange rate induce changes in the amounts of currency demanded and supplied in the foreign exchange market. Thus, the demand for currency and the supply of currency would tend to balance each other.

In spite of these advantages, there is strong opposition to the use of flexible exchange rates as an international monetary system. In fact, monetary authorities themselves are usually opposed to such an arrangement. Most countries prefer to fix the value of their currency in relation to the currencies of other nations because they fear that flexible exchange rates would leave the determination of the exchange rate to speculators rather than to free-market demand and supply forces.

With freely fluctuating exchange rates, if speculators expect the rates to decline, for example, they can force the decline by switching to a more valuable currency. Since a decline in the exchange rate decreases the ability of a currency to command other currencies in exchange, it pays the speculator to sell a currency before it depreciates. He simultaneously purchases other currencies. This action increases the supply relative to the demand for the depreciating currency, however, thereby providing the force needed to drive the exchange rate down.

When do the actions of the speculator actually tend to be destabilizing? Precisely when the internal conditions of a country warrant a continuing depreciation in the exchange rate. This is most likely to occur if domestic monetary and fiscal policies are causing continuing price rises relative to price levels abroad. Thus, it is chiefly domestic price inflation rather than the flexible exchange rates themselves, which triggers currency speculation that is destabilizing in terms of exchange rate determination.

In sharp contrast, when exchange rate movements appear to be temporary, the actions of the speculator may actually have a stabilizing influence. If the exchange rate has temporarily declined and speculators expect it to return to its old level, they will buy more of the depreciated currency because they expect to make a profit by selling the currency after it has returned to the higher level. This added demand for currency when it is depreciated will push exchange rates up.

Nonetheless, most countries are anxious to guard against the possibly destabilizing effects of speculative currency manipulation and, consequently, keep firm control of the value of their currency in the foreign exchange market. This effectively prevented flexible exchange rates from becoming a feasible international economic policy until recently.

Fixed exchange rates, on the other hand, are no guarantee that speculative currency manipulation will not occur. Speculation that the United States would devalue the dollar led to significant gold-reserve losses in the spring of 1968. Likewise, speculation that France would devalue the franc in late 1968 led to a halving of French gold reserves in late 1968; France finally devalued the franc, but not until August 1969. Again in both 1971 and 1973, a deterioration in the U.S. merchandise balance and rising prices induced speculators to sell dollars, thereby helping to cause the U.S. government to devalue the dollar in 1972 and 1973.

THE GOLD STANDARD

Many countries describe the value of their currencies in terms of gold. The dollar, for example, was defined in 1973 by our government as being equal to 1/42.22 ounce of gold. This presumably put the United States on the gold standard; that is, the U.S. Treasury supposedly stands ready to buy and sell gold at $42.22 an ounce. This is possible only for foreign governments, however. American citizens may soon be able to purchase gold in private markets. From 1933 to 1973 they were prohibited from owning gold except as jewelry, in coin collections, or for industrial purposes. Internationally, the United States buys and sells gold only in its transactions with other governments. Prior to March 1968, citizens of foreign nations could also buy and sell gold in dealings with the U.S. Treasury. A change in this policy was triggered by speculation regarding an increase in the dollar price of gold. Even the sale of gold between governments is severely limited under present international arrangements.

The following discussion describes how balance of payments adjustments *should* be made under the gold standard. They are *not* made in this manner in the real world because countries are unwilling to accept the internal consequences of the gold standard.

Under the gold standard, each country defines its money in terms of gold; consequently, governments should be prepared to exchange gold for currency and vice versa on demand. In addition, variations in the supply of gold should be permitted to affect the stock of money. The relationship of each unit of account to gold establishes the exchange rates between the different units of account. For example, if $1 = 1/42.22$ ounce of gold and 1 Deutsche mark $= 1/140$ ounce of gold, then the exchange rate between the two currencies would be $1 = 3.22$ Deutsche marks; the dollar would be worth 3.22 times as much gold as the Deutsche mark.

How would a balance of payments adjustment take place under such a gold standard? For simplicity, let us assume that there are only two currencies to deal with—the dollar and the Deutsche mark, the latter representing the unit of account for the rest of the world. Let us further assume that initially there is a balance of payments equilibrium. Now imagine that the American preferences for foreign goods and services increase. This leads to an increase in the demand for foreign goods and an increase in the supply of dollars in the foreign exchange market. The United States now has a balance of payments *deficit*. Further assume that the U.S. government is unwilling to decrease the gold content of the dollar and will not permit the exchange rate to decrease. Therefore, the United States must *lose gold* to the rest of the world. To protect itself against further gold losses the U.S. central bank *raises interest rates*. Other countries, in turn, decrease their interest rates in response to the gold inflow. As noted in Chapter 23, this change in interest rates would tend to improve the balance of payments position of the deficit country.

The loss of gold reduces commercial bank reserves in the United States and causes some contraction in deposit money. Deflationary forces are activated in the U.S. economy. At the same time in other countries, the gold inflow increases reserves and banks with the additional lending capacity expand loans. The lower interest rates abroad encourage foreigners to borrow more at home. In the United States, however, borrowing has become more expensive. Businesses must put a stop to capital expansion in plant and equipment because the margin between expected investment returns and the cost of funds has narrowed. As a result, employment decreases in the United States. In terms of our model of income determination, the gold loss has led to a shift to the left in *LM,* and consequently, to a rise in i and a decrease in Y.

If prices and wages are flexible in the United States, there also will be *downward pressure on the price level*. At the level of prices prior to the gold outflow, the demand for goods is less than the supply. With prices and wages flexible downward, however, some of the decrease in employment in the United States will be temporary. In time, declining prices will *stimulate demand for home-produced goods* by both Americans and foreigners.

Americans will also purchase fewer goods and services abroad. Thus the real demand for goods relative to the supply of goods will tend to be maintained.

Abroad, however, the situation is reversed. Lower interest rates have encouraged increased borrowing, expenditures on capital goods have risen, and income and output have increased. Since the rest of the world may be close to full employment, very little of the increased demand can be satisfied. As a consequence, there is upward pressure on prices and wages abroad. Thus the price level in the United States has decreased relative to prices abroad. This decrease, in turn, leads to an *increase in the demand for American currency and a decrease in its supply*. Conversely, the demand for the Deutsche mark (the unit of account we have posited for the rest of the world) decreases and its supply increases. In this fashion, the *balance of payments deficit* for the United States is *eliminated*.

This process makes the important assumption that there is downward price flexibility which assures full employment. Our theoretical analysis in Part IV showed that this typical nineteenth- and early twentieth-century economic assumption has proved unrealistic. We now know that it is possible to have less than full employment equilibrium. The flaw in the gold-standard mechanism for adjusting balance of payments differences is that it ignores this possibility.

If prices and wages are not flexible downward, changes must be made in income, output, or employment to achieve a balance of payments equilibrium. If prices do not decline in the United States as gold flows out, the money stock declines, interest rates rise, and, consequently, income, output, and employment fall. Decreases in income reduce the demand for foreign goods and this, in turn, means that the supply of American dollars in the foreign exchange market will decrease. So long as the deficit remains, however, gold will continue to flow out and domestic income and output will continue to drop. Once income has dropped sufficiently, the supply of American currency will again equal the demand, ending the balance of payments deficit. Internal stability will have been sacrificed for external stability.

Adherence to the gold standard would prevent national monetary authorities from exercising sufficient control over the domestic level of employment and prices. With wage and price rigidity, deficits tend to lead to unemployment; surpluses, during periods of full employment, tend to lead to inflation. Thus internal price and employment stability would be sacrificed for balance of payments stability.

This was roughly the state of affairs prior to World War I for those countries on the gold standard. Monetary authorities at the time were chiefly concerned with protecting their reserves. As gold flowed out, they increased interest rates; as gold flowed in, they decreased interest rates. Following World War I, however, central banks gradually became more and more interested in maintaining domestic equilibrium. Countries went off the rigid type of gold standard described here to improve domestic stability. Hence, although most economies of the Western world still maintain some fictitious external gold standard, most currencies are not convertible into gold internally. Even those countries that do not define their money in terms of gold frequently attempt to maintain a stable rate of exchange between their currency and the American dollar or the British pound sterling, which are still technically based on gold.

This adherence to the semblance of a gold standard in international trade creates difficulties in the contemporary economic world. We do not permit exchange rates to fluctuate freely in order to correct balance of payment difficulties. Nor do we permit an automatically functioning gold standard to compensate for balance of payments difficulties. How, then, do contemporary economies make adjustments in their balance of payments?

ADJUSTMENTS TO BALANCE OF PAYMENTS PROBLEMS UNDER RELATIVELY FIXED EXCHANGE RATES

No nation follows the rules of the gold standard or of fully flexible exchange rates. As a result, monetary authorities make many adjustments to balance of payments problems, some of them *ad hoc* and others somewhat more *permanent*. Most of these adjustments involve stimulating the demand for a country's currency and discouraging increases in the supply in the foreign exchange market when there is a continuing deficit in the balance of payments. A chronic surplus requires the reverse of these adjustments. Here we shall concentrate on policies for a deficit in the balance of payments, since this has been characteristic of the United States for some time. First we will consider policies that are primarily internal to a country, then those that involve direct controls, and finally those that require some form of international agreement.

Primarily Internal Policy Alternatives

Depressing domestic income growth. The first of the possible internal remedies for a balance of payments deficit — depressing the rate of domestic income growth — is dissatisfactory in the United States. Deliberately using contractionary monetary and fiscal policies to achieve an improvement in the balance of payments is not politically feasible, nor is it morally responsible when unemployment might ensue. No modern economy has chosen this route to correct payments imbalances. In any case, it is in the nature of economic growth that, as domestic income levels expand, increases occur in the demand for domestic and foreign goods and services.

Reducing inflation. A second regulatory method — reducing the growth rate of the price level — makes considerably more sense. Inflation, as we have stressed in this book, reduces the purchasing power of money, hitting fixed-income recipients most severely. Monetary and fiscal restraints that keep our commodity (*IS*) and money (*LM*) market equilibrium intersections from moving to the right of full employment output can help reduce a balance of payments deficit.

A slowdown in the rate of inflation might reduce the price level of the deficit country relative to those of surplus countries. Thus, foreign goods would become more expensive and domestic goods cheaper in the deficit country. The effect, as Figure 24–1 illustrates, would be a shift to the right in the demand (from *DD* to *D'D'*) and a shift to the left in the supply (from *SS* to *S'S'*) of the deficit country's currency in international money markets, with a resultant reduction in the balance of payments deficit from $E_2 - E_1$ to $E_4 - E_3$ millions of dollars at the fixed exchange rate E_f. Hence, an anti-inflationary policy can have some beneficial effects on a deficit in the balance of payments.

The preceding conclusion needs to be carefully qualified, however. First, if prices are rigid downward, then an anti-inflationary policy may reduce the demand for goods and cause unemployment and lower income levels — not particularly desirable domestic accomplishments. Under these circumstances, it would be best to try to reduce the rate of inflation, not the absolute level of prices. This is why an appropriate anti-inflationary policy should only prevent *IS* and *LM* from intersecting to the right of full employment output. Usually when there is inflation and unemployment, the anti-inflationary portion of economic policy is not adaptable to the international situation. Instead, balance of payments difficulties are handled by such devices as devaluation, trade controls, etc., all of which will be discussed subsequently.

Second, it is possible for a country to have less inflation than other countries and still have a deficit in its merchandise balance and in its balance of

Figure 24–1. Shifting *DD* and *SS* to reduce balance of payments difficulties.

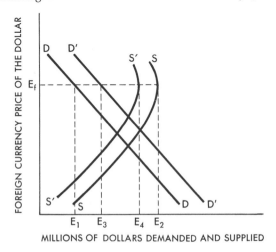

MILLIONS OF DOLLARS DEMANDED AND SUPPLIED

payments. Such has recently been the case for the United States. The prices of our exports have risen more rapidly than those of foreign countries. This is in part a result of the fact that other nations subsidize the producers of their exports more than we do. No matter what the source of this difference in price behavior, however, the important factor is the price of internationally-traded goods and services, not the relative price levels of all goods and services.

Raising interest rates. The third policy to reduce a balance of payments deficit — raising interest rates — is popular in many nations. The purpose of raising interest rates at home relative to those abroad is to make domestic securities more attractive both internally and abroad. As noted in Chapter 23, this action should shift DD and SS to the right and left, respectively. In terms of Figure 24–1, at a fixed exchange rate E_f, a deficit in the balance of payments is reduced from $E_2 - E_1$ to $E_4 - E_3$ (just as occurred when relative prices were changed in the preceding section).

The United States has used monetary policy to raise interest rates in order to reduce the balance of payments deficit several times in the last 13 years. For example, the Federal Reserve abandoned its "bills only" policy in 1961 in an effort to *keep long-term interest rates low and short-term rates relatively high.* By buying long-term securities, the Federal Reserve provided funds needed to stimulate an economy operating at less than full employment. By selling short-term securities, the Fed tried to keep short-term rates high and thereby induce individuals and businesses with temporarily idle funds to purchase short-term securities in the United States rather than abroad. This policy fell into disuse in 1965 when the higher short-term rates accompanying the Vietnam war financing efforts made such operations no longer necessary.

The Federal Reserve has also used the discount rate to help relieve balance of payments deficits. For example, the Fed increased the discount rate in July 1963 in an effort to relieve a balance of payments deficit. It was hoped that this action would not depress the economy internally. The discount rate was increased again in November 1964. The aim then was to counter a rise in the British short-term rate from 5 to 7 percent. Britain had increased its rate in order to reduce pressure on the pound resulting from an adverse balance of trade and payments. The American action was designed principally to prevent an increased flow of U.S. dollars to Britain pursuant to a widened spread of interest rates in Britain's favor. Further discount rate increases in March and April of 1968 were also in part designed to offset speculation on the dollar and thereby help reduce outflows of U.S. gold reserves.

More recent discount rate increases in early 1973 were aimed primarily at keeping the rate in line with private rates and were not intended to be either anti-inflationary or international instruments of policy. As our balance of payments difficulties mounted in the early 1970s, foreign governments attempted to pressure the United States into raising its interest rate structure. The Fed was reluctant to do this prior to early 1973 because unemployment rates were still in excess of 5 percent. Another consideration may have been political—given the existence of wage and price guidelines, the Fed may have felt it was inappropriate to permit interest rates (the price of borrowing money) to rise markedly. The Fed even forced some large commercial banks to rescind increases in the prime rates at which they lent to their better customers. This policy was abandoned by May 1973 when the Fed began following a restrictive monetary policy.

Reducing U.S. government expenditures and loans abroad. U.S. government expenditures, grants, and loans abroad are essentially noneconomic forces determined by military and foreign policy considerations, as we noted at the end of Chapter 23. Yet these dollar outflows may be, and actually have been, manipulated to reduce the supply of U.S. currency in international money markets. *The rate of military expenditures* abroad was reduced in the early 1960s, for example. Some American military installations in other countries were closed, and regulations permitting military dependents to live abroad were tightened. Our allies were encouraged to increase their armament purchases from the United States. Military expenditures, of course, increased with the intensification of the Vietnam war in 1965. Subsequently, as the U.S. commitment in Vietnam was reduced, so were our military expenditures. These actions in Vietnam had no direct connection with our balance of payments policy.

In addition, some effort has been made to require recipients of American foreign aid to spend these funds in the United States. Dollars provided other nations by the Agency for International Development must be spent in the United States, even if the price of goods is cheaper abroad.

Direct Controls

The U.S. government does not usually endorse controls as a means of adjusting the balance of payments deficit. Our government is officially and ideologically committed to the removal of trade barriers, and favors a free flow of goods, services, and funds throughout the world. To Americans, the economic common sense of such a policy is obvious: if other countries can be persuaded to reduce their trade barriers, then foreign demand for American goods, services, and securities will expand, thereby increasing the demand for American currency and decreasing the national balance of payments deficit.

The position of the United States on this matter, however, has become more and more ambivalent. On one hand, it has *taken the lead in reducing trade barriers* to encourage the free flow of goods and funds among nations. On the other hand, it has increasingly restricted the ability of Americans to purchase the foreign goods, services, and securities they desire. Three groups of direct governmental control will be considered in this section.

The interest equalization tax. The interest equalization tax—a control policy designed to make domestic securities more attractive—applies to all new or outstanding foreign securities purchased by Americans (Canadian securities are exempted). The tax is designed to reduce the interest differential between American and foreign securities in order to decrease the supply of American currency in the foreign exchange market. Thus *DD* is left unchanged, but a deficit in the balance of payments is reduced by shifting *SS* to the left. In terms of Figure 24–2, for example, a shift of *SS* to *S'S'* at E_f would eliminate a deficit entirely.

The interest equalization tax was first adopted as a temporary measure in 1964. Since that time, it has been repeatedly renewed by Congress at the President's request, the most recent extension occurring in 1973. The tax in 1973 was 0.75 percent on the interest paid to a bondholder and 11.25 percent on the purchase price of a foreign stock.

Voluntary foreign credit restraint guidelines. Closely related to the use of the interest equalization tax in making foreign investments less attractive to Americans is the Voluntary Foreign Credit Restraint (VFCR) policy of the Federal Reserve. Under this type of program, the Federal Reserve attempts to relieve balance of payments deficits in the United States by issuing restrictive guidelines on foreign lending by American banks and nonbank financial institutions. These guidelines are really a direct control program and have been used as such increasingly in recent years. The Fed has

Figure 24–2.   Correcting a balance of payments deficit.

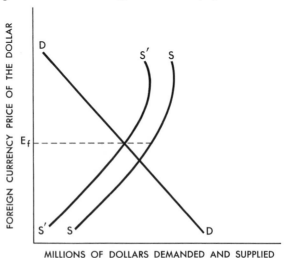

MILLIONS OF DOLLARS DEMANDED AND SUPPLIED

made these regulations mandatory (not voluntary) and has extended them to more and more types of foreign operations by American financial institutions.

For example, Federal Reserve regulations cover such diverse operations as (1) lending to foreign companies who wish to lease U.S. equipment to be used in the United States by its U.S. subsidiaries, (2) extending credit to finance the freight of foreign products carried in U.S. operated vessels, and (3) purchasing export credits from foreign financial institutions. A particularly striking example of the Fed's involvement in limiting American lending abroad is its attempt to define export credit. The VFCR program applies to loans by banks when less than 85 percent of the loan (export credit) finances U.S. exports. This means that U.S. exports must be defined in a variety of cases and given different interpretations, one of which reads:

When an article exported is manufactured in the United States in whole or in part from foreign raw materials or with foreign components that are not substantial or clearly identifiable, a determination must be made as to whether the resulting product has been "substantially transformed" in the United States.

To illustrate the question: a generator manufactured in the United States utilizes substantial amounts of Chilean copper and is manufactured according to engineering designs produced in the United Kingdom. A determination would have to be made as to whether the resulting generator should be considered a U.S. article. In a case such as this, it would not be feasible or perhaps useful to ascertain the portion of final value attributable to the foreign raw materials or to the foreign engineering services. However, it might be feasible to determine whether the U.S. manufacture resulted in a "substantial transformation" in the United States of the foreign materials.[2]

The VFCR policy is designed to shift the supply curve of American currency to the left and thereby reduce a balance of payments deficit. Figure 24–2 illustrates this. At the fixed exchange rate E_f, there is a deficit in the balance of payments. A shift to the left in the supply curve by employing such measures as restraining the amount of foreign lending by American banks, can presumably eliminate the deficit. This is illustrated in Figure 24–2 by a movement of the supply curve SS to $S'S'$.

Trade and exchange controls. Trade and exchange controls can also be used to decrease a balance of payments deficit. Tariffs and import restrictions are trade controls. An increase in tariffs raises the price of foreign goods and services to importers. This decreases the demand for foreign goods and services, reduces the supply of the importing country's currency on the foreign exchange market, and reduces that country's balance of payments deficit. Import quotas also restrict the supply of a country's cur-

[2] *Federal Reserve Bulletin* (February 1973), pp. 124–25.

rency. Under import quotas, only a given amount of foreign goods can be imported, regardless of the demand for the product. Exchange controls work somewhat differently. They restrict the use that nationals and foreigners may make of funds acquired in trade. For example, a foreign nation may be required to spend a given portion of its exchange receipts in the importing country, or the exporters of the country with the controls may be forced to sell their receipts of foreign currency at an official rate to their government in exchange for domestic currency.

The United States has had tariffs and import quotas throughout much of its history, but, since the 1930s, it has also taken the lead in reducing these barriers to trade. There was, for example, the Kennedy Round of negotiated tariff reductions of the early 1960s. Yet there have been numerous recent examples of increasing U.S. restrictionism due to balance of payments difficulties. In 1961, the United States reduced the duty-free exemption for returning tourists to $100 per person. In effect, this raised the price of foreign goods to American tourists and caused the demand for foreign goods and the supply of American dollars going abroad to decrease. These restrictions on American tourism continue today—more than a decade later. Another example of increased U.S. reliance on trade restrictions occurred in 1971 when a 10 percent import surcharge was placed on all U.S. imports for a period of four months. This action was part of an overall policy of economic controls designed to deal with inflation and the deficit in the balance of payments—a contradictory policy since the surcharge raised the domestic prices of foreign goods to Americans while wage and price controls were being ennacted by the government. This surcharge was removed when the United States agreed to devalue the dollar in December 1971.

Still another form of direct control has been the attempt to restrict foreign investments by nonfinancial U.S. corporations. Under this program, American businesses are limited in the amount of foreign investments they may make each year.

Policy Alternatives Requiring International Cooperation

As the United States experienced balance of payments difficulties, it developed numerous techniques for dealing with central banks and governments. The first of these was the gold pool and, subsequently, a two-tier gold system. The second was the development of a swap network. Thirdly, the United States experimented with devaluation and floating exchanges. Each of these will be considered in turn in this section.

Gold, the gold pool, and the development of a two-tier gold system. Internally, gold has little significance for the U.S. economy. The average citizen has not been able to redeem his money at the U.S. Treasury for the money metal gold since 1933. Today gold is important to the United States chiefly as a source of international reserves. By defining the dollar as equal to 1/42.22 ounce of gold, the United States has obligated itself to relinquish 1/42.22 ounce of gold to foreign monetary authorities in exchange for every U.S. dollar they accumulate. Since the volume of dollar claims to gold increases with a balance of payments deficit and decreases with a balance of payments surplus, gold flows are likely to increase with deficits in the U.S. balance of payments and decrease with surpluses in the absence of restrictions on world gold flows.

Because of successive balance of payments deficits, the United States experienced continual gold outflows until 1968. The net effect was to reduce the gold stock of the United States from $22.9 billion at the end of 1957 to $10.9 billion at the end of 1968.[3] These large losses led to speculation that the dollar would be devalued. Both Democrats and Republicans felt that a reduction in the exchange rate (devaluation) was not politically feasible in the 1960s; the United States was committed to keeping the dollar freely interchangeable with gold at what was at that time the legal price of gold — $35 an ounce. U.S. authorities also believed that if we devalued, other countries would retaliate by reducing their exchange rates, thereby negating any economic benefits to the United States. To minimize the effects of speculation, the gold pool was created.

The *Gold Pool* was an arrangement whereby various central banks operated in the London gold market to stabilize the price of gold. Previously, in the absence of efforts to stabilize the price of gold, speculation had caused serious fluctuations in the gold market. In the fall of 1960, for example, when the continuing U.S. balance of payments deficit led to the expectation of a decrease in the gold content of the dollar, many speculators rushed to get out of dollars and into gold. As a consequence, the dollar price of gold in the London market began to hover around $40 an ounce instead of close to $35 an ounce. By selling and buying gold defensively, the Gold Pool helped to stabilize the world price of gold and to minimize the effects of private speculation from 1961 to 1968. The Gold Pool was unable to halt speculative buying of gold in March of 1968, however. As previously noted, the United States was willing to buy and sell gold to everyone except American citizens. In the spring of 1968, when foreigners speculated that the American dollar would be devalued, they rushed to purchase gold at $35 an ounce. The U.S. Treasury supplied gold to private markets at this price through the London Gold Pool. However, the increased supply of American gold going into the gold market could not keep the private market price of gold from rising to almost $45 an ounce. The effect was to end the London Gold Pool, and the United States began to initiate new policies regarding the purchase and sale of gold.

The policies initiated in 1968 led to what has been called the *two-tier gold system*. The two tiers are (1) that for governments, and (2) that for

---

[3] *Economic Report of the President* (January 1973), p. 299.

individuals and businesses. The United States will still sell gold to foreign governments in exchange for dollars at a fixed price (now $42.22 an ounce), but, along with other major nations, not to governments that buy and sell gold in the free market (except for South Africa). In addition, the U.S. government no longer conducts transactions with individuals in the private-world gold market, since this would be a violation of the two-tier system. (Private citizens and businesses purchase gold in private markets; the price in 1973 sometimes rose as high as $125 an ounce.) As a result of these policies, the volume of U.S. gold holdings has been virtually constant since 1968.

The swap network. In addition to the preceding policies, during the 1960s, the Federal Reserve developed a technique known as the *swap network* or *reciprocal currency arrangements* for dealing with speculative pressures on the currencies of various nations. In general, a *swap* is an arrangement whereby a central bank agrees to exchange its currency for another currency for a limited period of time. This enables a country experiencing a temporary balance of payments deficit to use the foreign currency it acquires in a swap to buy back its own currency in the foreign exchange market, thus reducing the possibility that expanding foreign claims will result in a loss of international reserves. When we buy up our own currency in this fashion, the demand for dollars expands and the supply of other currencies in the foreign exchange market increases. This disappoints speculators who had counted on a deterioration in the price of the dollar relative to other currencies.

Swap arrangements for the United States are handled by the Federal Reserve. All purchases and sales of foreign currency are conducted by the special manager for foreign currency of the Federal Reserve Bank of New York. The Fed presently has arrangements with the Austrian National Bank, the National Bank of Belgium, the Bank of Canada, the Bank of Denmark, the Bank of England, the Bank of France, the German Federal Bank, the Bank of Italy, the Bank of Japan, the Bank of Mexico, the Netherlands Bank, the Bank of Norway, the Bank of Sweden, the Swiss National Bank, and the Bank for International Settlements. Swap arrangements have been particularly helpful in relieving pressure on the U.S. balance of payments caused by short-term capital flows.

Unfortunately, the swap network — like the gold pool, the two-tier gold system, and direct controls — is a technique that can only temporarily meet a crisis arising in connection with a balance of payments problem. Once the ad hoc remedy is removed, the underlying economic problem of a chronically undervalued currency (for a country with a continuing surplus in its balance of payments) or a chronically overvalued currency (for a country with a continuing deficit in its balance of payments) is apparent. Reciprocal currency arrangements and controls are impermanent, merely shifting the demand and supply of currency. Ultimately, more significant remedies are needed.

Devaluation and floating exchanges. An effort to arrive at a more permanent solution to the U.S. balance of payments deficit began in August of 1971. At that time, the United States went off the gold standard in its dealings with other governments, stating that it would no longer redeem in gold those dollars presented to it by foreign central banks. This meant that we were on a freely fluctuating exchange rate, but, unfortunately (from the viewpoint of the author), this was only a transitory measure until a new and more appropriate relationship between gold and the dollar could be found. That new relationship was temporarily established by what is now called the *Smithsonian agreement of December 1971,* under which exchange rates among the principal financial free-world powers were realigned. For Germany and Japan, this meant a revaluation of their currencies. For the United States, it meant the devaluation of the dollar from $35 to $38 for an ounce of gold. Once Congress approved the measure in March 1972, we were again willing to deal in gold with foreign central banks; this factor was unimportant, however, since there was almost no trading of gold among nations. The realignment of exchange rates was the key to the agreement, for it meant an increase in the price of foreign goods for Americans and a decrease in the price of our goods for foreigners. This should have improved our balance of trade and hence our balance of payments. But, as our earlier discussion demonstrated, the balance of payments deficit continued and the balance of trade actually worsened until it became negative in 1972.

At the same time the United States devalued, it tried to arrange for other nations to remove their barriers to the importation of U.S. goods in exchange for the removal of the temporary surcharge on foreign goods. Agreements with Japan were particularly notable on this score.

The U.S. trade deficit of 1972 and fear of additional inflation in the United States spelled the collapse of the Smithsonian currency realignments. Increasingly in early 1973, foreigners and American businesses and individuals who held dollars abroad for both speculative and business transactions attempted to exchange their dollars in foreign markets for such currencies as the German mark and the Japanese yen. Both the West German and the Japanese governments sought to support the U.S. dollar by buying billions of dollars, but the United States did surprisingly little to support its own currency directly. Obviously, another international monetary crisis was upon us. The United States finally responded in February 1973 by announcing it would again devalue the dollar—this time to $42.22 an ounce.

This decision to devalue led to tentative agreements among the principal financial nations in March 1973. According to these arrangements, the exchange rates of many nations are to be *floating exchange rates*—that is, free to float against the dollar. The United States is to have a fixed exchange rate, but the value of other currencies will float around the dollar in accordance with the demand and supply for each currency. This is a system somewhat similar to freely fluctuating exchange rates. For example,

Figure 24–3. Achieving balance of payments equilibrium with a change in exchange rates.

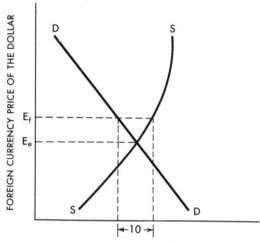

BILLIONS OF DOLLARS DEMANDED AND SUPPLIED

if there is a deficit in the U.S. balance of payments and an accompanying excess supply of American dollars, the value of the currencies in countries with surplus balance of payments would increase. Even though the gold price of the dollar were fixed, its foreign currency price would change. As can be seen from Figure 24–3, with exchange rate flexibility of the sort described, a U.S. deficit of $10 billion could be reduced to zero by a drop in the foreign currency price of the dollar from E_f to E_e. Remember that dropping the foreign currency price of the dollar stimulates the demand for U.S. goods and services and, accordingly, for the number of dollars demanded in international money markets. Similarly, this action raises the dollar price of foreign goods for Americans and reduces the number of dollars entering international money markets (assuming the U.S. demand for foreign goods and services is price elastic).

Hopefully, more fluctuations in exchange rates will correct underlying U.S. balance of payments difficulties. It remains to be seen, however, just how much freedom in international money markets will be permitted by the principal trading nations of the world. One dismaying note should be sounded with respect to the March 1973 arrangements. One of the agreements was that the United States would support the dollar more actively in the future by using the swap network frequently in the foreign exchange markets. This means that the United States would meet speculative runs on the dollar by borrowing foreign currency to buy surplus dollars. Such action, as noted earlier, is a means of eliminating speculation since, when accompanied by no change in the dollar price of the gold, it reduces speculative profits. Speculation shifts the demand curve for U.S. dollars to the left and the supply curve for dollars to the right. Government borrowing of foreign currencies and purchases of dollars, in turn, move the demand back to the right and the supply to the left. These actions by governments and speculators do not correct any underlying problems, however.

Fixed Rates, Controls, and Floating Exchange Rates

Whether an elimination of a balance of payments deficit can be permanent depends on the underlying economic and psychological variables that help to determine the demand for and supply of currency: relative interest rates, relative price levels, relative rates of growth in income, and confidence in the dollar relative to confidence in foreign currencies. Measures that restrict lending and trade are merely temporary accommodations. When such restrictions are removed, the balance of payments deficit will recur unless internal inflation is controlled, interest rates have increased relative to those abroad, or the exchange rate has been changed.

With fixed exchange rates, no automatic force can *continually* adjust for persistent balance of payments deficits or surpluses. Governments are forced to manipulate the position of the demand for and supply of currency schedules in foreign exchange markets. The international goal of all governments often appears to be an end to balance of payments deficits and the achievement of permanent balance of payments surpluses. This is a self-contradictory goal, however, since surpluses must always be matched by deficits. One way to correct chronic deficits and/or surpluses is to provide some form of flexible international exchange rate determination. As shown in Figure 24–3, with exchange rate flexibility, the exchange rate could move down to E_e. This would effectively eliminate the need to artificially manipulate the position of demand and supply schedules to maintain the exchange rate at the arbitrarily fixed rate of E_f. The argument that a country needs fixed exchange rates in order to guard against the destabilizing effects of currency speculation is no longer acceptable. Certainly the recent experience of the United States provides ample evidence of this.

THE PROBLEM OF INTERNATIONAL LIQUIDITY

The term *international liquidity* refers to the distribution and quantity of the gold reserves, SDRs, and foreign exchange holdings of all the countries of the world. Just as in our domestic economy commercial banks need more reserves in order to create additional money for a growing economy, so in the world as a whole more funds, are needed to carry on increased international trade. International liquidity in recent decades has been provided principally through deficits in the U.S. balance of payments. American deficits mean foreign surpluses and hence more international liquidity with which to conduct international trade and financial transactions.

As noted in the preceding discussion continued American deficits are not desirable. In spite of the fact that dollars are used in transactions throughout the world and, accordingly, serve both as international money and reserves, many nations have argued that dollars constitute too large a fraction of their international reserves. Continual deficits in the U.S. balance of payments have caused the dollar to decline as a universally acceptable form of international money. Yet some means of settling international transactions is needed, particularly since world trade, even with American deficits, has expanded more rapidly than the total supply of international reserves. *To many economists this means that there is a shortage of international liquidity.* The shortage would have been even worse without the deficit in the U.S. balance of payments.

There would, of course, be no problem of international liquidity if exchange rates were allowed to fluctuate freely. With flexible exchange rates, the currency of every country could be used to buy goods and services internationally. As noted earlier, however, most countries fear currency speculation and therefore prefer to keep relatively firm control over their currencies in the foreign exchange market. This forces some countries to accumulate extra reserves in order to meet speculative drains, and thereby aggravates any shortage of international liquidity.

How, then, is additional international liquidity to be provided? Gold production annually adds little to international reserves and we have too many dollars abroad. Most proposals concentrate on improving international monetary cooperation, and, of these, we shall touch on three here: (1) strengthening the International Monetary Fund (IMF), (2) increasing the price of gold, and (3) the Triffin plan.

Strengthening the International Monetary Fund

The *International Monetary Fund (IMF)* is an international financial institution designed to help provide international liquidity. The Fund, established after World War II by the principal western powers, seeks to promote free trade, to stabilize exchange rates at equilibrium levels, and to sell foreign currencies to countries experiencing deficits in their balance of payments. There were 124 members of the International Monetary Fund in 1973. Each member nation is assigned a quota of gold and currency that it must contribute to the Fund on request. The quota also indicates how much foreign currency a member nation may buy from the Fund when it experiences a balance of payments deficit.

The Fund acts to assist members when they experience temporary difficulties in their balance of payments. For example, when a country has a balance of payments deficit, it can draw (buy) foreign exchange from the IMF to the extent of its quota. This helps to reduce pressure on the deficit country to lower its exchange rate. The drawing must be repaid to the Fund within five years. Presumably the deficit country will undertake measures in the meantime to correct its balance of payments deficit. It cannot be forced to do so, however, and this weakens the power of the IMF.

Drawing rates are limited by a country's quota. Because of this limitation and the general belief in the shortage of international liquidity, the "Group of Ten" (ten countries: Belgium, Canada, France, West Germany, Italy, Japan, the Netherlands, Sweden, the United Kingdom, and the United States) implemented a program in 1970 to provide for *supplementary international reserves* through the IMF. These supplementary reserves are in the form of SDRs in the Fund and are in proportion to the IMF quota for each member nation. When used, they need be repaid only in part. Countries with deficits draw on both their quotas and their SDRs to acquire the foreign currencies needed. In effect, the measure is a means of expanding a country's international liquidity without requiring the borrower to make an additional contribution of gold to the IMF. This is why SDRs are sometimes called *paper gold.*

SDRs have been a valuable, but insufficient, supplement to the reserve assets of IMF members. The U.S. devaluations of 1972 and 1973 and the floating of many currencies around the dollar have demonstrated that international reserves are still inadequate. The continuing U.S. balance of payments deficit adds too many dollars to international reserves, and other nations and individuals have attempted to get into currencies such as the West German mark and the Japanese yen which are in short supply. The volume of U.S. gold reserves and SDRs is too small in relation to foreign government claims against the dollar for the United States to be willing to convert those claims into gold or SDRs.

Because of insufficient reserves, the United States has proposed that the IMF be strengthened and that SDRs be increased in importance. Additionally we have suggested that the IMF rules be changed so that both chronic deficit and surplus nations are required to correct their imbalances.[4] It remains to be seen just how well the international financial community responds to such proposals.

Revaluation of Gold

Some economists feel that freely fluctuating exchange rates are incompatible with political realities, that such a system needs "political cohesion and mutual acceptance of adjustment responsibility that does not exist in the world today."[5] They also believe that a system of SDRs is no substitute for the reserve growth formerly provided by the dollar. Milton Gilbert, for example, develops the thesis that there is nothing basically wrong with the U.S. balance of payments, that it only appears to be out of balance because of a world gold shortage and the political decision to maintain a comparatively low price of gold. After all, at the time Gilbert was writing (1970), the cost of living in the United States had increased two and one-

[4] See Arthur F. Burns. "Some Essentials of International Monetary Reform." *Monthly Review.* Federal Reserve Bank of New York (June 1972), pp. 131–34.
[5] Milton Gilbert, in Arthur Okun, Henry Fowler, and Milton Gilbert. *Inflation: The Problems It Creates and the Policies It Requires.* (New York University Press, 1970), p. 179.

half times since 1933, while the price of gold had officially remained at $35 an ounce. His solution is to have a worldwide revaluation of gold – that is, raise the price of gold for all countries. In this way, the fraction of gold in a country's international reserves would increase and there would be less pressure to convert foreign holdings of dollars into gold, SDRs, or other reserve currencies.

Gilbert believes that the dollar price of gold should not be frozen by the United States because this action would require a flexibility in the exchange rates of other nations that would be very difficult to manage. The United States has now revalued gold twice by devaluing the dollar, but it still seems committed to fixed exchanges, and other nations, as we have seen, are now allowing their currency to float in relation to the dollar. In the next several years, we shall see if such a system will be as difficult to maintain as Gilbert contends.

There are several problems in connection with a worldwide revaluation of gold. One is political. If freely fluctuating exchange rates are not politically feasible, why should revaluation of gold be any more so? After all, for the system to work, all nations must agree to it. In addition, revaluing gold does not give a nation any greater amount of real gold. Revaluation increases the dollar value of a given amount of gold, not the actual amount. International liquidity is increased by the scheme, but wouldn't many nations consider this an illusion and refuse to revalue?

The Triffin Plan

Many economists feel that the preceding ideas are still inadequate to meet long-run liquidity needs. Various alternative proposals that seem radical, at least to international bankers, have been made. A well-known American economist, Robert Triffin, for example, argued as early as the 1950s that the International Monetary Fund needed to be strengthened so that it would be comparable to a central world bank. The arrangement for SDRs bears some relationship to Triffin's ideas. According to Triffin's plan, all nations would turn over part of their holdings of international currencies to a reorganized Fund in exchange for new reserves – deposits with the Fund. International reserves would then consist only of gold and deposits with the Fund. Reserves would expand as the Fund made loans to member nations and thus enhance the ability of member nations to trade in an expanding world economy. Actually, the reorganized Fund would operate in much the same way that the Federal Reserve System does when it expands Federal Reserve credit which, in turn, expands member bank reserves and thus increases their lending ability. Triffin does not propose an unlimited expansion of international liquidity, of course; he would limit expansion to 3 or 4 percent a year, just enough to cover the need for additional international money as trade expands.

The principal objection to plans of this nature is political: nations would have to comply with IMF international financial policies. It seems most unlikely that countries still accustomed to thinking in terms of "the defense of the national interest" will comply, as a group, to a supranational Fund.

As long as proposals such as the Triffin plan or flexible exchange rates are politically unpalatable, it seems likely that we must continue to limp from one international financial crisis to another.

Supplementary Readings

American Economic Association. "International Liquidity." *American Economic Review, Papers and Proceedings* (May 1968), pp. 586–651.

Kindleberger, Charles P. "Flexible Exchange Rates." In Commission on Money and Credit, *Monetary Management*. Prentice-Hall, 1963.

Krause, Lawrence B. "Fixed, Flexible, and Gliding Exchange Rates." *Journal of Money, Credit and Banking* (May 1971), pp. 339–55.

Kreinin, Mordechai E. *International Economics: A Policy Approach.* Harcourt Brace Jovanovich, Inc., 1971, Chapters 8–9.

Posner, Michael V. "The World Monetary System: A Minimal Reform Program." *Essays in International Finance, No. 96.* Princeton University Press, 1972.

Triffin, Robert. *Gold and the Dollar Crisis.* Yale University Press, 1960.

25 Alternative Fiscal Policies

Fiscal policy posits the same goals as monetary policy: full employment, price stabilization, economic growth, and a balance in the flow of international payments. Fiscal policy is both discretionary and automatic, however, whereas monetary policy today is wholly discretionary. The instruments of fiscal policy are the government expenditure, tax, and debt management practices of Congress and the administration.

Chapter 25 will consider the tax and spending instruments of fiscal policy as they are used to help stabilize the economy. Some mention will also be made of the relationship between fiscal policy and economic growth. Debt management practices, already discussed in Chapter 13, will not be examined here, because debt management and Federal Reserve policy instruments are fairly well coordinated. This is important, of course. Discretionary management of the national debt by the Treasury can have a powerful influence on commercial bank reserve positions, necessitating coordination between Federal Reserve and treasury policies with regard to debt management.

FISCAL POLICY AND ECONOMIC STABILITY

Fiscal Policy in Recession

Variation in government expenditures is one way in which fiscal policy can be used to cure a recession. Let us assume that there is an increase in government expenditures. Let us further assume that federal tax collections are constant and that there has been a balanced budget prior to the present situation. Under circumstances such as these, increased government expenditures will directly raise the level of spending in the economy. To the extent that consumption and investment expenditure increases are induced by a rise in income resulting from new government spending, the total rise in the level of income will be some multiple of the government expenditure increase. If the increase in government spending is not accompanied by an increase in the stock of money, however, there will be some rise in interest rates and some dampening of the potential rise in income and output. Interest rates increase because increased spending means an increased demand for money relative to the supply. In our income expenditure model in Chapter 21, this assumes that the *IS* schedule intersects the rising portion of the *LM* schedule.

If the recession were severe, it would probably be best to finance the additional government expenditures by increasing the money stock. This would shift both *IS* and *LM* to the right, with monetary forces reinforcing the increase in government expenditures.

On the other hand, in a mild recession, when unemployment is not particularly high, there is a danger that an increase in government spending may result in price inflation. A shifted *IS* may intersect *LM* to the right of full employment output. For this reason, money stock increases should not be permitted to reinforce government spending increases during mild recessions. A decision to correct a minor downward cyclical disturbance by increasing government expenditures can be self-defeating unless financed through the least inflationary channel — borrowing from the nonbank public. Full employment and stable prices are not necessarily compatible goals.

Fiscal policy can also combat a recession by *decreasing government tax collections*. In an economy with a balanced budget, a decrease in government personal-tax collections will lead to an increase in disposable income, and in consumption spending. If business taxes are also lowered, the resultant increase in business saving should stimulate business investment expenditures. These additional consumption and investment expenditures will lead to a rise in income and output that is a multiple of the decrease in government tax collections. Thus decreased tax collections, like increased government expenditures, can lead to increased income and output.

Decreased government tax collections may also have money market effects. The way a deficit (whether expenditure- or tax-induced) is financed will lead to changes in the stock of money if securities are sold to either the central bank or commercial banks.

There is at least one important *difference between decreased tax collections and increased government spending* as tools for promoting economic recovery. Increased government expenditures directly cause increased spending, whereas tax decreases indirectly cause increased spending. Assume, for example, that the marginal propensity to consume is 0.80. A $1 billion increase in government spending directly increases gross national product by that amount. Subsequently, the marginal propensity to consume comes into play, and, barring money market effects, there will be $800 million, $640 million, etc., increases in the level of income. A decrease of $1 billion in government tax collections, however, will not directly affect spending in this manner. Instead, disposable income is increased by the amount of the tax decrease — $1 billion. This then induces $800 million, $640 million, etc., increases in the level of income. The difference in the effects of these two policies is in the initial effect of the $1 billion of government spending increase on the gross national product. A billion-dollar rise in spending has a greater overall effect on the economy than a billion-dollar decrease in tax collections. Thus *government spending changes are more potent than tax changes as a contracyclical policy instrument.* Government spending increases are also more likely to cause price inflation than tax decreases of comparable dollar amounts. As a curative for a mild recession, therefore, a decrease in taxes seems preferable to an increase in government spending.

The Revenue Act of 1964 and the Excise Tax Reduction Act of 1965 are examples of tax decreases that occurred during periods of continuing economic expansion. This is not to say that these actions were entirely inappropriate, since the unemployment rate in 1964 was still in excess of 5 percent while in 1965 it averaged $4\frac{1}{2}$ percent. The Revenue Act of 1964 provided for a permanent cut in income tax rates for all individual and corporate taxpayers. The maximum marginal personal income tax rate was cut from 91 to 70 percent, and the tax rate for most corporations fell from 52 to 48 percent. The Excise Tax Reduction Act of 1965 repealed federal excise taxes on various appliances, radios, television sets, jewelry, furs, and luggage, and reduced rates on automobiles and telephone services. The 1964 action was somewhat belated, since there had been discussions in the Kennedy administration concerning possible tax decreases in early 1961. Nevertheless, it is generally felt that the Revenue Act of 1964 did help to maintain economic expansion with relatively little price change. The Excise Tax Reduction Act of 1965, however, did not become effective until July 1965, and it coincided with an increase in Vietnam war expenditures. Although unemployment was still in excess of 4 percent at that time, the excise tax reduction, overall, does not seem to have been appropriate.

Additional decreases in tax rates occurred in 1971 — a year of gradual expansion but high unemployment (5.9 percent). The Nixon administration recommended and Congress passed a 7 percent investment credit designed to improve the profit positions of U.S. businesses, stimulate investment, and thereby reduce unemployment. A comparable action was the repeal of the 7 percent excise tax on automobiles. Income tax personal exemptions were increased at the same time.

Fiscal Policy for Inflation

During periods of full employment and rising prices, fiscal policy may be reversed to offset inflation. *Government expenditures may be reduced or government tax collections increased.* If either occurs, then, at a given level of income planned $I + G + F$ becomes less than planned $S_p + S_b + T$ and the *IS* line shifts to the left. This will lead to a reduction of income and output amounting to some multiple of the reduction in government spending or the increase in tax collections. If the decrease in government spending or the rise in tax collections occurs without any change in the money supply, interest rates will also decline (unless, of course, price rises continue through the period of income decline).

Decreases in government spending directly reduce income and thereby induce consumption and investment expenditure decreases. Raising taxes also reduces disposable income, thereby inducing consumption and investment expenditure decreases. A government spending decrease exerts a more powerful downward influence on income, however, than a comparable dollar increase in tax collections.

The degree of inflation present in the economy should dictate which anti-inflationary fiscal measure is appropriate. For a runaway inflation, a reduction in government spending might be more desirable because of its swifter and greater impact. On the other hand, for a mild inflation, the less depressive effects of a tax increase might be preferable. In either case, aggregate demand should not be allowed to fall so sharply that it causes less than full employment equilibrium.

Anti-inflationary fiscal measures can also have an important effect on the money supply. A drop in government spending or an increase in taxes may lead to a treasury surplus, for example. If these funds are held idle or are used to retire government securities held by the central bank, the money supply is decreased. This, in turn, sets up forces that keep interest rates high (*LM* shifts to the left), reinforcing the effects of the increasing government surplus on income. (Chapter 13 treated the mechanics of tax surpluses in some detail.)

In the 1960s there were two tax increases designed to offset inflationary pressures during periods of full employment. The Tax Adjustment Act of 1966 restored excise tax rates on automobiles and telephone services to the pre-1965 level. This action was taken rather quickly by Congress. In June 1968, Congress then passed a temporary 10 percent surcharge on individual and corporate income taxes. Economists had discussed the need for an income tax rate increase as early as 1966, but President Johnson did not recommend the surcharges until January 1967 and Congress was obviously very slow in responding to this recommendation.

The 1968 surcharge on individual and corporate income taxes provides one example, however, of the coordination between fiscal and monetary action. Following the enactment of the surcharge in June 1968, the Federal Reserve moved to a policy of monetary ease. It is evident the Fed believed the tax rate increase would significantly reduce demand in the economy and thereby give rise to a less than full employment situation. One infers that the Federal Reserve considered the tax increase too large, and, to offset possible unemployment in the economy, returned to a policy of monetary ease in the summer of 1968. In the recession of 1970, the surcharge was allowed to lapse.

Effects of Changes in Tax Rates

The relationship between discretionary spending policy and a stabilizing tax structure. In the preceding analysis, government tax changes were accomplished without reference to the tax structure of the nation. Our approach assumed that the government could deliberately vary the *amount* of its tax collections to help stabilize the economy. No mention was made as to *how* the tax collections would be varied, however. In point of fact, the *amount* of tax collections, as indicated in earlier chapters, varies automatically with the level of income. As gross national product increases, the amount of government tax collections increases; as gross national product decreases, tax collections decrease.

Assume, for example, that there is a proportional income tax of 20 percent. For simplicity, imagine this tax rate to be geared to gross national product. Under these circumstances, for every $1 billion change in gross national product, there will be a $200 million change in tax collections. Thus *the nature of the tax structure itself tends to dampen whatever phase of the cycle is current.* For this reason, our federal tax system is frequently called an *automatic stabilizer.* Changes in government tax collections occur automatically, without the need for discretionary action by Congress or the president.

The income expenditure model developed in Chapters 18–21 assumed a tax structure that was geared to the level of income. Under this model, the federal actions affecting equilibrium income are changes in government spending and changes in the tax rate. The *IS* line does not necessarily shift with changes in the amount of tax collections, as was assumed earlier in this chapter. Only when the amount of tax collections changes as a result of changes in the tax rate will the *IS* curve shift.

How much of a change in government expenditures is needed to change aggregate economic activity by a given amount when tax collections are not fixed but are geared to the level of income? More than is needed when tax collections are fixed! Assume, for example, that the government wants to increase disposable income directly by $1 billion. Ignoring the effects on business income and the induced effects on consumption and investment, we find that only a $1 billion increase in spending is needed. If taxes are stated in fixed amounts, a $1 billion increase in government spending will induce an equivalent increase in disposable income throughout the economy. If taxes are stated in proportion to personal income, however, at a uniform rate of 20 percent, then a $1 billion increase in government spending will cause disposable income to rise by only $800 million and $200 million will come back to the government in the form of taxes. Thus, with a proportional personal income tax, government spending will have to be increased by $1.25 billion in order to produce a $1 billion increase in disposable income. Similarly, in reverse, a reduction of $1.25 billion in government spending is needed to cause a $1 billion decrease in disposable income.[1]

A change in the tax rate. What happens when tax rates are changed? In terms of the analysis in Chapter 19, an increase in the tax rate will move

---

[1] If $\Delta Y_d = \Delta G - 0.2\Delta G$, then $\Delta G = \Delta Y_d/0.8$ and $\Delta G = \$1$ billion$/0.8 = \$1.25$ billion.

Figure 25–1. Effects of a change in the tax rate.

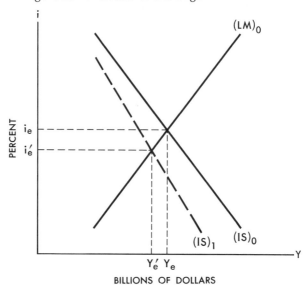

the $S_p + S_b + T$ line up and to the left, leading to a movement of the IS line down and to the left. This shift is from $(IS)_0$ to $(IS)_1$ in Figure 25–1. Notice that the IS lines intersect the upward sloping part of LM. Thus, assuming that there has been no change in the stock of money resulting from a tax surplus, an increase in the tax rate decreases disposable income and this, in turn, induces reductions in consumption and investment expenditures. Equilibrium income is reduced from Y_e to Y'_e in Figure 25–1, with a drop in the interest rate from i_e to i'_e. If full employment and rising prices existed prior to the tax rate change, the increase in the tax rate will reverse the increase in prices, halting the shifts to the left in LM that were probably taking place. If this tax increase is timed properly, the resultant equilibrium income Y'_e should also provide full employment income and output.

Lowering the tax rate should have the reverse effects. If no money stock changes result from a deficit, and if Y_e is full employment output and the initial IS line is $(IS)_1$, then a decrease in the tax rate will push the line from $(IS)_1$ to $(IS)_0$. This leads to increased disposable income and induces increases in consumption and investment spending. Equilibrium moves up from Y'_e to Y_e and the rate of interest rises from i'_e to i_e.

Like government spending changes, tax rate changes must be carefully planned because many offsets are possible. For example, a tax cut designed to stabilize the economy could lead people to believe that the government anticipated a severe recession. As a result, expectations for the economic future would worsen. In anticipation of declining incomes, personal saving would increase and business investment plans would be postponed or scaled down. Clearly, these events could more than offset the desirable effects of a tax cut. On the other hand, a tax cut or increased government spending may lead people to believe that the government is willing to do almost anything to offset a possible recession. They may assume that severe recession is impossible, that the government will take care of everything. In this case, spending plans, instead of being revised downward, would be revised upward. In the aggregate, this increase in demand might overshoot the point of full employment and cause price inflation.

Another reason for careful government planning of contracyclical fiscal policy is that it can have a serious impact on the money market. As previously noted, the stock of money can fluctuate with surpluses and deficits. Therefore, debt management should attempt to complement tax and spending changes.

FISCAL POLICY AND ECONOMIC GROWTH

Poorly planned fiscal policy can also inhibit economic growth. During periods of inflation, for example, appropriate contracyclical fiscal policy calls for an increase in tax rates. If the tax increase is imposed on businesses, the expected after-tax rate of return from investment projects is thereby reduced. In the absence of offsetting reductions in the cost of funds (interest rate), investment expenditures will decline. A decrease in investment expenditures may lead to real plant and equipment production decreases as well. Thus economic growth is retarded, for to raise the productive capacity of the economy, there must be an expansion of real investment, technological change, and an improved work force.

With this in mind, some have argued that during inflation and full employment the appropriate contracyclical fiscal policy would be to increase consumer taxes rather than to raise business taxes. This, it is suggested, would restrain consumption demand and possibly cause a redistribution of output from consumer to producer goods, helping to stem inflation and increasing the productive capacity of the economy simultaneously. A complementary monetary policy would be to keep interest rates high for consumers by means of selective credit controls and to maintain low interest rates on long-term credit to encourage business expansion.

During a recession, on the other hand, there is normally no conflict between stabilization and growth policies. Increased government expenditures and decreased tax rates promote expansion in both demand and growth.

Fiscal action was taken several times in the 1960s and 1970s to stimulate economic growth. In October 1962, Congress passed an Investment Tax Credit Bill which provided an incentive for new investment in depreciable equipment. This measure was temporarily repealed in the full employment years at the height of the Vietnam conflict. New investment tax credits were extended by Congress in 1971, as previously mentioned. In July 1962, the Treasury established new depreciation guidelines. This permitted businesses to write off the cost of new plant and equipment over a shorter period of time. Since depreciation expenses are regarded as a cost of production for tax purposes, the shortened depreciation period increased recorded production costs and thereby reduced business taxes. This made a greater volume of funds available to business enterprises for investment in new plant and equipment. Similar action was taken by the Nixon administration in 1971.

FISCAL POLICY AND THE BALANCE OF PAYMENTS

As we noted in Chapter 24, government expenditure and tax policies can influence the balance of payments. For example, government lending and spending abroad by the United States contributes to the supply of American dollars in the foreign exchange market. On the other hand, the interest equalization tax, lending guidelines, surcharges on imports, and tourist import limitations represent attempts to restrict the flow of dollars out of the United States.

In addition, the contracyclical timing of government spending and taxing may also influence the balance of payments. For example, a period of less than full employment calls for increased government spending and/or a decrease in government tax collections. This action will stimulate demand in the economy: *IS* schedules will shift to the right. Unfortunately, expanded demand means an increase in the demand for foreign as well as domestic goods and services. Hence, it is possible for the supply of a country's currency in foreign exchange markets to expand relative to the demand.

This expansion in the supply of currency is somewhat offset by the fact that expanding the demand for goods and services increases the amount of money demanded for transactions purposes. Interest rates therefore increase; that is, so long as the new *IS* schedule intersects a rising *LM* schedule, interest rates will rise. This can be seen in Figure 25–1 if we consider $(IS)_1$ as the original *IS*, and $(IS)_0$ as the new *IS* line. Here the interest rate rises from i'_e to i_e and helps to reduce a balance of payments deficit. But if the rise in domestic interest rates is not sufficient to eliminate the balance of payments deficit, restrictive monetary action may be necessary. This would shift the *LM* curve to the left, but hopefully not enough to choke off the beneficial effects on employment that are expected to stem from the expansive fiscal policy. We therefore see that *a fiscal policy designed to increase income and employment may contribute to a balance of payments deficit if the increase in the supply of currency described in the preceding paragraph is greater than the beneficial effects of the rise in interest rates.*

On the other hand (ignoring interest rate effects), *the fiscal policy of raising taxes and/or reducing government spending to fight inflationary pressures during a period of full employment is consistent with a policy of reducing a balance of payments deficit.* However, if the restrictive policy is

implemented in a nation experiencing continual balance of payments surpluses, then that country's restrictive fiscal policy (again ignoring interest
rate effects) is inconsistent with what its international economic policy
should be – a reduction in a continuing balance of payments surplus.

PROBLEMS OF DISCRETIONARY FISCAL POLICY

Our analysis points toward discretionary decreases in government
spending and increases in tax rates during periods of full employment and
rising prices and the reverse of these policies during recession. These policies are not easy to implement, however. Many of the problems that plague
monetary policy in this regard also affect fiscal policy. We have already
pointed out the dangers of overshooting the full employment mark when
carrying out anti-recessionary fiscal policy. There are also problems of
allocation and lag.

The Allocation Problem

When the federal government spends funds, it can alter the structure of
national production by creating a demand for specific goods and services;
businesses then respond by producing those goods and services. On the
other hand, tax measures affect the disposable income of consumers and
businesses; a change in disposable income leads to changes in investment
and consumption demands for specific goods and services. In this way, tax
and spending policies are comparable in their impact on production. There
is one difference, however: tax measures permit the private sector of the
economy to determine what goods are produced. If one values an economy
in which free choice determines the allocation of resources, then a contracyclical tax policy is to be preferred to a contracyclical spending policy.
Of course, the government must undertake those projects that have been
approved by a social consensus (e.g., defense, public education, highways,
social security). The doctrine of individual choice simply suggests that
there should be a minimum of interference with the allocation of resources
chosen by the free market for privately-produced goods *and* by social consensus for social goods.

The Lag Problem

The problem of lags can also affect fiscal policy. There are three main
lags in economic policy: (1) the lag between the time when economic action
becomes necessary and the time this need is recognized, (2) the lag
between the recognition of the need and the remedial action, and (3) the lag
between the action and the time when the effects of the action are felt in
the economy.

The first lag is as long for discretionary monetary policy as it is for fiscal policy. However, the second lag is much longer for fiscal policy than for monetary policy. Monetary action can be taken quickly by the Board of Governors, but discretionary fiscal action usually involves an act of Congress, and the legislative wheels grind slowly. As we noted earlier, a personal income tax increase was proposed in January 1967 but not passed until July 1968.

In some matters, discretionary response to need can be swift. The administration, so long as it operates within the confines of the budget passed by Congress, can increase or decrease the rate of government expenditures simply by issuing an order. Several presidents have impounded congressional appropriations. Most recently, in 1972, President Nixon stated that he would impound 45 percent of the money authorized for building sewage treatment plants in order to reduce inflationary pressures on construction costs. But this action, along with others, led congressional critics of the president to argue that he was subverting the Constitution.

The third lag—the lag between the action and the time when the effects of the action are felt in the economy—lasts either six to nine months or 12–16 months for monetary policy. In tax matters, the lag is considerably shorter. The effects of tax action are usually felt within the first six months.[2] Changes in government expenditures, however (public works and defense projects, for example) take time to plan. If expenditures are already planned, contracts introduce a delay. "The steps in appropriation, allocation of funds, bidding, contract award, and construction are of such length that only a small fraction of construction can be expected within a year from the initiation of a program."[3] Changes in the rate of defense spending "take a considerable period before they register themselves in output. . . . Aircraft contracts, for example, change output by only 20 percent of the contract by the end of six months, 55 percent by the end of three quarters, and are nearly fully reflected in output change by the end of a year."[4]

The length of these government spending lags suggests that changes in government spending are not really a suitable means of economic stabilization, at least for mild recessions and short-lived inflations. For such problems, discretionary taxes or monetary policy actions appear to be more appropriate. However, as we noted above, the lag between recognition of the need and the action is usually very long for tax measures. In addition, while tax cuts are always politically palatable, peacetime tax increases are almost impossible to pass through Congress. This means that, in practice, tax changes can seldom be used to correct peacetime inflation.

[2] Albert Ando, E. Cary Brown, Robert M. Solow, and John Kareken. "Lags in Fiscal and Monetary Policy." In Commission on Money and Credit. *Stabilization Policies*. (Prentice-Hall, 1963), p. 2.
[3] *Ibid.*, p. 11.
[4] *Ibid.*

FISCAL POLICY AS AN AUTOMATIC STABILIZER

Automatic fiscal action is at least a partial solution to the lag dilemma; it helps to stabilize the economy without direct action by government authorities, thus eliminating the first two lags, and the third lag is of comparatively short duration. In this regard, automatic fiscal policy appears to be superior to both discretionary fiscal and discretionary monetary policy. There is no automatic monetary policy.

There are two principal automatic fiscal stabilizers at work in the U.S. economy: (1) the federal income tax system, and (2) the social security program.

The Federal Income Tax System

We have already mentioned that as incomes increase, government tax collections rise, thereby restricting the growth of disposable personal and business income. Actually, our personal income tax is progressively scaled: as incomes rise, the tax collections increase more than proportionately to the growth in income. Thus, disposable income becomes an increasingly smaller percentage of gross national product as GNP rises. This helps restrain inflationary forces in the economy. On the other hand, as incomes fall, government tax collections decrease more than proportionately to the decline in income, people move into lower tax brackets, and disposable income becomes a greater fraction of GNP. This helps reduce the severity of an economic downturn.

The Social Security Program

Our second automatic fiscal stabilizer is the social security program. As income and employment drop, employee contributions to social security decline and increasing amounts of unemployment compensation are paid to the unemployed. This tends to maintain disposable income and thereby lessens the impact of recession. As economic recovery gets under way, unemployment drops, unemployment compensation decreases, and social security tax collections increase. This, in turn, helps to prevent a recovery from becoming a boom.

Automatic Stabilizers and Less than Full Employment Equilibrium

To the extent that automatic stabilizers dampen upward and downward movements in the economy, they seem to be an effective means of combating both inflation and deflation. However, there is also a possibility that automatic stabilizers may dampen recovery. Gross national product and full employment output expand over time. With a progressive income tax structure, people move into higher income tax brackets as GNP increases. Thus, the average income tax rate increases. This means that at higher levels of income and output more of an effort is needed to keep the economy at full employment output. For example, a $1 billion increase in government expenditures directly increases disposable income by $1 billion when taxes are unchanged, by $800 million when the average income tax rate is 20 percent, and by only $700 million when the average income tax rate drifts up with economic growth to 30 percent. Thus, larger injections of government spending are needed to keep the economy at full employment as the average tax rate climbs.

It is possible that occasional downward revisions of the tax rate structure might solve this problem. This was one of the arguments behind the 1964 tax reduction. There is one drawback, however. *Lowering the tax rate structure makes the economy more subject to volatile upward and downward movements in economic activity.* Government control of the economy is weakened. As consumption and investment expenditures increase because of a favorable business outlook, the accompanying increase in government tax collections at the new lower tax rate may not be enough to thwart inflation. Similarly, in a recession, the accompanying decrease in government tax collections will be less than the decrease under higher tax rates; thus, a lower tax rate structure may not be sufficient to cushion decreases in disposable income either.

SUMMARY AND EVALUATION OF FISCAL POLICY

Discretionary fiscal policy is subject to long lags arising from the slowness inherent in the legislative and administrative decision-making processes. Discretionary monetary policy works much faster in this respect. Once tax changes have been made, however, discretionary tax policy operates more rapidly than monetary policy. Automatic fiscal policy can be very helpful in stabilizing the economy, but possibly at the expense of high employment levels; periodic downward adjustments in tax rates may be the solution to this.

Conclusions concerning the potential effectiveness of fiscal policy are mixed. In a deep depression, there is no policy problem; the obvious course is to raise government expenditures and cut taxes. In a runaway inflation, the need to lower government expenditures and increase taxes is equally obvious. Of course, if a wise economic policy were followed in the first place, we would never have deep depressions or runaway inflations. Policy problems arise when mild inflations or recessions occur, however. Particular care must be taken, for example, in the discretionary use of both monetary and fiscal policy measures when the economy is close to the full employment. Because of lags, there is a danger of aggravating ensuing phases of economic fluctuations.

In practice, there has been little use of discretionary fiscal policy by Congress since the end of World War II. Congress and the president have seldom deliberately changed government expenditures for purposes of economic stabilization. Government expenditure changes are usually prompted by changing national defense commitments and pressing community needs. Tax cuts have not usually been considered anti-recessionary legislation either. There have been three principal tax cuts in the last two decades. The tax cuts of 1949 and 1954 were fortunately executed in the midst of recessions, but were not planned as a means of pulling the economy out of a slump. The 1964 tax cut, however, was officially justified as a means of increasing spending and reducing unemployment during the then current economic expansion. The 1968 tax increase was clearly planned as a means of reducing the rate of increase in spending and stemming inflationary pressures in the economy. This was designed to be a temporary tax surcharge during the Vietnam war, and, by 1970, Congress had already removed it.

Supplementary Readings

Ando, Albert, E. Cary Brown, Robert M. Solow, and John Kareken. "Lags in Fiscal and Monetary Policy." In Commission on Money and Credit. *Stabilization Policies*. Prentice-Hall, 1963, pp. 1–163.

"Federal Fiscal Policy in the 1960s." *Federal Reserve Bulletin* (September 1968), pp. 701–18.

"Federal Fiscal Policy, 1965–72." *Federal Reserve Bulletin* (June 1973), pp. 383–402.

26 Alternative Monetary Theories and Policies

INTRODUCTION

ECONOMIC GOALS AND FEDERAL RESERVE POLICY

Monetary Controls in Recession
Monetary Controls in Inflation

**THE EXTREME KEYNESIAN POSITION
ON MONEY AND POLICY**

**THE CONTEMPORARY QUANTITY THEORY POSITION
ON MONEY AND POLICY**

The Quantity Theory and Its Differences from the Keynesian Position
Automatic Monetary Policy Proposals of the Quantity Theorists
    Discretionary monetary policy and political philosophy
    Rules and economic empiricism
    100 percent reserve banking
    The rule of stabilization of the price level
    Stable money growth rules
    Economists' reactions to the variable lag

**THE NEO-KEYNESIAN POSITION
ON MONEY AND POLICY**

A Moderate Keynesian Approach to Theory and Policy
The Neo-Keynesian Portfolio Approach to Money,
    Money Substitutes, and Policy
    The theoretical position
    The policy position
    The empirical problem
Money and Optimum Portfolios
    The transactions demand for money and interest rates
    The speculative demand for money, risk,
        and interest rates

MONEY AND THE ECONOMY

INTRODUCTION

Monetary policy in the United States is administered and executed by the Federal Reserve System. As you will recall, the capstone to the decision to set up a system of central banking in the United States was the financial panic of 1907. This demonstrated conclusively the inherent defects of the national banking system: the lack of an elastic currency system, the pyramiding of reserves, the inadequate check-clearing facilities, and the overly rigid reserve requirements. The Federal Reserve System had as its original purpose the rectification of these shortcomings. By correcting the inadequacies of the national banking system, it was thought that financial panic could be eliminated forever.

The depression of the 1930s proved otherwise, of course. As a result, various additional monetary reforms were instituted: Federal Deposit Insurance was inaugurated; the Federal Reserve Board was given the power to change reserve requirements; open market operations became recognized as an important tool of contracyclical economic policy; and currency was no longer redeemable in gold. Because of these reforms in the 1930s and because of the present character of the Federal Reserve System, many economists today believe that the economy is depression-proof. Others, however, point to nonbank financial institutions as potential sources of economic difficulty. The dangers of discretionary policies have also been compared with automatic policies. Debates on how to improve policy, the financial system, and the economy in general are countless These debates take place in Congress, within the administration, in academic circles, among the lay public, and within the Federal Reserve System itself.

Debates on policy, insofar as they occur among economists, exist because of conflicting monetary theories. It is true that for most economists, today monetary theory is part of the theory of income determination and that a common basic framework of analysis exists (see Chapters 18–21). Yet differences persist, principally because economists have varying value systems and make conflicting interpretations of economic data.

This chapter will explore some of the differing contemporary views on the importance of money in the economy, placing particular emphasis on the policy implications of each theoretical position. We shall examine various economic proposals concerned with changing the goals and strategy of monetary policy. Three different views on the role of money will be examined: the Keynesian position, the contemporary quantity theory view (sometimes called the monetarist model), and the portfolio or neo-Keynesian position (sometimes called the fiscalist model).[1] Our discussion will begin with a very general statement on the relationship between economic goals and Federal Reserve policy—an apparently uncluttered enunciation of policy. Then we shall consider the alternative theories and policies of differing economists and see just why it is so difficult to make viable and clear-cut statements about the appropriate strategies of economic policy.

ECONOMIC GOALS AND FEDERAL RESERVE POLICY

Present monetary policy, as administered by the Federal Reserve System, recognizes four main goals: (1) full employment, (2) stable prices, (3) economic growth, and (4) a balance in the flow of payments to and from foreign countries. To accomplish these ends, the Fed relies principally on general monetary control techniques.

Monetary Controls in Recession

The logic of the control techniques is quite simple, as we pointed out in Chapters 11 and 12. To eliminate unemployment and the accompanying sluggishness in economic growth, the Federal Reserve is empowered to lower discount rates, reduce reserve requirements, and purchase U.S. government securities. The use of some combination of these policies should result in an increase in the stock of money. In terms of our income expenditure model and Figure 26–1, the LM schedule shifts to the right from $(LM)_0$ to $(LM)_1$ with an increase in the stock of money. Theoretically, interest rates then decline and consumption and investment expenditures rise. Income and output increase from Y_1 to Y_f in the figure. Economic growth is restored through rising investment expenditures; the productive capacity of the economy expands. Unemployment drops as businesses respond to increased demands for goods and services, and recession ends.

Although this appears to be a perfectly logical chain of analysis, it contains several hidden assumptions. If these policies are to work in the prescribed manner, the IS schedule must be sufficiently responsive to interest rate changes to intersect an LM schedule somewhere close to full employment output Y_f. If the economy is deeply depressed, however, these

---

[1] The views presented here as representative of the various groups of monetary theorists are the views of the majority of the members of each group, not the entire group. Thus, the Keynesian position presented here is articulated in the works of Alvin Hansen. Similarly, Milton Friedman has been selected as the spokesman for contemporary quantity theorists, whereas some 25 years ago Lloyd Mints would have been considered the leading exponent of this position. The "portfolio" neo-Keynesians are represented by James Tobin.

Figure 26–1. Shifts in the *IS* and *LM* curves caused by monetary and fiscal policy changes.

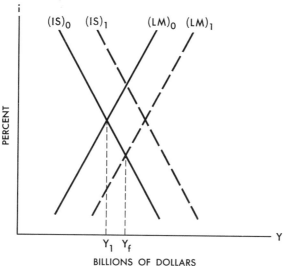

BILLIONS OF DOLLARS

conditions are not likely to be met. As a result, many economists recommend stronger fiscal policy measures that will directly increase spending and thereby shift the *IS* schedule to the right from $(IS)_0$ to $(IS)_1$. This type of control does not rely on indirect influences on consumption and investment spending via interest rate changes.

Will the suggested monetary techniques for correcting slow growth and recession also promote the other two goals of monetary policy: stable prices and a balanced flow of payments on the international market? To the extent that spending is generated by these money stock increases and directed toward the goods and services produced by depressed industries, little price-level change is to be expected. However, should spending increases occur in industries that are already operating close to capacity, then the increase in the money stock will result in some price inflation and, as a result, the real stock of money will decline. Thus, the shift to the right in the *LM* schedule resulting from money stock increases will be offset by a shift to the left in the *LM* schedule due to the price-level increase. Interest rate increases may also occur. Thus, an easy money policy may not be compatible with both price stability and the elimination of unemployment.

Balance in the flow of payments may also be adversely affected by these monetary techniques. A decrease in interest rates, by expanding the supply of currency relative to the demand for it in foreign exchange markets, tends to increase any existent balance of payments deficit. For this reason, it might be advisable to use fiscal measures to increase spending directly and simultaneously to use restrictive monetary measures to keep interest rates relatively high.

Monetary Controls in Inflation

The logic of inflation control techniques is also rather straightforward: sell U.S. government securities, raise discount rates, increase reserve requirements, and the result should be a decrease in the stock of money. This would shift the *LM* schedule to the left. Inflation usually occurs during periods of high employment, and investment and consumption expenditures, other things being equal, are somewhat likely to be interest-responsive in such periods. As a result, the shift in *LM* should induce interest rate increases and investment and consumption expenditure decreases. The fall in the demand for goods and services, relative to a stable rate of output, should then help stop the increase in prices.

The assumption "other things being equal," however, tends to conceal offsetting forces. Expectations for continued growth in income and prices, for example, may lead to continual increases in demand (shifts to the right in the *IS* schedule). As a result, the Federal Reserve might have to resort to repeated use of its control techniques. Should not fiscal techniques be used to reduce the rising demand for goods and services directly? A reduction in government expenditures or a rise in taxes would shift the *IS* line back to the left and possibly eliminate price inflation as well.

The use of monetary techniques to stem inflation calls for considerable care. If monetary restrictions are too severe, the result can be a deficiency of demand relative to the productive capacity of the economy. In terms of our income expenditure model, if *LM* is shifted to intersect with *IS* at some point to the left of full employment output, less than full employment equilibrium may result. Thus, anti-inflationary techniques are not always compatible with the full employment goal of economic policy.

If a monetary policy is too restrictive, it may also discourage needed investment expenditure in new plant and equipment. By decreasing this investment, a restrictive monetary policy can also impede economic growth.

How effective are these policy techniques in controlling inflation if the source of inflation is an increase in costs rather than an increase in the demand for goods and services? Assume, for example, that unions have been successful in securing wage increases. Firms will pass some of the increased costs on to consumers in the form of higher prices. This is a factor that may lead to recession. Higher prices mean reduced real purchasing power of money balances (*LM* shifts to the left) and induced rises in interest rates. Consumption and investment expenditures may decline as a result, and these reduced expenditures will mean less employment and output. Clearly, under such circumstances a restrictive monetary policy would be disastrous. Reductions in the money stock would shift the *LM* schedule further to the left. Thus, it is extremely important for the Federal Reserve to determine carefully whether the inflation is caused by demand or cost increases.

An anti-inflationary monetary policy will help to eliminate an unfavorable balance of payments. As previously noted, a restrictive monetary policy will raise interest rates and thereby tend to reduce a balance of payments deficit. It should be recognized that a restrictive monetary policy is inappropriate for a country with a balance of payments surplus, however. A rise in interest rates simply tends to widen an existing favorable balance of payments. This is an acceptable situation only when the surplus in the balance of payments is merely a temporary phenomenon. A surplus country, like a deficit country, needs to take measures to restore equilibrium in its balance of payments.

THE EXTREME KEYNESIAN POSITION ON MONEY AND POLICY

We shall begin our discussion of conflicting views on economic theory and policy with a discussion of the extreme Keynesians and then move to a consideration of the contemporary quantity theorists. Subsequently, we shall return to a consideration of the Keynesian position as it relates to the neo-Keynesian portfolio theorists. The discussion will be presented in roughly the chronological order of the development of the theory.

The extreme Keynesian position is that output is determined by consumption, investment, and government demand for goods and services. Consumption is seen as a function of income, and investment as a function of the rate of interest and the marginal efficiency of investment. In periods of less than full employment, investment demand is relatively interest-inelastic; government demand is autonomous (that is, it is determined primarily on noneconomic grounds); the rate of interest is determined by monetary supply and demand forces; the supply of money is autonomous, being determined by the monetary authorities; and the demand for money is a function of income and the rate of interest, becoming perfectly elastic at some low rate of interest. Since consumption is determined by the level of income and output and since the investment schedule is relatively interest-inelastic, it follows that the economy will not be significantly affected by money stock changes, at least during periods of less than full employment.[2] Consequently, many Keynesians feel that fiscal policy should be the principal means of influencing total demand and total output in the economy.

There are three important differences between the Keynesian position described above and the model presented in Chapters 19 and 20: many Keynesians (1) do not agree that interest rate changes are a major source of consumption and saving change, (2) do not believe that investment is responsive to the interest rate, at least during periods of less than full employment, and (3) believe that at low rates of interest there may be a liquidity trap. These disagreements result in *IS* and *LM* schedules different from those presented thus far. The Keynesian *IS* line is vertical, or perfectly

[2] For a concise statement of this position, see Alvin H. Hansen. *Monetary Theory and Fiscal Policy* (McGraw-Hill, 1949), Chapters 4 and 5.

Figure 26–2. The Keynesian *IS* and *LM* curves.

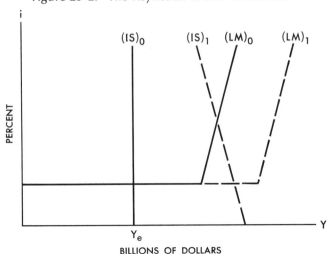

inelastic, showing that savings and investment do not respond at all to interest rate changes. The Keynesian *LM* line becomes perfectly horizontal at some low rate of interest, showing that all the money stock is demanded. *This position may be described as the extreme Keynesian model of* IS *and* LM. It is illustrated graphically by the solid *LM* and *IS* lines in Figure 26–2.

Two important policy implications may be drawn from this Keynesian position. First, if the *IS* schedule is interest-inelastic, then money stock changes are unimportant. There is only one possible level of equilibrium income, which is dictated by the position of the *IS* schedule. In Figure 26–2, for example, that income level is at Y_e. Second, fiscal policy—changes in government spending and taxation—becomes important. An increase in government spending, for example, will shift the *IS* line to the right by a multiple of the change in government expenditures. The change in income and output will be determined by the shift in the *IS* line.

THE CONTEMPORARY QUANTITY THEORY POSITION ON MONEY AND POLICY

The Quantity Theory and Its Differences from the Keynesian Position

Contemporary quantity theorists, unlike their neoclassical predecessors, no longer focus on the relationship between money and prices in their analysis and they no longer assume that full employment is the normal state of the economy. Instead, quantity theorists today stress the relation between money and income. In this respect, their views are comparable to those of

Keynesian economists. In many other respects, however, their views differ, and it is these differences that make the money supply, on the whole, a more important variable for the quantity theorist than it is for his Keynesian counterpart.

Many economists today hold the central thesis of the quantity theory to be:

in the first instance a theory of the *demand* for money. It is not a theory of output, or of money income, or of the price level. Any statement about these variables requires combining the quantity theory with some specifications about the conditions of supply of money and perhaps about other variables as well.[3]

In some ways, this definition is not completely in the quantity theory tradition. Early quantity theorists frequently discussed the relationship between money and prices; more recent quantity theorists like Lloyd Mints related money to income. The money supply, to these economists, was the crucial variable because they assumed that the demand for money was stable. The statement just cited, for example, places the emphasis on the demand for money, rather than on the economic policy variable—the money supply. Therefore, a more complete statement might be that *the quantity theory of money argues that there is a predictable relationship between money stock changes and gross national product changes. This follows from the fact that the supply of money is determined independently of the demand for money and that the demand for money is stable relative to its determinants.* Actually, however, no matter which statement of the quantity theory one prefers, the demand for money is an important variable.

According to the quantity theorist, the demand for money and its inverse, velocity, have a stable functional relationship with their determinants. He uses much the same determinants of demand as those discussed earlier—*income, wealth, and rate of interest.* The demand for money is not a constant for the quantity theorist. He merely states that *there is a predictable relationship* between the demand for money and its determinants.

The Keynesian would also agree that the demand for money is a function of income, wealth, and the rate of interest, since he believes that the transactions and precautionary components of demand are positively related to the level of income and that the speculative demand for money is inversely related to the rate of interest. For those Keynesians who have become "portfolio" theorists, wealth is an important determinant of the demand for money, although money itself is regarded as only one of a whole group of competing financial assets. What, then, is the difference between the quan-

---

[3] Milton Friedman. "The Quantity Theory of Money: A Restatement." In *Studies in the Quantity Theory of Money.* Milton Friedman, ed. (University of Chicago Press, 1956), p. 4.

tity theorist and the Keynesian economist? *First,* the quantity theorist regards the demand for money as more stable relative to expenditures than the marginal propensity to consume ($\Delta C/\Delta Y_d$). We said in Chapter 19 that the slope of the S_pS_p line is determined by the marginal propensity to save $\Delta S_p/\Delta Y_d$. The slope of the S_pS_p line, in turn, determines the position of the *IS* line. In essence, therefore, the quantity theorist argues that $\Delta S_p/\Delta Y_d$ and *IS* are comparatively unstable. As a result, he feels that although the income expenditure model is useful for demonstrating economic relationships and for indicating the direcon of movements in income, it is not helpful in making accurate quantitative predictions of gross national product. As an alternative, the quantity theorist proposes that the economist approach the matter by working from money stock changes to changes in gross national product, since velocity exhibits some regularity of behavior. As Figure 26–3 indicates, money supply changes and gross national product changes seem to correspond quite closely to each other over time.

In addition, quantity theorists argue that empirical work tends to support the view that velocity possesses greater stability than the marginal propensity to save.[4] On the other hand, Keynesian economists have contended that the tests made of their models have been performed only on the simplest and crudest versions, rather than on the more sophisticated econometric models.[5] Still other economists argue that it is incorrect to stress either the marginal propensity to save or the velocity of money to the exclusion of the other variables.[6] Finally, one recent econometric study developed a set of dynamic multipliers to test the importance of money supply and autonomous spending forces in determining aggregate demand during our most recent inter-war period, post-Korea (1954) to pre-Vietnam (1963). This study concluded that forces ". . . were often destabilizing, the record of monetary policy being even poorer than that of autonomous expenditures."[7]

A *second* area of disagreement between quantity and some Keynesian economists concerns the liquidity trap. Whereas many early extreme Keynesians generally believed that the liquidity trap existed, at least during periods of deep depression and low interest rates, most quantity theorists questioned its existence at all. The empirical evidence seems conclusive. on this issue. Studies conducted since the end of World War II show that we have experienced no liquidity trap—that the demand for money sched-

---

[4] Milton Friedman and David Meiselman. "The Relative Stability of Monetary Velocity and the Investment Multiplier in the United States, 1897–1958." In Commission on Money and Credit, *Stabilization Policies.* (Prentice-Hall, 1963).

[5] L. R. Klein. "The Friedman-Becker Illusion." *Journal of Political Economy* (1958), pp. 539–45.

[6] For a professional free-for-all on this issue involving Albert Ando, Franco Modigliani, Michael De Prano, Thomas Mayer, Milton Friedman, and David Meiselman, see *American Economic Review* (September 1965), pp. 693–792.

[7] J. Kmenta and P. E. Smith. "Autonomous Expenditures versus Money Supply: An Application of Dynamic Multipliers." *Review of Economics and Statistics* (August 1973), pp. 299–307.

Figure 26–3. Gross national product, money stock, and ratio of money stock to GNP in the United States.

* Change in series.

SOURCE: 1900–1971: Board of Governors of the Federal Reserve System. *Federal Reserve Historical Chart Book* (1972), p. 66; 1972–73: estimated by author.

ule does not become interest-elastic at some low rate of interest.[8] Of course, this does not preclude the possibility that at some time in the future we could be confronted with such a situation.

[8] Martin Bronfenbrenner and Thomas Mayer. "Liquidity Functions in the American Economy." *Econometrica* (1960), pp. 810–34; and Karl Brunner and Allan Meltzer, "Liquidity Traps for Money, Bank Credit, and Interest Rates." *Journal of Political Economy* (1968), pp. 1–37.

A *third* area of disagreement has to do with the quantity theorist contention that Keynesians treat the price level as an institutional datum in their theoretical analysis.[9] If this were so, then conceptually all nominal stock of money changes during periods of less than full employment would lead to output changes. Some quantity-oriented economists, the author included, do not accept this interpretation of the Keynesian position. Obviously, both the early extreme Keynesians and the current neo-Keynesians (James Tobin, among the latter) have been quite vocal in their belief that quantity theorists like Milton Friedman misinterpret their position.[10] Even Professor Friedman has backtracked a bit on this issue:

I did not intend . . . to mean that neo-Keynesians assert that prices and wages are in fact constant, or even that in their empirical work they do not introduce relations designed to predict the movement of prices and wages. . . . Treating the price level or the wage level as an institutional datum . . . is not equivalent to saying that wages or prices are constant. It means, rather, that the theory in question has nothing to say about what determines the wage level.[11]

Related to the views of quantity theorists and Keynesians concerning treating the price level as an institutional datum are debates concerning the importance of price expectations for the *Phillips curve*. It was argued in Chapter 21 that expectations of rising prices have pushed the Phillips curve to the right, thereby offsetting the beneficial effects upon unemployment ensuing from an expansionist monetary-fiscal policy. This is the typical view of many quantity theory oriented monetarists. On the other hand, Keynesians are more likely to feel that increased union power and an increased percentage of the work force becoming unemployable because of a lack of demand for their particular (if any) job skills have pushed the Phillips curve to the right.

Automatic Monetary Policy Proposals of the Quantity Theorists

Our present use of monetary controls is discretionary. Deliberate decisions are made by the monetary authorities to use their powers in particular ways to offset economic disturbances. The presumption of discretionary policy advocates is that, in a free society, the authorities can be counted upon to use their powers skillfully without usurping individual freedom.

Less optimistic economists reject discretionary controls and advocate automatic monetary policies. These economists are usually quantity theorists, but there is no reason why they could not be Keynesians. Op-

[9] Milton Friedman. "A Theoretical Framework for Monetary Analysis." *Journal of Political Economy* (1970), pp. 206, 211.

[10] James Tobin, "Friedman's Theoretical Framework." *Journal of Political Economy* (1972), pp. 852–63.

[11] Milton Friedman. "Comments on the Critics." *Journal of Political Economy* (1972), p. 918.

position to discretionary policy is on two levels, that of political philosophy and that of empirical economics.

Discretionary monetary policy and political philosophy. Those who quarrel with discretionary monetary policy on *political* grounds are opposed to all types of discretionary government policies. Their political position is typically that of the nineteenth-century liberal who wanted freedom from government interference: individuals should be free to go their own way, he felt, so long as they did not interfere with the rights of others to do likewise. Present-day critics view extensive regulation of the economy by the government as a hindrance to individual free choice and initiative. The American productive process is based largely on free product and resource markets. Interfere too much with these processes and you restrict individual freedom of action and set up authorities who coerce rather than act in response to the social consensus. Even the implementation of a social consensus decision must be carefully watched, lest there be a tyranny of the majority. The advocates of this position, however, do not feel that free enterprise and individual freedom of action should be left entirely unrestricted. And they are not saying that political anarchy is a superior form of government. Rather, they seek rules of law to implement the liberal philosophy—rules that authorities cannot change at their discretion.

Stability in the value of money and the lessening of economic fluctuations are important policy goals to all economists. They guarantee the individual an opportunity to have a measure of control over his own economic decisions, something he does not have when inflation reduces the purchasing power of money or when inadequate demand leads to lack of employment. Some type of regulation is needed, but what type will best preserve political liberty and economic freedom of action—authorities or rules? The "liberal" economists suggest the latter.

Rules have the merit of being simple and easy to understand. The realities of our economic and political world may make such simple rules impractical, however. We have a plurality of goals that occasionally conflict with one another. As demonstrated earlier, price stability and full employment are not always compatible: a rule to impose price stability on the economy may lead to unemployment; a rule to maintain full employment may lead to rising prices. A discretionary authority might solve this dilemma. If the goals are not in conflict, there may be conflict among several means to arrive at the goals. Discretionary decisions have to be made concerning the correct "package" of means and when it should be implemented. As one economist has argued, "The nature of economic progress, the plurality of goals, the plurality of authorities, the plurality of tools, all of these operate to make impracticable the conduct of monetary management in conformity with a 'rule.'"[12]

---

[12] Jacob Viner. "The Necessary and the Desirable Range of Discretion to Be Allowed to a Monetary Authority." In Leland B. Yeager, *In Search of a Monetary Constitution* (Harvard University Press, 1962), p. 273.

Rules and economic empiricism. The principal reason for advocating "rules" instead of "authorities" on the basis of *economic empiricism* is that, in the past, monetary authorities have often made the wrong policy decisions. This was particularly true during the 1930s and 1940s. Recently, the record has been better. To some economists, however, the present improved performance record does not alter the picture. They remember how the wrong policy decisions of the past intensified monetary instability and, in their view, discretionary policy remains a continuing source of economic instability. As solutions they propose automatic monetary policies and various other banking reforms.

100 percent reserve banking. One such reform that is sometimes proposed is the elimination of fractional reserve banking and the creation of *100 percent reserve banking.* Commercial banks would be required to maintain reserves equal in value to 100 percent of their demand-deposit liabilities. Thus, they could no longer be lenders of funds unless they were themselves permitted to issue stocks and bonds on a large scale. In effect, this proposal would eliminate commercial banking as we know it today.[13]

Experiences during the early 1930s gave rise to this proposal for 100 percent reserves since bank reserves were (and are today) only a fraction of deposit liabilities, banks were unable to redeem their deposit liabilities in response to financial panic. There were widespread bank failures and perverse decreases in the stock of money occurred.

A 100 percent reserve system would remove a major source of economic instability: people would know that their deposits could be immediately converted into currency. Deposit insurance has produced almost the same degree of confidence, however, and with far less revamping of our financial institutions. For this reason, most economists consider the 100 percent reserve proposal impractical. The Federal Deposit Insurance Corporation, established in 1935, assures the safety of bank deposit liabilities. In addition, it is generally felt that the 100 percent money proposal would not be politically feasible since such a proposal would encounter widespread opposition from both bankers and borrowers.

The 100 percent money proposal is frequently an assumption behind the rules suggested for an automatic monetary policy. It is not, however, an indispensable ingredient of an automatic policy.

The rule of stabilization of the price level. In past decades, the most widely acclaimed rule for automatic monetary action was what is known as the *stabilization of the price level.* Henry Simons and Lloyd Mints, the architects of this rule, suggested that the central bank be instructed to buy government securities whenever the price index fell beneath some particular level. The resultant increase in the stock of money would decrease the

---

[13] For a discussion of how this policy change could be instituted, see George Tolley. "100 Per Cent Reserve Banking." In Yeager, *op. cit.,* pp. 275–304.

deflationary forces at work in the economy. Mints and Simons hoped "that the announced policy, when implemented by annual additions to the stock of money, would result in an autonomous maintenance of a high average level of output and an absence of serious movements in the price index."[14] On the other hand, during periods of rising prices, they suggested that the central bank be instructed to sell government securities once the price level rose above some particular level. The decrease in the stock of money was expected to put downward pressures on the price level. Mints and Simons recognized the limitations of their system, however: "If price-level stabilization is a poor system, it is still, from a liberal viewpoint, infinitely better than no system at all."[15]

The promised advantages of this policy lie in the fact that it corresponds to the most understandable meaning of the concept of monetary stability, and it affords the opportunity for prompt and ample action to offset disturbances. However, from this latter fact also arises a possible drawback. Of necessity, discretionary control over the extent of open market operations would be given to the monetary agency, and the lag in effect might conceivably cause an unwanted magnification of autonomous developments.[16]

One of the chief economic advantages of a monetary policy involving a rule such as that recommended by Mints and Simons is its automatism; hence, it is called an *automatic monetary policy*. Once the specified conditions for action are met, the monetary authority must take appropriate corrective measures. Thus, there is no delay resulting from the deliberations and hesitations of a discretionary monetary authority. Some discretionary lag would remain, of course, but action should still be prompter with the rule than without it.

In addition to the stable prices rule, Mints and Simons also considered "increasing the stock of money at a rate roughly equivalent to the rate of increase in the volume of transactions."[17] By stabilizing the money supply, they thought that perverse variations in money would be eliminated as a source of economic instability. Velocity changes could still cause instability, of course. Thus they felt that the stable price-level rule was superior since "A price-index rule . . . defines . . . appropriate measures for dealing with velocity changes."[18]

Stable money growth rules. More recently, however, various *stable money growth* rules have been reexamined by Milton Friedman. The stable money growth rule recommended by Friedman states:

---

[14] Lloyd W. Mints. *Monetary Policy for a Competitive Society* (McGraw-Hill, 1951), p. 225.
[15] Henry Simons. *Economic Policy for a Free Society* (University of Chicago Press, 1948), p. 174.
[16] Mints, *op. cit.*, pp. 224–25.
[17] *Ibid.*, p. 123.
[18] Henry Simons. "Rules Versus Authorities in Monetary Policy." Reprinted in American Economic Association. *Readings in Monetary Theory* (Irwin, 1951), p. 355.

Instruct the System to use its open market powers to produce a 4 percent per year rate of growth in the total of currency held by the public and adjusted deposits in commercial banks. The System should be instructed to keep the rate of growth as steady as it can week by week and month by month and to introduce no seasonal movement in the money stock.[19]

The proposed policy changes would remove from the Federal Reserve System the burden of determining discretionary contracyclical monetary policy. For Friedman and other quantity theorists, there is a close relationship between changes in the money supply and changes in economic activity. Empirically:

The rate of change of the money supply shows well-marked cycles that match closely those in economic activity in general and precede the latter by a long interval. On the average, the rate of change of the money supply has reached its peak nearly sixteen months before the peak in general business and has reached its trough over the twelve months before the trough in general business.[20]

If this relationship is so steady, then possibly the Federal Reserve, instead of stabilizing the growth of the money supply, should change the rate of growth of the money supply to attain a predetermined rate of economic activity. This might be an equally acceptable rule for stable monetary growth were it not for the qualification "on the average" in Friedman's empirical work:

This is highly consistent behavior as such observations go and sufficient to pin down the *average* lead within a rather narrow range. But it is highly variable behavior for the individual episode with which policy must be concerned. . . . monetary changes have their effect only after a considerable lag and over a long period, and . . . the lag is rather variable.[21]

For Friedman, it is the *variable lag* that makes discretionary monetary policy impractical and rules out the advisability of Federal Reserve manipulation of variations in the rate of growth of the money stock. Why? Because it cannot be precisely predicted when a change in the rate of growth in the money stock will have its economic effects. It is entirely possible that the first effects of stepping up the rate of growth of the money supply in a recession would be felt during a subsequent boom. Similarly, the first effects of a decrease in the rate of growth of money during an inflation might be felt in a subsequent recession, thereby aggravating the current crisis. Thus, changes in the money stock remain a source of economic instability.

[19] Milton Friedman. *A Program for Monetary Stability* (Fordham University Press, 1960), p. 100.
[20] Milton Friedman. "The Supply of Money and Changes in Prices and Output." In Joint Economic Committee, *The Relationship of Prices to Economic Stability and Growth: Compendium*. Document No. 23734 (Washington, D.C.: 1958), pp. 249–50.
[21] Milton Friedman. *A Program for Monetary Stability,* pp. 87–88.

It should be noted, however, that Friedman's policy recommendation is not for a stable money supply, but rather for stable *growth* in the money supply. The reason for providing for a steady increase in the money supply is simple. As income and output expand with economic growth, more money is needed to carry on the increasing volume of transactions. If the money supply is not permitted to expand, price deflation can occur unless there is a velocity offset; this could lead to general unemployment.

Economists' reactions to the variable lag. Many economists disagree with Friedman's policy recommendations and empirical results. They contend that the lag in monetary policy (and fiscal policy as well) is short enough for a change in policy to have a stabilizing influence on income and output. For example, J. M. Culbertson has stated:

The broad record of experience seems to me to support the view that anticyclical monetary, debt management, and fiscal adjustments can be counted on to have their predominant direct effects within three to six months, soon enough that if they are undertaken moderately early in a cyclical phase they will not be destabilizing.[22]

Robert Solow and John Kareken, in an empirical study, also reach conclusions different from Friedman's:

Our conclusion is that it [monetary policy] works neither so slowly as Friedman thinks nor as quickly and surely as the Federal Reserve itself seems to believe. We find that the effect of monetary policy on the flow of expenditures is far from overwhelming, though it exists and is of a magnitude worth exploiting in the interests of economic stability. We also find that though the *full* results of policy changes on the flow of expenditures may be a long time coming, nevertheless the chain of effects is spread out over a fairly wide interval. This means that *some* effect comes reasonably quickly and that the effects build up over time so that some substantial stabilizing power results after a lapse of time of the order of six or nine months.[23]

In 1967, one economist, after reviewing the empirical literature concluded:

There is overwhelming evidence of a substantial lag in the effect of monetary policy, but there is no convincing evidence that the variance of the lag is great. Whether or not the lag is long and variable enough to make discretionary policy [as currently conducted] less desirable than a fixed rule depends in good part upon which of the several studies of the lag turns out to be correct.[24]

---

[22] J. M. Culbertson. "Friedman on the Lag in Effect of Monetary Policy." *Journal of Political Economy* (1960), p. 621.

[23] Albert Ando, E. Cary Brown, Robert M. Solow, and John Kareken. "Lags in Fiscal and Monetary Policy." In Commission on Money and Credit, *Stabilization Policies* (Prentice-Hall, 1963), p. 2.

[24] Thomas Mayer. "The Lag in the Effect of Monetary Policy: Some Criticisms." *Western Economic Journal* (September 1967), p. 342.

Debate on the variable lag continued into the 1970s, but with some change in emphasis. It was obvious to everyone that there was a lag in the effect of monetary policy on the economy, but it became increasingly important to correctly specify which variable represented monetary policy. It will be recalled that when we evaluated the performance of the Federal Reserve policy in Chapter 12, we used free reserves and the stock of money as indicators of policy. The components of the money stock as presented in this book have been currency and demand-deposit holdings of the nonbank public. This selection reflects the view of the author that money, while only one of a spectrum of liquid assets, is still unique since it is the only asset that can be used directly to purchase goods and services. Put another way, the author has emphasized the transactions function of money and, accordingly, has selected a *narrow definition* of money (sometimes called the M_1 definition) to represent monetary policy actions.

Other economists place more emphasis on the store of value function of money. Among them is Milton Friedman, who uses a *broad definition* of money (sometimes called the M_2 definition) which includes currency and the demand- and time-deposit liabilities of commercial banks to the nonbank public. Friedman also feels that he obtains a better statistical fit between changes in the stock of money and the level of income with this definition. Still other economists will, from time to time, use even broader definitions. For example, all federally insured deposits of non-bank financial institutions may be included in the definition of money.[25]

In addition, many econometric models have been built using nonborrowed reserves (total reserves less borrowings at the Fed) as the target variable. A recent survey of the literature stated:

Use of nonborrowed reserves as the exogenous monetary variable suggests that less than 40 percent of the impact of a monetary action occurs within five quarters and that the full effect is distributed over two and a half years. On the other hand, use of the money supply, the monetary base, or total reserves suggests that most of the effect occurs within four or five quarters.[26]

In the midst of all of this debate, the Federal Reserve has discarded the free reserve policy variable and, in the 1970s, has moved toward controlling monetary aggregates. Thus, the Fed now looks at both the narrow and broad measures of money when considering its policies. Recognizing, however, that it does not have direct control over the stock of money (no matter how defined), the Fed looks very carefully at the reserve base of the banking system, principally what it calls RPDs (reserves available to sup-

---

[25] V. K. Chetty. "On Measuring the Nearness of Near-Moneys." *American Economic Review* (June 1969), pp. 270–80.

[26] Michael J. Hamburger. "The Lag in the Effect of Monetary Policy: A Survey of the Recent Literature." Federal Reserve Bank of New York. *Monthly Review* (December 1971), pp. 289–98.

port private nonbank deposits). In any event, the Federal Reserve still follows discretionary, not automatic monetary policy.

Possibly the best conclusion that can be drawn from this debate was made by two Friedman disciples:

The evidence which has accumulated on monetary lags since Milton Friedman first proposed a constant rate of monetary growth as the wisest policy has by and large supported his case. While the estimates of the lag reviewed here all indicate similar difficulties for policy, they differ sufficiently to indicate that we still lack knowledge which might, if it were available, partially overcome those difficulties.[27]

THE NEO-KEYNESIAN POSITION ON MONEY AND POLICY

A Moderate Keynesian Approach to Theory and Policy

Earlier in this chapter, we discussed an extreme Keynesian view of theory which de-emphasized the importance of money in the economy. That view is no longer held by most Keynesians. These economists concede that money has a role to play, arguing that the money supply influences interest rates and thereby investment demand. According to this view, investment demand is responsive in some degree to interest rate changes, particularly as firms approach capacity output. Under these circumstances, moderate Keynesians believe that the *IS* line slopes downward and to the right.

By referring again to Figure 26–2, we can directly view the alternative Keynesian models of *IS* and *LM*. Recall that the solid lines represent the extreme Keynesian position. The broken lines illustrate the moderate Keynesian model. Money supply changes have no economic effect only so long as the *IS* line intersects *LM* where there is a liquidity trap. The higher the income and the output of the economy become, however, the more likely the *IS* curve will be interest-elastic and will not intersect the *LM* curve in the area of the liquidity trap. Under these circumstances, money supply changes can have an economic effect; an increase in the money supply may shift the *LM* line to a new position at $(LM)_1$ in the figure. Given the $(IS)_1$ line, this will lead to interest rate decreases, investment expenditure increases, and hence increased consumption spending. The increase in the stock of money will be absorbed partly by an increase in output and partly by an increase in the price level.[28] As noted earlier and as illustrated in Chapter 21, the closer we are to full employment, the stronger will be the effect of money stock increases on the price level. A restrictive

[27] Phillip Cagan and Anna J. Schwartz. "How Feasible is a Flexible Monetary Policy?" Paper prepared for the Conference on Capitalism and Freedom in honor of Milton Friedman, October 1972.
[28] See James Tobin. "Friedman's Theoretical Framework." *Journal of Political Economy* (1972), pp. 852–63 for the neo-Keynesian position on the relation of money, output, and prices.

monetary policy, on the other hand, would shift the LM line from $(LM)_1$ to $(LM)_0$ in Figure 26-2. This would lead to increases in the rate of interest and, consequently, decreases in investment, consumption, and income. If prices were relatively rigid downward, most of the decrease in demand would result in decreased real output, rather than in significantly lower prices.

Under these moderate Keynesian assumptions, fiscal measures, unaccompanied by money stock changes, would be affected by money market conditions when IS intersects the nonhorizontal or elastic portion of LM. Increased government expenditures would cause some interest rate increases, thereby dampening investment expenditures. However, government spending increases financed by an increase in the stock of money would lead to simultaneous shifts to the right in IS and LM. Thus, money stock increases would reinforce the effects of the increased government spending on income and output.

The Neo-Keynesian Portfolio Approach to Money, Money Substitutes, and Policy

The theoretical positon. The quantity theorist tends to regard money as a financial asset that is uniquely important for income determination. Portfolio theorists who are neo-Keynesians, however, regard money as only one of a group of competing financial assets. For these economists, the more types of financial assets there are in the economy in addition to money, the less important money is and the more difficult the task of the monetary authorities becomes.

Considerable discussion was devoted to the development of this concept in Chapters 5 and 7. There it was argued that nonbank financial institutions create forms of liquid wealth that compete with money for a place in the portfolios of individuals. Thus, people are confronted with a choice between these alternative forms. The more successful nonbank financial institutions are inducing people to maintain their liquid-wealth holdings in the form of savings bank deposits, savings and loan association share accounts, or life insurance policies instead of money, the less control monetary authorities may have over the economy.

To the portfolio economist, relative interest rates are key variables. When the yield on asset x, for example, rises relative to that on other assets, there will be an increase in the amount of x demanded and a decrease in the demand for other assets. Money is only one form of liquid asset. While it has no measurable yield, it is the safest of all liquid-wealth forms. Hence, as the yield on other assets increases, there will be a decrease in the demand for money and an increase in the amount demanded of other assets, and vice versa. This occurs because money and other assets are substitutes for one another. While other assets do not function as a medium of exchange, they do serve to satisfy the asset demand for money and hence, as their interest yields change, there will be a substitution between these other assets and money.

In terms of the model developed in Chapters 19 and 20, this *portfolio theory* suggests that W' (total wealth) and X' (other variables that may influence the demand for money) change as a result of the proliferation of financial assets and variations in relative interest yields. Thus, it is difficult for anyone to predict the behavior of velocity and even harder for the monetary authorities to control the position of *LM* by money stock changes. To be effective, monetary controls must be extended to the forms of liquid wealth created by nonbank financial intermediaries. Thus, the quantity theorist questions the stability of *IS*: the portfolio theorist questions the stability of *LM*.

The policy position. The liquid assets created by nonbank financial intermediaries have steadily increased in dollar volume relative to the stock of money. Aside from Regulation Q, the Federal Reserve's economic control techniques directly affect only commercial banks, however. Nonbank financial institutions are regulated, but by agencies whose principal function is to safeguard the claims of the depositors and account holders. In recognition of these changes in our financial system, proposals have been made by portfolio economists to expand economic control techniques to include the financial activities of nonbank financial intermediaries.

These proposals are related to the velocity effects of nonbank financial intermediary operations. As you will recall, these institutions create liquid wealth when they tap the idle funds of savers. The funds come to the financial institutions in the form of demand deposits, these deposits are then loaned to borrowers, and the borrowers spend these funds for goods and services. Thus, velocity—the turnover of the money supply—is increased.

As in commercial banks, the ratio of cash assets to liabilities and capital accounts created by nonbank financial institutions is fractional. There are required reserve ratios for nonbank financial institutions, but they are usually quite low and, unlike commercial banks, often include such assets as U.S. government securities. These reserve requirements are not normally adjusted in a contracyclical manner; they remain fixed. Thus, in periods of restrictive monetary policy, nonbank financial intermediaries sometimes continue to expand their lending activity to enhance their competitive position vis-à-vis commercial banks. This occurs, of course, only if the nonbank institutions are successful in their efforts to induce people to change the composition of their liquid-wealth holdings. A switch from demand and time deposits at commercial banks to savings and loan association share accounts, time deposits at mutual savings banks, or life insurance policies must then take place.

The ideas of the portfolio economists have extended widely into the financial community and were part of a group of recommendations presented by the *Hunt Commission,* a presidential commission on financial structure and regulation.[29] Among the specific proposals were (1) require mandatory Federal Reserve membership for all commercial banks, mutual savings banks, and savings and loan associations that offer third-party payment services, (2) impose comparable reserve requirements upon all institutions that are required to join the system, (3) expand the types of loans nonbank financial institutions may make (this was subsequently done, as we saw in Chapter 7); (4) eliminate reserve requirements on time deposits, and (5) equalize the tax treatment of banks and savings institutions. Ultimately, all of these proposals would make nonbank financial institutions more comparable to commercial banks both operationally and regulatively. Some of the previously discussed perverse variations in velocity could thereby be eliminated.

Let us briefly examine the proposal to extend the reserve requirement to various nonbank financial institutions. Nonbank financial intermediaries now operate with actual reserves far below those required for commercial banks. Considerable adjustments would be necessary if nonbank financial intermediaries were to have exactly the same reserve requirements as commercial banks. Some nonbank financial intermediaries would be forced to liquidate large volumes of earning assets, and this could have deflationary repercussions. The Hunt Commission therefore included the following recommendation for preferential treatment:

The Commission recommends that: the legally required deposit reserves for any existing commercial bank and any mutual savings bank required to join the Federal Reserve System . . . be set at a preferentially low initial rate, with gradual increases so that at the end of five years these rates are the same as those for all other members of the system.[30]

Assuming that the extension of the legal reserve requirement to nonbank financial institutions can actually become part of the program of economic control measures, will the new controls entirely eliminate undesired changes in velocity as a source of economic instability? No, because it will be recalled from Chapter 5 that, like commercial banks, nonbank financial institutions engage in asset and liability management. For example, changing the asset composition of a financial institution's portfolio from U.S. government securities to risky high-yield loans would increase velocity and possibly threaten the safety and solvency of that institution's assets.

These proposals to the president have since been revised and were forwarded to Congress in September of 1973. Among the most important proposals made to the Congress are: (1) eliminate interest rate ceilings on savings deposits; (2) permit savings and loan associations to offer checking accounts; (3) permit savings and loan associations to make consumer

---

[29] *The Report of the President's Commission on Financial Structure and Regulation*. Reed O. Hunt, Chairman. Washington D.C., December 1971.
[30] *Ibid.*, p. 65.

loans; (4) broaden the sources of funds for credit unions; (5) equalize the tax treatment of banks and savings institutions.

The empirical problem.   The empirical problem confronting the economists making the above recommendations is much like the one facing the quantity theorists. If the liabilities created by nonbank financial institutions are very close substitutes for money — if, in fact, they are equivalent to money — then it is clearly appropriate to bring these institutions under Federal Reserve control, to treat them like banks. Over the years, empirical results on this issue have been very mixed however, since they vary with the nature of the statistical techniques employed and the definition of money used. Studies based upon time series data indicate a high degree of substitutability, whereas those based upon cross-section data (data taken at some point in time) show poor substitutability. One very recent study shows ". . . . findings of very low or zero substitutability between money and near moneys, . . . findings of substitutability between bank and non-bank savings deposits."[31] In other words, near moneys are poor substitutes for money, but good substitutes for one another.

The policy implication of the first part of this statistical finding is that to affect aggregate economic activity the monetary authorities should concentrate on controlling the money stock rather than a broader spectrum of assets. This would make the quantity theorists right and the portfolio theorists wrong. The policy implication of the second part is that changes in the yield on the liabilities of nonbank financial institutions will cause a change in the demand for the time deposits of commercial banks. For example, an increased yield on savings and loan share accounts relative to savings accounts at commercial banks will lead to a diminution of the latter accounts, an increase in demand deposits owned by savings and loan associations, a decrease in t (the nonbank public's desired ratio of time to demand deposits at commercial banks) in equation 20–2 (the money multiplier), an increase in the money multiplier, an increase in the stock of money (if commercial banks have excess reserves), and a decrease in commercial bank lending ability. All of this follows because the reserve requirement on time deposits is less than it is on demand deposits. Remember, however, that one of the Hunt Commission's recommendations was the elimination of reserve requirements on time deposits. If this occurred, then the preceding chain of events would not ensue. In any case, given the possible policy outcomes, it might be advisable for some of the Hunt Commission recommendations to be shelved until additional and more conclusive evidence on the substitutability of money and near moneys becomes available.

---

[31] Franklin R. Edwards. "More on Substitutability Between Money and Near Moneys." *Journal of Money, Credit and Banking* (1972), p. 567.

Money and Optimum Portfolios

Underlying the logic of the portfolio position on money are ideas closely related to the analysis in Chapter 15. It will be recalled that investors may be viewed as seeking to hold an optimum portfolio of liquid-wealth forms that maximizes returns and utility and minimizes risk. This same type of theorizing may also be applied to the demand for money. We shall first consider the transactions demand for money and then the speculative demand for money.

The transactions demand for money and interest rates. As shown in Chapters 1, 17, and 20, money is held as a medium of exchange in order to carry on transactions, extinguish debt, avoid the inconveniences of barter exchange, and even out discrepancies between receipt and expenditure of money balances. As noted earlier, other liquid assets can perform these same services, albeit only indirectly. For example, savings accounts can be quickly converted into money and have the added advantage of earning interest. Bonds also earn interest and, if they are readily marketable, can be converted into money quickly. Stocks that are traded on the national exchanges can be sold quickly, although the possibility of loss exists. If these assets and others have yield advantages over money balances, why should anyone hold money balances idle to satisfy the transactions demand for money? Because there are costs connected with purchasing and selling liquid assets. There are brokerage fees for the purchase and sale of stocks and bonds. There is the delay and inconvenience involved in traveling to or mailing orders to savings and loan associations, and so on. *Thus, if one holds transactions balances in interest-yielding assets, there is a cost for conversion into money when payments must be made; but if one holds transactions balances in idle money, yield is foregone.* The right combination (portfolio) of money and yield-earning assets must be found—one that maximizes return and minimizes lost return and conversion costs.

It would appear logical that the greater the difficulties and costs of converting liquid assets into money, the greater the demand for money to hold. Similarly, the lower the return from liquid assets, the greater the demand for idle money. Hence, we can posit an inverse relationship between interest and the demand for money for transactions purposes and a positive relationship between the costs of acquiring competing liquid assets and the demand for transactions balances.[32]

This line of reasoning is most often applied to the demand for money by business firms, and most statistical tests center on corporate cash balances. The analysis assumes that firms treat cash as an inventory of a commodity to be held at a minimum cost until the right moment to relinquish it. The

---

[32] This position was first developed by William Baumol in "The Transactions Demand for Cash: An Inventory Theoretic Approach." *Quarterly Journal of Economics* (1952), pp. 545–56.

simplest approach defines the cost of portfolio management as the combined effects of the interest earnings foregone and the brokerage payments. One conceptual outcome of this approach is that there should be economies of scale in the holding of cash balances—that is, the larger the volume of transactions to be made, the smaller the required ratio of transactions balances to total transactions.[33] Much empirical work has been done to test this proposition and most of it has been unfavorable; witness the title of one article: "The Uselessness of Transactions Demand Models."[34] At the moment, the economics profession seems left with a much analyzed theoretical idea with little empirical content. Yet, as often happens, a more appropriate specification of transactions demand models may eventually yield useful results.

Although the empirical foundations of this analysis are at present weak, there are nevertheless some important policy implications that should be emphasized in the event the hypotheses ultimately prove to be valid. It is important, for example, that the transactions demand for money as well as the speculative demand for money is a function of the rate of interest. This means that monetary policy increases in importance. In terms of our income expenditure model, the *LM* curve is flatter than that yielded when only the speculative demand for money is a function of the interest rate. If commodity market demands for consumer durables and investment goods are a function of the interest rate, then the monetary authority needs to consider the effects of its actions on the economy even more closely. Put another way, under the Baumol hypothesis, the task of the monetary authority becomes more complex, since not only are commodity market and speculative demand for money forces affected by the interest rate, but so is the transactions demand for money itself. Finally and most important, if there are economies of scale in the holding of money balances, monetary policy becomes more potent. A given increment in the stock of money will support a greater increment in transactions (and hence in *Y*) with economies of scale. In terms of our model of income determination, a given increase in the stock of money induced by the monetary authority will shift the *LM* curve further to the right with economies of scale prevalent.[35]

The speculative demand for money, risk, and interest rates. The essential problem in portfolio selection, as argued in Chapter 15, is to determine one's optimum portfolio—the one that yields the greatest return and satis-

---

[33] Those with some training in mathematics will recognize that the economies of scale referred to follow from the form of the optimum cash-holding equations developed by Professor Baumol. His simplest equation is $C = \sqrt{2bT/i}$ where C is the optimum cash withdrawals from one's return-yielding liquid assets, b is the dollar brokerage fee of each cash withdrawal, T is the value of transactions to be made (it is T which necessitates the cash withdrawals), and i is the cost of giving up interest-yielding assets to acquire cash.

[34] Case M. Sprenkle. "The Uselessness of Transactions Demand Models." *The Journal of Finance* (1969), pp. 835–47.

[35] I am grateful to Daniel McCarty for reviewing and helping to improve the analysis of this section. Any error that remains is strictly the responsibility of the author.

faction at the lowest possible risk. The analysis of Chapter 15 was presented in connection with making a selection among alternative portfolios as developed in contemporary finance theory in contrast to monetary theory. Now we shall see how portfolio analysis is used in monetary theory, concentrating primarily upon the theory developed by James Tobin in his classic article "Liquidity Preference as Behavior Towards Risk."[36] Our discussion here will be considerably simpler, however.

The essential problem in monetary theory portfolio analysis is to determine the optimum proportion of money and other liquid assets in one's portfolio. Figure 26–4 illustrates the main ingredients of this theoretical approach to the demand for money. In the lower quadrant, on the vertical axis of the figure we measure the fraction of bonds in an individual's portfolio. On the horizontal axis we measure the degree of risk attached to having bonds in one's portfolio. For the sake of simplicity, assume that only two choices are open for inclusion in a portfolio—bonds and money. Naturally, the greater the fraction of bonds in a portfolio (and the smaller the fraction of money), the greater the degree of risk—that is, the greater the chances of either gain or loss. The line OB in the lower quadrant represents the individual's view of how his risk will vary with the number of bonds.

The vertical axis in the upper quadrant measures return. Again, risk is measured on the horizontal axis. I_0, I_1, and I_2 are indifference curves representing higher levels of satisfaction. Along any one indifference curve, we can see the trade-off between risk and return. (These curves are the same as those in Figure 15-3, but here the axes are reversed.) In addition to the indifference curves, there is an opportunity locus line OC in the upper quadrant. This line shows that, at a given interest rate on bonds, the amount of return will increase as the degree of risk increases and as the fraction of bonds in the portfolio increases (and the amount of money held decreases).

We are now in a position to see how risk, interest, and the distribution of a portfolio between money and bonds maximizes return and satisfaction. Assume that the fraction of bonds in the portfolio is OA_0. At this fraction, the degree of risk is v_0 and the return on the bonds is r_0 when the opportunity locus is OC_0. This is not the satisfaction maximizing portfolio, however, since the individual could get greater satisfaction by increasing the number of bonds in his portfolio. The satisfaction maximizing fraction of bonds is OA_1, where the opportunity locus OC_0 is just tangent to the highest indifference curve I_1 where r and v are r_1 and v_1.

Now assume that the interest rate on bonds changes, that it rises and that the OC line shifts up to OC_1 from OC_0. The individual can now obtain a greater return from an increase in risk than before. He will therefore

---

[36] James Tobin, "Liquidity Preference as Behavior Towards Risk." *Review of Economic Studies.* Vol. 25, No. 67 (February 1958), pp. 65–86.

Figure 26-4. Portfolio determination.

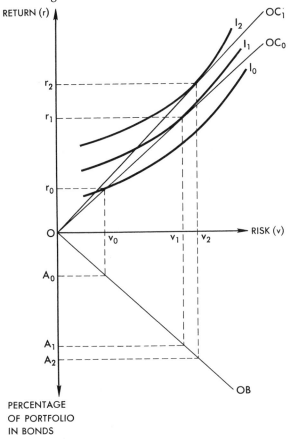

increase his demand for bonds to OA_2 and decrease his demand for money. Interest return and risk will be r_2 and v_2, respectively.

This type of analysis establishes an inverse relationship between the demand for money and the interest rate and a positive relationship between the demand for bonds and interest, other things being equal. People will hold higher-risk portfolios the higher the interest rate. An important given, of course, is the original estimate of risk—the OB line. Should this estimate be in error (if risk were underestimated, for example), then the OB line would rotate outward, the demand for bonds would decrease, and the demand for money would increase at any given interest rate.

The obvious *policy implication* of this analysis is one that has been stressed so often in this book: the interest rate and monetary policy are very important in determining the demand for money, the demand for other liquid assets, and the substitution between money and other liquid assets. Earlier comments on the problems of measuring substitutability naturally apply with equal force here.

MONEY AND THE ECONOMY

Although, as we have seen, there are the conflicting theoretical views and disparate empirical results, it is not impossible to arrive at wise policy choices among discretionary and automatic monetary policy proposals. The controversies mentioned here are the outward manifestations of a healthy scientific discipline. Setting up alternative hypotheses and policy prescriptions is part of the process of seeking to understand the nature of the world more fully. In many respects, the more we learn about the world and about economics, the more we recognize the complexity of apparently simple phenomena. Frequently, when we investigate problems, instead of solving them we find new questions to be answered.

There does seem to be general agreement today that monetary policy influences income and employment through interest rate and wealth (portfolio) effects. Variations in the stock of money influence interest rates and, accordingly, investment demand, the demand for consumer durables, and the balance of payments. In addition, variations in the stock of money disturb its given distribution among wealth forms. Therefore, an increase in the nominal stock of money, given the price level, will increase the level of one form of wealth—real cash balances. If businesses and consumers desire to maintain a given distribution among wealth forms, there will be an increase in the demand for goods and services.

This brief description of the process by which money stock changes affect the economy is consistent with the Keynesian, portfolio, and quantity theory approaches to monetary theory and policy. Moderate Keynesians stress interest rate effects on investment demand. Neo-Keynesian portfolio economists stress substitution effects among wealth forms that occur as a result of changing interest rate differentials. Quantity theorists stress wealth effects that occur as a result of changes in the level of real cash balances.

Overall, no matter what their theoretical position, economists believe that money is important for the economy. Through any of the mechanisms described, variations in the stock of money will affect income and spending. A decline in the quantity of money will reduce the level of employment, output, and prices, and an increase in the quantity of money will raise them. The closer we are to full employment, the more money stock variations are likely to affect the price level; the closer we are to having a significant amount of unemployment, the more money stock variations are likely to affect real output and employment.

Supplementary Readings

ON MONETARY THEORY

The debate between the quantity theorists and the neo-Keynesians is best summarized in "Symposium on Friedman's Theoretical Framework." Articles by

Karl Brunner and Allan H. Meltzer, James Tobin, Paul Davidson, Don Patinkin, and Milton Friedman. *Journal of Political Economy* (1972), pp. 837–950.

See also:

Friedman, Milton. (ed.) *Studies in the Quantity Theory of Money.* University of Chicago Press, 1956.

———. "A Theoretical Framework for Monetary Analysis." *Journal of Political Economy* (1970), pp. 193–238.

———. "A Monetary Theory of Nominal Income." *Journal of Political Economy* (1971), pp. 323–37.

Gurley, J. G., and Edward Shaw. *Money in a Theory of Finance.* The Brookings Institution, 1960.

Laumas, Gurcharan S. "The Degree of Moniness of Savings Deposits." *American Economic Review* (1968), pp. 501–503.

Patinkin, Don. *Money, Interest, and Prices,* 2nd ed. Harper & Row, 1965.

Pesek, Boris P., and Thomas R. Saving. *Money, Wealth, and Economic Theory.* Macmillan, 1967.

Ritter, Lawrence S. "The Role of Money in Keynesian Theory." In *Banking and Monetary Studies,* D. Carson (ed.). Irwin, 1963, pp. 134–50.

Tobin, James. "Money, Capital, and Other Stores of Value." *American Economic Review* (May 1961), pp. 26–37.

———. "A General Equilibrium Approach to Monetary Theory." *Journal of Money, Credit and Banking* (1969), pp. 15–29.

———. *Essays in Economics, Volume 1: Macroeconomics.* Markham Publishing Company, 1971.

ON MONETARY POLICY

Board of Governors of the Federal Reserve System, *Open Market Policies And Operating Procedures — Staff Studies.* Washington D.C., 1971.

Corrigan, E. Gerald. "Income Stabilization and Short-run Variability in Money." *Federal Reserve Bank of New York Monthly Review* (April 1973), pp. 87–98.

Fand, David I. "A Monetarist Model of the Monetary Process." *Journal of Finance* (1970), pp. 275–90.

Friedman, Milton. *A Program for Monetary Stability.* Fordham University Press, 1960.

Friedman, Milton., J. G. Gurley, and Arthur M. Okun, "Have Fiscal and/or Monetary Policy Failed?" *American Economic Review Papers and Proceedings* (May 1972), pp. 10–30.

Gurley, J. G., and Edward Shaw. "Financial Intermediaries and the Saving-Investment Process." *Journal of Finance* (1956), pp. 257–76.

Mann, Maurice. "How Does Monetary Policy Affect the Economy?" *Federal Reserve Bulletin* (1968), pp. 803–809.

Mints, Lloyd W. *Monetary Policy for a Competitive Society.* McGraw-Hill, 1950.

Simons, Henry. *Economic Policy for a Free Society.* University of Chicago Press, 1948.

Additional references can be found in the footnotes to this chapter.

Author Index

Subject Index